THE RANDOM HOUSE CONCISE

WORLD ATLAS

THE RANDOM HOUSE CONCISE

WORLD ATLAS

RANDOM HOUSE NEW YORK

All inquiries should be addressed to Random House, Inc., 201 East 50th Street, New York, N.Y. 10022. Published in the United States by Random House, Inc., New York, and simultaneously in Canada by Random House of Canada Limited, Toronto. Originally published in Great Britain by John Bartholomew & Son Ltd., Edinburgh.

Library of Congress Catalog Card Number: 84-43168

ISBN: 0-394-74007-6

Manufactured in Great Britain

First American Edition

CONTENTS

viii-ix World Physical
x-xi World Political
xii-xiii World Time Zones
xiv-xv World Environment
xvi Key to Symbols

1 Arctic Ocean 1:40M
2-3 North America – Political 1:35M
4-5 Canada, West 1:15M
6-7 Canada, East 1:15M
8-9 USA, West 1:12·5M
10-11 USA, East 1:12·5M
12 USA, Alaska 1:10M
13 Canada Pacific 1:7·5M
14-15 Lower Canada, USA North-East 1:5M
16 Washington – New York – Boston 1:2·5M
17 USA, South-East 1:5M
18-19 USA, South-Central 1:5M
20 USA, Pacific NW 1:5M
21 USA, Pacific S 1:5M
22 San Francisco & Los Angeles 1:2·5M
23 Central Mexico 1:5M
24-25 Mexico & Central America 1:15M
26-27 Caribbean 1:10M

28 South America - Political 1:40M
29 South America, South 1:15M
30 South America, Central 1:15M
31 South America, NE 1:15M
32-33 South America, North 1:15M
34 Central Argentina 1:7·5M
35 South-East Brazil 1:7·5M

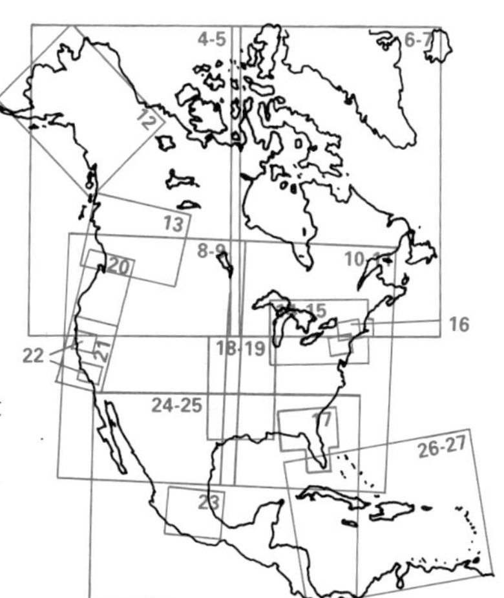

4-5
6-7
12
13
8-9
10-11
15
16
22
21
20
18-19
24-25
17
26-27
23

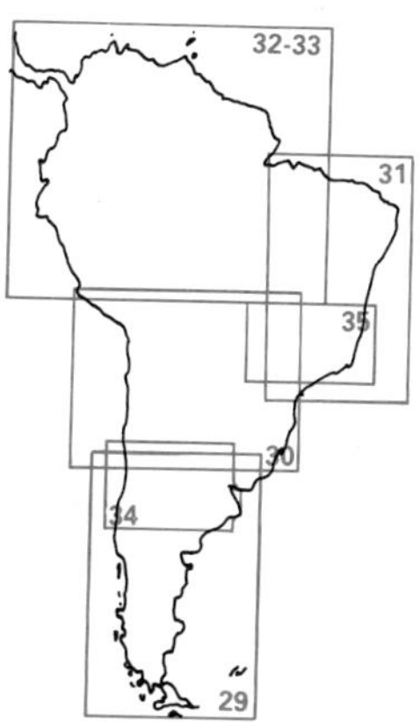

32-33
31
35
30
34
29

36–37 Europe – Political 1:16M
38–39 Scandinavia 1:7·5M
40–41 British Isles 1:5M
42–43 England & Wales 1:2·5M
44 Scotland, North 1:2·5M
45 Ireland 1:2·5M
46 Paris - Brussels – Ruhr 1:2·5M
47 Alps 1:2·5M
48–49 France 1:5M
50–51 Spain 1:5M
52–53 Italy 1:5M
54–55 The Balkans 1:5M
56–57 Germany & Austria 1:5M
58–59 East-Central Europe 1:5M
60–61 Central European Russia 1:10M
62 USSR – Political 1:45M
63 USSR, East 1:20M
64–65 USSR, West 1:20M
66–67 South Asia – Political 1:40M
68–69 East Asia 1:20M
70–71 South-East Asia 1:20M
72–73 Central China 1:10M
74 Japan & Korea 1:10M
75 Central Japan 1:5M
76–77 Indo-China & Singapore 1:10M
78 Indonesia, Central 1:10M
79 Philippines 1:10M
80–81 Middle East 1:20M
82–83 India & West China 1:20M
84–85 India, NW & Pakistan 1:7·5M

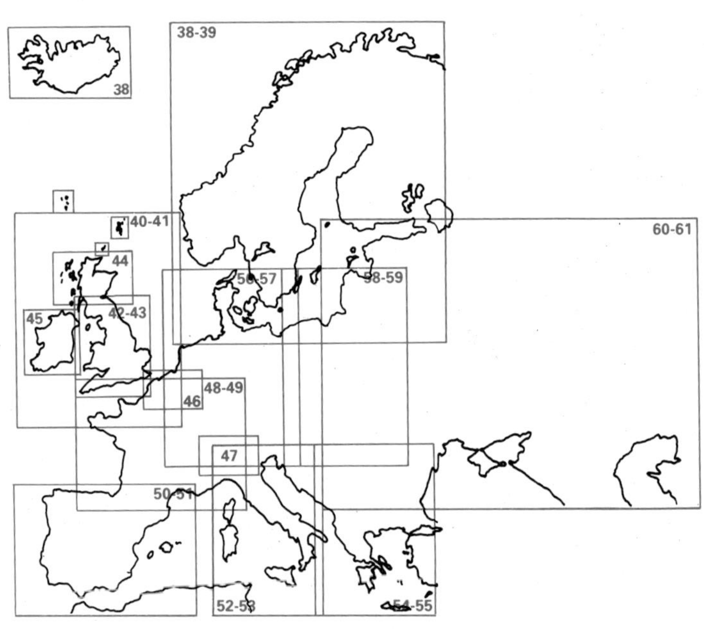
38
38-39
40-41
44
42-43
45
46
48-49
47
50-51
52-53
54-55
56-57
58-59
60-61

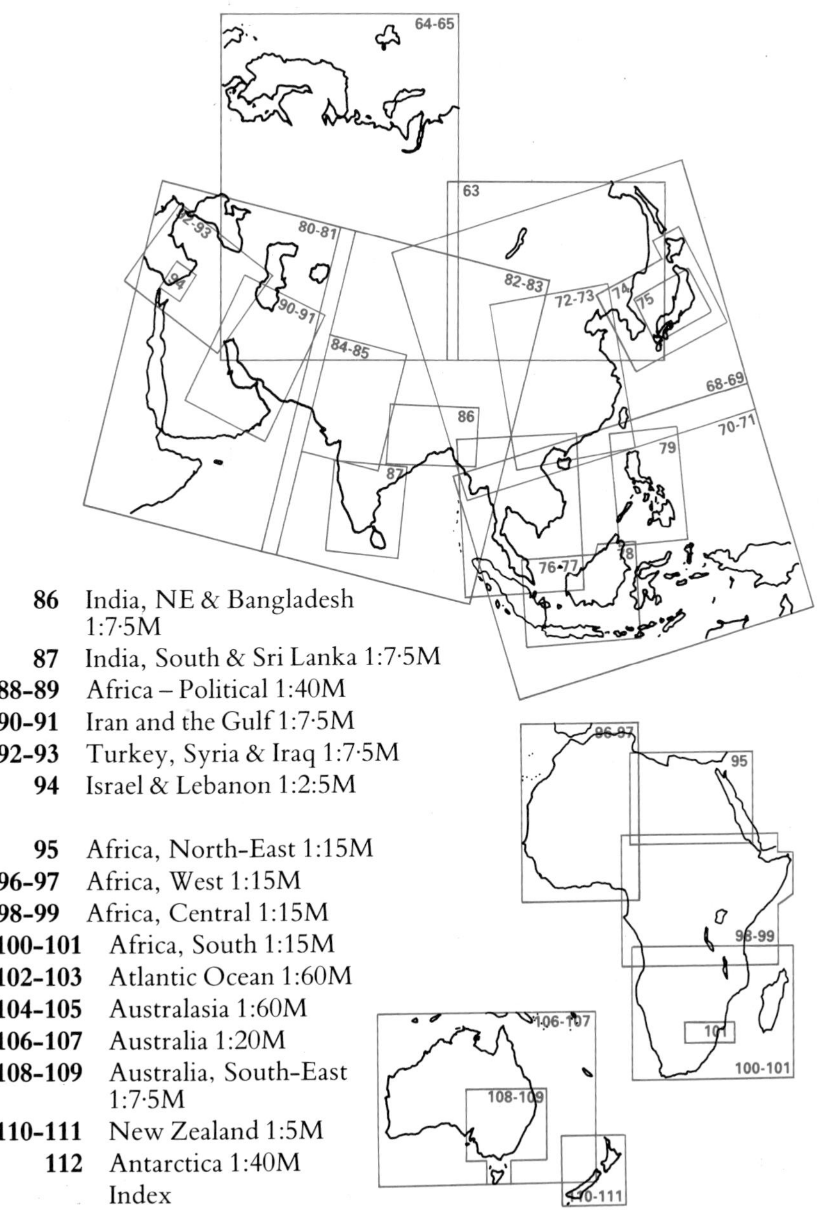
64-65
63
80-81
82-83
94
90-91
72-73
74
75
84-85
68-69
86
70-71
79
87
76-77
96-97
95
98-99
101
100-101
106-107
108-109
110-111

86 India, NE & Bangladesh 1:7·5M
87 India, South & Sri Lanka 1:7·5M
88-89 Africa – Political 1:40M
90-91 Iran and the Gulf 1:7·5M
92-93 Turkey, Syria & Iraq 1:7·5M
94 Israel & Lebanon 1:2:5M

95 Africa, North-East 1:15M
96-97 Africa, West 1:15M
98-99 Africa, Central 1:15M
100-101 Africa, South 1:15M
102-103 Atlantic Ocean 1:60M
104-105 Australasia 1:60M
106-107 Australia 1:20M
108-109 Australia, South-East 1:7·5M
110-111 New Zealand 1:5M
112 Antarctica 1:40M
Index

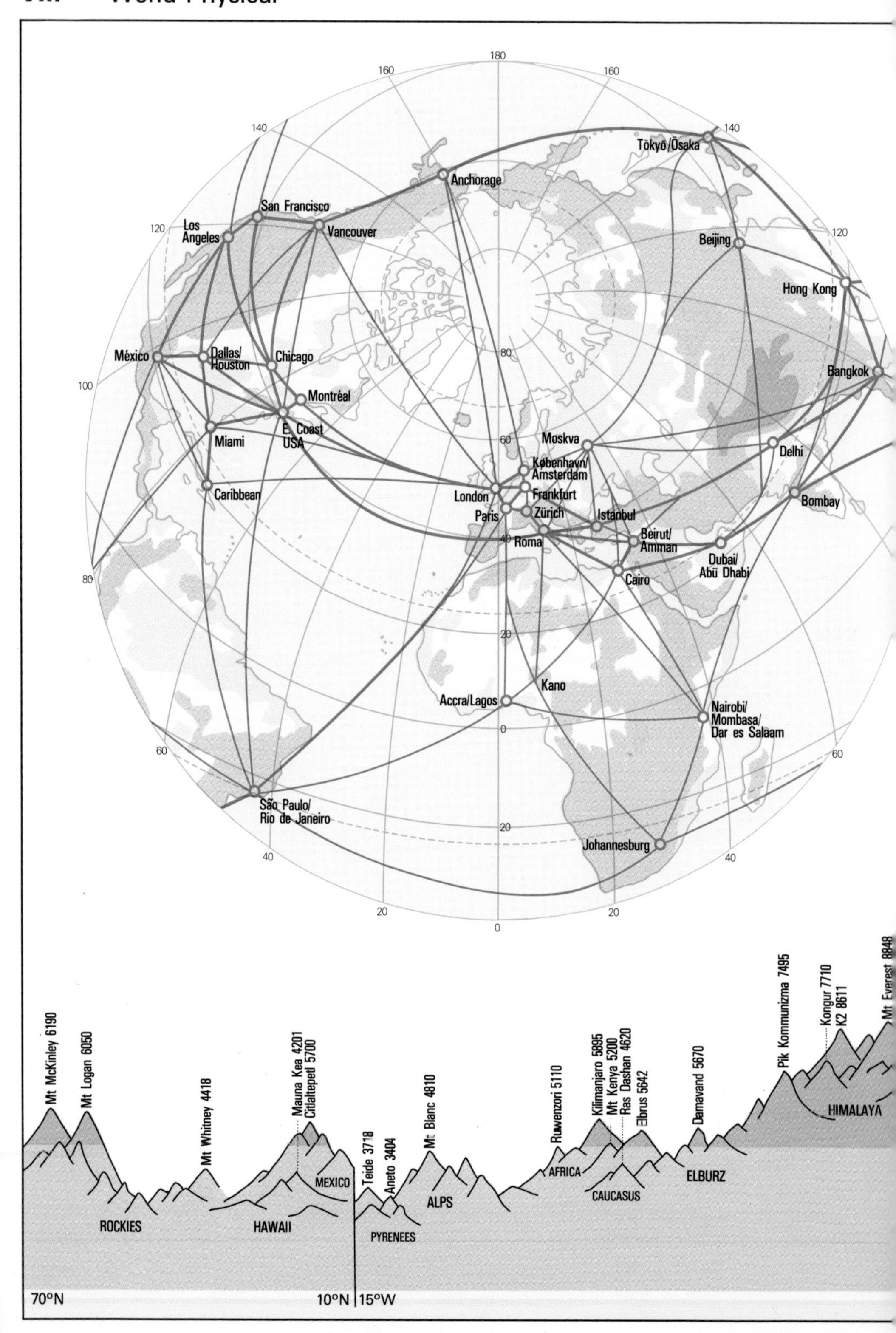
Anchorage
San Francisco
Los Angeles
Vancouver
Tōkyō/Ōsaka
Beijing
Hong Kong
Bangkok
México
Dallas/ Houston
Chicago
Montréal
E. Coast USA
Miami
Caribbean
Moskva
København/ Amsterdam
Frankfurt
London
Paris
Zürich
Roma
Istanbul
Beirut/ Amman
Dubai/ Abū Dhabi
Cairo
Delhi
Bombay
Kano
Accra/Lagos
Nairobi/ Mombasa/ Dar es Salaam
São Paulo/ Rio de Janeiro
Johannesburg
Mt McKinley 6190
Mt Logan 6050
Mt Whitney 4418
Mauna Kea 4201
Citlaltepetl 5700
Teide 3718
Aneto 3404
Mt Blanc 4810
Ruwenzori 5110
Kilimanjaro 5895
Mt Kenya 5200
Ras Dashan 4620
Elbrus 5642
Damavand 5670
Pik Kommunizma 7495
Kongur 7710
K2 8611
Mt Everest 8848
ROCKIES
HAWAII
MEXICO
PYRENEES
ALPS
AFRICA
CAUCASUS
ELBURZ
HIMALAYA
70°N
10°N
15°W

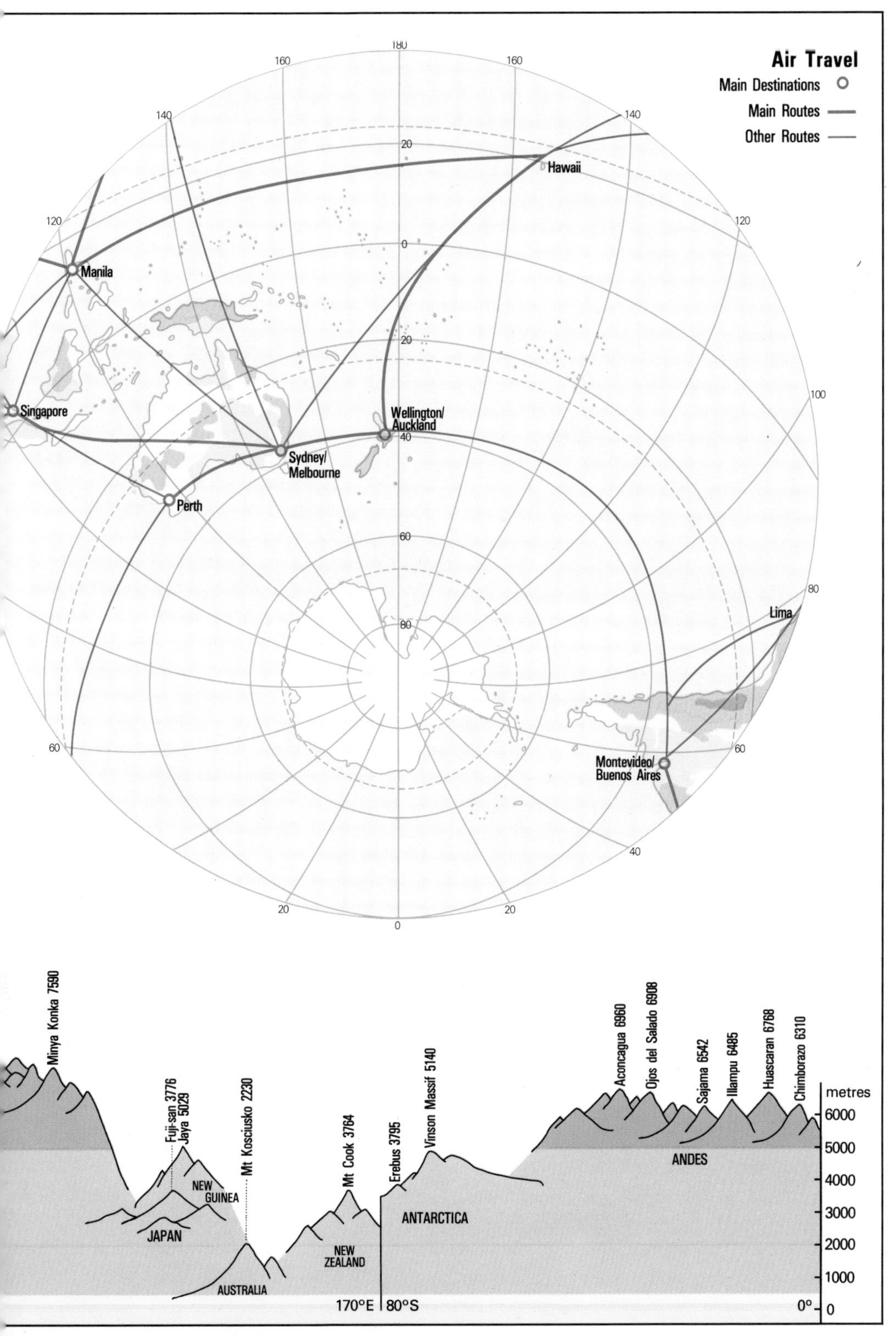
Air Travel
Main Destinations
Main Routes
Other Routes
Manila
Singapore
Sydney/
Melbourne
Perth
Wellington/
Auckland
Hawaii
Lima
Montevideo/
Buenos Aires
180
160
140
120
100
80
60
40
20
0
Minya Konka 7590
Fuji-san 3776
Jaya 5029
Mt Kosciusko 2230
Mt Cook 3764
Erebus 3795
Vinson Massif 5140
Aconcagua 6960
Ojos del Salado 6908
Sajama 6542
Illampu 6485
Huascaran 6768
Chimborazo 6310
NEW
GUINEA
JAPAN
AUSTRALIA
NEW
ZEALAND
ANTARCTICA
ANDES
metres
6000
5000
4000
3000
2000
1000
0
170°E
80°S
0°

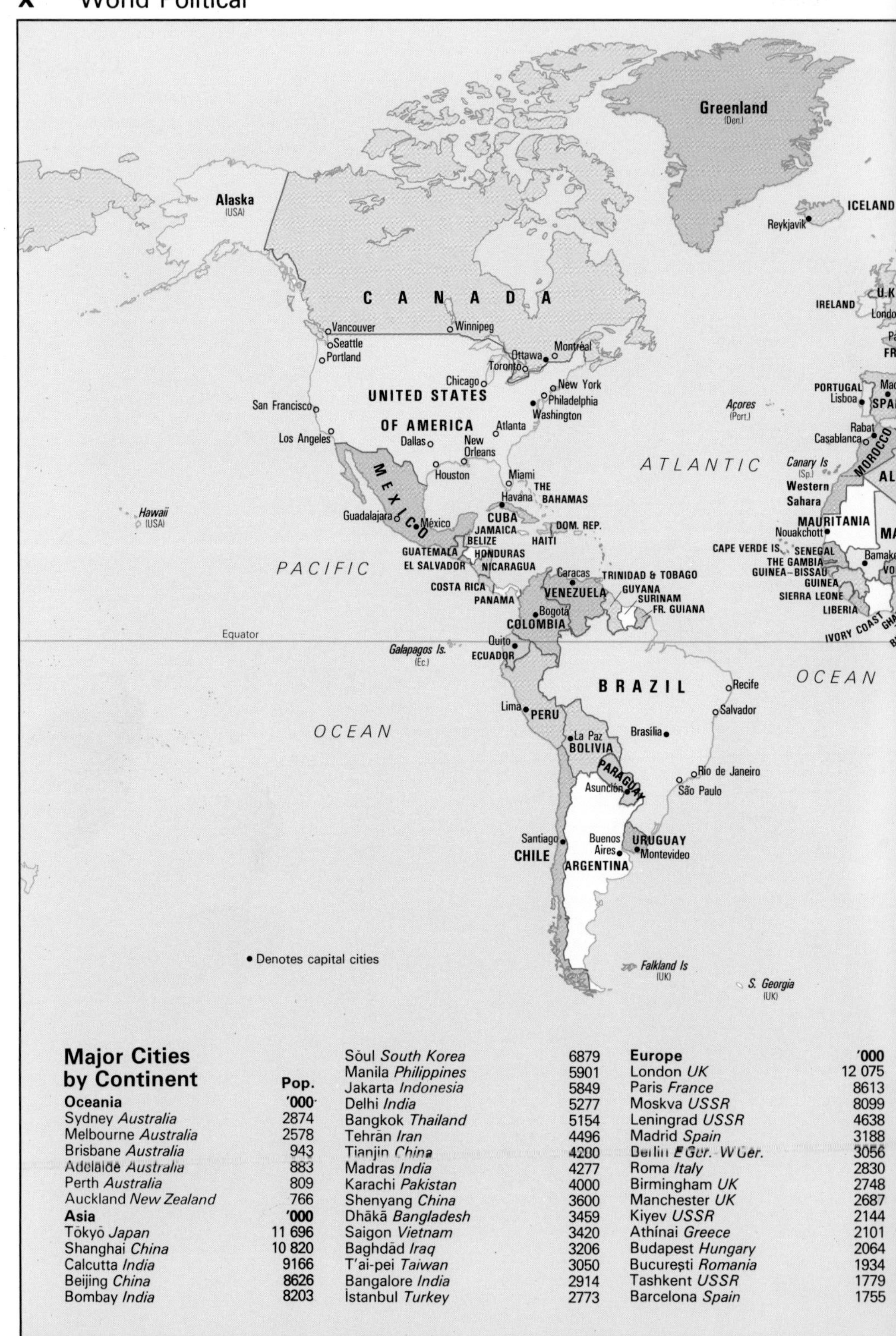

Major Cities by Continent

	Pop.
Oceania	**'000**
Sydney *Australia*	2874
Melbourne *Australia*	2578
Brisbane *Australia*	943
Adelaide *Australia*	883
Perth *Australia*	809
Auckland *New Zealand*	766
Asia	**'000**
Tōkyō *Japan*	11 696
Shanghai *China*	10 820
Calcutta *India*	9166
Beijing *China*	8626
Bombay *India*	8203
Sŏul *South Korea*	6879
Manila *Philippines*	5901
Jakarta *Indonesia*	5849
Delhi *India*	5277
Bangkok *Thailand*	5154
Tehrān *Iran*	4496
Tianjin *China*	4280
Madras *India*	4277
Karachi *Pakistan*	4000
Shenyang *China*	3600
Dhākā *Bangladesh*	3459
Saigon *Vietnam*	3420
Baghdād *Iraq*	3206
T'ai-pei *Taiwan*	3050
Bangalore *India*	2914
İstanbul *Turkey*	2773
Europe	**'000**
London *UK*	12 075
Paris *France*	8613
Moskva *USSR*	8099
Leningrad *USSR*	4638
Madrid *Spain*	3188
Berlin *E Ger.-W Ger.*	3056
Roma *Italy*	2830
Birmingham *UK*	2748
Manchester *UK*	2687
Kiyev *USSR*	2144
Athínai *Greece*	2101
Budapest *Hungary*	2064
București *Romania*	1934
Tashkent *USSR*	1779
Barcelona *Spain*	1755

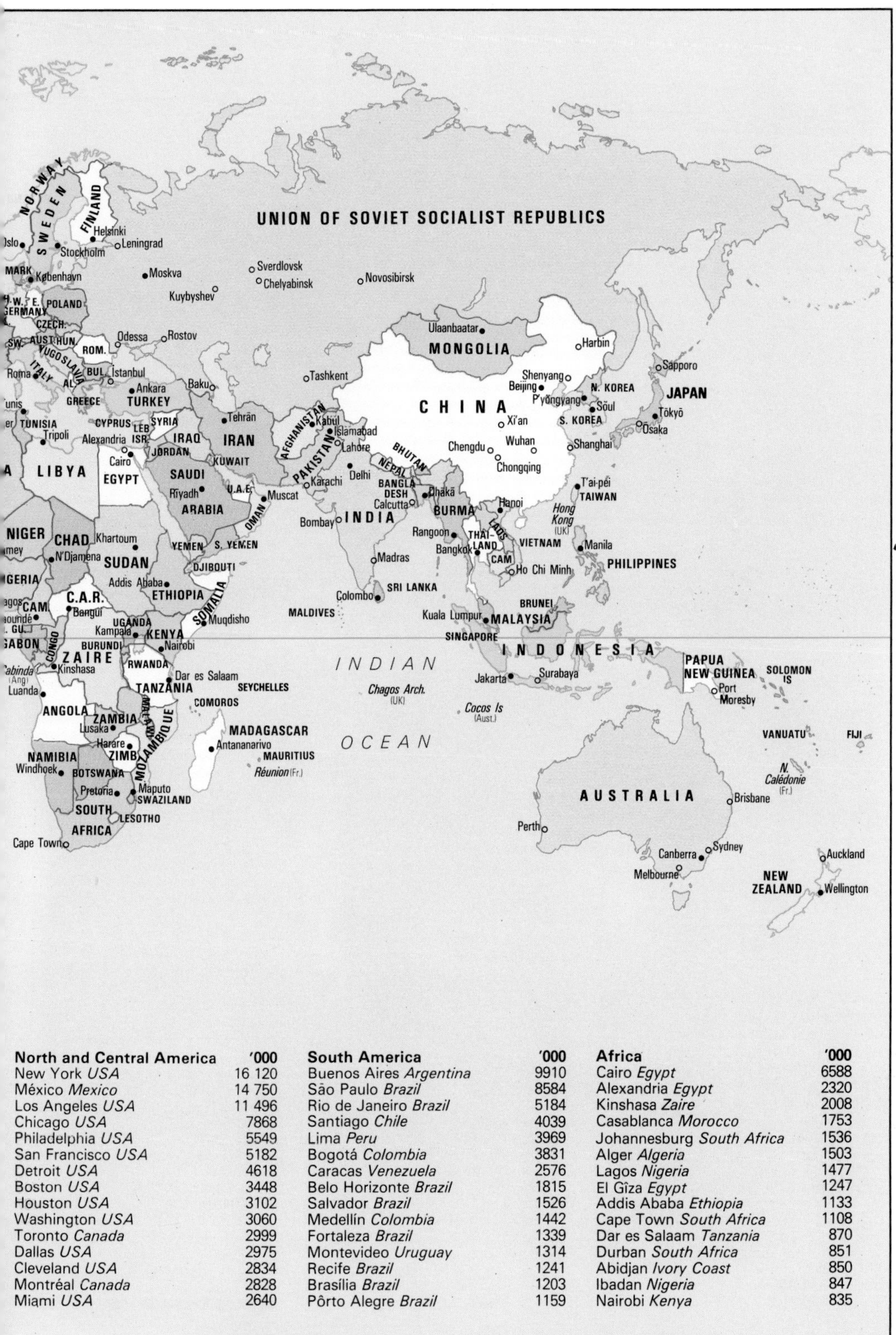

North and Central America	'000
New York *USA*	16 120
México *Mexico*	14 750
Los Angeles *USA*	11 496
Chicago *USA*	7868
Philadelphia *USA*	5549
San Francisco *USA*	5182
Detroit *USA*	4618
Boston *USA*	3448
Houston *USA*	3102
Washington *USA*	3060
Toronto *Canada*	2999
Dallas *USA*	2975
Cleveland *USA*	2834
Montréal *Canada*	2828
Miami *USA*	2640

South America	'000
Buenos Aires *Argentina*	9910
São Paulo *Brazil*	8584
Rio de Janeiro *Brazil*	5184
Santiago *Chile*	4039
Lima *Peru*	3969
Bogotá *Colombia*	3831
Caracas *Venezuela*	2576
Belo Horizonte *Brazil*	1815
Salvador *Brazil*	1526
Medellín *Colombia*	1442
Fortaleza *Brazil*	1339
Montevideo *Uruguay*	1314
Recife *Brazil*	1241
Brasília *Brazil*	1203
Pôrto Alegre *Brazil*	1159

Africa	'000
Cairo *Egypt*	6588
Alexandria *Egypt*	2320
Kinshasa *Zaire*	2008
Casablanca *Morocco*	1753
Johannesburg *South Africa*	1536
Alger *Algeria*	1503
Lagos *Nigeria*	1477
El Gîza *Egypt*	1247
Addis Ababa *Ethiopia*	1133
Cape Town *South Africa*	1108
Dar es Salaam *Tanzania*	870
Durban *South Africa*	851
Abidjan *Ivory Coast*	850
Ibadan *Nigeria*	847
Nairobi *Kenya*	835

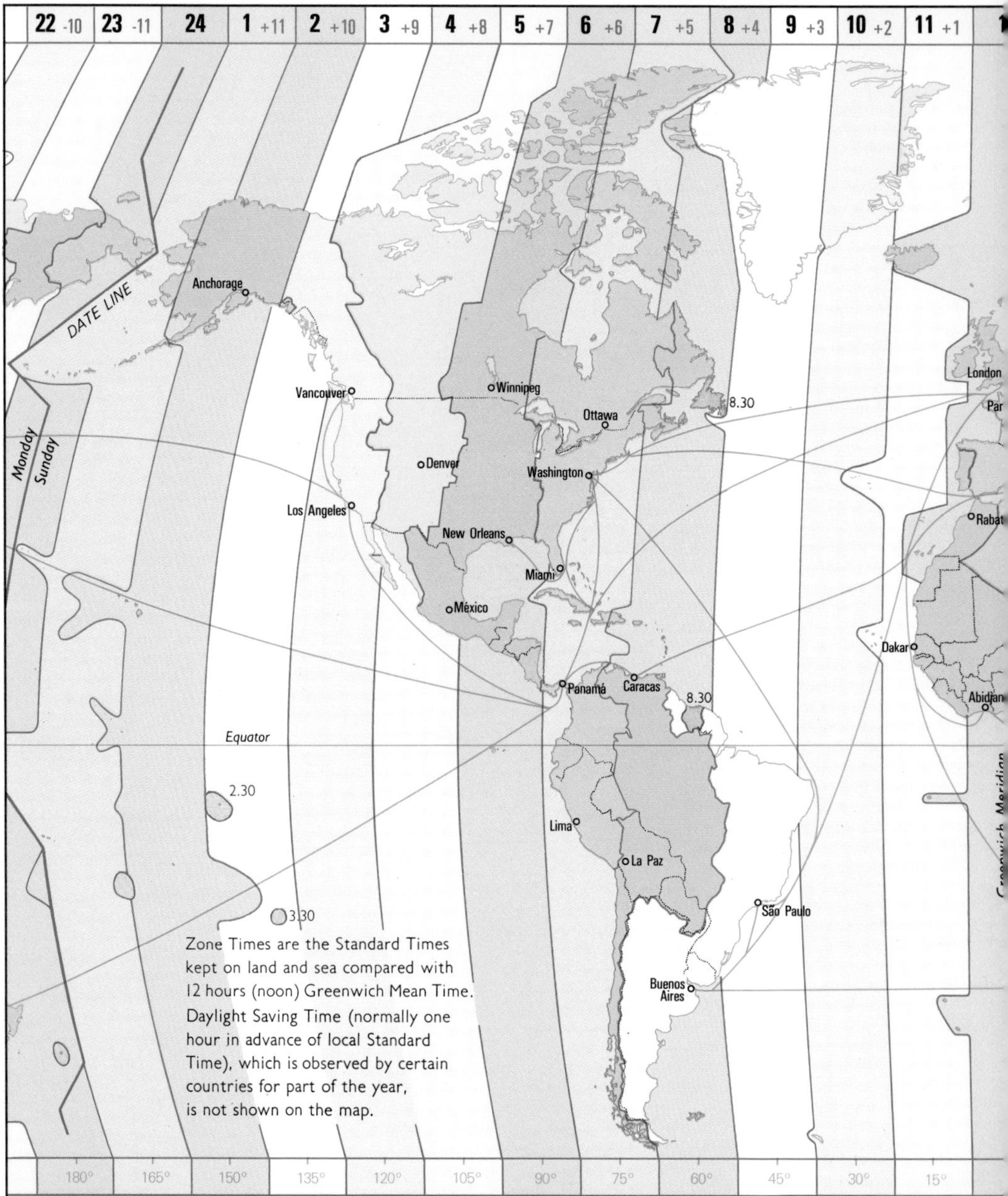

22 -10
23 -11
24
1 +11
2 +10
3 +9
4 +8
5 +7
6 +6
7 +5
8 +4
9 +3
10 +2
11 +1
DATE LINE
Monday
Sunday
Anchorage
Vancouver
Winnipeg
Ottawa
8.30
London
Denver
Washington
Los Angeles
New Orleans
Miami
México
Rabat
Dakar
Panamá
Caracas
8.30
Abidjan
Equator
2.30
Lima
La Paz
3.30
São Paulo
Buenos Aires
Greenwich Meridian
180°
165°
150°
135°
120°
105°
90°
75°
60°
45°
30°
15°

Zone Times are the Standard Times kept on land and sea compared with 12 hours (noon) Greenwich Mean Time. Daylight Saving Time (normally one hour in advance of local Standard Time), which is observed by certain countries for part of the year, is not shown on the map.

Journey Times

Sail (via Cape) 164 days

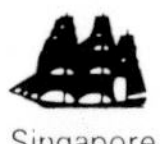

Steam (via Cape) 43 days

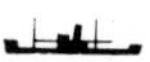

Steam (via Suez) 30 days

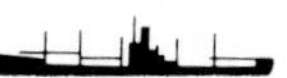

Supertanker (via Cape) 28 days

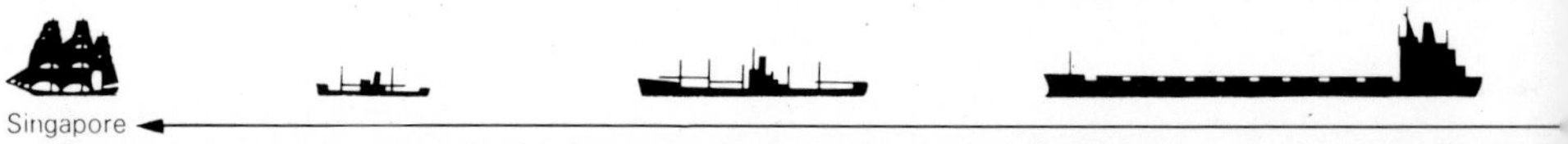

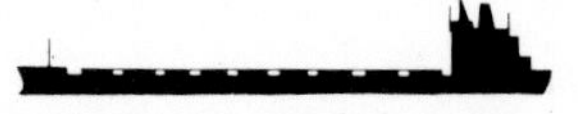

Singapore

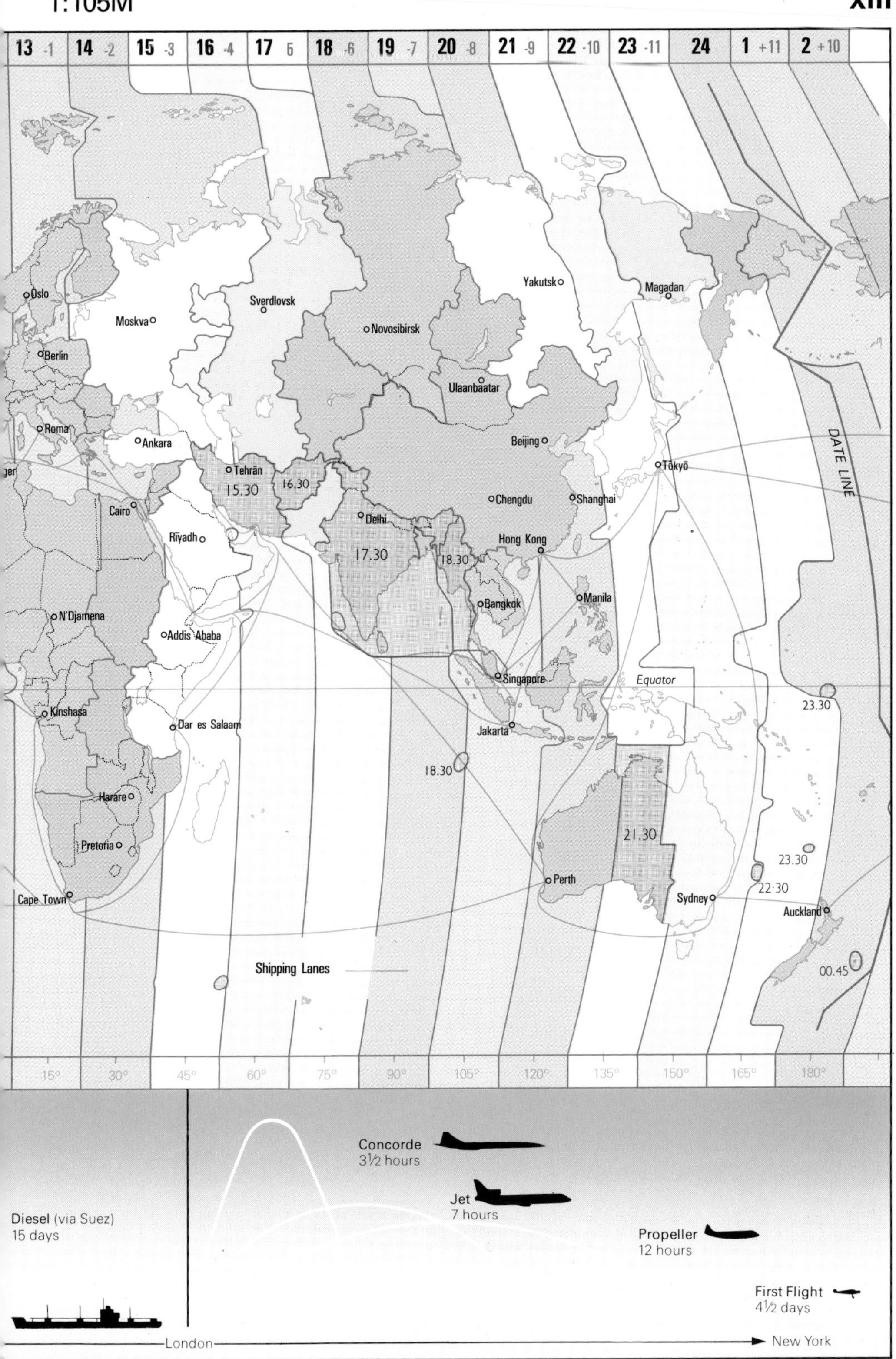
13 -1
14 -2
15 -3
16 -4
17 -5
18 -6
19 -7
20 -8
21 -9
22 -10
23 -11
24
1 +11
2 +10
Oslo
Moskva
Sverdlovsk
Novosibirsk
Yakutsk
Magadan
Berlin
Ulaanbaatar
Roma
Ankara
Beijing
Tokyo
DATE LINE
Tehrān
15.30
16.30
Cairo
Chengdu
Shanghai
Delhi
Riyadh
Hong Kong
17.30
18.30
Bangkok
Manila
N'Djamena
Addis Ababa
Singapore
Equator
23.30
Kinshasa
Dar es Salaam
Jakarta
18.30
Harare
21.30
Pretoria
23.30
Perth
22.30
Cape Town
Sydney
Auckland
Shipping Lanes
00.45
15°
30°
45°
60°
75°
90°
105°
120°
135°
150°
165°
180°
Concorde
3½ hours
Jet
7 hours
Diesel (via Suez)
15 days
Propeller
12 hours
First Flight
4½ days
London
New York

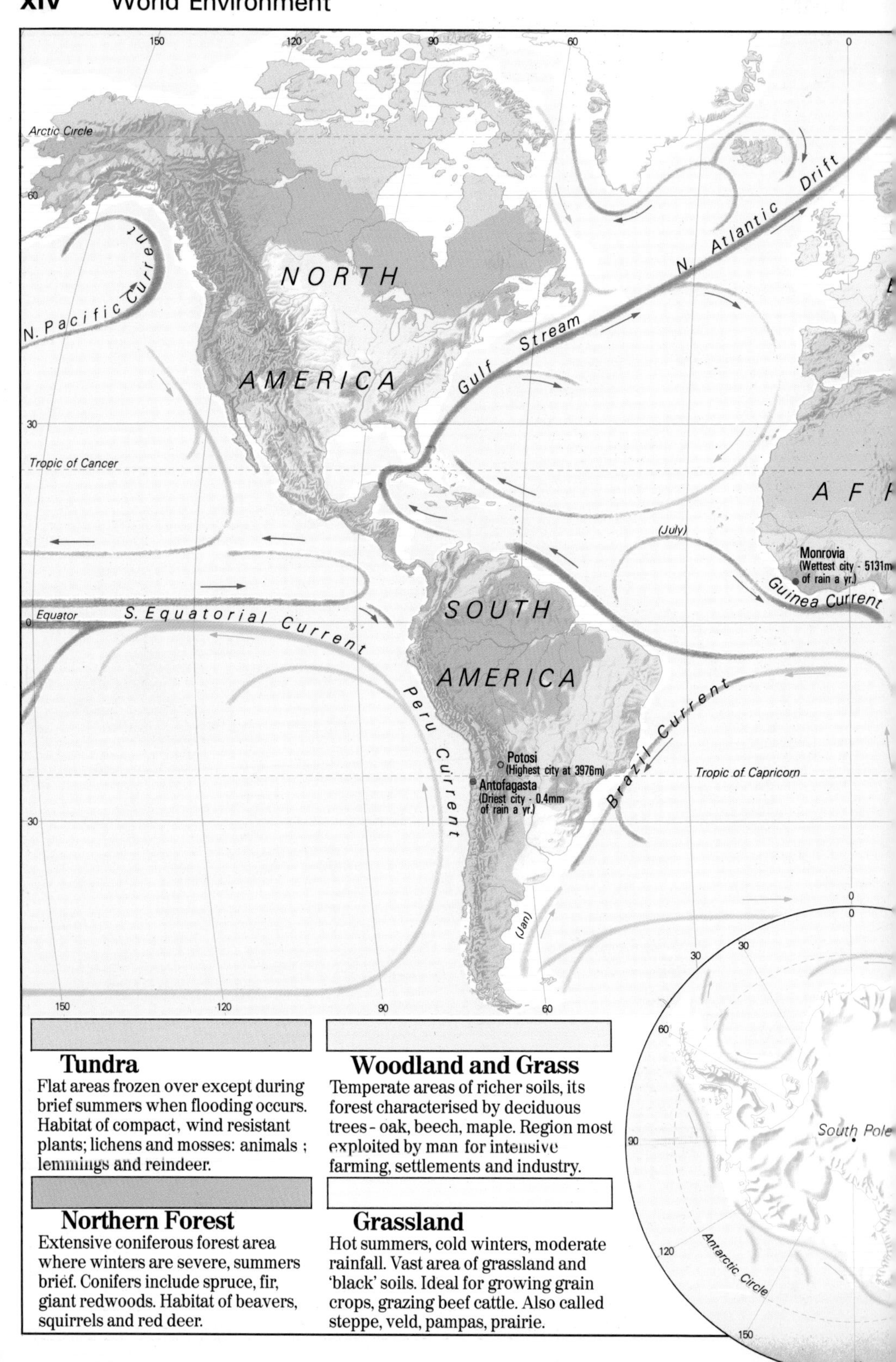

Arctic Circle
Tropic of Cancer
Equator
Tropic of Capricorn
Antarctic Circle
NORTH AMERICA
SOUTH AMERICA
A F
N. Pacific Current
N. Atlantic Drift
Gulf Stream
S. Equatorial Current
Peru Current
Brazil Current
Guinea Current
(July)
(Jan)
Monrovia
(Wettest city - 5131mm of rain a yr.)
Potosi
(Highest city at 3976m)
Antofagasta
(Driest city - 0.4mm of rain a yr.)
South Pole
Tundra
Flat areas frozen over except during brief summers when flooding occurs. Habitat of compact, wind resistant plants; lichens and mosses: animals ; lemmings and reindeer.
Woodland and Grass
Temperate areas of richer soils, its forest characterised by deciduous trees - oak, beech, maple. Region most exploited by man for intensive farming, settlements and industry.
Northern Forest
Extensive coniferous forest area where winters are severe, summers brief. Conifers include spruce, fir, giant redwoods. Habitat of beavers, squirrels and red deer.
Grassland
Hot summers, cold winters, moderate rainfall. Vast area of grassland and 'black' soils. Ideal for growing grain crops, grazing beef cattle. Also called steppe, veld, pampas, prairie.

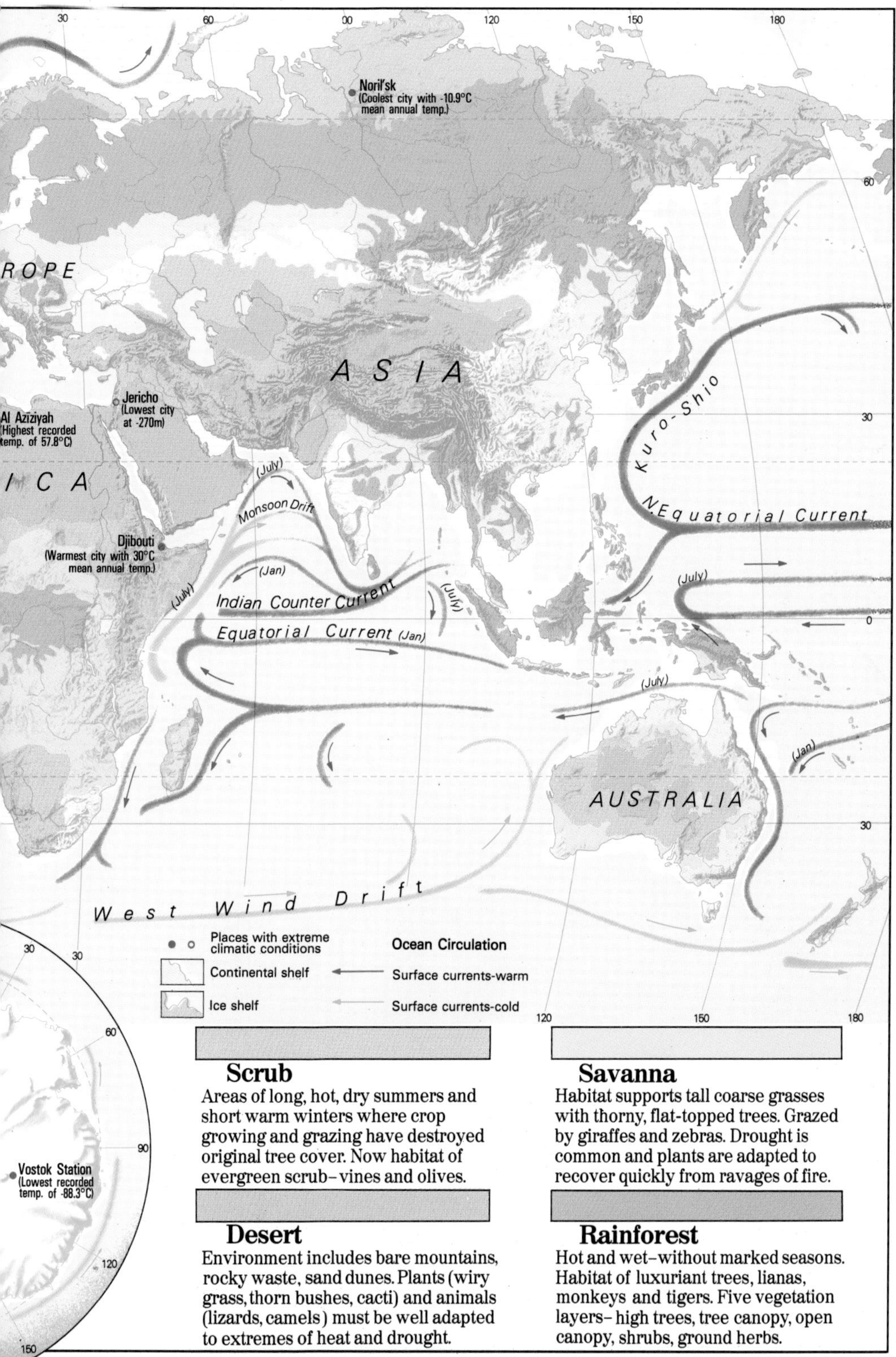

Scrub

Areas of long, hot, dry summers and short warm winters where crop growing and grazing have destroyed original tree cover. Now habitat of evergreen scrub–vines and olives.

Desert

Environment includes bare mountains, rocky waste, sand dunes. Plants (wiry grass, thorn bushes, cacti) and animals (lizards, camels) must be well adapted to extremes of heat and drought.

Savanna

Habitat supports tall coarse grasses with thorny, flat-topped trees. Grazed by giraffes and zebras. Drought is common and plants are adapted to recover quickly from ravages of fire.

Rainforest

Hot and wet–without marked seasons. Habitat of luxuriant trees, lianas, monkeys and tigers. Five vegetation layers– high trees, tree canopy, open canopy, shrubs, ground herbs.

BOUNDARIES

International
International under Dispute
Cease Fire Line
Autonomous or State/ Administrative
Maritime (National)
International Date Line

COMMUNICATIONS

Motorway/Under Construction
Major/Other Road
Under Construction
Track
Road Tunnel
Car Ferry
Main/Other Railway
Under Construction
Rail Ferry
Rail Tunnel
Canal
International/Other Airport

LANDSCAPE FEATURES

Glacier, Ice Cap
Marsh, Swamp
Sand Desert, Dunes
Freshwater
Saltwater
Seasonal
Salt Pan

OTHER FEATURES

River/Seasonal
Pass, Gorge
Dam, Barrage
Waterfall, Rapid
Aqueduct
Reef
.217 ▲4231 Spot Height, Depth/ Summit, Peak
Well
Oil/Gas Field
Gas / Oil — Oil/Natural Gas Pipeline
Gemsbok Nat. Pk — National Park
∴UR — Historic Site

LETTERING STYLES

CANADA	Independent Nation
FLORIDA	State, Province or Autonomous Region
Gibraltar (U.K.)	Sovereignty of Dependent Territory
Lothian	Administrative Area
LANGUEDOC	Historic Region
Loire *Vosges*	Physical Feature or Physical Region

TOWNS AND CITIES

Square symbols denote capital cities — *Population*

■ ●	**New York**	over 5 000 000
■ ●	**Montréal**	over 1 000 000
□ ○	Ottawa	over 500 000
■ ●	Québec	over 100 000
□ ○	St John's	over 50 000
□ ○	Yorkton	over 10 000
□ ○	Jasper	under 10 000

Built-up-area

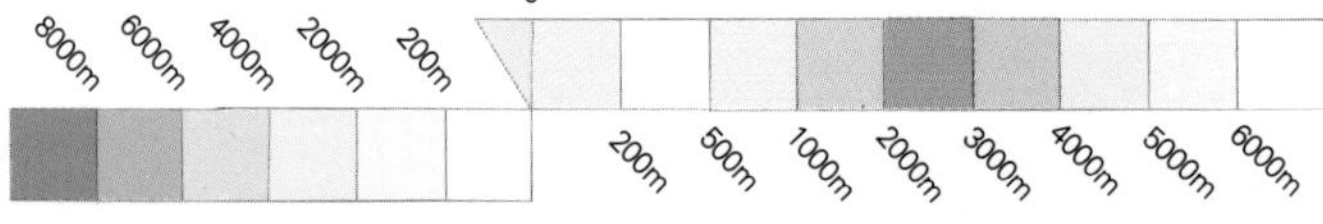

ARCTIC OCEAN
North Pole
Chukchi Sea
E. Siberian Sea
Laptev Sea
Kara Sea
Barents Sea
Greenland Sea
Norwegian Sea
Beaufort Sea
Lincoln Sea
Baffin Bay
Hudson Bay
Foxe Basin
Davis Str.
Hudson Str.
Denmark Strait
ATLANTIC OCEAN
Arctic Circle
Tree Limit
average minimum extent of sea ice
Novaya Zemlya
Severnaya Zemlya
Novosibirskiye Ostrova
O. Vrangelya
Zemlya Frantsa Iosifa
Svalbard (Spitsbergen) (Nor.)
Bjørnøya (Bear I.) (Nor.)
Jan Mayen (Nor.)
Nordkapp
Greenland (Den.)
ICELAND
Reykjavik
Queen Elizabeth Islands
Ellesmere I.
Banks I.
Victoria I.
Baffin I.
Southampton I.
N. Magnetic Pole (1980)
Alaska (U.S.A.)
Mt McKinley 6194
CANADA
ROCKY MTS
U.S.S.R.
CHINA
FINLAND
SWEDEN
NORWAY
Newfoundland
Uralskiy Khrebet
Gt Bear L.
Gt Slave L.
L. Athabasca
L. Winnipeg
James B.
Gulf of St Lawrence
Watkins Bjerge 3700
K. Farvel
Seattle
Vancouver
Calgary
Edmonton
Saskatoon
Prince Rupert
Juneau
Dawson
Fairbanks
Prudhoe Bay
Barrow
Teller
Inuvik
Norman Wells
Yellowknife
Coppermine
Resolute
Eureka
Alert
Thule
Pond Inlet
Upernavik
Godhavn
Søndre Strømfjord
Godthåb
Julianehåb
Angmagssalik
Scoresbysund
Nord
Churchill
Flin Flon
Inukjuac
Fort George
Schefferville
Hebron
Nain
Gander
Pevek
Vankarem
Ambarchik
Polyarnyy
Kazach'ye
Tiksi
Ust'Nera
Verkhoyansk
Zhigansk
Yakutsk
Aldan
Skovorodino
Chul'man
Blagoveshchensk
Chita
Ust'Kut
Oz. Baykal
Krasnoyarsk
Novosibirsk
Omsk
Tobol'sk
Sverdlovsk
Magnitogorsk
Orsk
Aktyubinsk
Perm'
Ufa
Kuybyshev
Serov
Kazan'
Gor'kiy
Kirov
Yaroslavl'
Syktyvkar
Kotlas
Berezovo
Nadym
Salekhard
Vorkuta
Turukhansk
Dudinka
Noril'sk
Khatanga
Nordvik
Dikson
Mezen'
Arkhangel'sk
Murmansk
Leningrad
Oulu
Umeå
Tromsø
Narvik
Lena
Yenisey
Ob'
Irtysh
Kolyma
Indigirka
Amur
Mackenzie
Yukon
Sev. Dvina
G. of Boothia
McClure Str.
Nares Str.
Bering

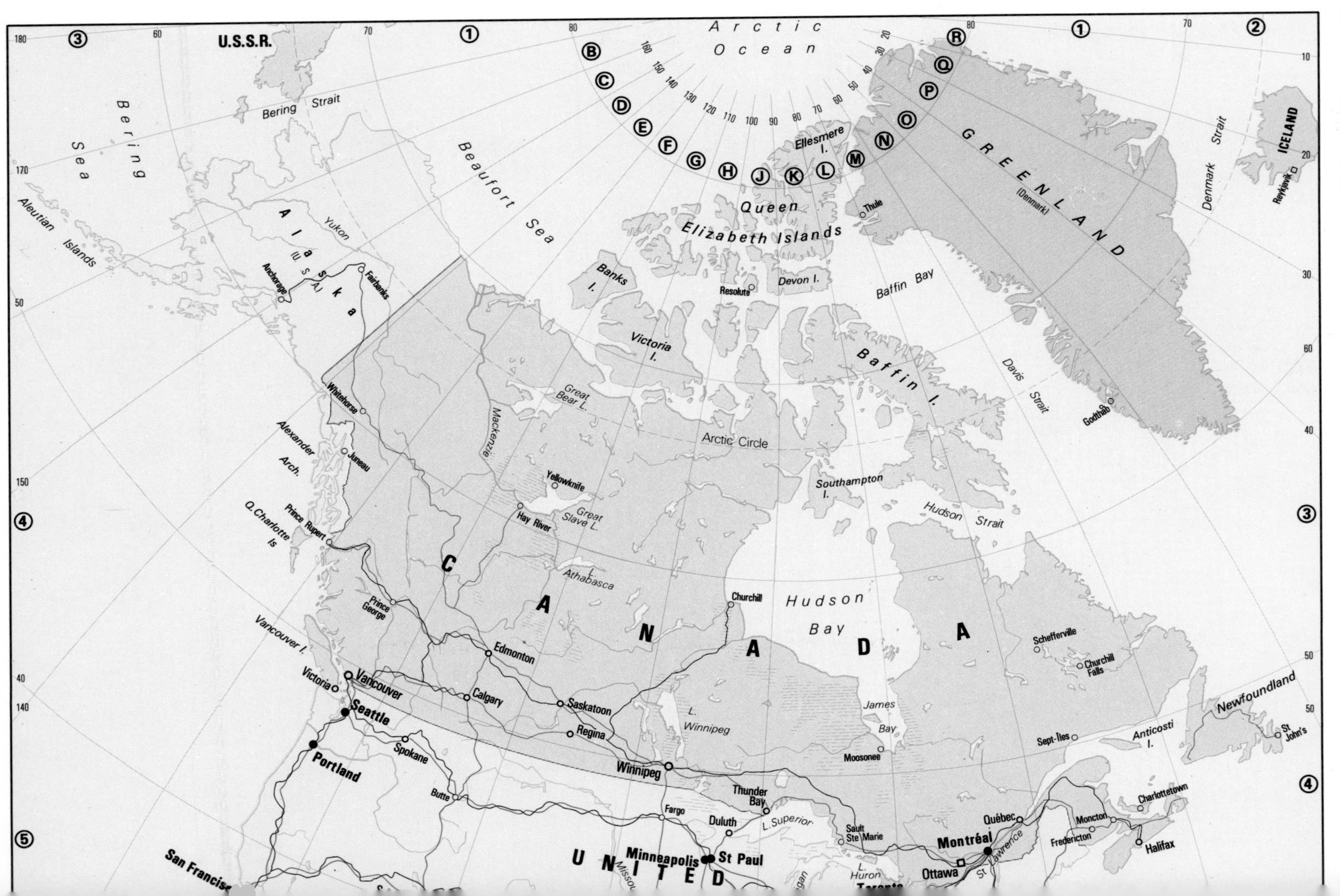
U.S.S.R.
Arctic Ocean
Bering Strait
Bering Sea
Aleutian Islands
Alaska
(U. S. A.)
Yukon
Anchorage
Fairbanks
Beaufort Sea
Queen Elizabeth Islands
Ellesmere I.
Banks I.
Resolute
Devon I.
Baffin Bay
Thule
GREENLAND
(Denmark)
Denmark Strait
ICELAND
Reykjavik
Victoria I.
Baffin I.
Davis Strait
Godthab
Whitehorse
Great Bear L.
Mackenzie
Arctic Circle
Alexander Arch.
Juneau
Yellowknife
Southampton I.
Hay River
Great Slave L.
Hudson Strait
Prince Rupert
Q. Charlotte Is
CANADA
L. Athabasca
Churchill
Hudson Bay
Prince George
Edmonton
Schefferville
Churchill Falls
Vancouver I.
Victoria
Vancouver
Calgary
Saskatoon
L. Winnipeg
James Bay
Newfoundland
St John's
Seattle
Regina
Sept-Îles
Anticosti I.
Portland
Spokane
Winnipeg
Moosonee
Thunder Bay
Butte
Fargo
Duluth
L. Superior
Sault Ste Marie
Québec
Charlottetown
Moncton
Fredericton
Halifax
Montréal
St Lawrence
Ottawa
L. Huron
San Francisco
UNITED
Minneapolis
St Paul
Missou

1:35M

0 250 500 750 1000 1250 km

0 250 500 750 mls

ATLANTIC OCEAN

Bermuda (U.K.)

UNITED STATES OF AMERICA

New York
Philadelphia
Washington
Baltimore
Norfolk
Cleveland
Detroit
Indianapolis
Charleston
Jacksonville
Miami
Atlanta
Nashville
Ohio
Memphis
Birmingham
St Louis
Mississippi
New Orleans
Kansas City
Dallas
Houston
Fort Worth
San Antonio
Tampa
Denver
Albuquerque
El Paso
Colorado
Phoenix
Tucson
Los Angeles
San Diego

Rio Grande

MEXICO

Chihuahua
Monterrey
Torreón
Tampico
Veracruz
México
Guadalajara
Mazatlán
Acapulco
Mérida

G. de California
Guadalupe (Mex.)
Is Revilla Gigedo (Mex.)
Clipperton (Fr.)

Gulf of Mexico

THE BAHAMAS
Nassau
CUBA
Habana
Guantánamo
HAITI
Port-au-Prince
DOMINICAN REP.
Sto Domingo
Pto Rico (U.S.A.)
JAMAICA
Kingston

DOMINICA
ST LUCIA
BARBADOS
ST VINCENT
GRENADA
TRINIDAD & TOBAGO
Netherlands Antilles

CARIBBEAN SEA

BELIZE
Belmopan
GUATEMALA
Guatemala
S.Salvador
EL SALVADOR
HONDURAS
Tegucigalpa
NICARAGUA
Managua
COSTA RICA
S.José
PANAMA
Panamá

VENEZUELA
Caracas
Maracaibo
COLOMBIA
Bogotá
Medellín
Barranquilla
Sta Marta
ECUADOR
Quito
PERU
BRAZIL
Negro

Malpelo (Col.)
I.del Coco (C.R)
Galapagos Is (Ecu.)

PACIFIC OCEAN

Tropic of Cancer
Equator

30 20 10 0
130 120 110 100 90 80 70 60

G H J K L M
5 6 7 8

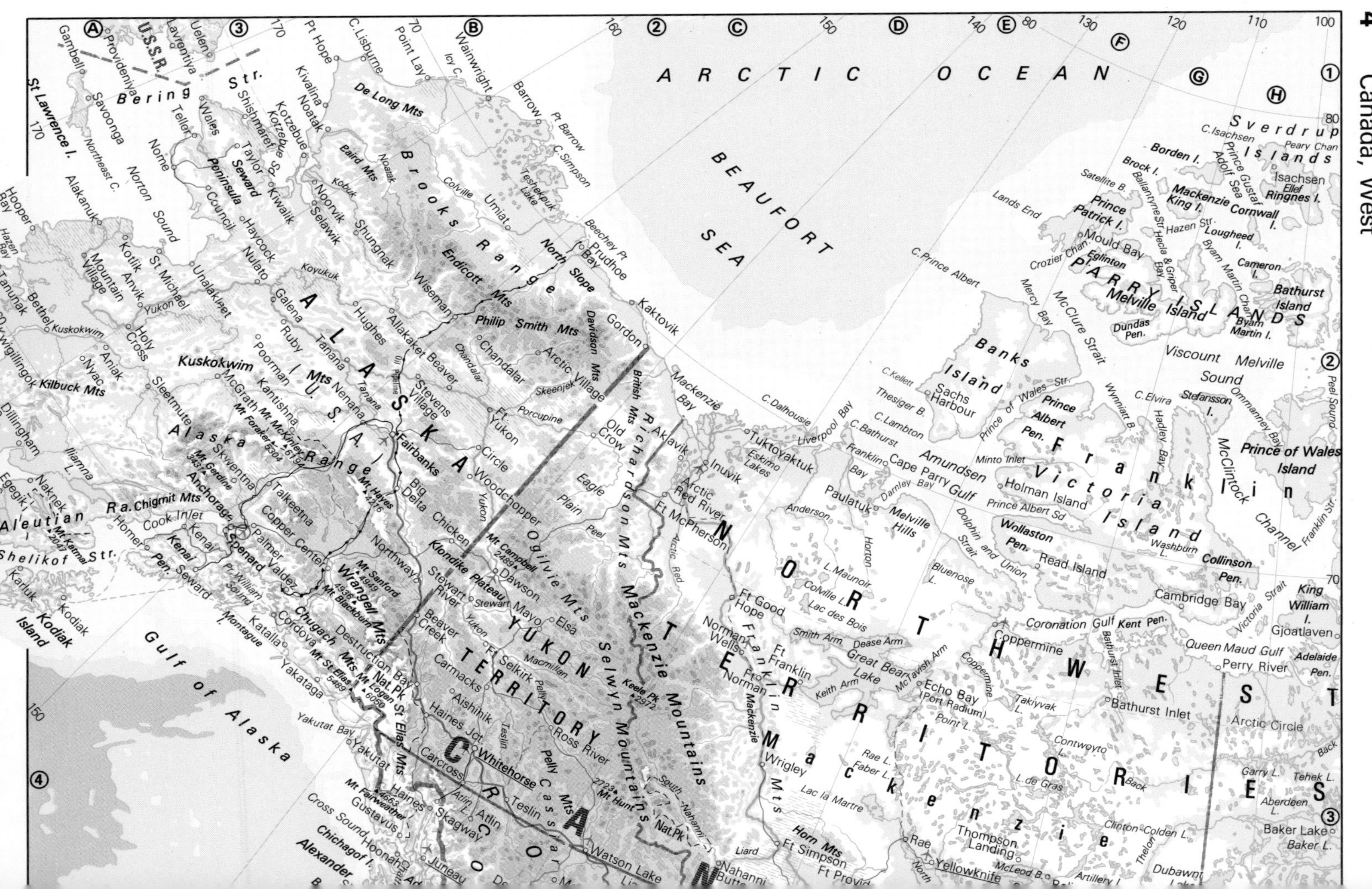
ARCTIC OCEAN
BEAUFORT SEA
Sverdrup Islands
PARRY ISLANDS
Prince of Wales Island
Victoria Island
Banks Island
Melville Island
Prince Patrick I.
Bathurst Island
Cornwall I.
Ellef Ringnes I.
Mackenzie King I.
Borden I.
Brock I.
Lougheed I.
Cameron I.
Byam Martin I.
Isachsen
Mould Bay
Sachs Harbour
Holman Island
McClure Strait
Viscount Melville Sound
McClintock Channel
Amundsen Gulf
Dolphin and Union Strait
Coronation Gulf
Queen Maud Gulf
Bathurst Inlet
Cambridge Bay
Gjoatlaven
Perry River
Arctic Circle
Baker Lake
NORTHWEST TERRITORIES
Mackenzie
Franklin
Great Bear Lake
Coppermine
Echo Bay (Port Radium)
Paulatuk
Tuktoyaktuk
Inuvik
Aklavik
Arctic Red River
Ft McPherson
Ft Good Hope
Norman Wells
Ft Norman
Ft Franklin
Wrigley
Ft Simpson
Rae
Yellowknife
Mackenzie Mountains
Richardson Mts
Selwyn Mountains
Keele Pk 2972
Mt Hunt 2723
Ogilvie Mts
Mt Campbell 2489
YUKON TERRITORY
Dawson
Mayo
Elsa
Ross River
Ft Selkirk
Carmacks
Whitehorse
Teslin
Watson Lake
Haines Jct.
Beaver Creek
Old Crow
Eagle Plain
Klondike Plateau
St Elias Mts
Mt Logan 6050
Mt St Elias 5489
Cassiar Mts
Pelly Mts
Carcross
Atlin
Skagway
Haines
Juneau
Yakutat
Mt Fairweather 4663
Gustavus
Hoonah
Chichagof I.
Alexander
Cross Sound
Gulf of Alaska
ALASKA
U.S.A.
U.S.S.R.
Brooks Range
North Slope
British Mts
Davidson Mts
Philip Smith Mts
Endicott Mts
De Long Mts
Baird Mts
Barrow
Pt Barrow
Teshekpuk Lake
Prudhoe Bay
Kaktovik
Umiat
Wainwright
Point Lay
C. Lisburne
Pt Hope
Kivalina
Noatak
Kotzebue
Kotzebue Sd
Noorvik
Selawik
Shungnak
Kiwalik
Shishmaref
Taylor
Seward Peninsula
Council
Wales
Teller
Nome
Norton Sound
Bering Str.
Uelen
Lavrentiya
Provideniya
Gambell
Savoonga
Northeast C.
St Lawrence I.
Unalakleet
St Michael
Kotlik
Alakanuk
Mountain Village
Anvik
Holy Cross
Aniak
Nyac
Bethel
Tununak
Hooper Bay
Hazen Bay
Kwigillingok
Kilbuck Mts
Dillingham
Iliamna L.
Naknek
Egegik
Mt Katmai 2047
Aleutian Ra.
Shelikof Str.
Kodiak Island
Kodiak
Karluk
Cook Inlet
Kenai Pen.
Kenai
Homer
Seward
Chigmit Mts
Anchorage
Spenard
Palmer
Valdez
Cordova
Katalla
Yakataga
Chugach Mts
Wrangell Mts
Mt Sanford 4949
Mt Blackburn 4936
Copper Center
Talkeetna
Skwentna
Alaska Range
Mt McKinley 6194
Mt Foraker 5304
Mt Gerdine 3431
Mt Hayes 4216
McGrath
Kantishna
Poorman
Ruby
Galena
Nulato
Haycock
Tanana
Nenana
Fairbanks
Big Delta
Chicken
Northway
Hughes
Allakaket
Wiseman
Stevens Village
Beaver
Chandalar
Ft Yukon
Circle
Woodchopper
Arctic Village
Kuskokwim Mts
Sleetmute
Oil Pipeline
Destruction Bay
Yakutat Bay
Montague I.
Pt William Sound

1:15M 0 200 400 600 km 0 100 200 300 mls

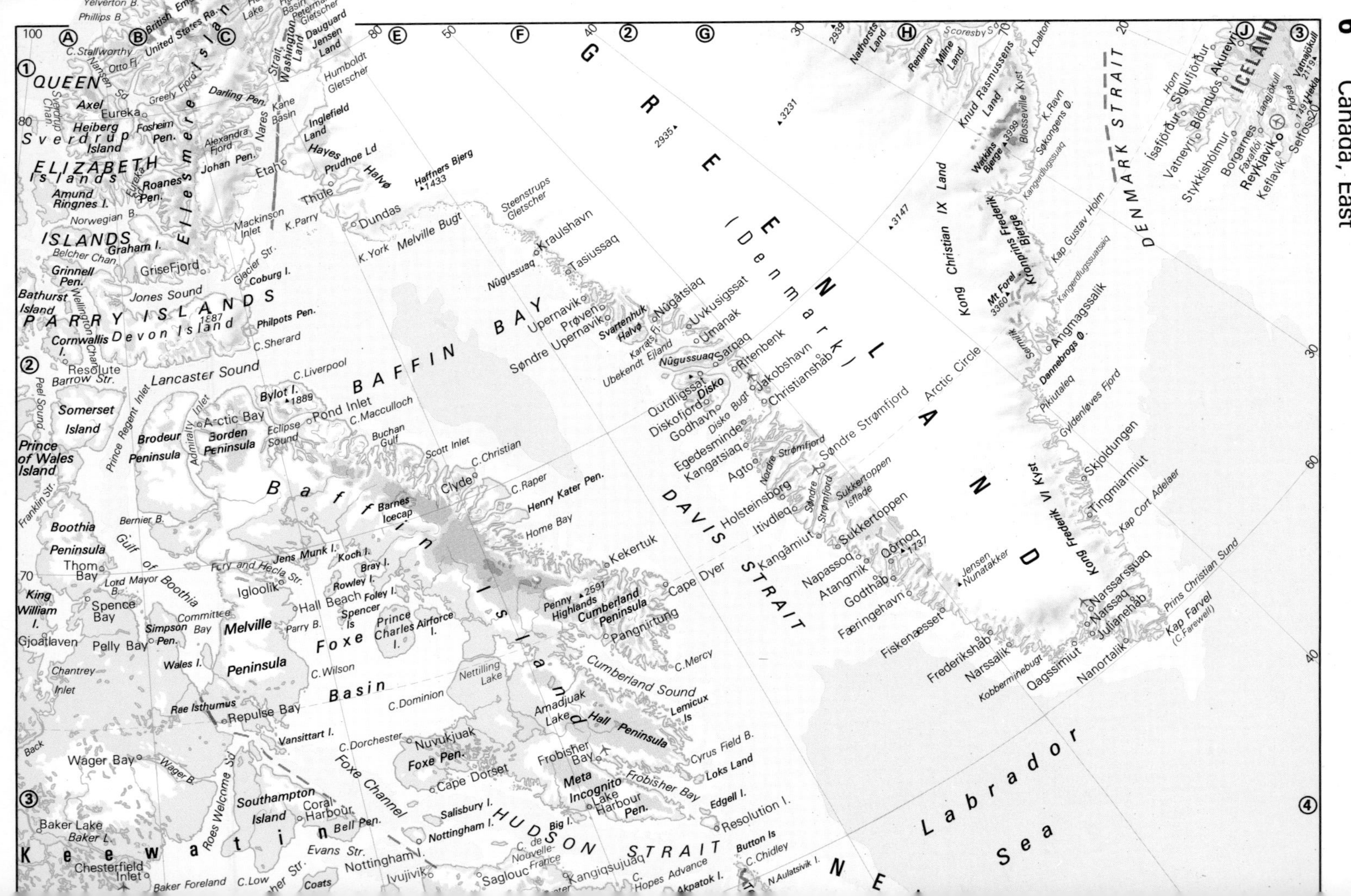
GREENLAND (Denmark)
BAFFIN BAY
DAVIS STRAIT
DENMARK STRAIT
ICELAND
Labrador Sea
HUDSON STRAIT
Baffin Island
Foxe Basin
Foxe Channel
Keewatin
QUEEN ELIZABETH ISLANDS
PARRY ISLANDS
Sverdrup Islands
Ellesmere Island
Devon Island
Lancaster Sound
Jones Sound
Cumberland Sound
Frobisher Bay
Melville Peninsula
Southampton Island
Boothia Peninsula
Gulf of Boothia
Somerset Island
Prince of Wales Island
Bathurst Island
Cornwallis I.
Axel Heiberg Island
Amund Ringnes I.
Graham I.
Bylot I.
Borden Peninsula
Brodeur Peninsula
Cumberland Peninsula
Hall Peninsula
Meta Incognito Pen.
Foxe Pen.
Resolution I.
Thule
Dundas
Melville Bugt
Upernavik
Umanak
Jakobshavn
Christianshåb
Godthåb
Sukkertoppen
Holsteinsborg
Frederikshåb
Julianehåb
Nanortalik
Angmagssalik
Kap Farvel (C. Farewell)
Reykjavík
Akureyri
Keflavík
Ísafjörður
Resolute
Grise Fiord
Pond Inlet
Arctic Bay
Clyde
Igloolik
Hall Beach
Repulse Bay
Coral Harbour
Chesterfield Inlet
Baker Lake
Wager Bay
Frobisher Bay
Pangnirtung
Cape Dorset
Cape Dyer
Arctic Circle
Kong Christian IX Land
Kong Frederik VI Kyst
Knud Rasmussens Land
Kronprins Frederik Bjerge
Watkins Bjerge
Prudhoe Ld
Inglefield Land
Washington Land
Nares Str.
Kane Basin
Barnes Icecap
Nettilling Lake
Amadjuak Lake

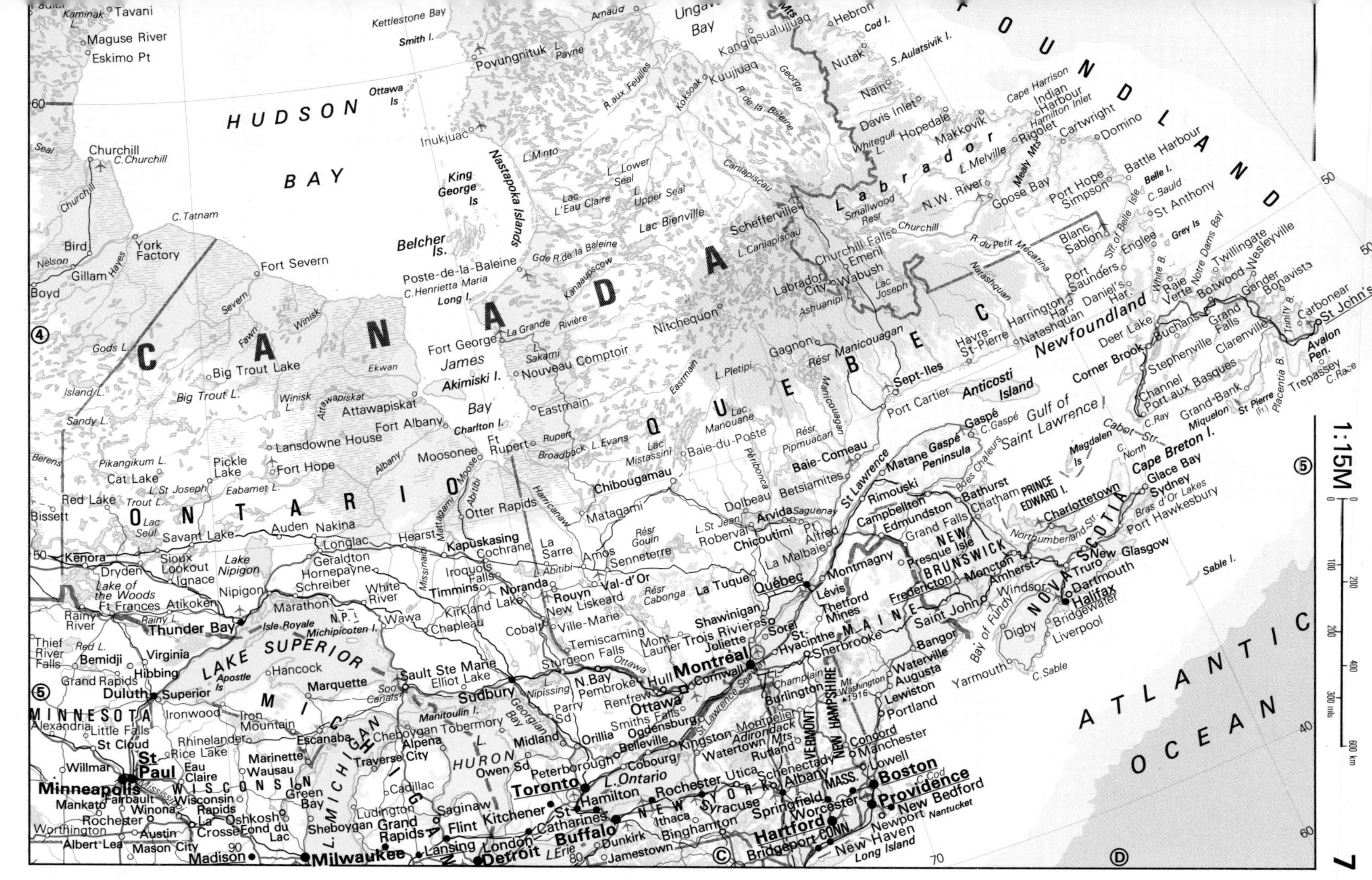
1:15M
0 100 200 300 mls
0 200 400 600 km
7
C A N A D A
HUDSON BAY
ATLANTIC OCEAN
NEWFOUNDLAND
Labrador
QUEBEC
ONTARIO
NOVA SCOTIA
NEW BRUNSWICK
PRINCE EDWARD I.
MAINE
NEW HAMPSHIRE
VERMONT
NEW YORK
MASS.
CONN.
MICHIGAN
WISCONSIN
MINNESOTA
LAKE SUPERIOR
L. HURON
L. Ontario
L. Erie
L. Michigan
James Bay
Ungava Bay
Gulf of Saint Lawrence
Anticosti Island
Gaspé Peninsula
Cape Breton I.
Avalon Pen.
Nastapoka Islands
Belcher Is.
Akimiski I.
Manitoulin I.
Long Island
Sable I.
Bay of Fundy
Montreal
Québec
Ottawa
Toronto
Hamilton
Buffalo
Detroit
Boston
Providence
Hartford
Halifax
St John's
Corner Brook
Sept-Iles
Baie-Comeau
Thunder Bay
Duluth
Minneapolis
St Paul
Milwaukee
Madison
Sudbury
Sault Ste Marie
Churchill
York Factory
Fort Severn
Moosonee
Chibougamau
Schefferville
Labrador City
Goose Bay
Fredericton
Saint John
Moncton
Charlottetown
Sydney
Gander
Kapuskasing
Timmins
Rouyn
Val-d'Or
Chicoutimi
Trois Rivieres
Sherbrooke
Portland
Bangor
Albany
Syracuse
Rochester
Kenora
Nipigon
Marquette
Green Bay
Grand Rapids
Lansing
Flint
London
Kitchener
Windsor
Yarmouth
Digby
Iron Mountain
Escanaba
50
60
70
80
90
40

1:12.5M

0 100 200 300 400 500 km

0 100 200 300 mls

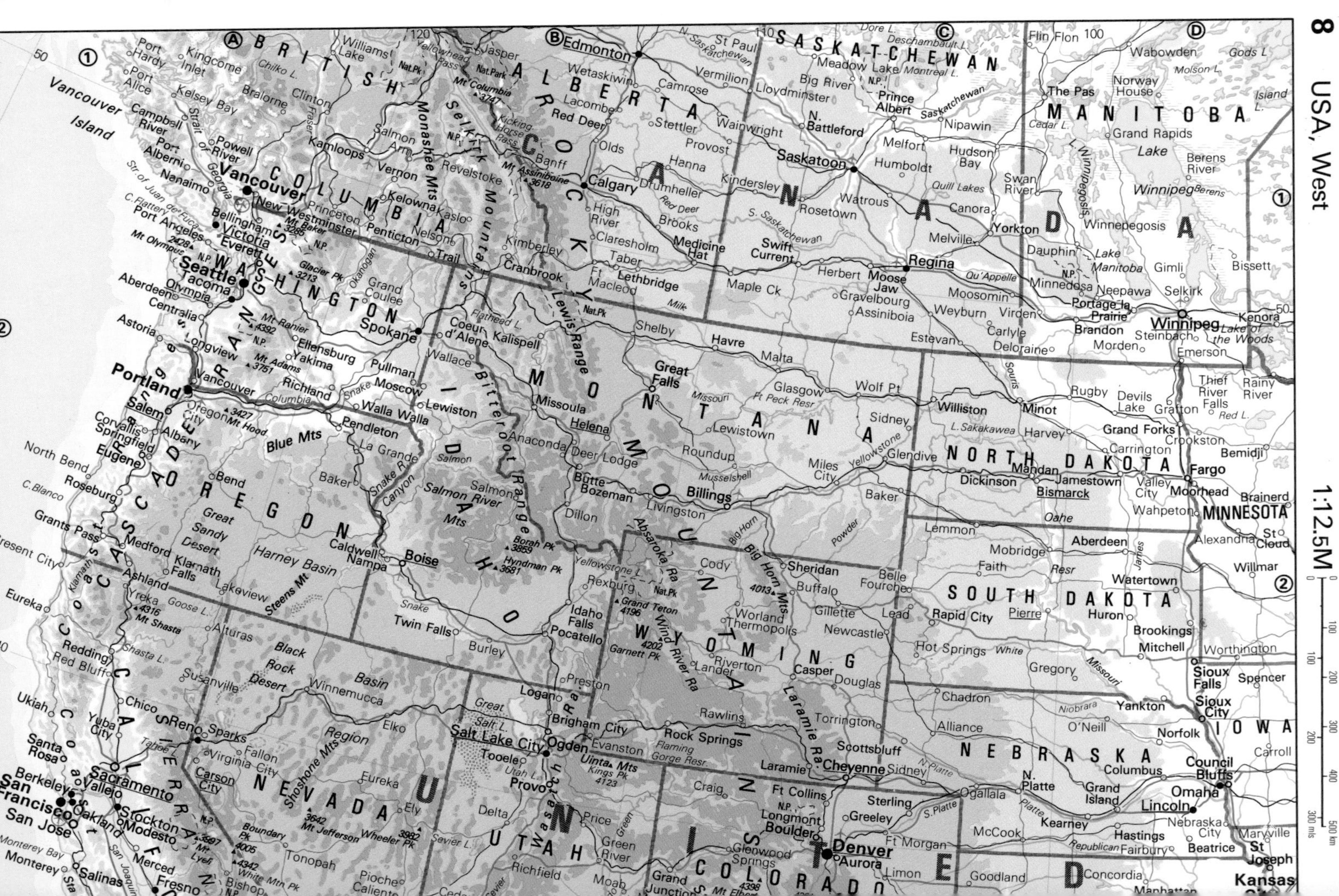

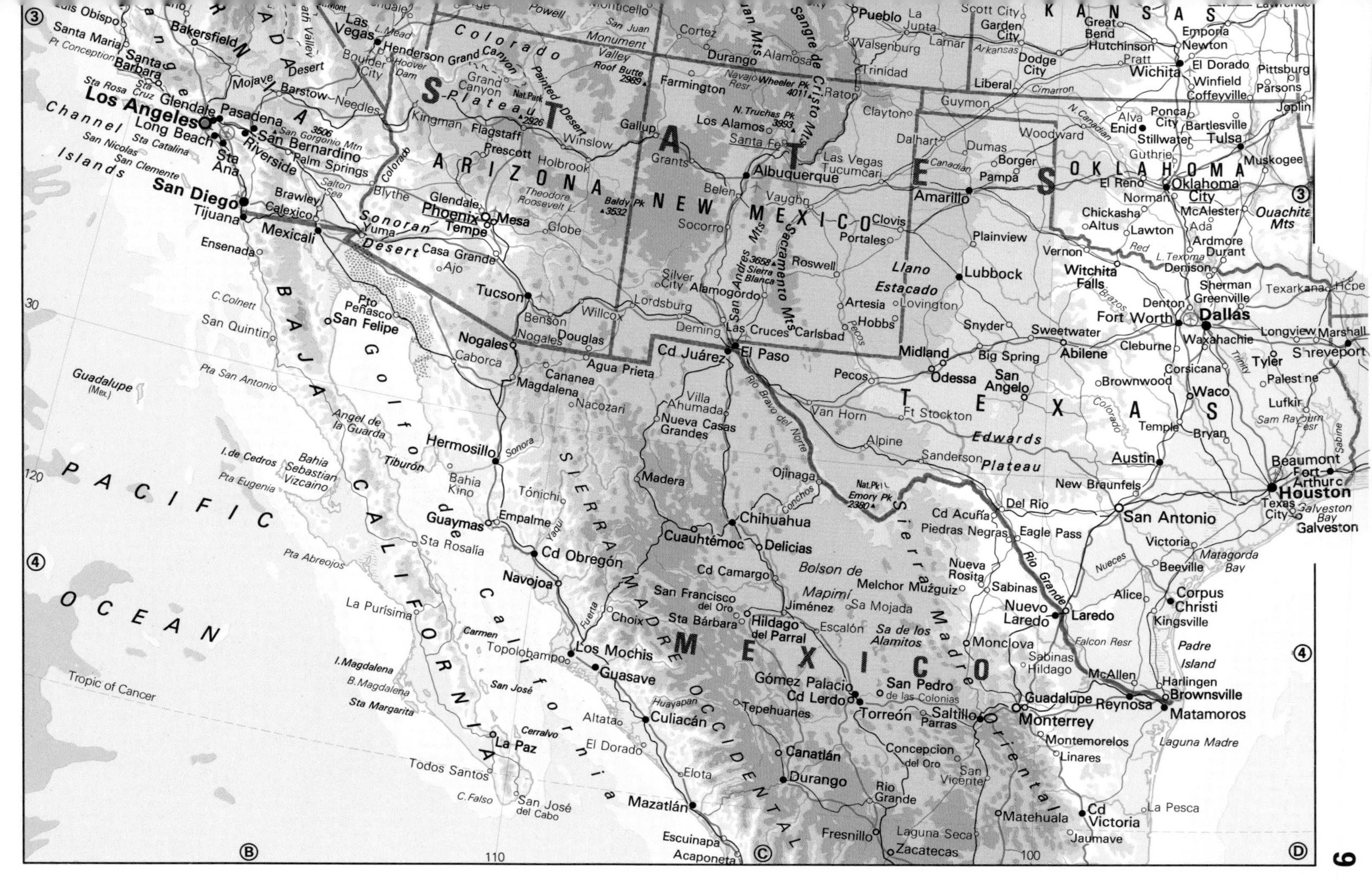
PACIFIC OCEAN
ARIZONA
NEW MEXICO
OKLAHOMA
KANSAS
TEXAS
MEXICO
STATES
Los Angeles
San Diego
Tijuana
Mexicali
Ensenada
San Quintin
Santa Maria
Santa Barbara
Bakersfield
Pasadena
Glendale
Long Beach
Sta Ana
San Bernardino
Riverside
Palm Springs
Mojave
Barstow
Needles
Las Vegas
Henderson
Boulder City
Hoover Dam
L. Mead
Kingman
Flagstaff
Prescott
Winslow
Holbrook
Grand Canyon
Colorado Plateau
Painted Desert
Phoenix
Mesa
Tempe
Glendale
Yuma
Sonoran Desert
Casa Grande
Ajo
Globe
Tucson
Benson
Willcox
Nogales
Douglas
Albuquerque
Santa Fe
Los Alamos
Gallup
Grants
Farmington
Durango
Cortez
Pueblo
Walsenburg
Trinidad
Raton
Las Vegas
Tucumcari
Clovis
Portales
Roswell
Alamogordo
Las Cruces
Carlsbad
Hobbs
Artesia
Silver City
Lordsburg
Deming
Socorro
Belen
Vaughn
Sacramento Mts
San Andres Mts
Sangre de Cristo Mts
Wheeler Pk 4011
N. Truchas Pk 3993
Baldy Pk 3532
Llano Estacado
Amarillo
Lubbock
Midland
Odessa
Big Spring
Abilene
San Angelo
El Paso
Cd Juárez
Pecos
Van Horn
Ft Stockton
Alpine
Edwards Plateau
Dallas
Fort Worth
Waco
Austin
San Antonio
Houston
Galveston
Beaumont
Corpus Christi
Laredo
Brownsville
Del Rio
Eagle Pass
Oklahoma City
Tulsa
Wichita
Wichita Falls
Lawton
Chihuahua
Cd Obregón
Hermosillo
Guaymas
Los Mochis
Culiacán
Mazatlán
Durango
Torreón
Saltillo
Monterrey
Nuevo Laredo
Matamoros
Reynosa
Cd Victoria
Zacatecas
Fresnillo
La Paz
Golfo de California
Baja California
Sierra Madre Occidental
Sierra Madre Oriental
Rio Grande
Tropic of Cancer
30
120
110
100

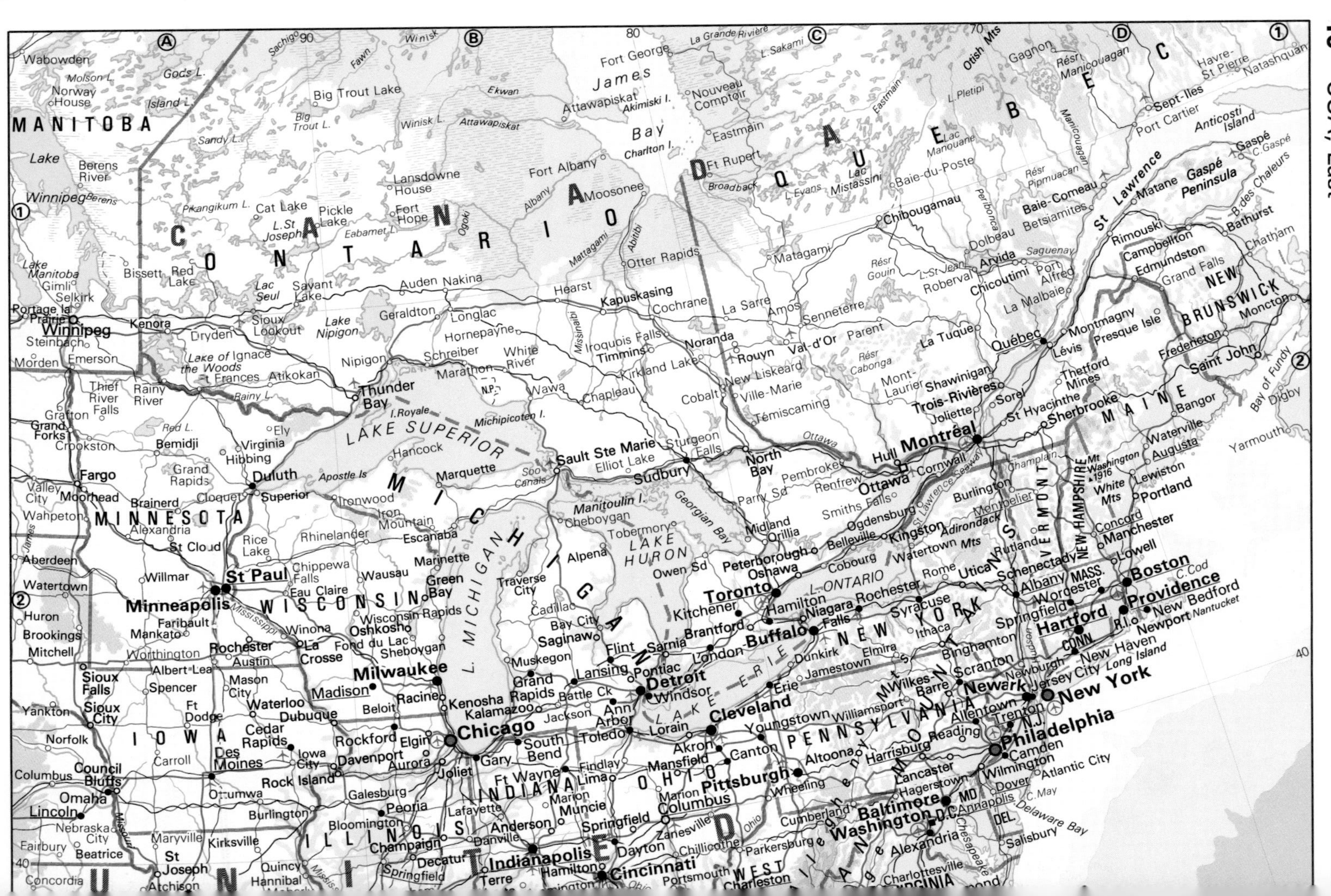
MANITOBA
ONTARIO
QUEBEC
NEW BRUNSWICK
MAINE
VERMONT
NEW HAMPSHIRE
MASS.
CONN.
R.I.
NEW YORK
PENNSYLVANIA
OHIO
INDIANA
ILLINOIS
MICHIGAN
WISCONSIN
MINNESOTA
IOWA
N.J.
DEL.
MD
D.C.
James Bay
LAKE SUPERIOR
LAKE HURON
L. MICHIGAN
L. ONTARIO
LAKE ERIE
Georgian Bay
Lake Nipigon
Lake of the Woods
Bay of Fundy
St Lawrence
Gaspé Peninsula
Anticosti Island
Winnipeg
Thunder Bay
Duluth
Minneapolis
St Paul
Milwaukee
Chicago
Detroit
Toronto
Ottawa
Montréal
Québec
Boston
Providence
Hartford
New York
Philadelphia
Baltimore
Washington
Pittsburgh
Cleveland
Buffalo
Columbus
Cincinnati
Indianapolis
Sault Ste Marie
Sudbury
Fargo
Omaha
Lincoln
Des Moines

ATLANTIC
OCEAN
GULF OF MEXICO
THE BAHAMAS
CUBA
Straits of Florida
Tropic of Cancer
STATES
MISSOURI
KENTUCKY
TENNESSEE
NORTH CAROLINA
SOUTH CAROLINA
GEORGIA
FLORIDA
ALABAMA
MISSISSIPPI
LOUISIANA
ARKANSAS
OKLAHOMA
TEXAS
Ozark Plateaus
Boston Mts
Ouachita Mts
Wichita
Tulsa
Oklahoma City
Dallas
Fort Worth
Houston
Galveston
Beaumont
Port Arthur
Austin
Waco
Corpus Christi
Brownsville
Matamoros
Laguna Madre
Padre Island
Little Rock
Memphis
Nashville
Knoxville
Chattanooga
Atlanta
Birmingham
Montgomery
Mobile
New Orleans
Baton Rouge
Jackson
Shreveport
Pensacola
Tallahassee
Jacksonville
Savannah
Charleston
Columbia
Charlotte
Raleigh
Greensboro
Wilmington
Orlando
Tampa
St Petersburg
Miami
Miami Beach
Ft Lauderdale
West Palm Beach
Key West
Nassau
Habana (Havana)
Matanzas
Camagüey
Holguín
Grand Bahama
Great Abaco
Little Abaco
Eleuthera
Andros
Great Exuma
Long
Cat
San Salvador
C. Hatteras
C. Lookout
C. Fear
C. Canaveral
Apalachee Bay
Mobile Bay
Lake Okeechobee
The Everglades
Florida Keys
Arch. de Camagüey
Great Bahama Bank
Exuma Sound
G. de Batabanó
90
80
70
30

1:10M

0 100 200 300 400 km
0 100 200 mls

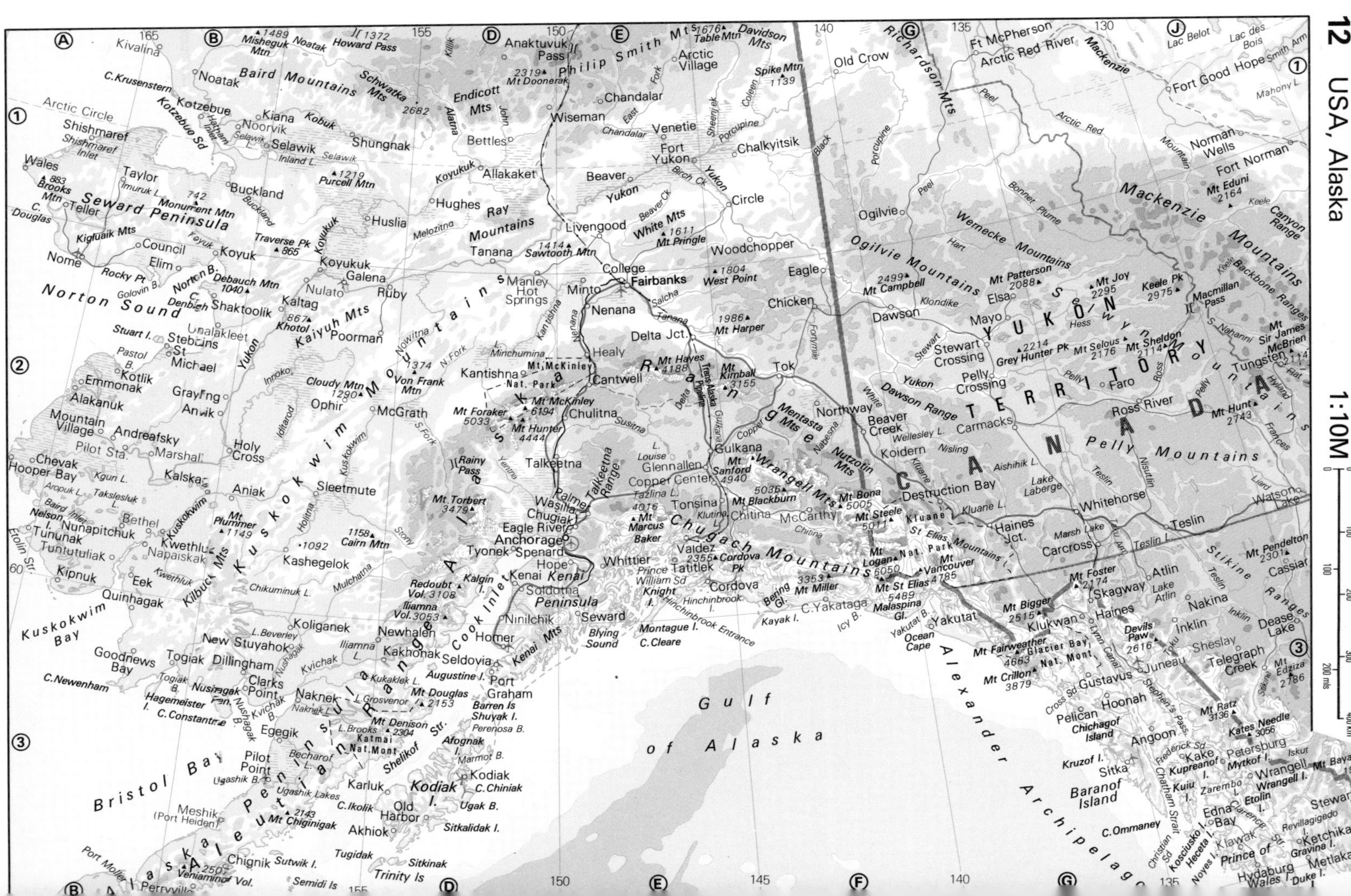

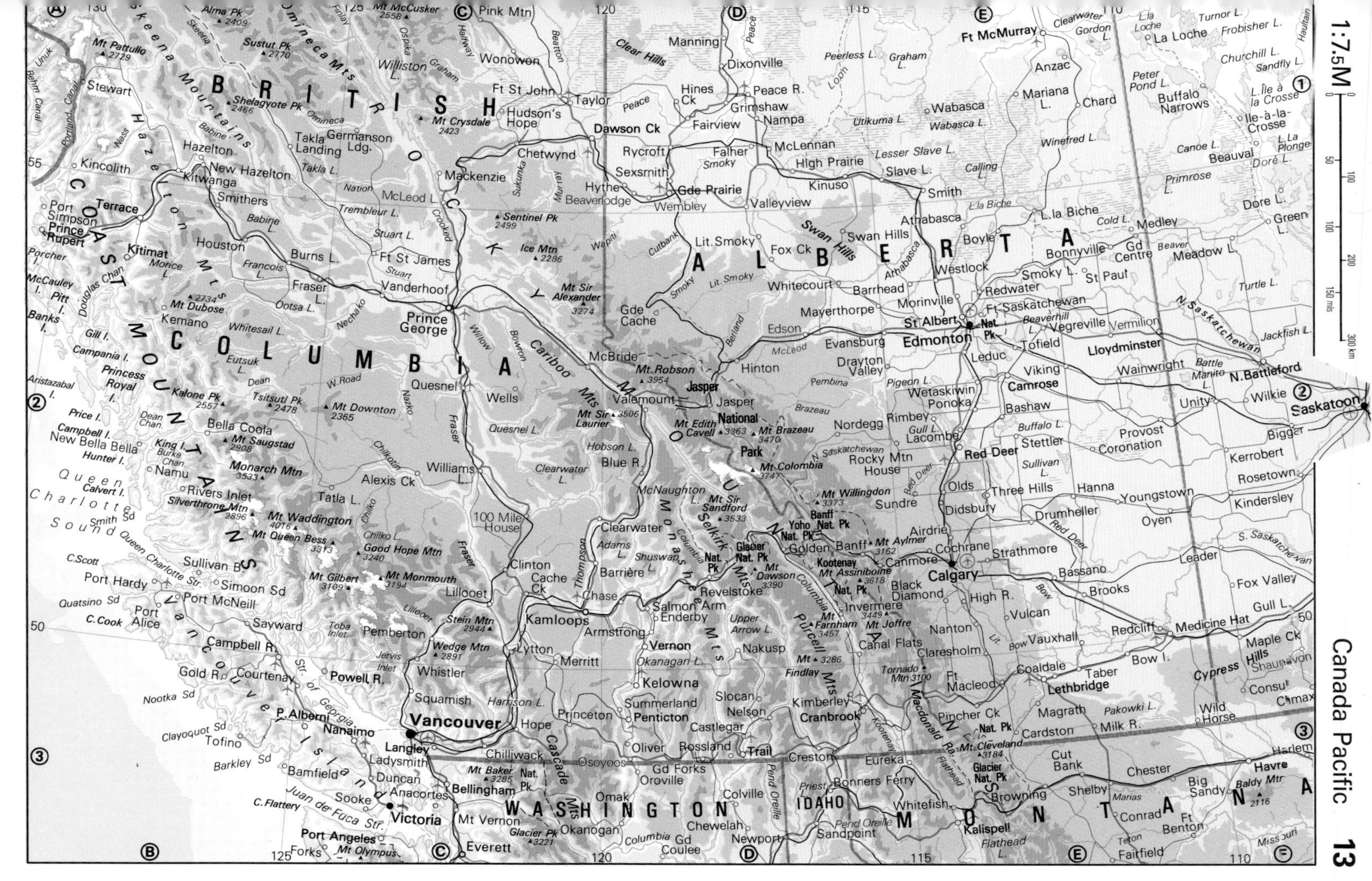
BRITISH COLUMBIA
ALBERTA
MONTANA
WASHINGTON
IDAHO
COAST MOUNTAINS
ROCKY MOUNTAINS
Hazelton Mts
Skeena Mountains
Omineca Mts
Cariboo Mts
Monashee Mts
Selkirk Mts
Purcell Mts
Cascade Mts
Swan Hills
Clear Hills
Cypress Hills
Queen Charlotte Sound
Vancouver Island
Str. of Georgia
Juan de Fuca Str.
Jasper National Park
Banff Nat. Pk
Yoho Nat. Pk
Kootenay Nat. Pk
Glacier Nat. Pk
Vancouver
Victoria
Prince George
Prince Rupert
Kamloops
Kelowna
Edmonton
Calgary
Red Deer
Lethbridge
Medicine Hat
Saskatoon
N. Battleford
Lloydminster
Camrose
Ft McMurray
Dawson Ck
Ft St John
Gde Prairie
Jasper
Banff
Revelstoke
Nelson
Cranbrook
Penticton
Vernon
Nanaimo
Kitimat
Terrace
Kalispell
Havre
N. Saskatchewan
Fraser
Thompson
Columbia
Peace
Smoky
Athabasca
Red Deer
Bow

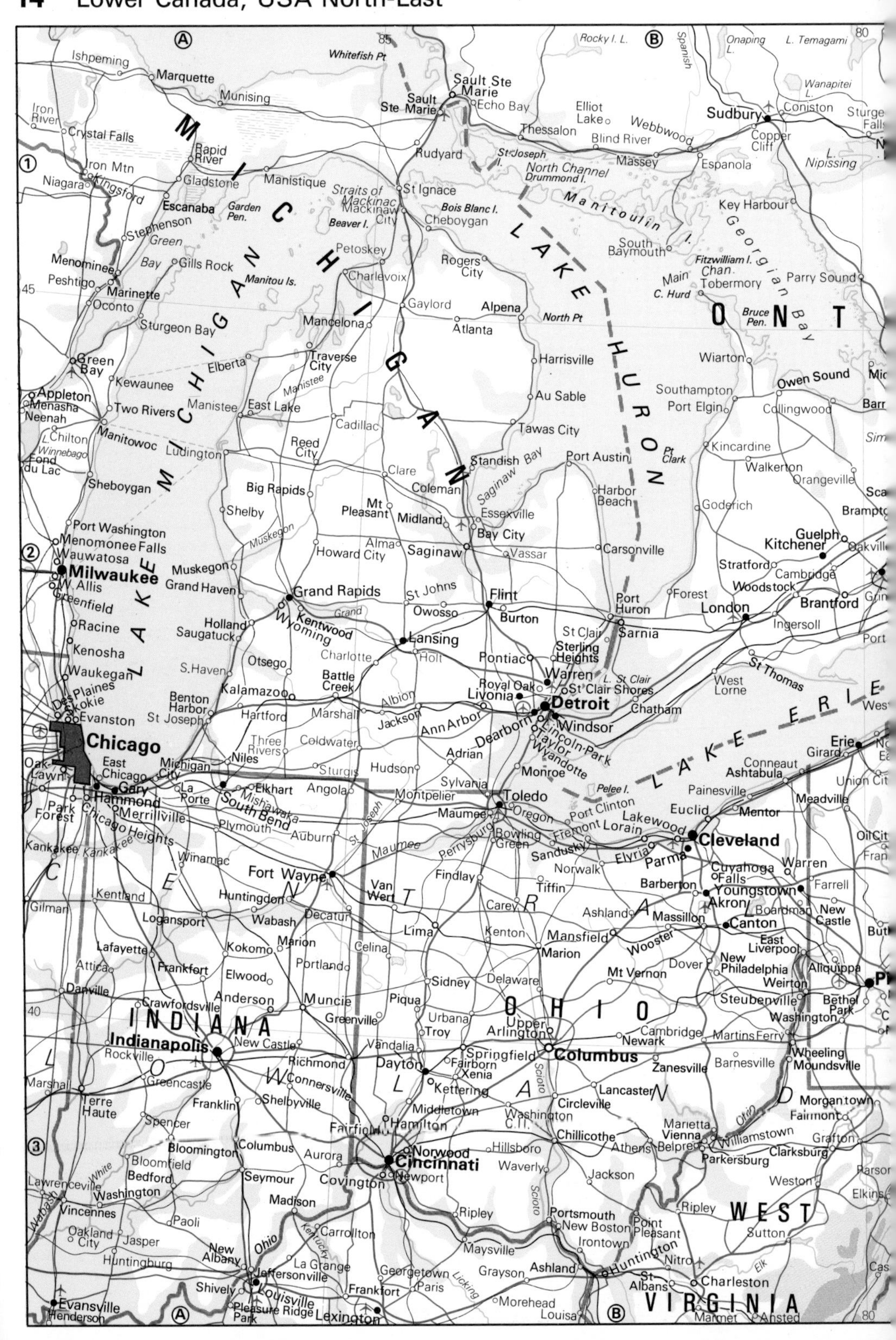

A
B
85
80
45
40
1
2
3
Rocky I. L.
Spanish
Onaping L.
L. Temagami
Wanapitei L.
Whitefish Pt
Ishpeming
Marquette
Munising
Sault Ste Marie
Sault Ste Marie
Echo Bay
Elliot Lake
Webbwood
Sudbury
Coniston
Sturgeon Falls
Iron River
Crystal Falls
Thessalon
Blind River
Copper Cliff
Rapid River
Rudyard
St Joseph I.
Massey
Espanola
L. Nipissing
Iron Mtn
North Channel
Drummond I.
Niagara
Kingsford
Gladstone
Manistique
Straits of Mackinac
St Ignace
Escanaba
Garden Pen.
Mackinaw City
Bois Blanc I.
Manitoulin I.
Key Harbour
Beaver I.
Cheboygan
Stephenson
Green Bay
Petoskey
South Baymouth
Georgian Bay
Menominee
Gills Rock
Rogers City
Fitzwilliam I.
Peshtigo
Marinette
Manitou Is.
Charlevoix
Main Chan.
Tobermory
Parry Sound
Oconto
C. Hurd
Gaylord
Alpena
Sturgeon Bay
Mancelona
Atlanta
North Pt
Bruce Pen.
ONT
Green Bay
Traverse City
Harrisville
Wiarton
Elberta
Kewaunee
Manistee
Southampton
Owen Sound
Appleton
Menasha
Neenah
Two Rivers
Manistee
East Lake
Au Sable
Port Elgin
Collingwood
Barrie
Cadillac
L. Chilton
L. Winnebago
Manitowoc
Ludington
Reed City
Tawas City
Fond du Lac
Port Austin
Pt Clark
Kincardine
Simcoe
Clare
Standish
Saginaw Bay
Walkerton
Sheboygan
Big Rapids
Coleman
Harbor Beach
Orangeville
Mt Pleasant
Midland
Goderich
Shelby
Essexville
Brampton
Port Washington
Bay City
Guelph
Menomonee Falls
Muskegon
Alma
Vassar
Kitchener
Wauwatosa
Howard City
Saginaw
Carsonville
Milwaukee
Muskegon
Stratford
Cambridge
W. Allis
Grand Haven
Grand Rapids
St Johns
Woodstock
Brantford
Greenfield
Flint
Port Huron
Forest
London
Owosso
Burton
Racine
Holland
Grand
Kentwood
Sarnia
Ingersoll
Saugatuck
Wyoming
Lansing
St Clair
Kenosha
Charlotte
Holt
Pontiac
Sterling Heights
St Thomas
Otsego
Waukegan
S.Haven
Battle Creek
Warren
West Lorne
Royal Oak
L. St Clair
Des Plaines
Kalamazoo
Albion
Livonia
St Clair Shores
Skokie
Benton Harbor
Detroit
Chatham
Evanston
St Joseph
Hartford
Marshall
Jackson
Ann Arbor
Dearborn
Windsor
Lincoln Park
Chicago
Three Rivers
Coldwater
Adrian
Taylor
Wyandotte
LAKE ERIE
Erie
Oak Lawn
East Chicago
Michigan City
Niles
Sturgis
Hudson
Monroe
Girard
Conneaut
Ashtabula
Gary
La Porte
Elkhart
Angola
Sylvania
Pelee I.
Painesville
Union City
Park Forest
Hammond
South Bend
Mishawaka
Montpelier
Toledo
Meadville
Merrillville
Chicago Heights
Plymouth
Maumee
Oregon
Port Clinton
Euclid
Mentor
Auburn
St Joseph
Bowling Green
Perrysburg
Fremont
Lakewood
Lorain
Cleveland
Oil City
Kankakee
Kankakee
Maumee
Sandusky
Elyria
Parma
Winamac
Fort Wayne
Findlay
Norwalk
Cuyahoga Falls
Warren
Tiffin
Farrell
Van Wert
Barberton
Youngstown
Kentland
Huntingdon
Akron
Gilman
Wabash
Decatur
Carey
Ashland
Massillon
Boardman
New Castle
Logansport
Lima
Kenton
Mansfield
Canton
Wooster
Lafayette
Kokomo
Marion
Celina
Marion
East Liverpool
Butler
Attica
Frankfort
Portland
Dover
New Philadelphia
Aliquippa
Elwood
Sidney
Delaware
Mt Vernon
Danville
Weirton
Crawfordsville
Anderson
Muncie
Piqua
Steubenville
Bethel Park
INDIANA
Greenville
Urbana
OHIO
Washington
Indianapolis
New Castle
Troy
Upper Arlington
Cambridge
Newark
Martins Ferry
Rockville
Vandalia
Springfield
Columbus
Wheeling
Richmond
Dayton
Fairborn
Zanesville
Barnesville
Moundsville
Marshall
Greencastle
Connersville
Xenia
Scioto
Kettering
Lancaster
Terre Haute
Franklin
Shelbyville
Circleville
Morgantown
Middletown
Washington C.H.
Fairmont
Spencer
Fairfield
Hamilton
Marietta
Vienna
Chillicothe
Williamstown
Grafton
Bloomington
Columbus
Norwood
Hillsboro
Athens
Belpre
Parkersburg
Clarksburg
Bloomfield
Aurora
Cincinnati
Waverly
Bedford
Seymour
Covington
Newport
Jackson
Weston
Lawrenceville
White
Washington
Madison
Elkins
Wabash
Vincennes
Ripley
Ripley
WEST
Paoli
Kentucky
Portsmouth
Point Pleasant
Oakland City
Jasper
Carrollton
Scioto
New Boston
Sutton
New Albany
Ohio
Maysville
Irontown
Huntington
Huntingburg
La Grange
Elk
Nitro
Jeffersonville
Georgetown
Grayson
Ashland
St. Albans
Charleston
Shively
Frankfort
Paris
Licking
Evansville
Louisville
Morehead
VIRGINIA
Henderson
Pleasure Ridge Park
Lexington
Louisa
Marmet
Ansted
LAKE MICHIGAN
MICHIGAN
LAKE HURON
CENTRAL
LOWLAND

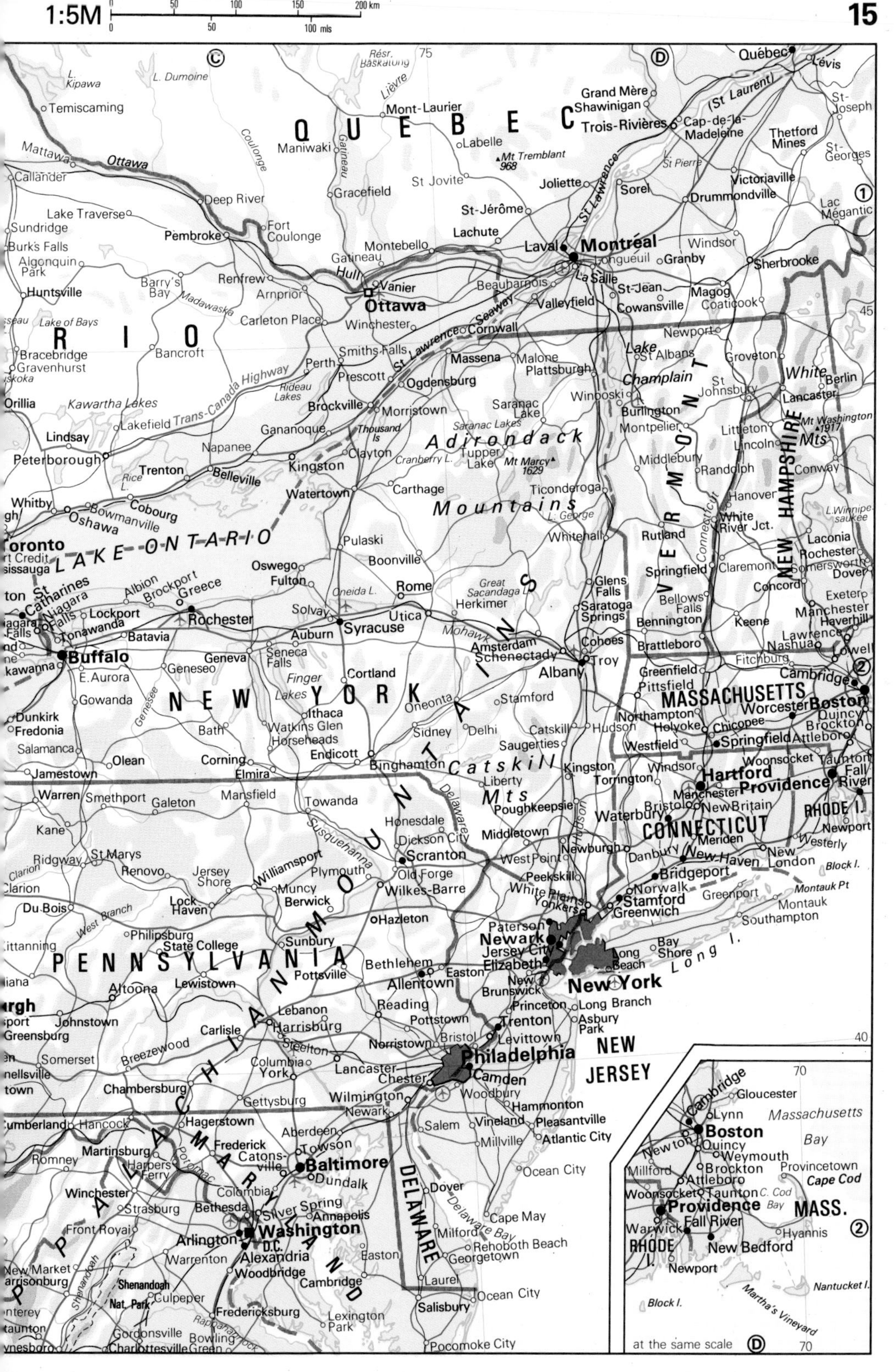
Ⓒ
Ⓓ
75
Résr. Baskatong
Québec
Lévis
L. Kipawa
L. Dumoine
Lièvre
Grand Mère
Shawinigan
(St Laurent)
St-Joseph
Temiscaming
Mont-Laurier
QUEBEC
Trois-Rivières
Cap-de-la-Madeleine
Thetford Mines
Coulonge
Gatineau
Labelle
Mattawa
Ottawa
Maniwaki
Mt Tremblant 968
St Pierre
St-Georges
Callander
St Jovite
Joliette
Sorel
Victoriaville
Deep River
Gracefield
St Lawrence
Drummondville
①
Lake Traverse
St-Jérôme
Lac Mégantic
Sundridge
Pembroke
Fort Coulonge
Lachute
Windsor
Burk's Falls
Montebello
Laval
Montréal
Granby
Algonquin Park
Gatineau
Longueuil
Sherbrooke
Hull
Huntsville
Barry's Bay
Renfrew
Vanier
Beauharnois
La Salle
St-Jean
Magog
Coaticook
Arnprior
Ottawa
Valleyfield
Cowansville
Madawaska
Seaway
45
Lake of Bays
Carleton Place
Winchester
Cornwall
Newport
RIO
Bancroft
St Lawrence
Smiths Falls
Massena
Malone
Lake
St Albans
Groveton
Bracebridge
Perth
Plattsburgh
Champlain
White
Berlin
Gravenhurst
Trans-Canada Highway
Prescott
Ogdensburg
St Johnsbury
Lancaster
Rideau Lakes
Orillia
Kawartha Lakes
Brockville
Morristown
Saranac Lake
Winooski
Burlington
Mt Washington 1917
Mts
Lakefield
Saranac Lakes
Montpelier
Littleton
Lindsay
Gananoque
Thousand Is
Adirondack
Lincoln
Napanee
Clayton
Tupper Lake
Middlebury
Peterborough
Kingston
Cranberry L.
Mt Marcy 1629
Randolph
Conway
Trenton
Rice L.
Belleville
VERMONT
NEW HAMPSHIRE
Ticonderoga
Carthage
Hanover
Whitby
Cobourg
Watertown
Mountains
Bowmanville
Oshawa
L. George
Connecticut
White River Jct.
L. Winnipesaukee
Toronto
LAKE ONTARIO
Whitehall
Rutland
Laconia
Pulaski
Rochester
Oswego
Boonville
Springfield
Claremont
Somersworth
Dover
Fulton
Albion
Brockport
Greece
Great Sacandaga L.
Glens Falls
Concord
St Catharines
Niagara Falls
Rome
Oneida L.
Herkimer
Saratoga Springs
Bellows Falls
Exeter
Manchester
Haverhill
Lockport
Rochester
Solvay
Utica
Bennington
Keene
Tonawanda
Batavia
Auburn
Syracuse
Mohawk
Amsterdam
Cohoes
Lawrence
Lowell
Nashua
Seneca Falls
Schenectady
Troy
Brattleboro
Buffalo
Geneva
Albany
Fitchburg
②
Geneseo
Cortland
Greenfield
Cambridge
E. Aurora
Finger Lakes
Pittsfield
MASSACHUSETTS
Gowanda
NEW YORK
Oneonta
Stamford
Worcester
Boston
Quincy
Genesee
Ithaca
Northampton
Brockton
Dunkirk
Fredonia
Bath
Watkins Glen
Sidney
Delhi
Catskill
Hudson
Holyoke
Chicopee
Horseheads
Saugerties
Westfield
Springfield
Attleboro
Salamanca
Endicott
Woonsocket
Taunton
Olean
Corning
Binghamton
Catskill
Kingston
Windsor
Hartford
Fall River
Jamestown
Elmira
Liberty
Torrington
Providence
Warren
Smethport
Galeton
Mansfield
Towanda
Mts
Manchester
Bristol
New Britain
RHODE I.
Poughkeepsie
Honesdale
Delaware
Hudson
Waterbury
CONNECTICUT
Kane
Dickson City
Middletown
Meriden
Newport
Susquehanna
Scranton
Newburgh
Danbury
New Haven
Westerly
St Marys
Ridgway
Renovo
Williamsport
Old Forge
West Point
New London
Block I.
Clarion
Jersey Shore
Plymouth
Peekskill
Bridgeport
Montauk Pt
Muncy
Wilkes-Barre
White Plains
Norwalk
Greenport
Lock Haven
Berwick
Yonkers
Stamford
Greenwich
Montauk
Du Bois
West Branch
Hazleton
Southampton
Paterson
Philipsburg
Sunbury
Newark
Bay Shore
Long I.
State College
Jersey City
PENNSYLVANIA
Bethlehem
Elizabeth
Long Beach
Easton
Pottsville
New Brunswick
New York
Allentown
Altoona
Lewistown
Long Branch
Reading
Princeton
Johnstown
Lebanon
Asbury Park
Greensburg
Harrisburg
Pottstown
Trenton
Carlisle
Levittown
Steelton
Bristol
Norristown
NEW JERSEY
40
Somerset
Breezewood
Philadelphia
Columbia
Lancaster
York
Chester
Camden
Chambersburg
Woodbury
Hammonton
Gettysburg
Wilmington
Newark
Pleasantville
Hancock
Hagerstown
Salem
Vineland
Atlantic City
Cumberland
Aberdeen
Millville
Martinsburg
Frederick
Towson
Romney
Harpers Ferry
Catonsville
Baltimore
Dundalk
Ocean City
Potomac
Columbia
DELAWARE
Dover
Winchester
Strasburg
Bethesda
Silver Spring
Annapolis
Delaware Bay
Cape May
Front Royal
Arlington
Washington D.C.
Milford
Rehoboth Beach
Alexandria
MARYLAND
Easton
Georgetown
New Market
Warrenton
Harrisonburg
Woodbridge
Cambridge
Laurel
Shenandoah
Shenandoah Nat. Park
Culpeper
Ocean City
Salisbury
Fredericksburg
Lexington Park
Rappahannock
Gordonsville
Bowling Green
Charlottesville
Pocomoke City
APPALACHIAN MOUNTAINS
70
Cambridge
Gloucester
Lynn
Massachusetts Bay
Boston
Newton
Quincy
Weymouth
Millford
Brockton
Provincetown
Attleboro
Cape Cod
Woonsocket
Taunton
C. Cod Bay
Providence
MASS.
Fall River
Warwick
Hyannis
RHODE I.
New Bedford
Newport
Nantucket I.
Block I.
Martha's Vineyard
at the same scale
Ⓓ
70

1:2.5M

0 25 50 75 100 km
0 25 50 mls

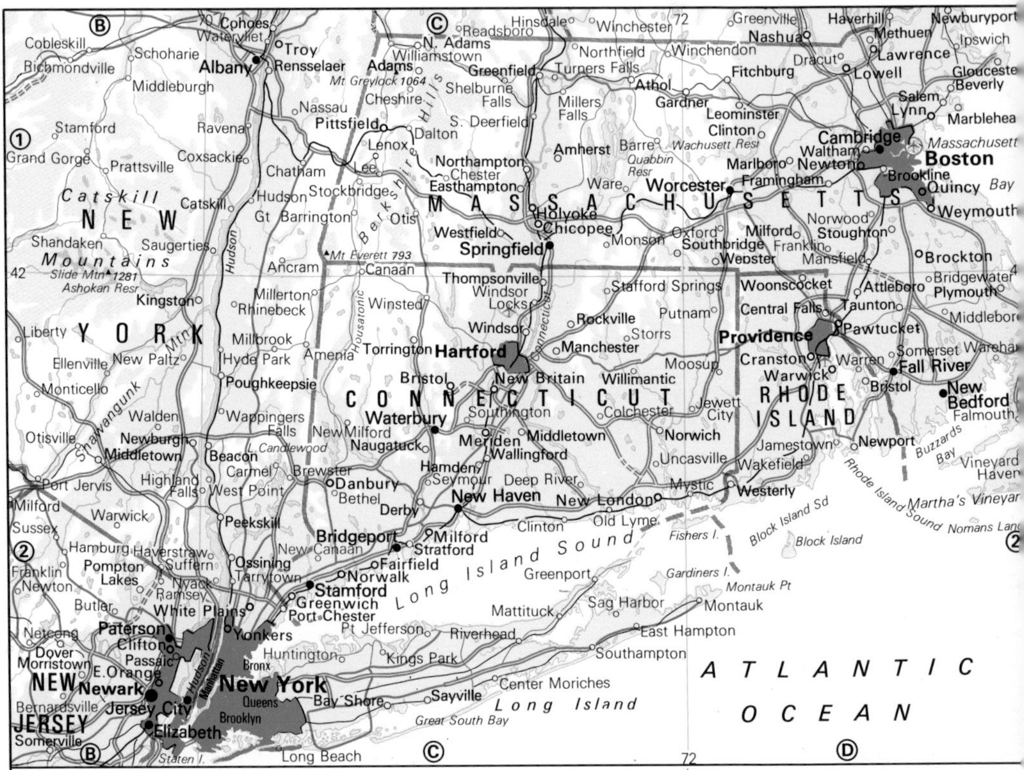

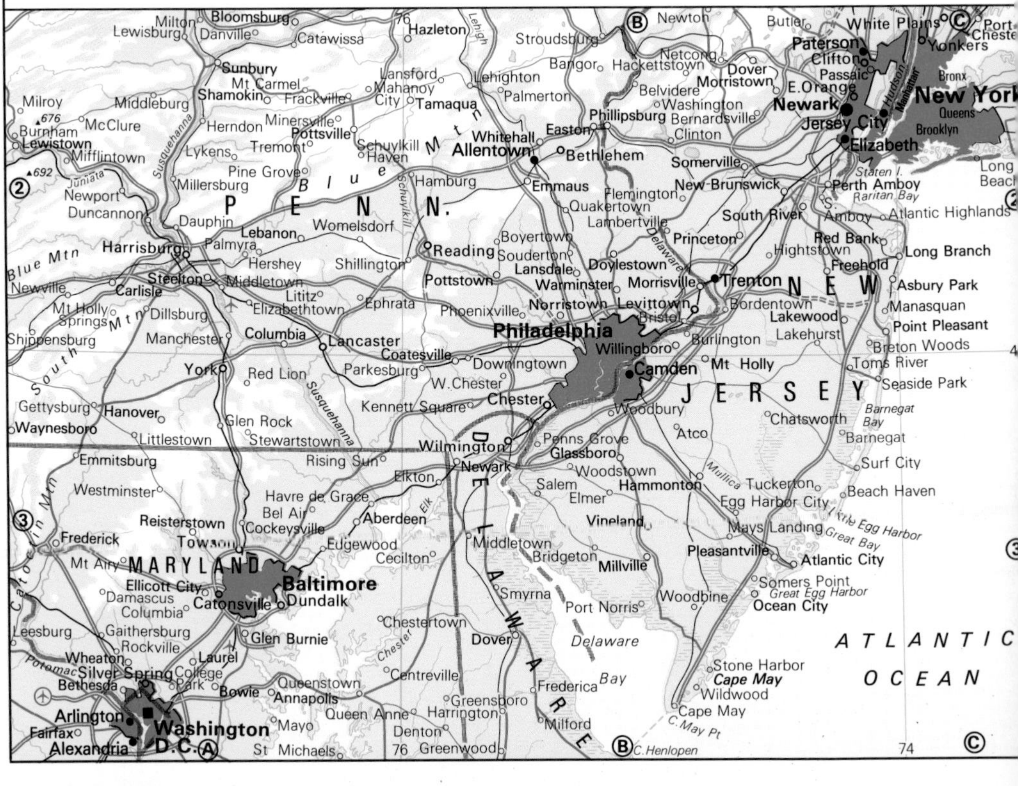

B C 70 72 D 1 2 42

Cohoes Waterveliet Troy Albany Rensselaer Cobleskill Schoharie Richmondville Middleburgh Adams N. Adams Williamstown Readsboro Hinsdale Winchester Northfield Winchendon Greenville Nashua Haverhill Methuen Newburyport Ipswich Lawrence Dracut Lowell Gloucester Beverly Salem Lynn Marblehead

Mt Greylock 1064 Greenfield Turners Falls Athol Gardner Fitchburg Leominster Clinton Shelburne Falls Cheshire Nassau Pittsfield Dalton S. Deerfield Millers Falls Stamford Ravena Grand Gorge Prattsville Coxsackie Chatham Lenox Lee Northampton Chester Easthampton Amherst Barre Wachusett Resr Quabbin Resr Cambridge Waltham Newton Massachusetts Boston Brookline Quincy Bay Weymouth Marlboro Framingham Worcester Ware

Catskill Mountains NEW YORK Catskill Hudson Stockbridge Berkshire Hills Gt Barrington Otis MASSACHUSETTS Holyoke Chicopee Westfield Springfield Monson Oxford Southbridge Webster Milford Franklin Mansfield Norwood Stoughton Brockton Bridgewater Plymouth Middleboro

Shandaken Saugerties Slide Mtn 1281 Ashokan Resr Mt Everett 793 Ancram Canaan Thompsonville Windsor Locks Stafford Springs Woonsocket Attleboro Taunton Central Falls Pawtucket Kingston Millerton Rhinebeck Winsted Housatonic Windsor Rockville Putnam Storrs Providence Liberty Millbrook Hyde Park Amenia Torrington Hartford Manchester Cranston Somerset Wareham Ellenville New Paltz Mink Bristol New Britain Willimantic Moosup Warwick Warren Fall River Poughkeepsie Monticello Shawangunk CONNECTICUT RHODE ISLAND Bristol New Bedford Falmouth Walden Wappingers Falls Waterbury Southington Colchester Jewett City Otisville Newburgh Middletown New Milford Naugatuck Meriden Wallingford Middletown Norwich Jamestown Newport Buzzards Bay Beacon L. Candlewood Uncasville Wakefield Vineyard Haven Port Jervis Highland Falls Carmel Brewster Hamden Seymour Deep River Mystic Westerly West Point Danbury Bethel Derby New Haven New London Milford Martha's Vineyard Rhode Island Sound Nomans Land Sussex Warwick Peekskill Clinton Old Lyme Block Island Sd Block Island Fishers I. Hamburg Haverstraw Bridgeport Milford Stratford Long Island Sound Franklin Pompton Lakes Suffern Ossining New Canaan Fairfield Greenport Gardiners I. Montauk Pt Newton Nyack Tarrytown Norwalk Ramsey Stamford Greenwich Port Chester Mattituck Sag Harbor Montauk Butler White Plains Pt Jefferson Riverhead East Hampton Netcong Paterson Yonkers Clifton Huntington Kings Park Southampton Dover Morristown Passaic Bronx E. Orange Manhattan Hudson NEW JERSEY Newark New York Center Moriches ATLANTIC OCEAN Bernardsville Jersey City Queens Bay Shore Sayville Long Island Elizabeth Brooklyn Great South Bay Somerville Staten I. Long Beach

Milton Bloomsburg Lewisburg Danville Catawissa 76 Hazleton Lehigh Newton Butler White Plains Port Chester Sunbury Stroudsburg Yonkers Paterson Mt Carmel Lansford Mahanoy City Lehighton Bangor Hackettstown Netcong Dover Clifton Passaic Milroy Middleburg Shamokin Frackville Tamaqua Palmerton Belvidere Morristown E. Orange Bronx Manhattan New York 676 Burnham McClure Minersville Washington Newark Hudson Queens Lewistown Herndon Pottsville Phillipsburg Bernardsville Jersey City Brooklyn Mifflintown Lykens Tremont Schuylkill Haven Blue Mtn Whitehall Easton Clinton Elizabeth Long Beach 692 Juniata Pine Grove Allentown Bethlehem Somerville Staten I. Newport Millersburg Hamburg Emmaus Flemington New Brunswick Perth Amboy Raritan Bay Duncannon PENN. Quakertown Lambertville Amboy Atlantic Highlands Dauphin Lebanon Womelsdorf Delaware South River Red Bank Long Branch Harrisburg Palmyra Boyertown Princeton Hightstown Blue Mtn Hershey Shillington Reading Souderton Lansdale Doylestown Freehold Asbury Park Newville Steelton Middletown Carlisle Lititz Ephrata Pottstown Warminster Morrisville Trenton NEW Manasquan Mt Holly Springs Dillsburg Elizabethtown Phoenixville Norristown Levittown Bristol Bordentown Lakewood Point Pleasant Shippensburg South Mtn Manchester Columbia Lancaster Philadelphia Burlington Lakehurst Breton Woods Coatesville Willingboro Toms River York Red Lion Parkesburg Downingtown Camden Mt Holly Seaside Park Susquehanna W. Chester Chester JERSEY Gettysburg Hanover Kennett Square Woodbury Barnegat Bay Waynesboro Glen Rock Chatsworth Littlestown Stewartstown Atco Barnegat Emmitsburg Wilmington Penns Grove Glassboro Rising Sun Newark Surf City Elkton Woodstown Westminster Salem Mullica Tuckerton Havre de Grace DELAWARE Elmer Hammonton Beach Haven Bel Air Elk Egg Harbor City Little Egg Harbor Reisterstown Cockeysville Aberdeen Vineland Great Bay Frederick Towson Mays Landing Edgewood Middletown Pleasantville Mt Airy MARYLAND Cecilton Bridgeton Millville Atlantic City Catoctin Mtn Ellicott City Baltimore Somers Point Damascus Catonsville Dundalk Smyrna Port Norris Woodbine Great Egg Harbor Columbia Ocean City Leesburg Gaithersburg Glen Burnie Chestertown Dover Rockville Chester Delaware ATLANTIC OCEAN Wheaton Laurel Potomac Silver Spring College Park Centreville Stone Harbor Bethesda Queenstown Frederica Bay Cape May Bowie Annapolis Wildwood Arlington Greensboro Cape May Harrington C. May Pt Fairfax Washington D.C. Mayo Queen Anne Denton Milford Alexandria St Michaels 76 Greenwood C. Henlopen 74 A B C 2 3 4

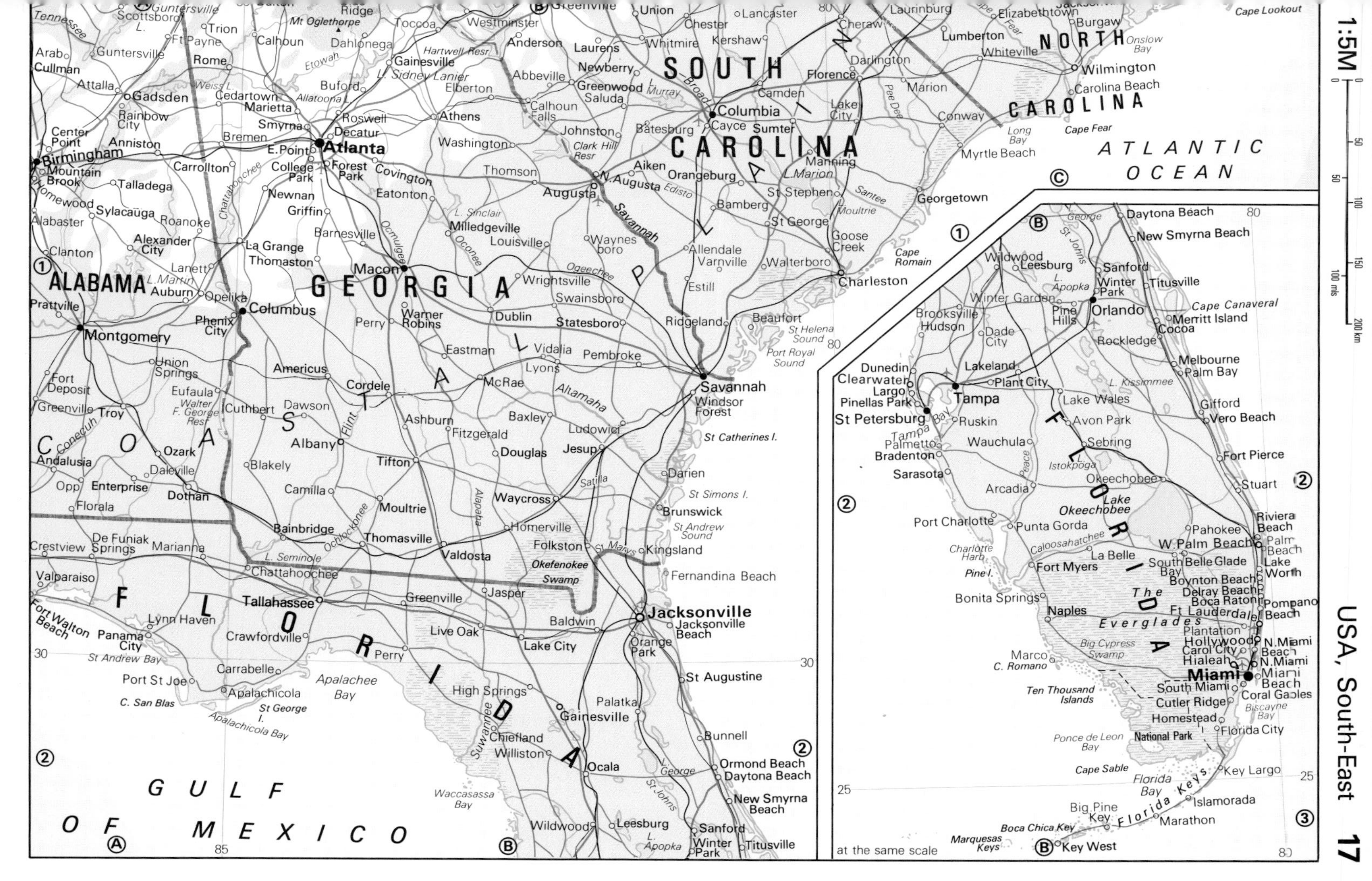
NORTH CAROLINA
SOUTH CAROLINA
GEORGIA
ALABAMA
FLORIDA
ATLANTIC OCEAN
GULF OF MEXICO
Atlanta
Savannah
Jacksonville
Tallahassee
Montgomery
Birmingham
Columbia
Charleston
Tampa
St Petersburg
Miami
Orlando
Key West
Florida Keys
Lake Okeechobee
The Everglades
at the same scale

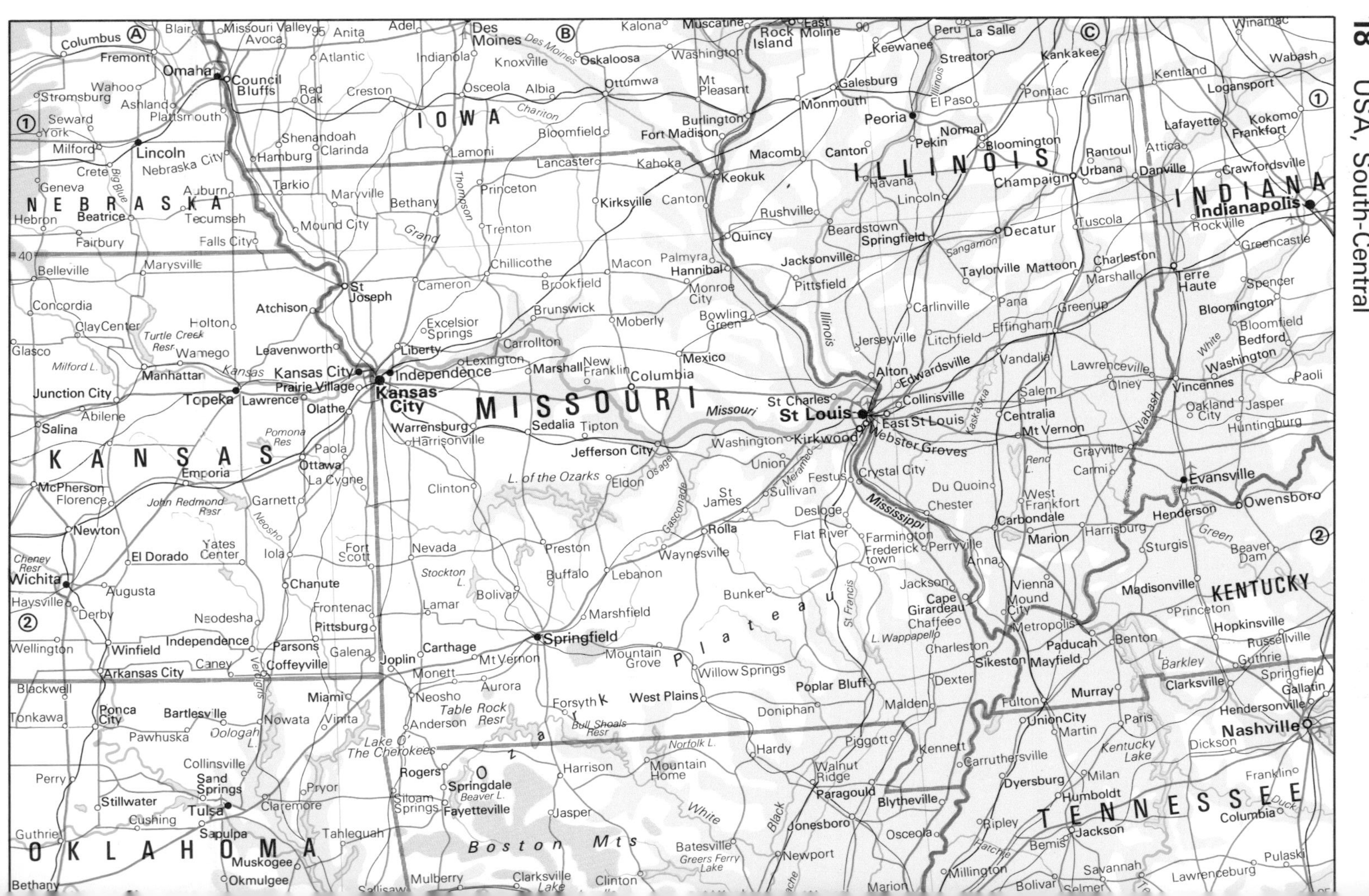
IOWA
NEBRASKA
ILLINOIS
INDIANA
MISSOURI
KANSAS
KENTUCKY
TENNESSEE
OKLAHOMA
Omaha
Lincoln
Des Moines
Peoria
Indianapolis
Springfield
St Louis
Kansas City
Topeka
Wichita
Tulsa
Evansville
Nashville
Jefferson City
L. of the Ozarks
Plateau
Boston Mts
Mississippi
Missouri
Illinois
Wabash

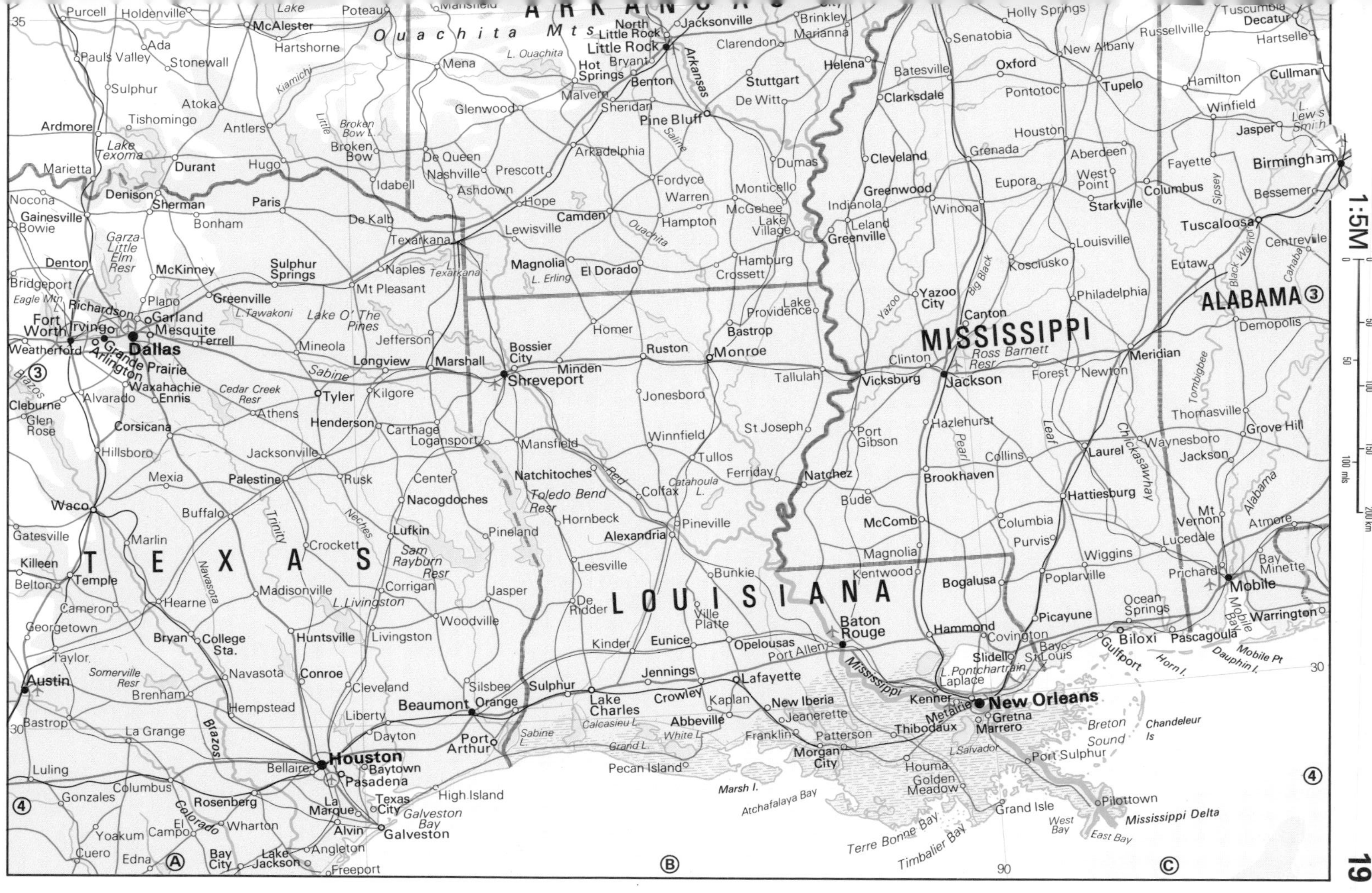
ARKANSAS
Ouachita Mts
TEXAS
LOUISIANA
MISSISSIPPI
ALABAMA ③
Little Rock
North Little Rock
Jacksonville
Hot Springs
Pine Bluff
El Dorado
Texarkana
Dallas
Fort Worth
Arlington
Grand Prairie
Waco
Austin
Houston
Pasadena
Galveston
Beaumont
Port Arthur
Tyler
Longview
Marshall
Shreveport
Bossier City
Monroe
Ruston
Alexandria
Natchitoches
Lafayette
Lake Charles
Baton Rouge
New Orleans
Houma
Thibodaux
Morgan City
New Iberia
Vicksburg
Jackson
Hattiesburg
Laurel
Meridian
Gulfport
Biloxi
Pascagoula
Mobile
Tuscaloosa
Birmingham
Tupelo
Oxford
Greenville
Greenwood
Cleveland
Natchez
McComb
Brookhaven
Lufkin
Nacogdoches
Bryan
College Sta.
Temple
Killeen
Sherman
Denison
Ardmore
McAlester
Paris
Lake Texoma
L. Ouachita
Toledo Bend Resr
Sam Rayburn Resr
L. Livingston
Ross Barnett Resr
L. Pontchartrain
Arkansas
Red
Sabine
Trinity
Brazos
Colorado
Navasota
Neches
Mississippi
Pearl
Big Black
Yazoo
Tombigbee
Alabama
Chickasawhay
Leaf
Ouachita
Saline
Galveston Bay
Atchafalaya Bay
Terre Bonne Bay
Timbalier Bay
Marsh I.
Mississippi Delta
Breton Sound
Chandeleur Is
Horn I.
Dauphin I.
Mobile Pt
Mobile Bay
Ⓐ
Ⓑ
Ⓒ
③
④
30
35
90
1:5M
0 50 100 150 200 km
0 50 100 mls
19

1:5M 0 50 100 150 200 km 0 50 100 mls

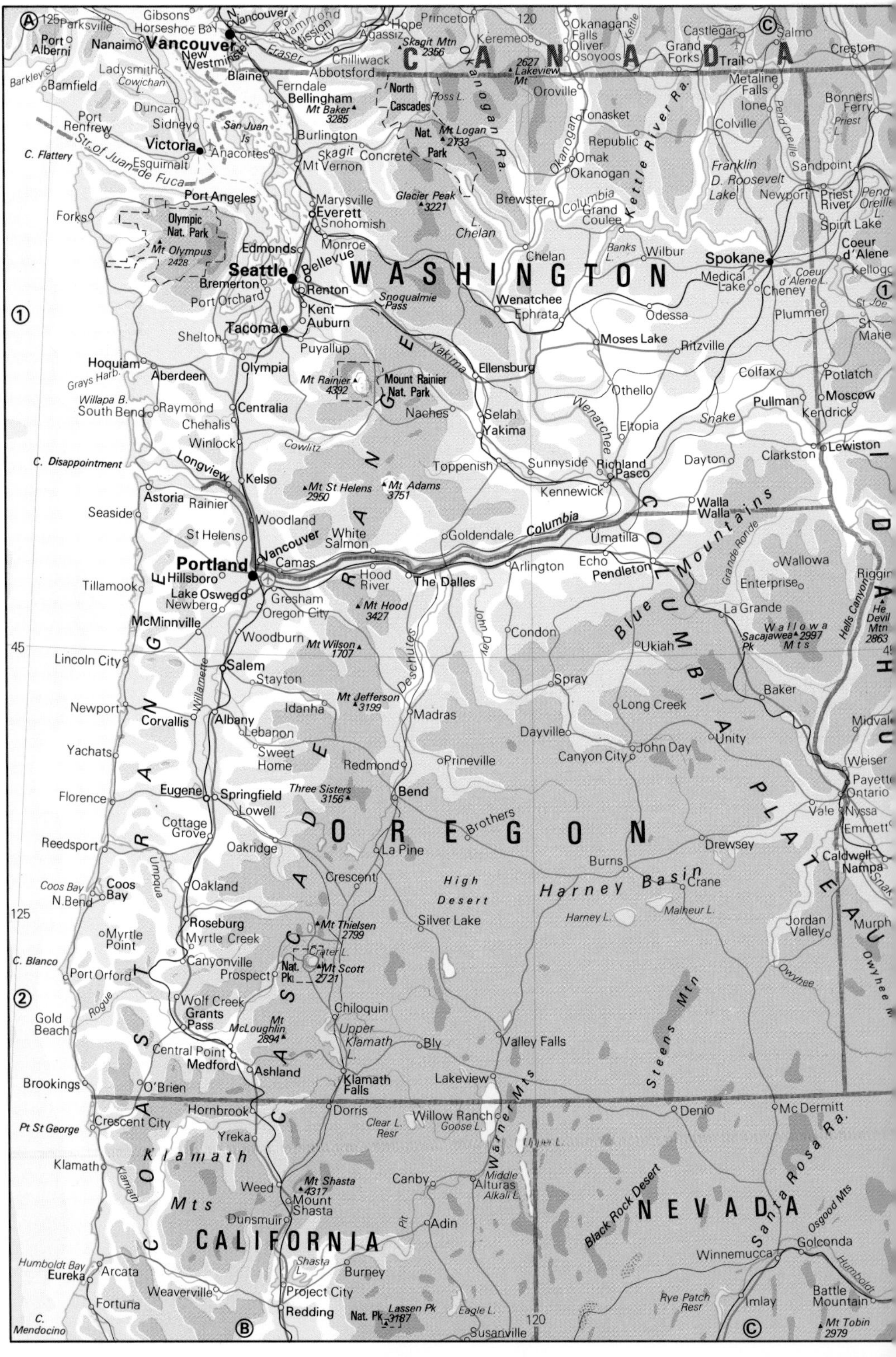

A B C 1 2

CANADA
WASHINGTON
OREGON
CALIFORNIA
NEVADA
IDAHO

Parksville Port Alberni Nanaimo Gibsons Horseshoe Bay Vancouver North Vancouver New Westminster Port Hammond Mission City Hope Agassiz Chilliwack Abbotsford Fraser Princeton Skagit Mtn 2356 Keremeos Okanagan Falls Oliver Osoyoos Kettle Castlegar Salmo Grand Forks Trail Creston 120 125
Ladysmith Cowichan L. Barkley Sd Bamfield Duncan Port Renfrew Sidney San Juan Is Victoria Esquimalt Str. of Juan de Fuca C. Flattery Anacortes Blaine Ferndale Bellingham Mt Baker 3285 North Cascades Nat. Park Ross L. Mt Logan 2133 2627 Lakeview Mt Okanogan Ra. Oroville Tonasket Republic Kettle River Ra. Metaline Falls Ione Pend Oreille Colville Bonners Ferry Priest L.
Burlington Skagit Concrete Mt Vernon Okanogan Omak Franklin D. Roosevelt Lake Sandpoint Priest River Newport Pend Oreille Spirit Lake
Port Angeles Olympic Nat. Park Mt Olympus 2428 Forks Marysville Everett Snohomish Monroe Glacier Peak 3221 L. Chelan Brewster Columbia Grand Coulee Banks L. Wilbur Chelan Spokane Coeur d'Alene Coeur d'Alene L. Kellogg
Edmonds Bellevue Seattle Bremerton Renton Port Orchard Kent Auburn Snoqualmie Pass Wenatchee Ephrata Medical Lake Cheney Odessa St Joe Plummer St Maries
Shelton Tacoma Puyallup Moses Lake Ritzville Yakima Ellensburg Colfax Potlatch
Hoquiam Grays Harb. Aberdeen Olympia Mt Rainier 4392 Mount Rainier Nat. Park Othello Moscow Pullman Kendrick
Willapa B. South Bend Raymond Centralia Chehalis Winlock Cowlitz Naches Selah Yakima Wenatchee Eltopia Snake
C. Disappointment Longview Kelso Toppenish Sunnyside Richland Pasco Dayton Clarkston Lewiston
Astoria Rainier Seaside Mt St Helens 2950 Mt Adams 3751 Kennewick Walla Walla Blue Mountains Grande Ronde Wallowa
Woodland St Helens Vancouver White Salmon Goldendale Columbia Umatilla Camas Arlington Echo Pendleton Riggins
Portland Hillsboro Tillamook Lake Oswego Newberg Gresham Oregon City Hood River The Dalles Mt Hood 3427 Enterprise La Grande He Devil Mtn 2863 Hells Canyon
McMinnville Woodburn Mt Wilson 1707 Deschutes John Day Condon Ukiah Wallowa Mts Sacajawea Pk 2997
45 Lincoln City Salem Stayton Willamette Spray Baker
Newport Corvallis Albany Idanha Mt Jefferson 3199 Madras Long Creek Lebanon Midvale
Yachats Sweet Home Redmond Prineville Dayville John Day Canyon City Unity Weiser
Florence Eugene Springfield Three Sisters 3156 Bend Payette Ontario Lowell Vale Nyssa
Cottage Grove Brothers Emmett
Reedsport Oakridge La Pine Drewsey Caldwell Nampa
Coos Bay N. Bend Umpqua Oakland Crescent Burns High Desert Harney Basin Crane Snake
125 Roseburg Myrtle Creek Mt Thielsen 2799 Silver Lake Harney L. Malheur L. Jordan Valley Murphy
Myrtle Point Crater L. C. Blanco Canyonville Nat. Pk Mt Scott 2721 Port Orford Prospect Owyhee Owyhee Mts
Gold Beach Rogue Wolf Creek Grants Pass Chiloquin Steens Mtn
Mt McLoughlin 2894 Upper Klamath L. Bly Valley Falls
Central Point Medford Ashland Klamath Falls Lakeview Warner Mts
Brookings O'Brien
Pt St George Crescent City Hornbrook Dorris Clear L. Resr Willow Ranch Goose L. Denio Mc Dermitt
Yreka Klamath Mts Upper L. Santa Rosa Ra.
Klamath Weed Mt Shasta 4317 Mount Shasta Canby Middle Alturas Alkali L. Black Rock Desert Osgood Mts
Dunsmuir Pit Adin
Humboldt Bay Eureka Arcata Shasta L. Burney Winnemucca Golconda Humboldt
Weaverville Project City Rye Patch Resr Imlay Battle Mountain
Fortuna C. Mendocino Redding Nat. Pk Lassen Pk 3187 Eagle L. 120 Susanville Mt Tobin 2979

Cascade Range
Coast Ranges
Columbia Plateau

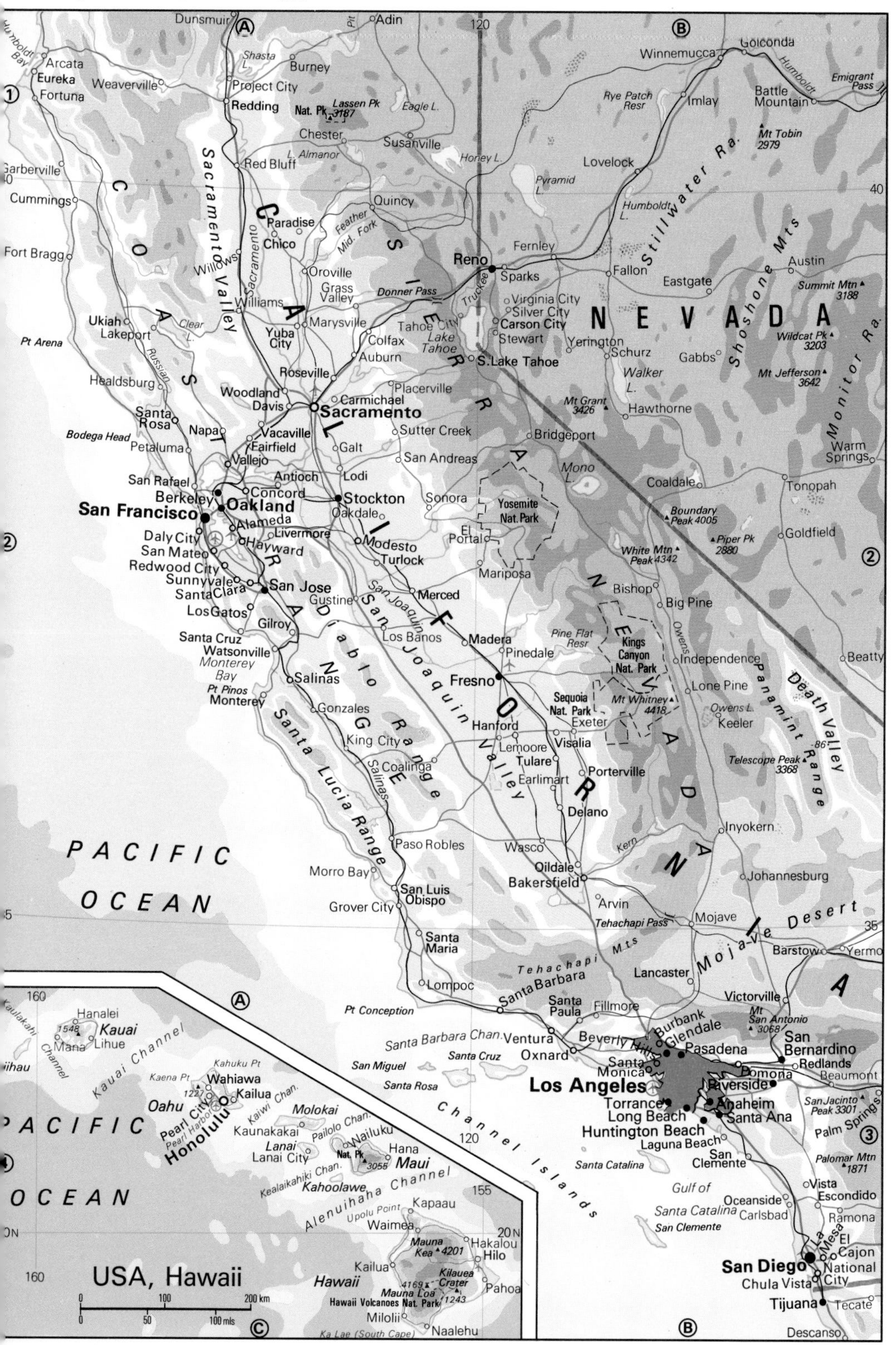
Dunsmuir
A
Adin
120
B
Golconda
Humboldt Bay
Arcata
Eureka
Fortuna
1
Weaverville
Shasta L.
Burney
Project City
Redding
Nat. Pk
Lassen Pk 3187
Eagle L.
Winnemucca
Humboldt
Emigrant Pass
Rye Patch Resr
Imlay
Battle Mountain
Mt Tobin 2979
Chester
Susanville
Garberville
Sacramento Valley
L. Almanor
Red Bluff
Honey L.
Lovelock
Pyramid L.
Stillwater Ra.
40
Cummings
C O A S T
Quincy
Humboldt L.
Paradise
Chico
Feather
Mid. Fork
Shoshone Mts
Fort Bragg
Willows
Sacramento
Reno
Fernley
Sparks
Fallon
Austin
Oroville
Grass Valley
Donner Pass
Truckee
Eastgate
Summit Mtn 3188
Williams
Virginia City
Silver City
Carson City
N E V A D A
Ukiah
Lakeport
Clear L.
Marysville
Yuba City
Tahoe City
Lake Tahoe
Stewart
Yerington
Colfax
Wildcat Pk 3203
Monitor Ra.
Pt Arena
Russian
Auburn
S. Lake Tahoe
Schurz
Gabbs
Healdsburg
Roseville
Walker L.
Mt Jefferson 3642
Woodland
Carmichael
Placerville
Davis
Sacramento
Mt Grant 3426
Hawthorne
Santa Rosa
Napa
Vacaville
Sutter Creek
Bodega Head
Petaluma
Fairfield
Galt
Bridgeport
Warm Springs
Vallejo
San Andreas
Mono L.
San Rafael
Antioch
Lodi
Coaldale
Tonopah
Berkeley
Concord
Sonora
San Francisco
Oakland
Stockton
Yosemite Nat. Park
Boundary Peak 4005
Oakdale
Alameda
Daly City
Livermore
El Portal
Piper Pk 2880
Goldfield
2
San Mateo
Hayward
Modesto
White Mtn Peak 4342
Redwood City
Turlock
Mariposa
Sunnyvale
Santa Clara
San Jose
Bishop
Merced
Gustine
San Joaquin
Los Gatos
Big Pine
Gilroy
Diablo Range
Owens
Santa Cruz
Los Banos
Madera
Pine Flat Resr
Kings Canyon Nat. Park
Watsonville
Independence
Beatty
Monterey Bay
Pinedale
Salinas
Fresno
Panamint Range
Death Valley
Pt Pinos
Monterey
Lone Pine
Sequoia Nat. Park
Mt Whitney 4418
Gonzales
San Joaquin Valley
Owens L.
Exeter
Hanford
Keeler
Santa Lucia Range
King City
Lemoore
Visalia
-86
Tulare
Telescope Peak 3368
Coalinga
Salinas
Porterville
Earlimart
Delano
C A L I F O R N I A
S I E R R A N E V A D A
Inyokern
P A C I F I C
Paso Robles
Wasco
Kern
O C E A N
Oildale
Morro Bay
Bakersfield
Johannesburg
San Luis Obispo
Arvin
Grover City
Mojave
Tehachapi Pass
35
Santa Maria
Mojave Desert
Barstow
Yermo
Tehachapi Mts
Lancaster
Lompoc
Santa Barbara
Victorville
Pt Conception
Santa Paula
Fillmore
Mt San Antonio 3068
Burbank
Glendale
Santa Barbara Chan.
Ventura
San Bernardino
Pasadena
Beverly Hills
Santa Cruz
Oxnard
Santa Monica
Redlands
San Miguel
Pomona
Beaumont
Los Angeles
Riverside
Santa Rosa
Torrance
Anaheim
San Jacinto Peak 3301
Long Beach
Santa Ana
Channel Islands
Huntington Beach
Palm Springs
3
120
Laguna Beach
San Clemente
Santa Catalina
Palomar Mtn 1871
Gulf of Santa Catalina
Vista
Escondido
Oceanside
Carlsbad
San Clemente
Ramona
La Mesa
El Cajon
San Diego
National City
Chula Vista
Tijuana
Tecate
B
Descanso
160
Hanalei
Kauai
1548
Mana
Lihue
Kaulakahi Channel
Kauai Channel
Niihau
Kahuku Pt
Kaena Pt
Wahiawa
1227
Kailua
Oahu
Pearl City
Pearl Harbor
Honolulu
Kaiwi Chan.
Molokai
PACIFIC
Kaunakakai
Pailolo Chan.
Wailuku
Lanai
Lanai City
Nat. Pk
Hana
3055
Maui
Kealaikahiki Chan.
Kahoolawe
OCEAN
Alenuihaha Channel
155
Kapaau
Upolu Point
Waimea
20N
Mauna Kea 4201
Hakalau
Hilo
Kailua
Kilauea Crater
160
USA, Hawaii
4169
Mauna Loa
1243
Pahoa
Hawaii
Hawaii Volcanoes Nat. Park
0 100 200 km
0 50 100 mls
Milolii
C
Ka Lae (South Cape)
Naalehu

1:2.5M 0 25 50 75 100 km
0 25 50 mls

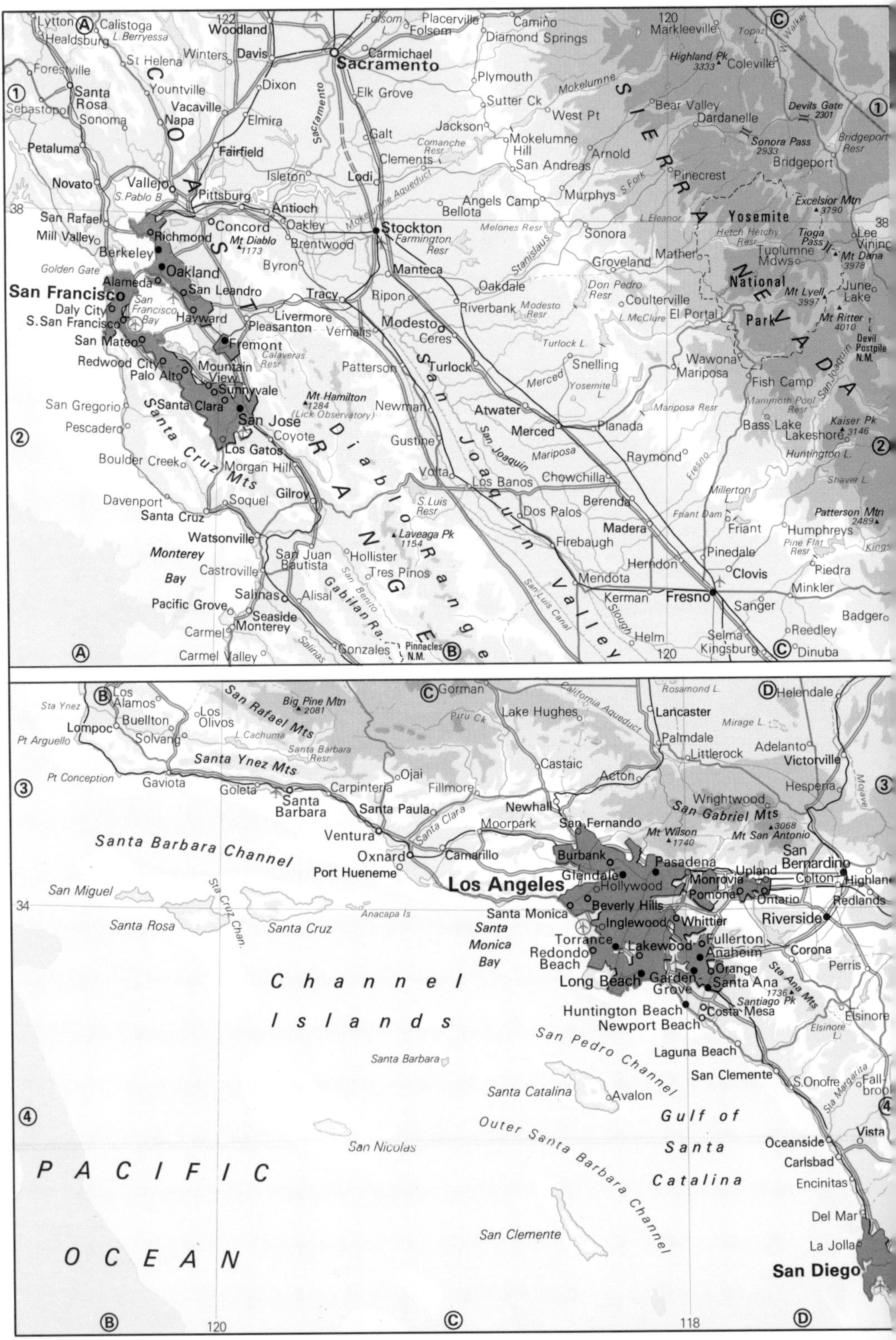

Lytton
Calistoga
Healdsburg
L. Berryessa
Woodland
Folsom L.
Placerville
Folsom
Camino
Diamond Springs
Markleeville
Topaz L.
W. Walker
St Helena
Winters
Davis
Carmichael
Sacramento
Highland Pk 3333
Coleville
Forestville
Yountville
Dixon
Plymouth
Santa Rosa
Sebastopol
Sonoma
Vacaville
Napa
Elmira
Sacramento
Elk Grove
Sutter Ck
Mokelumne
Bear Valley
West Pt
Dardanelle
Devils Gate 2301
Petaluma
Fairfield
Galt
Jackson
Comanche Resr
Mokelumne Hill
Arnold
Sonora Pass 2933
Bridgeport Resr
Bridgeport
Novato
Vallejo
S. Pablo B.
Pittsburg
Isleton
Lodi
Clements
San Andreas
Pinecrest
Antioch
Oakley
Mokelumne Aqueduct
Bellota
Angels Camp
Murphys
S. Fork
Excelsior Mtn 3790
San Rafael
Mill Valley
Richmond
Concord
Mt Diablo 1173
Brentwood
Stockton
Farmington Resr
Melones Resr
Sonora
L. Eleanor
Yosemite National Park
Hetch Hetchy Resr
Tioga Pass
Lee Vining
Berkeley
Golden Gate
Oakland
Byron
Manteca
Stanislaus
Groveland
Mather
Tuolumne Mdws
Mt Dana 3978
San Francisco
Alameda
San Leandro
Tracy
Ripon
Oakdale
Don Pedro Resr
Coulterville
June Lake
Daly City
S. San Francisco
San Francisco Bay
Hayward
Livermore
Pleasanton
Vernalis
Modesto
Ceres
Riverbank
Modesto Resr
L. McClure
El Portal
Mt Lyell 3997
Mt Ritter 4010
San Mateo
Fremont
Calaveras Resr
Turlock L.
Devil Postpile N.M.
Redwood City
Palo Alto
Mountain View
Sunnyvale
Patterson
Turlock
Snelling
Merced
Yosemite L.
Wawona
Mariposa
Fish Camp
San Gregorio
Santa Clara
Mt Hamilton 1284 (Lick Observatory)
Newman
Atwater
Mariposa Resr
Mammoth Pool Resr
San Joaquin
Pescadero
San Jose
Coyote
Merced
Planada
Bass Lake
Kaiser Pk 3146
Lakeshore
Gustine
San Joaquin
Mariposa
Raymond
Huntington L.
Boulder Creek
Los Gatos
Morgan Hill
Santa Cruz Mts
Diablo Range
Volta
Los Banos
Chowchilla
Fresno
Shaver L.
Davenport
Santa Cruz
Soquel
Gilroy
S. Luis Resr
Dos Palos
Berenda
Millerton L.
Friant Dam
Patterson Mtn 2489
Watsonville
Laveaga Pk 1154
Madera
Friant
Humphreys
Monterey Bay
Firebaugh
Pine Flat Resr
Kings
Castroville
San Juan Bautista
Hollister
Tres Pinos
Herndon
Pinedale
Clovis
Piedra
Mendota
San Benito
San Luis Canal
Salinas
Alisal
Kerman
Fresno
Minkler
Pacific Grove
Seaside
Monterey
Gabilan Ra.
Slough
Sanger
Badger
Carmel
Salinas
Gonzales
Pinnacles N.M.
Helm
Selma
Kingsburg
Reedley
Carmel Valley
Dinuba
Coast Ranges
Sierra Nevada
San Joaquin Valley
38
122
120
A
B
C
1
2

Los Alamos
Sta Ynez
San Rafael Mts
Big Pine Mtn 2081
Gorman
California Aqueduct
Rosamond L.
Helendale
Lompoc
Buellton
Los Olivos
Piru Ck
Lake Hughes
Lancaster
Pt Arguello
Solvang
L. Cachuma
Santa Barbara Resr
Mirage L.
Palmdale
Littlerock
Adelanto
Victorville
Santa Ynez Mts
Castaic
Pt Conception
Gaviota
Ojai
Acton
Mojave
Hesperia
Goleta
Carpinteria
Fillmore
Santa Barbara
Santa Paula
Newhall
Wrightwood
San Gabriel Mts
Santa Clara
Ventura
Moorpark
San Fernando
Mt Wilson 1740
3068
Mt San Antonio
Santa Barbara Channel
Oxnard
Camarillo
Burbank
Pasadena
San Bernardino
Port Hueneme
Glendale
Hollywood
Upland
Colton
Highland
Los Angeles
Monrovia
Pomona
Ontario
Redlands
San Miguel
Sta Cruz Chan.
Beverly Hills
Santa Rosa
Santa Cruz
Anacapa Is
Santa Monica
Inglewood
Whittier
Riverside
Santa Monica Bay
Torrance
Redondo Beach
Lakewood
Fullerton
Anaheim
Corona
Perris
Long Beach
Garden Grove
Orange
Santa Ana
Sta Ana Mts
1736
Santiago Pk
Channel Islands
Huntington Beach
Costa Mesa
Elsinore
Newport Beach
San Pedro Channel
Elsinore L.
Laguna Beach
Santa Barbara
San Clemente
Santa Catalina
Avalon
S. Onofre
Fallbrook
Sta Margarita
Gulf of Santa Catalina
Outer Santa Barbara Channel
Vista
San Nicolas
Oceanside
Carlsbad
Encinitas
PACIFIC OCEAN
Del Mar
San Clemente
La Jolla
San Diego
34
120
118
B
C
D
3
4

GULF OF MEXICO
Cd Madero
Tampico
Poza Rica
Veracruz
Jalapa
Córdoba
Orizaba
Puebla
Tlaxcala
México
Xochimilco
Toluca
Cuernavaca
Pachuca
Querétaro
Celaya
Salamanca
Irapuato
León
Guanajuato
San Luis Potosí
Aguascalientes
Guadalajara
Tlaquepaque
Morelia
Uruapan
Zamora
Colima
Manzanillo
Tepic
Acapulco
Chilpancingo
Iguala
Taxco
Oaxaca
Tehuacán
Tuxtepec
Tehuantepec
Salina Cruz
Lázaro Cárdenas
QUERÉTARO
HIDALGO
GUANAJUATO
MORELOS
TLAXCALA
JALISCO
COLIMA
MICHOACÁN
GUERRERO
OAXACA
NAYARIT
VERACRUZ
Nev. de Toluca 4558
Popocatepetl 5450
Vol. Citlaltepetl 5700
L. de Chapala

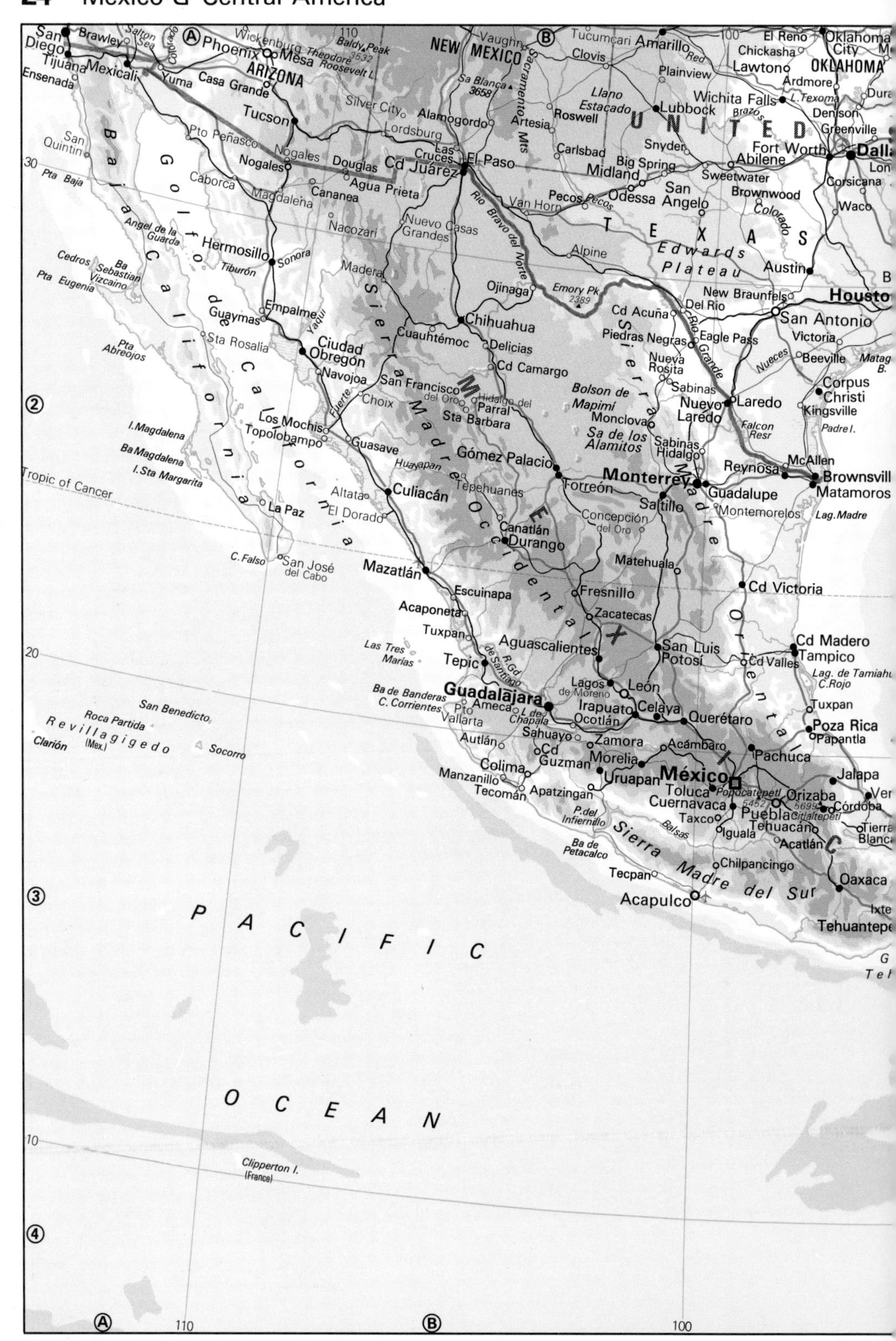

San Diego
Tijuana
Ensenada
Brawley
Salton Sea
Colorado
Mexicali
Yuma
Phoenix
Mesa
Baldy Peak 3532
Theodore Roosevelt L.
ARIZONA
Casa Grande
Tucson
Silver City
Lordsburg
Alamogordo
NEW MEXICO
Sa Blanca 3658
Sacramento Mts
Vaughn
Artesia
Roswell
Tucumcari
Clovis
Amarillo
Red
Llano Estacado
Lubbock
Plainview
Chickasha
El Reno
Oklahoma City
Lawton
OKLAHOMA
Ardmore
Wichita Falls
L. Texoma
Denison
Greenville
Brazos
UNITED
Dallas
Fort Worth
Abilene
Snyder
Big Spring
Midland
Odessa
Sweetwater
San Angelo
Brownwood
Colorado
Corsicana
Waco
Pecos
Van Horn
Carlsbad
Las Cruces
El Paso
Cd Juárez
Douglas
Agua Prieta
Nogales
Cananea
Nacozari
Magdalena
Caborca
Pto Peñasco
San Quintín
Pta Baja
Baja California
Golfo de California
Hermosillo
Sonora
Tiburón
Angel de la Guarda
Cedros
Ba Sebastián Vizcaíno
Pta Eugenia
Guaymas
Empalme
Yaqui
Sta Rosalía
Pta Abreojos
Ciudad Obregón
Navojoa
Nuevo Casas Grandes
Madera
Rio Bravo del Norte
Alpine
Emory Pk. 2389
TEXAS
Edwards Plateau
Austin
Houston
New Braunfels
Del Rio
San Antonio
Cd Acuña
Piedras Negras
Eagle Pass
Rio Grande
Victoria
Nueces
Beeville
Corpus Christi
Kingsville
Padre I.
Ojinaga
Chihuahua
Cuauhtémoc
Delicias
Cd Camargo
Sierra Madre Occidental
MEXICO
Nueva Rosita
Sabinas
Bolson de Mapimí
Monclova
Sa de los Alamitos
Nuevo Laredo
Laredo
Falcon Resr
Sabinas Hidalgo
McAllen
Reynosa
Brownsville
Matamoros
Lag. Madre
San Francisco del Oro
Hidalgo del Parral
Sta Barbara
Choix
Fuerte
Los Mochis
Topolobampo
Guasave
I. Magdalena
Ba Magdalena
I. Sta Margarita
Tropic of Cancer
Gómez Palacio
Torreón
Monterrey
Guadalupe
Saltillo
Montemorelos
Sierra Madre Oriental
Huayapan
Tepehuanes
Altata
Culiacán
El Dorado
La Paz
C. Falso
San José del Cabo
Mazatlán
Canatlán
Durango
Concepción del Oro
Matehuala
Cd Victoria
Escuinapa
Fresnillo
Acaponeta
Zacatecas
Tuxpan
Las Tres Marías
Tepic
R. Gd de Santiago
Aguascalientes
San Luis Potosí
Cd Madero
Tampico
Cd Valles
Lag. de Tamiahua
C. Rojo
Guadalajara
Ba de Banderas
C. Corrientes
Pto Vallarta
Ameca
L. de Chapala
Lagos de Moreno
León
Irapuato
Celaya
Ocotlán
Querétaro
Tuxpan
Poza Rica
Papantla
San Benedicto
Roca Partida
Revillagigedo (Mex.)
Clarión
Socorro
Autlán
Sahuayo
Zamora
Cd Guzman
Morelia
Acámbaro
Pachuca
Colima
Manzanillo
Tecomán
Apatzingan
Uruapan
México
Toluca
Popocatépetl 5452
Cuernavaca
Taxco
Iguala
Puebla
Orizaba
Citlaltépetl 5699
Córdoba
Jalapa
Tehuacán
Acatlán
Tierra Blanca
P. del Infiernillo
Balsas
Sierra Madre del Sur
Ba de Petacalco
Tecpan
Chilpancingo
Acapulco
Oaxaca
Tehuantepec
PACIFIC OCEAN
Clipperton I. (France)
110
100
30
20
10

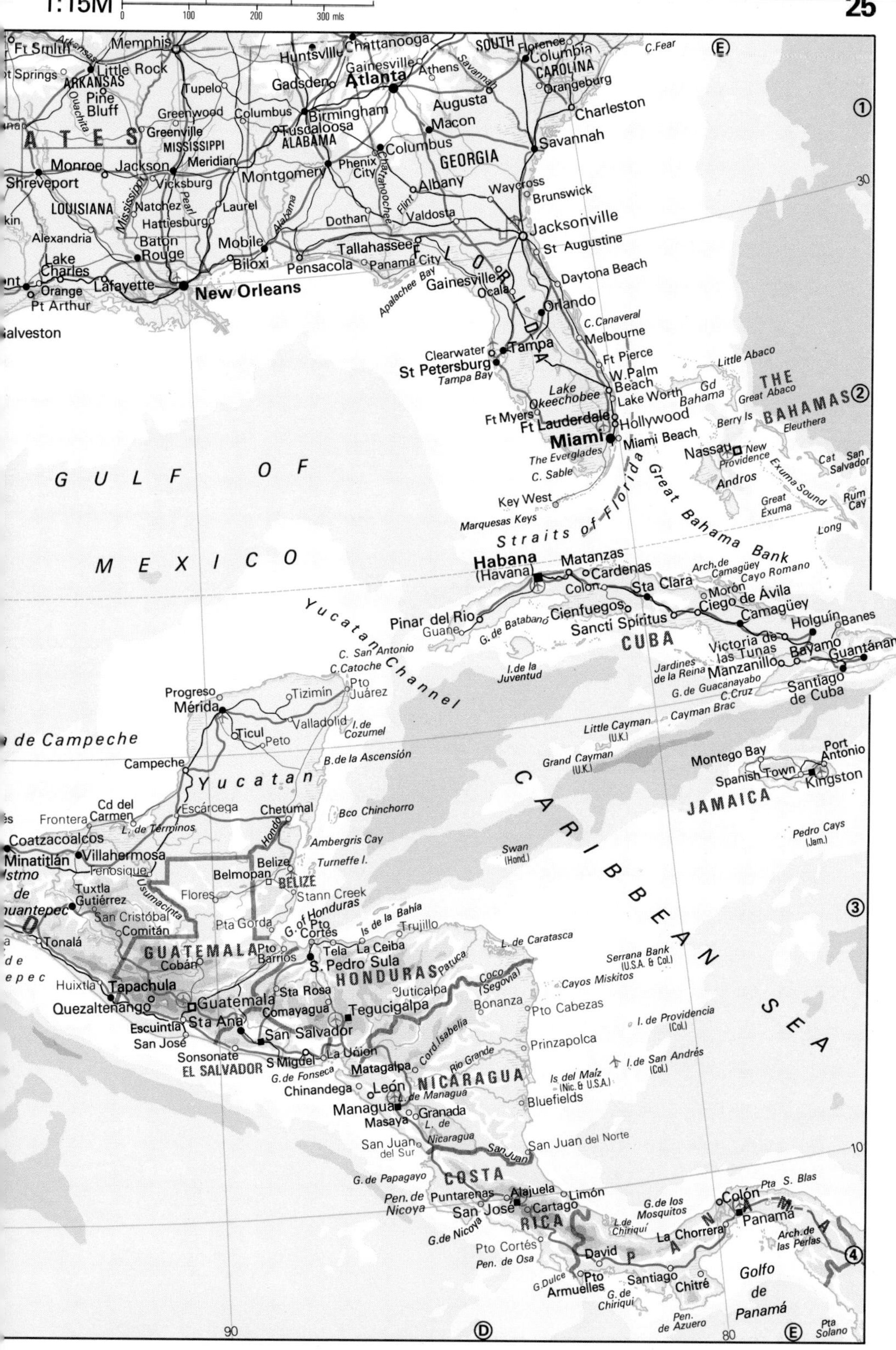
Ft Smith
Memphis
Chattanooga
Huntsville
SOUTH
Florence
Columbia
CAROLINA
C.Fear
Little Rock
ARKANSAS
Pine Bluff
Gainesville
Atlanta
Athens
Gadsden
Orangeburg
Tupelo
Augusta
Charleston
Greenwood
Columbus
Birmingham
Macon
Greenville
Tuscaloosa
ALABAMA
MISSISSIPPI
Savannah
Columbus
GEORGIA
Monroe
Jackson
Meridian
Phenix City
Shreveport
Vicksburg
Montgomery
Albany
Waycross
Brunswick
LOUISIANA
Natchez
Laurel
Hattiesburg
Dothan
Valdosta
Jacksonville
Alexandria
Baton Rouge
Mobile
Tallahassee
St Augustine
Lake Charles
Biloxi
Pensacola
Panama City
FLORIDA
Daytona Beach
Orange
Lafayette
New Orleans
Apalachee Bay
Gainesville
Ocala
Pt Arthur
Orlando
C. Canaveral
Melbourne
Clearwater
Tampa
St Petersburg
Tampa Bay
Ft Pierce
Little Abaco
W.Palm Beach
THE
Lake Okeechobee
Lake Worth
Gd Bahama
Great Abaco
BAHAMAS
Ft Myers
Ft Lauderdale
Hollywood
Berry Is
Eleuthera
Miami
Miami Beach
Nassau
New Providence
Cat
San Salvador
The Everglades
C. Sable
Andros
Exuma Sound
GULF OF MEXICO
Key West
Great Exuma
Rum Cay
Marquesas Keys
Straits of Florida
Great Bahama Bank
Long
Habana (Havana)
Matanzas
Cardenas
Arch. de Camagüey
Cayo Romano
Colon
Sta Clara
Morón
Ciego de Ávila
Yucatan Channel
Pinar del Rio
G. de Batabanó
Cienfuegos
Camagüey
Holguín
Banes
Guane
Sancti Spíritus
CUBA
Victoria de las Tunas
Bayamo
Guantánamo
C. San Antonio
C.Catoche
I. de la Juventud
Jardines de la Reina
Manzanillo
Santiago de Cuba
G. de Guacanayabo
C.Cruz
Progreso
Mérida
Tizimín
Pto Juárez
Valladolid
I. de Cozumel
Little Cayman (U.K.)
Cayman Brac
Ticul
Peto
de Campeche
Campeche
B. de la Ascensión
Grand Cayman (U.K.)
Montego Bay
Port Antonio
Yucatan
Spanish Town
Kingston
Cd del Carmen
Frontera
Escárcega
Chetumal
Bco Chinchorro
JAMAICA
L. de Términos
Coatzacoalcos
Hondo
Ambergris Cay
Pedro Cays (Jam.)
Minatitlán
Villahermosa
Belize
Turneffe I.
Swan (Hond.)
Tenosique
Belmopan
BELIZE
Tuxtla Gutiérrez
Usumacinta
Flores
Stann Creek
CARIBBEAN SEA
San Cristóbal
Pta Gorda
G. of Honduras
Is de la Bahía
Trujillo
Comitán
Pto Cortés
Tonalá
L. de Caratasca
GUATEMALA
Pto Barrios
Tela
La Ceiba
Serrana Bank (U.S.A. & Col.)
Cobán
S. Pedro Sula
HONDURAS
Patuca
Coco (Segovia)
Huixtla
Tapachula
Juticalpa
Cayos Miskitos
Sta Rosa
Guatemala
Comayagua
Tegucigalpa
Bonanza
Quezaltenango
Pto Cabezas
Escuintla
Sta Ana
I. de Providencia (Col.)
San José
San Salvador
Cord. Isabelia
Prinzapolca
Sonsonate
La Unión
S Miguel
Rio Grande
I. de San Andrés (Col.)
EL SALVADOR
G. de Fonseca
Matagalpa
NICARAGUA
Is del Maíz (Nic. & U.S.A.)
Chinandega
León
L. de Managua
Bluefields
Managua
Granada
Masaya
L. de Nicaragua
San Juan del Sur
San Juan
San Juan del Norte
G. de Papagayo
COSTA RICA
Pta S. Blas
Alajuela
Limón
Pen. de Nicoya
Puntarenas
Cartago
G. de los Mosquitos
Colón
San José
L. de Chiriquí
Panamá
G. de Nicoya
La Chorrera
Arch. de las Perlas
Pto Cortés
David
PANAMA
Pen. de Osa
G. Dulce
Pto Armuelles
Santiago
Chitré
Golfo de Panamá
G. de Chiriquí
Pen. de Azuero
Pta Solano
30
10
90
80

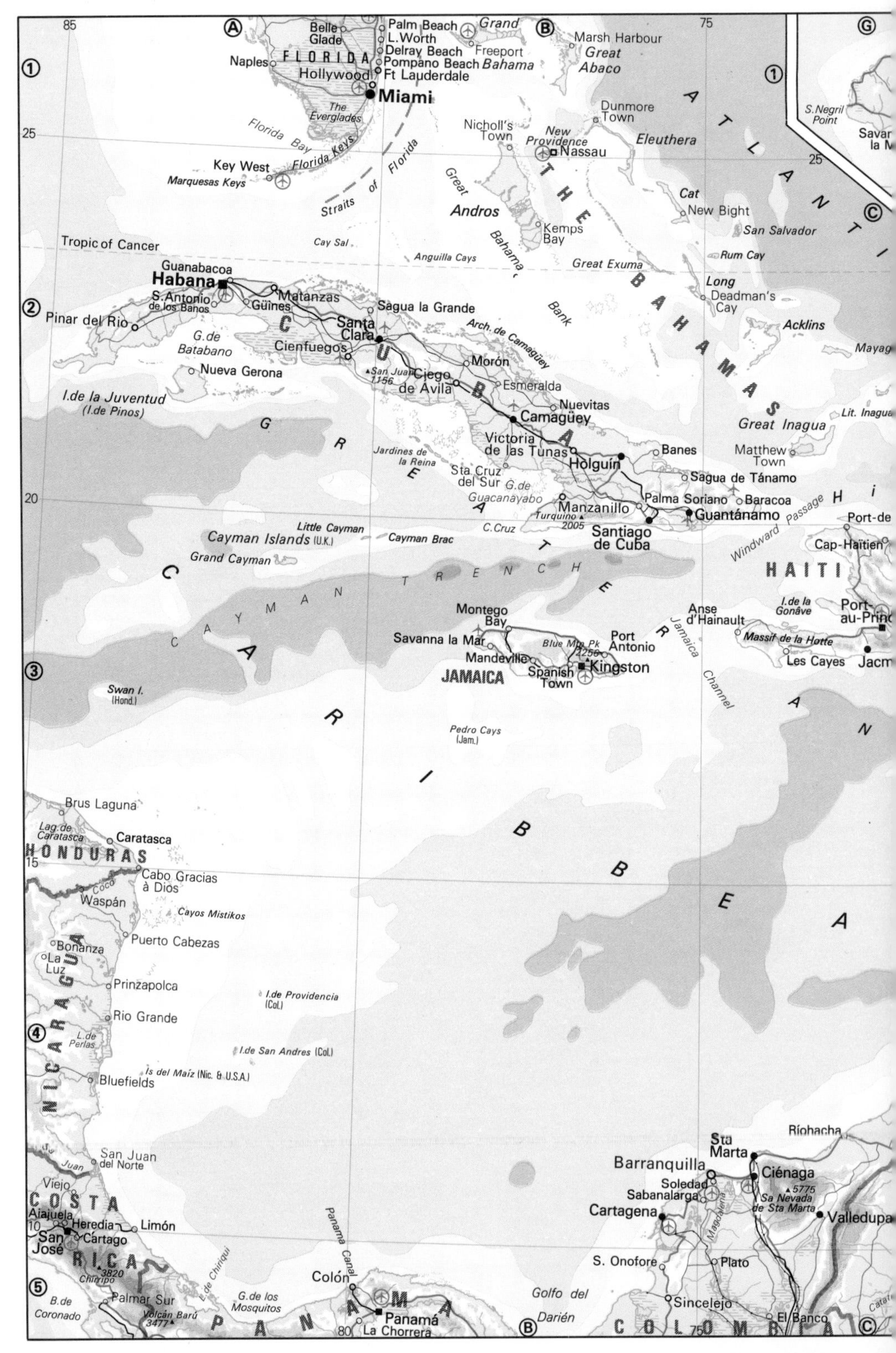
FLORIDA
Belle Glade
Palm Beach
L. Worth
Delray Beach
Pompano Beach
Ft Lauderdale
Hollywood
Naples
Miami
The Everglades
Florida Bay
Florida Keys
Key West
Marquesas Keys
Straits of Florida
Grand Bahama
Freeport
Marsh Harbour
Great Abaco
Dunmore Town
Nicholl's Town
New Providence
Nassau
Eleuthera
Great Andros
Great Bahama Bank
Kemps Bay
Cat
New Bight
San Salvador
Rum Cay
Great Exuma
Long
Deadman's Cay
Acklins
Mayag
Lit. Inagua
Great Inagua
Matthew Town
THE BAHAMAS
ATLANTIC
Tropic of Cancer
Cay Sal
Anguilla Cays
Guanabacoa
Habana
S. Antonio de los Baños
Matanzas
Güines
Pinar del Rio
Sagua la Grande
Santa Clara
Cienfuegos
G. de Batabano
Nueva Gerona
I. de la Juventud (I. de Pinos)
Arch. de Camagüey
CUBA
San Juan 1156
Ciego de Avila
Morón
Esmeralda
Nuevitas
Camagüey
Jardines de la Reina
Victoria de las Tunas
Banes
Holguín
Sagua de Tánamo
Sta Cruz del Sur
G. de Guacanayabo
Manzanillo
Turquino 2005
Palma Soriano
Baracoa
Guantánamo
Santiago de Cuba
C. Cruz
Windward Passage
Port-de
Cap-Haïtien
HAITI
Little Cayman
Cayman Islands (U.K.)
Cayman Brac
Grand Cayman
CAYMAN TRENCH
GREATER ANTILLES
I. de la Gonâve
Port-au-Princ
Anse d'Hainault
Massif de la Hotte
Les Cayes
Jacm
Montego Bay
Savanna la Mar
Blue Mt. Pk 2256
Port Antonio
Mandeville
Kingston
Spanish Town
JAMAICA
Jamaica Channel
Swan I. (Hond.)
Pedro Cays (Jam.)
CARIBBEAN
Brus Laguna
Lag. de Caratasca
Caratasca
HONDURAS
Cabo Gracias à Dios
Coco
Waspán
Cayos Mistikos
Puerto Cabezas
Bonanza
La Luz
Prinzapolca
I. de Providencia (Col.)
Rio Grande
L. de Perlas
I. de San Andres (Col.)
Is del Maíz (Nic. & U.S.A.)
Bluefields
NICARAGUA
San Juan del Norte
Juan
Viejo
COSTA RICA
Alajuela
Heredia
Limón
San José
Cartago
Chirripó 3820
E. de Chiriquí
B. de Coronado
Palmar Sur
Volcán Barú 3477
G. de los Mosquitos
Panama Canal
Colón
Panamá
La Chorrera
PANAMA
Golfo del Darién
Ríohacha
Sta Marta
Barranquilla
Ciénaga
Soledad
Sabanalarga
5775 Sa Nevada de Sta Marta
Cartagena
Magdalena
Valledupa
S. Onofore
Plato
Sincelejo
El Banco
COLOMBIA
S. Negril Point
Savar la M
85
80
75
25
20
15
10
A
B
C
G
1
2
3
4
5

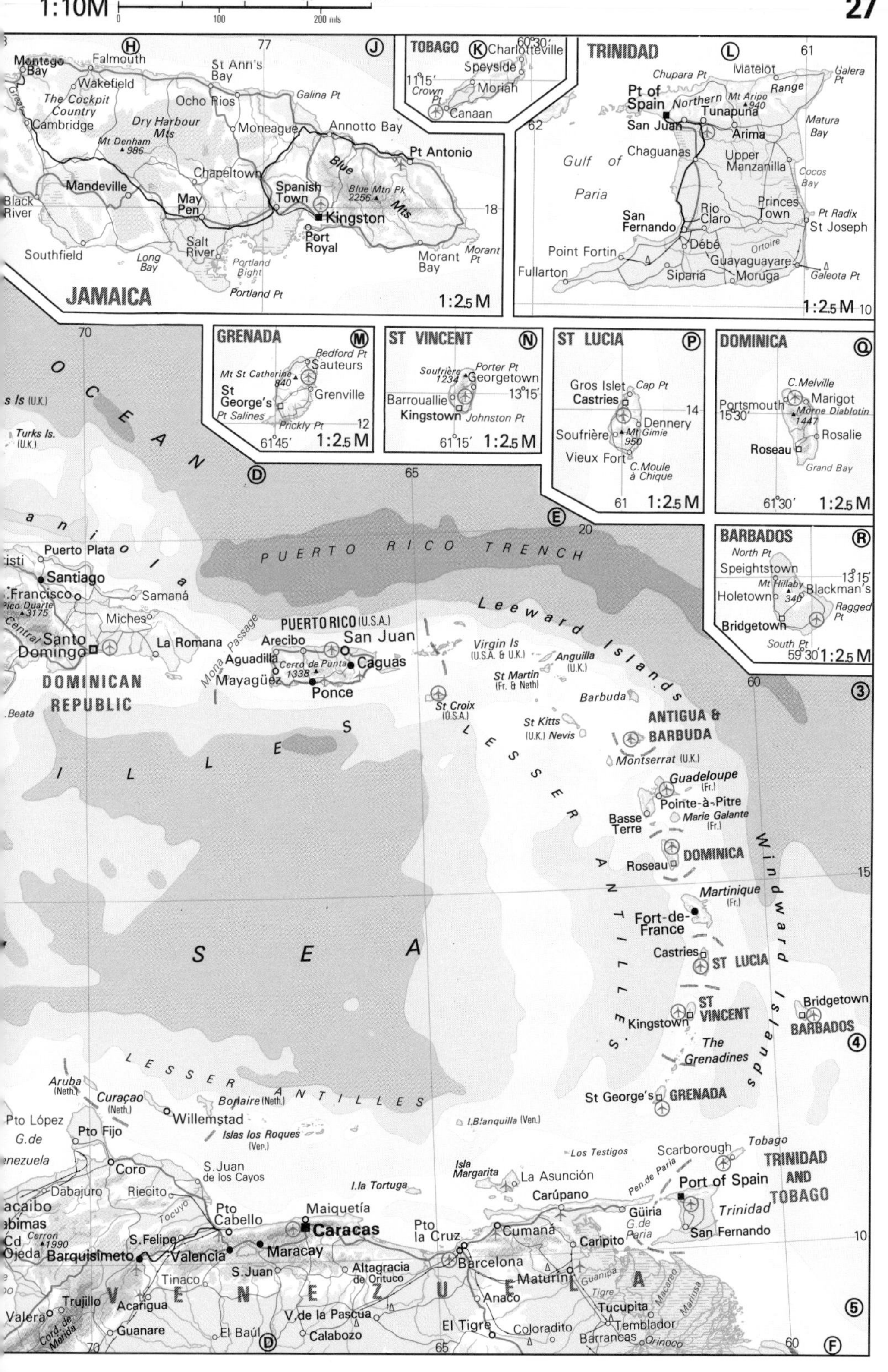
1:10M
JAMAICA
1:2.5 M
TOBAGO
TRINIDAD
GRENADA
ST VINCENT
ST LUCIA
DOMINICA
BARBADOS
Montego Bay
Falmouth
St Ann's Bay
Ocho Rios
Kingston
Spanish Town
Mandeville
May Pen
Port Royal
Pt Antonio
Annotto Bay
Blue Mts
Port of Spain
San Fernando
Arima
Chaguanas
Gulf of Paria
Scarborough
Charlotteville
St George's
Kingstown
Castries
Roseau
Bridgetown
PUERTO RICO TRENCH
Leeward Islands
Windward Islands
LESSER ANTILLES
PUERTO RICO (U.S.A.)
San Juan
Ponce
Mayagüez
Caguas
DOMINICAN REPUBLIC
Santo Domingo
Santiago
Virgin Is (U.S.A. & U.K.)
St Croix (U.S.A.)
Anguilla (U.K.)
St Martin (Fr. & Neth)
St Kitts (U.K.) Nevis
ANTIGUA & BARBUDA
Montserrat (U.K.)
Guadeloupe (Fr.)
Pointe-à-Pitre
Basse Terre
Marie Galante (Fr.)
Martinique (Fr.)
Fort-de-France
The Grenadines
TRINIDAD AND TOBAGO
S E A
Aruba (Neth.)
Curaçao (Neth.)
Bonaire (Neth.)
Willemstad
Caracas
Maracay
Valencia
Barquisimeto
Barcelona
Cumaná
Maturín
Ciudad Bolívar
V E N E Z U E L A
Isla Margarita
I. la Tortuga
Los Testigos
I. Blanquilla (Ven.)
Islas los Roques (Ven.)

1:40M 0 400 800 1200 1600 km / 0 400 800 mls

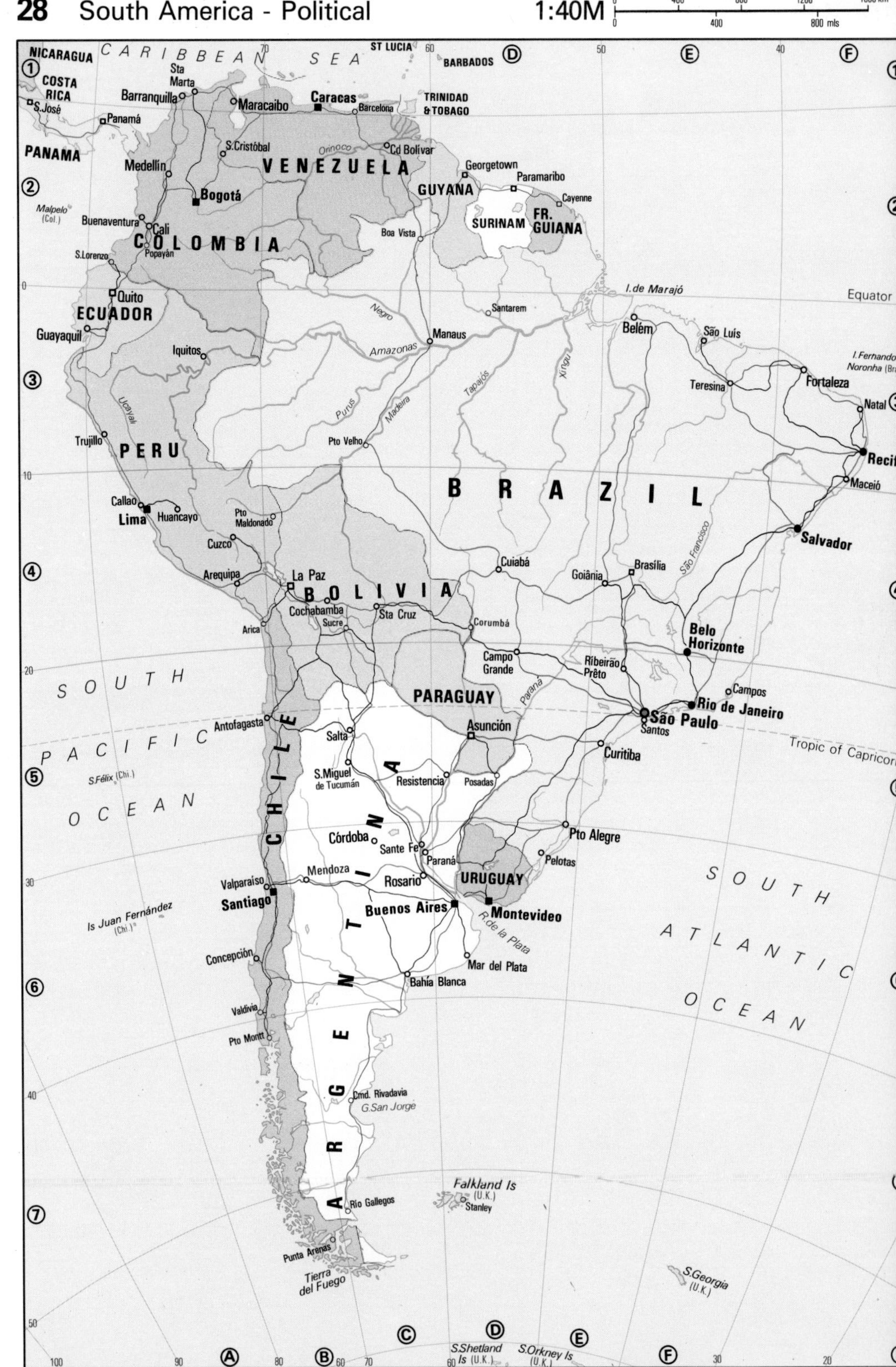

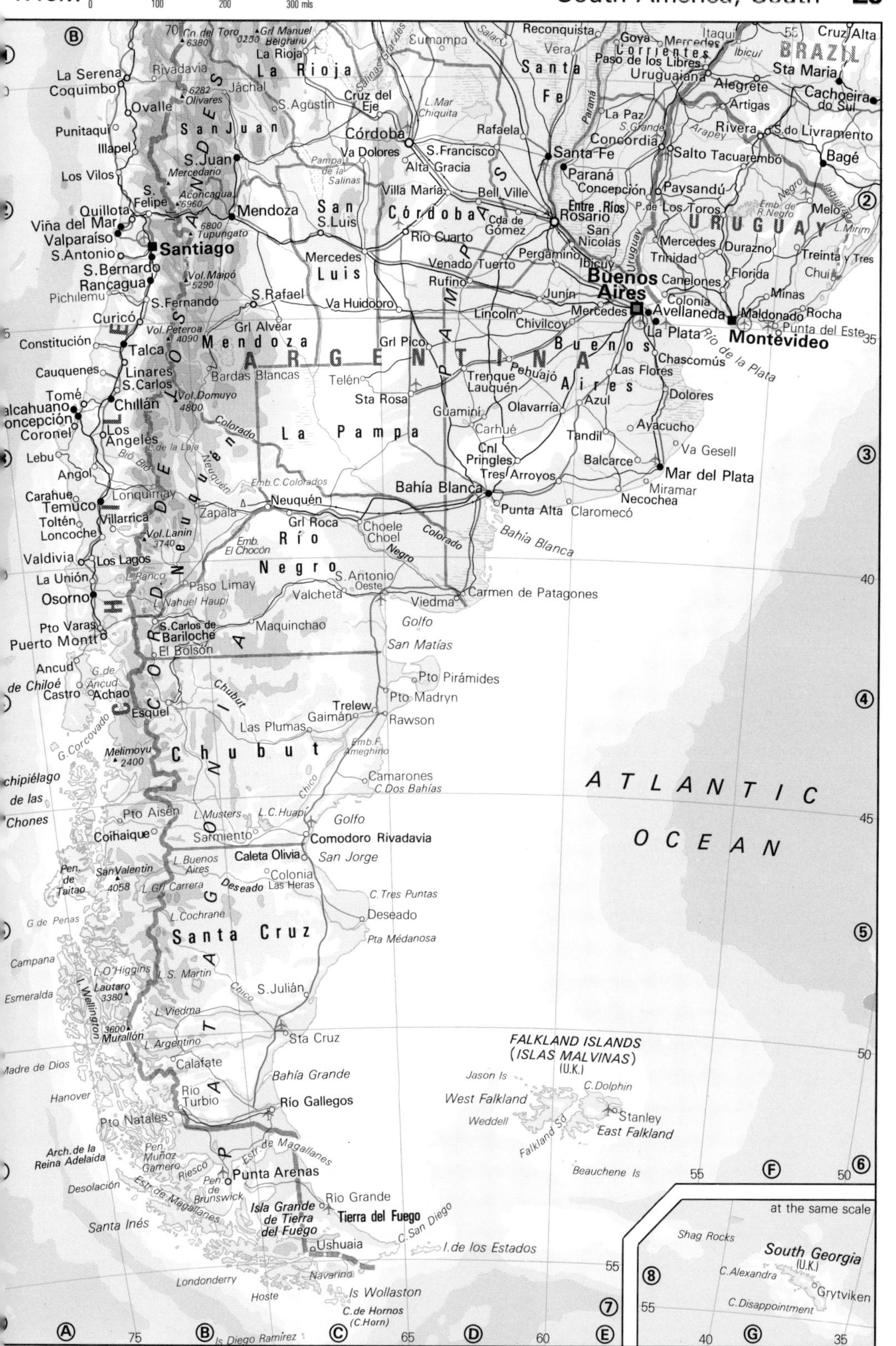
La Serena
Coquimbo
Ovalle
Punitaqui
Illapel
Los Vilos
Quillota
Viña del Mar
Valparaíso
S.Antonio
Santiago
S.Bernardo
Rancagua
Pichilemu
Curicó
Constitución
Talca
Cauquenes
Linares
S.Carlos
Tomé
Chillán
Coronel
Los Angeles
Lebu
Angol
Carahue
Temuco
Toltén
Villarrica
Loncoche
Valdivia
Los Lagos
La Unión
Osorno
Pto Varas
Puerto Montt
Ancud
Castro
Achao
Esquel
Coihaique
Pto Aisén
Calafate
Río Turbio
Pto Natales
Punta Arenas
Río Grande
Ushuaia
La Rioja
Rivadavia
Jáchal
S.Agustín
Cruz del Eje
Córdoba
Va Dolores
S.Francisco
Alta Gracia
Villa María
Bell Ville
Río Cuarto
Mendoza
S.Luis
Mercedes
S.Rafael
Grl Alvear
Va Huidobro
Venado Tuerto
Rufino
Junín
Lincoln
Chivilcoy
Pergamino
Rosario
San Nicolas
Santa Fe
Paraná
Rafaela
Reconquista
Vera
Goya
Corrientes
Paso de los Libres
Uruguaiana
Alegrete
Sta Maria
Cachoeira do Sul
Artigas
Rivera
S.do Livramento
Bagé
Salto
Tacuarembó
Paysandú
Concordia
La Paz
Concepción
Melo
Mercedes
Durazno
Trinidad
Treinta y Tres
Florida
Canelones
Colonia
Minas
Maldonado
Rocha
Montevideo
Punta del Este
Buenos Aires
Avellaneda
La Plata
Chascomús
Las Flores
Dolores
Azul
Olavarría
Tandil
Ayacucho
Balcarce
Va Gesell
Mar del Plata
Miramar
Necochea
Claromecó
Tres Arroyos
Cnl Pringles
Carhué
Guaminí
Trenque Lauquén
Pehuajó
Grl Pico
Telén
Sta Rosa
Bahía Blanca
Punta Alta
Neuquén
Zapala
Grl Roca
Choele Choel
S.Antonio Oeste
Valcheta
Viedma
Carmen de Patagones
Maquinchao
S.Carlos de Bariloche
El Bolsón
Paso Limay
Pto Pirámides
Pto Madryn
Trelew
Gaimán
Rawson
Las Plumas
Camarones
Comodoro Rivadavia
Sarmiento
Caleta Olivia
Colonia Las Heras
Deseado
S.Julián
Sta Cruz
Río Gallegos
ARGENTINA
URUGUAY
BRAZIL
La Rioja
San Juan
San Luis
Córdoba
Santa Fe
Entre Ríos
Buenos Aires
La Pampa
Mendoza
Neuquén
Río Negro
Chubut
Santa Cruz
Tierra del Fuego
Isla Grande de Tierra del Fuego
PAMPAS
PATAGONIA
CORDILLERA
ANDES
Aconcagua 6960
Tupungato 6800
Mercedario
Vol. Maipó 5290
Vol. Peteroa 4090
Vol. Domuyo 4800
Vol. Lanín 3740
Melimoyu 2400
San Valentín 4058
Lautaro 3380
Murallón 3600
Golfo San Matías
Golfo San Jorge
Bahía Blanca
Bahía Grande
Río de la Plata
Estr. de Magallanes
C. San Diego
I. de los Estados
Navarino
Is Wollaston
C. de Hornos (C. Horn)
Is Diego Ramírez
ATLANTIC OCEAN
FALKLAND ISLANDS (ISLAS MALVINAS) (U.K.)
West Falkland
East Falkland
Stanley
Jason Is
Weddell
C. Dolphin
Falkland Sd
Beauchene Is
at the same scale
Shag Rocks
South Georgia (U.K.)
C. Alexandra
Grytviken
C. Disappointment
Arch. de la Reina Adelaida
Desolación
Santa Inés
Hanover
Madre de Dios
Esmeralda
Campana
G. de Penas
Pen. de Taitao
Archipiélago de las Chones
G. Corcovado
Londonderry
Hoste

1:15M

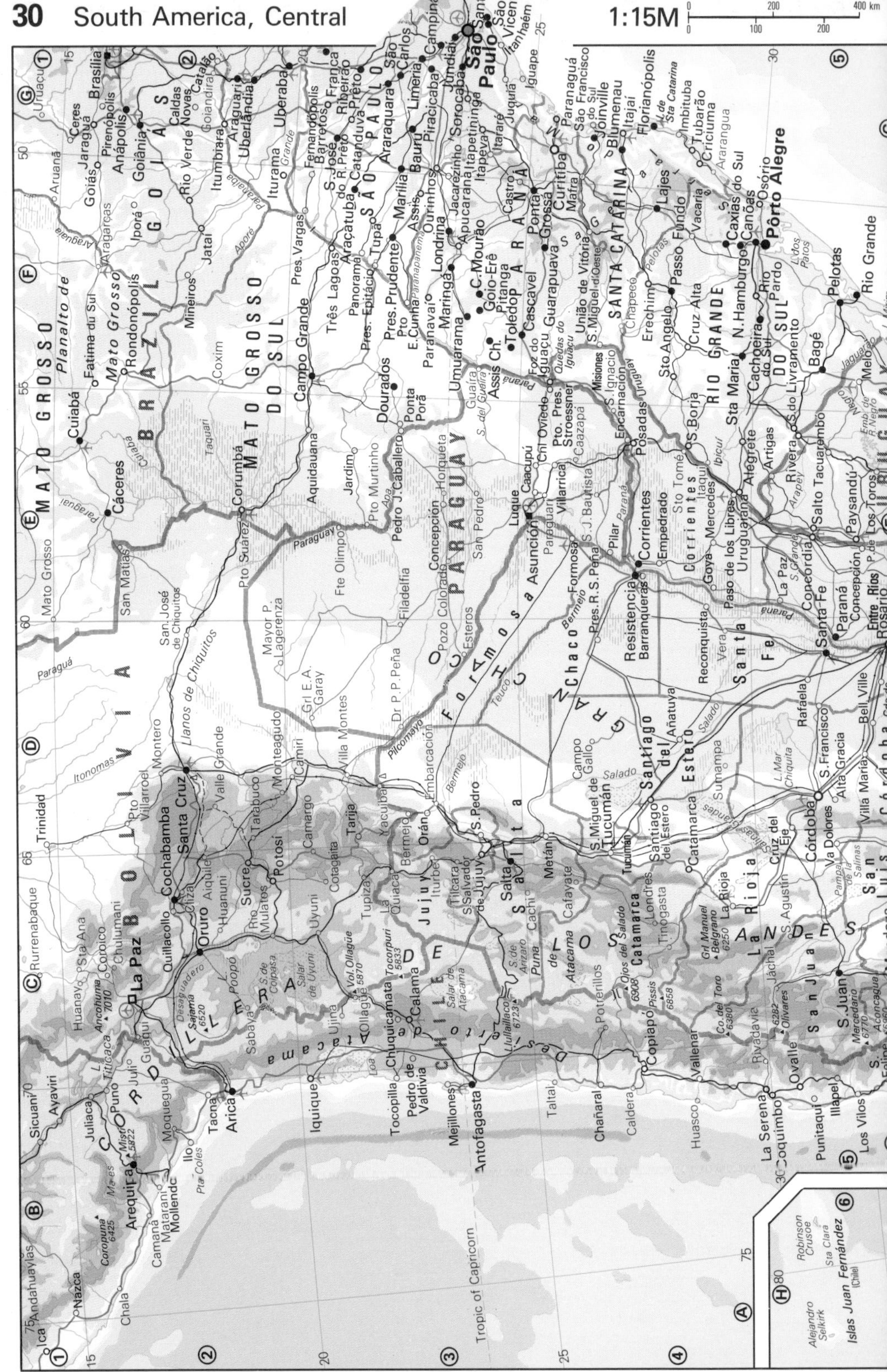

MATO GROSSO
MATO GROSSO DO SUL
BRAZIL
GOIÁS
SÃO PAULO
PARANÁ
SANTA CATARINA
RIO GRANDE DO SUL
BOLIVIA
PARAGUAY
URUGUAY
CHILE
GRAN CHACO
Planalto de Mato Grosso
Llanos de Chiquitos
Desierto de Atacama
ANDES
São Paulo
Santos
Campinas
Curitiba
Pôrto Alegre
Florianópolis
Brasília
Goiânia
Anápolis
Uberaba
Uberlândia
Cuiabá
Campo Grande
Corumbá
Londrina
Maringá
Asunción
Concepción
Corrientes
Resistencia
Posadas
Santa Fe
Rosario
Paraná
Córdoba
Tucumán
Salta
Santiago del Estero
Catamarca
La Rioja
San Juan
Mendoza
La Paz
Oruro
Cochabamba
Santa Cruz
Sucre
Potosí
Tarija
Arequipa
Arica
Iquique
Antofagasta
Calama
Copiapó
La Serena
Coquimbo
Tropic of Capricorn
Islas Juan Fernández (Chile)
Robinson Crusoe
Alejandro Selkirk

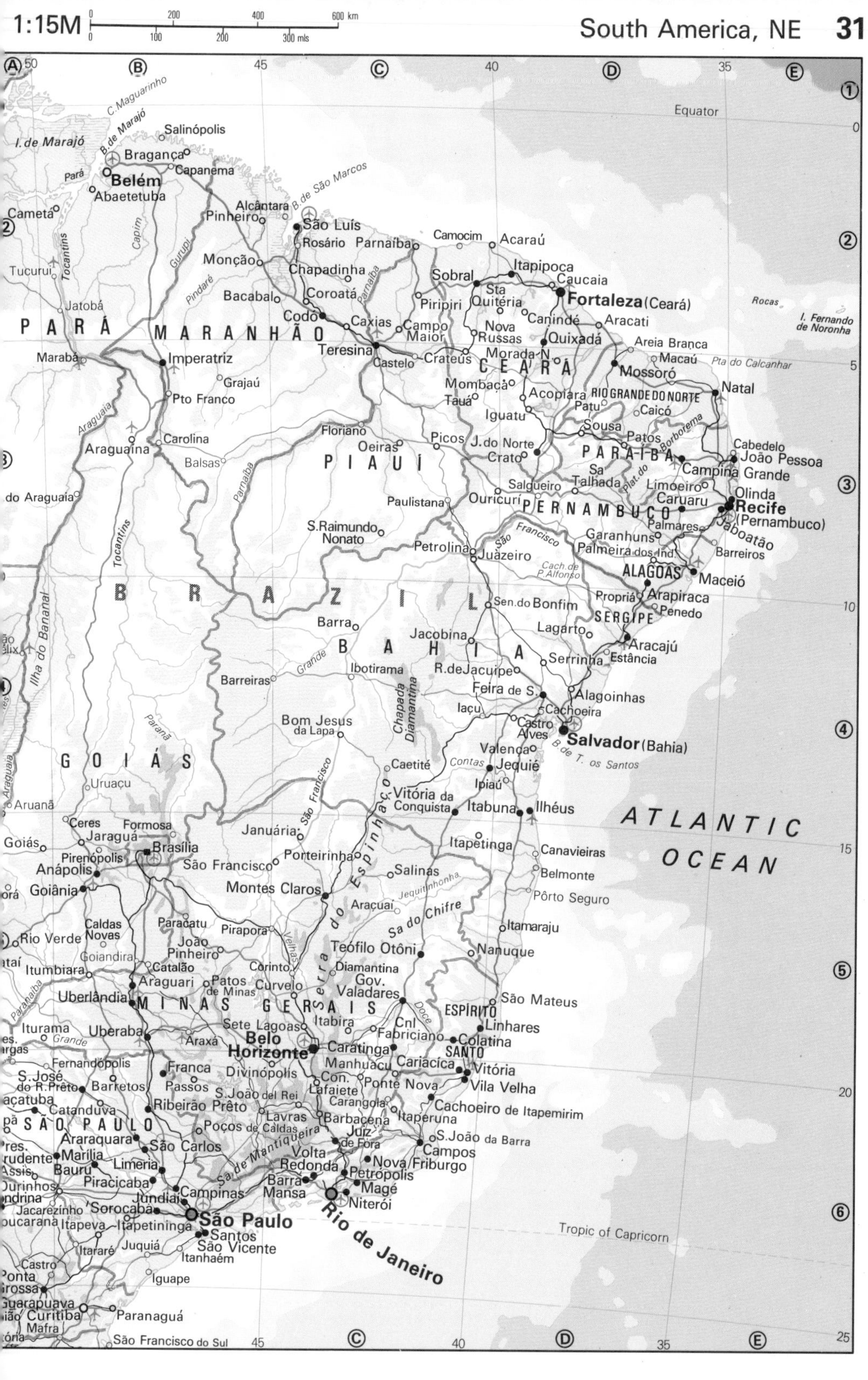
A B C D E
50 45 40 35
1 2 3 4 5 6
0 5 10 15 20 25
Equator
C. Maguarinho
B. de Marajó
I. de Marajó
Salinópolis
Bragança
Capanema
Pará
Belém
Abaetetuba
Cametá
Alcântara
B. de São Marcos
Pinheiro
São Luís
Rosário
Parnaíba
Camocim
Acaraú
Tucuruí
Tocantins
Capim
Gurupi
Monção
Chapadinha
Itapipoca
Sobral
Caucaia
Pindaré
Bacabal
Coroatá
Parnaíba
Piripiri
Sta Quitéria
Fortaleza (Ceará)
Rocas
I. Fernando de Noronha
Jatobá
Codó
Caxias
Campo Maior
Canindé
Aracati
PARÁ
MARANHÃO
Nova Russas
Quixadá
Teresina
Areia Branca
Marabá
Imperatriz
Castelo
Crateús
Morada N.
CEARÁ
Macaú
Pta do Calcanhar
Mossoró
Grajaú
Mombaça
Natal
Tauá
Acopiara
RIO GRANDE DO NORTE
Pto Franco
Patu
Caicó
Iguatu
Araguaia
Sousa
Carolina
Floriano
Picos
J. do Norte
Patos
Plat. da Borborema
Cabedelo
Araguaína
Oeiras
Crato
PARAÍBA
João Pessoa
Balsas
PIAUÍ
Sa Talhada
Campina Grande
Salgueiro
Limoeiro
do Araguaia
Paulistana
Ouricuri
PERNAMBUCO
Caruaru
Olinda
Recife (Pernambuco)
Palmares
Jaboatão
S. Raimundo Nonato
São Francisco
Garanhuns
Tocantins
Petrolina
Juazeiro
Palmeira dos Índ.
Barreiros
Cach. de P. Afonso
ALAGOAS
Maceió
BRAZIL
Propriá
Arapiraca
Sen. do Bonfim
Penedo
SERGIPE
Ilha do Bananal
Barra
Jacobina
Lagarto
Aracajú
BAHIA
Estância
Serrinha
Ibotirama
R. de Jacuípe
Barreiras
Grande
Feira de S.
Alagoinhas
Chapada Diamantina
Iaçu
Cachoeira
Paranã
Bom Jesus da Lapa
Castro Alves
Salvador (Bahia)
Valença
B. de T. os Santos
GOIÁS
Caetité
Contas
Jequié
São Francisco
Uruaçu
Ipiaú
Aruanã
Vitória da Conquista
Itabuna
Ilhéus
ATLANTIC OCEAN
Ceres
Formosa
Januária
Goiás
Jaraguá
Brasília
Itapetinga
Pirenópolis
Porteirinha
Canavieiras
Anápolis
São Francisco
Salinas
Belmonte
Goiânia
Montes Claros
Jequitinhonha
Pôrto Seguro
Araçuaí
Serra do Espinhaço
Caldas Novas
Paracatu
Sa do Chifre
Itamaraju
Rio Verde
Pirapora
Velhas
João Pinheiro
Teófilo Otôni
Goiandira
Nanuque
Itumbiara
Catalão
Corinto
Diamantina
Araguari
Patos de Minas
Curvelo
Gov. Valadares
Paranaíba
Uberlândia
MINAS GERAIS
Doce
ESPÍRITO SANTO
São Mateus
Iturama
Grande
Uberaba
Sete Lagoas
Itabira
Cnl Fabriciano
Linhares
Araxá
Belo Horizonte
Colatina
Caratinga
Fernandópolis
Franca
Divinópolis
Manhuaçu
Cariacica
Vitória
S. José do R. Prêto
Barretos
Passos
Con. Lafaiete
Ponte Nova
Vila Velha
S. João del Rei
Carangola
Catanduva
Ribeirão Prêto
Cachoeiro de Itapemirim
SÃO PAULO
Lavras
Barbacena
Itaperuna
Poços de Caldas
Sa da Mantiqueira
Araraquara
Juiz de Fora
S. João da Barra
Marília
São Carlos
Volta Redonda
Campos
Bauru
Limeira
Nova Friburgo
Petrópolis
Piracicaba
Barra Mansa
Magé
Campinas
Jundiaí
Niterói
Jacarezinho
Sorocaba
Rio de Janeiro
Itapeva
Itapetininga
São Paulo
Santos
Tropic of Capricorn
Itararé
Juquiá
São Vicente
Itanhaém
Castro
Iguape
Ponta Grossa
Guarapuava
Curitiba
Paranaguá
Mafra
São Francisco do Sul

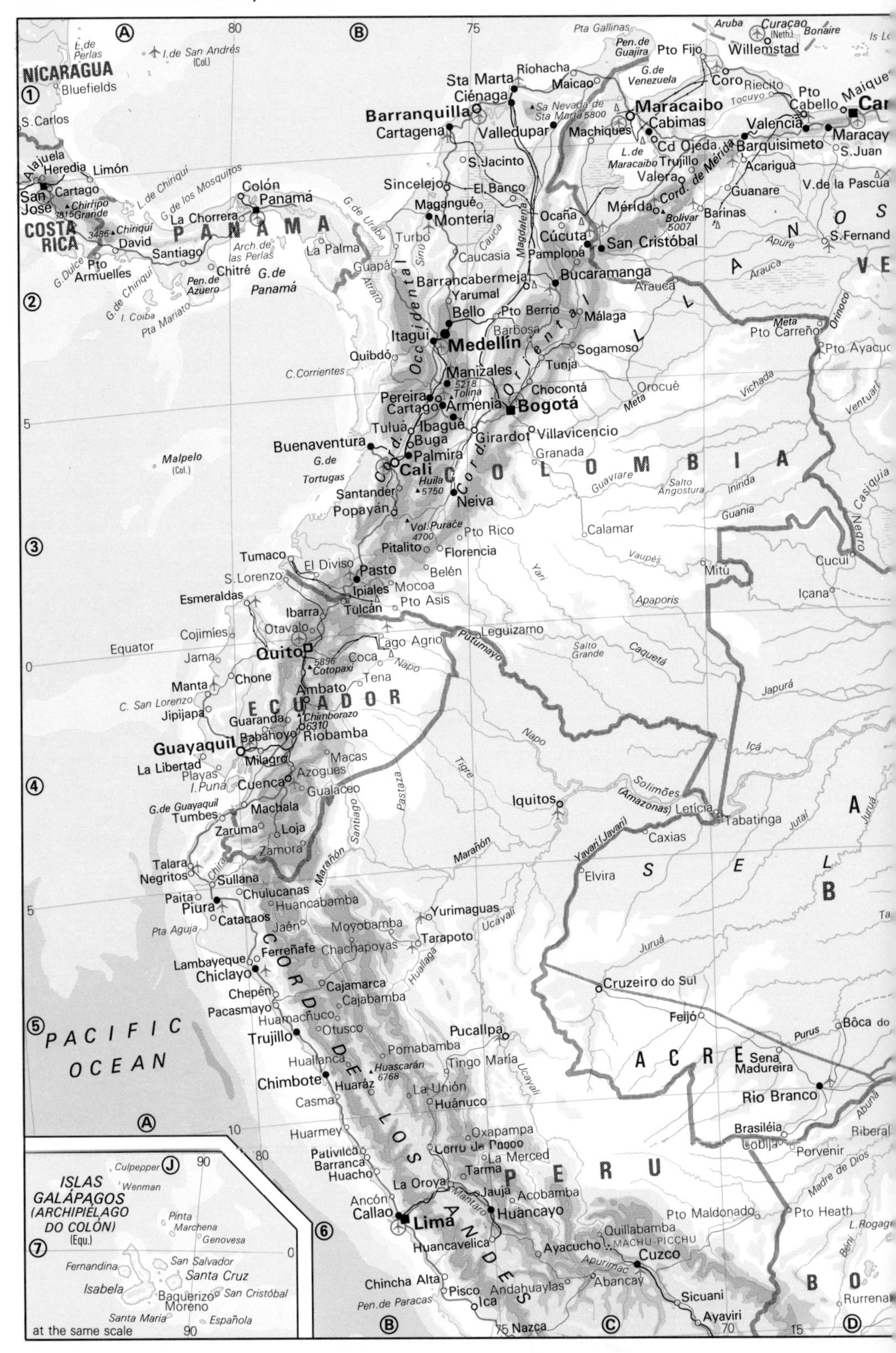

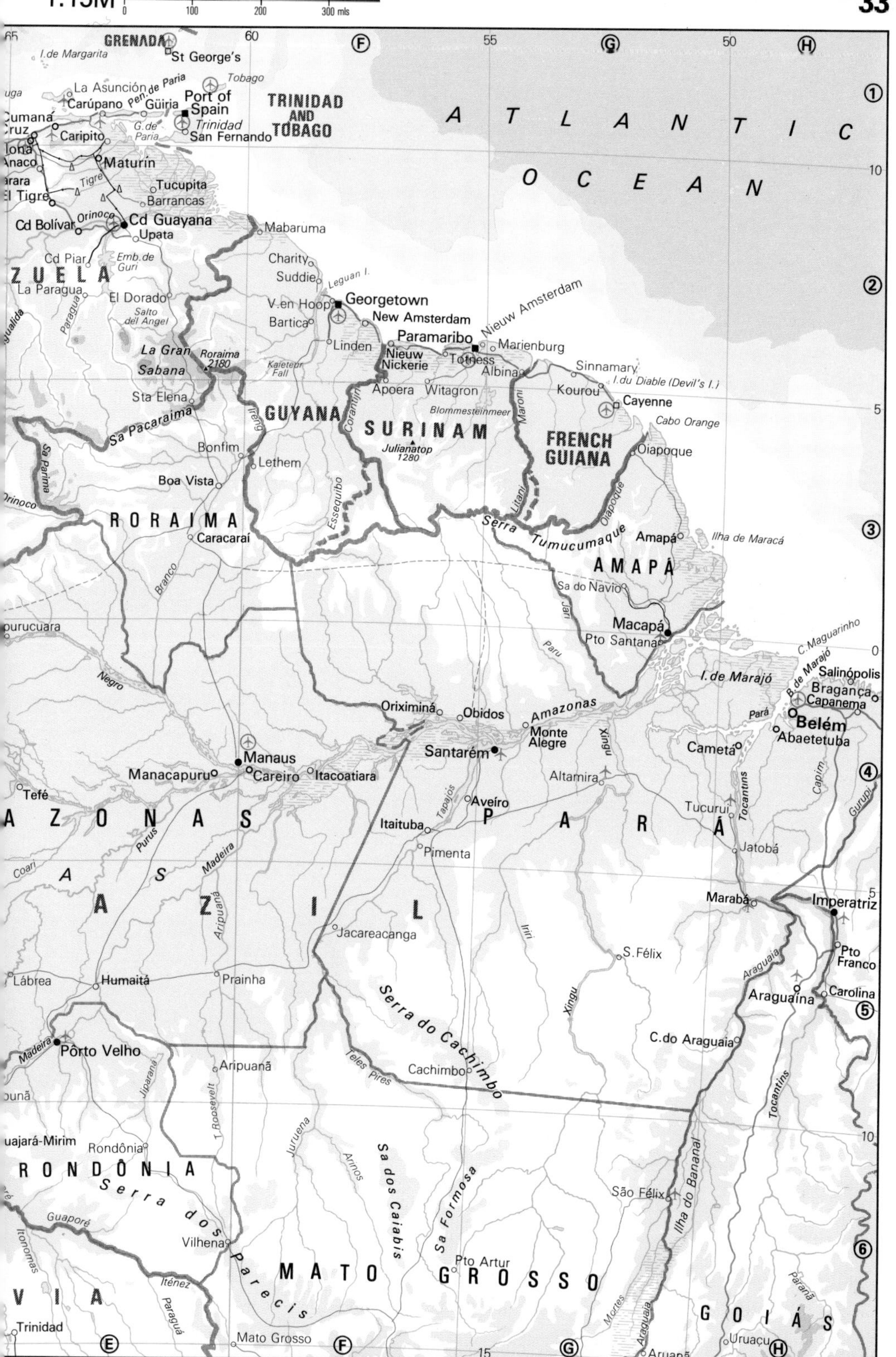
1:15M
0 200 400 600 km
0 100 200 300 mls
ATLANTIC
OCEAN
GRENADA
St George's
I.de Margarita
La Asunción
Carúpano
Pen. de Paria
Güiria
Port of Spain
Tobago
Trinidad
San Fernando
TRINIDAD AND TOBAGO
G. de Paria
Cumaná
Caripito
Maturín
Anaco
El Tigre
Tigre
Tucupita
Barrancas
Orinoco
Cd Bolívar
Cd Guayana
Upata
Mabaruma
Cd Piar
Emb.de Guri
ZUELA
La Paragua
El Dorado
Salto del Angel
Paragua
Charity
Suddie
Leguan I.
Georgetown
V.en Hoop
New Amsterdam
Bartica
Linden
Nieuw Amsterdam
Paramaribo
Marienburg
Nieuw Nickerie
Totness
Albina
Sinnamary
I.du Diable (Devil's I.)
Kourou
Cayenne
La Gran Sabana
Roraima 2180
Kaieteur Fall
Apoera
Witagron
Sta Elena
GUYANA
SURINAM
Blommesteinmeer
Julianatop 1280
FRENCH GUIANA
Cabo Orange
Oiapoque
Sa Pacaraima
Bonfim
Lethem
Sa Parima
Boa Vista
Orinoco
Corantijn
Maroni
Essequibo
Litani
Oiapoque
Ireng
RORAIMA
Caracaraí
Branco
Serra Tumucumaque
Amapá
Ilha de Maracá
AMAPÁ
Sa do Navio
Jari
Macapá
Pto Santana
Paru
C. Maguarinho
I. de Marajó
B. de Marajó
Salinópolis
Bragança
Capanema
Pará
Belém
Abaetetuba
Cametá
Negro
Oriximiná
Obidos
Amazonas
Monte Alegre
Santarém
Xingu
Manaus
Manacapuru
Careiro
Itacoatiara
Altamira
Tefé
AZONAS
Purus
Tapajós
Aveíro
Itaituba
PARÁ
Tucuruí
Tocantins
Capim
Gurupi
Jatobá
Pimenta
Coari
Madeira
ASAZIL
Aripuanã
Marabá
Imperatriz
Jacareacanga
Iriri
S.Félix
Pto Franco
Lábrea
Humaitá
Prainha
Serra do Cachimbo
Xingu
Araguaia
Araguaína
Carolina
Pôrto Velho
Madeira
C.do Araguaia
Aripuanã
Jiparaná
Teles Pires
Cachimbo
T. Roosevelt
Tocantins
Guajará-Mirim
Rondônia
RONDÔNIA
Serra dos Parecis
Juruena
Arinos
Sa dos Caiabis
Sa Formosa
São Félix
Ilha do Bananal
Guaporé
Vilhena
Pto Artur
MATO GROSSO
Iténez
Paraguá
Mortes
Araguaia
Paranã
GOIÁS
VIA
Trinidad
Mato Grosso
Aruanã
Uruaçu
E F G H
1 2 3 4 5 6
65 60 55 50
10 5 0 5 10 15

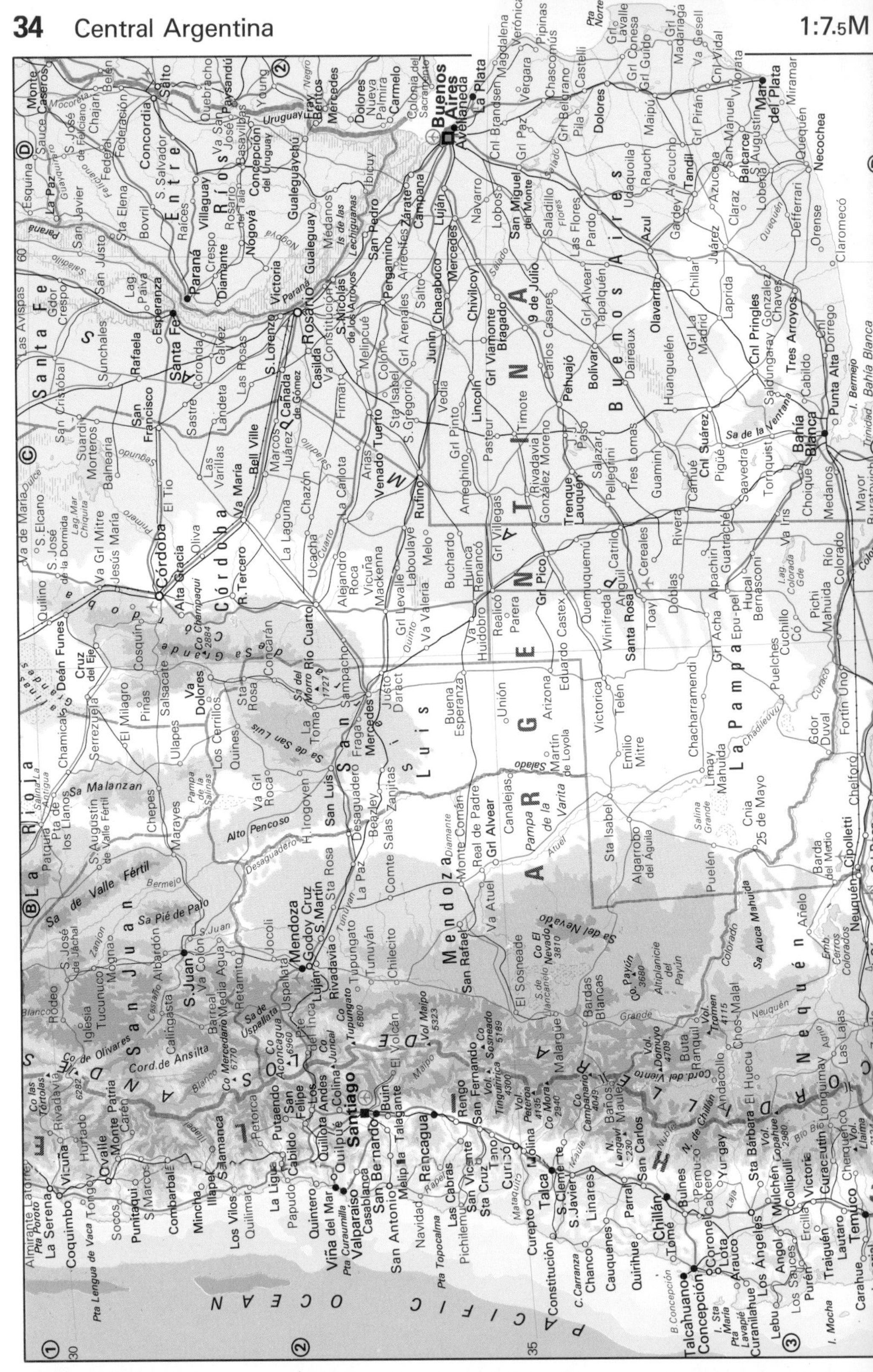

Santa Fe
Entre Ríos
Córdoba
San Luis
Mendoza
San Juan
La Rioja
Buenos Aires
La Pampa
Neuquén
ARGENTINA
CHILE
OCEANO PACIFICO
Buenos Aires
La Plata
Rosario
Santa Fe
Paraná
Córdoba
Mendoza
San Juan
San Luis
Santiago
Valparaíso
Concepción
Temuco
Mar del Plata
Bahía Blanca
Neuquén
Santa Rosa
Río Cuarto
Concordia
Montevideo

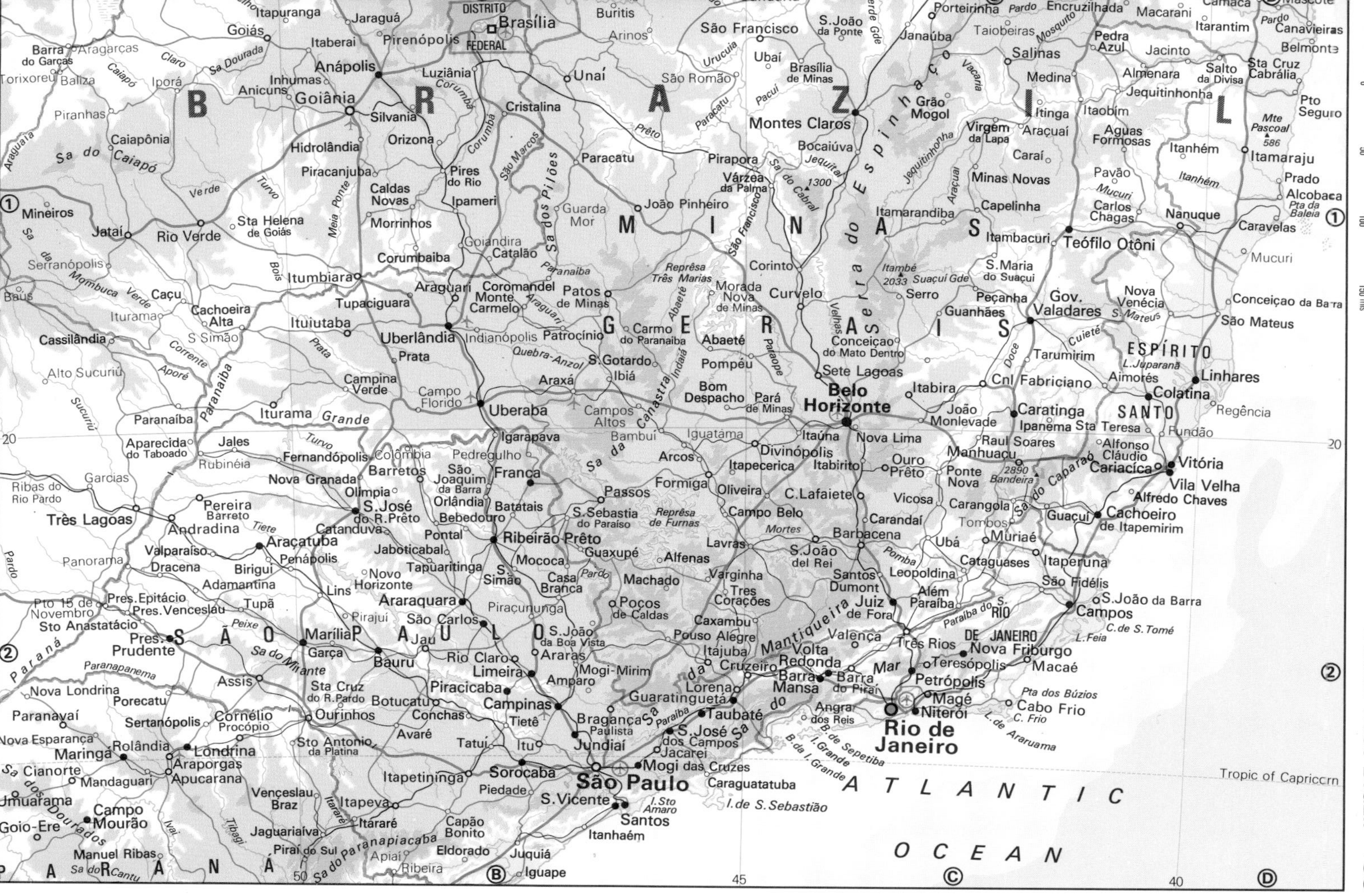
BRAZIL
MINAS GERAIS
SÃO PAULO
ESPÍRITO SANTO
RIO DE JANEIRO
PARANÁ
ATLANTIC OCEAN
Tropic of Capricorn
DISTRITO FEDERAL
Brasília
Goiânia
Anápolis
Belo Horizonte
Rio de Janeiro
São Paulo
Vitória
Vila Velha
Niterói
Campinas
Santos
Uberlândia
Uberaba
Ribeirão Prêto
Juiz de Fora
Montes Claros
Gov. Valadares
Teófilo Otôni
Londrina
Maringá
Bauru
Marília
Campos
Sorocaba
Taubaté
Serra do Espinhaço
Serra da Mantiqueira
Sa da Canastra
Paranaíba
São Francisco
Doce
Grande
Tietê

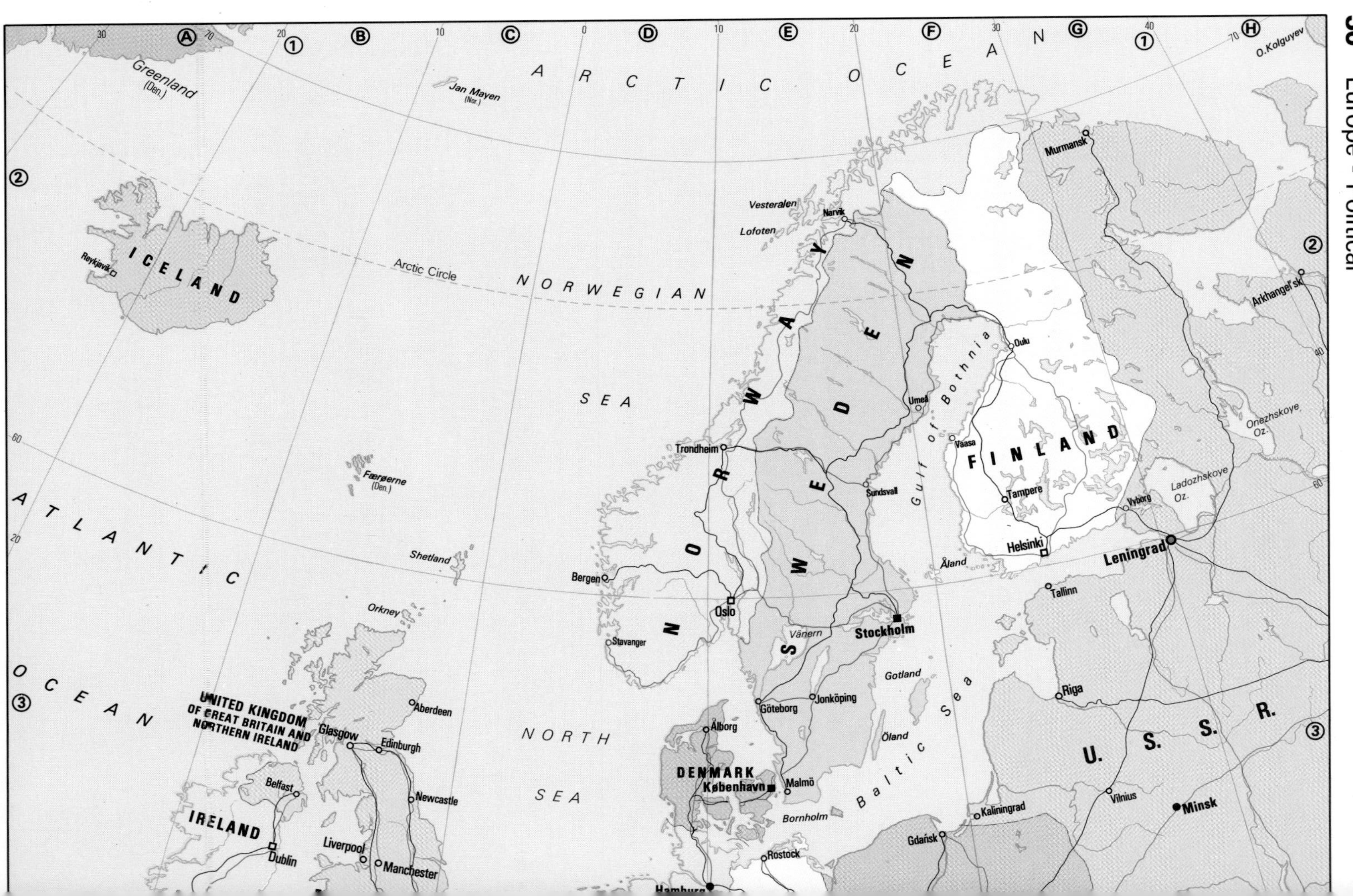
ARCTIC OCEAN
Greenland (Den.)
Jan Mayen (Nor.)
O. Kolguyev
ICELAND
Reykjavík
Arctic Circle
NORWEGIAN SEA
Færøerne (Den.)
Shetland
Orkney
ATLANTIC OCEAN
NORTH SEA
NORWAY
SWEDEN
FINLAND
DENMARK
U. S. S. R.
UNITED KINGDOM OF GREAT BRITAIN AND NORTHERN IRELAND
IRELAND
Vesterålen
Lofoten
Narvik
Murmansk
Arkhangel'sk
Onezhskoye Oz.
Ladozhskoye Oz.
Gulf of Bothnia
Oulu
Umeå
Vaasa
Tampere
Sundsvall
Vyborg
Helsinki
Leningrad
Åland
Trondheim
Bergen
Oslo
Stavanger
Vänern
Stockholm
Tallinn
Gotland
Riga
Göteborg
Jönköping
Öland
Baltic Sea
Ålborg
København
Malmö
Bornholm
Rostock
Hamburg
Kaliningrad
Gdańsk
Vilnius
Minsk
Aberdeen
Glasgow
Edinburgh
Newcastle
Belfast
Dublin
Liverpool
Manchester

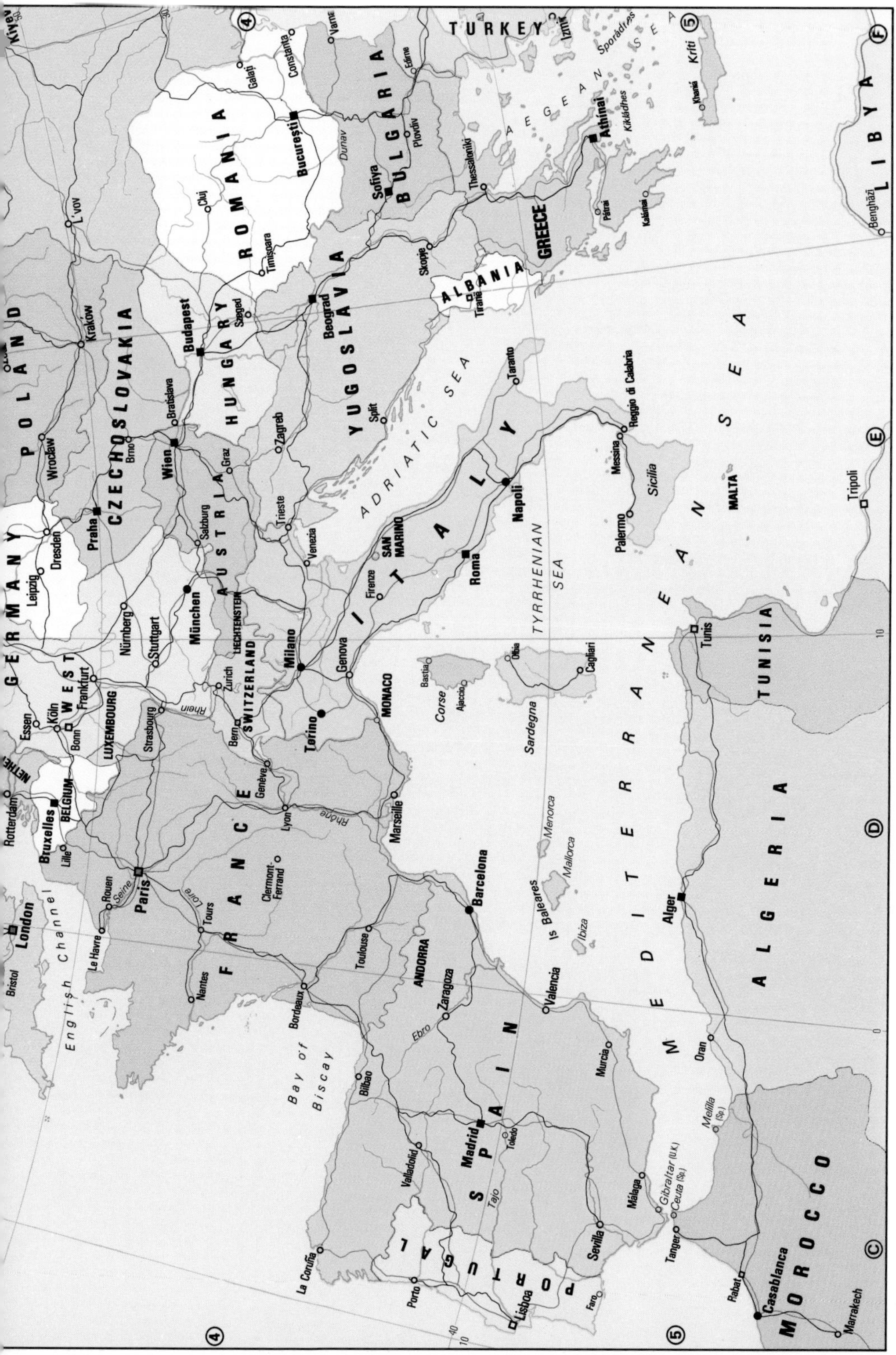

WEST GERMANY
POLAND
CZECHOSLOVAKIA
ROMANIA
HUNGARY
AUSTRIA
YUGOSLAVIA
BULGARIA
TURKEY
ALBANIA
GREECE
ITALY
SAN MARINO
SWITZERLAND
LIECHTENSTEIN
LUXEMBOURG
BELGIUM
NETHERLANDS
FRANCE
MONACO
ANDORRA
SPAIN
PORTUGAL
MOROCCO
ALGERIA
TUNISIA
LIBYA
MALTA
AEGEAN SEA
ADRIATIC SEA
TYRRHENIAN SEA
MEDITERRANEAN SEA
Bay of Biscay
English Channel
Kiyev
L'vov
Kraków
Wrocław
Dresden
Leipzig
Praha
Brno
Wien
Bratislava
Budapest
Szeged
Timișoara
Cluj
București
Galați
Constanța
Varna
Sofiya
Plovdiv
Edirne
İzmir
Thessaloníki
Athínai
Pátrai
Kalámai
Khaniá
Kríti
Kikládhes
Sporádhes
Skopje
Tiranë
Beograd
Zagreb
Split
Graz
Salzburg
München
Nürnberg
Stuttgart
Frankfurt
Köln
Essen
Bonn
Strasbourg
Rhein
Zurich
Bern
Genève
Lyon
Rhône
Marseille
Milano
Torino
Genova
Venezia
Trieste
Firenze
Roma
Napoli
Taranto
Reggio di Calabria
Messina
Palermo
Sicilia
Corse
Bastia
Ajaccio
Sardegna
Olbia
Cagliari
Tunis
Tripoli
Benghāzī
Rotterdam
Bruxelles
Lille
London
Bristol
Paris
Rouen
Seine
Le Havre
Tours
Loire
Nantes
Clermont-Ferrand
Bordeaux
Toulouse
Barcelona
Is Baleares
Menorca
Mallorca
Ibiza
Valencia
Zaragoza
Ebro
Bilbao
Madrid
Toledo
Tajo
Valladolid
La Coruña
Porto
Lisboa
Faro
Sevilla
Málaga
Murcia
Gibraltar (U.K.)
Ceuta (Sp.)
Melilla (Sp.)
Tanger
Rabat
Casablanca
Marrakech
Oran
Alger
Dunav
C D E F
4 5
0 10 40 50

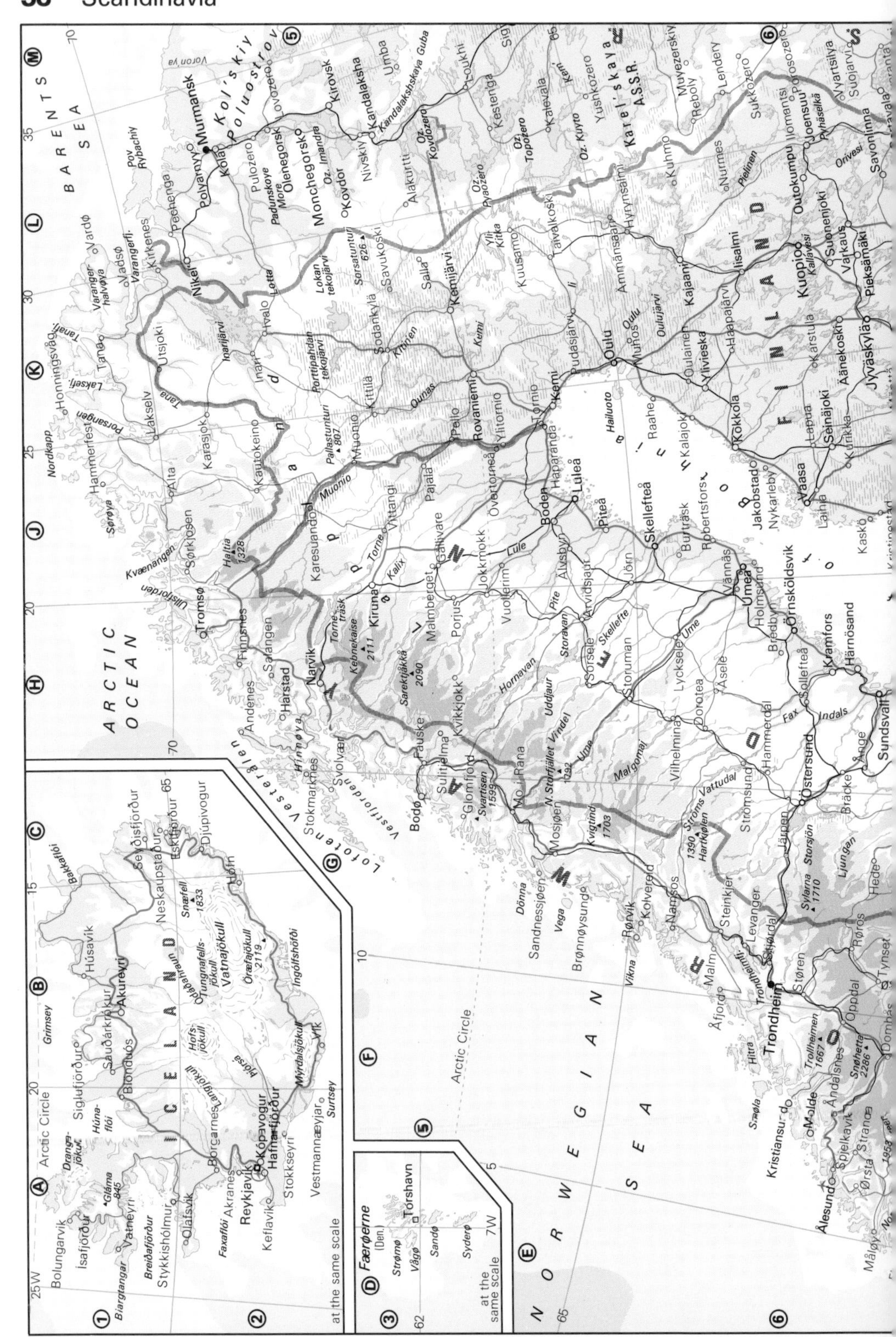
ARCTIC OCEAN
BARENTS SEA
NORWEGIAN SEA
ICELAND
FINLAND
Færøerne (Den.)
at the same scale
Arctic Circle
Karel'skaya A.S.S.R.
Kol'skiy Poluostrov
Lofoten
Vesterålen
Vestfjorden
Reykjavík
Akureyri
Tórshavn
Tromsø
Narvik
Kiruna
Bodø
Murmansk
Oulu
Luleå
Umeå
Skellefteå
Trondheim
Östersund
Sundsvall
Vaasa
Kuopio
Jyväskylä
Rovaniemi
Kemi
Hammerfest
Nordkapp
Kebnekaise 2111
Sarektjåkkå 2090
Haltia 1328
Vatnajökull
Öræfajökull 2119
Snæfell 1833
Snøhetta 2286
Sylarna 1710

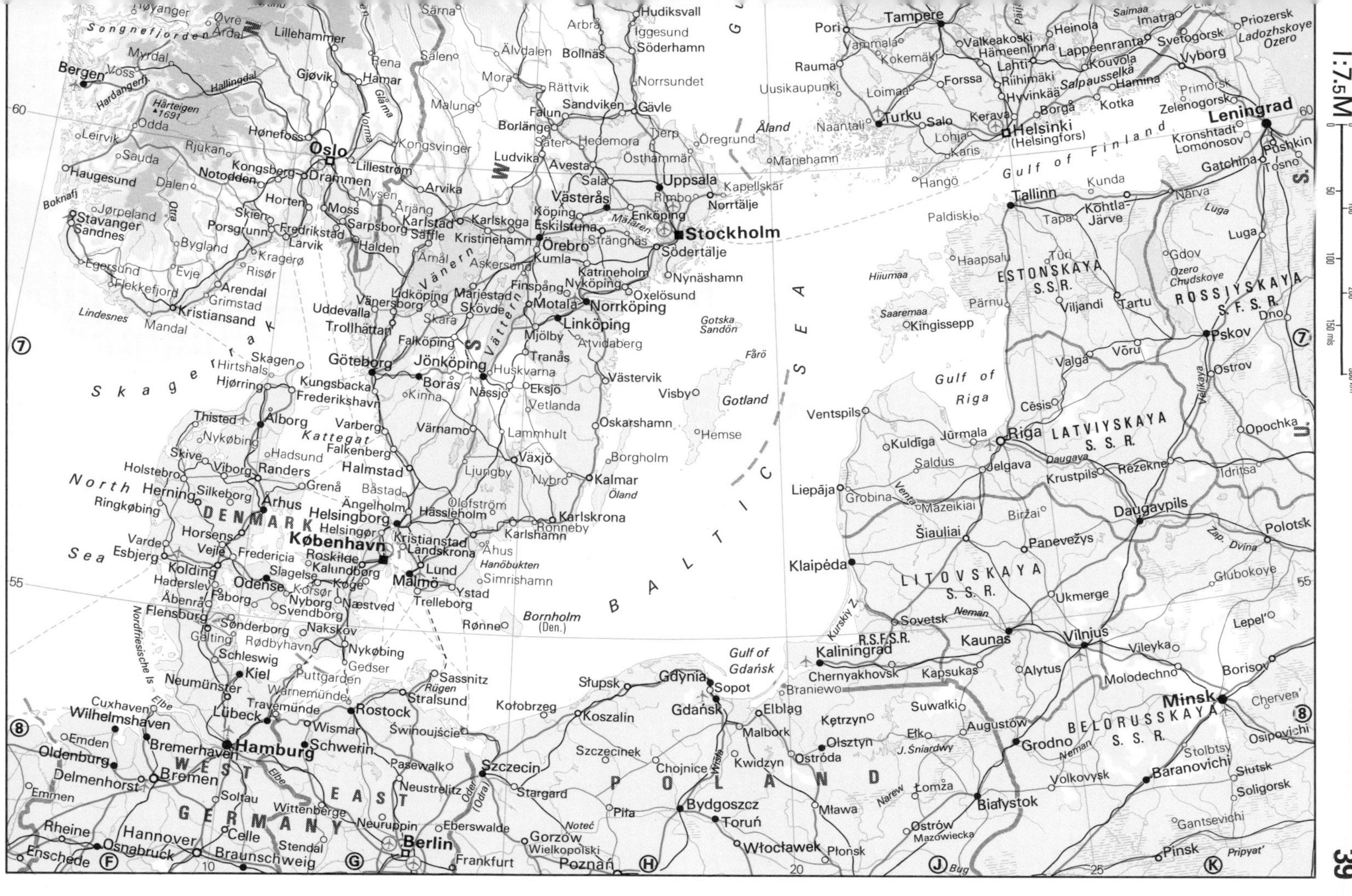
Leningrad
Helsinki (Helsingfors)
Gulf of Finland
Tallinn
ESTONSKAYA S.S.R.
ROSSIYSKAYA S.F.S.R.
Pskov
Tartu
Riga
Gulf of Riga
LATVIYSKAYA S.S.R.
Daugavpils
Vilnius
Kaunas
LITOVSKAYA S.S.R.
Minsk
BELORUSSKAYA S.S.R.
Grodno
Kaliningrad
R.S.F.S.R.
Klaipėda
Liepāja
Ventspils
Gotland
Visby
Stockholm
Uppsala
Västerås
Örebro
Norrköping
Linköping
Jönköping
Göteborg
Malmö
Kalmar
Karlskrona
Öland
Åland
Turku
Tampere
Pori
Oslo
Bergen
Stavanger
Kristiansand
Skagerrak
Kattegat
København
DENMARK
Århus
Odense
Ålborg
North Sea
Bornholm (Den.)
BALTIC SEA
Gdańsk
Gdynia
Gulf of Gdańsk
POLAND
Białystok
Bydgoszcz
Toruń
Szczecin
Poznań
Berlin
EAST GERMANY
WEST GERMANY
Hamburg
Bremen
Kiel
Lübeck
Rostock
Hannover
Braunschweig
Osnabrück

1:5M

0 50 100 150 200 km
0 50 100 mls
NORWAY
Nordhordland
Dale
Bergen
Sotra
Sunnhordland
Stord
Leirvik
Bømlo
Skjold
Haugesund
Karmøy
NORTH SEA
Shetland
Herma Ness
Unst
Fetlar
Yell
Isbister
St Magnus B.
Whalsay
Foula
Lerwick
Sumburgh Hd
Fair Isle
Orkney
Westray
Sanday
Rousay
Stronsay
Sule Skerry
Stromness
Kirkwall
Stack Skerry
Hoy
Scapa Flow
N.Rona
Sula Sgeir
C. Wrath
Butt of Lewis
Thurso
Duncansby Hd
Wick
Ben Hope 927
Ben More Assynt 998
Helmsdale
Dornoch Firth
Dornoch
Ullapool
Moray Firth
Dingwall
Elgin
Banff
Fraserburgh
Peterhead
Buchan Ness
Inverness
L. Ness
Spey
Don
Aberdeen
Fort Augustus
Ben Macdui 1309
Dee
Braemar
Stonehaven
SCOTLAND
Grampian Mts
Ben Nevis 1344
Fort William
Mallaig
Kyle of Lochalsh
Skye
Portree
Pitlochry
Montrose
Arbroath
F. of Tay
St Andrews
Perth
Kirkcaldy
F. of Forth
Edinburgh
St Abbs Hd
Berwick-upon-Tweed
Holy I.
Galashiels
White Coomb 822
Hawick
Alnwick
Cheviots
Moffat
Nith
Morpeth
Blyth
Newcastle upon Tyne
S.Shields
Sunderland
Gateshead
Carlisle
Merrick 843
Dumfries
Kirkcudbright
Oban
L.Awe
Mull
L.Lomond
Stirling
Greenock
Glasgow
Paisley
Motherwell
Clyde
Irvine
Kilmarnock
Ayr
Arran
F. of Clyde
Girvan
Campbeltown
Stranraer
Larne
F. of Lorn
Colonsay
Jura
Islay
Coll
Tiree
Rum
Barra
S. Uist
N. Uist
Harris
Lewis
Stornoway
The Minch
Outer Hebrides
Flannan Is
St Kilda
Malin Hd
Rathlin I.
L. Foyle
Coleraine
N. IRELAND
Ballymena
Errigal 752
Londonderry
Aran I.
Rossan Pt
Donegal

Sligo
Armagh
Monaghan
Ballina
L. Conn
L. Allen
Newry
Achill I.
Castlebar
Boyle
Cavan
Dundalk
Clew B.
L. Mask
Roscommon
Longford
Drogheda
L. Ree
Slyne Hd
L. Corrib
Athlone
Mullingar
Galway
Dublin
(Baile Atha Cliath)
Dun Laoghaire
Bray
Galway B.
Aran Is
Shannon
Monastereven
Wicklow Mts
Wicklow
REP. OF IRELAND
Port Laoise
Carlow
Ennis
L. Derg
Nenagh
Kilrush
Limerick
Kilkenny
Arklow
Tipperary
Suir
Barrow
Tralee
Clonmel
Dingle
Waterford
Wexford
Dingle B.
Blackwater
Rosslare
Killarney
Carrauntoohill
1041
Cork
Dungarvan
Youghal
Bantry
Bantry B.
Old Hd of Kinsale
C. Clear
St George's Chan.
IRISH SEA
Douglas
Isle of Man
Kendal
Barrow-in-Furness
Morecambe
Lancaster
Blackpool
Preston
Harrogate
York
Leeds
Bradford
Huddersfield
Bolton
Manchester
Liverpool
Birkenhead
Holyhead
Anglesey
Bangor
1085
Snowdon
Cambrian Mts
Dee
Warrington
Chester
Crewe
Stoke-on-Trent
Pwllheli
Cardigan Bay
Aberystwyth
WALES
Shrewsbury
Wolverhampton
Birmingham
Builth Wells
Brecon
Fishguard
Carmarthen
St David's Hd
Pembroke
Swansea
Newport
Cardiff
Wye
Severn
Worcester
Gloucester
Bristol Chan.
Lundy I.
Barnstaple
Bude
Taunton
Exeter
Dartmoor
Newquay
Plymouth
Torbay
Truro
Penzance
Land's End
Falmouth
Isles of Scilly
Lizard Pt
Prawle Pt
Yorkshire Moors
Scarborough
Flamborough Hd
Ouse
Hull
Spurn Hd
Humber
Grimsby
Trent
Doncaster
Sheffield
Lincoln
The Wash
Nottingham
Derby
King's Lynn
Norwich
Great Yarmouth
Lowestoft
Leicester
Nene
Peterborough
Coventry
ENGLAND
Newmarket
Cambridge
Ipswich
Felixstowe
Harwich
Northampton
Bedford
Colchester
Luton
Oxford
Swindon
Bristol
Bath
Weston-super-Mare
Windsor
London
Chelmsford
Southend-on-Sea
Thames
Reading
Canterbury
Maidstone
Dover
Guildford
Winchester
Crawley
Salisbury
Southampton
Folkestone
Hastings
Brighton
Eastbourne
Str. of Dover
Bournemouth
Portsmouth
Weymouth
Isle of Wight
English Channel
Esbjerg
's-Gravenhage
(Den Haag)
Rotterdam
NETHERLANDS
Vlissingen
Zeebrugge
Antwerpen
Brugge
Oostende
Mechelen
BELGIUM
Gent
Schelde
Bruxelles
(Brüssel)
Dunkerque
Kortrijk
Calais
St-Omer
Tourcoing
Roubaix
Tournai
Mons
Lille
Bethune
Boulogne
Valenciennes
Montreuil
Douai
Arras
Denain
Cambrai
ARTOIS
Abbeville
Le Tréport
Dieppe
Amiens
St-Quentin
PICARDIE
Neufchâtel
Montdidier
Laon
Oise
Compiègne
Fécamp
Le Havre
Bolbec
Beauvais
Soissons
Senlis
Château-Thierry
Rouen
Deauville
Seine
Elbeuf
Louviers
Bayeux
Lisieux
Caen
St-Lô
NORMANDIE
Mantes
Cergy-Pontoise
ILE-DE-FRANCE
Evreux
Eure
Versailles
Paris
Meaux
Sézanne
Dreux
Orne
Argentan
FRANCE
Rambouillet
Provins
Chartres
Étampes
Melun
Romilly-s.-S
Fontainebleau
Sens
C. de la Hague
Pte de Barfleur
Alderney
Cherbourg
Guernsey
Sark
Valognes
Channel Is
(U.K.)
Jersey
St Helier
Coutances
Golfe de St-Malo
Granville
Roscoff
Morlaix
St-Malo
Mont-St-Michel
Domfront
Brest
I.d'Ouessant
St-Brieuc
Carhaix-Plouguer
Dinan
Fougères
Mayenne
Alençon
B
C
D
3
4
5
50

N O R T H
S E A
I R I S H
S E A
North Channel
Glasgow
Edinburgh
Newcastle upon Tyne
Sunderland
Middlesbrough
York
Leeds
Bradford
Hull
Manchester
Liverpool
Sheffield
Carlisle
Dumfries and Galloway
Borders
Lothian
Fife
Central
Strathclyde
Northumberland
Durham
Cumbria
N. Yorkshire
Lancashire
Humberside
Cleveland
Tyne and Wear
Merseyside
Gtr Man.
S. Yorkshire
W. Yorkshire
Isle of Man
Douglas
Belfast
Pennines
Cheviot Hills
Firth of Forth
Firth of Clyde
Solway Firth
Morecambe B.
Liverpool Bay
Anglesey
Holyhead
Blackpool
Preston
Lancaster
Barrow in-Furness
Whitehaven
Workington
Scarborough
Whitby
Bridlington
Grimsby
Doncaster
Stockport
Warrington
Birkenhead
Wigan
Bolton
Blackburn
Burnley
Oldham
Rochdale
Huddersfield
Halifax
Wakefield
Barnsley
Rotherham
Harrogate
Ripon
Darlington
Stockton
Hartlepool
Gateshead
Tynemouth
Sth Shields
Berwick -upon-Tweed
Stirling
Dunfermline
Kirkcaldy
Paisley
Greenock
Kilmarnock
Ayr
Stranraer
Kintyre
Islay
Jura
Down
Farne Deep
Flamborough Hd
Spurn Hd
Rough
West Sole
Humber
Trent
Ouse
Tweed
Eden
Tyne
Tees
Mersey
Dee
Esbjerg
Bergen
Dublin
Dun Laoghaire

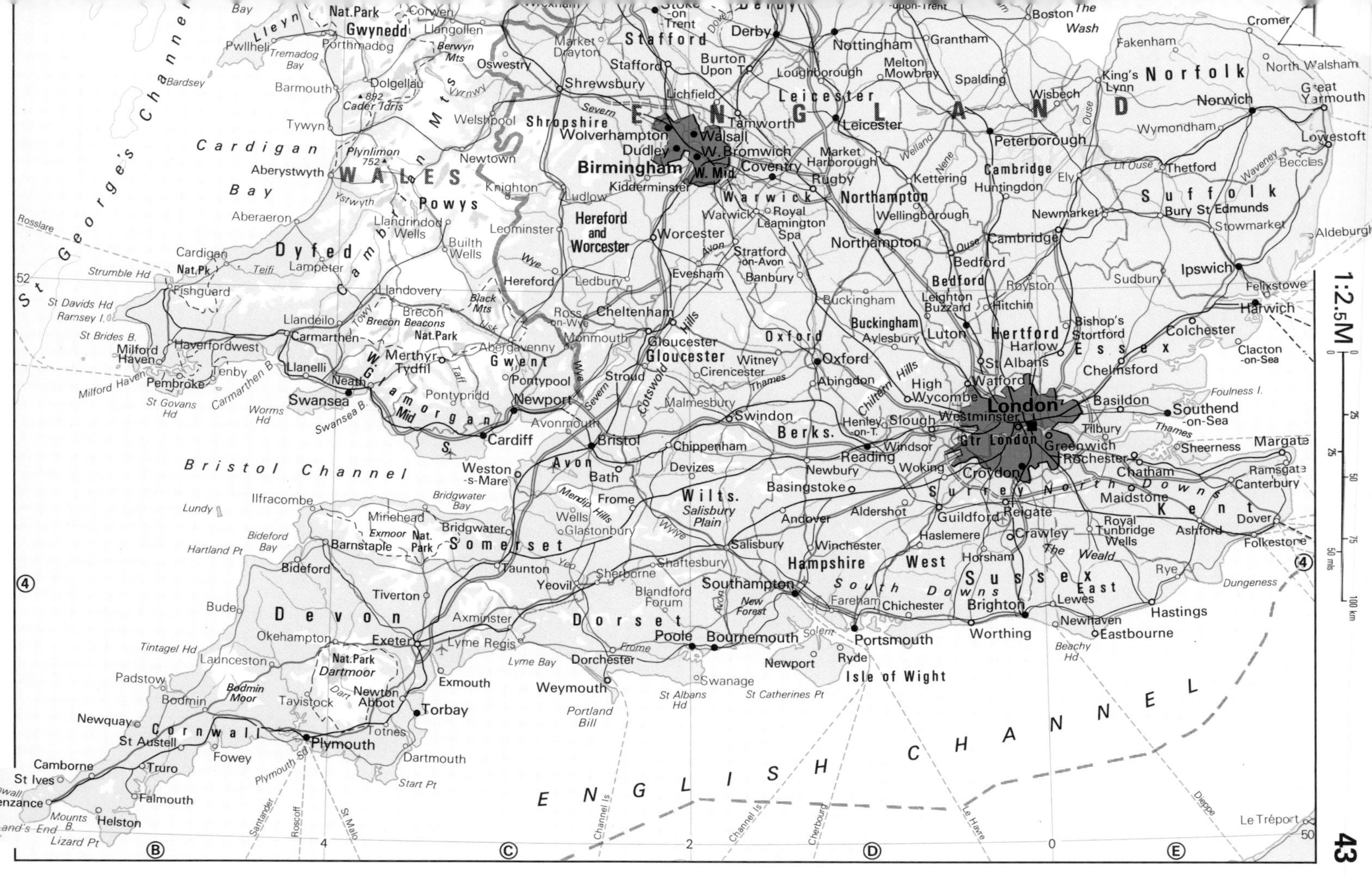
E N G L I S H   C H A N N E L
Bristol Channel
Cardigan Bay
St George's Channel
E N G L A N D
W A L E S
London
Gtr London
Westminster
Birmingham
W. Mid.
Norfolk
Suffolk
Essex
Kent
Surrey
East Sussex
West Sussex
Hampshire
Isle of Wight
Dorset
Devon
Cornwall
Somerset
Avon
Wilts.
Berks.
Oxford
Gloucester
Hereford and Worcester
Shropshire
Stafford
Leicester
Northampton
Cambridge
Bedford
Hertford
Buckingham
Warwick
Powys
Dyfed
Gwynedd
Gwent
Mid Glamorgan
W. Glamorgan
S. Glamorgan
Norwich
Ipswich
Great Yarmouth
Lowestoft
Cromer
King's Lynn
Peterborough
Nottingham
Leicester
Derby
Coventry
Oxford
Reading
Swindon
Bristol
Bath
Cardiff
Newport
Swansea
Southampton
Portsmouth
Bournemouth
Poole
Brighton
Hastings
Dover
Folkestone
Canterbury
Margate
Ramsgate
Southend-on-Sea
Colchester
Chelmsford
Cambridge
Exeter
Plymouth
Torbay
Penzance
Land's End
Lizard Pt
Weymouth
Salisbury
Winchester
Guildford
Croydon
Luton
Watford
Gloucester
Cheltenham
Worcester
Hereford
Shrewsbury
Wolverhampton
Walsall
Dudley
Stafford
Aberystwyth
Carmarthen
Pembroke
Milford Haven
Fishguard
Dartmoor
Exmoor
Bodmin Moor
Brecon Beacons
Salisbury Plain
New Forest
Cotswold Hills
Chiltern Hills
North Downs
South Downs
The Weald
The Wash
Thames
Severn
Dieppe
Le Havre
Cherbourg
St Malo
Roscoff
Le Tréport
Channel Is
Rosslare

1:2.5M

0 25 50 75 100 km

0 25 50 mls

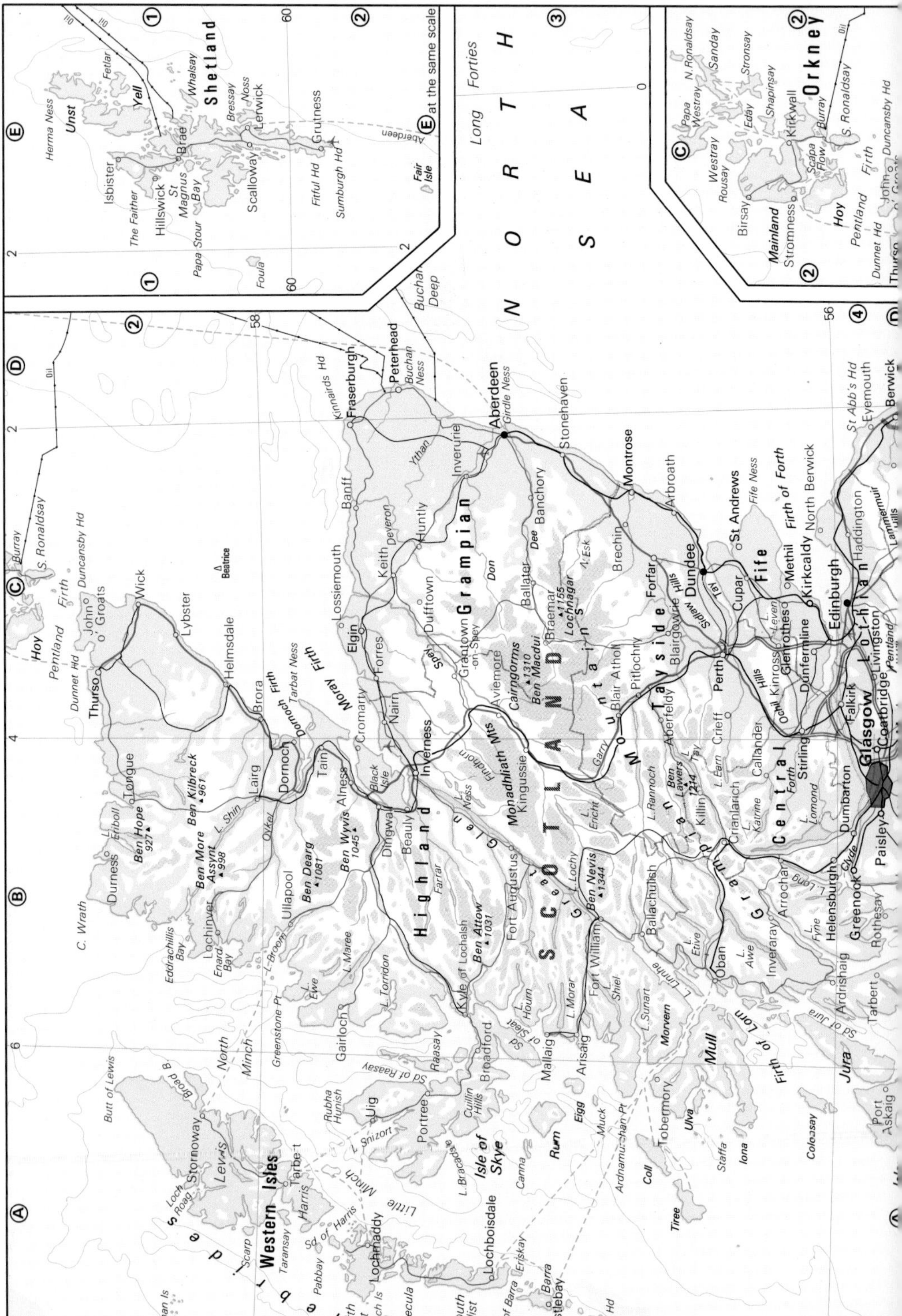

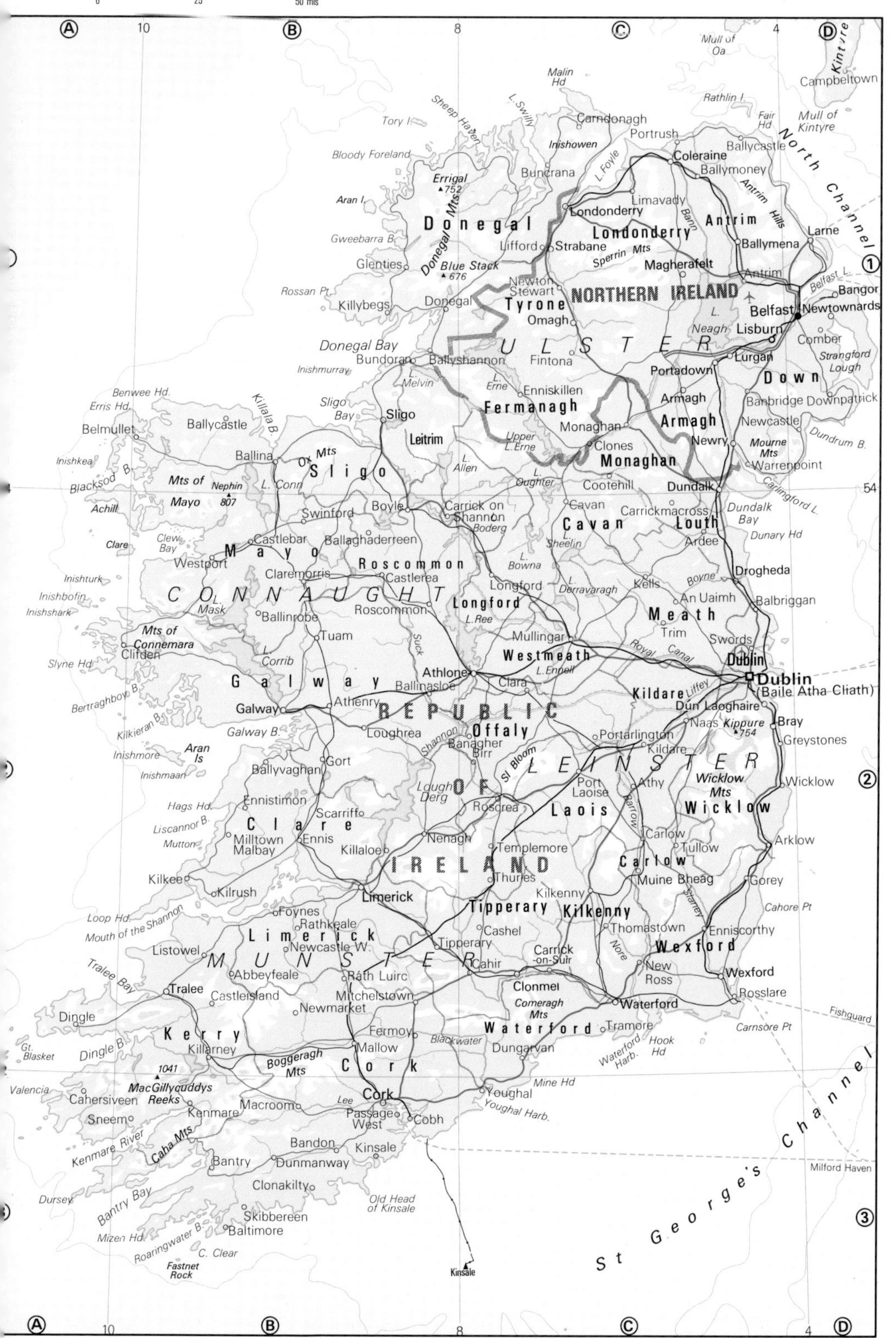

A
B
C
D
10
8
4
Mull of Oa
Kintyre
Campbeltown
Malin Hd
Rathlin I.
Fair Hd
Mull of Kintyre
North Channel
Sheep Haven
L. Swilly
Tory I.
Carndonagh
Portrush
Ballycastle
Inishowen
Bloody Foreland
Coleraine
Ballymoney
Errigal 752
Buncrana
L. Foyle
Aran I.
Limavady
Antrim Hills
Londonderry
Bann
Donegal
Londonderry
Antrim
Larne
Gweebarra B.
Lifford
Strabane
Ballymena
Sperrin Mts
Donegal Mts
Blue Stack 676
Magherafelt
Glenties
Antrim
Belfast L.
Newton Stewart
Bangor
Rossan Pt.
NORTHERN IRELAND
Killybegs
Donegal
Tyrone
Belfast
Newtownards
Omagh
L. Neagh
Lisburn
Comber
Donegal Bay
ULSTER
Bundoran
Ballyshannon
Fintona
Lurgan
Strangford Lough
Inishmurray
Portadown
L. Melvin
Down
L. Erne
Enniskillen
Benwee Hd.
Armagh
Killala B.
Banbridge
Downpatrick
Erris Hd.
Sligo Bay
Fermanagh
Sligo
Armagh
Newcastle
Belmullet
Ballycastle
Monaghan
Leitrim
Newry
Dundrum B.
Upper L. Erne
Clones
Mourne Mts
Ballina
Ox Mts
Monaghan
Inishkea
L. Allen
Warrenpoint
Sligo
Mts of Mayo
Nephin 807
Blacksod B.
L. Conn
L. Oughter
Cootehill
Dundalk
54
Carlingford L.
Achill
Boyle
Swinford
Carrick on Shannon
Cavan
Carrickmacross
Dundalk Bay
L. Boderg
Cavan
Louth
Clew Bay
Dunany Hd
Castlebar
Ballaghaderreen
Clare
Ardee
L. Sheelin
Mayo
Westport
Roscommon
Claremorris
L. Bowna
Drogheda
Inishturk
Castlerea
Longford
Kells
Boyne
L. Derravaragh
CONNAUGHT
Inishbofin
An Uaimh
Balbriggan
Longford
Inishshark
L. Mask
Roscommon
Ballinrobe
Meath
L. Ree
Trim
Mts of Connemara
Tuam
Suck
Mullingar
Swords
Clifden
Royal Canal
Westmeath
L. Corrib
Slyne Hd
Dublin
Athlone
L. Ennell
Dublin (Baile Atha Cliath)
Galway
Clara
Kildare
Liffey
Bertraghboy B.
Ballinasloe
Dún Laoghaire
Athenry
REPUBLIC
Galway
Naas
Kippure 754
Bray
Kilkieran B.
Offaly
Portarlington
Loughrea
Shannon
Galway B.
Banagher
Greystones
Birr
Kildare
Aran Is
Inishmore
Gort
Sl Bloom
LEINSTER
OF
Ballyvaghan
Inishmaan
Port Laoise
Athy
Wicklow Mts
Wicklow
Lough Derg
Ennistimon
Hags Hd.
Roscrea
Barrow
Laois
Wicklow
Scarriff
Clare
Liscannor B.
Carlow
Milltown Malbay
Ennis
Nenagh
Tullow
Arklow
Mutton
Killaloe
Templemore
Carlow
IRELAND
Thurles
Muine Bheag
Kilkee
Gorey
Kilkenny
Kilrush
Limerick
Slaney
Tipperary
Kilkenny
Cahore Pt
Loop Hd.
Foynes
Cashel
Mouth of the Shannon
Rathkeale
Thomastown
Enniscorthy
Limerick
Nore
Newcastle W.
Tipperary
Listowel
Carrick -on-Suir
Wexford
MUNSTER
Cahir
Abbeyfeale
New Ross
Tralee Bay
Ráth Luirc
Wexford
Tralee
Clonmel
Castleisland
Mitchelstown
Rosslare
Fishguard
Comeragh Mts
Newmarket
Waterford
Dingle
Carnsore Pt
Waterford
Tramore
Fermoy
Kerry
Blackwater
Hook Hd
Gt. Blasket
Waterford Harb.
Dingle B.
Killarney
Mallow
Dungarvan
Boggeragh Mts
Cork
1041
St George's Channel
Mine Hd
Valencia
MacGillycuddys Reeks
Youghal
Cahersiveen
Cork
Lee
Kenmare
Macroom
Youghal Harb.
Sneem
Passage West
Cobh
Kenmare River
Caha Mts
Bandon
Kinsale
Bantry
Dunmanway
Milford Haven
Clonakilty
Bantry Bay
Old Head of Kinsale
Dursey
Skibbereen
3
Mizen Hd.
Baltimore
Roaringwater B.
C. Clear
Fastnet Rock
Kinsale
1
2

1:2.5M

0 25 50 75 100 km

0 25 50 mls

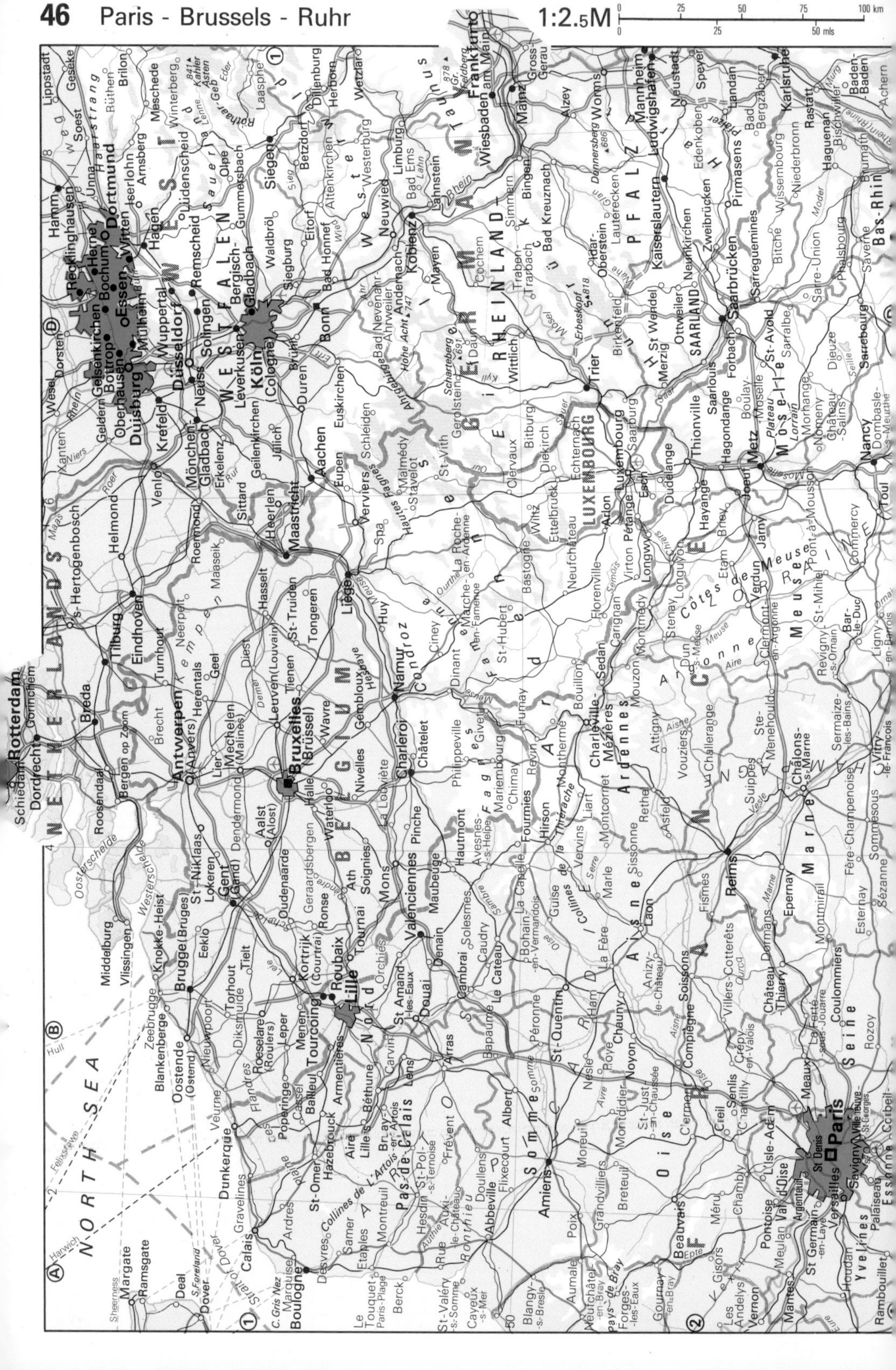

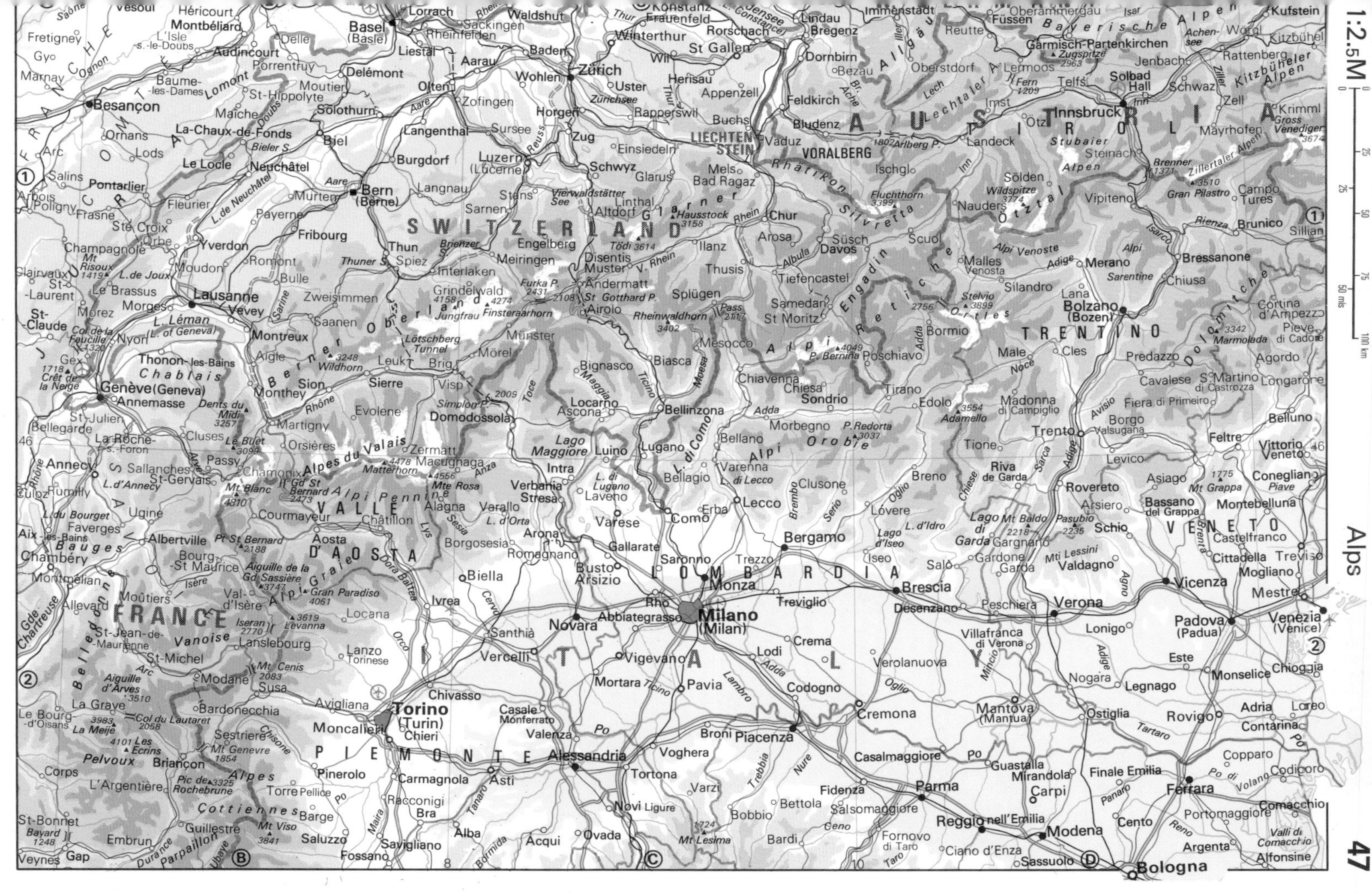
0 25 50 75 100 km
0 25 50 mls
Kufstein
Innsbruck
Bolzano (Bozen)
Trento
Venezia (Venice)
Padova (Padua)
Vicenza
Verona
Ferrara
Bologna
Modena
Parma
Brescia
Bergamo
Milano (Milan)
Como
Lecco
Sondrio
Piacenza
Pavia
Novara
Alessandria
Asti
Torino (Turin)
Aosta
Chur
Zürich
Luzern (Lucerne)
Bern (Berne)
Basel (Basle)
Lausanne
Genève (Geneva)
Besançon
Annecy
Chambéry
Briançon
Gap
Lago Maggiore
Lago di Garda
L. di Como
SWITZERLAND
LIECHTENSTEIN
AUSTRIA
TIROL
VORALBERG
TRENTINO
VENETO
LOMBARDIA
PIEMONTE
VALLE D'AOSTA
FRANCE
ITALY

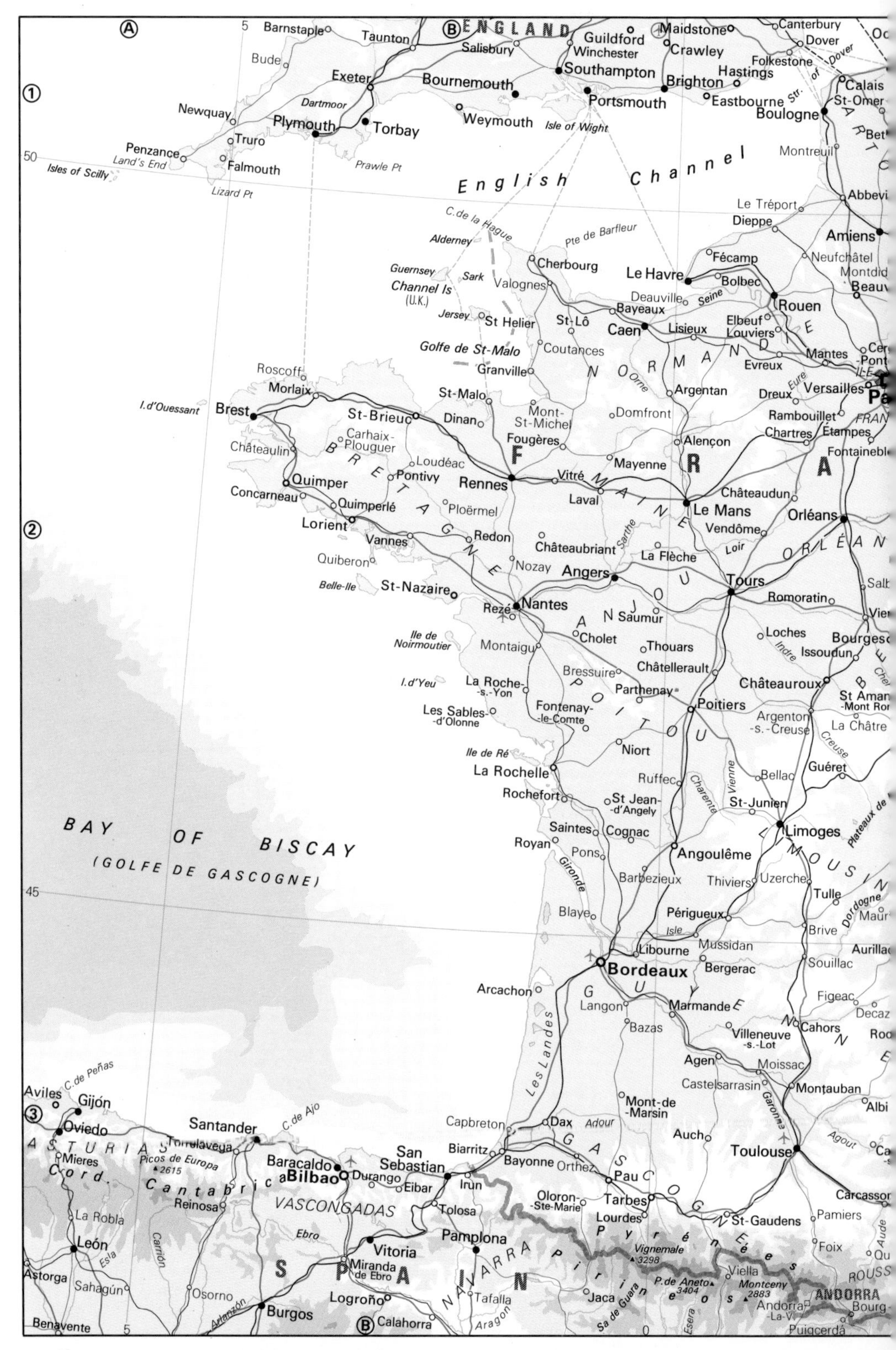
A
B
1
2
3
5
0
50
45
ENGLAND
Barnstaple
Taunton
Bude
Salisbury
Maidstone
Canterbury
Guildford
Winchester
Crawley
Dover
Folkestone
Str. of Dover
Exeter
Bournemouth
Southampton
Brighton
Hastings
Calais
St-Omer
Newquay
Dartmoor
Portsmouth
Eastbourne
Boulogne
Plymouth
Torbay
Weymouth
Isle of Wight
Penzance
Land's End
Truro
Falmouth
Prawle Pt
Montreuil
Isles of Scilly
Lizard Pt
English Channel
Abbevi
Le Tréport
Dieppe
Amiens
C. de la Hague
Alderney
Pte de Barfleur
Fécamp
Neufchâtel
Guernsey
Sark
Cherbourg
Le Havre
Bolbec
Montdid
Channel Is
(U.K.)
Valognes
Deauville
Seine
Beauv
Rouen
Jersey
St Helier
St-Lô
Bayeux
Caen
Lisieux
Elbeuf
Louviers
Golfe de St-Malo
Coutances
Evreux
Mantes
Granville
NORMANDIE
Orne
Roscoff
Morlaix
Argentan
Dreux
Eure
Versailles
Pa
St-Malo
Domfront
Rambouillet
I. d'Ouessant
Brest
St-Brieuc
Dinan
Mont-St-Michel
Chartres
Étampes
Carhaix-Plouguer
Fougères
Alençon
Fontainebl
Châteaulin
BRETAGNE
F
R
A
Loudéac
Mayenne
Quimper
Pontivy
Rennes
Vitré
MAINE
Concarneau
Laval
Châteaudun
Quimperlé
Ploërmel
Le Mans
Orléans
Lorient
Vendôme
Vannes
Redon
Châteaubriant
Sarthe
La Flèche
Loir
ORLÉANAIS
Quiberon
Nozay
Angers
Belle-Ile
St-Nazaire
Tours
Sal
Nantes
Rezé
ANJOU
Saumur
Romoratin
Vie
Ile de Noirmoutier
Cholet
Loches
Bourges
Montaigu
Thouars
Indre
Issoudun
Châtellerault
Bressuire
Châteauroux
I. d'Yeu
La Roche-s.-Yon
Parthenay
POITOU
Poitiers
St Aman -Mont Ro
Les Sables-d'Olonne
Fontenay-le-Comte
Argenton-s.-Creuse
La Châtre
Creuse
Ile de Ré
Niort
Guéret
La Rochelle
Ruffec
Vienne
Bellac
Charente
Rochefort
St Jean-d'Angely
St-Junien
Plateaux de
BAY OF BISCAY
(GOLFE DE GASCOGNE)
Saintes
Cognac
Limoges
Royan
Pons
Angoulême
LIMOUSIN
Gironde
Barbezieux
Thiviers
Uzerche
Tulle
Dordogne
Blaye
Périgueux
Maur
Isle
Brive
Libourne
Mussidan
Aurilla
Bordeaux
Bergerac
Souillac
Arcachon
GUYENNE
Langon
Figeac
Marmande
Decaz
Les Landes
Bazas
Cahors
Villeneuve-s.-Lot
Rod
Agen
Moissac
Castelsarrasin
Montauban
C. de Peñas
Aviles
Gijón
Mont-de-Marsan
Garonne
Albi
Oviedo
Santander
C. de Ajo
Capbreton
Dax
Adour
Auch
ASTURIAS
Torrelavega
San Sebastian
Biarritz
GASCOGNE
Toulouse
Agout
Ca
Mieres
Picos de Europa
2615
Baracaldo
Bayonne
Orthez
Cord. Cantabrica
Bilbao
Durango
Irun
Pau
Eibar
Carcasso
Reinosa
VASCONGADAS
Tolosa
Oloron-Ste-Marie
Tarbes
La Robla
Lourdes
St-Gaudens
Pamiers
Ebro
Pamplona
Pyrénées
Vignemale
3298
León
Vitoria
Foix
Carrión
Esla
NAVARRA
Pirineos
Astorga
Sahagún
S
P
A
I
N
Miranda de Ebro
Viella
P. de Aneto
3404
Montceny
2883
ROUSS
Osorno
Logroño
Tafalla
Jaca
Andorra-La-V.
ANDORRA
Arlanzón
Burgos
Sa de Guara
Esera
Bourg
Benavente
Calahorra
Aragon
Puigcerdá
Aude
Qu
Chartres
Orthez

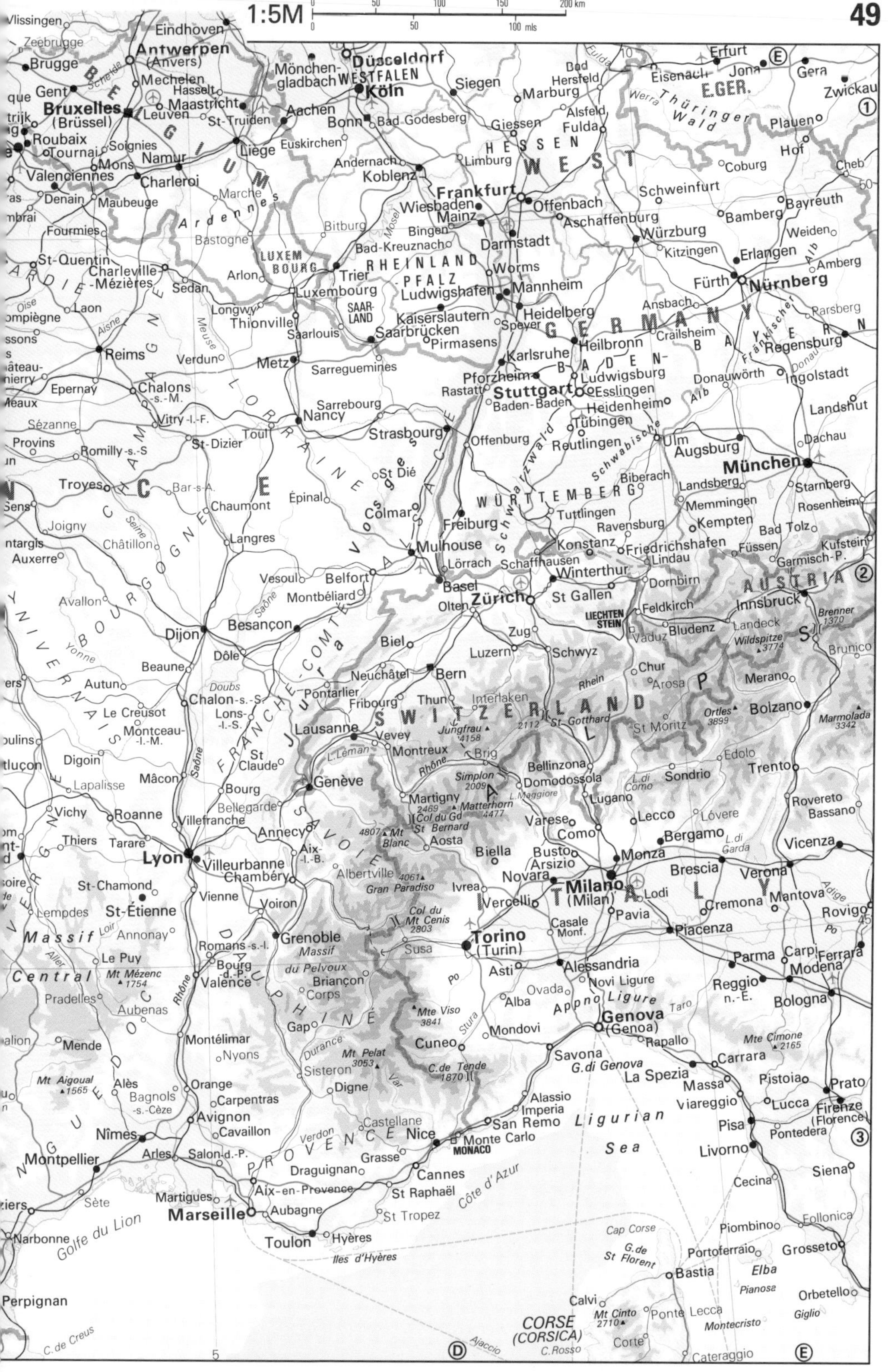

1:5M
0 50 100 150 200 km
0 50 100 mls
Vlissingen
Eindhoven
Zeebrugge
Antwerpen
(Anvers)
Brugge
Düsseldorf
Mönchen-gladbach
WESTFALEN
Köln
Mechelen
Hasselt
Gent
Bruxelles
(Brüssel)
Leuven
Maastricht
St-Truiden
Aachen
Bonn
Bad Godesberg
Siegen
Marburg
Bad Hersfeld
Eisenach
Erfurt
Jena
Gera
Zwickau
E.GER.
Thüringer Wald
Werra
Fulda
Alsfeld
Giessen
Plauen
Hof
Roubaix
Tournai
Soignies
Mons
Namur
Liège
Euskirchen
Valenciennes
Charleroi
Andernach
Koblenz
Limburg
HESSEN
WEST
Coburg
Cheb
Denain
Maubeuge
Marche
Ardennes
Frankfurt
Offenbach
Schweinfurt
Wiesbaden
Mainz
Aschaffenburg
Bamberg
Bayreuth
Fourmies
Bitburg
Bingen
Mosel
Würzburg
Weiden
Bastogne
Bad-Kreuznach
Darmstadt
Kitzingen
Erlangen
Amberg
St-Quentin
Charleville-Mézières
LUXEMBOURG
RHEINLAND-PFALZ
Worms
Arlon
Trier
Sedan
Luxembourg
Ludwigshafen
Mannheim
Fürth
Nürnberg
Alb
Laon
Oise
Aisne
Compiègne
Longwy
Thionville
SAAR-LAND
Kaiserslautern
Heidelberg
Ansbach
Parsberg
Saarlouis
Saarbrücken
Speyer
GERMANY
Crailsheim
Fränkischer
Pirmasens
Heilbronn
Regensburg
Reims
Verdun
Meuse
Metz
Karlsruhe
BADEN-
BAYERN
Donau
Sarreguemines
Ludwigsburg
Donauwörth
Ingolstadt
Epernay
Chalons-s.-M.
Pforzheim
Rastatt
Stuttgart
Esslingen
Meaux
Sarrebourg
Nancy
LORRAINE
Baden-Baden
Heidenheim
Landshut
Sézanne
Vitry-l.-F.
Toul
Strasbourg
Tübingen
Ulm
Dachau
Provins
Romilly-s.-S
St-Dizier
Offenburg
Reutlingen
Schwäbische
Augsburg
München
Schwarzwald
Vosges
St Dié
Biberach
Landsberg
Starnberg
Troyes
Bar-s-A.
CHAMPAGNE
Épinal
WÜRTTEMBERG
Memmingen
Rosenheim
Sens
Chaumont
Colmar
Freiburg
Tuttlingen
Ravensburg
Kempten
Bad Tolz
Joigny
Seine
Châtillon
Langres
Mulhouse
Konstanz
Friedrichshafen
Füssen
Kufstein
Montargis
Auxerre
Lörrach
Schaffhausen
Lindau
Garmisch-P.
Vesoul
Belfort
Basel
Winterthur
Dornbirn
AUSTRIA
Avallon
Saône
Montbéliard
Olten
Zürich
St Gallen
Innsbruck
Feldkirch
LIECHTENSTEIN
Brenner 1370
Dijon
Besançon
Vaduz
Bludenz
Landeck
Wildspitze 3774
NIVERNAIS
BOURGOGNE
Yonne
Dôle
FRANCHE-COMTÉ
Jura
Biel
Zug
Luzern
Schwyz
Brunico
Beaune
Neuchâtel
Bern
Chur
Arosa
Rhein
Merano
Autun
Doubs
Chalon-s.-S.
Pontarlier
Fribourg
Thun
Interlaken
SWITZERLAND
St Gotthard 2112
Ortles 3899
Bolzano
Marmolada 3342
Le Creusot
Lons-l.-S.
Lausanne
Vevey
Jungfrau 4158
St Moritz
Montceau-l.-M.
St Claude
Montreux
L. Léman
Rhône
Brig
Edolo
Trento
Digoin
Bellinzona
Sondrio
Mâcon
Genève
Simplon 2009
Domodossola
L. di Como
Lapalisse
Bourg
Bellegarde
Martigny
L. Maggiore
Lugano
Rovereto
Vichy
Roanne
Villefranche
Annecy
2469 Col du Gd St Bernard
Matterhorn 4477
Varese
Lecco
Lóvere
Bassano
Thiers
Tarare
4807 Mt Blanc
Aosta
Como
Bergamo
L. di Garda
Lyon
Villeurbanne
Aix-l.-B.
Biella
Busto Arsizio
Monza
Vicenza
Chambéry
SAVOIE
Albertville
4061 Gran Paradiso
Brescia
Verona
St-Chamond
Vienne
Ivrea
Novara
Milano (Milan)
Lodi
ITALY
Mantova
Adige
St-Étienne
Voiron
Col du Mt Cenis 2803
Vercelli
Pavia
Cremona
Rovigo
Lempdes
Massif Central
Annonay
Grenoble
Massif du Pelvoux
Casale Monf.
Piacenza
Po
Romans-s.-I.
Susa
Torino (Turin)
Parma
Carpi
Ferrara
Le Puy
Bourg-d.-P.
DAUPHINÉ
Asti
Alessandria
Modena
Mt Mézenc 1754
Valence
Briançon
Novi Ligure
Reggio n.-E.
Pradelles
Corps
Ovada
Appno Ligure
Bologna
Aubenas
Alba
Taro
Mte Viso 3841
Genova (Genoa)
Gap
Mondovi
Stura
Mte Cimone 2165
Montélimar
Durance
Cuneo
Rapallo
Mende
Nyons
Mt Pelat 3053
Savona
G. di Genova
Carrara
LANGUEDOC
Sisteron
C. de Tende 1870
La Spezia
Massa
Pistoia
Prato
Mt Aigoual 1565
Alès
Orange
Digne
Var
Alassio
Imperia
Viareggio
Lucca
Bagnols-s.-Cèze
Carpentras
Firenze (Florence)
Avignon
Castellane
San Remo
Ligurian Sea
Pisa
Nîmes
Cavaillon
Verdon
PROVENCE
Nice
Monte Carlo
MONACO
Pontedera
Montpellier
Arles
Salon-d.-P.
Grasse
Livorno
Draguignan
Cannes
Siena
Aix-en-Provence
St Raphaël
Côte d'Azur
Sète
Martigues
Cecina
Marseille
Aubagne
St Tropez
Follonica
Golfe du Lion
Cap Corse
Piombino
Narbonne
Toulon
Hyères
Iles d'Hyères
G. de St Florent
Portoferraio
Grosseto
Bastia
Elba
Pianosa
Orbetello
Perpignan
Calvi
Mt Cinto 2710
Ponte Lecca
Montecristo
Giglio
CORSE (CORSICA)
Corte
C. de Creus
Ajaccio
C. Rosso
Cateraggio

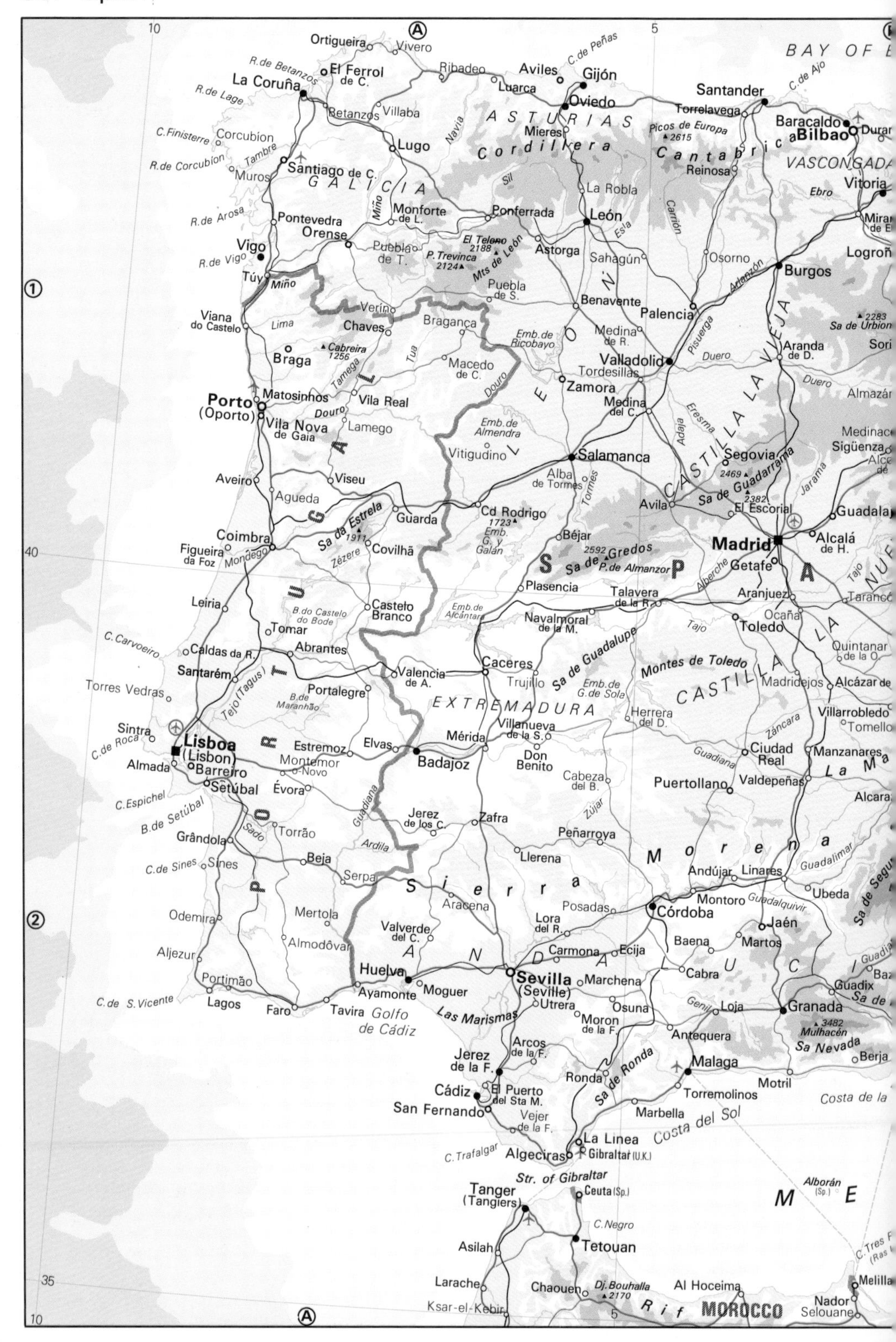
BAY OF B
La Coruña
El Ferrol de C.
Ortigueira
Vivero
Ribadeo
Luarca
Aviles
Gijón
Oviedo
Santander
Torrelavega
Baracaldo
Bilbao
Vitoria
ASTURIAS
Cordillera Cantabrica
VASCONGADA
GALICIA
Lugo
Santiago de C.
Betanzos
Villaba
Corcubíon
Muros
Pontevedra
Orense
Vigo
Túy
Monforte de L.
Ponferrada
León
Astorga
Mieres
La Robla
Reinosa
Picos de Europa
Burgos
Logroño
Osorno
Sahagún
Benavente
Palencia
Valladolid
Tordesillas
Zamora
Medina del C.
Medina de R.
Aranda de D.
Soria
CASTILLA LA VIEJA
LEÓN
Segovia
Salamanca
Avila
El Escorial
Madrid
Getafe
Alcalá de H.
Guadalajara
Aranjuez
Toledo
Ocaña
Talavera de la R.
Plasencia
Béjar
Cd Rodrigo
Vitigudino
Sa de Gredos
Viana do Castelo
Braga
Chaves
Verín
Bragança
Macedo de C.
Porto
(Oporto)
Matosinhos
Vila Nova de Gaia
Vila Real
Lamego
Viseu
Aveiro
Agueda
Guarda
Coimbra
Figueira da Foz
Covilhã
Sa da Estrela
Leiria
Tomar
Castelo Branco
Abrantes
Caldas da R.
Santarém
Torres Vedras
Sintra
Lisboa
(Lisbon)
Almada
Barreiro
Setúbal
Évora
Estremoz
Montemor-o-Novo
Elvas
Portalegre
Badajoz
Mérida
Caceres
Trujillo
Valencia de A.
EXTREMADURA
Navalmoral de la M.
Villanueva de la S.
Don Benito
CASTILLA LA NUEVA
Montes de Toledo
Ciudad Real
Puertollano
Valdepeñas
Manzanares
Madridejos
Alcázar
Villarrobledo
Tomelloso
Quintanar de la O.
Grândola
Sines
Beja
Serpa
Odemira
Aljezur
Mertola
Almodôvar
Portimão
Lagos
Faro
Tavira
Ayamonte
Huelva
Moguer
Golfo de Cádiz
Valverde del C.
Aracena
Sierra Morena
Jerez de los C.
Zafra
Llerena
Peñarroya
Cabeza del B.
Posadas
Lora del R.
Córdoba
Montoro
Andújar
Linares
Ubeda
Jaén
Baena
Martos
Cabra
Sevilla
(Seville)
Carmona
Ecija
Marchena
Utrera
Osuna
Moron de la F.
Las Marismas
Arcos de la F.
Jerez de la F.
Cádiz
El Puerto del Sta M.
San Fernando
Vejer de la F.
Ronda
Sa de Ronda
Antequera
Loja
Granada
Mulhacén
Sa Nevada
Malaga
Torremolinos
Marbella
Motril
Berja
Costa del Sol
La Linea
Gibraltar (U.K.)
Algeciras
C. Trafalgar
Str. of Gibraltar
Tanger
(Tangiers)
Ceuta (Sp.)
Tetouan
Asilah
Larache
Ksar-el-Kebir
Chaouen
Al Hoceima
MOROCCO
Rif
Melilla
Nador
Selouane
Alborán (Sp.)
ANDALUCIA
PORTUGAL
SPAIN
M E
① ②
10 5 40 35

FRANCE
Mont-de-Marsin
Albi
Nîmes
Arles
Salon-d.-P.
Montpellier
Aix-en-Provence
Capbreton
Dax
Adour
Auch
Garonne
Toulouse
Tarn
Agout
Castres-s.l'A
Martigues
Marseille
Aubagne
San Sebastian
Biarritz
Bayonne
Orthez
Pau
GASCOGNE
Béziers
Sète
Toulon
Hyères
Irun
Tarbes
Carcassonne
Narbonne
Golfe du Lion
Oloron-Ste-Marie
Lourdes
St-Gaudens
Pamiers
Tolosa
Pyrénées
Foix
Aude
Quillan
Pamplona
Vignemale 3298
Viella
ROUSSILLON
Perpignan
NAVARRA
P.de Aneto 3404
Montceny 2883
ANDORRA
Andorra-La-V.
Bourg-Madame
C. de Creus
Jaca
Tafalla
Sa de Guara
Puigcerdá
Figueras
Calahorra
Aragon
Esera
Sa del Codi
CATALUÑA
Costa Brava
Alfaro
Tudela
Huesca
Gallego
Barbastro
Segre
Ter
Gerona
Tarazona
Ebro
Vich
San Felíu de G.
Alagón
Jalón
Zaragoza
Cinca
Lérida
Sabadell
Granollérs
Matanó
Tarrasa
Badalona
ARAGÓN
Emb. de Mequinenza
Barcelona
Calatayud
Valls
Villanueva-y-G.
Jiloca
Daroca
Caspe
Reus
Tarragona
Alcaniz
Golfo de San Jorge
Monreal del C.
Tortosa
Guadalope
Amposta
C. de Tortosa
Sa de Albarracín
Sa de Gudar
Vinaroz
Benicarló
C. de Caballeria
Teruel
2019 Penarroya
Torreblanca
C. Formentor
Menorca
40
de Cuenca
Sarrion
Ciudadela
Mahón
Cuenca
Castellon de la P.
Alcudia
Villarreal
Is Columbretes
Mallorca
1445 Mayor
C. Binibeca
Capdepera
Segorbe
Emb. de Alarcón
Palma de Mallorca
Manacor
Sagunto
Golfo de Valencia
Turia
Motilla del P.
Utiel
Cabriel
Valencia
Santañy
VALENCIA
C. de Salinas
Cabrera
La Roda
Alcira
Ibiza
Játiva
S. Antonio Abad
Jucar
Albacete
Gandia
Ibiza
ISLAS BALEARES
(BALEARIC ISLANDS)
(Sp.)
Onteniente
Denia
Almansa
C. de la Nao
Formentera
Villena
Alcoy
Benidorm
Hellín
MURCIA
Elda
Alicante
Segura
Cieza
Elche
Costa Blanca
Orihuela
Caravaca
Murcia
Totana
Lorca
C. de Palos
Cartagena
G. de Mazarrón
Aguilas
Vera
C. de Gata
MEDITERRANEAN SEA
Alger (Algiers)
El Harrach
Dellys
Bejaïa (Bougie)
Tizi Ouzou
Djurdjura
Soummam
Kherrata
Cherchell
Boufarik
Ténès
Blida
Isser
Beni Mansour
Sétif
Miliana
Bouira
Médéa
Bir Rabalou
Bj bou Arréridj
Khemis
Dahra
Bosquet
Cheliff
El Asnam
Mts du Hodna
C. Ferrat
Massif de l'Ouarsenis
Ksar El Boukhari
Sbisseb
M'Sila
Mostaganem
Arzew
ALGERIA
Aïn Oussera
Aïn el Hadjel
Chott el Hodna
Barika
Mers el Kebir
Relizane
Oran
Sig
Ouassel
O. Tlélat
Mohammadia
Z. Chergui
Bou Saâda
Mina
Plat. du Sersou
Mascara
Tiaret
35
Beni-Saf
Aïn Témouchent
Monts des Ouled Nail
Sidi-bel-Abbès
Frenda
0
5

HUNGARY
AUSTRIA
W. GER.
SWITZERLAND
LIECHTENSTEIN
FRANCE
YUGOSLAVIA
SAN MARINO
MONACO
CROATIA
DALMATIA
ADRIATIC
SAVOIE
Ligurian Sea
G. di Venezia
G. di Genova
Appno Ligure
Appno Tosco-Emilliano
Appno Umbro-Marchigiano
Alpi Dolomitiche
Velebit
Wien
Budapest
Bratislava
Győr
Sopron
Szombathely
Veszprém
Székesfehérvár
Pécs
Kaposvár
Nagykanizsa
Graz
Maribor
Klagenfurt
Villach
Innsbruck
Salzburg
München
Zagreb
Ljubljana
Trieste
Rijeka (Fiume)
Split (Spalato)
Zadar
Šibenik
Sarajevo
Mostar
Dubrovnik
Banja Luka
Zenica
Tuzla
Bolzano
Trento
Udine
Venezia (Venice)
Mestre
Chioggia
Padova
Vicenza
Verona
Treviso
Mantova
Ferrara
Bologna
Modena
Parma
Ravenna
Rimini
Pesaro
Ancona
Pescara
L'Aquila
Perugia
Terni
Firenze (Florence)
Prato
Pisa
Livorno
Lucca
Siena
Grosseto
Viterbo
Milano (Milan)
Bergamo
Brescia
Como
Monza
Pavia
Piacenza
Cremona
Novara
Vercelli
Alessandria
Genova (Genoa)
Savona
La Spezia
Cuneo
Aosta
Zürich
Basel
Bern
Luzern
Lausanne
Genève
Nice
Cannes
Monte Carlo
San Remo
Bastia
Ajaccio
Corte
Elba
Lugano
St Moritz
Grossglockner 3798
Brenner 1370
Marmolada 3342
Mte Cimone 2165
Mte Viso 3841
Gran Paradiso 4061
Mt Blanc 4807
Mte Amiata 1738
Mte Corno 2914

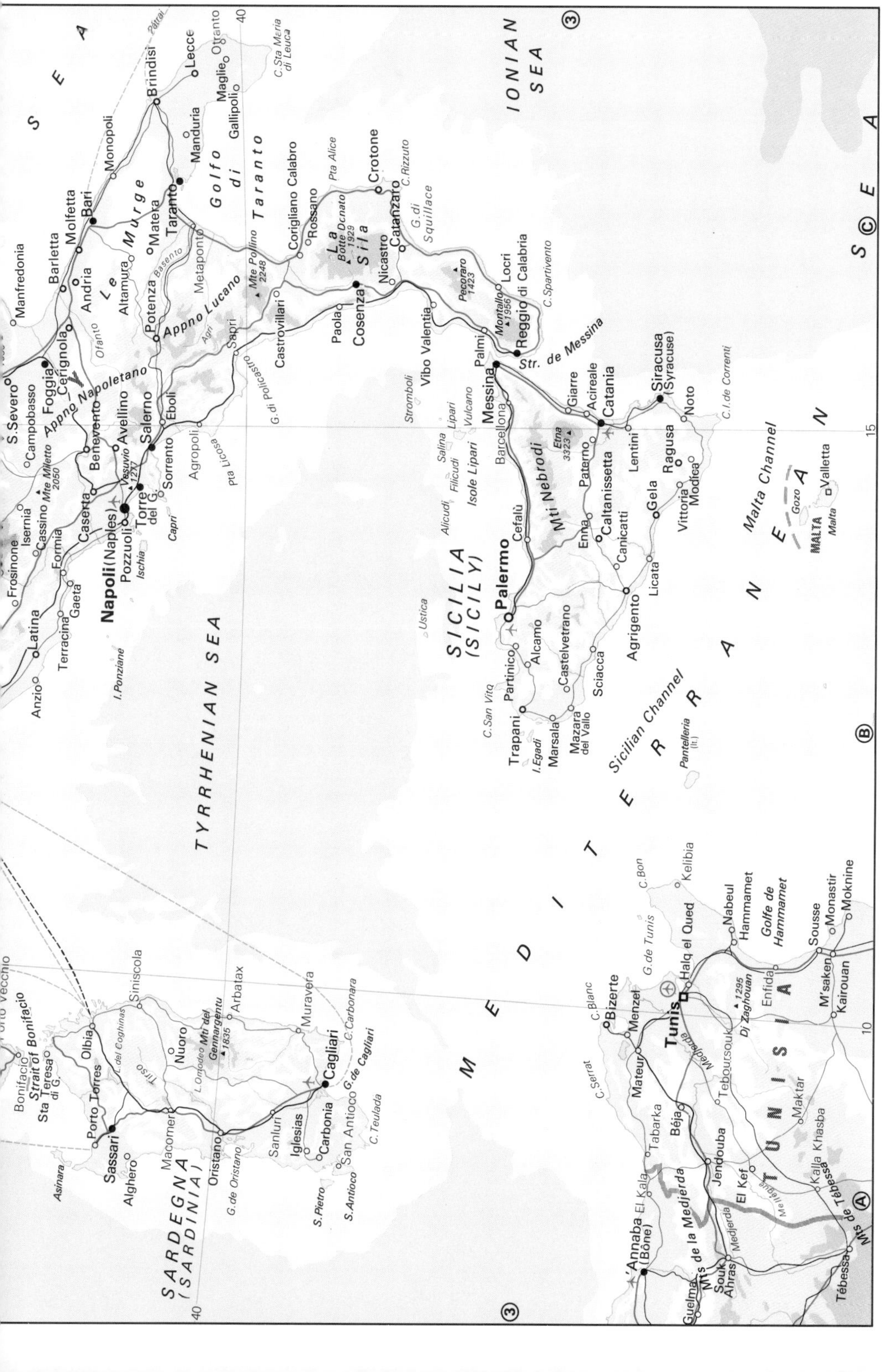

1:5M
0 50 100 150 200 km
0 50 100 mls

Porto Vecchio
Bonifacio
Strait of Bonifacio
Sta Teresa di G.
Asinara
Porto Torres
Olbia
Sassari
Alghero
L.del Coghinas
Siniscola
Tirso
Macomer
Nuoro
SARDEGNA (SARDINIA)
L.Omodeo
Mti del Gennargentu
1835
Oristano
G.de Oristano
Arbatax
Sanluri
Iglesias
Muravera
S.Pietro
Carbonia
Cagliari
S.Antioco
San Antioco
G.de Cagliari
C.Carbonara
C.Teulada
40
TYRRHENIAN SEA
Frosinone
Isernia
Anzio
Latina
Cassino
Mte Miletto 2050
Terracina
Gaeta
Formia
Caserta
I.Ponziane
Napoli (Naples)
Pozzuoli
Ischia
Torre del G.
Capri
Vesuvio 1277
Sorrento
S.Severo
Campobasso
Foggia
Appno Napoletano
Cerignola
Benevento
Avellino
Salerno
Eboli
Agropoli
Pta Licosa
Manfredonia
Barletta
Molfetta
Andria
Bari
Ofanto
Le Murge
Altamura
Monopoli
Matera
Potenza
Basento
Appno Lucano
Agri
Brindisi
Pátrai
Taranto
Manduria
Lecce
Metaponto
Golfo di Taranto
Maglie
Otranto
Gallipoli
C.Sta Maria di Leuca
Sapri
G.di Policastro
Mte Pollino 2248
Castrovillari
Corigliano Calabro
Rossano
Pta Alice
La Sila
Botte Donato 1929
Paola
Cosenza
Crotone
Nicastro
Catanzaro
C.Rizzuto
G.di Squillace
Stromboli
Vibo Valentia
Ustica
Alicudi
Filicudi
Salina
Lipari
Vulcano
Isole Lipari
SICILIA (SICILY)
Pecoraro 1423
Palmi
Messina
Montallo 1956
Locri
Reggio di Calabria
C.Spartivento
IONIAN SEA
C.San Vito
Trapani
Partinico
Palermo
Barcellona
Cefalù
Alcamo
I.Egadi
Marsala
Mti Nebrodi
Etna 3323
Castelvetrano
Mazara del Vallo
Giarre
Enna
Paterno
Acireale
Sciacca
Caltanissetta
Catania
Str. de Messina
Canicatti
Agrigento
Lentini
Licata
Gela
Siracusa (Syracuse)
Ragusa
Vittoria
Modica
Noto
C.I.de Correnti
Sicilian Channel
Pantelleria (It.)
Malta Channel
Gozo
MALTA
Malta
Valletta
MEDITERRANEAN SEA
C.Serrat
C.Blanc
Bizerte
'Annaba (Bône)
El Kala
Menzel
Mateur
G.de Tunis
C.Bon
Tabarka
Tunis
Béja
Halq el Qued
Kelibia
Guelma
Mts de la Medjerda
Medjerda
Souk Ahras
Jendouba
Teboursouk
Nabeul
1295
Dj Zaghouan
Hammamet
El Kef
Enfida
Golfe de Hammamet
Mellègue
TUNISIA
Maktar
Sousse
Kalla Khasba
M'saken
Monastir
Tébessa
Mts de Tébessa
Kairouan
Moknine
10
15
Ⓐ
Ⓑ
Ⓒ
③

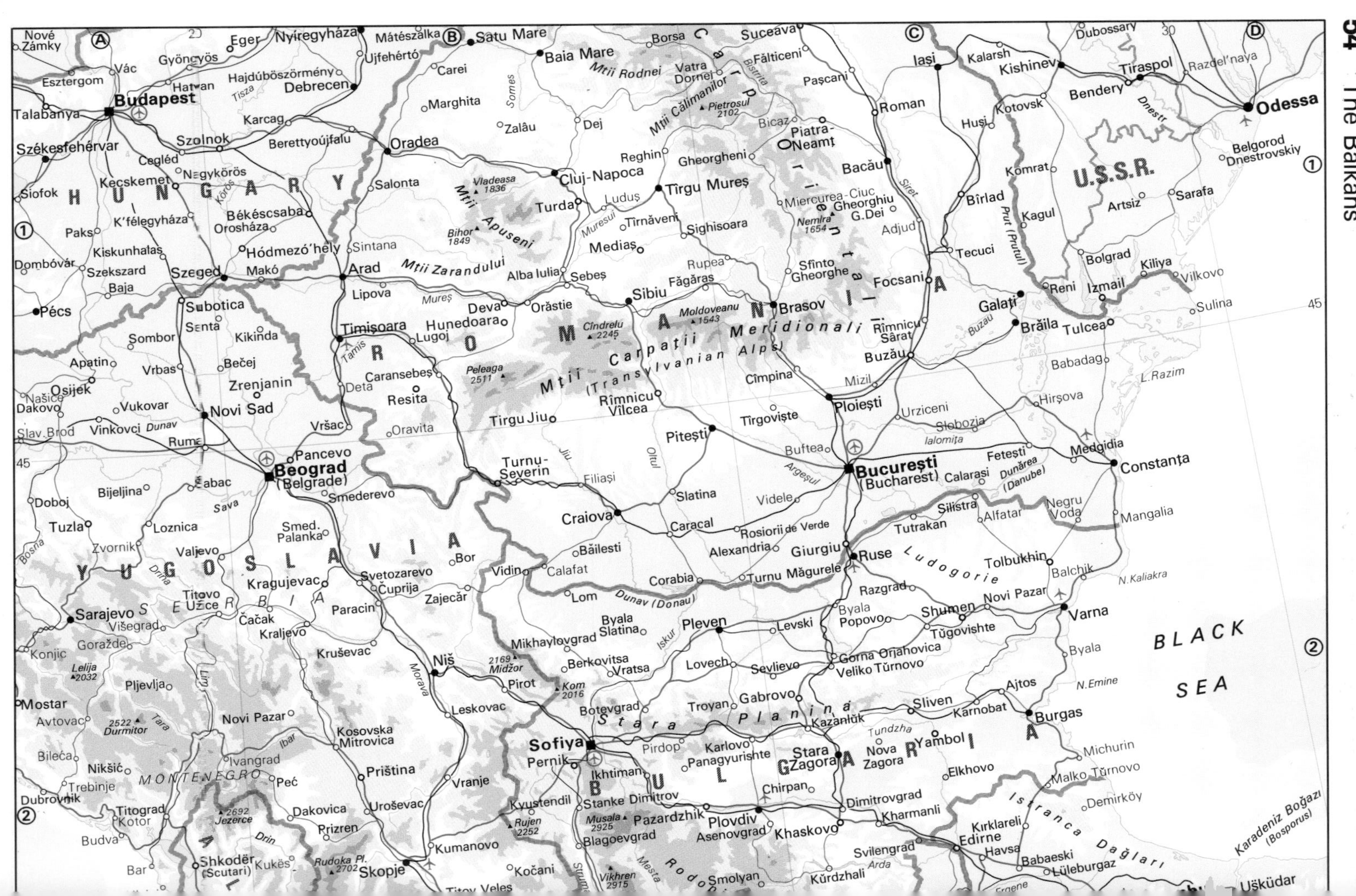
BLACK SEA
U.S.S.R.
HUNGARY
ROMANIA
YUGOSLAVIA
BULGARIA
Odessa
Belgorod Dnestrovskiy
Tiraspol
Bendery
Kishinev
Izmail
Sulina
Constanţa
Mangalia
Tulcea
Brăila
Galaţi
Iaşi
Roman
Bacău
Suceava
Focşani
Buzău
Ploieşti
Bucureşti (Bucharest)
Giurgiu
Ruse
Varna
Burgas
Shumen
Tolbukhin
Silistra
Pleven
Sofiya
Plovdiv
Stara Zagora
Khaskovo
Edirne
Karadeniz Boğazi (Bosporus)
Üsküdar
Braşov
Sibiu
Tîrgu Mureş
Cluj-Napoca
Oradea
Satu Mare
Baia Mare
Arad
Timişoara
Deva
Craiova
Piteşti
Rîmnicu Vîlcea
Turnu-Severin
Vidin
Niš
Skopje
Priština
Beograd (Belgrade)
Novi Sad
Subotica
Szeged
Debrecen
Budapest
Pécs
Osijek
Sarajevo
Mostar
Dubrovnik
Titograd
Shkodër (Scutari)
Carpaţii Meridionali (Transylvanian Alps)
Stara Planina
Ludogorie
Rodopi
Istranca Dağlari
Mţii Apuseni
Dunav (Donau)
Dunărea (Danube)
Prut (Prutul)
Dnestr
Siret
Oltul
Morava
Sava
Drina
Mureş
Tisza

A B C 3 4

20 25 35 40

TURKEY
Sea of Marmara
Marmara Adı
Yalova
Gemlik
Bursa
Iznik G.
Karacabey
Mustafa-Kemalpaşa
Orhaneli
Tavşanlı
Dursunbey
Simav
Ak Dağ 2089
Bigadiç
Bandırma
Kuş G.
Gönen
Biga
Balıkesir
Sındırgı
Soma
Akhisar
Gediz
Kula
Alaşehir
Salihli
Turgutlu
Manisa
Edremit
Burhaniye
Kırkağaç
Ayvalık
Bergama
Menemen
Bornova
İzmir
Boz Dağları 2157
Ödemiş
Tire
Nazilli
Buldan
Denizli
Urla
Çeşme
Torbalı
Selçuk
Aydın
Söke
Çine
Muğla
Milas
Bodrum
Marmaris
Ak
Tekir D.
Keşan
İpsala
Saros Körfezi
Gelibolu (Gallipoli)
Eceabat
Çanakkale
Ezine
Ayvacık
Edremit K.
Çandarlı K.
İzmir K.
Kuşadası K.
Mandalya K.
Kerme K.
Gökçeada
Bozcaada
Samothráki
Alexandroúpolis
Sápai
Xánthi
Kaválla
Dráma
Sérrai
Thásos
Límnos
Kástron
Áyios Evstrátios
Lésvos
Mitilíni
Kallonis K.
Khíos
Psará
Sámos
Ikaría
Pagóndhas
Foúrnoi
Pátmos
Léros
Kálimnos
Kós
Tílos
Sími
Alimniá
Khálki
Ródhos
Líndos
Kárpathos
Kásos
SPORÁDHES
(DODECANESE)
Armagós
Astipálaia
Anáfi
AEGEAN SEA
Kikládhes (Cyclades)
Ándros
Tínos
Míkonos
Náxos
Páros
Íos
Thíra
Síkinos
Mílos
Sífnos
Sérifos
Kíthnos
Kéa
Síros
Sea of Crete
Kríti
Iráklion
Dhíkti Óri 2148
Sitía
Ierápetra
Akr. Sídheros
K. Merabéllou
Réthimnon
Ídhi Óros 2456
Timbákion
Akr. Líthinon
Khaniá
Lévka Óri 2452
Akr. Spátha
Kastélli
Andikíthira
Kíthira
Mirtoan Sea
Ídhra
Aíyna
Saronikós K.
Argolikós K.
Akr. Maléa
Neápolis
Lakonikós Kólpos
Akr. Taínaron
Messiniakós Kólpos
Athínai (Athens)
Piraiévs
Akharnái
Mégara
Kórinthos
Korinthiakós K.
Thívai
Khalkís
Kími
Káristos
Akr. Kafirévs
Évvoia
Skíros
Skópelos
Skíathos
Iliodhrómia
Istiáia
Livanátais
Vólos
Almirós
Fársala
Lárisa
Tírnavos
Thessaloníki (Salonica)
Khalkidhíki
Thermaïkós Kólpos
K. Strimonikós
K. Singitikós
K. Toronaíos
Áthos 2033
Políyiros
Nigríta
Kilkís
Yiannitsá
Gevgelija
Edhessa
Véroia
Kateríni
Ólimbos (Olympus) 2917
Ptolemaís
Kozáni
Aliákmon
Piniós
Kalabáka
Kardhítsa
Dhomokós
Lamía
Tímfristós 2316
Óthris 1726
Gióna 2510
Ámfissa
Levádhia
GREECE
Píndhos
Prilep
Bitola
Flórina
Prespansko Jez.
Kastoría
Grámmos 2503
Smólikas 2633
Tzouměrka 2429
Ioánnina
Árta
Amfilokhía
Agrínion
Návpaktos
Mesolóngion
Pátrai
Aíyion
Sikionía
Killíni 2376
Árgos
Návplion
Párnon Ó. 1935
Trípolis
Megalópolis
Spartí
Moláoi
Yíthion
Kalámai
Messíni
Pílos
Kiparissía
Filiatrá
Kiparissiakós Kólpos
Pírgos
Amaliás
Alfiós
Zákinthos
Argostólion
Kefallinía
Levkás
Préveza
Igoumenítsa
IÓNIOI NÍSOI (Ionian Islands)
Kérkira
Kérkira (Corfu)
Sarandë
Gjirokastër
Vijosë
Ohrid
Ohridsko Jez.
Korçë
Devoll
Tomorrit 2480
ALBANIA
Tiranë
Elbasan
Durrës
Kavajë
Lushnjë
Fier
Berat
Vlorë
Strait of Otranto
IONIAN SEA
Brindisi
Lecce
Otranto
Maglie
Gallipoli
C. Sta Maria di Leuca
Bari

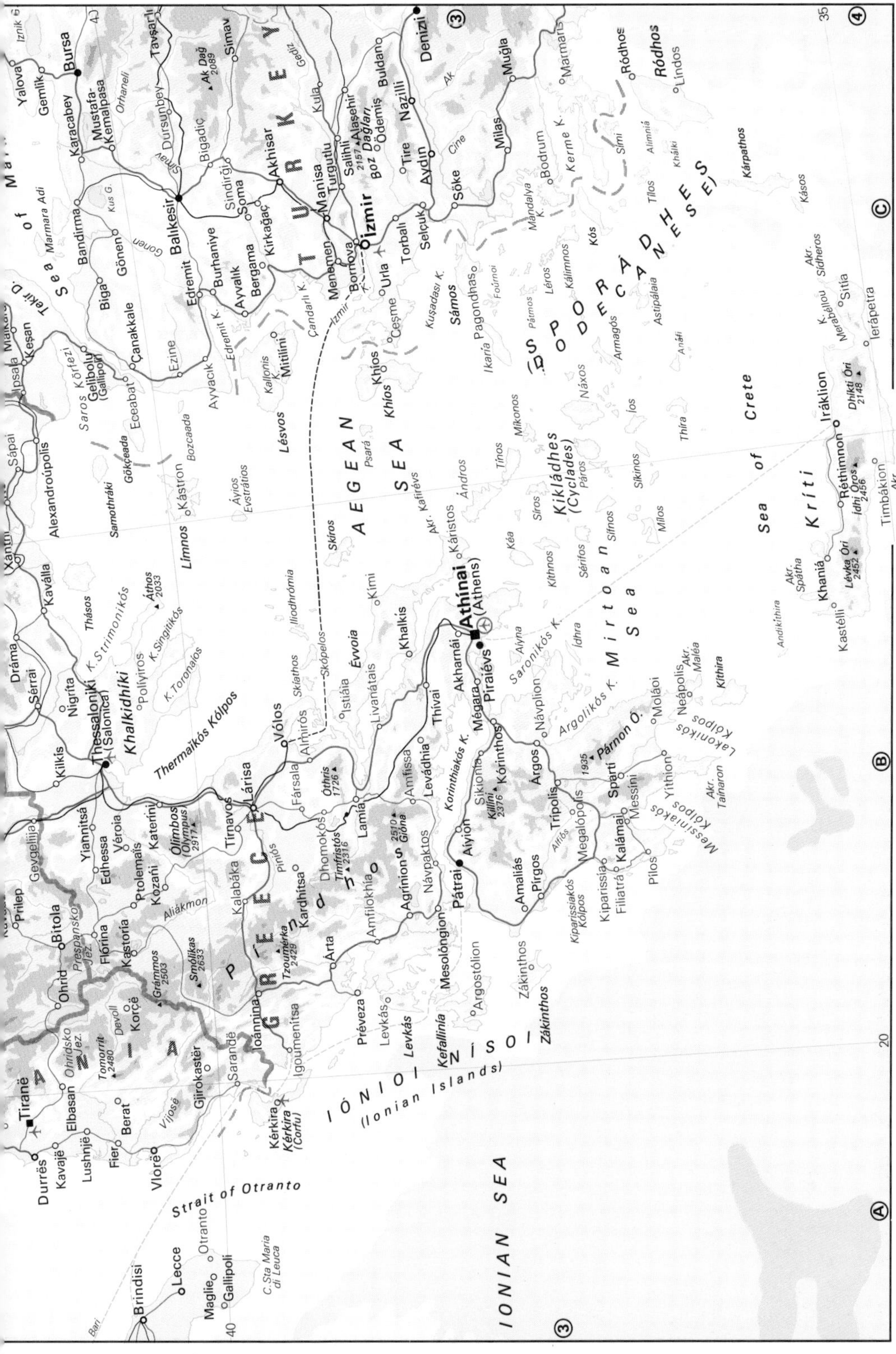

NORTH SEA
BALTIC SEA
SWEDEN
DENMARK
POLAND
EAST GERMANY
NIEDERSACHSEN
NORDRHEIN-
SCHLESWIG-HOLSTEIN
Kattegat
Jylland (Jutland)
Sjælland
Fyn
Lolland
Falster
Bornholm
Rügen
Öland
Göteborg
Borås
Jönköping
Malmö
Lund
Helsingborg
Helsingør
København (Copenhagen)
Roskilde
Odense
Århus
Ålborg
Esbjerg
Kolding
Flensburg
Kiel
Lübeck
Hamburg
Bremen
Bremerhaven
Hannover
Berlin
Potsdam
Rostock
Stralsund
Greifswald
Schwerin
Wismar
Magdeburg
Braunschweig
Wolfsburg
Szczecin
Poznań
Koszalin
Amsterdam
Rotterdam
's-Gravenhage (Den Haag)
Utrecht
Groningen
Dortmund
Essen
Duisburg
Antwerpen (Anvers)
Brugge
Oostende
Dunkerque

WEST GERMANY
AUSTRIA
SWITZERLAND
ITALY
FRANCE
YUGOSLAVIA
LUXEMBOURG
LIECHTENSTEIN
Praha (Prague)
Wien (Vienna)
Bratislava
München (Munich)
Nürnberg
Frankfurt
Stuttgart
Zürich
Bern
Genève
Lyon
Dijon
Milano (Milan)
Torino (Turin)
Venezia (Venice)
Zagreb
Ljubljana
Dresden
Karl Marx Stadt
Salzburg
Innsbruck
Graz
Linz
Brno
Strasbourg
Basel
Besançon
Grenoble
Trieste
Bolzano
Verona
Reims
Metz
Nancy
Koblenz
Bonn
Mannheim
Regensburg
Augsburg

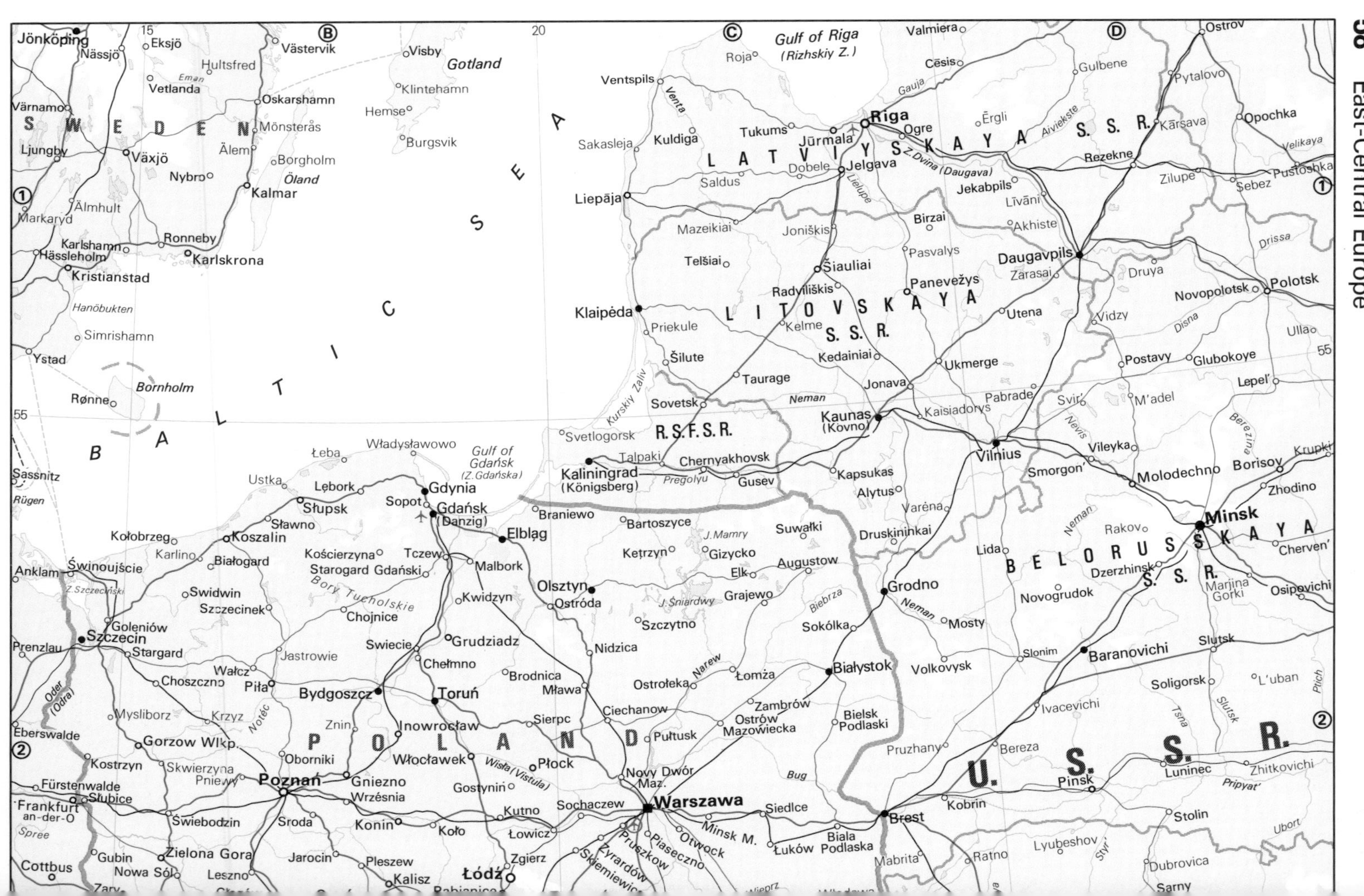

Gulf of Riga
(Rizhskiy Z.)
Gulf of Gdańsk
(Z. Gdańska)
Kurskiy Zaliv
Hanöbukten
B A L T I C S E A
S W E D E N
L A T V I Y S K A Y A S. S. R.
L I T O V S K A Y A S. S. R.
B E L O R U S S K A Y A S. S. R.
U. S. S. R.
R.S.F.S.R.
P O L A N D
Gotland
Öland
Bornholm
Rügen
Jönköping
Nässjö
Eksjö
Värnamo
Vetlanda
Hultsfred
Eman
Västervik
Oskarshamn
Mönsterås
Borgholm
Kalmar
Nybro
Ålem
Växjö
Ljungby
Markaryd
Älmhult
Ronneby
Karlskrona
Karlshamn
Hässleholm
Kristianstad
Simrishamn
Ystad
Rønne
Visby
Klintehamn
Hemse
Burgsvik
Sassnitz
Ventspils
Venta
Roja
Kuldiga
Sakasleja
Liepāja
Saldus
Tukums
Jūrmala
Riga
Jelgava
Dobele
Lielupe
Ogre
Cēsis
Valmiera
Gauja
Ērgli
Jekabpils
Z. Dvina (Daugava)
Aiviekste
Līvāni
Gulbene
Rezekne
Kārsava
Zilupe
Daugavpils
Ostrov
Pytalovo
Opochka
Sebez
Pustoshka
Velikaya
Drissa
Polotsk
Novopolotsk
Ulla
Lepel'
Glubokoye
Postavy
M'adel
Druya
Disna
Vidzy
Svir'
Nevis
Berezina
Borisov
Zhodino
Krupki
Minsk
Cherven'
Osipovichi
Marjina Gorki
Molodechno
Vileyka
Smorgon'
Dzerzhinsk
Rakov
Neman
Novogrudok
Baranovichi
Slutsk
Soligorsk
L'uban
Ptich
Tsna
Luninec
Zhitkovichi
Pripyat'
Stolin
Pinsk
Ivacevichi
Slonim
Lida
Vilnius
Kaunas (Kovno)
Šiauliai
Radviliškis
Kelme
Joniškis
Mazeikiai
Telšiai
Klaipėda
Priekule
Šilute
Taurage
Sovetsk
Kedainiai
Jonava
Ukmerge
Panevežys
Pasvalys
Birzai
Akhiste
Utena
Zarasai
Kaisiadorys
Pabrade
Alytus
Kapsukas
Varėna
Druskininkai
Grodno
Mosty
Volkovysk
Brest
Kobrin
Pruzhany
Bereza
Lyubeshov
Ratno
Mabrita
Dubrovica
Sarny
Chernyakhovsk
Gusev
Talpaki
Kaliningrad (Königsberg)
Svetlogorsk
Pregolyu
Braniewo
Bartoszyce
J. Mamry
Kętrzyn
Giżycko
Suwałki
Augustów
Ełk
Grajewo
Biebrza
J. Śniardwy
Szczytno
Olsztyn
Ostróda
Nidzica
Elbląg
Malbork
Kwidzyn
Grudziądz
Gdańsk (Danzig)
Gdynia
Sopot
Władysławowo
Tczew
Starogard Gdański
Kościerzyna
Chojnice
Bory Tucholskie
Lębork
Łeba
Słupsk
Ustka
Sławno
Koszalin
Białogard
Kołobrzeg
Karlino
Świdwin
Szczecinek
Wałcz
Piła
Jastrowie
Noteć
Bydgoszcz
Świecie
Chełmno
Toruń
Inowrocław
Gniezno
Września
Konin
Koło
Kalisz
Pleszew
Jarocin
Środa
Poznań
Oborniki
Znin
Włocławek
Gostynin
Kutno
Łowicz
Łódź
Zgierz
Płock
Sierpc
Mława
Ciechanów
Pułtusk
Ostrołęka
Łomża
Zambrów
Ostrów Mazowiecka
Białystok
Sokółka
Bielsk Podlaski
Biała Podlaska
Siedlce
Łuków
Minsk M.
Otwock
Warszawa
Nowy Dwór Maz.
Piaseczno
Pruszków
Żyrardów
Skierniewice
Sochaczew
Brodnica
Narew
Bug
Wisła (Vistula)
Szczecin
Stargard
Goleniów
Świnoujście
Choszczno
Myślibórz
Gorzów Wlkp.
Krzyż
Pniewy
Skwierzyna
Świebodzin
Zielona Gora
Leszno
Nowa Sól
Gubin
Kostrzyn
Słubice
Frankfurt an-der-O
Fürstenwalde
Eberswalde
Prenzlau
Anklam
Cottbus
Spree
Oder (Odra)
Z. Szczeciński

Praha (Prague)
Wien (Vienna)
Budapest
Bratislava
Kraków
Wrocław (Breslau)
L'vov
Chernovtsy
Debrecen
Miskolc
Košice
Cluj-Napoca
Zagreb
Ljubljana
Graz
Linz
Brno
Ostrava
Katowice
Szeged
Arad
Timişoara
Oradea
Braşov
Bacău
Iaşi
Ploieşti
Novi Sad
Rijeka (Fiume)
Rovno
Ternopol
Khmel'nitskiy
Ivano-Frankovsk
Uzhgorod
Mukachevo
Satu Mare
Baia Mare
Sibiu
Tîrgu Mureş
Pécs
Györ
Sopron
Maribor
Klagenfurt
České Budějovice
Olomouc
Opole
Częstochowa
Kielce
Rzeszów
Tarnów
Przemys'l
Nyíregyháza
Kecskemet
Szolnok
Székesfehérvar
AUSTRIA
HUNGARY
YUGOSLAVIA
ROMANIA
SLOVENSKO
ČESKÉ ZEMĚ
UKRAINSKAYA S.S.R.
Carpaţii Meridionali (Transylvanian Alps)
Beskidy Zachodnie
Dunav
Donau
Siret
Prut (Prutul)
Dnestr
Tisza
Balaton

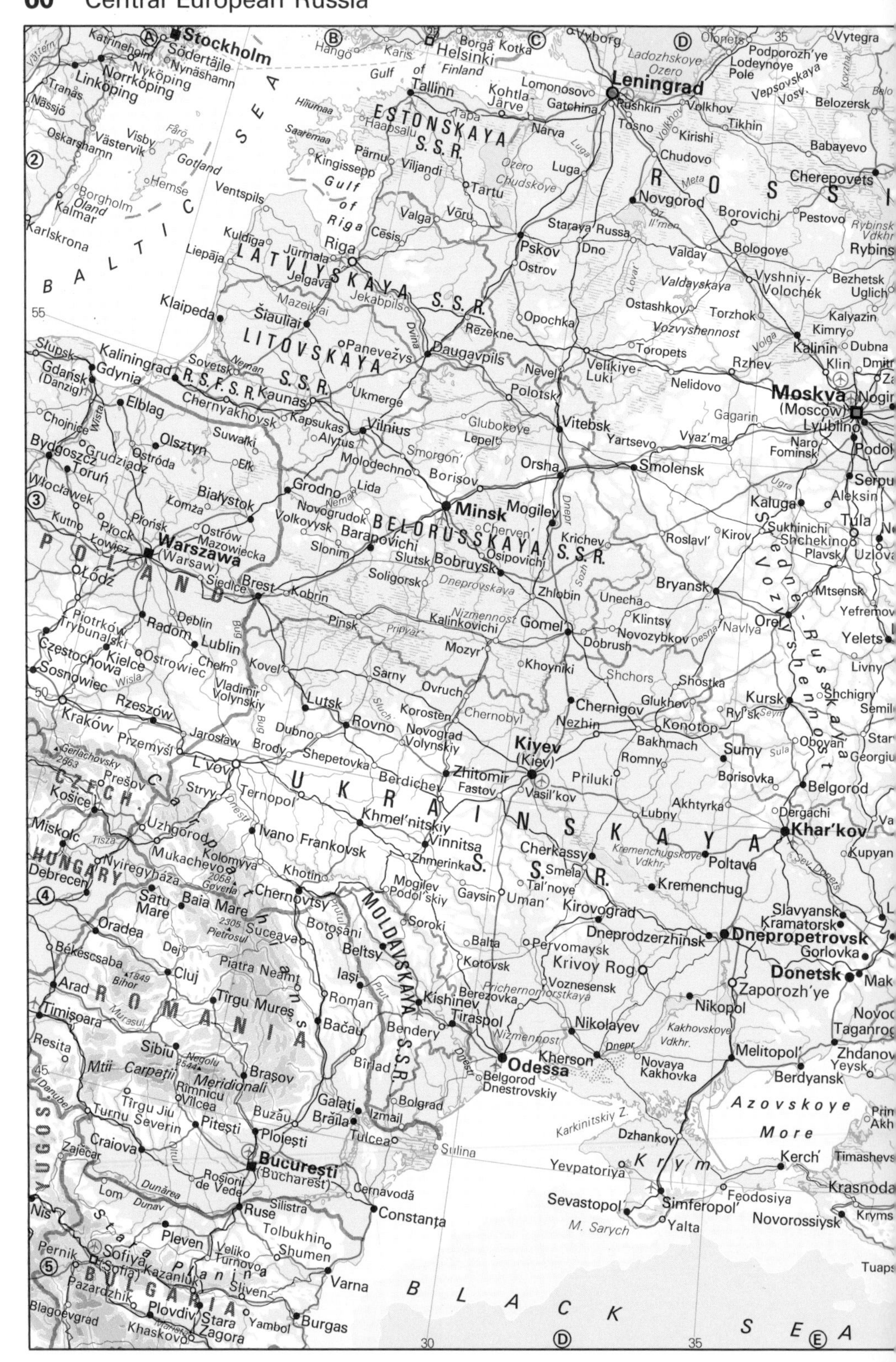

Stockholm
Södertälje
Nynäshamn
Nyköping
Norrköping
Linköping
Tranås
Nässjö
Katrineholm
Västervik
Visby
Oskarshamn
Fårö
Gotland
Hemse
Borgholm
Öland
Kalmar
Karlskrona
B A L T I C   S E A
Hangö
Karis
Helsinki
Borgå
Kotka
Vyborg
Gulf of Finland
Tallinn
Kohtla-Järve
Lomonosov
Gatchina
Leningrad
Pushkin
Volkhov
Olonets
Podporozh'ye
Lodeynoye Pole
Vytegra
Vepsovskaya Vosv.
Belozersk
Ladozhskoye Ozero
Tosno
Kirishi
Tikhin
Chudovo
Babayevo
Cherepovets
Hiiumaa
Saaremaa
Haapsalu
Tapa
ESTONSKAYA S.S.R.
Narva
Luga
Pärnu
Viljandi
Kingissepp
Ventspils
Gulf of Riga
Ozero Chudskoye
Tartu
Novgorod
R O S S I
Borovichi
Pestovo
Rybinsk
Valga
Võru
Cēsis
Staraya Russa
Il'men
Kuldiga
Liepāja
Riga
Jūrmala
Jelgava
LATVIYSKAYA S.S.R.
Pskov
Dno
Valday
Bologoye
Ostrov
Valdayskaya
Vyshniy-Volochek
Bezhetsk
Uglich
Klaipeda
Šiauliai
Mazeikiai
Jekabpils
Dvina
Rēzekne
Opochka
Ostashkov
Torzhok
Vozvyshennost
Kalyazin
Kimry
Dubna
Kalinin
LITOVSKAYA S.S.R.
Panevežys
Daugavpils
Toropets
Velikiye-Luki
Nevel
Rzhev
Klin
Sovetsk
Kaliningrad
R.S.F.S.R.
Kaunas
Neman
Słupsk
Gdańsk (Danzig)
Gdynia
Elbląg
Chernyakhovsk
Ukmerge
Polotsk
Nelidovo
Moskva (Moscow)
Gagarin
Lyublino
Chojnice
Suwałki
Kapsukas
Alytus
Vilnius
Glubokoye
Lepel
Vitebsk
Yartsevo
Vyaz'ma
Naro Fominsk
Podolsk
Bydgoszcz
Grudziądz
Toruń
Olsztyn
Ostróda
Ełk
Smorgon'
Molodechno
Borisov
Orsha
Smolensk
Serpukhov
Włocławek
Białystok
Łomża
Grodno
Lida
Minsk
Mogilev
Ugra
Kaluga
Aleksin
Kutno
Płock
Płońsk
Ostrów Mazowiecka
Novogrudok
Volkovysk
BELORUSSKAYA S.S.R.
Cherven'
Krichev
Dnepr
Roslavl'
Kirov
Sukhinichi
Tula
Shchekino
Plavsk
Uzlovaya
POLAND
Łowicz
Warszawa (Warsaw)
Baranovichi
Slonim
Slutsk
Bobruysk
Osipovichi
Łódź
Siedlce
Brest
Kobrin
Soligorsk
Dneprovskaya
Zhlobin
Sozh
Unecha
Bryansk
Mtsensk
Yefremov
Piotrków Trybunalski
Dęblin
Radom
Lublin
Bug
Pinsk
Pripyat'
Nizmennost
Kalinkovichi
Gomel'
Klintsy
Novozybkov
Dobrush
Desna
Navlya
Orel
Yelets
Częstochowa
Kielce
Ostrowiec
Chełm
Kovel'
Mozyr'
Khoyniki
Livny
Sosnowiec
Wisła
Vladimir Volynskiy
Sarny
Ovruch
Shchors
Shostka
Kursk
Shchigry
Semiluki
Kraków
Rzeszów
Lutsk
Sluch
Korosten
Chernobyl
Chernigov
Glukhov
Ryl'sk
Seym
Gerlachovský 2663
Przemyśl
Jarosław
Dubno
Rovno
Novograd Volynskiy
Nezhin
Konotop
Bakhmach
Oboyan'
Staryy Oskol
Brody
Shepetovka
Kiyev (Kiev)
Romny
Sumy
Sula
CZECH.
Prešov
L'vov
Berdichev
Zhitomir
Priluki
Borisovka
Košice
Stryy
Ternopol'
Fastov
Vasil'kov
Belgorod
UKRAINSKAYA S.S.R.
Uzhgorod
Dnestr
Khmel'nitskiy
Akhtyrka
Lubny
Dergachi
Miskolc
Tisza
Ivano Frankovsk
Vinnitsa
Kremenchugskoye Vdkhr.
Khar'kov
Kupyansk
HUNGARY
Nyíregyháza
Mukachevo
Kolomyya
Zhmerinka
Cherkassy
Poltava
Debrecen
2058 Goverla
Khotin
Mogilev Podol'skiy
Smela
Sev. Donets
Satu Mare
Baia Mare
Chernovtsy
Prut
Gaysin
Tal'noye
Uman'
Kremenchug
Kirovograd
Slavyansk
Kramatorsk
Oradea
2305 Pietrosul
Suceava
Botoşani
MOLDAVSKAYA S.S.R.
Soroki
Dneprodzerzhinsk
Dnepropetrovsk
Gorlovka
Dej
Bel'tsy
Balta
Pervomaysk
Krivoy Rog
Békéscsaba
1849 Bihor
Cluj
Piatra Neamţ
Kotovsk
Voznesensk
Donetsk
Arad
ROMANIA
Iaşi
Prichernomorskaya
Zaporozh'ye
Timişoara
Mureşul
Tîrgu Mureş
Roman
Kishinev
Berezovka
Nikopol
Bacău
Tiraspol
Bendery
Nikolayev
Kakhovskoye Vdkhr.
Taganrog
Resita
Sibiu
2544 Negolu
Bîrlad
Nizmennost
Kherson
Melitopol'
Zhdanov
Yeysk
Mtii Carpaţii Meridionali
Braşov
Odessa
Novaya Kakhovka
Berdyansk
Danube
Rimnicu Vîlcea
Belgorod Dnestrovskiy
Tîrgu Jiu
Turnu Severin
Galaţi
Brăila
Bolgrad
Izmail
Azovskoye More
Buzău
Piteşti
Ploieşti
Karkinitskiy Z.
Craiova
Tulcea
Sulina
Dzhankoy
Zaječar
Olt
Bucureşti (Bucharest)
Yevpatoriya
Krym
Kerch'
Timashevsk
YUGOSLAVIA
Roşiori de Vede
Dunărea
Lom
Dunav
Cernavodă
Sevastopol'
Simferopol'
Feodosiya
Krasnodar
Niš
Silistra
Ruse
Constanţa
M. Sarych
Yalta
Novorossiysk
Krymsk
Pleven
Tolbukhin
Shumen
Veliko Turnovo
Pernik
Sofiya (Sofia)
Kazanlŭk
Stara Planina
Varna
Tuapse
BULGARIA
Pazardzhik
Sliven
BLACK SEA
Blagoevgrad
Plovdiv
Stara Zagora
Yambol
Burgas
Khaskovo
Maritsa
55
50
45
30
35

F
H
J
K
45
50
55
60
2
3
4
Konosha
Vel'sk
Velikiy Ustyug
Krasavino
Luza
Griva
Kazhim
Gayny
Solikamsk
Serov
Sos'va
Nov. Lyalya
Pinyug
Lesnoy
Kizel
Brusenets
Tot'ma
Kharovsk
Roslyatino
Oparino
Kirs
Kudymkar
Kachkanar
Kushva
Turinsk
Alapayevsk
Irbit
Sokol
Sukhona
Nikol'sk
Murashi
Chusovoy
Nizhniy Tagil
Artemovskiy
Vologda
Gryazovets
Omutninsk
S. F. S. R.
Lys'va
Nev'yansk
Rezh
Asbest
Kamyshlov
S K A Y A
Khalturin
Kirov
Zuyevka
Vereshchagino
Ochër
Krasnokamsk
Perm'
Kungur
Kirovgrad
Sverdlovsk
Bogdanovich
Buy
Manturovo
Kotel'nich
Novo-Vyatsk
Glazov
Balezino
Shamary
Pervoural'sk
Revda
Kamensk-Ural'skiy
Galich
Neya
Sharya
Bogorodskoye
Osa
Kostroma
Makaryev
Shakhun'ya
Nolinsk
Igra
Udmurtskaya A.S.S.R.
Votkinsk
Chaykovskiy
Krasnoufimsk
Nizhniye Sergi
Sysert'
Kasli
Kineshma
Sovetsk
Yaransk
Urzhum
Izhevsk
Sarapul
Chernushka
Kyshtym
Vichuga
Uren'
Sanchursk
Yoshkar Ola
Kil'mez'
Agryz
Nyazepetrovsk
G. Yurma
Chelyabinsk
Shuya
Gor'kovskoye Vdkhr.
Mozhga
Kambarka
Kusa
Semenov
Mariyskaya A.S.S.R.
Malmyzh
Zlatoust
Kopeysk
Miass
Korkino
Gorodets
Brezhnev
Menzelinsk
Pavlovka
Satka
Kovrov
Dzerzhinsk
Gor'kiy
Koz'modem'yansk
Cheboksary
Arsk
Birsk
Belaya
Vyazniki
Zelenodol'sk
Kazan'
Mamadysh
Asha
Ust'-Katav
Bakal
Plast
Gus'-Khrustalnyy
Pavlovo
Chuvashkaya
Tatarskaya A.S.S.R.
Zainsk
Ufa
Shumerlya
Kanash
Chistopol'
Al'met'yevsk
Bashkirskaya
Tirlyanskiy
Beloretsk
Verkhneural'sk
Murom
Arzamas
Sergach
A.S.S.R.
Kuybyshevskoye Vdkhr.
Leninogorsk
Oktyabr'skiy
Davlekanovo
Krasnousol'skiy
Magnitogorsk
Alatyr'
Tetyushi
Bugul'ma
Kasimov
Pervomaysk
Nurlat
Belebey
A.S.S.R.
Kartaly
Ryazan'
Moksha
Mordovskaya A.S.S.R.
Ul'yanovsk
Sterlitamak
Salavat
Sasovo
Dimitrovgrad
Sernovodsk
Bugulma
Abdulino
Saransk
Kovylkino
Bugurusian
Meleuz
Sibay
Shilovo
Privolzhskaya
Tol'yatti
Kumertau
Baymak
Bredy
Yuzhnyy Ural
Ryazhsk
Nizhniy Lomov
Nikol'sk
Barysh
Kinel'
Jok
Morshansk
Syzran'
Kuybyshev
Chaplygin
Kamenka
Penza
Kuznetsk
Buzuluk
Sorochinsk
Michurinsk
Vozvyshennost
Khvalynsk
Saratovskoye Vdkhr.
Syrt
Orenburg
Saraktash
Mednogorsk
Orsk
Tambov
Serdobsk
Rasskazovo
Petrovsk
Vol'sk
Balakovo
Bol. Irgiz
Obshchiy
Kuvandyk
Novotroitsk
Gryazi
Rtishchevo
Pugachev
Ural
Sol'-Iletsk
Akbulak
Dombarovskiy
Arkadak
Atkarsk
Ilek
Zherdevka
Balashov
Saratov
Yershov
Ural'sk
Aksay
Engel's
Aktyubinsk
Mugodzhary
Borisoglebsk
Povorino
Krasnyy Kut
Alga
Krasnoarmeysk
Buturlinovka
Uryupinsk
Kushum
Novoalekseyevka
Oktyabr'sk
Volgogradskoye Vdkhr.
Novo Uzensk
Novoanninskiy
Pavlovsk
Chapayevo
Shubar-Kuduk
Medvedista
Kalach
Pallasovka
Emba
Bol. Uzen'
Mikhaylovka
Kamyshin
Mal. Uzen'
Nikolayevsk
Prikaspiyskaya
Uil
Frolovo
Don
Masteksay
Nizmennost'
Inderborskiy
Perelazovskiy
Zharkamys
Millerovo
Volzhskiy
Saykhin
Kalach-na-Donu
Volgograd (Stalingrad)
KAZAKHSKAYA S.S.R.
Akhtubinsk
Emba
Voroshilovgrad
Ryn Peski
Makat
Kulakshi
Morozovsk
Tsimlyanskoye Vdkhr.
Gur'yev
Balykshi
Kul'šary
Aktumsyk
Shakhty
Kotel'nikovo
Kharabali
Volgodonsk
Sal
Volga
Kalmytskaya
Sarykamys
Rostov-na-Donu
Proletarskaya
Krasnyy Yar
Astrakhan'
Sal'sk
Yegorlyk
Yashkul'
Elista
A.S.S.R.
Sor Mertvyy Kultuk
Beyneu
Burynshik
Chernyye Zemli
Tikhoretsk
Divnoye
Mumra
Ipatovo
Kaspiyskiy
Plato
Kropotkin
Ova Tyuleni
Stavropol'
Ustyurt
UZBEKSKAYA S.S.R.
Armavir
Budennovsk
Kuma
M. Tyub-Karagan
Say-Utes
Ft Shevchenko
Poluostrov
Mangyshlak
Labinsk
Cherkessk
Georgiyevsk
Shevchenko
Novyy Uzen
Kislovodsk
Pyatigorsk
Prokhladnyy
CASPIAN SEA
Groznyy
Fetisovo
Elbrus 5642
Nal'chik
Dykh Tau 5203
Makhachkala
Abkhazskaya
Alagir
Ordzhonikidze
Buynaksk

1:45M

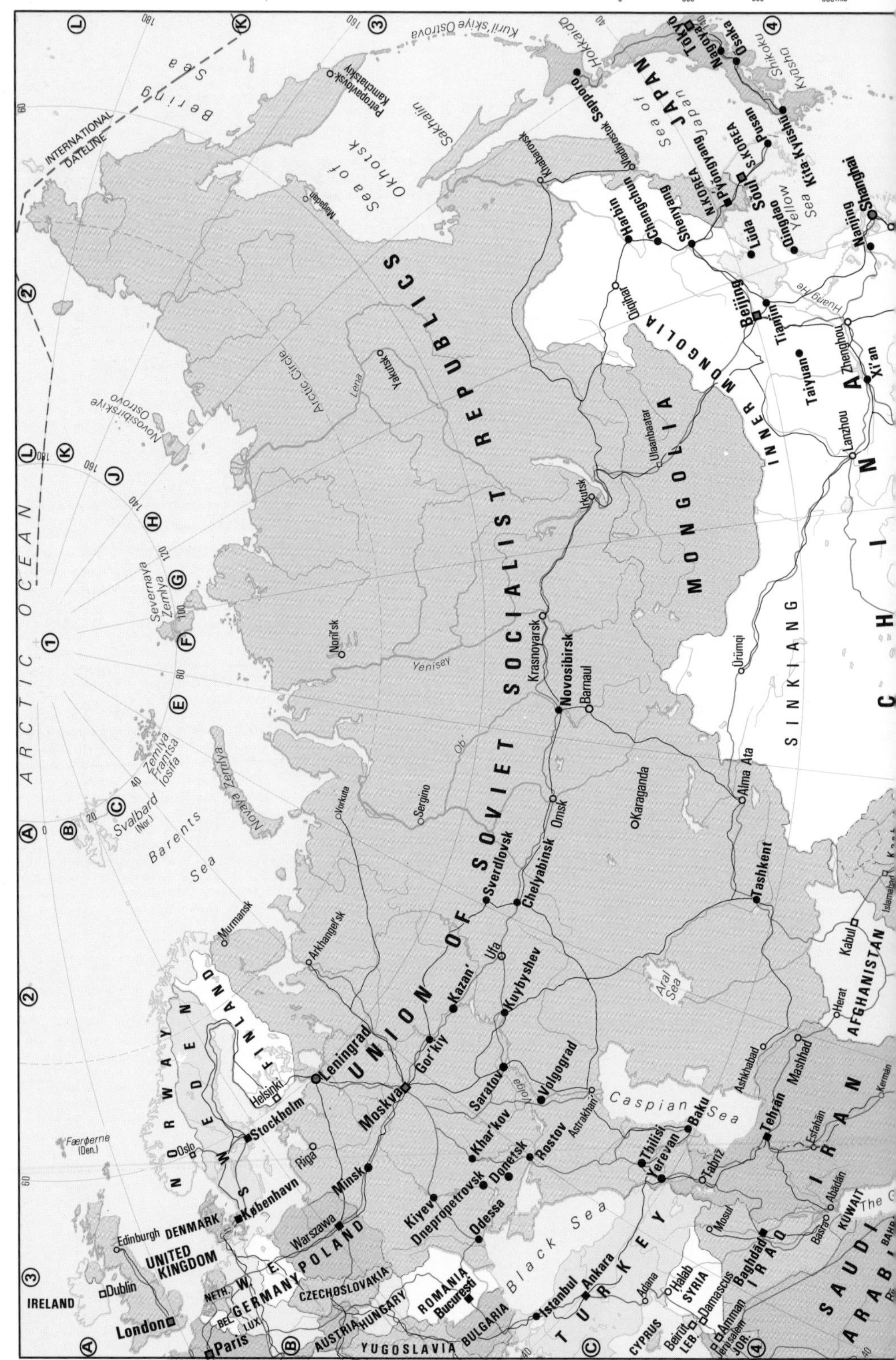
0
600
1200
1800 km
300
600
900 mls
UNION OF SOVIET SOCIALIST REPUBLICS
ARCTIC OCEAN
Bering Sea
Sea of Okhotsk
Sea of Japan
Yellow Sea
Barents Sea
Caspian Sea
Aral Sea
Black Sea
INTERNATIONAL DATELINE
Arctic Circle
Kuril'skiye Ostrova
Sakhalin
Hokkaido
Shikoku
Kyushu
Novosibirskiye Ostrova
Severnaya Zemlya
Zemlya Frantsa Iosifa
Novaya Zemlya
Svalbard (Nor.)
Færøerne (Den.)
Lena
Yenisey
Ob
Volga
Huang He
Petropavlovsk-Kamchatskiy
Magadan
Yakutsk
Noril'sk
Vorkuta
Sergino
Murmansk
Arkhangel'sk
Leningrad
Moskva
Gor'kiy
Kazan'
Kuybyshev
Ufa
Sverdlovsk
Chelyabinsk
Omsk
Novosibirsk
Barnaul
Krasnoyarsk
Irkutsk
Khabarovsk
Vladivostok
Karaganda
Alma Ata
Tashkent
Ashkhabad
Saratov
Volgograd
Astrakhan'
Kharkov
Donetsk
Rostov
Dnepropetrovsk
Kiyev
Odessa
Minsk
Riga
Tbilisi
Yerevan
Baku
MONGOLIA
Ulaanbaatar
INNER MONGOLIA
SINKIANG
Ürümqi
CHINA
Lanzhou
Xi'an
Zhengzhou
Taiyuan
Beijing
Tianjin
Qiqihar
Harbin
Changchun
Shenyang
Lüda
Qingdao
Nanjing
Shanghai
N.KOREA
Pyŏngyang
S.KOREA
Sŏul
Pusan
JAPAN
Sapporo
Tokyo
Nagoya
Osaka
Kita-Kyushu
AFGHANISTAN
Kabul
Herat
Islamabad
IRAN
Tehrān
Mashhad
Esfahān
Kermān
Tabrīz
Abādān
IRAQ
Baghdād
Mosul
Basra
KUWAIT
SAUDI ARABIA
SYRIA
Halab
Damascus
LEB.
Beirut
JOR.
Amman
Jerusalem
CYPRUS
TURKEY
Ankara
Istanbul
Adana
BULGARIA
ROMANIA
Bucureşti
YUGOSLAVIA
HUNGARY
AUSTRIA
CZECHOSLOVAKIA
POLAND
Warszawa
W. GERMANY
LUX.
BEL.
NETH.
Paris
London
UNITED KINGDOM
Edinburgh
IRELAND
Dublin
DENMARK
København
NORWAY
Oslo
SWEDEN
Stockholm
FINLAND
Helsinki

0 200 400 600 800 km
0 200 400 mls

ARCTIC OCEAN
ZEMLYA FRANTSA IOSIFA
(FRANZ-JOSEF-LAND)
Zemlya Aleksandry
Zemlya Georga
Ostrov Rudol'fa
Ostrov Green Bell
Zemlya Vil'cheka
M.Zhelaniya
NOVAYA ZEMLYA
KARA SEA
Dikson
Yeniseyskiy Zal
Gydanskiy Poluostrov
Tazovskiy
Ostrov Belyy
Pov Yamal
Obskaya Guba
Nyda
Novyy Port
Labytnangi
Baydaratskaya G.
O. Vaygach
Amderma
Khrebet Pay Khoy
Vorkuta
Karskiye Vorota
Proliv Karskiye Vorota
Pechorskoye More
Krasino
O.Mezhdusharskiy
Nar'yan Mar
Usa
Muzhi
Berezovo
Nordaustlandet
Kong Karls Land
Barentsøya
Edgeøya
Hopen
Prins Karls Forland
Spitsbergen
Sørkapp
SVALBARD
(SPITSBERGEN)
(Nor.)
Bjørnøya
BARENTS SEA
Ostrov Kolguyev
Kanin Nos
Pov Kanin
Cheshskaya Guba
Belush'ye
Ust'Tsil'ma
Izhma
Ukhta
Timanskiy Kryazh
Mezen'
Ponoy
Gremikha
Kol'skiy Poluostrov
Murmansk
Pov Rybachiy
Vardø
Nikel
Kirkenes
Kirovsk
Kandalaksha
Beloye More
(White Sea)
Arkhangel'sk
Severodvinsk
Onega
Pinega
Usogorsk
Syktyvkar
Kotlas
Sev Dvina
Vel'sk
Nyandoma
Shenkursk
Medvezh'yegorsk
Kem
Belomorsk
Karel'skaya A.S.S.R.
Petrozavodsk
Vytegra
Lodeynoye Pole
Konosha
Sokol
Vologda
Sharya
Nordkapp
Hammerfest
Tromsø
Narvik
Kiruna
Muonio
Lappland
Inari
Kelloselka
Kemi
Oulu
Haparanda
Luleå
Kajaani
FINLAND
Kuopio
Vaasa
Tampere
Lahti
Vyborg
Turku
Helsinki
Pori
Gulf of Bothnia
Vesterålen
Lofoten
Vestfjorden
Bodø
Mo
NORWEGIAN SEA
Arctic Circle
Namsos
Östersund
Umeå
Sundsvall
Trondheim
Kristiansund
Ålesund
Jotunheimen
2481
Gävle
Uppsala
Stockholm
Örebro
Norrköping
Oslo
Drammen
Bergen
Stavanger
Kristiansand
Vänern
Vättern
Jönköping
Göteborg
Helsingborg
Malmö
Skagerrak
Frederikshavn
Ålborg
København
Odense
DENMARK
Esbjerg
Kiel
Hamburg
Bremen
GERMANY
Berlin
Sassnitz
Bornholm
Öland
Gotland
BALTIC SEA
Faerøerne
(Den.)
Shetland Is
Orkney Is
Wick
Hebrides
Inverness
Aberdeen
U.K.
SCOTLAND
Edinburgh
Glasgow
NORTH SEA
Leningrad
Ladozhskoye Ozero
Onezhskoye Ozero
Chudovo
Cherepovets
Rybinsk
Rybinskoye Vdkhr
Yaroslavl'
Bologoye
Kalinin
Vladimir
Novgorod
Ozero Il'men
Moskva
(Moscow)
Rzhev
Velikiye Luki
Vyaz'ma
Smolensk
Roslavl'
Bryansk
Tallinn
ESTONSKAYA S.S.R.
Gulf of Finland
Tartu
Chudskoye Oz.
Pskov
Ostrov
Pärnu
Gulf of Riga
Riga
LATVIYSKAYA S.S.R.
Daugavpils
Polotsk
Vitebsk
Orsha
Dnepr
Mogilev
Ventspils
Liepaja
LITOVSKAYA S.S.R.
Vilnius
Kaunas
Minsk
BELORUSSKAYA S.S.R.
Bobruysk
Gomel'
Mozyr'
Pripyat'
Klaipeda
Sovetsk
Kaliningrad
R.S.F.S.R.
Grodno
Białystok
Pinsk
Brest
Kovel'
Rovno
Korosten'
Zhitomir
Gdańsk
Szczecin
Bydgoszcz
Wista
Warszawa
POLAND
Poznań
Łódź
Lublin
Radom
Kraków
Wrocław
Oder
Warta
L'vov
Przemyśl
Ivano-Frankovsk
Carpathian Mts
Chernovtsy
Vinnitsa

R.S.F.S.R.

1 Chuvashskaya A.S.S.R.
2 Checheno-Ingushskaya A.S.S.R.
3 Severo-Osetinskaya A.S.S.R.
4 Kabardino-Balkarskaya A.S.S.R.

GRUZINSKAYA S.S.R.

5 Abkhazskaya A.S.S.R.
6 Adzharskaya A.S.S.R.

AZERBAYDZHANSKAYA S.S.R.

7 Nakhichevanskaya A.S.S.R.

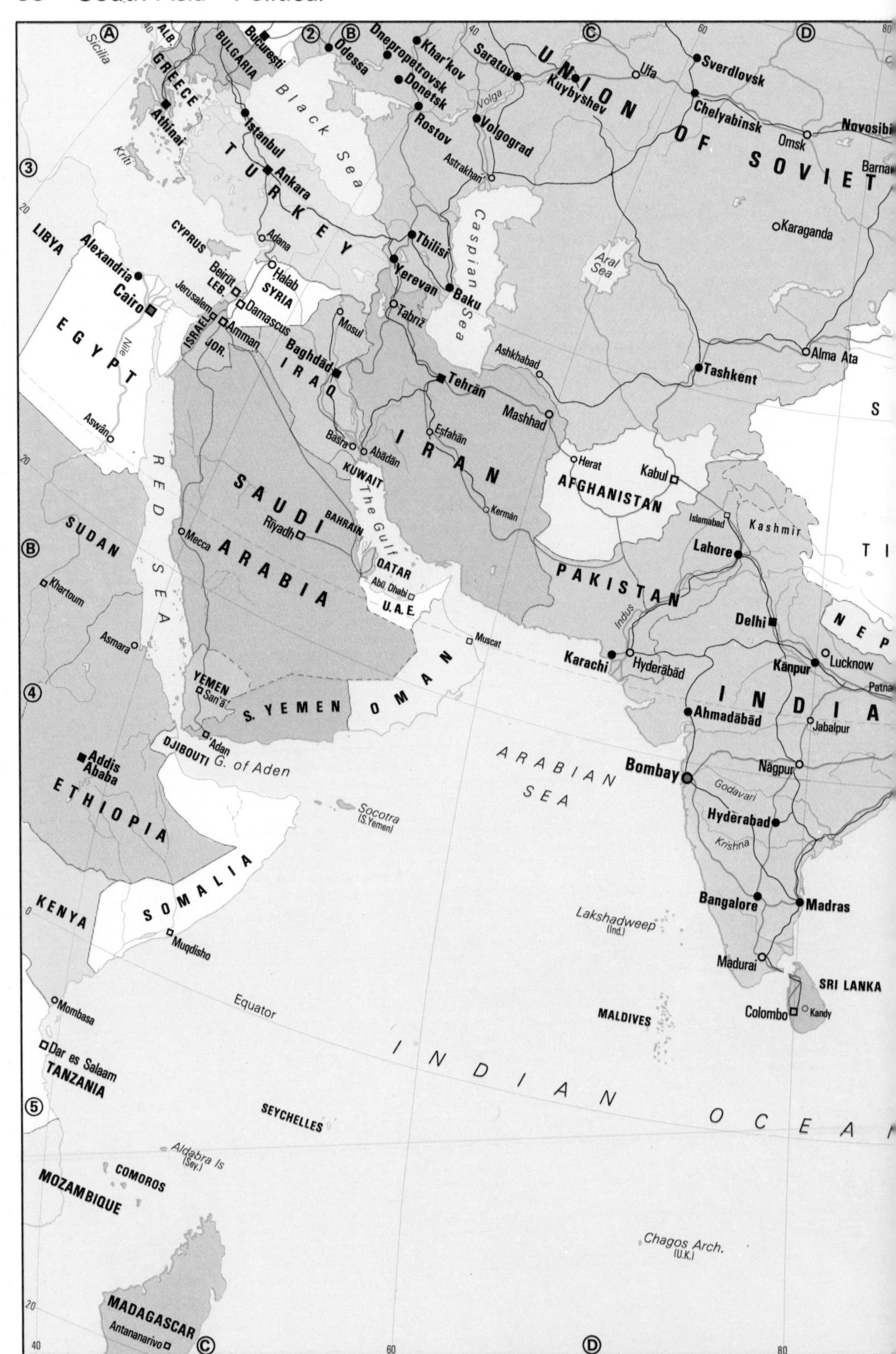
Sicilia
ALB.
BULGARIA
Bucureşti
Odessa
Dnepropetrovsk
Khar'kov
Donetsk
Rostov
Saratov
UNION OF SOVIET
Kuybyshev
Ufa
Sverdlovsk
Chelyabinsk
Omsk
Novosibi
Barna
Volga
Volgograd
Astrakhan'
GREECE
Athínai
Kriti
Istanbul
TURKEY
Ankara
Black Sea
Caspian Sea
Karaganda
Aral Sea
LIBYA
Alexandria
Cairo
CYPRUS
Adana
Tbilisi
Yerevan
Baku
Beirūt
LEB.
Halab
SYRIA
Jerusalem
Damascus
ISRAEL
Amman
JOR.
Mosul
Tabrīz
EGYPT
Nile
Baghdād
IRAQ
Ashkhabad
Alma Ata
Tashkent
Tehrān
Mashhad
S
Aswân
Basra
Abādān
Eşfahān
IRAN
Herat
Kabul
AFGHANISTAN
KUWAIT
RED SEA
SAUDI ARABIA
Riyadh
BAHRAIN
The Gulf
Kermān
Islamabad
Kashmir
SUDAN
Mecca
Lahore
TI
QATAR
Abū Dhabi
U.A.E.
PAKISTAN
Khartoum
Indus
Delhi
NEP
Asmara
Muscat
Karachi
Hyderābād
Kānpur
Lucknow
Patna
YEMEN
San'ā'
S. YEMEN
OMAN
INDIA
Ahmadābād
Jabalpur
'Adan
DJIBOUTI
G. of Aden
ARABIAN SEA
Bombay
Nāgpur
Addis Ababa
ETHIOPIA
Socotra
(S.Yemen)
Godavari
Hyderabad
Krishna
SOMALIA
KENYA
Bangalore
Madras
Lakshadweep
(Ind.)
Muqdisho
Madurai
SRI LANKA
Colombo
Kandy
Equator
MALDIVES
Mombasa
Dar es Salaam
TANZANIA
INDIAN OCEAN
SEYCHELLES
Aldabra Is
(Sey.)
COMOROS
MOZAMBIQUE
Chagos Arch.
(U.K.)
MADAGASCAR
Antananarivo

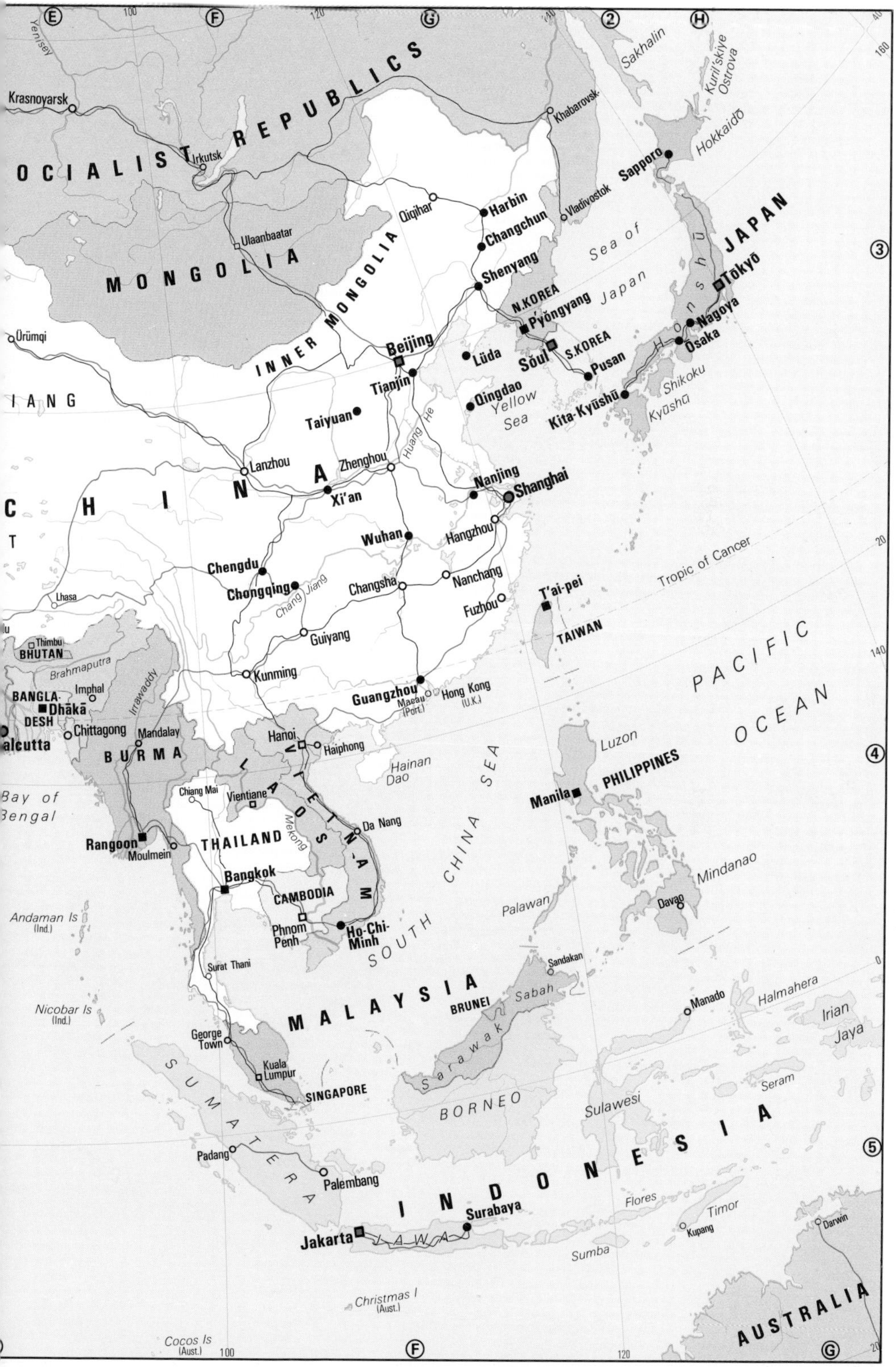

E F G 2 H 3 4 5 F G

100 120 140 160 40 20 0

SOCIALIST REPUBLICS

Yenisey
Krasnoyarsk
Irkutsk
Ulaanbaatar
MONGOLIA
Khabarovsk
Sakhalin
Kuril'skiye Ostrova
Hokkaidō
Sapporo
Vladivostok
Qiqihar
Harbin
Changchun
Shenyang
INNER MONGOLIA
Sea of Japan
JAPAN
Honshu
Tōkyō
Nagoya
Ōsaka
N.KOREA
Pyongyang
S.KOREA
Sŏul
Pusan
Kita-Kyūshū
Shikoku
Kyūshū
Ürümqi
Beijing
Tianjin
Lüda
Qingdao
Yellow Sea
IANG
Taiyuan
Huang He
Lanzhou
Zhenghou
Xi'an
CHINA
Nanjing
Shanghai
Hangzhou
Wuhan
Chengdu
Chongqing
Chang Jiang
Changsha
Nanchang
Fuzhou
T'ai-pei
TAIWAN
Tropic of Cancer
Lhasa
Thimbu
BHUTAN
Brahmaputra
Guiyang
Kunming
PACIFIC OCEAN
BANGLADESH
Dhākā
Imphal
Irrawaddy
Guangzhou
Macau (Port.)
Hong Kong (U.K.)
Calcutta
Chittagong
Mandalay
BURMA
Hanoi
Haiphong
Hainan Dao
Luzon
PHILIPPINES
Manila
Bay of Bengal
Chiang Mai
Vientiane
LAOS
VIETNAM
Mekong
Da Nang
SOUTH CHINA SEA
Rangoon
Moulmein
THAILAND
Bangkok
CAMBODIA
Phnom Penh
Ho-Chi-Minh
Mindanao
Davao
Palawan
Andaman Is (Ind.)
Surat Thani
Sandakan
Sabah
BRUNEI
MALAYSIA
Nicobar Is (Ind.)
Manado
Halmahera
Irian Jaya
George Town
Sarawak
Kuala Lumpur
SINGAPORE
BORNEO
Sulawesi
Seram
SUMATERA
INDONESIA
Padang
Palembang
Flores
Timor
Surabaya
Kupang
Darwin
Jakarta
JAWA
Sumba
Christmas I (Aust.)
AUSTRALIA
Cocos Is (Aust.)

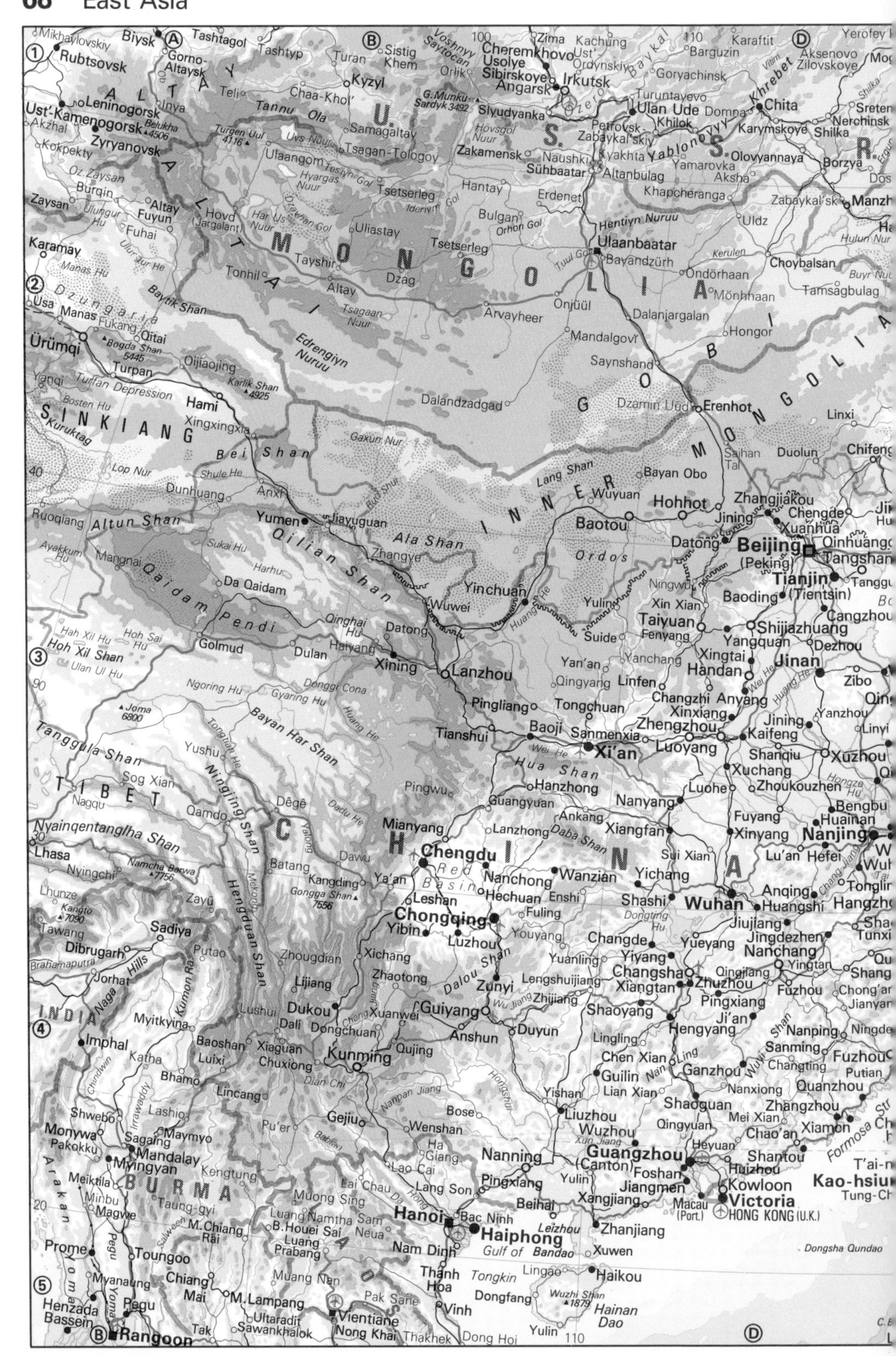
Mikhaylovskiy
Biysk
Tashtagol
Tashtyp
Sistig Khem
Turan
Voshnyy Saytocan
Zima
Kachug
Baykal
Barguzin
Karaftit
Yerofey
Rubtsovsk
Gorno-Altaysk
Kyzyl
Cheremkhovo
Usolye
Sibirskoye
Angarsk
Irkutsk
Ust'-Ordynskiy
Goryachinsk
Aksenovo Zilovskoye
Mog
Leninogorsk
Teli
Chaa-Khol'
Orlik
G. Munku-Sardyk 3492
Turuntayevo
Ulan Ude
Domna
Chita
Shilka
Sreten
Nerchinsk
Ust'-Kamenogorsk
Akzhal
Belukha 4506
Inya
Tannu Ola
Sylyudyanka
Petrovsk-Zabaykal'skiy
Khilok
Yablonovyy
Khrebet
Karymskoye
Shilka
Kokpekty
Zyryanovsk
Turgen Uul 4116
Uvs Nuur
Samagaltay
Tsagan-Tologoy
Hövsgöl Nuur
Zakamensk
Naushki
Kyakhta
Olovyannaya
Borzya
Oz. Zaysan
Burqin
Ulaangom
Hyargas Nuur
Tesiyn Gol
Sühbaatar
Altanbulag
Yamarovka
Aksha
Dos
Zaysan
Ulungur Hu
Altay
Fuyun
Tsetserleg
Hantay
Erdenet
Khapcheranga
Zabaykal'sk
Manzh
Fuhai
Hovd (Jargalant)
Har Us Nuur
Dzavhan Gol
Ideriyn Gol
Bulgan
Orhon Gol
Uldz
Karamay
Uliastay
Hentiyn Nuruu
Hulun Nur
Ulur Jur He
Manas Hu
Tayshir
Tsetserleg
Ulaanbaatar
Tuul Gol
Bayandzürh
Kerulen
Choybalsan
Buyr Nur
Tonhil
Dzag
Ondörhaan
Mönhhaan
Tamsagbulag
Dzungaria
Baytik Shan
Altay
Onjüül
Usa
Manas
Fukang
Qitai
Tsagaan Nuur
Arvayheer
Dalanjargalan
Ürümqi
Bogda Shan 5445
Edrengiyn Nuruu
Mandalgovĭ
Hongor
Turpan
Oijiaojing
Saynshand
Yanqi
Turfan Depression
Karlik Shan 4925
Hami
Bosten Hu
Dalandzadgad
Dzamin Uüd
Erenhot
Linxi
SINKIANG
Kuruktag
Xingxingxia
Gaxun Nur
Saihan Tal
Duolun
Chifeng
Bei Shan
Lop Nur
Shule He
Lang Shan
Bayan Obo
Dunhuang
Anxi
Ruo Shui
Wuyuan
Hohhot
Zhangjiakou
Chengde
Ruoqiang
Altun Shan
Yumen
Jiayuguan
Jining
Xuanhua
Qinhuangd
Ala Shan
Baotou
Datong
Beijing (Peking)
Tangshan
Ayakkum Hu
Sukai Hu
Qilian Shan
Zhangye
Ordos
Mangnai
Harhu
Tianjin (Tientsin)
Tanggu
Qaidam Pendi
Da Qaidam
Yinchuan
Ningwu
Baoding
Wuwei
Huang He
Yulin
Xin Xian
Cangzhou
Qinghai Hu
Taiyuan
Fenyang
Shijiazhuang
Hah Xil Hu
Hoh Sai Hu
Datong
Suide
Yangquan
Dezhou
Hoh Xil Shan
Golmud
Dulan
Haiyang
Xining
Xingtai
Handan
Jinan
Ulan Ul Hu
Lanzhou
Yan'an
Yanchang
Zibo
Donggi Cona
Qingyang
Linfen
Wei He
Ngoring Hu
Gyaring Hu
Pingliang
Tongchuan
Changzhi
Anyang
Joma 6800
Xinxiang
Yanzhou
Bayan Har Shan
Jining
Linyi
Tanggula Shan
Tianshui
Baoji
Sanmenxia
Zhengzhou
Kaifeng
Tongtian He
Xi'an
Luoyang
Yushu
Hua Shan
Shangiu
Xuzhou
Sog Xian
Ningjing Shan
Xuchang
TIBET
Pingwu
Hanzhong
Luohe
Zhoukouzhen
Hongze Hu
Nagqu
Dêqê
Guangyuan
Nanyang
Bengbu
Qamdo
Dadu He
Ankang
Fuyang
Huainan
Nyainqentanglha Shan
Mianyang
Lanzhong
Daba Shan
Xiangfan
Xinyang
Nanjing
Lhasa
Yalong
Chengdu
Dawu
Sui Xian
Lu'an
Hefei
Wuh
Nyingchi
Namcha Barwa 7756
Batang
Red Basin
Nanchong
Wanzian
Yichang
Kangding
Ya'an
Tongli
Lhunze
Kangto 7090
Zayü
Gongga Shan 7556
Leshan
Hechuan
Enshi
Shashi
Wuhan
Anqing
Huangshi
Hangzh
Tawang
Mekong
Chongqing
Fuling
Dongting Hu
Jiujiang
Chang Jiang
Sadiya
Yibin
Luzhou
Youyang
Changde
Yueyang
Jingdezhen
Tunxi
Dibrugarh
Putao
Hengduan Shan
Zhougdian
Xichang
Dalou Shan
Yuanling
Yiyang
Nanchang
Brahamaputra
Naga Hills
Kumon Ra.
Zhaotong
Changsha
Qingjiang
Yingtan
Jorhat
Lijiang
Zunyi
Lengshuijiang
Xiangtan
Zhuzhou
Fuzhou
INDIA
Dukou
Guiyang
Wu Jiang
Zhijiang
Pingxiang
Chong'an
Jianyar
Myitkyina
Lushui
Xuanwei
Shaoyang
Ji'an
Imphal
Dali
Dongchuan
Anshun
Duyun
Hengyang
Nanping
Ningde
Baoshan
Xiaguan
Qujing
Lingling
Wuyi Shan
Sanming
Katha
Luixi
Chuxiong
Kunming
Chen Xian
Nan Ling
Ganzhou
Changting
Fuzhou
Putian
Chindwin
Bhamo
Dian Chi
Hongshui
Guilin
Lincang
Yishan
Lian Xian
Nanxiong
Quanzhou
Irrawaddy
Lashio
Nanpan Jiang
Bose
Liuzhou
Shaoguan
Zhangzhou
Shwebo
Pu'er
Gejiu
Wenshan
Wuzhou
Qingyuan
Mei Xian
Xiamen
Monywa
Sagaing
Maymyo
Babian
Xun Jiang
Heyuan
Chao'an
Formosa Str
Pakokku
Mandalay
Ha Giang
Nanning
Guangzhou (Canton)
Shantou
Myingyan
Kengtung
Lao Cai
Foshan
Huizhou
T'ai-n
Meiktila
BURMA
Lai Chau
Lang Son
Pingxiang
Yulin
Jiangmen
Kowloon
Kao-hsiu
Minbu
Taung-gyi
Muong Sing
Beihai
Xangjiang
Macau (Port.)
Victoria
Tung-Ch
Magwe
Luang Namtha
Sam Neua
Hanoi
Bac Ninh
Leizhou
HONG KONG (U.K.)
Arakan
Salween
M. Chiang Rai
B. Houei Sai
Haiphong
Zhanjiang
Prome
Pegu Yoma
Toungoo
Luang Prabang
Nam Dinh
Gulf of Tongkin
Bandao
Xuwen
Dongsha Qundao
Chiang Mai
Muang Nan
Thanh Hoa
Lingao
Haikou
Myanaung
Pegu
M. Lampang
Pak Sane
Vinh
Dongfang
Wuzhi Shan 1879
Hainan Dao
Henzada
Bassein
Rangoon
Uttaradit
Sawankhalok
Tak
Vientiane
Nong Khai
Thakhek
Dong Hoi
Yulin
LAOS
CHINA
INNER MONGOLIA
GOBI
MONGOLIA
ALTAY
ALTAI
U.S.S.R.

Skovorodino
Zeya
Ovsyanka
Dzhalinda
Tygda
Ushumun
Ekimchan
Tugur
Moskal'vo
Okha
Nikolayevsk-na-Amure
Bogorodskoye
Poliny Osipento
Amgun'
Oz. Chukchagirskoye
Oz. Evoron
De Kastri
Katangli
SEA OF
Opala
Mys Lopatka
Paramushir
Guqigu
Shimanovsk
Huma
Norsk
Ust'-Umal'ta
Aleksandrovsk-Sakhalinskiy
Tymovskoye
OKHOTSK
Mangui
Kumara
Svobodnyy
Belogorsk
Chekunda
Bureinskiy Khrebet
Komsomol'sk na-Amure
SAKHALIN
Proliv
Onekotan
Ergun Zuoqi
Xiao
Blagoveshchensk
Bolon'
Pobedino
Shiashkotan
Anhui
Zavitinsk
Bureya
Litovko
Oz. Bolon'
Uglegorsk
Poronaysk
Vanino
Zaliv Terpeniya
Rasshua
Hinggan
Xunke
Obluch'ye
Sovetskaya Gavan'
Tartarskiy
Il'inskiy
Kuril'skiye Ostrova (Kuril Islands)
Nenjiang
Khabarovsk
Simushir
Butha Qi
Bei'an
Ling
Birobidzhan
Leninskoye
Khor
Yuzhno-Sakhalinsk
Yichun
Fujin
Nel'ma
Urup
Qiqihar
Hailun
Hegang
Vyazemskiy
Bikin
Gornozavodsk
Korsakov
Mys Aniva
Suihua
Jiamusi
Shuangyashan
Svetlaya
Anda
Dal'nerechensk
Amgu
La Perouse Strait
Harbin
Hulin
Lesozavodsk
Wakkanai
Iturup
Vityaz Depth 10542
Da'an
Songhua
Jixi
Turiy Rog
Plastun
Oz. Khanka
Spassk Dal'niy
Rudnaya Pristan'
Abashiri
Kunashir
Shikotan
Wuchang
Mudanjiang
Sikhote Alin'
Rumoi
Asahi Dake 2290
Nemuro
Changchun
Jilin
Ussuriysk
Olga
Asahikawa
Otaru
Kushiro
Shuangliao
Songhua Hu
Vladivostok
Nakhodka
Sapporo
Muroran
HOKKAIDŌ
Siping
Liaoyuan
Zaliv Petra Velikogo
Uchiura-wan
Erimo-misaki
Tieling
Yanji
Hakodate
Fushun
Linjiang
Najin
Ch'ŏngjin
Tsugaru-kaikyō
Aomori
Benxi
Tonghua
Hyesan
Hirosaki
Hachinohe
Anshan
Yalu
Manpo
Samsu
Songjin
Noshiro
Dandong
Hŭich'ŏn
Sŏho-ri
SEA OF
Akita
Morioka
Liaodong
Hamhŭng
NORTH
Sinuiju
Anju
Hŭngnam
JAPAN
Sakata
Ishinomaki
Korea Bay
KOREA
Yamagata
Sendai
Lüda
P'yŏngyang
Wŏnsan
Sado
Fukushima
Haeju
Ch'unch'ŏn
Niigata
Kaesŏng
Kangnŭng
Nagaoka
HONSHŪ
Yantai
Sŏul (Seoul)
SOUTH
Ullung do
Tok-do
Takaoka
Utsunomiya
Inch'ŏn
Mito
Chengshan Jiao
Chŏnan
Ch'ŏngju
Kanazawa
Oki
Fukui
Tōkyō
Taejŏn
KOREA
Gifu
Fuji-san 3776
Yokohama
Kunsan
Taegu
Matsue
Tottori
Kyōto
Nagoya
YELLOW
Chŏnju
Korea Strait
Ōsaka
Shizuoka
Kwangju
Pusan
Kōbe
Toyohashi
Mokp'o
Masan
Hiroshima
Sakai
SEA
Tsushima
Kure
Wakayama
Miyake
Shimonoseki
Matsuyama
Cheju haehyŏp
Kita-Kyūshū
Kōchi
Kii-suidō
Hachijo
Fukuoka
Cheju
Sasebo
Shikoku
Cheju do
Bungo-suidō
Nagasaki
Kumamoto
Myojin
Kyūshū
Sumisu
Miyazaki
Kagoshima
Tori
Ramapo Deep 10374
Ōsumi-kaikyō
Shanghai
Tanega
Sofu Gan
Hangpan Yang
EAST
Yaku
Ningbo
Tokara Retto
Muko-jima
Chichi-jima
CHINA SEA
Amami
Amami gunto
RETTO
Nishino-shima
Ogasawara Gunto (Bonin Islands) (Jap.)
Wenzhou
Tokuno
Haha-jima
Okinawa
Kitalo
Naha
Okinawa gunto
Senkaku Gunto
Daitō Is
Kazan Retto (Volcano Is) (Jap.)
Iwo Jima
Fleming Deep 8651
Chi-lung
Sakishima guntō
Miyako
Tropic of Cancer
T'ai-pei
Hsueh Shan 3884
Ishigaki
RYŪKYŪ
Iriomote
Hua-lien
TAIWAN (FORMOSA) (China Nat. Rep.)
PACIFIC
Farallon de Pajaros
Maug Is
Asuncion
Agrihan
Parece Vela
MARIANAS
Batan Is
Pagan
Alamagan
Strait
OCEAN
Guguan
Babuyan Is
C. Engaño
Northern Marianas
Sarigan
Anatahan
Aparri
130
140
150
50
40
30
20
E
F
G
H

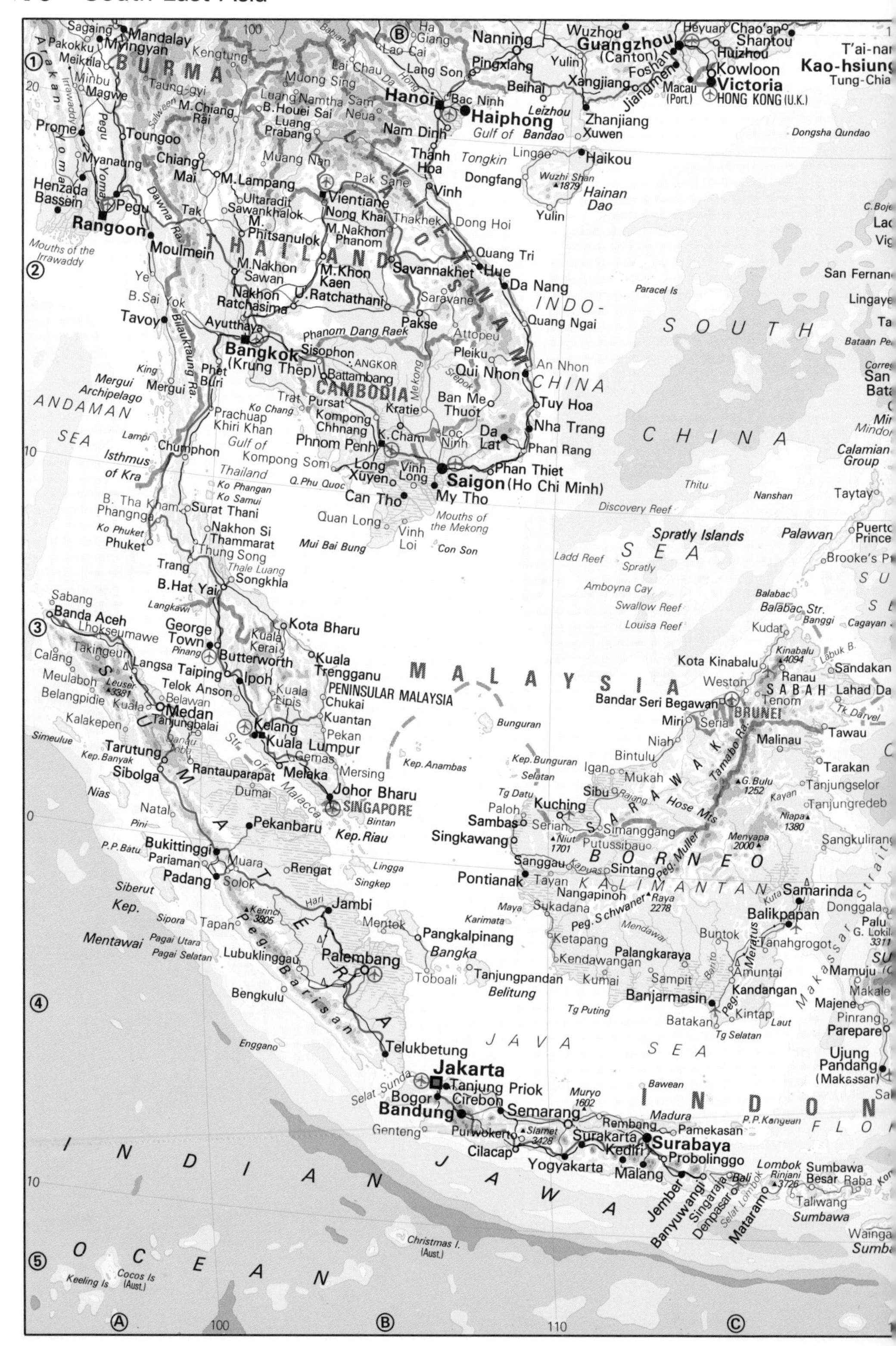

BURMA
Sagaing
Mandalay
Myingyan
Pakokku
Meiktila
Minbu
Magwe
Taunggyi
Kengtung
Prome
Toungoo
Myanaung
Henzada
Bassein
Pegu
Rangoon
Mouths of the Irrawaddy
Moulmein
Ye
Tavoy
Mergui
Mergui Archipelago
Irrawaddy
Salween
Yoma
Pegu
Arakan
Chiang Mai
M. Lampang
M. Chiang Rai
Tak
Dawna Ra.
THAILAND
Ultaradit
Sawankhalok
M. Phitsanulok
M. Nakhon Sawan
Nakhon Ratchasima
Ayutthaya
Bangkok (Krung Thep)
Phet Buri
Prachuap Khiri Khan
Chumphon
Bilauktaung Ra.
B. Sai Yok
King
Lampi
Isthmus of Kra
Gulf of Thailand
Ko Phangan
Ko Samui
B. Tha Kham
Phangnga
Ko Phuket
Phuket
Surat Thani
Nakhon Si Thammarat
Thung Song
Trang
Thale Luang
Songkhla
B. Hat Yai
Langkawi
ANDAMAN SEA
Hanoi
Haiphong
Bac Ninh
Nam Dinh
Thanh Hoa
Vinh
Dong Hoi
Quang Tri
Hue
Da Nang
Quang Ngai
Qui Nhon
An Nhon
Tuy Hoa
Nha Trang
Phan Rang
Phan Thiet
Da Lat
Pleiku
Ban Me Thuot
Loc Ninh
Saigon (Ho Chi Minh)
My Tho
Can Tho
Vinh Long
Long Xuyen
Mouths of the Mekong
Vinh Loi
Con Son
Quan Long
Mui Bai Bung
Lao Cai
Ha Giang
Lai Chau
Lang Son
Muong Sing
Luang Namtha
B. Houei Sai
Sam Neua
Luang Prabang
Muang Nan
Pak Sane
Vientiane
Nong Khai
Thakhek
M. Nakhon Phanom
M. Khon Kaen
U. Ratchathani
Savannakhet
Saravane
Pakse
Attopeu
Phanom Dang Raek
Sisophon
ANGKOR
Battambang
CAMBODIA
Pursat
Trat
Ko Chang
Kompong Chhnang
Kratie
K. Cham
Phnom Penh
Kompong Som
Q. Phu Quoc
Mekong
Srepok
Tongkin
Gulf of Bandao
Nanning
Pingxiang
Beihai
Yulin
Wuzhou
Guangzhou (Canton)
Foshan
Jiangmen
Xangjiang
Macau (Port.)
Heyuan
Chao'an
Shantou
Huizhou
Kowloon
Victoria
HONG KONG (U.K.)
Kao-hsiung
Tung-Chia
T'ai-nan
Leizhou
Zhanjiang
Xuwen
Dongsha Qundao
Lingao
Haikou
Dongfang
Wuzhi Shan 1879
Hainan Dao
Yulin
Paracel Is
INDO-CHINA
SOUTH CHINA SEA
San Fernando
Lingayen
Calamian Group
Taytay
Nanshan
Thitu
Discovery Reef
Spratly Islands
Spratly
Ladd Reef
Amboyna Cay
Swallow Reef
Louisa Reef
Palawan
Puerto Princesa
Brooke's Point
Balabac
Balabac Str.
Banggi
Cagayan
Kudat
Kota Kinabalu
Kinabalu 4094
Labuk B.
Sandakan
Ranau
SABAH
Lahad Datu
Tenom
Weston
Bandar Seri Begawan
BRUNEI
Miri
Seria
Niah
Bintulu
Tawau
Malinau
Tarakan
Tamabo Ra.
Mukah
Igan
SARAWAK
Sibu
Kuching
Sambas
Paloh
Tg Datu
Serian
Simanggang
Hose Mts
G. Bulu 1252
Kayan
Tanjungselor
Tanjungredeb
Niapa 1380
Niut 1701
Putussibau
Menyapa 2000
Sangkulirang
Singkawang
Sanggau
Kapuas
Sintang
Peg. Muller
BORNEO
KALIMANTAN
Pontianak
Tayan
Nangapinoh
Raya 2278
Peg. Schwaner
Sukadana
Maya
Karimata
Ketapang
Kendawangan
Mendawai
Palangkaraya
Sampit
Kumai
Buntok
Barito
Meratus
Banjarmasin
Kandangan
Amuntai
Tanahgrogot
Balikpapan
Samarinda
Kuta
Donggala
Palu
G. Lokilalaki 3311
Mamuju
Majene
Makale
Pinrang
Parepare
Ujung Pandang (Makassar)
Kintap
Batakan
Laut
Tg Selatan
Tg Puting
Makassar Strait
MALAYSIA
PENINSULAR MALAYSIA
Kota Bharu
Kuala Kerai
Kuala Trengganu
Kuala Lipis
Chukai
Kuantan
Pekan
Mersing
Johor Bharu
SINGAPORE
Kuala Lumpur
Kelang
Gemas
Melaka
Ipoh
Taiping
Butterworth
George Town
Pinang
Telok Anson
Bunguran
Kep. Anambas
Kep. Bunguran Selatan
Str. of Malacca
Sabang
Banda Aceh
Lhokseumawe
Takingeun
Langsa
Calang
Meulaboh
Leuser 3381
Belangpidie
Kuala
Medan
Belawan
Tanjungbalai
Kalakepen
Simeulue
Danau Toba
Tarutung
Kep. Banyak
Sibolga
Rantauparapat
Nias
Natal
Dumai
Pekanbaru
Bintan
Kep. Riau
Pini
P.P. Batu
Bukittinggi
Pariaman
Padang
Muara
Solok
Rengat
Lingga
Singkep
Siberut
Kep. Mentawai
Sipora
Pagai Utara
Pagai Selatan
Tapan
Kerinci 3805
Hari
Jambi
Mentok
Pangkalpinang
Bangka
Toboali
Tanjungpandan
Belitung
Lubuklinggau
Palembang
Bengkulu
Peg. Barisan
SUMATERA
Enggano
Telukbetung
Selat Sunda
Jakarta
Tanjung Priok
Bogor
Bandung
Cirebon
Semarang
Genteng
Purwokerto
Slamet 3428
Cilacap
Yogyakarta
Surakarta
Kediri
Madiun
Malang
Rembang
Muryo 1602
Bawean
Madura
Pamekasan
Surabaya
Probolinggo
Jember
Banyuwangi
Singaraja
Bali
Denpasar
Selat Lombok
Mataram
Lombok
Rinjani 3726
Sumbawa Besar
Raba
Taliwang
Sumbawa
P.P. Kangean
JAVA SEA
INDONESIA
INDIAN OCEAN
JAWA
Christmas I. (Aust.)
Cocos Is (Aust.)
Keeling Is
Flores
Waingapu
Sumba

1:20M
0 200 400 600 800 km
0 200 400 mls
TAIWAN (FORMOSA)
(China Nat. Rep.)
PACIFIC
OCEAN
Parece Vela
Farallon de Pajaros
Maug Is
Asuncion
Agrihan
Pagan
Alamagan
Guguan
Sarigan
Anatahan
Farallon de Medinilla
Saipan
Tinian
Rota
Northern Marianas
MARIANAS
Guam (U.S.A.)
Nero Deep 9637
Challenger Deep 11033
Mansyu Deep 9818
Batan Is
Babuyan Is
C. Engaño
Aparri
Tuguegarao
Ilagan
LUZON
Baler
Cabanatuan
Quezon City
Polillo Is
Manila
PHILIPPINES
Daet
Catanduanes
Naga
Boac
Legazpi
Bulan
Catarman
Masbate
Samar
Roxas
Catbalogan
Guiuan
Iloilo
Bacolod
Tacloban
Leyte
10497
Negros
Cebu
Bohol
Dinaget
10265
Siargao
Surigao
Siaton
Bohol Sea
Butuan
Manukan
Cagayan de Oro
Ozamiz
Marawi
MINDANAO
L. Lanao
Malanbang
Cotabato
Zamboanga
Davao
Basilan
Moro Gulf
Digos
Davao G.
Jolo
General Santos
Tinaca Pt
Sulu Arch
PHILIPPINE SEA
Ulithi
Fais
Gaferut
Yap
Faraulep
Ngulu
Sorol
Lamotrek
Trust Terr. of the PACIFIC ISLANDS (USA)
Woleai
Ifalik
Eauripik
Palau Islands
Koror
Rep. of Belau
CAROLINE ISLANDS
Fed. States of Micronesia
Sonsorol
Pulo Anna
Merir
Tobi
Helen Reef
Kepulauan Talaud
Karakelong
Tahuna
Sangine
Kepulauan Sangihe
CELEBES SEA
Morotai
Tobelo
Manado
Buol
Kuandang
Belang
Gorontalo
Ternate
Halmahera
Molucca Sea
Teluk Weda
Mapia
Equator
Waigeo
Selat Dampier
Kwoka 3000
Manokwari
Supiori
Biak
Ninigo Group
Wuvulu
Kep. Togian
Luwuk
Bacan
MOLUCCAS
Sorong
Cendrawasih
Peg Arfak 2939
Numfoor
Yapen
Tg d'Urville
Sarmi
Jayapura
Mamberamo
Peleng
Taliabu
Mangole
Misoöl
Teluk Cendrawasih
Dom 1340
Aitape
Schouten Is
Wewak
Kep. Banggai
Obi
Teluk Tolo
Kep Sula
CERAM SEA
Teluk Berau
IRIAN JAYA
Angemuk 3741
PAPUA
Sepik
Karkar
Danau Towuti
Piru
3019
Bula
Fakfak
Kaimana
Pegunungan Maoke
Pk Jaya 5029
Pk Mandala 4702
NEW GUINEA
Long I.
Ramu
Madang
Namlea
Seram
Ambon
Buru
Kendari
Wowoni
Adi
Kokonau
Central Ra.
Mt Hagen
Goroka
Finschhafen
Kolaka
Kep. Banda
Mendi
Kubor 4359
Lae
Muna
Butung
Baubau
BANDA SEA
Kep. Kai
Dobo
Wokam
Tk Flamingo
Tanahmerah
Bulolo
Wau
Salamaua
Kep. Tukangbesi
Kep. Aru
Kobroör
Digul
L. Murray
PAPUA
Kikori
Kerema
Morobe
Albert Edward 3993
4073
ASIA
Nila
Trangan
Fly
Teun
Damar
P. Kolepom
Gulf of Papua
Mt Victoria
Kokoda
Wetar
Romang
Yamdena
Kepulauan Tanimbar
Merauke
Daru
Port Moresby
Lomblen
Alor
Kep. Leti
Babar
Saumlaki
Selaru
Tg Vals
Komoran
Saibai
Flores
Dili
Selat Wetar
Sermata
ARAFURA SEA
Mulgrave I.
Banks I.
Ende
Atambua
TIMOR
Torres Strait
Thursday I.
C. York
Pr. of Wales I.
Somerset
Savu Sea
Great Barrier Rf
CORAL SEA
Kupang
C. Grenville
Roti
C.V. Diemen
Dundas Str.
Croker I.
Wessel Is
Melville I.
Coburg Pen.
AUSTRALIA
Iron Range
Bathurst I.
C. Arnhem
Weipa
Gove Pen.
Nhulunbuy
Albatross B.
Clarence Str.
Darwin
Arnhem Land
TIMOR SEA
130
140
20
10
0
D
E
F
2
3
4
5

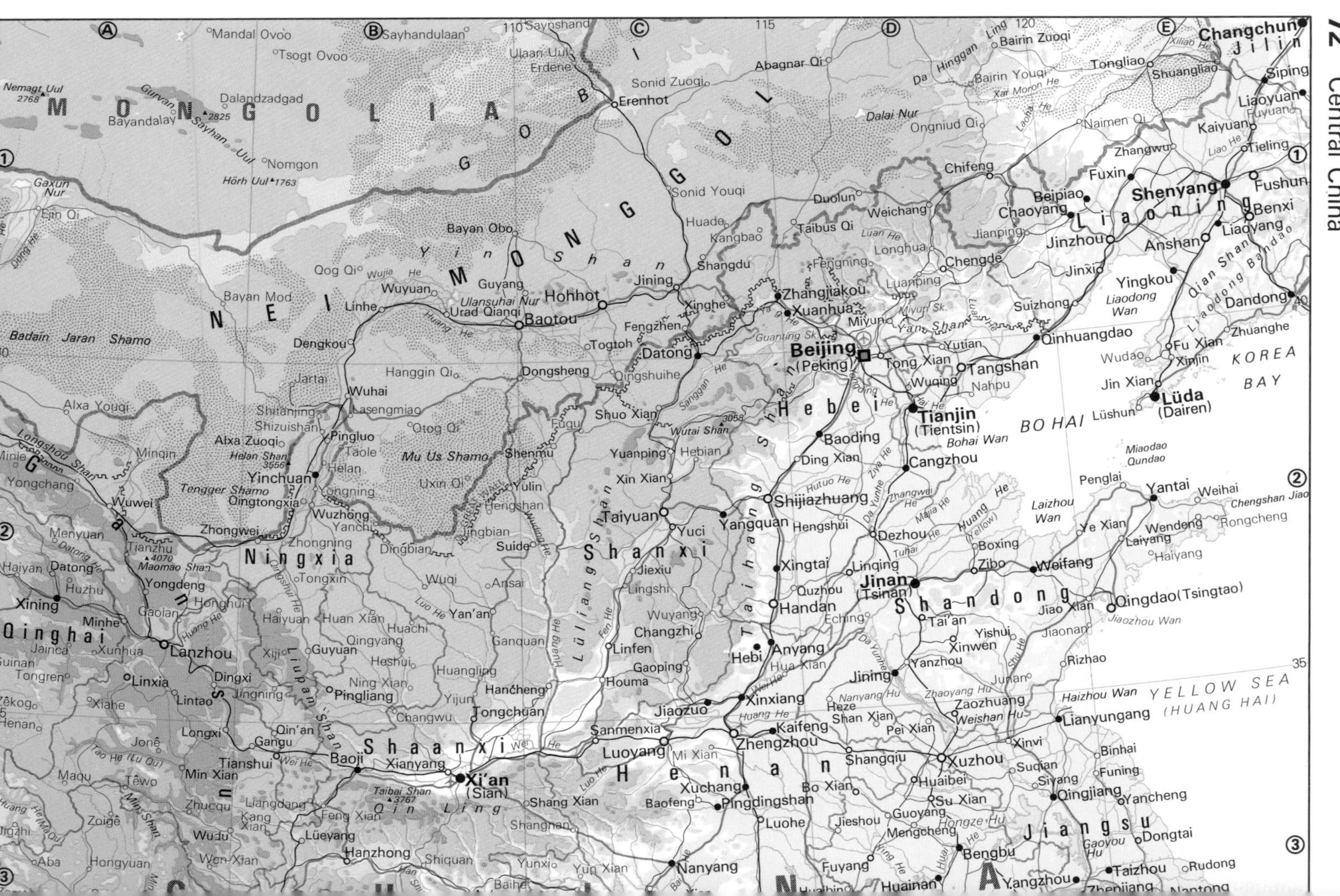
Changchun
Jilin
Siping
Liaoyuan
Tieling
Fushun
Shenyang
Benxi
Liaoyang
Anshan
Dandong
KOREA BAY
Yingkou
Lüda
(Dairen)
Lüshun
Jin Xian
Fu Xian
Liaodong Wan
Jinzhou
Fuxin
Beipiao
Chaoyang
Tongliao
Qinhuangdao
Tangshan
BO HAI
Bohai Wan
Tianjin
(Tientsin)
Beijing
(Peking)
Chengde
Chifeng
Zhangjiakou
Xuanhua
Baoding
Cangzhou
Shijiazhuang
Hebei
Xingtai
Handan
Anyang
Dezhou
Jinan
(Tsinan)
Shandong
Yantai
Weihai
Weifang
Zibo
Qingdao(Tsingtao)
Jiaozhou Wan
YELLOW SEA
(HUANG HAI)
Haizhou Wan
Lianyungang
Xuzhou
Jiangsu
Bengbu
Huainan
Yangzhou
Taizhou
Qingjiang
Jining
Zhengzhou
Kaifeng
Xinxiang
Henan
Luoyang
Pingdingshan
Nanyang
Xuchang
Luohe
Sanmenxia
Jiaozuo
Taiyuan
Shanxi
Yangquan
Datong
Linfen
Changzhi
Houma
Xi'an
(Sian)
Shaanxi
Baoji
Xianyang
Tongchuan
Yan'an
Yulin
Hohhot
Baotou
Erenhot
Wuhai
Linhe
Yinchuan
Ningxia
Shizuishan
Wuzhong
Zhongwei
Lanzhou
Tianshui
Xining
Qinghai
Wuwei
Pingliang
Guyuan
Hanzhong
Yin Shan
Lüliang Shan
Taihang Shan
Wutai Shan
Mu Us Shamo
Tengger Shamo
Badain Jaran Shamo
Huang He
Wei He
Fen He
Qin Ling
Liupan Shan
Helan Shan
Longshou Shan
Da Hinggan Ling
Dalai Nur
Nemagt Uul 2768
Hörh Uul 1763
Gurvan Sayhan Uul 2825
Mandal Ovoo
Dalandzadgad
Sayhandulaan
Saynshand
Tsogt Ovoo
Nomgon
Bayandalay
Ulaan Uul
Erdene
Zhangwu
Kaiyuan
Naimen Qi
Jinxi
Suizhong
Weichang
Duolun
Huade
Shangdu
Sonid Youqi
Sonid Zuoqi
Abagnar Qi
Bayan Obo
Guyang
Wuyuan
Dengkou
Togtoh
Dongsheng
Shenmu
Suide
Dingbian
Huan Xian
Qingyang
Xiji
Dingxi
Linxia
Lintao
Longxi
Min Xian
Wudu
Zoigê
Maqu
Henan
Tongren
Guinan
Jainca
Huzhu
Minhe
Menyuan
Yongdeng
Minqin
Alxa Youqi
Alxa Zuoqi
Yongchang
Ejin Qi
Gaxun Nur
Hanggin Qi
Otog Qi
Uxin Qi
Urad Qianqi
Ulansuhai Nur
Jartai
Yuci
Xin Xian
Fengzhen
Xinghe
Kangbao
Taibus Qi
Fengning
Luanping
Miyun
Tong Xian
Wuqing
Ding Xian
Hengshui
Linqing
Heze
Shangqiu
Fuyang
Bo Xian
Huaibei
Su Xian
Tai'an
Yishui
Rizhao
Jiaonan
Laiyang
Haiyang
Wendeng
Rongcheng
Penglai
Laizhou Wan
Chengshan Jiao
Miaodao Qundao
Yancheng
Dongtai
Binhai
Funing
Siyang
Suqian
Xinyi
Gaoyou Hu
Hongze Hu
Weishan Hu

Hubei
Sichuan
Guizhou
Hunan
Jiangxi
Zhejiang
Fujian
Guangdong
Guangxi
Yunnan
VIETNAM
LAOS
TAIWAN
SOUTH CHINA SEA
GULF OF TONGKIN
FORMOSA STRAIT
(TAIWAN HAIXIA)
Wuhan
Chongqing (Chungking)
Chengdu
Guiyang
Kunming
Changsha
Nanchang
Hangzhou
Fuzhou (Foochow)
Guangzhou (Canton)
Nanning
Hanoi
Haiphong
T'ai-pei
Kao-hsiung
Victoria
HONG KONG (U.K.)
Macau (Port.)
Kowloon
Shantou (Swatow)
Xiamen (Amoy)
Haikou
Dongsha Qundao (Prates)
Leizhou Bandao (Luichow Peninsula)
Nan Ling
Wuyi Shan
Miao Ling
Dabie Shan
Daxue Shan
Dongting Hu
Poyang Hu
Yangtze Gorges
Dashennongjia 3053

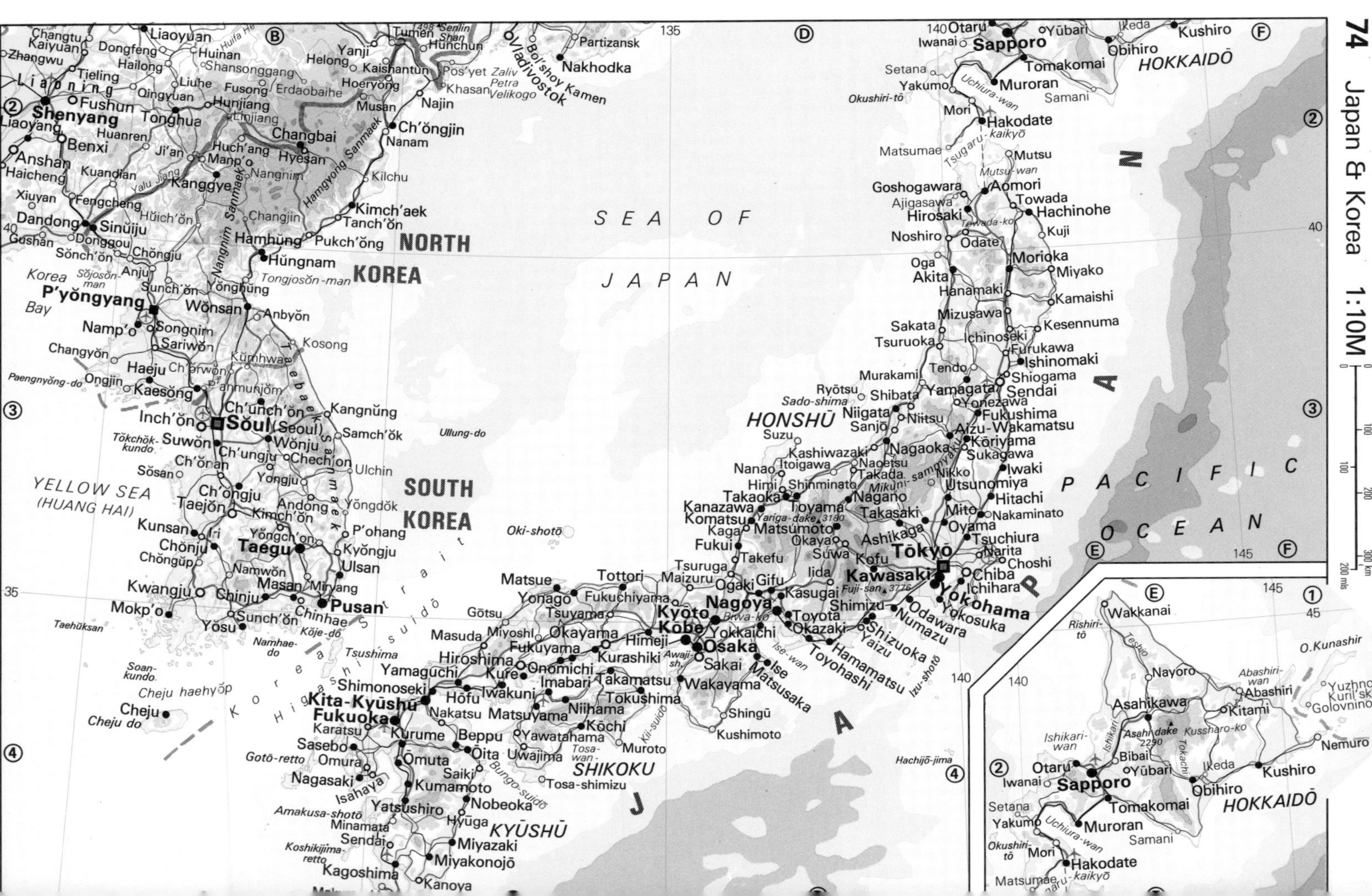

0 100 200 300 km
0 100 200 mls
PACIFIC OCEAN
SEA OF JAPAN
YELLOW SEA (HUANG HAI)
Korea Bay
Korea Strait
NORTH KOREA
SOUTH KOREA
HOKKAIDŌ
HONSHŪ
SHIKOKU
KYŪSHŪ
Sapporo
Hakodate
Aomori
Morioka
Sendai
Tōkyō
Yokohama
Kawasaki
Nagoya
Kyoto
Kobe
Ōsaka
Hiroshima
Kita-Kyūshū
Fukuoka
Nagasaki
Kagoshima
P'yŏngyang
Sŏul (Seoul)
Inch'ŏn
Pusan
Taegu
Kwangju
Taejŏn
Shenyang
Vladivostok
Nakhodka
Cheju
Cheju do
Oki-shotō
Sado-shima
Izu-shotō
Tsushima
Fuji-san 3776

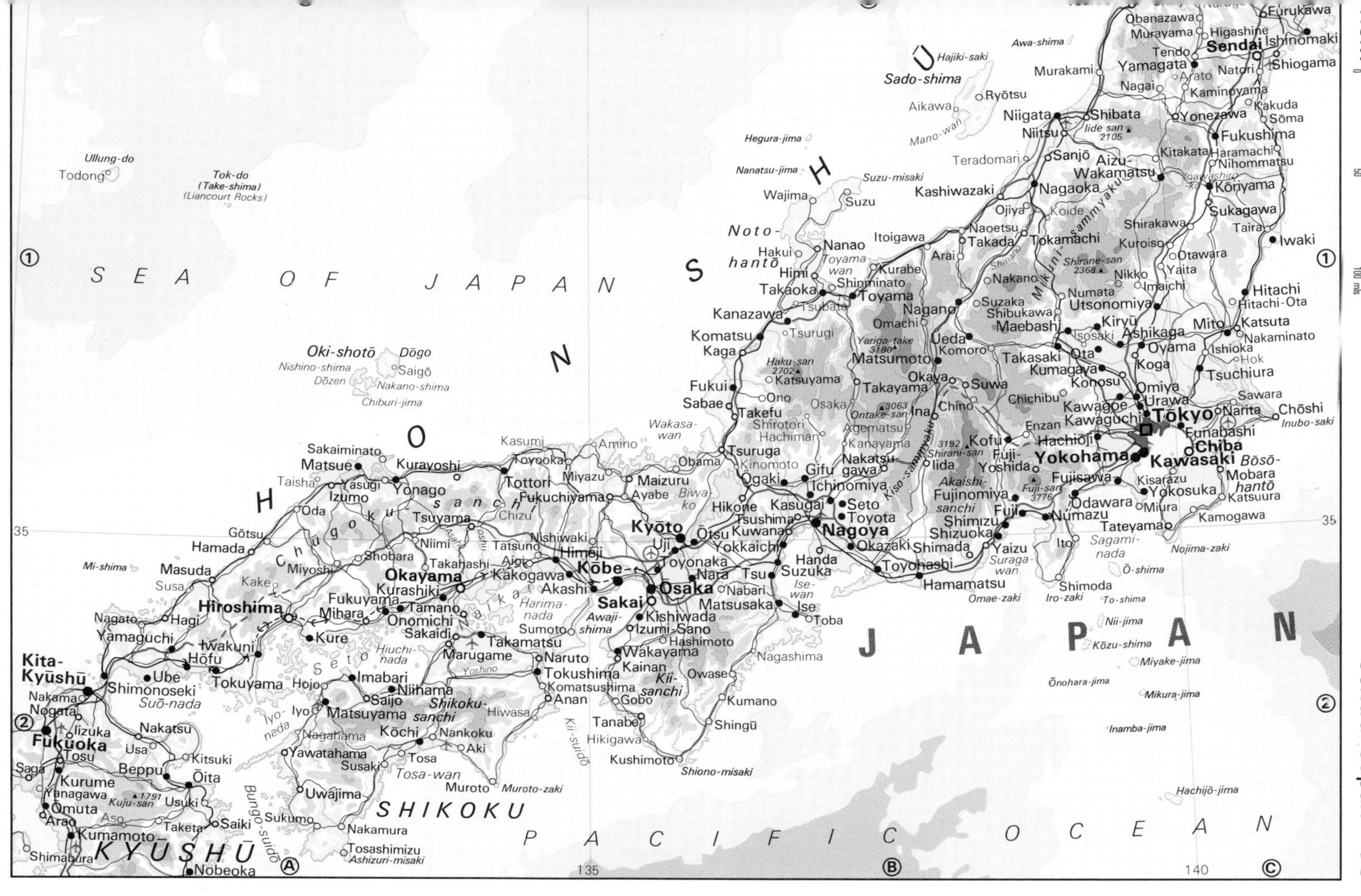
SEA OF JAPAN
HONSHU
JAPAN
SHIKOKU
KYŪSHŪ
PACIFIC OCEAN
Sado-shima
Hajiki-saki
Awa-shima
Ryōtsu
Aikawa
Mano-wan
Ullung-do
Todong
Tok-do
(Take-shima)
(Liancourt Rocks)
Oki-shotō
Dōgo
Saigō
Nishino-shima
Dōzen
Nakano-shima
Chiburi-jima
Hegura-jima
Nanatsu-jima
Suzu-misaki
Noto-hantō
Wajima
Suzu
Hakui
Nanao
Himi
Toyama-wan
Sendai
Ishinomaki
Shiogama
Furukawa
Obanazawa
Murayama
Higashine
Tendo
Yamagata
Natori
Nagai
Kaminoyama
Kakuda
Sōma
Murakami
Niigata
Niitsu
Shibata
Yonezawa
Fukushima
Iide san 2105
Teradomari
Sanjō
Aizu-Wakamatsu
Kitakata
Haramachi
Nihommatsu
Kōriyama
Kashiwazaki
Nagaoka
Sukagawa
Ojiya
Koide
Mikuni-sammyaku
Taira
Iwaki
Itoigawa
Naoetsu
Takada
Tokamachi
Shirakawa
Kuroiso
Otawara
Yaita
Shirane-san 2368
Nikko
Imaichi
Hitachi
Hitachi-Ota
Arai
Kurabe
Nakano
Shinminato
Takaoka
Toyama
Suzaka
Shibukawa
Nagano
Numata
Utsonomiya
Kanazawa
Tsubata
Omachi
Maebashi
Kiryū
Isosaki
Ashikaga
Mito
Katsuta
Nakaminato
Komatsu
Tsurugi
Yariga-take 3180
Ueda
Komoro
Takasaki
Ōta
Oyama
Ishioka
Kaga
Haku-san 2702
Matsumoto
Kumagaya
Koga
Tsuchiura
Fukui
Katsuyama
Okaya
Suwa
Konosu
Omiya
Sawara
Sabae
Ono
Takayama
Chichibu
Kawagoe
Urawa
Chōshi
Takefu
Osaka
Ontake-san 3063
Ina
Chino
Kawaguchi
Tōkyō
Narita
Inubo-saki
Shirotori
Agematsu
Enzan
Hachiōji
Funabashi
Hachiman
Kofu
Chiba
Wakasa-wan
Kanayama
Shirani-san 3192
Yokohama
Kawasaki
Bōsō-hantō
Tsuruga
Kinomoto
Nakatsugawa
Iida
Fuji-Yoshida
Mobara
Kisarazu
Yokosuka
Katsuura
Obama
Gifu
Kiso-sammyaku
Akaishi-sanchi
Fujisawa
Ogaki
Ichinomiya
Fujinomiya
Fuji-san 3776
Odawara
Miura
Kamogawa
Kasugai
Seto
Toyota
Fuji
Numazu
Tateyama
Hikone
Biwa-ko
Tsushima
Nagoya
Shimizu
Shizuoka
Ito
Sagami-nada
Nojima-zaki
Kyōto
Ōtsu
Kuwana
Yokkaichi
Okazaki
Shimada
Yaizu
Suruga-wan
Ō-shima
Uji
Handa
Toyohashi
Hamamatsu
Shimoda
Toyonaka
Nara
Tsu
Suzuka
Omae-zaki
Iro-zaki
To-shima
Ōsaka
Sakai
Nabari
Ise-wan
Matsusaka
Ise
Toba
Nii-jima
Kishiwada
Izumi-Sano
Hashimoto
Kōzu-shima
Wakayama
Nagashima
Miyake-jima
Kainan
Kii-sanchi
Owase
Ōnohara-jima
Komatsushima
Gobo
Kumano
Mikura-jima
Tanabe
Shingū
Hikigawa
Kii-suidō
Kushimoto
Shiono-misaki
Inamba-jima
Hachijō-jima
Kasumi
Amino
Miyazu
Maizuru
Ayabe
Toyooka
Kurayoshi
Tottori
Fukuchiyama
Sakaiminato
Matsue
Yasugi
Yonago
Taisha
Izumo
Chizu
Oda
Chūgoku-sanchi
Tsuyama
Nishiwaki
Tatsuno
Himeji
Kōbe
Gōtsu
Hamada
Niimi
Shobara
Aioi
Kakogawa
Akashi
Mi-shima
Masuda
Miyoshi
Takahashi
Okayama
Kurashiki
Harima-nada
Awaji-shima
Sumoto
Susa
Kake
Fukuyama
Tamano
Hiroshima
Mihara
Onomichi
Sakaidi
Takamatsu
Nagato
Hagi
Kure
Marugame
Naruto
Yamaguchi
Iwakuni
Hiuchi-nada
Seto Naikai
Yoshino
Tokushima
Hōfu
Imabari
Anan
Kita-Kyūshū
Ube
Tokuyama
Hojo
Niihama
Saijo
Shikoku-sanchi
Hiwasa
Shimonoseki
Suō-nada
Iyo
Matsuyama
Iyo-nada
Nakama
Nogata
Nagahama
Kōchi
Nankoku
Iizuka
Nakatsu
Aki
Fukuoka
Tosu
Usa
Yawatahama
Tosa
Kitsuki
Susaki
Tosa-wan
Saga
Beppu
Ōita
Kurume
Yanagawa
Uwajima
Muroto
Muroto-zaki
Omuta
Kuju-san 1791
Usuki
Arao
Aso
Taketa
Saiki
Bungo-suidō
Sukumo
Nakamura
Kumamoto
Shimabara
Nobeoka
Tosashimizu
Ashizuri-misaki
35
135
140

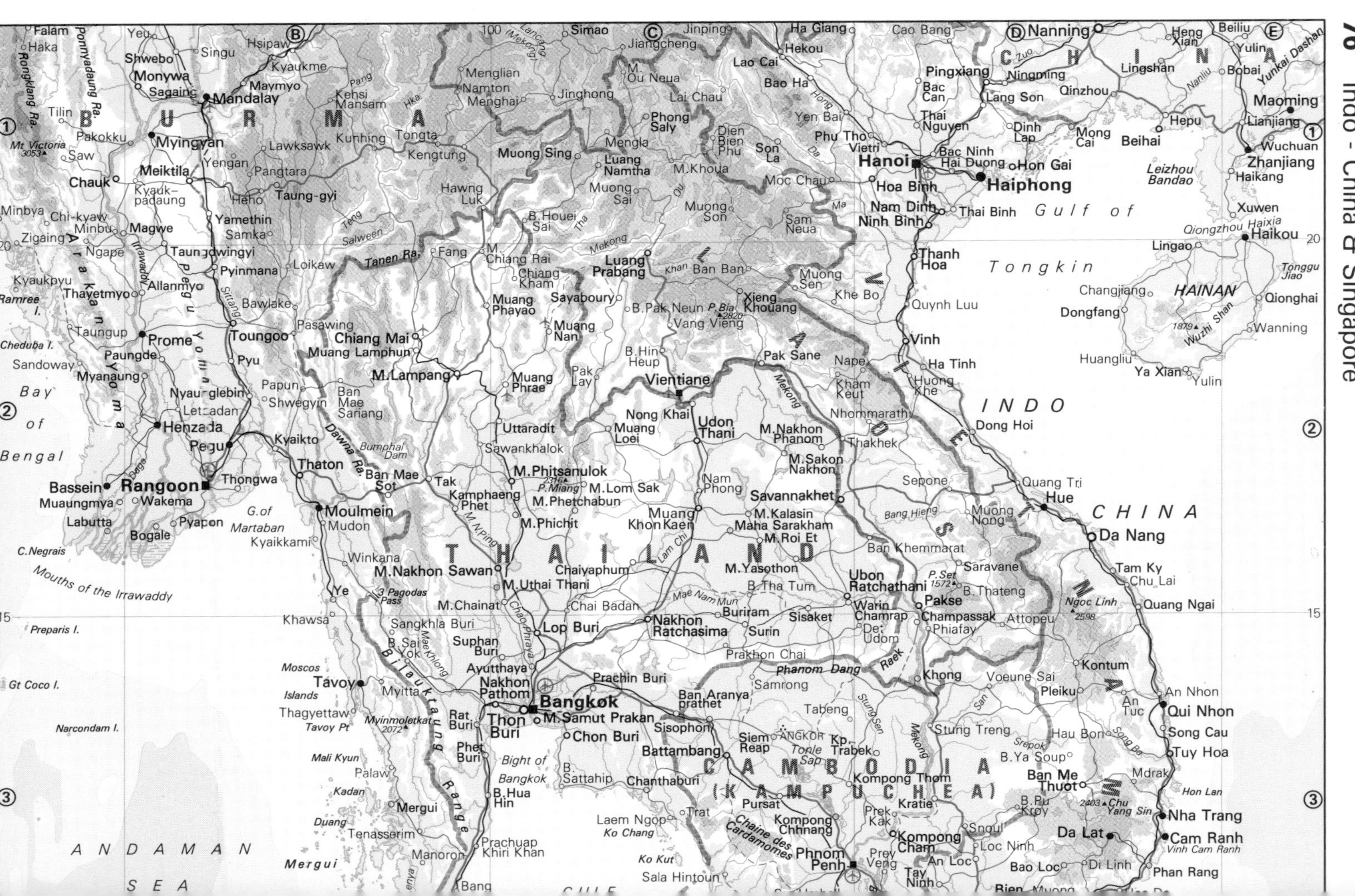
BURMA
THAILAND
LAOS
VIETNAM
CAMBODIA (KAMPUCHEA)
CHINA
INDO CHINA
HAINAN
Gulf of Tongkin
Bay of Bengal
ANDAMAN SEA
G. of Martaban
Bight of Bangkok
Mouths of the Irrawaddy
Rangoon
Bangkok
Hanoi
Haiphong
Vientiane
Phnom Penh
Mandalay
Moulmein
Chiang Mai
Luang Prabang
Hue
Da Nang
Haikou
Nanning
Zhanjiang
Maoming
Qui Nhon
Nha Trang
Cam Ranh
Da Lat
Ban Me Thuot
Pakse
Savannakhet
Udon Thani
Nakhon Ratchasima
Ubon Ratchathani
Battambang
Kompong Cham
Tavoy
Mergui
Bassein
Prome
Toungoo
Pegu
Henzada
Myingyan
Meiktila
Taung-gyi
Vinh
Nam Dinh
Thanh Hoa
Mekong
Arakan Yoma
Pegu Yoma
Dawna Ra.
Tanen Ra.
Bilauktaung Range
Phanom Dang
Chaine des Cardamomes
Ponnyadaung Ra.
Rongklang Ra.

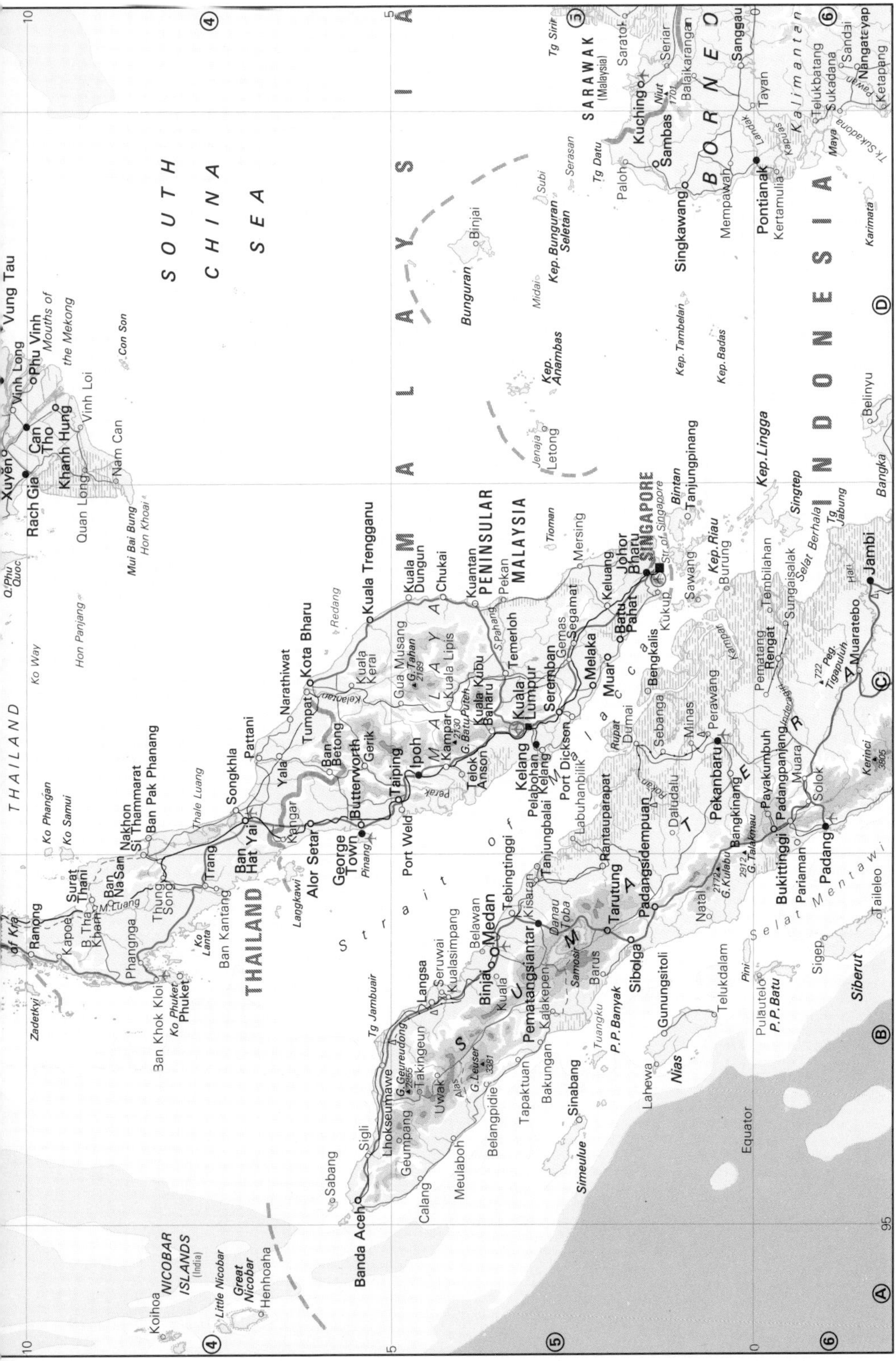

SOUTH CHINA SEA

THAILAND

MALAYSIA

PENINSULAR MALAYSIA

MALAYA

SARAWAK (Malaysia)

BORNEO

Kalimantan

INDONESIA

SUMATERA

Strait of Malacca

Selat Mentawai

NICOBAR ISLANDS (India)

Koihoa

Little Nicobar

Great Nicobar

Henhoaha

Banda Aceh

Sabang

Sigli

Lhokseumawe

Calang

Meulaboh

Geumpang

Takingeun

Uwak

G. Geureudong 2855

G. Leuser 3381

Alas

Belangpidie

Tapaktuan

Bakungan

Sinabang

Simeulue

Langsa

Seruwai

Kualasimpang

Binjai

Kuala

Medan

Belawan

Pematangsiantar

Tebingtinggi

Kisaran

Tanjungbalai

Kalakepen

Danau Toba

Samosir

Barus

Tuangku

Sibolga

Tarutung

Padangsidempuan

Rantauparapat

Labuhanbilik

P. P. Banyak

Nias

Gunungsitoli

Lahewa

Telukdalam

Pini

Pulautelo

P. P. Batu

Siberut

Sigep

Taileleo

Padang

Pariaman

Bukittinggi

Padangpanjang

Payakumbuh

Solok

Muara

Kerinci 3805

Natal

G. Kulabu 2172

G. Talakmau 2912

Bangkinang

Pekanbaru

Perawang

Minas

Daludalu

Rokan

Dumai

Rupat

Sebanga

Bengkalis

Kampar

Pematang

Rengat

Inderagiri

Peg. Tigapuluh 722

Muaratebo

Hari

Jambi

Tembilahan

Sungaisalak

Selat Berhala

Singtep

Tg Jabung

Kep. Lingga

Kep. Riau

Burung

Sawang

Bintan

Tanjungpinang

Bangka

Belinyu

Equator

of Kra

Zadetkyi

Ranong

Kapoe

B. Tha Kham

Surat Thani

M. Luang

Ban Na San

Phangnga

Ban Khok Kloi

Ko Phuket

Phuket

Ko Lanta

Ban Kantang

Thung Song

Trang

Nakhon Si Thammarat

Ban Pak Phanang

Ko Phangan

Ko Samui

Thale Luang

Songkhla

Ban Hat Yai

Pattani

Yala

Narathiwat

Langkawi

Kangar

Alor Setar

George Town

Pinang

Butterworth

Port Weld

Taiping

Ipoh

Gerik

Ban Betong

Tumpat

Kota Bharu

Kelantan

Kuala Krai

Redang

Kuala Trengganu

Gua Musang

G. Tahan 2189

Kuala Lipis

Kuala Dungun

Chukai

Kuantan

Pekan

S. Pahang

Temerloh

Perak

Kampar

G. Batu Puteh 2130

Telok Anson

Kuala Kubu Baharu

Kelang

Pelabohan Kelang

Kuala Lumpur

Seremban

Port Dickson

Gemas

Segamat

Melaka

Muar

Batu Pahat

Keluang

Mersing

Tioman

Johor Bharu

SINGAPORE

Kukup

Str. of Singapore

Tg Jambuair

Xuyen

Rach Gia

Can Tho

Vinh Long

Phu Vinh

Vung Tau

Mouths of the Mekong

Khanh Hung

Quan Long

Vinh Loi

Nam Can

Con Son

Mui Bai Bung

Hon Khoai

Q. Phu Quoc

Ko Way

Hon Panjang

Bunguran

Binjai

Jenaja

Letong

Kep. Anambas

Midai

Kep. Bunguran Seletan

Subi

Serasan

Tg Sirik

Tg Datu

Paloh

Kuching

Sambas

Niut 1701

Saratok

Seriar

Balaikarangan

Singkawang

Kep. Tambelan

Kep. Badas

Mempawah

Sanggau

Pontianak

Kertamulia

Landak

Kapuas

Tayan

Telukbatang

Maya

Sukadana

Sandai

Nangatayap

Pawan

Ketapang

Tk. Sukadona

Karimata

A B C D 4 5 6

10 5 0 95

1:10M

0 100 200 300 400 km
0 100 200 mls

INDONESIA
BORNEO
SARAWAK
Kalimantan
SULAWESI (CELEBES)
SUMATERA
JAWA
MALAYSIA
SINGAPORE
BRUNEI
SABAH

Celebes Sea
Selat Makassar
Java Sea
Bali Sea
Flores Sea
Selat Karimata
Selat Sunda
Selat Bangka
Selat Gaspar
Selat Berhala
Str. of Singapore

Kuala Lumpur
Kelang
Seremban
Port Dickson
Melaka
Muar
Batu Pahat
Gemas
Segamat
Keluang
Mersing
Johor Bharu
Kukup
Tioman
Bengkalis
Dumai
Rupat
Minas
Perawang
Pekanbaru
Kep. Riau
Bintan
Tanjungpinang
Sawang
Burung
Kep. Lingga
Singtep
Pematang
Rengat
Tembilahan
Sungaisalak
Tg Jabung
Jambi
Muaratebo
Peg. Tigapuluh
Bangko
Sarolangun
Surulangun
Muaralakitan
Gresik
Telangbetutu
Palembang
Prabumulih
Muaraenim
Lubuklinggau
Lahat
Baturaja
Martapura
G. Patah 2817
G. Dempo
Pgunungan Barisan
Bengkulu
Lais
Tais
Manna
Bintuhan
Krui
Kotaagung
Kotabumi
Menggala
Tulangbawang
Telukbetung
Tegineneng
Kalianda
Sukadana
G. Rasag 2232
Enggano
G. Gedang 2446
Tg Lumut
Bangka
Mentok
Belinyu
Pangkalpinang
Koba
Toboali
Belitung
Tanjungpandan
Manggar
Dendang
Karimata
Kep. Anambas
Kep. Tambelan
Kep. Badas
Kep. Bunguran Seletan
Midai
Subi
Serasan
Jenaja
Letong
Tg Datu
Paloh
Sambas
Singkawang
Mempawah
Pontianak
Kertamulia
Kuching
Serian
Balaikarangan
Sanggau
Tayan
Sintang
Nangapinoh
Semitau
Simanggang
Lubok Antu
Saratok
Sibu
Mukah
Igan
Tg Sirik
Bintulu
Kapit
Belaga
Hose Mts
Dulit Ra.
Long Akah
Pegunungan Iran
Penambo Ra.
Bt Batubrok 2240
Peg. Muller
Putussibau
Longnawan
Batukelau
Tanjungselor
Tanjungredeb
Tarakan
Seguntur
Sangkulirang
Merah
G. Bulu 1252
Kongkemul 2053
G. Njapa 1385
G. Menyapa 2000
Tg Mangkalihat
Maratua
Equator
Bangsalsembera
Samarinda
Tenggarong
Samboja
Balikpapan
Intu
Muaratewah
Tokung
Tewah
Buntok
Tanahgrogot
Tanjung
Amuntai
Barabai
G. Besar 1892
Peg. Meratus
Kandangan
Banjarmasin
Martapura
Pagatan
Kotabaru
Sungaiaiyar
Kintap
Jorong
Batakan
Tg Selatan
Laut
Tg Layar
Palangkaraya
Sampit
Kumai
Tg Puting
Kotabaharu
Sandai
Nangatayap
Sukaraya
Kendawangan
Ketapang
Telukbatang
Sukadana
Tg Sambar
Peg. Schwaner
Raya 2278
Tk. Sukadona
Tk. Sampit
Tk. Kumai
Maya
Pasangkayu
Karossa
Sampaga
Mamuju
Bk Gandadiwata 3074
Majene
Polewali
Onang
Teluk Mandar
Ujung Pandang (Makassar)
Pattallassang
P.P. Postilyon
P.P. Kangean
Kep. Sabalana
Salembu Besar
Kadapongan
Matasiri
Kalembau
Bawean
P.P. Karimunjawa
Tg Bugel
Madura
Sumenep
Pamekasan
Gresik
Surabaya
Pasuruan
Probolinggo
Situbondo
Jember
Banyuwangi
G. Raung 3332
Malang
Blitar
Kediri
Mojokerto
Madiun
Bangil
Tulungagung
Rembang
Blora
Cepu
Kudus
Semarang
Surakarta
Slaung
G. Lawu 3265
Pacitan
Yogyakarta
Purworejo
Magelang
G. Sumbing 3371
Pekalongan
Pemalang
Tegal
Brebes
Indramayu
Cirebon
Bandung
Tasikmalaya
Purwokerto
Cilacap
Cijulang
Garut
Pameungpeuk
Sukabumi
Cianjur
Bogor
Jakarta
Tanjung Priok
Serang
Labuhan
Tk. Pelabuanratu
Genteng
Rakata (Krakatau)
Bali
Denpasar
Singaraja
Lombok
Mataram
Praya
Bayan
Sumbawa
Sumbawa Besar
Taliwang
Alas
Tk. Saleh 1128
Dompu
Raba
Sape
Sangeang
Barung
Satengar

Kota Kinabalu
Labuan
Victoria
Weston
Bandar Seri Begawan
Muara
Seria
Miri
Marudi
Labi
Lawas
Pensiangan
Tenom
Tomani
Bingkor
Lumbis
Kalabakan
Mt. Magdalena 1346
Tawau
Malinau
Tarakan
Saang

A B C
120 125
1 2 3 4 5
20 15 10 5

PACIFIC OCEAN
Dongsha Qundao
Luzon Strait
Batan Islands
Basco
Balintang Channel
Babuyan Islands
Babuyan Channel
Cape Engaño
Cape Bojeador
Laoag
2234
Aparri
Cagayan
Cordillera Central
Sierra Madre
Bangued
Vigan
Tuguegarao
Ilagan
Santiago
Mt Pulog 2929
San Fernando
Solano
La Trinidad
Bayombang
Baguio
LUZON
PHILIPPINE SEA
PHILIPPINES
Lingayen
Dagupan
San Carlos
San Jose
Baler
Camiling
Tarlac
Cabanatuan
SOUTH CHINA SEA
Gapan
Angeles
San Fernando
Polillo Islands
San Antonio
Olongapo
Malolos
Manila
Quezon City
Cavite
Laguna de Bay
Lamon Bay
Corregidor
Calagua Islands
Santa Cruz
Jose Pañganiban
Daet
San Pablo
Lucban
Lipao
Lucena
Catanduanes
Lubang Islands
Batangas
Sipocot
Naga
Boac
Virac
Iriga
Mayon 2421
Legazpi
Calapan
2585
Mt Halcon
Marinduque
MINDORO
Sorsogon
Gubat
Sablayan
Mt Baco 2488
Burias
Sibuyan
Bulan
Mindoro Strait
Romblon
Sibuyan
Catarman
Tablas
Masbate
San Jose
Busuanga
Calamian Group
Culion
Sea
Masbate
Samar Sea
Calbayog
Oras
SAMAR
Semirara Islands
Kalibo
Linapacan Strait
Pandan
Roxas
Visayan Sea
Biliran
Catbalogan
San Isidro
Carigara
El Nido
Cuyo Islands
PANAY
Tacloban
Bogo
Ormoc
Guiuan
Taytay
Dalanganem Islands
Cadiz
Escalante
Burauen
LEYTE
Iloilo
Silay
Leyte Gulf
Baybay
Palawan Passage
Bacolod
Danao
.10497
.10265
Cleopatra Needle 1593
Dumaran
La Carlota
Cebu
Lapu-Lapu
Dinagat
Roxas
Binalbagan
Cebu
Maasin
PALAWAN
Negros
Bohol
Surigao
Siarao
Puerto Princesa
Sipalay
Tagbilaran
Cagayan Islands
Bais
Tanjay
Bohol Sea
Aborlan
1798
Siquijor
Dumaguete
Lazi
Diuat Mts
Camiguin
Butuan
Siaton
Gingoog
Agusan
Mt Mantalingajan 2054
Brooke's Point
Tubbataha Reefs
Dipolog
Dapitan
Lianga
Mañukan
Oroquieta
Cagayan de Oro
SULU SEA
Mt Ozamiz
Iligan
Bislig
Liloy
Dapiak 2560
Marawi
Malaybalay
Tangub
Lanao
Balabac
Pagadian
MINDANAO
2815
Malabang
Zamboanga Pen.
Illana Bay
Tagum
Balabac Strait
Sibuguay Bay
Banggi
Moro Gulf
Cotabato
Davao
Kudat
Cagayan Sulu
Zamboanga
Datu Piang
Mt Apo 2954
Mati
Isabela
Digos
Davao Gulf
Bandau
Basilan
1216 Mt Palin
Telok Labuk
Pangutaran Group
Lais
Kinabalu 4094
Ranau
General Santos
Cape San Agustin
Sandakan
Jolo
Jolo
Parang
Samales Group
Mt Melta 2000
SABAH (Malaysia)
Tapul Group
Tinaca Point
Bingkor
Kinabatangan
Tawitawi
CELEBES SEA
Sarangani Islands
Tenom
Kuamut
Lahad Datu
Tawitawi Group
Sibutu Passage
Sulu Archipelago
Tomani
1606
Brassey Ra.
Telok Darvel
Kepulauan Kawio
Kepulauan Nenusa
Mt Magdalena 1346
Bum Bum
Karakelong
Kalabakan
Semporna

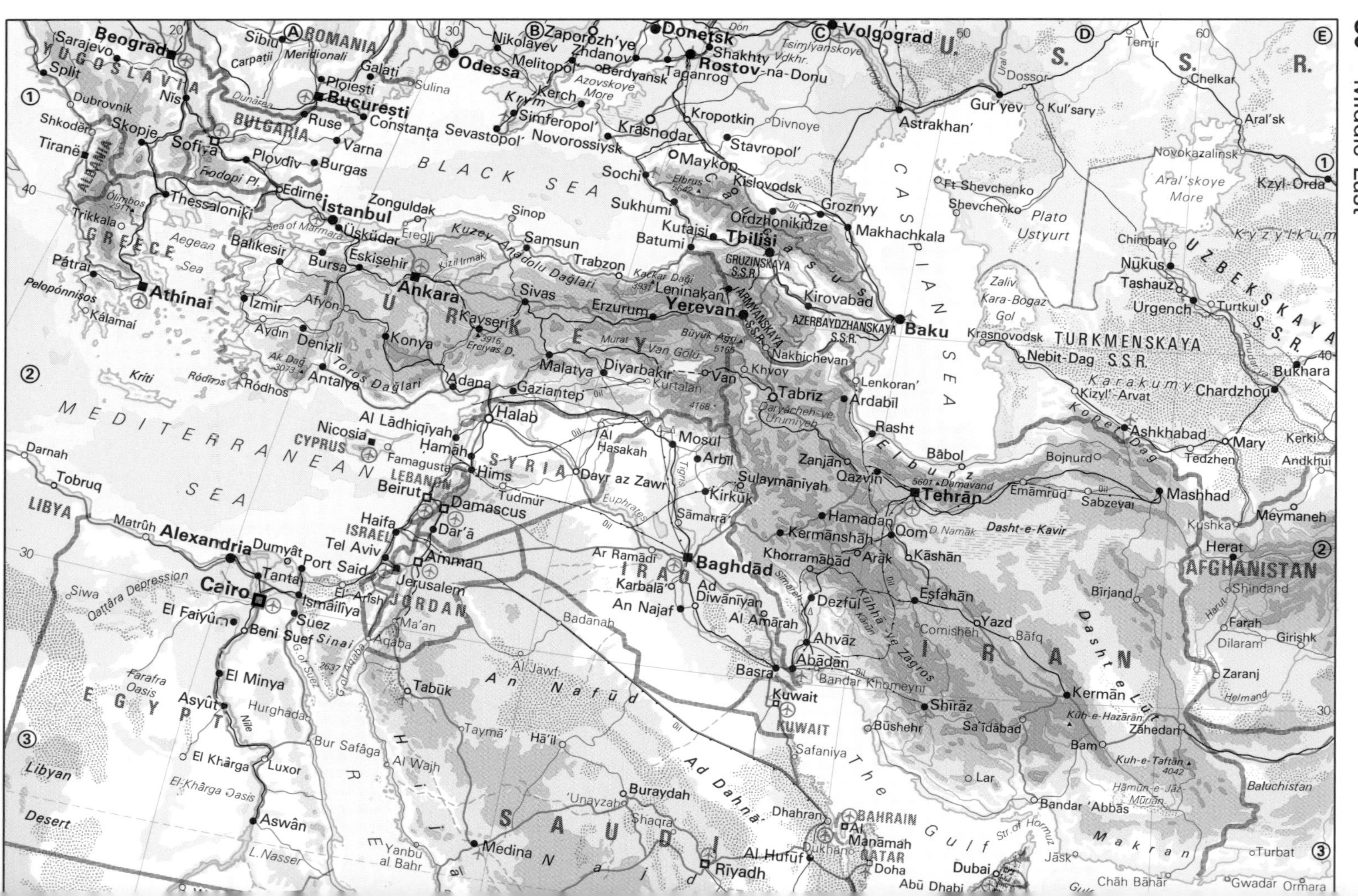
BLACK SEA
CASPIAN SEA
MEDITERRANEAN SEA
The Gulf
U. S. S. R.
YUGOSLAVIA
ROMANIA
BULGARIA
ALBANIA
GREECE
TURKEY
SYRIA
LEBANON
ISRAEL
JORDAN
CYPRUS
IRAQ
IRAN
KUWAIT
BAHRAIN
QATAR
SAUDI
AFGHANISTAN
LIBYA
EGYPT
GRUZINSKAYA S.S.R.
ARMYANSKAYA S.S.R.
AZERBAYDZHANSKAYA S.S.R.
TURKMENSKAYA S.S.R.
UZBEKSKAYA S.S.R.
Aral'skoye More
Plato Ustyurt
Kyzylkum
Karakumy
Kopet Dag
Elburz
Dasht-e-Kavir
Dasht-e-Lūt
Kūhhā-ye Zagros
Makran
Baluchistan
An Nafūd
Ad Dahnā
Najd
Hijaz
Libyan Desert
Qattâra Depression
Anadolu Dağlari
Toros Dağlari
Tigris
Euphrates
Nile
Beograd
Sarajevo
Split
Dubrovnik
Shkodër
Tiranë
Skopje
Niš
Sofiya
Bucureşti
Ploieşti
Galaţi
Constanţa
Varna
Burgas
Plovdiv
Edirne
Thessaloníki
Athínai
Pátrai
Odessa
Nikolayev
Zaporozh'ye
Donetsk
Rostov-na-Donu
Volgograd
Astrakhan'
Gur'yev
Aral'sk
Kzyl-Orda
Simferopol'
Sevastopol'
Novorossiysk
Krasnodar
Stavropol'
Sochi
Groznyy
Makhachkala
Tbilisi
Yerevan
Baku
Krasnovodsk
Nebit-Dag
Ashkhabad
Mary
Chardzhou
Bukhara
İstanbul
Bursa
Eskişehir
Ankara
İzmir
Konya
Kayseri
Samsun
Trabzon
Erzurum
Malatya
Diyarbakır
Adana
Gaziantep
Antalya
Nicosia
Halab
Ḥamāh
Ḥims
Beirut
Damascus
Haifa
Tel Aviv
Jerusalem
Amman
Mosul
Kirkūk
Baghdād
Basra
Tabrīz
Rasht
Tehrān
Mashhad
Herat
Hamadān
Qom
Eşfahān
Yazd
Kermān
Shīrāz
Abādān
Kuwait
Dhahran
Al Manāmah
Doha
Dubai
Abū Dhabi
Rīyadh
Medina
Tabūk
Cairo
Alexandria
Port Said
Suez
Tanta
El Minya
Asyût
Luxor
Aswân
Tobruq
Darnah
Siwa

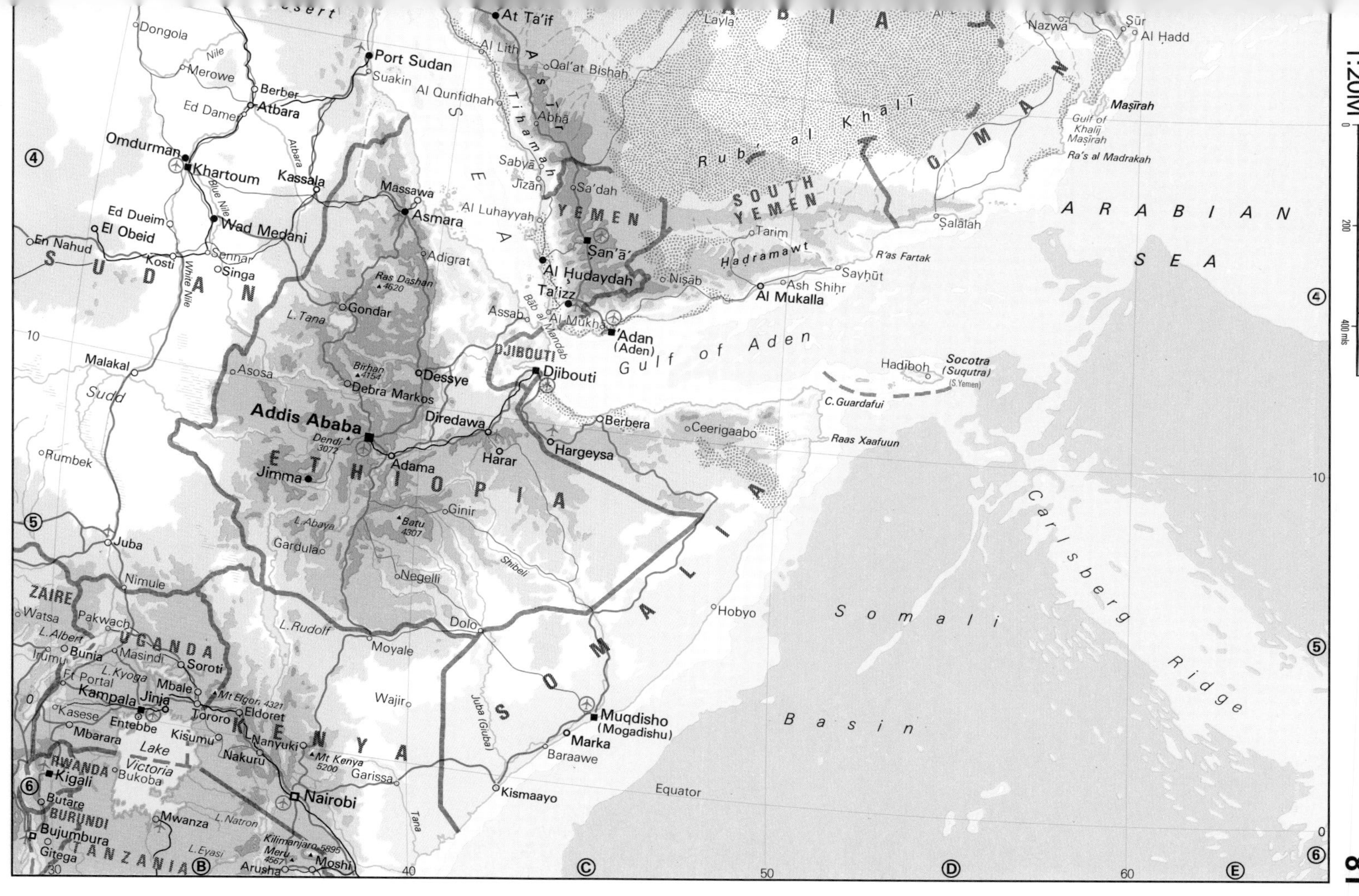
ARABIAN SEA
Gulf of Aden
Carlsberg Ridge
Somali Basin
Equator
Rub' al Khālī
OMAN
SOUTH YEMEN
YEMEN
DJIBOUTI
ETHIOPIA
SOMALIA
SUDAN
KENYA
UGANDA
TANZANIA
RWANDA
BURUNDI
ZAIRE
Socotra (Suqutra) (S.Yemen)
Hadībоh
C. Guardafui
Raas Xaafuun
Ra's Fartak
Masīrah
Gulf of Khalīj Masīrah
Ra's al Madrakah
Ṣūr
Al Ḥadd
Nazwa
Layla
Ṣalālah
Ḥaḍramawt
Tarim
Sayḥūt
Ash Shiḥr
Al Mukalla
Niṣāb
'Adan (Aden)
Al Mukhā
Bāb al Mandab
Ta'izz
Al Ḥudaydah
Ṣan'ā'
Ṣa'dah
Jīzān
Sabyā
Al Luḥayyah
Tihāmah
Abhā
Qal'at Bīshah
At Ta'if
Al Lith
Al Qunfidhah
Port Sudan
Suakin
Dongola
Merowe
Nile
Berber
Atbara
Ed Damer
Omdurman
Khartoum
Kassala
Blue Nile
White Nile
Wad Medani
Ed Dueim
El Obeid
En Nahud
Kosti
Sennar
Singa
Malakal
Sudd
Rumbek
Juba
Nimule
Massawa
Asmara
Adigrat
Assab
Ras Dashan 4620
Gondar
L. Tana
Asosa
Birhan 4154
Debra Markos
Dessye
Djibouti
Addis Ababa
Dendi 3072
Diredawa
Adama
Harar
Hargeysa
Berbera
Ceerigaabo
Jimma
Ginir
Batu 4307
Shibeli
L. Abaya
Gardula
Negelli
L. Rudolf
Dolo
Moyale
Hobyo
Wajir
Juba (Giuba)
Muqdisho (Mogadishu)
Marka
Baraawe
Kismaayo
Garissa
Tana
Watsa
Pakwach
L. Albert
Bunia
Irumu
Masindi
Soroti
L. Kyoga
Ft Portal
Mbale
Mt Elgon 4321
Kampala
Jinja
Tororo
Eldoret
Kasese
Entebbe
Kisumu
Mbarara
Nanyuki
Lake Victoria
Nakuru
Mt Kenya 5200
Kigali
Bukoba
Nairobi
Butare
Mwanza
L. Natron
Bujumbura
Gitega
L. Eyasi
Kilimanjaro 5895
Meru 4567
Moshi
Arusha

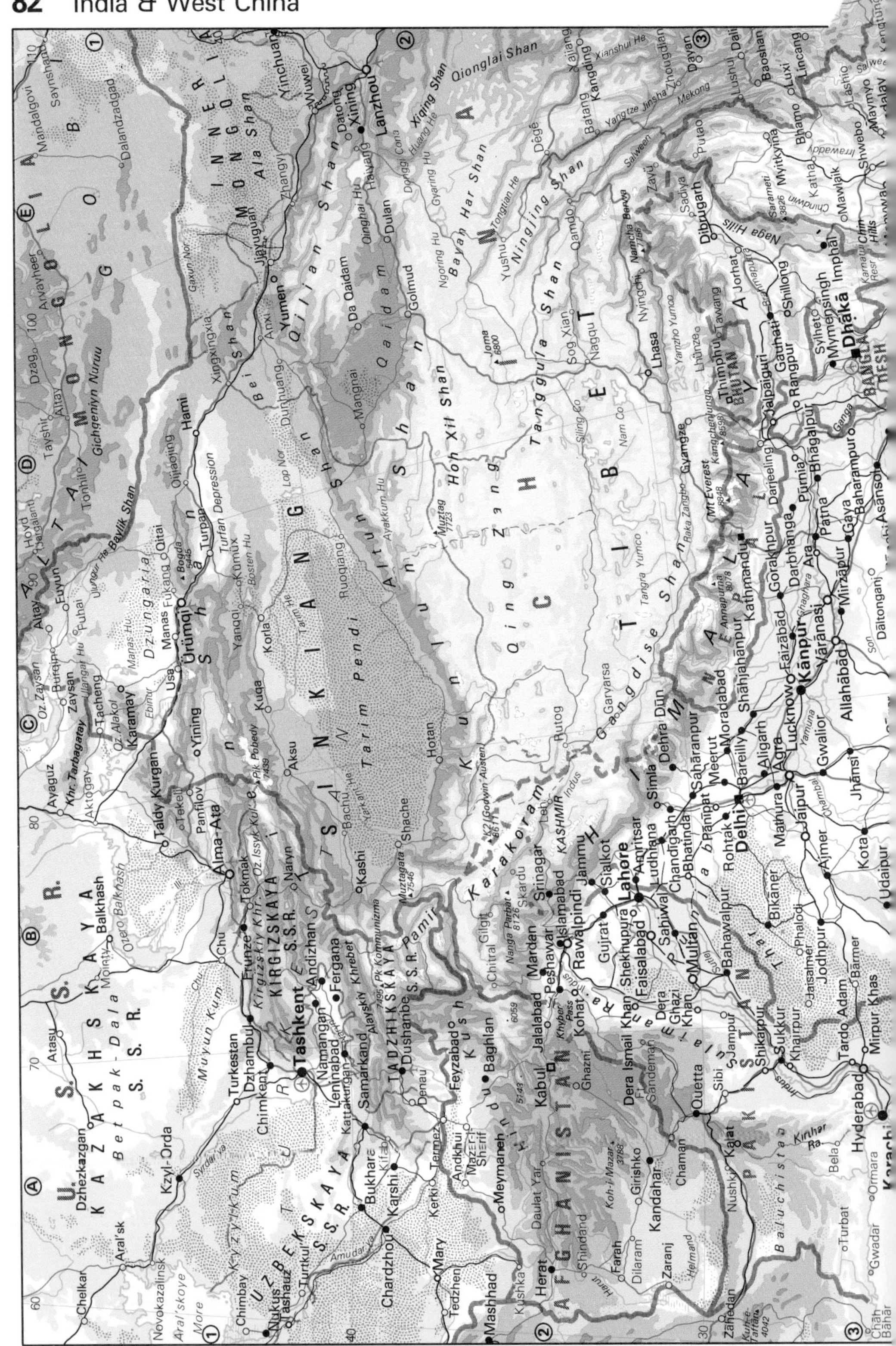
U.S.S.R.
KAZAKHSKAYA S.S.R.
UZBEKSKAYA S.S.R.
KIRGIZSKAYA S.S.R.
TADZHIKSKAYA S.S.R.
MONGOLIA
INNER MONGOLIA
SINKIANG
TIBET
QINGHAI
AFGHANISTAN
PAKISTAN
INDIA
NEPAL
BHUTAN
BANGLADESH
KASHMIR
Tashkent
Alma-Ata
Frunze
Dushanbe
Kabul
Islamabad
Lahore
Delhi
Kathmandu
Thimphu
Dhaka
Lhasa
Ürümqi
Lanzhou
Xining
Karachi
Quetta
Kandahar
Herat
Samarkand
Bukhara
Kashi
Hotan
Aksu
Golmud
Dunhuang
Hami
Turpan
Karakoram
Kunlun Shan
Tian Shan
Altun Shan
Qilian Shan
Tanggula Shan
Hindu Kush
Himalaya
Tarim Pendi
Qaidam
Dzungaria
Turfan Depression
Mt Everest 8848
K2 (Godwin Austen) 8611
Kanpur
Allahabad
Varanasi
Patna
Agra
Jaipur
Amritsar
Rawalpindi
Peshawar
Multan
Hyderabad
Sukkur

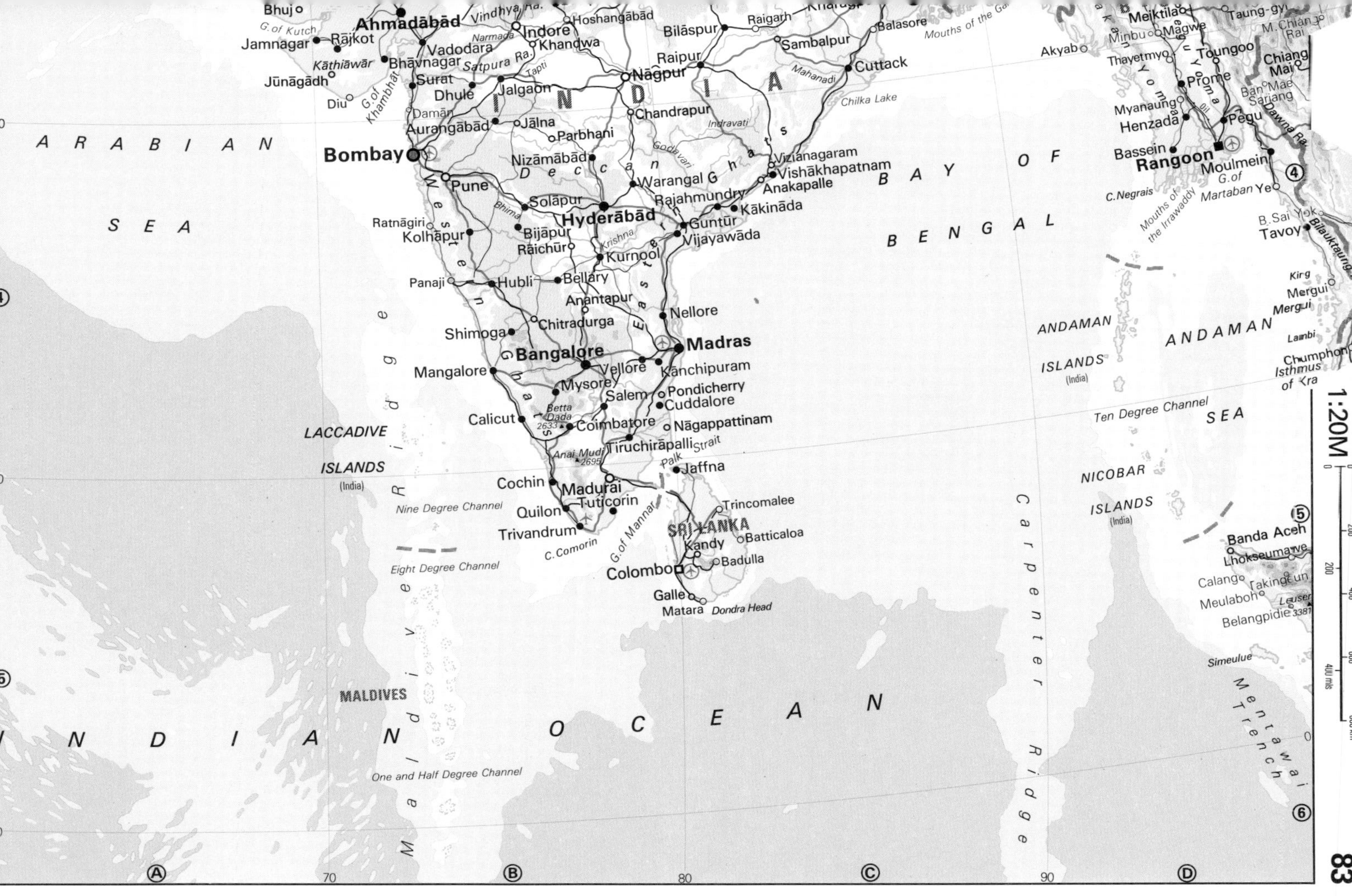
ARABIAN SEA
BAY OF BENGAL
ANDAMAN SEA
INDIAN OCEAN
INDIA
Deccan
Western Ghats
Eastern Ghats
SRI LANKA
LACCADIVE ISLANDS (India)
MALDIVES
Maldive Ridge
ANDAMAN ISLANDS (India)
NICOBAR ISLANDS (India)
Carpenter Ridge
Mentawai Trench
Ten Degree Channel
Nine Degree Channel
Eight Degree Channel
One and Half Degree Channel
Bombay
Ahmadābād
Hyderābād
Madras
Bangalore
Rangoon
Colombo
Bhuj
G. of Kutch
Jamnagar
Rājkot
Kāthiāwār
Jūnāgādh
Diu
G. of Khambhat
Bhāvnagar
Vadodara
Surat
Damān
Dhule
Aurangābād
Jalgaon
Indore
Khandwa
Hoshangābād
Bilāspur
Raigarh
Raipur
Nāgpur
Chandrapur
Parbhani
Jālna
Nizāmābād
Warangal
Solāpur
Pune
Kolhāpur
Ratnāgiri
Panaji
Hubli
Bijāpur
Rāichūr
Bellary
Kurnool
Guntūr
Vijayawāda
Rajahmundry
Kākināda
Vishākhapatnam
Vizianagaram
Anakapalle
Sambalpur
Cuttack
Balasore
Chilka Lake
Mouths of the Ganga
Anantapur
Chitradurga
Shimoga
Mangalore
Mysore
Betta Dada 2633
Calicut
Anai Mudi 2695
Cochin
Quilon
Trivandrum
C. Comorin
Madurai
Tuticorin
Coimbatore
Salem
Vellore
Kānchipuram
Pondicherry
Cuddalore
Nāgappattinam
Tiruchirāpalli
Nellore
Palk Strait
Jaffna
G. of Mannar
Trincomalee
Batticaloa
Kandy
Badulla
Galle
Matara
Dondra Head
Narmada
Tāpti
Sātpura Ra.
Vindhya Ra.
Godāvari
Krishna
Bhima
Mahānadi
Indrāvati
Akyab
Bassein
Henzada
Myanaung
Thayetmyo
Minbu
Magwe
Meiktila
Prome
Toungoo
Pegu
Moulmein
G. of Martaban
Ye
Tavoy
B. Sai Yok
Bilauktaung Ra.
Mergui
Lambi
Chumphon
Isthmus of Kra
Chiang Mai
Ban Mae Sariang
Dawna Ra.
C. Negrais
Mouths of the Irrawaddy
Banda Aceh
Lhokseumawe
Calang
Meulaboh
Takingeun
Leuser 3381
Belangpidie
Simeulue

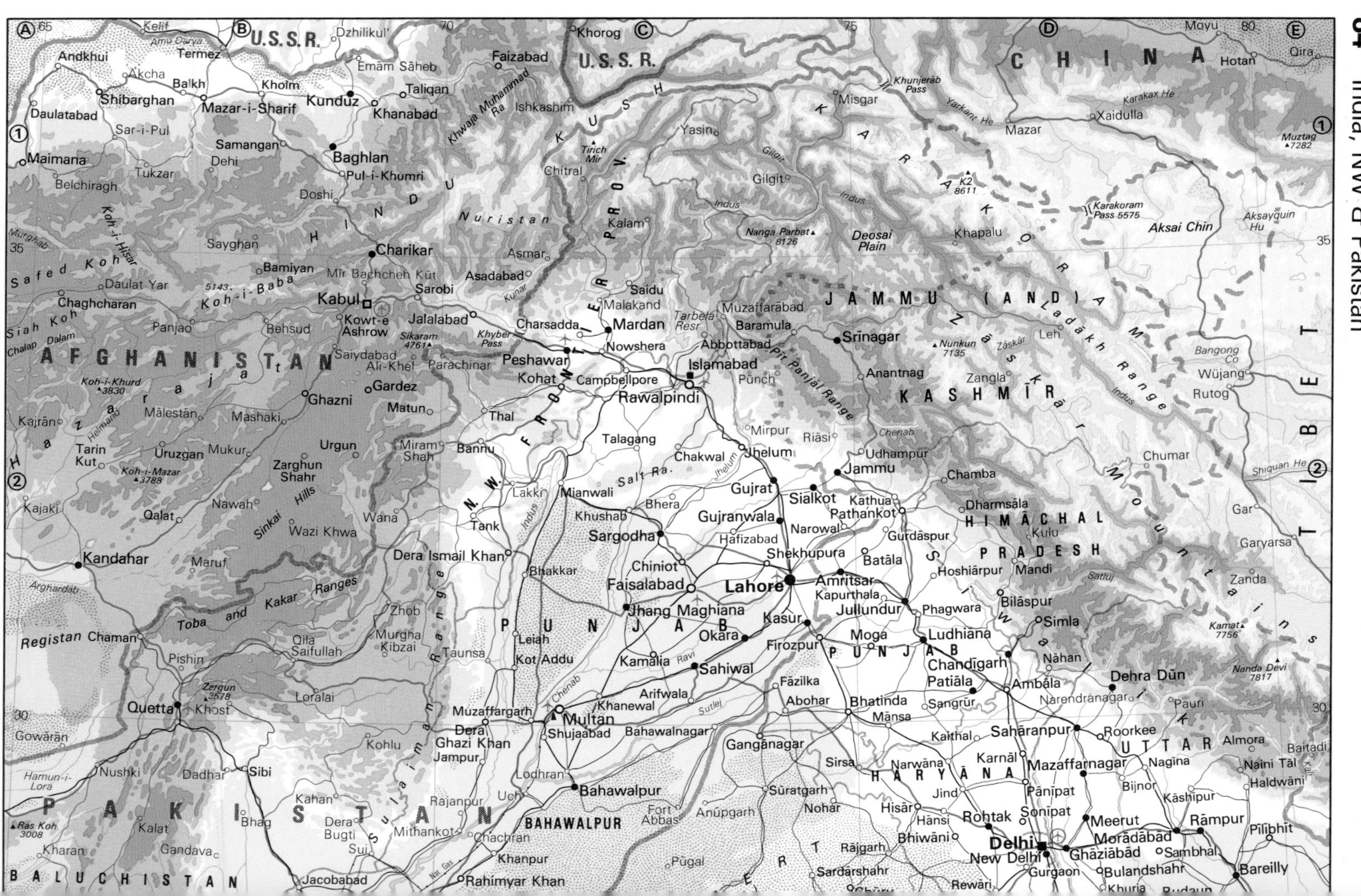
CHINA
U.S.S.R.
AFGHANISTAN
PAKISTAN
BALUCHISTAN
PUNJAB
JAMMU AND KASHMIR
HIMACHAL PRADESH
UTTAR
HARYANA
BAHAWALPUR
N.W. FRONTIER PROV.
HINDU KUSH
KARAKORAM
TIBET
Ladakh Range
Pir Panjal Range
Safed Koh
Koh-i-Baba
Toba and Kakar Ranges
Sulaiman Range
Siwalik
Salt Ra.
Registan
Aksai Chin
Deosai Plain
Nuristan
Kabul
Islamabad
Delhi
New Delhi
Lahore
Rawalpindi
Peshawar
Quetta
Kandahar
Multan
Faisalabad
Srinagar
Amritsar
Ludhiana
Chandigarh
Simla
Dehra Dun
Jammu
Sialkot
Gujranwala
Sargodha
Bahawalpur
Ghazni
Jalalabad
Mazar-i-Sharif
Kunduz
Termez
Hotan
Leh
Gilgit
K2 8611
Nanga Parbat 8126
Tirich Mir
Khyber Pass
Karakoram Pass 5575
Khunjerab Pass
Nanda Devi 7817
Indus
Chenab
Jhelum
Ravi
Sutlej
Helmand

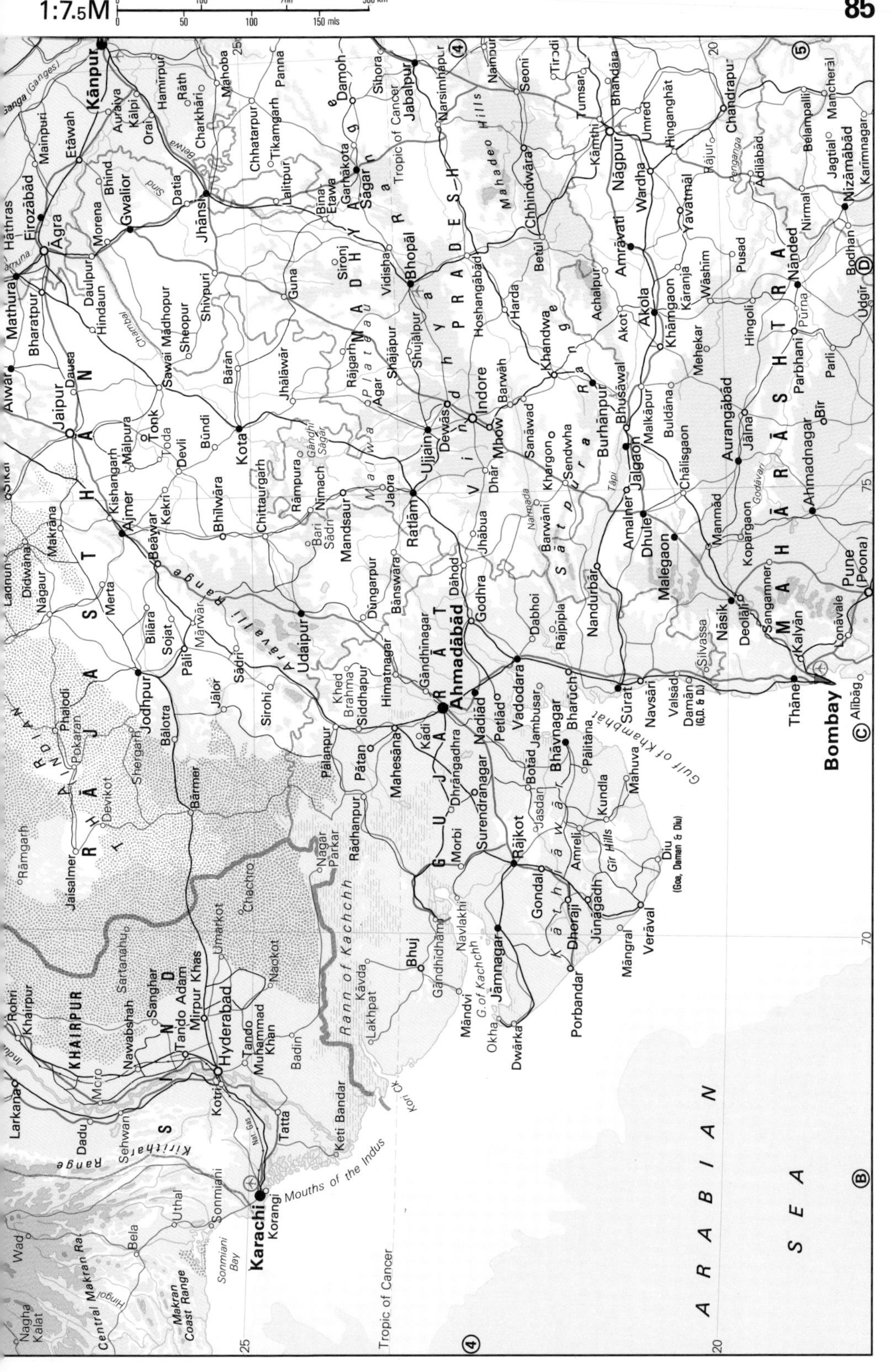
Kānpur
Ganga (Ganges)
Etāwah
Mainpuri
Firozābād
Hāthras
Āgra
Mathura
Bharatpur
Alwar
Jaipur
Dausa
Gwalior
Morena
Bhind
Datia
Jhānsi
Shivpuri
Guna
Sawai Mādhopur
Sheopur
Tonk
Kota
Būndi
Bārān
Jhālāwār
Ajmer
Kishangarh
Beāwar
Makrāna
Didwāna
Nāgaur
Merta
Jodhpur
Phalodi
Pokaran
Jaisalmer
Bārmer
Bālotra
Pāli
Sojat
Bilāra
Mārwār
Sirohi
Jālor
Udaipur
Chittaurgarh
Bhīlwāra
Aravalli Range
Mandsaur
Nimach
Rāmpura
Ratlām
Ujjain
Dewās
Indore
Mhow
Dhār
Jhābua
Dāhod
Godhra
Bānswāra
Dungarpur
Himatnagar
Gāndhinagar
Ahmadābād
Nadiād
Vadodara
Bharūch
Sūrat
Navsāri
Valsād
Damān (G.D. & D.)
Silvassa
Dabhoi
Rajpipla
Petlād
Bhāvnagar
Pālitāna
Mahuva
Amreli
Jūnāgadh
Verāval
Porbandar
Dwārka
Okha
Jāmnagar
Rājkot
Morbi
Surendranagar
Dhrāngadhra
Mahesāna
Pātan
Pālanpur
Rādhanpur
Bhuj
Māndvi
Gāndhīdhām
Kāvda
Lakhpat
Rann of Kachchh
G. of Kachchh
Gulf of Khambhat
Diu (Goa, Daman & Diu)
Gīr Hills
Bhopāl
Vidisha
Sāgar
Damoh
Jabalpur
Narsimhapur
Seoni
Chhindwāra
Betūl
Hoshangābād
Harda
Khandwa
Burhānpur
Bhusāwal
Jalgaon
Dhule
Malegaon
Nāsik
Deolāli
Kalyān
Thāne
Bombay
Pune (Poona)
Ahmadnagar
Aurangābād
Jālna
Akola
Amrāvati
Nāgpur
Wardha
Yavatmāl
Chandrapur
Nānded
Nizāmābād
Parbhani
Bīr
Arabian Sea
Karachi
Hyderabad
Mirpur Khas
Tando Adam
Nawabshah
Khairpur
Rohri
Larkana
Dadu
Sehwan
Kotri
Tatta
Keti Bandar
Badin
Umarkot
Chachro
Sonmiani
Sonmiani Bay
Bela
Uthal
Kirthar Range
Makran Coast Range
Mouths of the Indus
Tropic of Cancer
M A D H Y A P R A D E S H
R Ā J A S T H Ā N
G U J A R Ā T
M A H Ā R Ā S H T R A
S I N D
Vindhya Range
Sātpura Range
Mahadeo Hills
Mālwa Plateau

1:7.5M

0 100 200 300 km

0 50 100 150 mls

Thāna
Kalyān
Bombay
Lonāvale
Alībāg
Pune
(Poona)
MAHARASHTRA
Ahmadnajar
Parbhani
Pūrna
Nānded
Nirmal
Belampalli
Sironcha
Jagdalpur
Kotapad
Dantewāra
Bījāpur
Sukma
Bīr
Parli
Daund
Bodhan
Nizāmābād
Jagtial
Mancherāl
Udgīr
Lātūr
Karīmnagar
Mahād
Bārāmati
Wai
Shrīvardhan
Barsi
Mānjra
Siddipet
Warangal
Godāvari
Sabari
Phaltan
Bīdar
Koyna Resr
Sātāra
Solāpur
Homnābād
Sangāreddi
Yellandu
Bhadrāchalam
Chiplūn
Pandharpur
Akalkot
Gulbarga
Bhongir
Kottagūdem
Karād
Vite
Hyderābād
Ratnāgiri
Shāhābād
Tāndūr
Khammam
Rājahmundry
Sāngli
Miraj
Nalgonda
Suriāpet
Kākināda
Kolhāpur
Ichalkaranji
Bijāpur
Yādgīr
Mahbūbnagar
ANDHRA
Elūru
Yanam
Jamkhandi
Shorāpur
Nārāyanpet
Krishna
Vijayawāda
Māvalli
Mācherla
Guntūr
Bhīmavaram
Mālvan
Krishna
Rāichur
Wanparti
Tenāli
Machilīpatnam
Bāgalkot
Narasarāopet
Guledagudda
Nallamala Range
Chilakalūrupet
Vengurla
Belgaum
Tungabhadra
Kurnool
PRADESH
Bāpatla
Gajendragarh
Ādoni
Chīrāla
Panaji
Goa, Daman & Diu
KARNATAKA
Dhone
Nandyāl
Kani Giri
Ongole
Madgaon
Dandeli
Hubli
Gadag
Koppal
Hospet
Bellary
Guntakal
Giddalūr
Kondukūr
Kārwār
Gooty
15
Swāmihalli
Tādpatri
Proddatūr
Kavali
Hāveri
Sirsi
Kottūru
Rāyadurg
Rānībennur
Hirihar
Anantapur
Kumta
Dāvangere
Kalyandurg
Dhamavaram
Cuddapah
Penner
Nellore
Jog Falls
Chitradurga
Coast
Bhatkal
Kadiri
Gūdūr
Shimoga
Bhadrāvati
Venkatagiri
Tarikere
Sri Kālahasti
Coondapoor
Bhadra Resr
Sira
Hindupur
Pulicat L.
Kadūr
Tirupati
Arsikere
Tumkūr
Chik Ballāpur
Udupi
Kārkal
Chikmagalūr
Chittoor
Tiptūr
Dod Ballāpur
Kolār
Arakkonam
Hassan
Madras
Mangalore
Bangalore
Kolār Gold Fields
Vellore
Kānchipuram
Hole Narsipur
Āmbūr
Kāsaragod
Madikeri
Mandya
Krishnagiri
Javadi Hills
Tiruppattūr
Mysore
Tindivanam
Dharmapuri
Tiruvannāmalai
Nanjangūd
Cannanore
Tellicherry
Mahe
Chāmrājnagar
Stanley Resr
Villupuram
Pondicherry
Malabar
Mettūr
Salem
Cuddalore
Badagara
Doda Betta 2636
Calicut (Kozhikode)
Ootacamund
Coonoor
Erode
Vriddhāchalam
Beypore
Nilgiri Hills
TAMIL NĀDU
Chidambaram
Coimbatore
Tiruppur
Kumbakonam
Androth
Shoranūr
Pālghāt
Cauvery
Kāraikāl
Ponnāni
Tiruchchirāppalli
Thanjāvūr
Nāgappattinam
Pollāchi
Mannārgudi
Trichūr
Anaimalai Hills
Palani
Pudukkottai
Pt Calimera
Kalpeni
Dindigul
Kodikkarai
Bodināyakkanūr
Palk Strait
10
Cochin
Ernākulam
Vembanad L.
Madurai
Pt Pedro
Kambam
Virudunagar
Paramakkudi
Jaffna
Kottayam
Alleppey
Aruppukkottai
Rāmanāthapuram
Rājapālaiyam
Mullaittvu
Nine Degree Channel
Kāyankulam
Puliyangudi
Adam's Bridge
Talaimannar
Mannar
Tenkāsi
Quilon
Tuticorin
Vavuniya
Tirunelveli
Gulf of
Trincomalee
Palayankottai
Havankulam
Trivandrum
Tiruchchendūr
Anuradhapura
Minicoy
Nāgercoil
Mannār
Kanniyākumari
C.Comorin
Puttalam
Dambulla
Batticaloa
Eight Degree Channel
SRI LANKA
CEYLON
Chilaw
Matale
Kurunegala
Negombo
Kandy
Gampola
Colombo
Badulla
Adam's Pk 2243
Nuwara-Eliya
Dehiwala-Mt Lavinia
Ratnapura
Moratuwa
Opanake
MALDIVES
Ambalangoda
Galle
Hambantota
Matara
Dondra Hd
A
B
C
1
2
3
75
80

NORTH ATLANTIC OCEAN
UNITED KINGDOM
IRELAND
NORWAY
SWEDEN
FINLAND
DENMARK
NETH.
BELG.
LUX.
FRANCE
SPAIN
PORTUGAL
GERMANY EAST
GERMANY WEST
POLAND
CZECHOSLOVAKIA
AUSTRIA
SWITZ.
HUNGARY
ROMANIA
YUGOSLAVIA
BULGARIA
ALB.
GREECE
ITALY
U. S. S. R.
TURKEY
CYPRUS
SYRIA
LEB.
ISR.
JORDAN
IRAQ
IRAN
KUWAIT
BAHRAIN
QATAR
UNITED ARAB EMIRATES
OMAN
SAUDI ARABIA
YEMEN
SOUTH YEMEN
DJIBOUTI
AFGHANISTAN
PAK.
EGYPT
LIBYA
TUNISIA
ALGERIA
MOROCCO
MAURITANIA
MALI
NIGER
CHAD
SENEGAL
THE GAMBIA
GUINEA BISSAU
GUINEA
UPPER VOLTA
SAHARA
North Sea
Baltic Sea
Bay of Biscay
Mediterranean Sea
Adriatic Sea
Black Sea
Caspian Sea
Aral Sea
Red Sea
Gulf of Aden
The Gulf
Tropic of Cancer
Madeira (Port.)
Islas Canarias (Sp.)
Açores (Port.)
London
Paris
Madrid
Lisboa
Roma
Berlin
Warszawa
Moskva
Leningrad
Kiev
Praha
Wien
Budapest
Beograd
Sofiya
Bucureşti
Athinai
Istanbul
Ankara
Baghdād
Tehrān
Riyadh
Cairo
Alexandria
Tripoli
Tunis
Alger
Rabat
Casablanca
Dakar
Nouakchott
Khartoum
Niamey

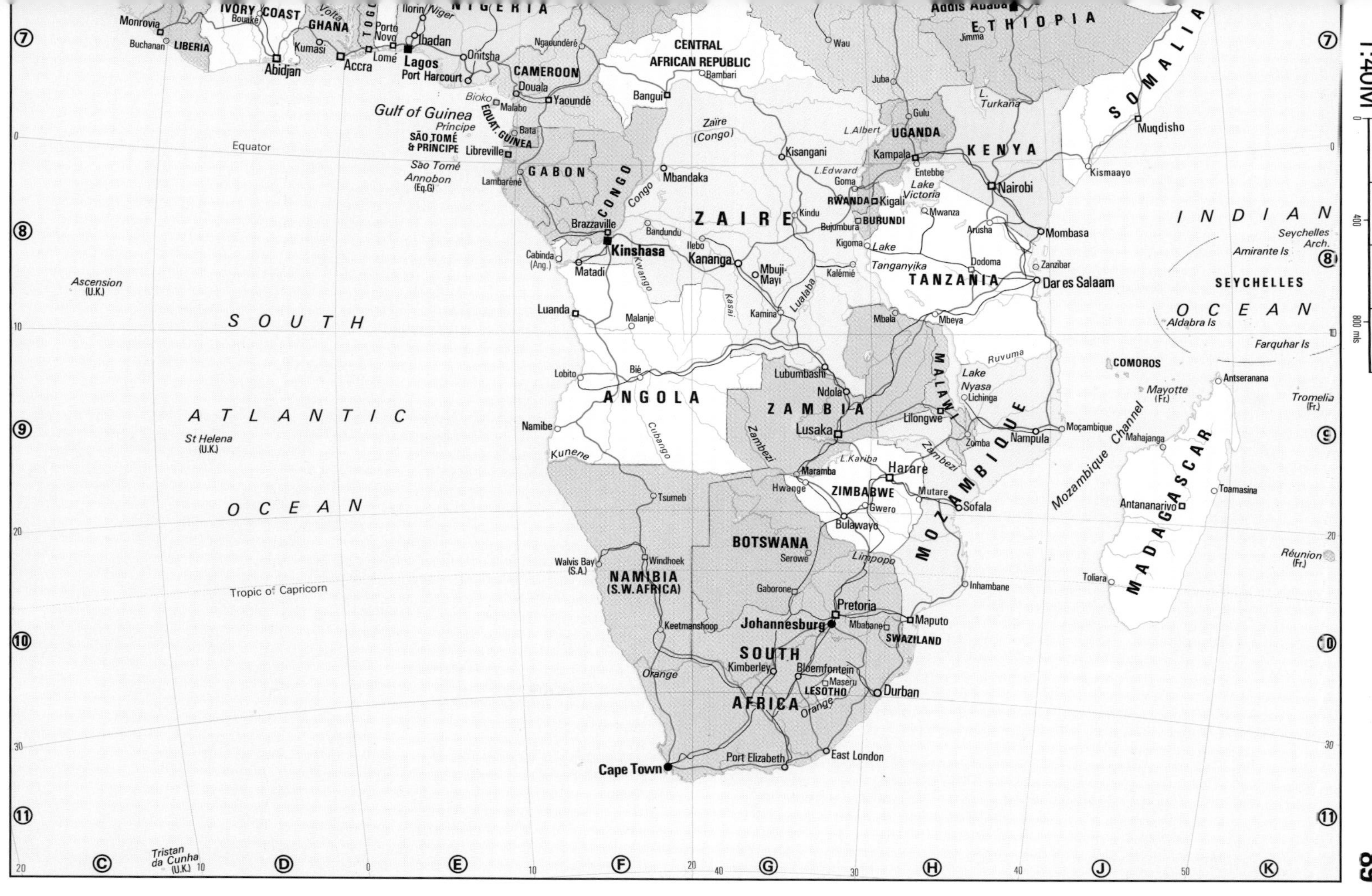
SOMALIA
Muqdisho
Kismaayo
ETHIOPIA
Jimma
KENYA
Nairobi
Mombasa
L. Turkana
UGANDA
Kampala
Entebbe
Gulu
Juba
Wau
Lake Victoria
Mwanza
Arusha
Dodoma
Zanzibar
Dar es Salaam
TANZANIA
Lake Tanganyika
Kigoma
Kigali
RWANDA
BURUNDI
Bujumbura
Goma
L.Edward
L.Albert
Kisangani
Kindu
Kalémié
Mbeya
Mbala
MALAWI
Lilongwe
Zomba
Lake Nyasa
Lichinga
Ruvuma
Nampula
Moçambique
MOZAMBIQUE
Sofala
Inhambane
Maputo
Mozambique Channel
COMOROS
Mayotte (Fr.)
Mahajanga
MADAGASCAR
Antananarivo
Toamasina
Toliara
Antseranana
Aldabra Is
Farquhar Is
SEYCHELLES
Amirante Is
Seychelles Arch.
Tromelin (Fr.)
Réunion (Fr.)
INDIAN OCEAN
ZAIRE
Zaïre (Congo)
Lualaba
Kasai
Mbuji-Mayi
Kamina
Kananga
Ilebo
Bandundu
Kinshasa
Kwango
Mbandaka
Congo
CONGO
Brazzaville
Matadi
Cabinda (Ang.)
GABON
Libreville
Lambaréné
EQUAT. GUINEA
Bata
Malabo
Bioko
CAMEROON
Douala
Yaoundé
Ngaoundéré
CENTRAL AFRICAN REPUBLIC
Bangui
Bambari
ZAMBIA
Lusaka
Ndola
Lubumbashi
Zambezi
L.Kariba
Harare
Mutare
ZIMBABWE
Gwero
Bulawayo
Hwange
Maramba
Limpopo
BOTSWANA
Serowe
Gaborone
ANGOLA
Luanda
Lobito
Malanje
Bié
Namibe
Cubango
Kunene
Tsumeb
NAMIBIA (S.W. AFRICA)
Windhoek
Walvis Bay (S.A.)
Keetmanshoop
Orange
SOUTH AFRICA
Pretoria
Johannesburg
Mbabane
SWAZILAND
Durban
Maseru
LESOTHO
Bloemfontein
Kimberley
East London
Port Elizabeth
Cape Town
NIGERIA
Ilorin
Niger
Ibadan
Lagos
Port Harcourt
Onitsha
TOGO
Porto Novo
Lomé
Accra
GHANA
Volta
Kumasi
IVORY COAST
Bouaké
Abidjan
LIBERIA
Monrovia
Buchanan
Gulf of Guinea
Principe
SÃO TOMÉ & PRINCIPE
São Tomé
Annobon (Eq.G)
Equator
SOUTH ATLANTIC OCEAN
St Helena (U.K.)
Ascension (U.K.)
Tristan da Cunha (U.K.)
Tropic of Capricorn

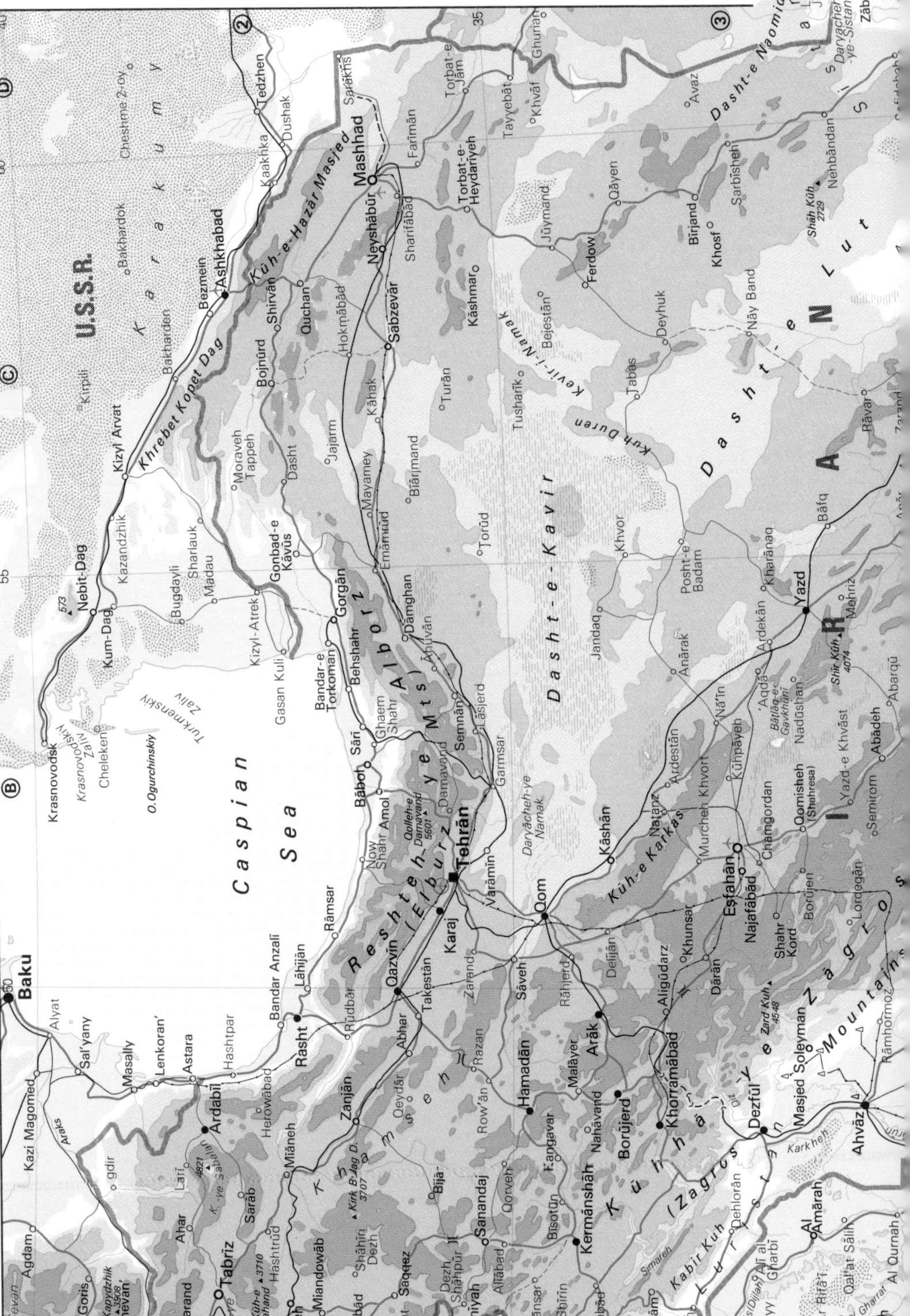

U.S.S.R.
Karakumy
Caspian Sea
Krasnovodskiy Zaliv
Turkmenskiy Zaliv
O. Ogurchinskiy
Khrebet Kopet Dag
Kūh-e-Hazār Masjed
Reshteh-ye Alborz (Elburz Mts)
Dasht-e-Kavīr
Dasht-e Lut
Dasht-e Naomid
Kavīr-i-Namak
Kuh Duren
Kūh-e Karkas
Kūhhā-ye Zāgros (Zagros Mountains)
Kabir Kuh
Luristan
IRAN
Qolleh-ye Damāvand 5601
Kūh-e Sahand 3710
K.-ye Sabalān 4821
Kapydzhik 3906
Kirk B. Jag D. 3707
Zard Kuh 4548
Shīr Kūh 4074
Shāh Kūh 2729
Daryācheh-ye Orūmīyeh
Daryācheh-ye Namak
Daryācheh-ye Sīstan
Bātlāq-e Gavkhūnī
Oz. Sevan
Araks
Tigris (Dijlah)
Karkheh
Diyala
Baku
Alyat
Sal'yany
Kazi Magomed
Masally
Lenkoran'
Astara
Krasnovodsk
Cheleken
Kum-Dag
Nebit-Dag
Kazandzhik
Kizyl Arvat
Bakharden
Bezmein
Ashkhabad
Kaakhka
Dushak
Tedzhen
Cheshme 2-oy
Bakhardok
Kirpili
Bugdayli
Sharlauk
Madau
Kizyl-Atrek
Gasan Kuli
Kamo
Agdam
Goris
Nakhichevan'
Julfa
Marand
Tabrīz
Ahar
Sarāb
Ardabīl
Lārī
Herowābād
Hashtpar
Bandar Anzalī
Rasht
Lāhījān
Rūdbār
Rāmsar
Now Shahr
Āmol
Bābol
Sārī
Ghaem Shahr
Behshahr
Bandar-e Torkoman
Gorgān
Gonbad-e Kāvūs
Moraveh Tappeh
Dasht
Bojnūrd
Shīrvān
Quchan
Hokmābād
Jajarm
Mayamey
Kāhak
Emāmrūd
Dāmghan
Āhuvān
Semnān
Lāsjerd
Garmsar
Damāvand
Tehrān
Karaj
Varāmīn
Qazvīn
Takestān
Abhar
Zanjān
Mīāneh
Hashtrūd
Marāgheh
Miandowāb
Shāhīn Dezh
Mahābād
Naqadeh
Sar Dasht
Saqqez
Bījār
Qeydār
Hamadān
Malāyer
Arāk
Sāveh
Zarand
Razan
Row'ān
Qom
Kāshān
Natanz
Dellījān
Rāhjerd
Khonsar
Alīgūdarz
Borūjerd
Nahāvand
Kangāvar
Khorramābād
Sanandaj
Qorveh
Kermānshāh
Bīsotūn
Dezh Shāhpūr
Sulaymānīyah
Halabja
Ravānsar
Qasr-e Shīrīn
Shāhābād
Eslāmābād
Ilām
Mehrān
Dehlorān
Dezfūl
Masjed Soleymān
Rāmhormoz
Ahvāz
Abādān
Eşfahān
Najafābād
Shahr Kord
Borūjen
Lordegān
Semirom
Qomisheh (Shahresa)
Chamgordān
Murcheh Khvort
Ardestān
Kūhpāyeh
Nā'īn
Nadūshan
'Aqdā
Anārak
Jandaq
Ardekān
Yazd
Mehrīz
Abarqū
Abādeh
Yazd-e Khvāst
Kharānaq
Posht-e Badam
Bāfq
Khvor
Tabas
Rāvar
Zarand
Deyhuk
Nāy Band
Bejestān
Tusharīk
Ferdow
Jūymand
Qāyen
Bīrjand
Khosf
Sarbīsheh
Nehbandan
Avaz
Khvāf
Tayyebāt
Torbat-e Jām
Torbat-e Heydarīyeh
Farīmān
Mashhad
Neyshābūr
Sharīfābād
Sabzevār
Kāshmar
Bīārjmand
Torūd
Turān
Sarakhs
Ghurian
Lash-e Joveyn
Zābol
Zaranj
Al Kūt
Al Hayy
'Alī al Gharbī
Al 'Amārah
Qal'at Sālih
Ar Rifā'ī
Ash Shatrah
An Nāsirīyah
Al Qurnah
Sūq
S. al Gharraf
Simareh
40
50
55
60
35
B
C
D
2
3

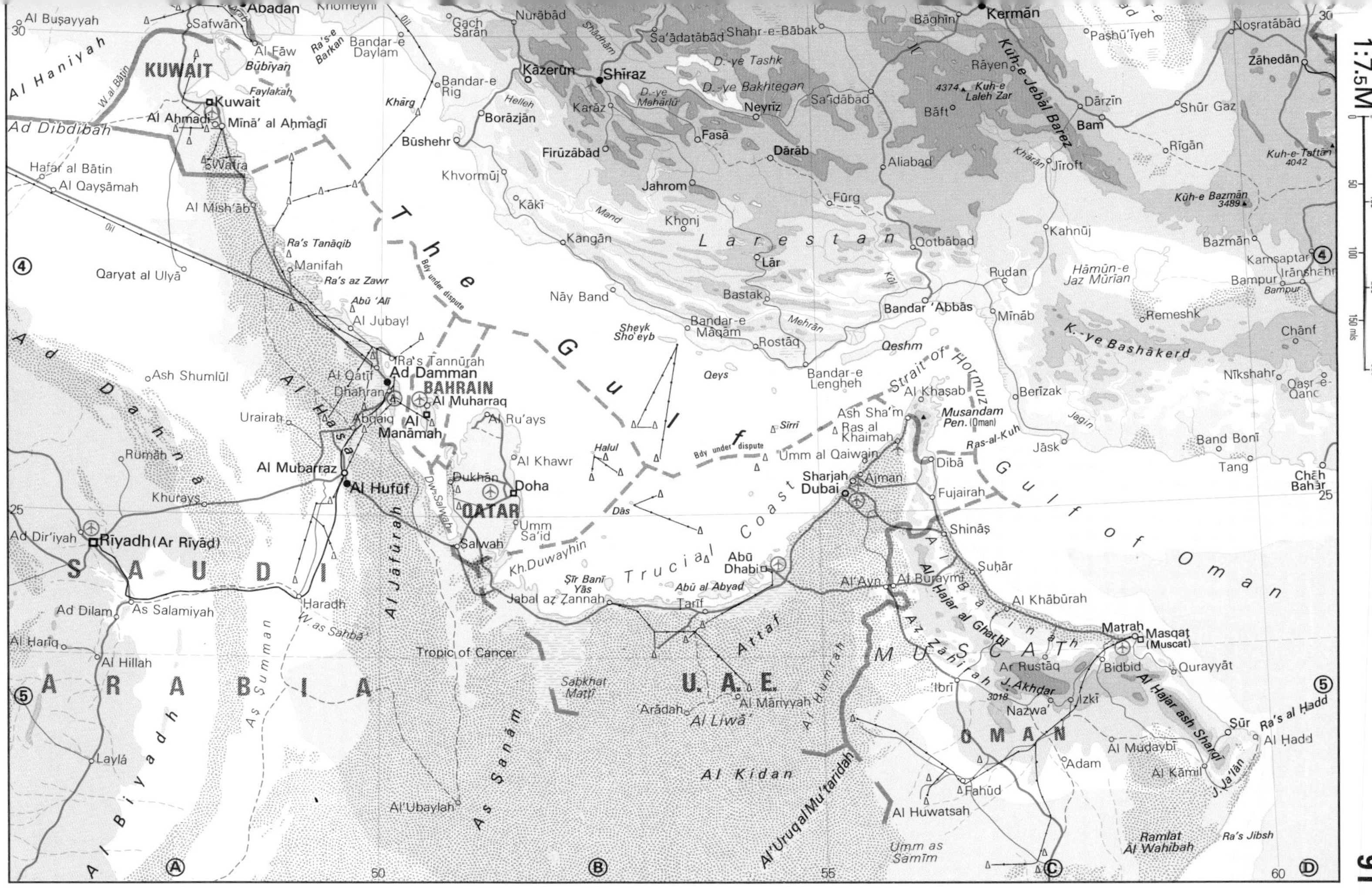
The Gulf
Gulf of Oman
Strait of Hormuz
Trucial Coast
Bdy under dispute
KUWAIT
Kuwait
BAHRAIN
QATAR
Doha
U.A.E.
OMAN
MUSCAT
SAUDI ARABIA
Riyadh (Ar Riyāḍ)
Larestan
Kermān
Shīraz
Bandar 'Abbās
Abū Dhabi
Dubai
Sharjah
Ajman
Umm al Qaiwain
Ras al Khaimah
Fujairah
Masqat (Muscat)
Maṭraḥ
Ṣūr
Ra's al Ḥadd
Al Ḥadd
Al Hajar ash Sharqī
Al Hajar al Gharbī
J. Akhḍar 3018
Al Bāṭinah
Aẓ Ẓāhirah
Musandam Pen. (Oman)
Ras-al-Kuh
Qeshm
Qeys
Sheyk Sho'eyb
Sīrrī
Halul
Dās
Ṣīr Banī Yās
Al Jāfūrah
Al Ḥasā
Ad Dahnā
Ad Dibdibah
Al Haniyah
W. al Bāṭin
As Summan
As Sanām
Al Biyāḍh
Al Kidan
Al Liwā'
'Arādah
Al Māriyyah
Al Humrah
'Attaf
Sabkhat Maṭṭī
Ramlat Al Wahibah
Ra's Jibsh
J. Ja'lān
Tropic of Cancer
Al 'Uruq al Mu'taridah
Umm as Samīm
Al Huwatsah
Fahūd
Adam
Al Muḍaybī
Al Kāmil
Nazwa
Izkī
Ar Rustāq
Ibrī
Bidbid
Qurayyāt
Al Khābūrah
Ṣuḥār
Shināṣ
Al Buraymī
Al 'Ayn
Dibā
Al Khaṣab
Ash Sha'm
Jask
Jagin
Band Bonī
Tang
Chāh Bahār
Nīkshahr
Qaṣr-e-Qand
Chānf
Remeshk
K.-ye Bashākerd
Hāmūn-e Jaz Mūrian
Bampur
Īrānshahr
Kamsaptar
Bazmān
Kūh-e Bazmān 3489
Kūh-e Taftān 4042
Zāhedān
Nosratābād
Shūr Gaz
Rīgān
Bam
Dārzīn
Jīroft
Khārān
Kahnūj
Rudan
Mīnāb
Berīzak
Pashū'īyeh
Kūh-e Jebāl Barez
Kūh-e Laleh Zar 4374
Rāyen
Bāft
Bāghīn
Aliabad
Ṣa'īdābād
Qotbābād
Fūrg
Dārāb
Neyrīz
Fasā
Jahrom
Khonj
Lār
Kūl
Bastak
Mehrān
Bandar-e Maqām
Rostāq
Bandar-e Lengheh
Nāy Band
Kangān
Mand
Kākī
Khvormūj
Fīrūzābād
Karāz
D.-ye Maharlū
D.-ye Bakhtegan
D.-ye Tashk
Sa'ādatābād
Shahr-e-Bābak
Shādhām
Helleh
Kāzerūn
Nūrābād
Gach Sārān
Borāzjān
Būshehr
Bandar-e Rig
Bandar-e Daylam
Ra's-e Barkan
Khārg
Khomeynī
Abadan
Oil
Al Fāw
Safwān
Būbīyan
Faylakah
Al Aḥmadī
Mīnā' al Aḥmadī
Wafra
Al Buṣayyah
Hafar al Bāṭin
Al Qayṣāmah
Al Mish'āb
Ra's Tanāqib
Manifah
Ra's az Zawr
Abū 'Alī
Al Jubayl
Ra's Tannūrah
Ad Damman
Al Qaṭīf
Dhahran
Al Muharraq
Al Manāmah
Abqaiq
Al Ru'ays
Al Khawr
Dukhān
Dw. Salwah
Umm Sa'īd
Salwah
Kh. Duwayhin
Jabal az Zannah
Abū al Abyaḍ
Ṭarīf
Al Mubarraz
Al Hufūf
Urairah
Ash Shumlūl
Qaryat al Ulyā
Rumāh
Khurays
Ad Dir'īyah
Haraḍh
W. as Sahbā'
Al 'Ubaylah
Ad Dilam
As Salamiyah
Al Hariq
Al Hillah
Laylá
30 25 50 55 60
A B C D
4 5

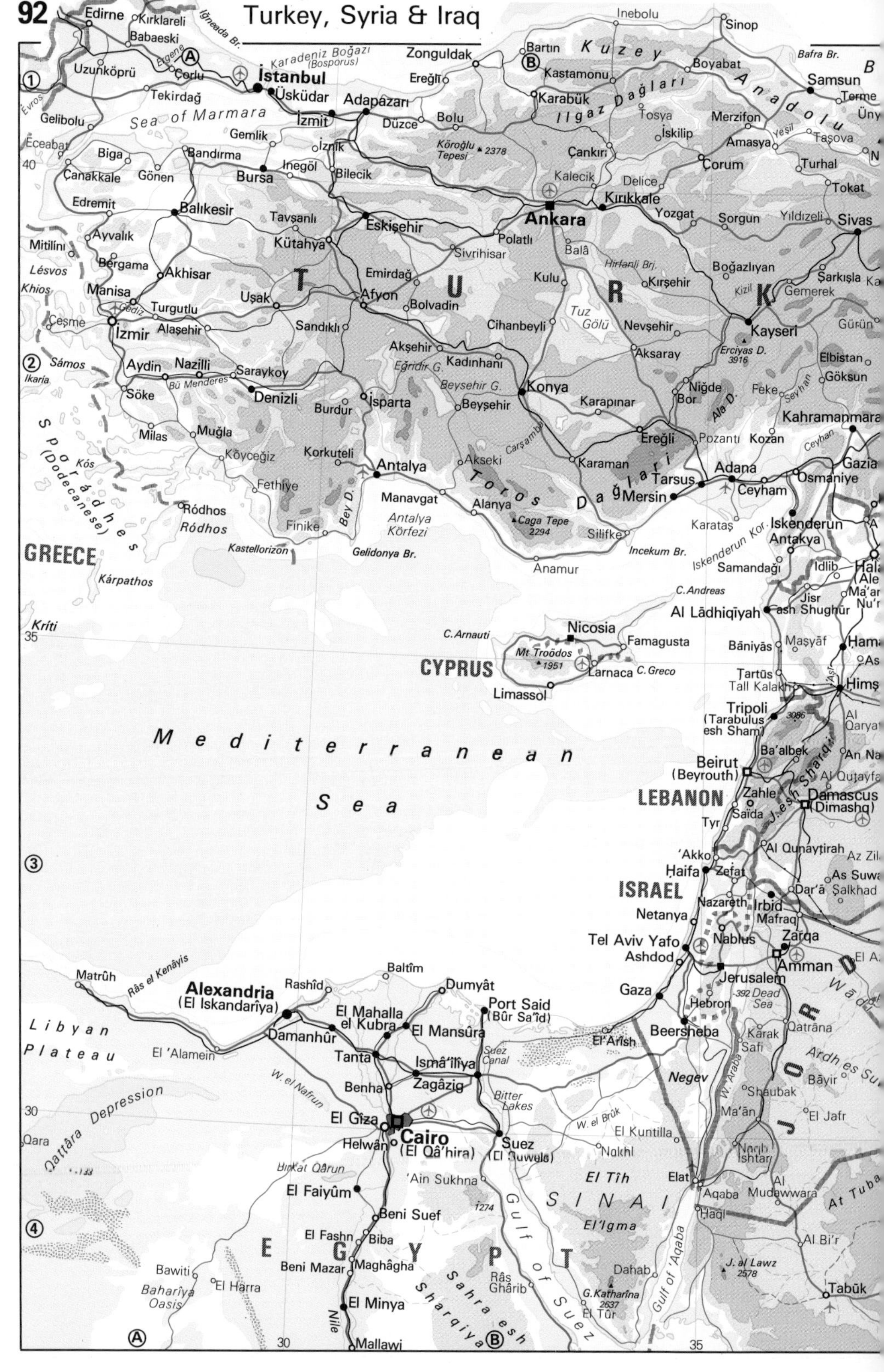
Edirne
Kırklareli
Babaeski
İğneada Br.
Ergene
Uzunköprü
Çorlu
Karadeniz Boğazı (Bosporus)
İstanbul
Üsküdar
Tekirdağ
Evros
Gelibolu
Sea of Marmara
İzmit
Adapazarı
Zonguldak
Ereğli
Düzce
Bolu
Bartın
Kuzey Anadolu
Inebolu
Sinop
Kastamonu
Karabük
Ilgaz Dağları
Boyabat
Tosya
Bafra Br.
Samsun
Terme
Ünye
Merzifon
Amasya
Yeşil
Taşova
İskilip
Çorum
Turhal
Tokat
Eceabat
Gemlik
İznik
Biga
Bandırma
Çanakkale
Gönen
Bursa
İnegöl
Bilecik
Köroğlu Tepesi 2378
Çankırı
Kalecik
Delice
Kırıkkale
Yozgat
Sorgun
Yıldızeli
Sivas
Edremit
Balıkesir
Tavşanlı
Eskişehir
Ankara
Polatlı
Balâ
Mitilíni
Ayvalık
Kütahya
Sivrihisar
Hirfanli Brj.
Kırşehir
Boğazlıyan
Şarkışla
Lésvos
Bergama
Akhisar
Emirdağ
Kulu
Kizil
Gemerek
Khíos
Manisa
T U R K
Uşak
Afyon
Bolvadin
Tuz Gölü
Nevşehir
Kayseri
Gürün
Turgutlu
Gediz
Çeşme
İzmir
Alaşehir
Sandıklı
Cihanbeyli
Aksaray
Erciyas D. 3916
Elbistan
Sámos
Ikaria
Aydin
Nazilli
Saraykoy
Akşehir
Kadınhanı
Eğridir G.
Beyşehir G.
Göksun
Bü Menderes
Söke
Denizli
Isparta
Burdur
Beyşehir
Konya
Karapınar
Niğde
Bor
Ala D.
Feke
Seyhan
Kahramanmaraş
Milas
Muğla
Çarşamba
Ereğli
Pozantı
Kozan
Ceyhan
Kós
Sporádhes (Dodecanese)
Köyceğiz
Korkuteli
Antalya
Akseki
Karaman
Tarsus
Adana
Osmaniye
Gaziantep
Fethiye
Toros Dağları
Mersin
Ceyham
Ródhos
Manavgat
Alanya
Bey D.
Antalya Körfezi
Caga Tepe 2294
Silifke
Karataş
Iskenderun
Antakya
Finike
Kastellorizon
Gelidonya Br.
Incekum Br.
Iskenderun Kor.
Samandağı
Idlib
GREECE
Kárpathos
Anamur
C. Andreas
Jisr esh Shughur
Al Lādhiqīyah
Kríti
C. Arnauti
Nicosia
Famagusta
Bāniyās
Maṣyāf
Ḥamā
Mt Troödos 1951
CYPRUS
Larnaca
C. Greco
Ṭarṭūs
Tall Kalakh
Ḥimṣ
Limassol
Tripoli (Tarabulus esh Sham)
3086
Mediterranean Sea
Ba'albek
Beirut (Beyrouth)
Zahle
Damascus (Dimashq)
LEBANON
Saida
J. esh Sharqi
Tyr
Al Qunayṭirah
'Akko
Ḥaifa
Zefat
As Suwayda
ISRAEL
Dar'ā
Şalkhad
Nazareth
Irbid
Netanya
Mafraq
Tel Aviv Yafo
Nablus
Zarqa
Ashdod
Amman
Jerusalem
Gaza
Matrûh
Râs el Kenâyis
Baltîm
Alexandria (El Iskandarîya)
Rashîd
Dumyât
Port Said (Bûr Sa'îd)
-392 Dead Sea
Hebron
El Mahalla el Kubra
El Mansûra
Beersheba
Qatrāna
Libyan Plateau
El 'Alamein
Damanhûr
El 'Arish
Karak
Ṣafi
Tanta
Ismâ'ilîya
Suez Canal
Negev
W. Araba
Ardh es Suwwan
Benha
Zagâzig
Bāyir
W. el Natrun
Shaubak
Qattâra Depression
Bitter Lakes
W. el Brûk
Ma'ān
El Jafr
El Gîza
Cairo (El Qâ'hira)
Suez (El Suweis)
El Kuntilla
JORDAN
Qara
Helwân
Nakhl
Naqb Ishtar
Birkat Qârûn
'Ain Sukhna
El Tîh
Elat
Al Mudawwara
El Faiyûm
1274
SINAI
Aqaba
Haql
At Tubayq
Beni Suef
Gulf of Suez
El'Igma
El Fashn
Biba
EGYPT
Al Bi'r
Bawiti
Beni Mazar
Maghâgha
Râs Ghârib
Dahab
J. al Lawz 2578
Baharîya Oasis
El Harra
Sahra esh Sharqîya
Gulf of 'Aqaba
G. Katharîna 2637
Tabūk
El Minya
El Tûr
Nile
Mallawi

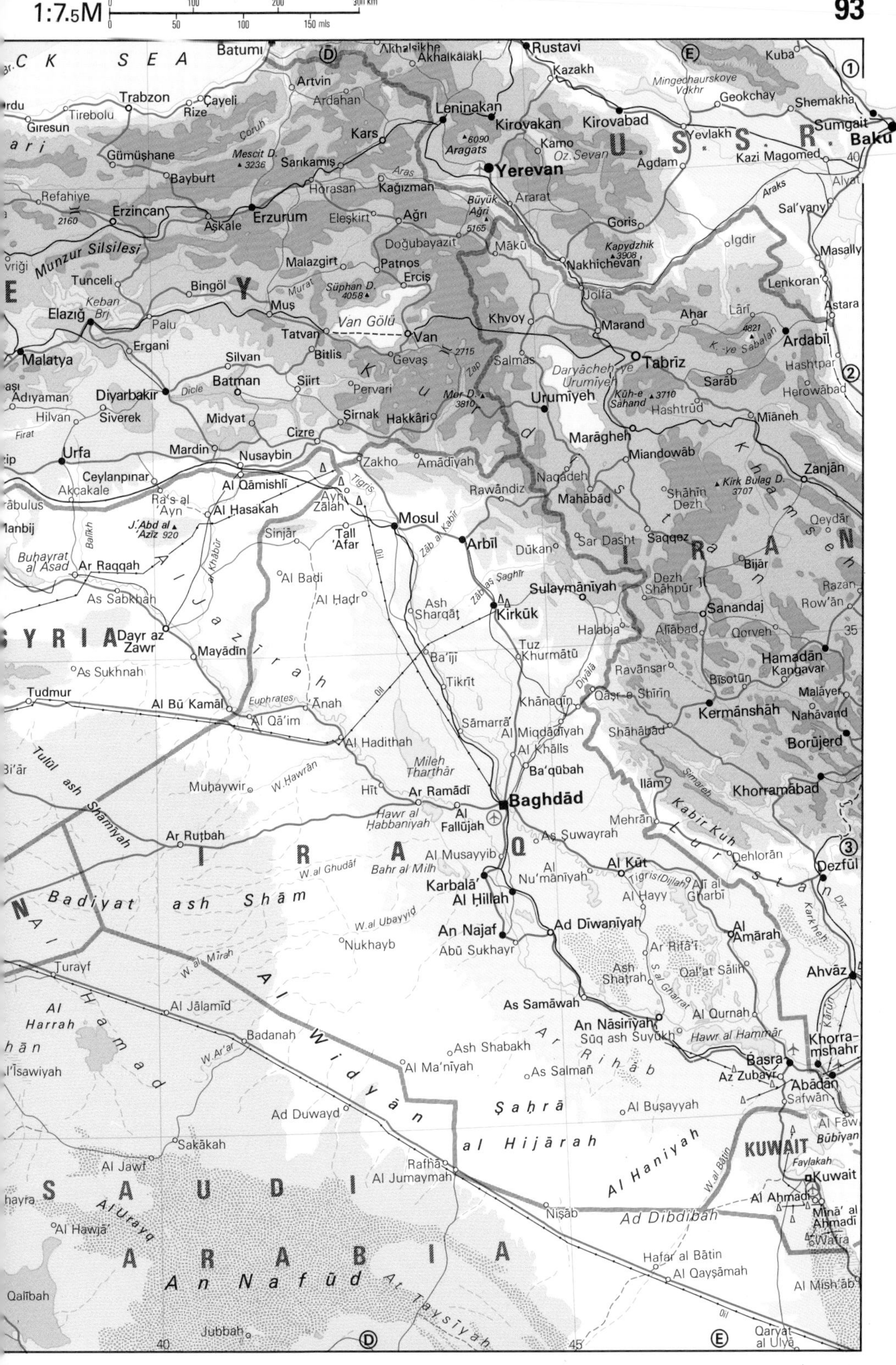

Batumi
D
E
1
2
3
Akhalsikhe
Akhalkalaki
Rustavi
Kuba
Kazakh
Mingechaurskoye Vdkhr
Artvin
Ardahan
Trabzon
Çayeli
Rize
Tirebolu
Giresun
Leninakan
Kirovakan
Kirovabad
Geokchay
Shemakha
Sumgait
Baku
Kars
6090 Aragats
Kamo
Oz. Sevan
Yevlakh
Agdam
Kazi Magomed
Gümüşhane
Mescit D. 3236
Sarıkamış
Yerevan
Coruh
Bayburt
Horasan
Aras
Kağızman
Ararat
Alyat
Araks
Sal'yany
Refahiye
2160
Erzincan
Aşkale
Erzurum
Eleşkirt
Ağrı
Büyük Ağrı 5165
Goris
Doğubayazit
Mākū
Igdir
Kapydzhik 3908
Masally
Munzur Silsilesi
Malazgirt
Patnos
Nakhichevan
Tunceli
Bingöl
Murat
Süphan D. 4058
Erciş
Jolfa
Lenkoran'
Astara
Keban Brj
Elazığ
Muş
Khvoy
Ahar
Lārī
Palu
Van Gölü
Marand
4821
Tatvan
Van
Ardabīl
Malatya
Ergani
Silvan
Bitlis
Geyaş
2715
Salmās
Tabrīz
K.-ye Sabalan
Hashtpar
Batman
Siirt
Zap
Daryācheh-ye Urumīyeh
Sarāb
Adıyaman
Diyarbakır
Dicle
Pervari
Mor D. 3810
Urumīyeh
Kūh-e Sahand 3710
Herowābad
Hilvan
Siverek
Midyat
Şirnak
Hakkâri
Hashtrūd
Mīāneh
Firat
Cizre
Marāgheh
Urfa
Mardin
Nusaybin
Miandowāb
Zanjān
Zakho
Amādīyah
Ceylanpınar
Al Qāmishlī
Naqadeh
Kirk Bulag D. 3707
Akçakale
Ra's al 'Ayn
Tigris
Rawāndiz
Mahābād
Shāhīn Dezh
Al Ḩasakah
Ayn Zālah
Mosul
Qeydār
J. Abd al 'Azīz 920
Balīkh
Sinjār
Tall 'Afar
Zāb al Kabīr
Arbīl
Dūkān
Sar Dasht
Saqqez
Buḩayrat al Asad
Ar Raqqah
al Khābūr
Oil
Al Badi
Bījār
Dezh Shāhpūr
Zāb aş Şaghīr
Sulaymānīyah
Razan
As Sabkhah
Al Ḩadr
Ash Sharqāţ
Kirkūk
Sanandaj
Row'ān
SYRIA
Dayr az Zawr
Al Jazīrah
Halabja
Alīābād
Qorveh
35
Mayādīn
Tuz Khurmātū
Ba'ījī
Hamadān
Kangavar
As Sukhnah
Ravānsar
Tikrīt
Diyālā
Bīsotūn
Tudmur
Al Bū Kamāl
Euphrates
'Ānah
Khānaqīn
Qaşr-e Shīrīn
Malāyer
Kermānshāh
Nahāvand
Al Qā'im
Sāmarrā'
Al Miqdādīyah
Shāhābād
Borūjerd
Al Hadithah
Al Khāliş
Bi'ār
Tulūl ash Shāmīyah
Mileh Tharthār
Ba'qūbah
Muḩaywir
W. Ḩawrān
Hīt
Ar Ramādī
Baghdād
Ilām
Simareh
Khorramābād
Hawr al Ḩabbānīyah
Al Fallūjah
Kabīr Kūh
Mehrān
Ar Ruţbah
IRAQ
As Şuwayrah
Luristan
Al Musayyib
Dehlorān
W. al Ghudāf
Bahr al Milh
Al Nu'mānīyah
Al Kūt
Dezfūl
Karbalā'
Tigris (Dijlah)
Alī al Gharbī
Badiyat ash Shām
Al Ḩillah
Al Ḩayy
Karkheh
W. al Ubayyiḑ
An Najaf
Ad Dīwānīyah
Al 'Amārah
Nukhayb
Abū Sukhayr
Ar Rifā'ī
Ahvāz
Turayf
W. al Mirah
Ash Shaţrah
S. al Gharraf
Qal'at Sālih
Al Ḩamad
Al Ḩarrah
Al Jalāmīd
As Samāwah
Al Qurnah
Kārūn
An Nāsirīyah
Sūq ash Suyūkh
Hawr al Hammār
Badanah
Ash Shabakh
Ar Rihāb
Khorramshahr
W. Ar'ar
Al Widyān
Basra
Al Ma'nīyah
As Salmān
Az Zubayr
Abādān
Safwān
Ad Duwayd
Şaḩrā al Ḩijārah
Al Buşayyah
Al Fāw
Būbiyān
Sakākah
KUWAIT
Faylakah
Rafḩā
Al Hanīyah
W. al Bāţin
Al Jawf
Al Jumaymah
Kuwait
SAUDI ARABIA
Al Ahmadī
Al 'Urayq
Nişāb
Ad Dibdibah
Mīnā' al Aḩmadī
Al Hawjā'
Wafra
Ḩafar al Bāţin
Al Qayşūmah
An Nafūd
At Taysīyah
Al Mish'āb
Qalībah
Oil
Jubbah
40
45
Qaryat al Ulyā

1:2.5M

0 25 50 75 100 km
0 25 50 mls

CYPRUS
Larnaca
Larnaca Bay
Paleokhorio
Lefkara
Zyyi
C.Kiti
C.Greco
Limassol
Akrotiri Bay
C.Gata

MEDITERRANEAN SEA

LEBANON
Tarțūs
Arwad
Duraykīsh
Kafrūn Bashūr
Şāfītā
Qal'at al Hişn (KRAK DES CHEVALIERS)
Ḥamīdīyah
Tall Kalakh
Kleiat
Qoubayat
Al Quşayr
Halba
El Mīna
Tripoli (Tarābulus esh Sham)
Zghorta
El Hermel
Qornet es Saouda 3086
Batroun
Amioune
Bcharre
Laboue
Deir el Ahmar
Jubail BYBLOS
Kartaba
Rhazīr
Ba'albek
Jounié
Baie de St Georges
Bikfaya 2628
Beirut (Beyrouth)
Ba'abda
Zahle
Rayak
Aley
Damour
Beit ed Dine
Saïda (Sidon)
Jezzine
Machgharab
Rachaya
Hāsbaiya
Marjayoun
Tyr (Tyre, Sour)
Enn Nâqoûra
Jebel Liban
Jebel esh Sharqi (Anti Lebanon)
El Beqa'a
Lītāni

SYRIA
Damascus (Dimashq)
Yabrūd
An Nabk
Az Zabdānī
Qutayfah
'Ayn al Fījah
At Tall
Dūmā
Qatanā
J. ash Shaykh (Mt Hermon)
Al Kiswah
Dayr 'Alī
Bāniyās
Mas'adah
CEASE FIRE LINES 1974
Al Qunayţirah
Aş Şanamayn
Khushnīyah
Nawā
Izra'
Shaykh Miskīn
Dar'a
As Suwaydā'
Al Lajāh 863
Ghabāghib
Mismīyah
Khabab
Busrá ash Shām

ISRAEL
Q. Shemona
Jouai'ya
Bennt Jbail
Yesud Hama'ala
1208 Har Meron
Nahariya
'Akko (Acre)
Ma'alot Tarshīhā
Zefat (Safad)
Rama
L. Tiberias (Yam Kinneret) (Sea of Galilee)
B. of Haifa
Q. Yam
Haifa (Hefa)
Shefar'am
Q. Ata
Tiberias
Tasīl
Fīq
'Atlit
528 Mt Carmel
Nazareth
Afula
Ma'agan
Zikhron Ya'aqov
MEGIDDO ARMAGEDDON
CAESAREA
Pardes Hanna
Hadera
Jenin
Beyt Shean
Qabatiya
Netanya
Tulkarm
Tubas
Plain of Sharon
ARMISTICE LINE
Sabastiya
Nablus
Herzliyya
Kefar Sava
Yargon
Bat Yam
Petah Tiqwa
Ramat Gan
Tel Aviv
Yafo (Jaffa)
Holon
Sarida
Ba'al Hazor 1016
Rishon le Zion
Lod
Ramallah
Rehovot
Ramla
Jericho (Arīḥā)
Latrun
Ashdod
Jerusalem (El Quds) (Yerushalayim)
Beit Jala
Bethlehem (Bayt Lahm)
Ashqelon
Qiryat Gat
Bet Guvrin
LACHISH
Gaza
Gaza Strip
Sederot
Hebron (El Khalil)
Dura
En Gedi
Yatta
Edh Dhahiriya
Khan Yunis
Rafah
Besor
Gerar
MEZADA
Beersheba (Be'er Sheva)
Ofaqim
Nevatim
'Arad
Zeelim
Be'er Sheva
HALUZA
Sedom
Dimona
MAMSHIT
Revivim
Yeroham
Queziot
SHIVTA
Oron
Sede Boqer
NIZANA
AVEDAT
Zin
Hazeva
Negev
El Quseima
Mizpe Ramon
Neqarot
Ein Yahav
1305 Har Ramon
Har Saggi 1006
Har Hakippa 467
Dead Sea (Bahrat Lut)

JORDAN
Irbid
Ramtha
Mafraq
Sabhā
Deir Abu Sa'id
Husn
Ajlūn
J. Umm ed Daraj 1247
Jarash
Es Samrā
Zarqa
Er Rummān
Suweilih
Salt
Karama
Marka
Amman
Wadi es Sir
Sahāb
Naur
Jiza
Mādabā
Qasr el Kharana
963 Jebel Mudeisisat
Dab'a
Dhībān
Khan ez Zabīb
Mazra
Rabba
El Lisān
Qatrāna
Karak
1253 T. el Mulse
Mazār
1305
J. Ed Dabāb
Safi
El Ghor
Manzil
Tafila
Ḥāsā
1356 J. Qasred Deir
Rashādīya
Danā
1641 J. el Atā'ita
Jurf ed Darāwīsh
W. Fidan
Shaubak
Nijil
1615 Jum Suwwāna
Uneisa
1082
GILEAD
MOAB
EDOM
CEASE FIRE LINE
Jordan
Yarmūk
Zarqa
Heidan
W. Mujib
W. el Hāsā
W. el Jeib
Qā'el Hafīra
Qa'el Jinz
W. el Janab

EGYPT
Râs Burûn
Sabkhet el Bardawîl
El 'Arîsh
Bîr Lahfân
W. Hareidin
W. el 'Arîsh
Abu 'Aweigila
G. Libni 463
G. Maghâra 735
892 G. Halâl
Bîr Hasana
Bîr Gifgâfa

34
32
36
A B C
1 2 3

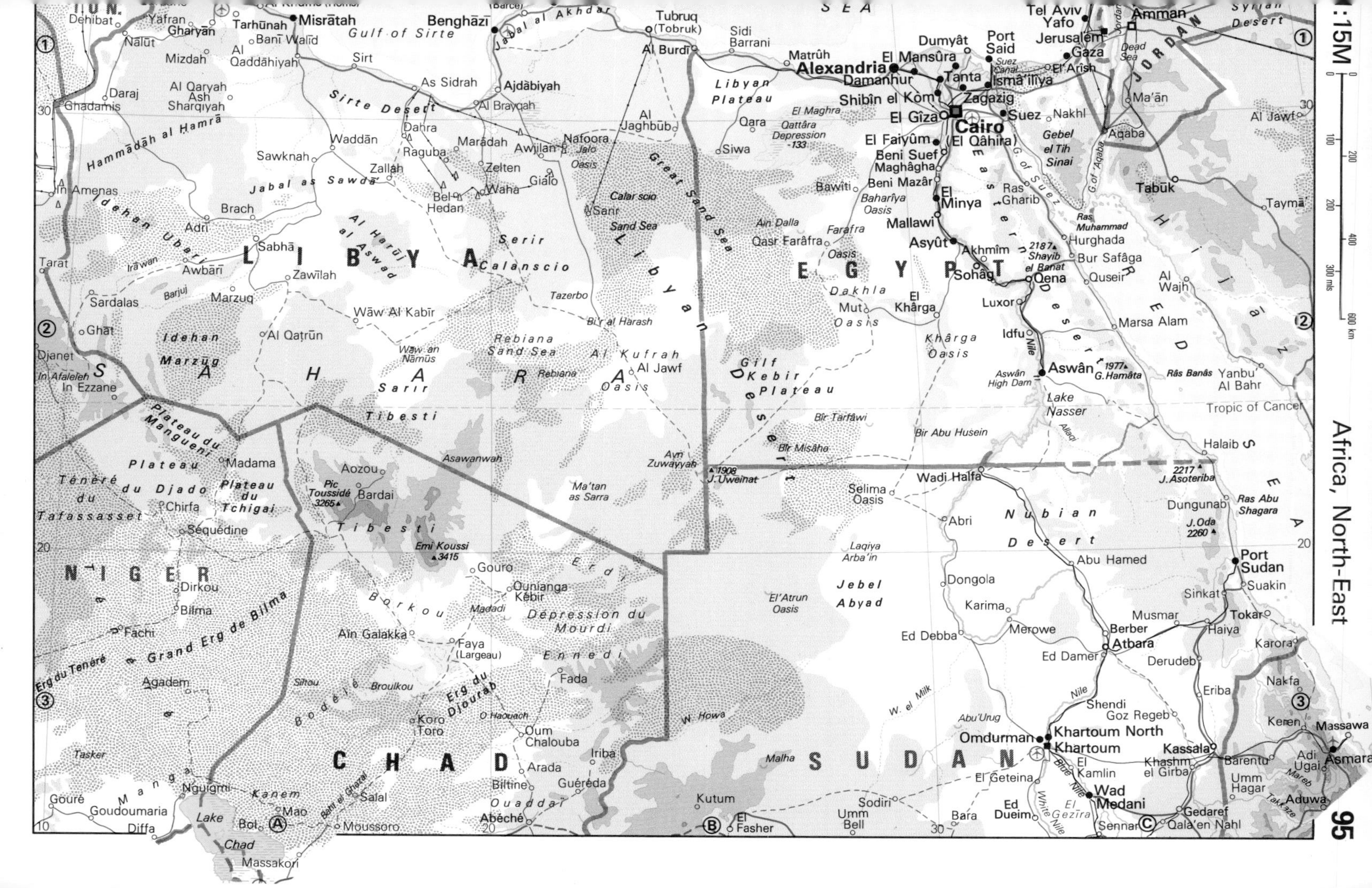
Alexandria
Cairo (El Qâhira)
Port Said
Suez
Aswân
Luxor
Wadi Halfa
Khartoum
Khartoum North
Omdurman
Port Sudan
Benghāzī
Misrātah
Tubruq (Tobruk)
Tabūk
Amman
Jerusalem
Gaza
Asmara
Massawa
Kassala
Wad Medani
El Fasher
Abéché
Faya (Largeau)
Sabhā
Ghadamis
Lake Nasser
Lake Chad
Tropic of Cancer
Great Sand Sea
Gulf of Sirte
Libyan Desert
Nubian Desert
Tibesti
Emi Koussi 3415
Pic Toussidé 3265
LIBYA
EGYPT
SUDAN
CHAD
NIGER

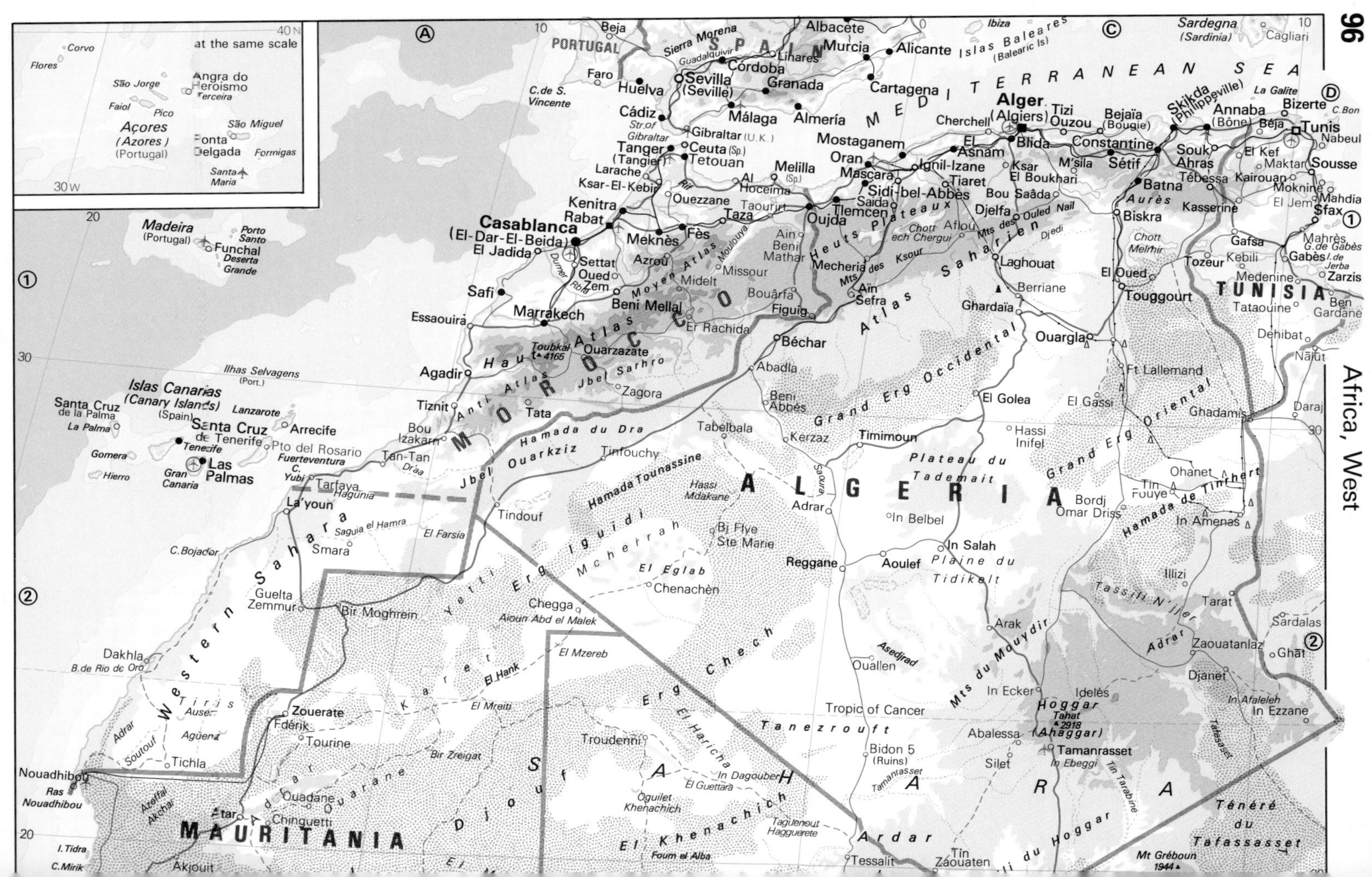
MEDITERRANEAN SEA
Sardegna (Sardinia)
Cagliari
Islas Baleares (Balearic Is)
Ibiza
SPAIN
PORTUGAL
MOROCCO
ALGERIA
TUNISIA
MAURITANIA
Western Sahara
Alger (Algiers)
Tunis
Casablanca (El-Dar-El-Beida)
Rabat
Marrakech
Fès
Meknès
Oran
Constantine
Annaba (Bône)
Skikda (Philippeville)
Bizerte
Sfax
Sousse
Gabès
Tanger (Tangier)
Ceuta (Sp.)
Melilla (Sp.)
Gibraltar (U.K.)
Sevilla (Seville)
Córdoba
Granada
Málaga
Almería
Murcia
Cartagena
Alicante
Albacete
Cádiz
Huelva
Faro
Beja
Agadir
Safi
Essaouira
Tiznit
Tan-Tan
Tarfaya
La'youn
Smara
Dakhla
Nouadhibou
Zouerate
Akjoujt
Atar
Chinguetti
Tindouf
Béchar
Figuig
Oujda
Tlemcen
Sidi-bel-Abbès
Mostaganem
Ghardaïa
Laghouat
Ouargla
Touggourt
Biskra
Batna
Sétif
Blida
El Golea
In Salah
Timimoun
Adrar
Reggane
Aoulef
Tamanrasset
Djanet
Ghadamis
Ghât
Illizi
In Amenas
Tessalit
Troudenni
Bir Moghrein
Hoggar (Ahaggar)
Tahat 2918
Toubkal 4165
Haut Atlas
Moyen Atlas
Anti Atlas
Grand Erg Occidental
Grand Erg Oriental
Plateau du Tademait
Tassili N'Ajjer
Tanezrouft
Erg Iguidi
Erg Chech
Hamada du Dra
Tropic of Cancer
Madeira (Portugal)
Funchal
Porto Santo
Islas Canarias (Canary Islands) (Spain)
Las Palmas
Santa Cruz de Tenerife
Lanzarote
Fuerteventura
Gran Canaria
Gomera
Hierro
La Palma
Ilhas Selvagens (Port.)
Açores (Azores) (Portugal)
at the same scale
Ponta Delgada
Angra do Heroísmo
São Miguel
Terceira
Pico
Faial
São Jorge
Flores
Corvo
Santa Maria
Formigas
C. Bojador
C. Bon
Mt Gréboun 1944
Ténéré du Tafassasset

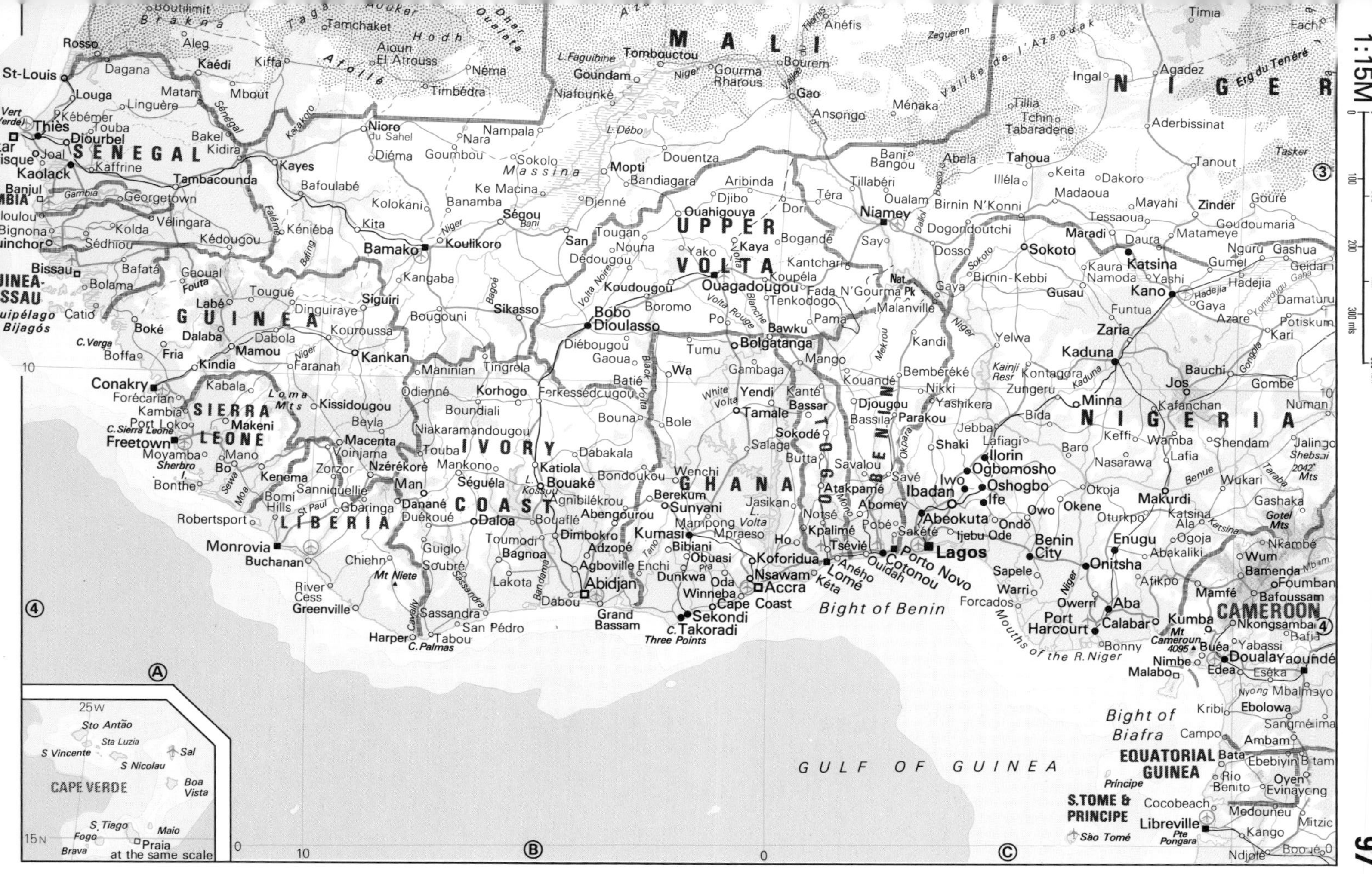
MALI
NIGER
UPPER VOLTA
NIGERIA
GHANA
TOGO
BENIN
IVORY COAST
LIBERIA
SIERRA LEONE
GUINEA
GUINEA-BISSAU
SENEGAL
THE GAMBIA
CAMEROON
EQUATORIAL GUINEA
S.TOME & PRINCIPE
CAPE VERDE
GULF OF GUINEA
Bight of Benin
Bight of Biafra
Mouths of the R. Niger
Dakar
Bamako
Niamey
Ouagadougou
Accra
Lomé
Porto Novo
Lagos
Abidjan
Monrovia
Freetown
Conakry
Bissau
Banjul
Malabo
Libreville
Yaoundé
Douala
Kano
Kaduna
Ibadan
Kumasi
Tombouctou
Gao
Mopti
Ségou
Sikasso
Bobo Dioulasso
Tamale
Bouaké
Niger
Volta
Benue
Praia
at the same scale

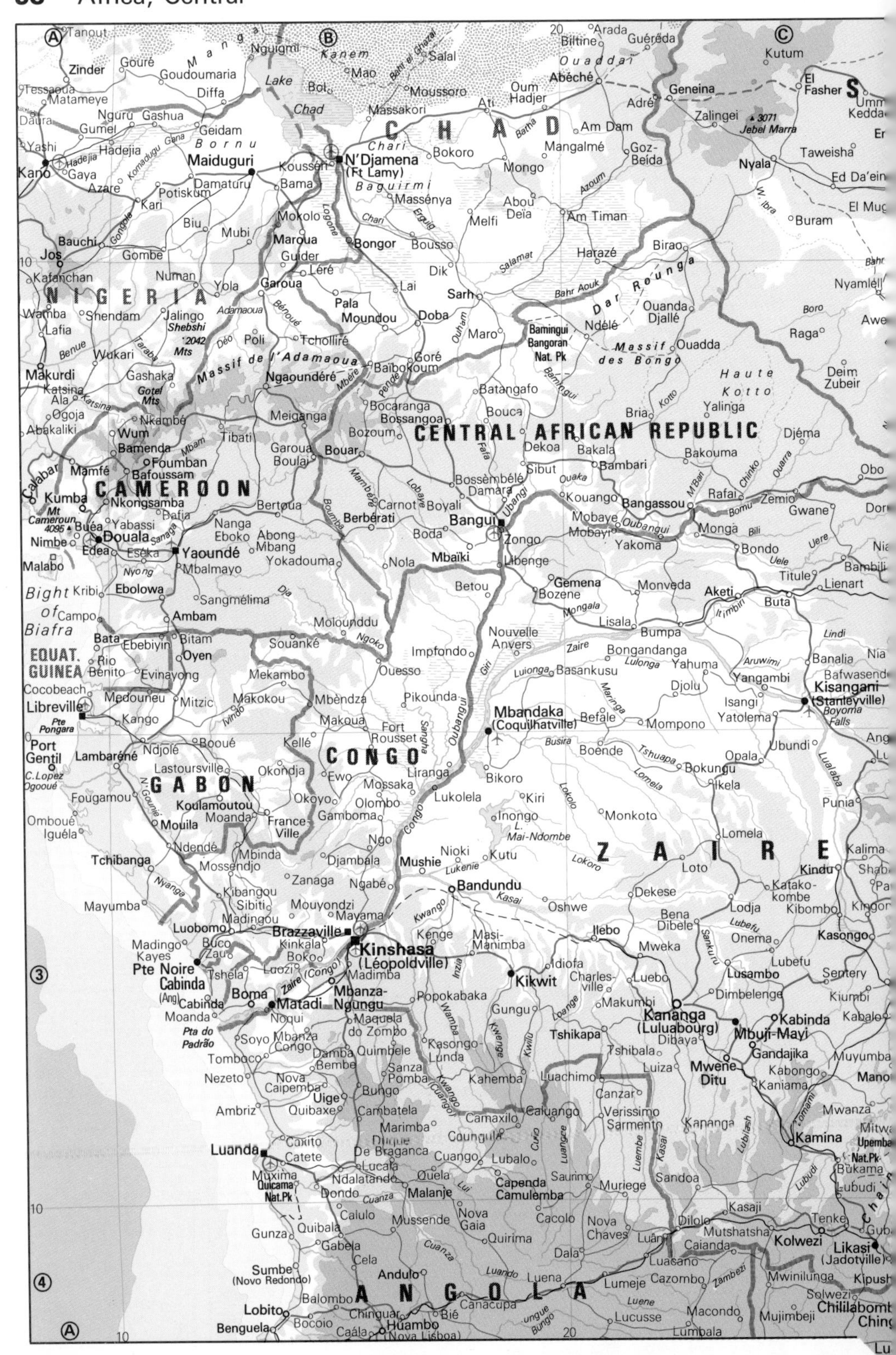
CHAD
NIGERIA
CAMEROON
CENTRAL AFRICAN REPUBLIC
EQUAT. GUINEA
GABON
CONGO
ZAIRE
ANGOLA
Lake Chad
Bight of Biafra
Tanout
Zinder
Gouré
Manga
Goudoumaria
Tessaoua
Matameye
Diffa
Nguigmi
Kanem
Mao
Bol
Bahr el Ghazal
Salal
Moussoro
Massakori
Arada
Biltine
Guéréda
Ouaddaï
Abéché
Oum Hadjer
Ati
Adré
Geneina
Kutum
El Fasher
Zalingei
3071 Jebel Marra
Daura
Nguru
Gashua
Gumel
Geidam
Yashi
Hadejia
Bornu
Kano
Gaya
Azare
Maiduguri
Damaturu
Potiskum
Kousseri
N'Djamena (Ft Lamy)
Chari
Bokoro
Batha
Am Dam
Mangalmé
Goz-Beïda
Nyala
Taweisha
Ed Da'ein
Bama
Baguirmi
Masséna
Mongo
Kari
Biu
Mubi
Mokolo
Maroua
Logone
Erguig
Melfi
Abou Deïa
Am Timan
Buram
Bauchi
Gombe
Jos
Kafanchan
Bongor
Bousso
Guider
Léré
Garoua
Lai
Dik
Salamat
Harazé
Birao
Dar Rounga
Numan
Yola
Wamba
Shendam
Lafia
Jalingo
Shebshi 2042 Mts
Adamaoua
Bénoué
Pala
Moundou
Doba
Sarh
Bahr Aouk
Ouanda Djallé
Ndélé
Nyamlell
Benue
Wukari
Déo
Poli
Tcholliré
Maro
Bamingui Bangoran Nat. Pk
Massif des Bongo
Ouadda
Raga
Makurdi
Gashaka
Gotel Mts
Massif de l'Adamaoua
Ngaoundéré
Baïbokoum
Goré
Mbéré
Pende
Batangafo
Haute Kotto
Deim Zubeir
Katsina Ala
Ogoja
Abakaliki
Nkambé
Wum
Bamenda
Mbam
Tibati
Meiganga
Bocaranga
Bossangoa
Bouca
Bria
Yalinga
Bozoum
Garoua Boulai
Bouar
Dekoa
Bakala
Bakouma
Djéma
Calabar
Mamfé
Foumban
Bafoussam
Sibut
Bambari
Obo
Kumba
Nkongsamba
Bafia
Mambéré
Lobaye
Bossèmbélé
Damara
Ouaka
Kouango
Bangassou
Rafai
Zemio
Mt Cameroun 4095
Buéa
Yabassi
Douala
Nimbe
Edea
Eséka
Sanaga
Bertoua
Nanga Eboko
Abong Mbang
Carnot
Boyali
Berbérati
Bangui
Boda
Zongo
Mobaye
Mobayi
Oubangui
Yakoma
Monga
Gwane
Bondo
Uele
Malabo
Yaoundé
Mbalmayo
Nyong
Yokadouma
Nola
Mbaïki
Libenge
Bambili
Titule
Lienart
Kribi
Ebolowa
Sangmélima
Dja
Betou
Gemena
Bozene
Monveda
Aketi
Buta
Campo
Ambam
Mongala
Lisala
Itimbiri
Bumpa
Lindi
Molounddu
Ngoko
Bata
Ebebiyin
Bitam
Oyen
Souanké
Nouvelle Anvers
Zaire
Bongandanga
Rio Benito
Evinayong
Impfondo
Ouesso
Basankusu
Lulonga
Yahuma
Aruwimi
Banalia
Bafwasende
Cocobeach
Libreville
Medouneu
Mitzic
Mekambo
Makokou
Mbèndza
Pikounda
Djolu
Yangambi
Isangi
Kisangani (Stanleyville)
Boyoma Falls
Pte Pongara
Kango
Ivindo
Makoua
Fort Rousset
Sangha
Mbandaka (Coquilhatville)
Befale
Maringa
Mompono
Yatolema
Port Gentil
Lambaréné
Ndjolé
Booué
Kellé
Oubangui
Giri
Busira
Boende
Tshuapa
Opala
Ubundi
Lualaba
C. Lopez
Ogooué
Lastoursville
Okondja
Ewo
Liranga
Mossaka
Bikoro
Bokungu
Ikela
Lomela
Fougamou
N'Gounié
Koulamoutou
Okoyo
Olombo
Lukolela
Kiri
Lokolo
Punia
Omboué
Iguéla
Mouila
Moanda
Franceville
Gamboma
Inongo
L. Mai-Ndombe
Monkoto
Tchibanga
Ndendé
Mbinda
Ngo
Congo
Djambala
Mushie
Nioki
Lukenie
Kutu
Lokoro
Lomela
Kalima
Shabunda
Nyanga
Mossendjo
Zanaga
Ngabé
Bandundu
Kasai
Loto
Kindu
Kibangou
Sibiti
Mouyondzi
Mayama
Kwango
Oshwe
Dekese
Katako-kombe
Kibombo
Mayumba
Madingou
Luobomo
Brazzaville
Kinshasa (Léopoldville)
Kenge
Masi-Manimba
Ilebo
Bena Dibele
Lubefu
Lodja
Onema
Kasongo
Madingo Kayes
Buco Zau
Kinkala
Boko
Luozi
Zaire (Congo)
Madimba
Idiofa
Mweka
Lubefu
Sankuru
Sentery
Pte Noire
Cabinda
Tshela
Boma
Matadi
Mbanza-Ngungu
Inzia
Kikwit
Charlesville
Luebo
Lusambo
Kiumbi
Cabinda (Ang)
Moanda
Noqui
Maquela do Zombo
Popokabaka
Wamba
Gungu
Loange
Makumbi
Dimbelenge
Kananga (Luluabourg)
Mbuji-Mayi
Kabinda
Kabalo
Pta do Padrão
Soyo
Mbanza Congo
Kasongo-Lunda
Kwenge
Kwilu
Tshikapa
Dibaya
Tshibala
Gandajika
Tomboco
Damba
Quimbele
Bembe
Luiza
Mwene-Ditu
Kabongo
Muyumba
Nezeto
Nova Caipemba
Sanza Pomba
Kwango (Cuango)
Kahemba
Luachimo
Canzar
Kaniama
Ambriz
Uige
Quibaxe
Bungo
Cambatela
Caluango
Camaxilo
Verissimo Sarmento
Kananga
Lubilash
Mwanza
Marimba
Cuango
Cuilo
Luangue
Luembe
Kasai
Kamina
Upemba Nat. Pk
Luanda
Caxito
Catete
Duque de Bragança
Cuango
Lubalo
Muxima
Quiçama Nat. Pk
Lucala
Ndalatando
Quela
Capenda Camulemba
Saurimo
Muriege
Sandoa
Lubudi
Bukama
Dondo
Cuanza
Malanje
Lui
Kasaji
Calulo
Mussende
Nova Gaia
Cacolo
Nova Chaves
Dilolo
Tenke
Mutshatsha
Kolwezi
Likasi (Jadotville)
Gunza
Quibala
Gabela
Quirima
Dala
Luau
Caianda
Cela
Luando
Luacano
Cazombo
Zambezi
Mwinilunga
Sumbe (Novo Redondo)
Andulo
Luena
Lumeje
Solwezi
Lobito
Balombo
Canacupa
Luene
Macondo
Chililabombwe
Benguela
Bocoio
Chinguar
Huambo (Nova Lisboa)
Caála
Bié
Bungo
Lucusse
Lumbala
Mujimbeji
Chingola
Kipushi
Kedda
Umm
Er
El Mug
Bahr
Awe
Boro
Dor
Nia
Bili
Bomu
Chinko
Ouarra
M'Bari
Kotto
Bamingui
Ouham
Fafa
Boumba
Bahr
Kwilu
Wamba
Lomami
Mano
Mitwaba
Kingombe
Pa
Ang
Lu
Gubi
Kalemie
20
10
A
B
C
3
4

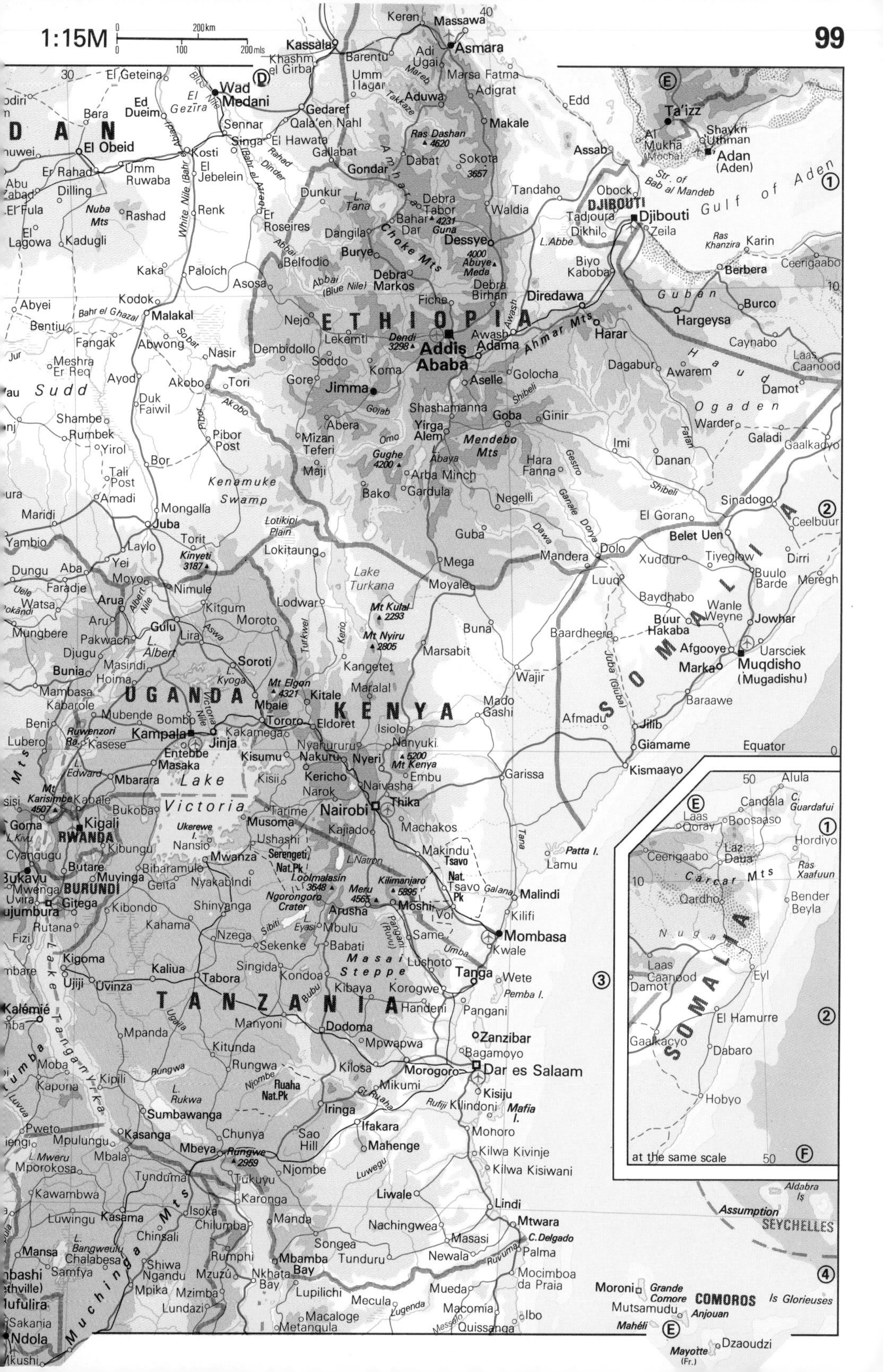

SUDAN
ETHIOPIA
DJIBOUTI
SOMALIA
UGANDA
KENYA
RWANDA
BURUNDI
TANZANIA
SEYCHELLES
COMOROS

Keren
Massawa
Asmara
Kassala
Barentu
Adi Ugai
Khashm el Girba
Umm Hagar
Marsa Fatma
Adigrat
Aduwa
Edd
Ta'izz
Al Mukha (Mocha)
Shaykh 'Uthman
Adan (Aden)
Assab
El Geteina
Wad Medani
El Gezira
Ed Dueim
Bara
El Obeid
Sennar
Gedaref
Qala'en Nahl
Singa
El Hawata
Kosti
Gallabat
Makale
Ras Dashan 4620
Gondar
Dabat
Sokota 3657
Er Rahad
Umm Ruwaba
El Jebelein
Abu Zabad
Dilling
El Fula
Nuba Mts
Rashad
Renk
El Lagowa
Kadugli
Er Roseires
Dunkur
L. Tana
Debra Tabor 4231 Guna
Bahar Dar
Waldia
Tandaho
Obock
Tadjoura
Djibouti
Dikhil
Str. of Bab al Mandeb
Gulf of Aden
Zeila
L. Abbe
Dangila
Choke Mts
Dessye
Burye
Belfodio
4000 Abuye Meda
Ras Khanzira
Karin
Biyo Kaboba
Berbera
Ceerigaabo
Kaka
Paloich
Asosa
Abbai (Blue Nile)
Debra Markos
Debra Birhan
Fiche
Awash
Diredawa
Guban
Burco
Hargeysa
Kodok
Abyei
Bahr el Ghazal
Malakal
Bentiu
Nejo
Dendi 3298
Addis Ababa
Adama
Ahmar Mts
Harar
Caynabo
Fangak
Sobat
Abwong
Nasir
Lekemti
Dembidollo
Soddo
Koma
Aselle
Golocha
Dagabur
Awarem
Haud
Laas Caanood
Damot
Meshra Er Req
Ayod
Akobo
Tori
Gore
Jimma
Shibeli
Sudd
Duk Faiwil
Gojab
Shashamanna
Goba
Ginir
Ogaden
Warder
Shambe
Rumbek
Abera
Mizan Teferi
Omo
Yirga Alem
Mendebo Mts
Imi
Galadi
Gaalkacyo
Yirol
Pibor Post
Gughe 4200
L. Abaya
Hara Fanna
Gestro
Danan
Tali Post
Bor
Maji
Arba Minch
Kenamuke Swamp
Bako
Gardula
Negelli
Ganale Dorya
Shibeli
Sinadogo
Amadi
Mongalla
Maridi
Juba
El Goran
Ceelbuur
Lotikipi Plain
Torit
Guba
Dawa
Belet Uen
Yambio
Laylo
Kinyeti 3187
Lokitaung
Mandera
Dolo
Xuddur
Tiyeglow
Dirri
Dungu
Aba
Yei
Mega
Lake Turkana
Buulo Barde
Meregh
Faradje
Moyo
Nimule
Moyale
Luuq
Watsa
Arua
Albert Nile
Kitgum
Lodwar
Mt Kulal 2293
Baydhabo
Wanle Weyne
Jowhar
Mungbere
Aru
Moroto
Buur Hakaba
Pakwach
Gulu
Lira
Aswa
Turkwel
Kerio
Mt Nyiru 2805
Buna
Baardheere
Djugu
L. Albert
Marsabit
Afgooye
Uarsciek
Bunia
Masindi
Soroti
Kangetet
Marka
Muqdisho (Mugadishu)
Hoima
L. Kyoga
Mt Elgon 4321
Maralal
Wajir
Juba (Giuba)
Mambasa
Kabarole
Kitale
Baraawe
Mubende
Bombo
Victoria Nile
Mbale
Mado Gashi
Beni
Ruwenzori Ra.
Kampala
Jinja
Tororo
Eldoret
Isiolo
Afmadu
Jilib
Lubero
Kasese
Kakamega
Nyahururu
Nanyuki
Giamame
Equator
Entebbe
Kisumu
Nakuru
Nyeri
5200 Mt Kenya
Kismaayo
L. Edward
Masaka
Kisii
Kericho
Embu
Garissa
Mbarara
Lake Victoria
Narok
Naivasha
Mt Karisimbe 4507
Kabale
Bukoba
Tarime
Nairobi
Thika
Goma
L. Kivu
Kigali
Ukerewe I.
Musoma
Kajiado
Machakos
Ushashi
Nansio
Serengeti Nat. Pk
L. Natron
Makindu
Tsavo Nat. Pk
Patta I.
Lamu
Cyangugu
Kibungu
Mwanza
Bukavu
Butare
Biharamulo
Loolmalasin 3648
Kilimanjaro 5895
Tsavo
Galana
Malindi
Mwenga
Muyinga
Geita
Nyakabindi
Ngorongoro Crater
Meru 4565
Moshi
Uvira
Gitega
Bujumbura
Kibondo
Shinyanga
Arusha
Kilifi
Voi
Rutana
Kahama
L. Eyasi
Mbulu
Pangani (Ruvu)
Same
Mombasa
Fizi
Nzega
Sibiti
Sekenke
Babati
Kwale
Lake Tanganyika
Kigoma
Singida
Masai Steppe
Lushoto
Umba
Ujiji
Uvinza
Kaliua
Tabora
Kondoa
Tanga
Wete
Kibaya
Korogwe
Pemba I.
Bubu
Handeni
Kalémié
Manyoni
Ugalla
Pangani
Dodoma
Mpanda
Mpwapwa
Zanzibar
Kitunda
Bagamoyo
Moba
Rungwa
Kilosa
Morogoro
Dar es Salaam
Kipili
Njombe
Ruaha Nat. Pk
Kapona
Mikumi
Kisiju
L. Rukwa
Gt. Ruaha
Rufiji
Kilindoni
Mafia I.
Iringa
Sumbawanga
Ifakara
Mohoro
Pweto
Kasanga
Chunya
Sao Hill
Mahenge
Mpulungu
Mbeya
Rungwe 2959
Kilwa Kivinje
L. Mweru
Mbala
Mporokosa
Luwegu
Kilwa Kisiwani
Tunduma
Tukuyu
Kawambwa
Karonga
Liwale
Muchinga Mts
Kasama
Isoka
Lindi
Luwingu
Chilumba
Manda
Nachingwea
Mtwara
Chinsali
L. Bangweulu
Songea
Masasi
C. Delgado
Mansa
Chalabesa
Rumphi
Mbamba Bay
Tunduru
Newala
Ruvuma
Palma
Samfya
Shiwa Ngandu
Mzuzu
Nkhata Bay
Mocimboa da Praia
Mpika
Mzimba
Lupilichi
Mueda
Mufulira
Lundazi
Mecula
Lugenda
Macomia
Sakania
Macaloge
Messalo
Ibo
Ndola
Metangula
Quissanga
Moroni
Grande Comore
Mutsamudu
Anjouan
Is Glorieuses
Mahéli
Mayotte (Fr.)
Dzaoudzi
Aldabra Is
Assumption

Alula
C. Guardafui
Candala
Laas Qoray
Boosaaso
Hordiyo
Laz Daua
Ceerigaabo
Carcar Mts
Ras Xaafuun
Qardho
Bender Beyla
Nugaal
Laas Caanood
Damot
Eyl
El Hamurre
Gaalkacyo
Dabaro
Hobyo
at the same scale

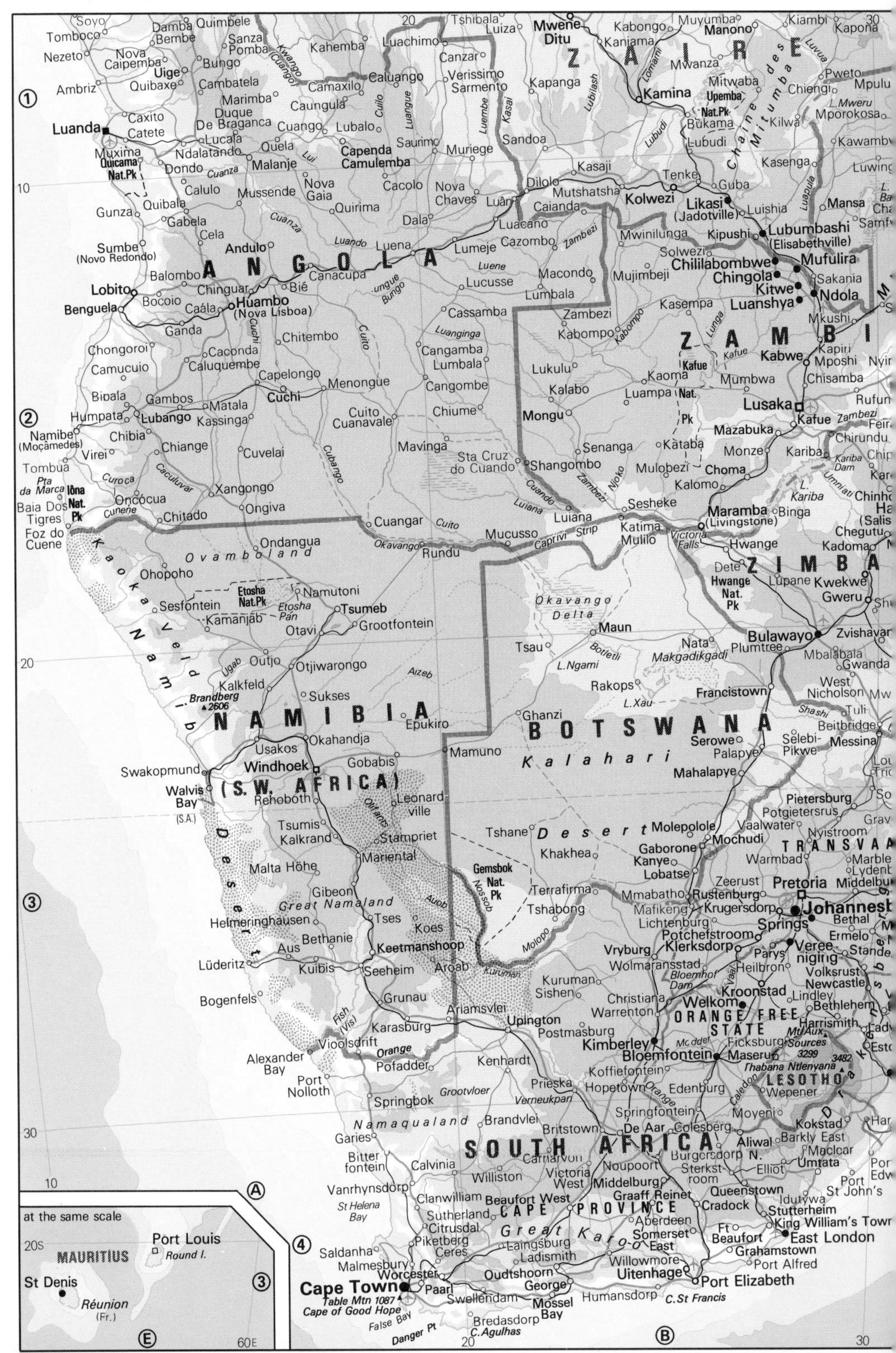
ANGOLA
ZAIRE
ZAMBIA
NAMIBIA
(S.W. AFRICA)
BOTSWANA
ZIMBABWE
SOUTH AFRICA
LESOTHO
TRANSVAAL
ORANGE FREE STATE
CAPE PROVINCE
Luanda
Lobito
Benguela
Huambo
(Nova Lisboa)
Namibe
(Moçâmedes)
Lubango
Menongue
Cuito Cuanavale
Saurimo
Malanje
Dilolo
Kolwezi
Likasi
(Jadotville)
Lubumbashi
(Elisabethville)
Kamina
Chililabombwe
Chingola
Kitwe
Ndola
Mufulira
Luanshya
Kabwe
Lusaka
Mongu
Livingstone
Hwange
Bulawayo
Francistown
Maun
Okavango Delta
Kalahari Desert
Gaborone
Mochudi
Pietersburg
Pretoria
Johannesburg
Tsumeb
Grootfontein
Windhoek
Swakopmund
Walvis Bay
(S.A.)
Rehoboth
Keetmanshoop
Lüderitz
Mariental
Etosha Nat.Pk
Etosha Pan
Brandberg
2606
Namib Desert
Kaokoveld
Ovamboland
Great Namaland
Gemsbok Nat. Pk
Upington
Kimberley
Bloemfontein
Maseru
Welkom
Kroonstad
Klerksdorp
Potchefstroom
Vereeniging
Springs
Mafikeng
Mmabatho
Rustenburg
Krugersdorp
Vryburg
Kuruman
Springbok
Namaqualand
Orange
Alexander Bay
Port Nolloth
Calvinia
Beaufort West
Great Karoo
Oudtshoorn
George
Mossel Bay
Worcester
Paarl
Cape Town
Table Mtn 1087
Cape of Good Hope
False Bay
Danger Pt
C.Agulhas
Bredasdorp
Saldanha
Port Elizabeth
Uitenhage
Grahamstown
Port Alfred
East London
King William's Town
Queenstown
Cradock
Graaff Reinet
Middelburg
De Aar
Colesberg
Aliwal N.
Umtata
Kokstad
Thabana Ntlenyana 3482
Mont Aux Sources 3299
Drakensberg
Victoria Falls
L. Kariba
Caprivi Strip
L. Ngami
Makgadikgadi
Zambezi
Okavango
Cunene
C.St Francis
at the same scale
MAURITIUS
Port Louis
Round I.
St Denis
Réunion
(Fr.)
20S
60E
10
20
30

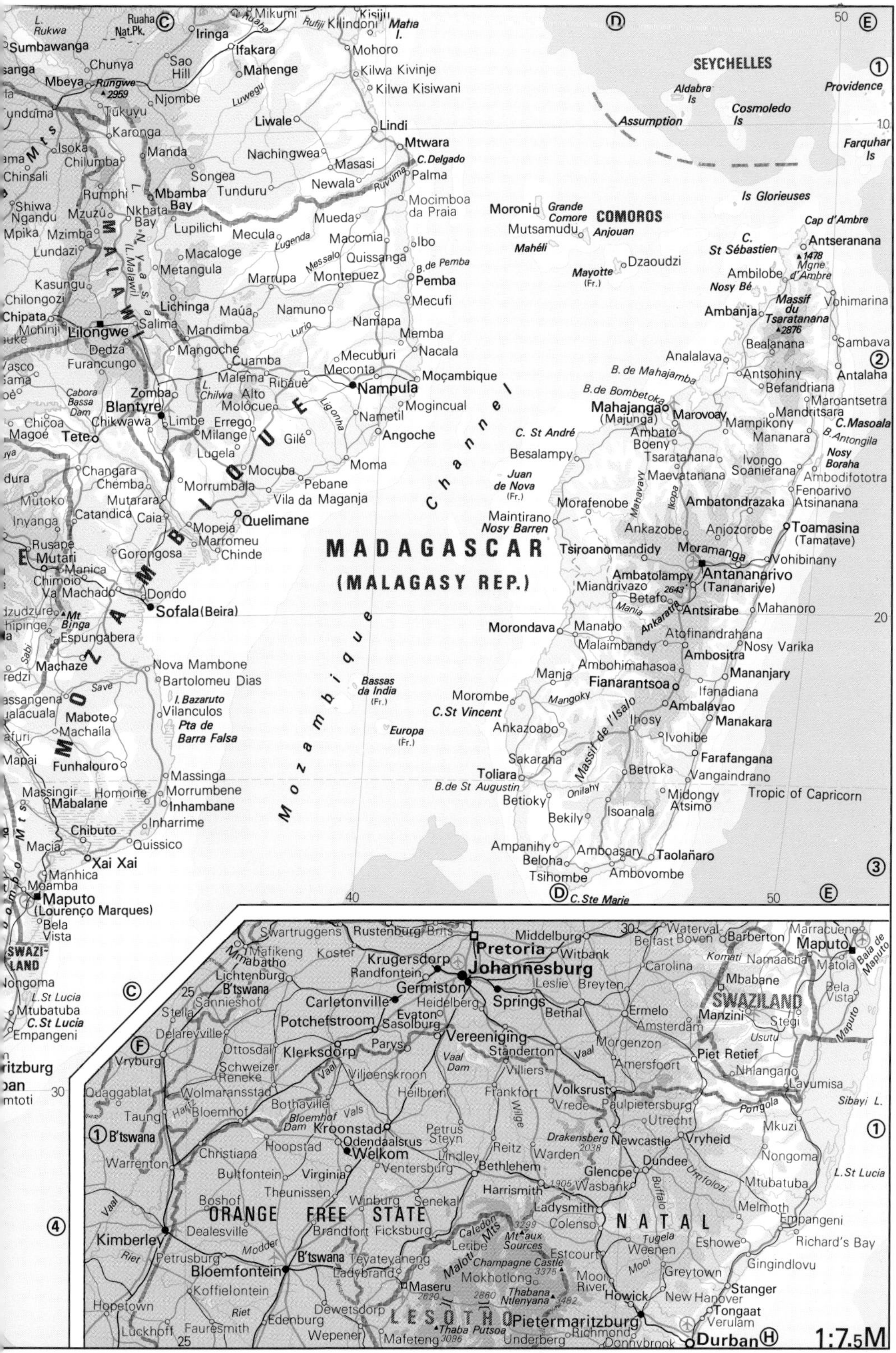

SEYCHELLES
Aldabra Is
Assumption
Cosmoledo Is
Providence
Farquhar Is
Is Glorieuses
COMOROS
Grande Comore
Moroni
Mutsamudu
Anjouan
Mohéli
Mayotte (Fr.)
Dzaoudzi
Cap d'Ambre
Antseranana
C. St Sébastien
1478 Mgne d'Ambre
Ambilobe
Nosy Bé
Massif du Tsaratanana
2876
Vohimarina
Ambanja
Sambava
Bealanana
Analalava
Antalaha
B. de Mahajamba
Antsohiny
Befandriana
B. de Bombetoka
Maroantsetra
Mahajangao (Majunga)
Marovoay
Mandritsara
Mampikony
C. Masoala
Ambato Boeny
Mananara
B. Antongila
C. St André
Tsaratanana
Ivongo Soanierana
Nosy Boraha
Besalampy
Maevatanana
Ambodifototra
Juan de Nova (Fr.)
Mahavavy
Ikopa
Fenoarivo Atsinanana
Morafenobe
Ambatondrazaka
Maintirano
Nosy Barren
Ankazobe
Anjozorobe
Toamasina (Tamatave)
MADAGASCAR
(MALAGASY REP.)
Tsiroanomandidy
Moramanga
Vohibinany
Antananarivo (Tananarive)
Ambatolampy
Miandrivazo
2643
Betafo
Mania
Ankaratra
Antsirabe
Mahanoro
Morondava
Manabo
Malaimbandy
Atofinandrahana
Nosy Varika
Ambositra
Ambohimahasoa
Manja
Fianarantsoa
Mananjary
Ifanadiana
Morombe
Mangoky
Ambalavao
C. St Vincent
Ankazoabo
Ihosy
Manakara
Massif de l'Isalo
Ivohibe
Sakaraha
Farafangana
Toliara
Betroka
Vangaindrano
B. de St Augustin
Onilahy
Midongy Atsimo
Tropic of Capricorn
Betioky
Isoanala
Bekily
Ampanihy
Amboasary
Taolañaro
Beloha
Tsihombe
Ambovombe
C. Ste Marie
Bassas da India (Fr.)
Europa (Fr.)
Mozambique Channel

L. Rukwa
Ruaha Nat. Pk.
Mikumi
Ruaha
Rufiji
Kisiju
Kilindoni
Mafia I.
Iringa
Sumbawanga
Ifakara
Mohoro
Chunya
Sao Hill
Mahenge
Kilwa Kivinje
Kilwa Kisiwani
Mbeya
Rungwe 2959
Njombe
Luwegu
Tunduma
Tukuyu
Liwale
Lindi
Karonga
Mtwara
Isoka
Manda
Nachingwea
Masasi
C. Delgado
Chilumba
Songea
Newala
Ruvuma
Palma
Chinsali
Rumphi
Mbamba Bay
Tunduru
Mocimboa da Praia
Shiwa Ngandu
Mzuzu
Nkhata Bay
Mueda
Mpika
Mzimba
Lupilichi
Mecula
Macomia
Lugenda
Ibo
Lundazi
Macaloge
Metangula
Messalo
Quissanga
B. de Pemba
Kasungu
Marrupa
Montepuez
Pemba
Chilongozi
Mecufi
Lichinga
Maúa
Namuno
Chipata
Salima
Mandimba
Namapa
Mchinji
Lilongwe
Lurio
Memba
Dedza
Mangoche
Mecuburi
Nacala
Furancungo
Cuamba
Meconta
Malema
Ribáuè
Moçambique
Cabora Bassa Dam
Zomba
L. Chilwa
Alto Molócue
Nampula
Blantyre
Ligonha
Mogincual
Chicoa
Chikwawa
Limbe
Erregó
Nametil
Magoé
Tete
Milange
Gilé
Angoche
Lugela
Changara
Mocuba
Moma
Chemba
Morrumbala
Pebane
Mutarara
Vila da Maganja
Mutoko
Catandica
Caia
Inyanga
Mopeia
Quelimane
Rusape
Marromeu
Mutari
Gorongosa
Chinde
Manica
Chimoio
Va Machado
Dondo
Mt Binga
Sofala (Beira)
Espungabera
Sabi
Machaze
Nova Mambone
Bartolomeu Dias
Save
I. Bazaruto
Mabote
Vilanculos
Machaíla
Pta de Barra Falsa
Mapai
Funhalouro
Massinga
Massingir
Homoine
Morrumbene
Mabalane
Inhambane
Chibuto
Inharrime
Macia
Quissico
Xai Xai
Manhica
Moamba
Maputo (Lourenço Marques)
Bela Vista
SWAZILAND
Jongoma
L. St Lucia
Mtubatuba
C. St Lucia
Empangeni
MALAWI
MOZAMBIQUE
L. Nyasa (L. Malawi)

Swartruggens
Rustenburg
Brits
Middelburg
Waterval-Boven
Marracuene
Mafikeng
Koster
Pretoria
Belfast
Barberton
Maputo
Mmabatho
Krugersdorp
Witbank
Baía de Maputo
Lichtenburg
Randfontein
Johannesburg
Carolina
Komati
Namaacha
Matola
B'tswana
Germiston
Leslie
Breyten
Mbabane
Sannieshof
Carletonville
Heidelberg
Springs
Bela Vista
Stella
Potchefstroom
Evaton
Bethal
Ermelo
SWAZILAND
Delareyville
Sasolburg
Amsterdam
Manzini
Stegi
Ottosdal
Klerksdorp
Parys
Vereeniging
Standerton
Morgenzon
Usutu
Maputo
Vryburg
Schweizer Reneke
Vaal
Vaal Dam
Villiers
Piet Retief
Amersfoort
Viljoenskroon
Nhlangano
Quaggablat
Wolmaransstad
Heilbron
Frankfort
Volksrust
Lavumisa
Bothaville
Vrede
Paulpietersburg
Sibayi L.
Taung
Harts
Bloemhof
Bloemhof Dam
Vals
Wilge
Pongola
Utrecht
B'tswana
Kroonstad
Petrus Steyn
Drakensberg
2038
Newcastle
Vryheid
Mkuzi
Christiana
Hoopstad
Odendaalsrus
Welkom
Reitz
Warden
Lindley
Nongoma
Warrenton
Bultfontein
Virginia
Ventersburg
Bethlehem
Glencoe
Dundee
Umfolozi
L. St Lucia
Buffalo
Theunissen
Harrismith
1905
Wasbank
Mtubatuba
Boshof
Winburg
Senekal
Ladysmith
Melmoth
ORANGE FREE STATE
Colenso
NATAL
Empangeni
Dealesville
Brandfort
Ficksburg
Caledon
Mts
3299
Mt aux Sources
Tugela
Kimberley
Modder
Eshowe
Richard's Bay
Riet
Petrusburg
B'tswana
Teyateyaneng
Leribe
Estcourt
Weenen
Bloemfontein
Ladybrand
Maloti
Champagne Castle
3375
Mooi
Gingindlovu
Mokhotlong
Greytown
Koffiefontein
Maseru
2620
2860
Thabana Ntlenyana
3482
Mooi River
Stanger
Hopetown
Riet
Dewetsdorp
Howick
New Hanover
Tongaat
Edenburg
LESOTHO
Pietermaritzburg
Verulam
Luckhoff
Fauresmith
Wepener
Mafeteng
Thaba Putsoa 3096
Underberg
Richmond
Donnybrook
Durban
1:7.5M

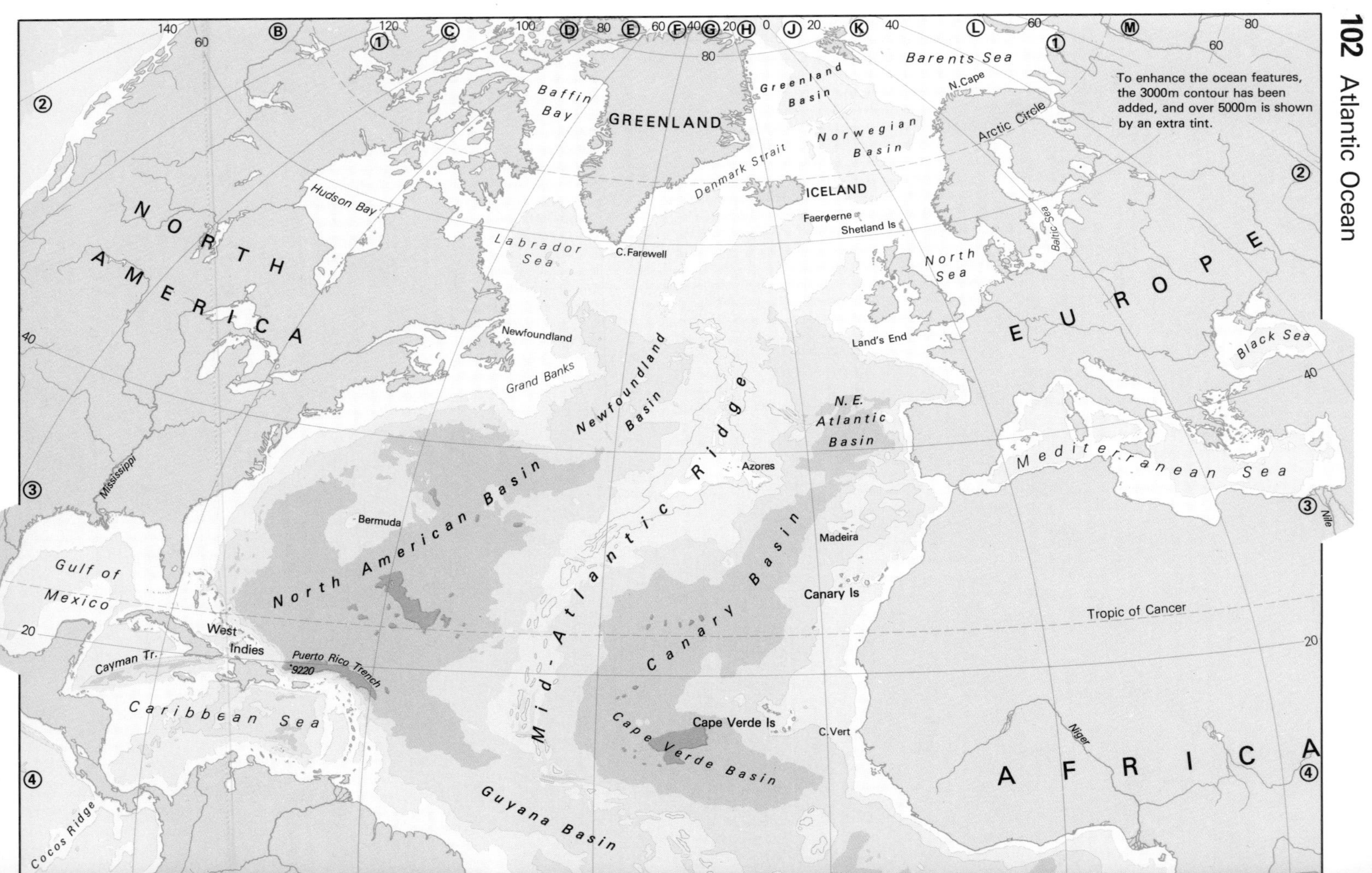
To enhance the ocean features, the 3000m contour has been added, and over 5000m is shown by an extra tint.
NORTH AMERICA
EUROPE
AFRICA
GREENLAND
ICELAND
Baffin Bay
Hudson Bay
Labrador Sea
C.Farewell
Denmark Strait
Greenland Basin
Norwegian Basin
Barents Sea
N.Cape
Arctic Circle
Baltic Sea
Faerøerne
Shetland Is
North Sea
Land's End
Black Sea
Mediterranean Sea
Nile
Newfoundland
Grand Banks
Newfoundland Basin
N.E. Atlantic Basin
Mid-Atlantic Ridge
Azores
Madeira
Canary Is
Canary Basin
Tropic of Cancer
Cape Verde Is
C.Vert
Cape Verde Basin
Niger
North American Basin
Bermuda
Mississippi
Gulf of Mexico
West Indies
Cayman Tr.
Puerto Rico Trench
9220
Caribbean Sea
Guyana Basin
Cocos Ridge

1:60M 0 600 1200 1800 2400 km 0 600 1200 mls

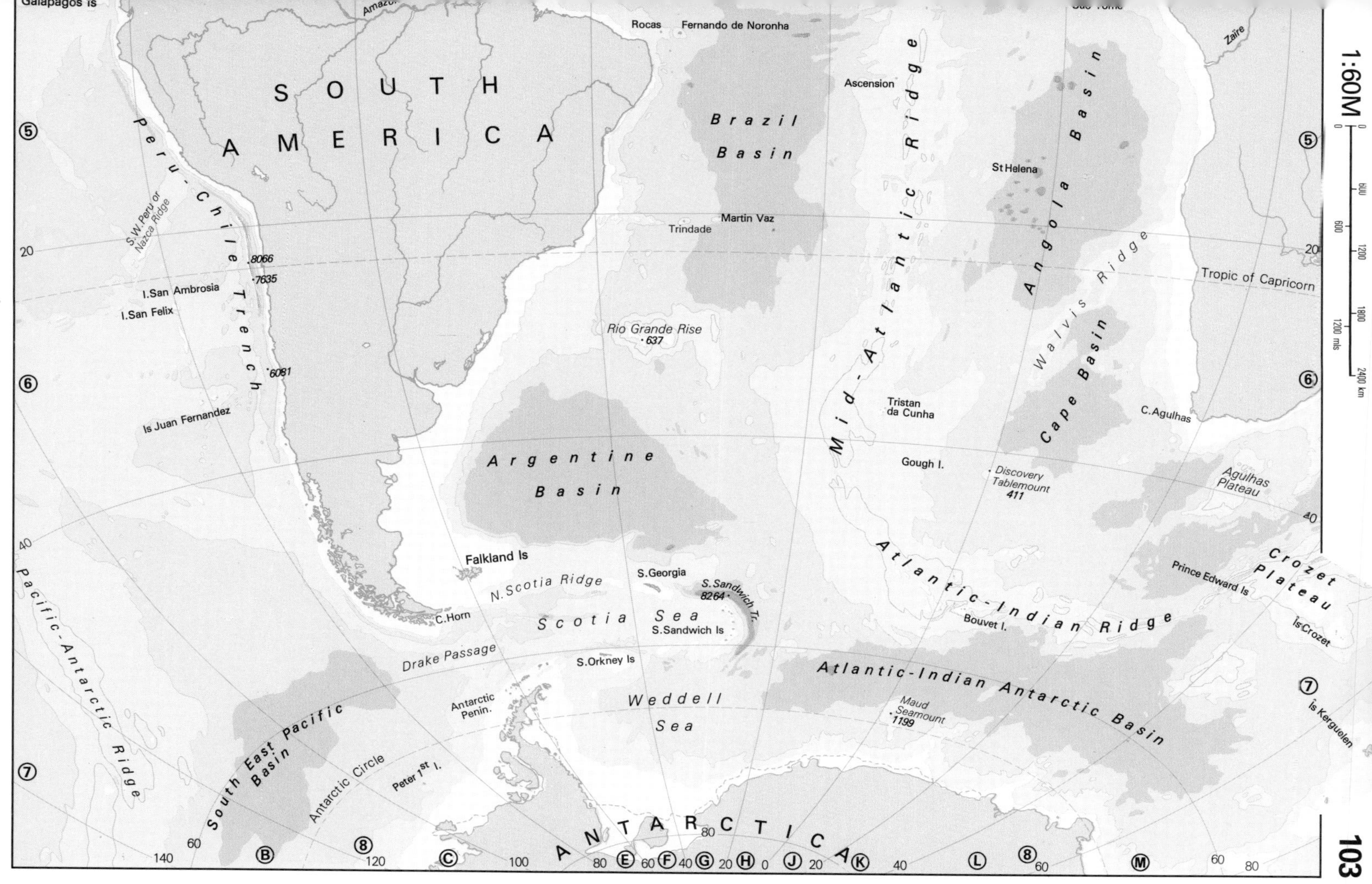

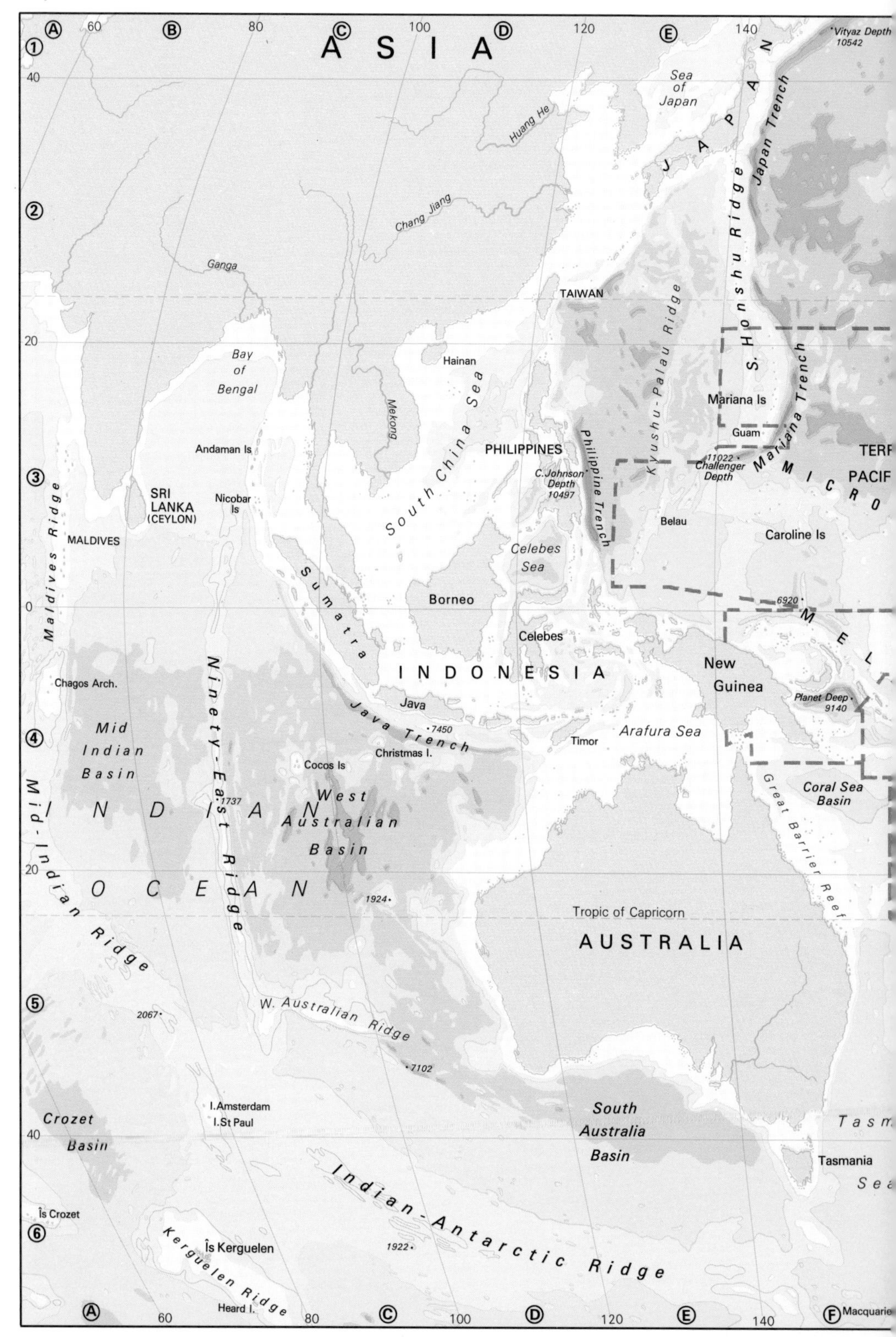
ASIA
Sea of Japan
JAPAN
Japan Trench
Vityaz Depth 10542
Huang He
Chang Jiang
Ganga
TAIWAN
Honshu Ridge
S. Honshu Ridge
Kyushu-Palau Ridge
Bay of Bengal
Hainan
Mekong
South China Sea
Mariana Is
Mariana Trench
Guam
Andaman Is
PHILIPPINES
Philippine Trench
11022 Challenger Depth
C.Johnson Depth 10497
SRI LANKA (CEYLON)
Nicobar Is
MALDIVES
Maldives Ridge
Belau
Caroline Is
Celebes Sea
Sumatra
Borneo
6920
Celebes
INDONESIA
New Guinea
Chagos Arch.
Java
Java Trench
7450
Christmas I.
Timor
Arafura Sea
Planet Deep 9140
Mid Indian Basin
Ninety-East Ridge
Cocos Is
Mid-Indian Ridge
INDIAN OCEAN
1737
West Australian Basin
Coral Sea Basin
Great Barrier Reef
1924
Tropic of Capricorn
AUSTRALIA
W. Australian Ridge
2067
7102
I.Amsterdam
I.St Paul
Crozet Basin
South Australia Basin
Tasmania
Tasman Sea
Indian-Antarctic Ridge
Îs Crozet
Îs Kerguelen
Kerguelen Ridge
1922
Heard I.
Macquarie

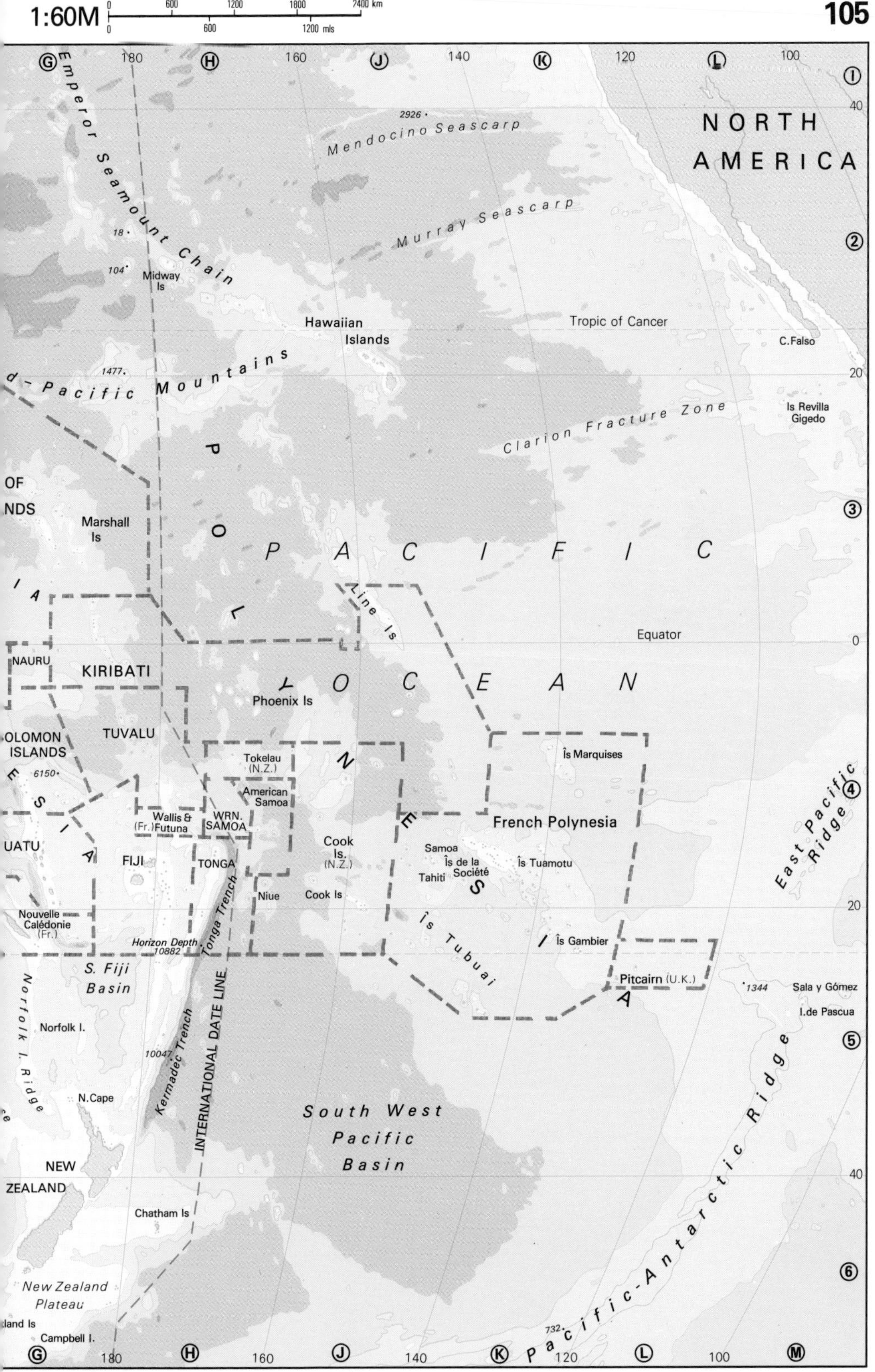
NORTH AMERICA
Emperor Seamount Chain
Mendocino Seascarp
Murray Seascarp
Midway Is
Hawaiian Islands
Tropic of Cancer
C.Falso
Mid-Pacific Mountains
Clarion Fracture Zone
Is Revilla Gigedo
Marshall Is
POLYNESIA
PACIFIC OCEAN
Line Is
Equator
NAURU
KIRIBATI
Phoenix Is
SOLOMON ISLANDS
TUVALU
Tokelau (N.Z.)
American Samoa
Îs Marquises
Wallis & Futuna (Fr.)
WRN. SAMOA
French Polynesia
East Pacific Ridge
VANUATU
FIJI
TONGA
Cook Is. (N.Z.)
Samoa
Îs de la Société
Tahiti
Îs Tuamotu
Niue
Cook Is
Nouvelle Calédonie (Fr.)
Tonga Trench
Horizon Depth 10882
Îs Tubuai
Îs Gambier
Pitcairn (U.K.)
S. Fiji Basin
Sala y Gómez
I.de Pascua
Norfolk I. Ridge
Norfolk I.
Kermadec Trench
INTERNATIONAL DATE LINE
N.Cape
South West Pacific Basin
Pacific-Antarctic Ridge
NEW ZEALAND
Chatham Is
New Zealand Plateau
Campbell I.

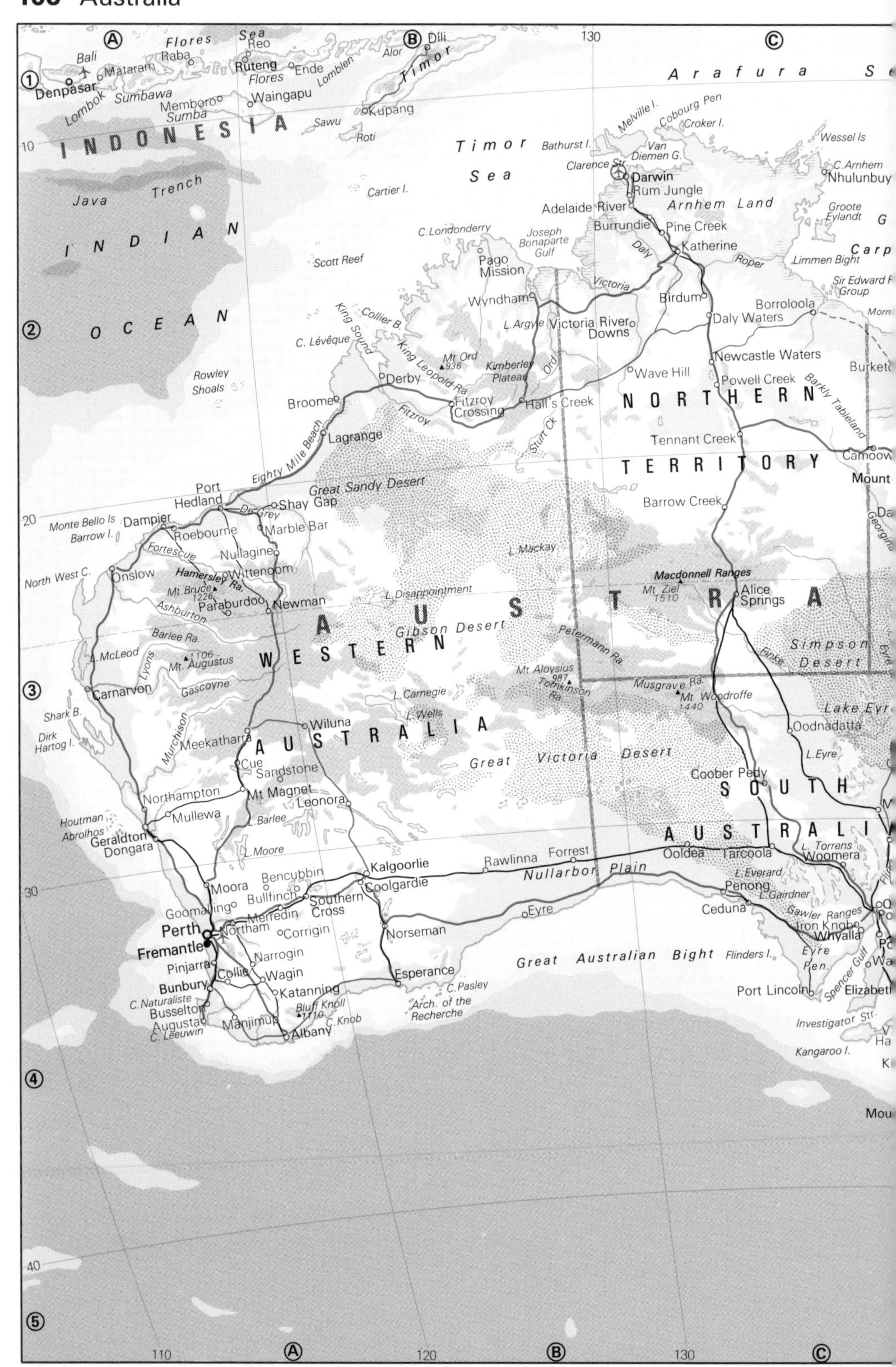
INDONESIA
INDIAN OCEAN
Java Trench
Timor Sea
Arafura Sea
WESTERN AUSTRALIA
NORTHERN TERRITORY
SOUTH AUSTRALIA
Great Sandy Desert
Gibson Desert
Great Victoria Desert
Simpson Desert
Nullarbor Plain
Great Australian Bight
Arnhem Land
Kimberley Plateau
Barkly Tableland
Macdonnell Ranges
Hamersley Ra.
Musgrave Ra.
Petermann Ra.
Darwin
Katherine
Alice Springs
Tennant Creek
Perth
Fremantle
Kalgoorlie
Coolgardie
Geraldton
Carnarvon
Port Hedland
Broome
Derby
Esperance
Albany
Bunbury
Port Lincoln
Whyalla
Woomera
Coober Pedy
Ceduna
Denpasar
Kupang
Dili
Timor
Flores
Sumbawa
Sumba
Lombok
Bali

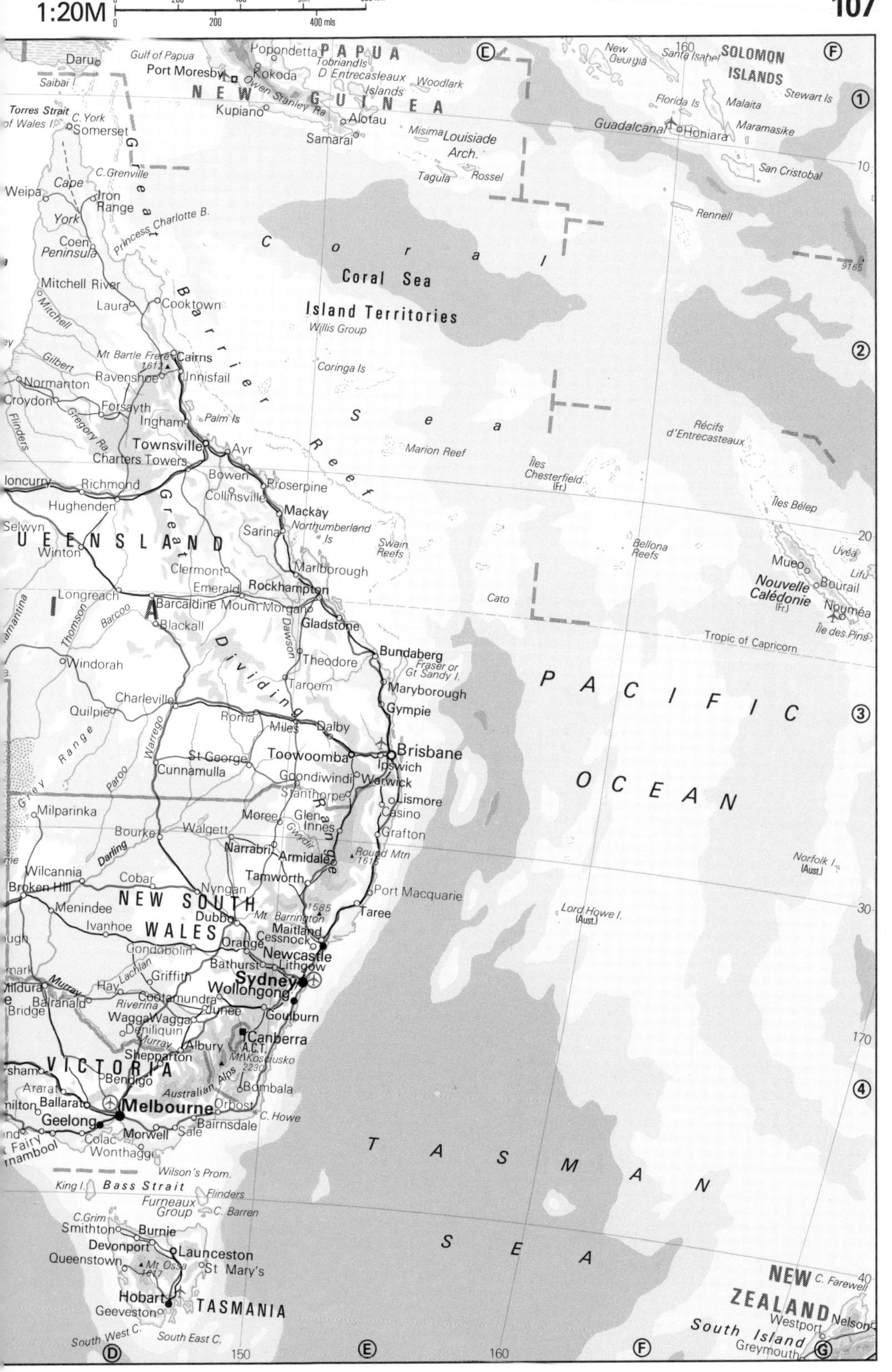
PAPUA NEW GUINEA
Port Moresby
Popondetta
Kokoda
Owen Stanley Ra.
Kupiano
Alotau
Samarai
Daru
Saibai I.
Gulf of Papua
Tobriand Is
D'Entrecasteaux Islands
Woodlark
Misima
Louisiade Arch.
Tagula
Rossel
SOLOMON ISLANDS
New Georgia
Santa Isabel
Florida Is
Malaita
Stewart Is
Guadalcanal
Honiara
Maramasike
San Cristobal
Rennell
Torres Strait
C. York
Somerset
Weipa
Cape York Peninsula
C. Grenville
Iron Range
Coen
Princess Charlotte B.
Great Barrier Reef
Coral Sea
Coral Sea Island Territories
Willis Group
Coringa Is
Mitchell River
Mitchell
Laura
Cooktown
Mt Bartle Frere 1612
Cairns
Innisfail
Gilbert
Normanton
Ravenshoe
Croydon
Forsayth
Gregory Ra.
Flinders
Ingham
Palm Is
Townsville
Charters Towers
Ayr
Bowen
Proserpine
Collinsville
Cloncurry
Richmond
Hughenden
Mackay
Sarina
Northumberland Is
Swain Reefs
Marion Reef
Îles Chesterfield (Fr.)
Récifs d'Entrecasteaux
Îles Bélep
Bellona Reefs
Selwyn
QUEENSLAND
Winton
Great Dividing Range
Clermont
Marlborough
Emerald
Rockhampton
Longreach
Barcaldine
Mount Morgan
Gladstone
Cato
Blackall
Barcoo
Thomson
Dawson
Bundaberg
Fraser or Gt Sandy I.
Theodore
Taroom
Maryborough
Gympie
Windorah
Charleville
Quilpie
Roma
Miles
Dalby
Brisbane
Ipswich
Toowoomba
Warrego
Grey Range
St George
Cunnamulla
Paroo
Goondiwindi
Warwick
Stanthorpe
Lismore
Casino
Milparinka
Moree
Glen Innes
Grafton
Bourke
Walgett
Gwydir
Narrabri
Armidale
Round Mtn 1615
Darling
Wilcannia
Broken Hill
Cobar
Nyngan
Tamworth
Port Macquarie
NEW SOUTH WALES
Menindee
Dubbo
Mt Barrington 1585
Taree
Ivanhoe
Maitland
Cessnock
Orange
Newcastle
Condobolin
Bathurst
Lithgow
Sydney
Wollongong
Mildura
Murray
Hay
Lachlan
Griffith
Balranald
Riverina
Cootamundra
Junee
Goulburn
Wagga Wagga
Deniliquin
Canberra
A.C.T.
Albury
Shepparton
Mt Kosciusko 2230
VICTORIA
Bendigo
Australian Alps
Bombala
Ararat
Ballarat
Melbourne
Orbost
Geelong
C. Howe
Colac
Morwell
Sale
Bairnsdale
Wonthaggi
Wilson's Prom.
King I.
Bass Strait
Flinders
Furneaux Group
C. Barren
C. Grim
Smithton
Burnie
Devonport
Launceston
Queenstown
Mt Ossa 1617
St Mary's
Hobart
Geeveston
TASMANIA
South West C.
South East C.
TASMAN SEA
PACIFIC OCEAN
Tropic of Capricorn
Mueo
Bourail
Nouvelle Calédonie (Fr.)
Nouméa
Île des Pins
Uvéa
Lifu
Norfolk I. (Aust.)
Lord Howe I. (Aust.)
NEW ZEALAND
C. Farewell
Nelson
Westport
South Island
Greymouth
9165
10
20
30
40
150
160
170
C
D
E
F
G
1
2
3
4

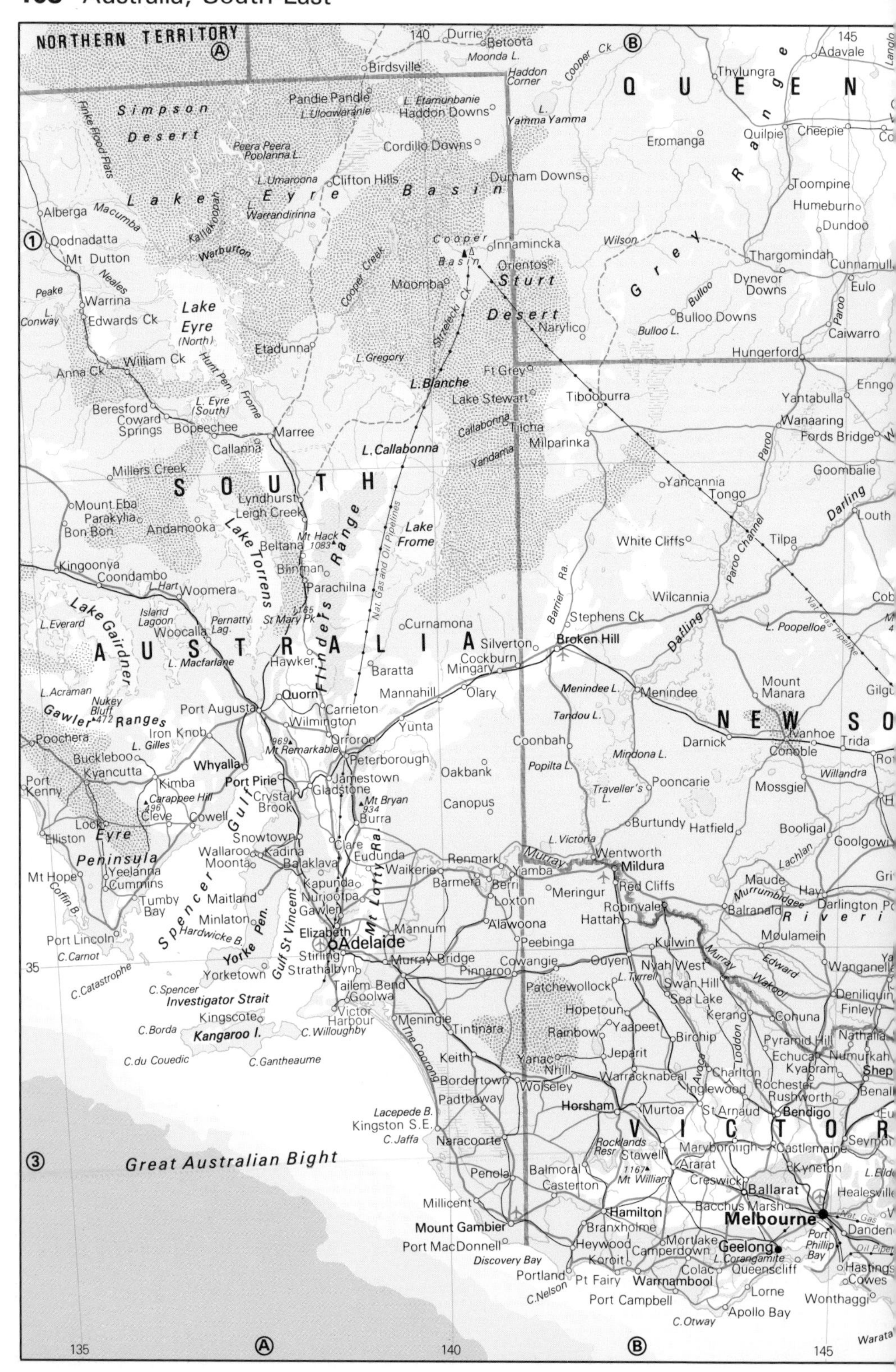
NORTHERN TERRITORY
QUEENSLAND
SOUTH AUSTRALIA
NEW SOUTH WALES
VICTORIA
Simpson Desert
Lake Eyre Basin
Sturt Desert
Grey Range
Lake Eyre (North)
L. Eyre (South)
Lake Torrens
Lake Gairdner
Lake Frome
Flinders Range
Mt Lofty Ra.
Gawler Ranges
Eyre Peninsula
Yorke Pen.
Spencer Gulf
Gulf St Vincent
Investigator Strait
Kangaroo I.
Great Australian Bight
Birdsville
Adelaide
Port Augusta
Whyalla
Port Pirie
Port Lincoln
Broken Hill
Mildura
Wilcannia
Horsham
Ballarat
Bendigo
Geelong
Melbourne
Mount Gambier
Warrnambool
Hamilton
Naracoorte
Murray
Darling
Cooper Creek
Nat. Gas and Oil Pipelines
135
140
145
35
A
B
1
3

Augathella
914 Mt Hutton
Injune
Eurombah
Dawson
Taroom
Mundubbera
Biggenden
Gayndah
Maryborough
Double Island Pt
155
LAND
Morven
Maranoa
Mitchell
Wandoan
Goomeri
Murgon
Wondai
Gympie
Tewantin
Cooroy
Nambour
Maroochydore
Caloundra
Caboolture
Moreton I.
Redcliffe
Guluguba
Mungallala
Muckadilla
Roma
Wallumbilla
Miles
Chinchilla
Kingaroy
Brooloo
Nanango
Yarraman
Kilcoy
Toogoolawah
Crows Nest
Jackson
Nat. Gas Pipeline
Bungil
Condamine
Jandowae
Surat
Tara
Dalby
Glenmorgan
Meandarra
Oakey
Gatton
Brisbane
Darling Downs
Moonie
Oil Pipeline
Toowoomba
Pittsworth
Ipswich
N. Stradbroke I.
Beenleigh
Millmerran
Clifton
Mt Domville 642
Allora
Boonah
Beaudesert
Gold Coast
Tweed Heads
St George
Bollon
Nebine
Mungallala
Neabul
Maranoa
Balonne
Moonie
Dirranbandi
Talwood
Inglewood
Goondiwindi
Warwick
Killarney
Murwillumbah
Mullumbimby
C. Byron
Thallon
Boggabilla
Stanthorpe
Kyogle
Lismore
Hebel
Mungindi
Macintyre
Texas
Goodooga
Garah
Yetman
Casino
Ballina
New Angledool
Croppa Ck
Tenterfield
PACIFIC
Lightning Ridge
Ashley
Ashford
Woodburn
Narran
Bokhara
Birrie
Moree
Collarenebri
Gwydir
Warialda
Deepwater
Clarence
Yamba
Maclean
Narran L.
Pokataroo
Gravesend
Barwon
Rowena
Bellata
Bingara
Inverell
Glen Innes
Grafton
Walgett
Burren Jct.
Pian
Namoi
Wee Waa
Nandewar Ra.
Bundarra
Glenreagh
Guyra
Dorrigo
Round Mtn 1615
Coff's Harbour
30
OCEAN
Byrock
Marra
Macquarie
Castlereagh
Narrabri
1508 Kaputar
Barraba
New England Ra.
Great Dividing Ra.
Bellingen
Gwabegar
Boggabri
Manilla
Uralla
Armidale
Nambucca Heads
Macksville
Smoky C.
Bogan
Baradine
Coonamble
Gunnedah
Moonbi Ra.
Walcha
Kempsey
Coonabarabran
Mullaley
Tamworth
Gulargambone
Werris Creek
Black Sugarloaf 1494
Wauchope
Port Macquarie
Nyngan
Gilgandra
Quirindi
Warren
Liverpool Ra.
Murrurundi
Kendall
Nevertire
Coolah
Wingham
Trangie
Dunedoo
Gloucester
Taree
Tottenham
Scone
Narromine
Dubbo
Merriwa
Gulgong
Muswellbrook
Forster
C. Hawke
573 Yellow Mtn
Wellington
Macquarie
Mudgee
Hunter
Dungog
Sugarloaf Pt
H WALES
Singleton
Maitland
Trundle
Peak Hill
Yeoval
Mt Coricudgy 1274
Kandos
Kurri Kurri
Port Stephens
Condobolin
Cessnock
Raymond Terrace
Molong
Newcastle
Parkes
Morisset
L. Macquarie
Orange
Blue Mts
Cargelligo
Forbes
Portland
Wyong
Burcher
L. Cowal
Lachlan
Bathurst
Lithgow
Tuggerah L.
Blayney
Richmond
Canowindra
Katoomba
Windsor
Cowra
Parramatta
Port Jackson
West Wyalong
Grenfell
Sydney
Camden
L. Burragorang
155
Campbelltown
Young
Picton
Ardlethan
Crookwell
Wollongong
Boorowa
Cootamundra
Murrumburrah
Bowral
Port Kembla
Shellharbour
Burrinjuck Resr
Goulburn
Coolamon
Junee
Yass
Nowra
Shoalhaven R.
Wagga Wagga
L. George
35
Gundagai
Rock
Canberra
Jervis B.
Tumut
A.C.T.
Queanbeyan
Ulladulla
Batlow
Tumut
Holbrook
Tumbarumba
Hume
Batemans Bay
L. Eucumbene
Australian Alps
Moruya
Wodonga
Corryong
Beechworth
Mt Kosciusko 2230
Snowy Mts
Cooma
Cobargo
Bright
Nimmitabel
1986 Mt Bogong
Bega
Bombala
Merimbula
Delegate
Eden
Gippsland
Genoa
C. Howe
Orbost
Bairnsdale
Cann River
Sale
Lakes Entrance
Pt Hicks
Ninety Mile Beach
150

145E
Wilson's Promontory
B
C
C. Wickham
Bass Strait
King I.
Currie
Naracoopa
Grassy
Stokes Pt
C. Frankland
Furneaux
Flinders I.
Whitemark
Lady Barron
Group
40S
Cape Barren I.
Hunter Is
Stanley
C. Grim
Smithton
Marrawah
Wynyard
Burnie
Ulverstone
Banks Strait
C. Portland
George Town
Gladstone
Eddystone Pt
Devonport
Latrobe
Scottsdale
Bridport
Launceston
St Helens
Waratah
Deloraine
1573 Ben Lomond
St Marys
Longford
Rosebery
1617 Mt Ossa
Great L.
Queenstown
Strahan
Derwent Br.
Macquarie Har.
Frenchmans Cap 1444
Oatlands
Freycinet Peninsula
TASMANIA
Tarraleah
Oyster Bay
New Norfolk
Sorell
Maria I.
Maydena
Hobart
Huonville
Tasman Pen.
Geeveston
Storm Bay
C. Pillar
Port Davey
S.W. Cape
Bruny I.
S.E. Cape
at the same scale

① ② ④

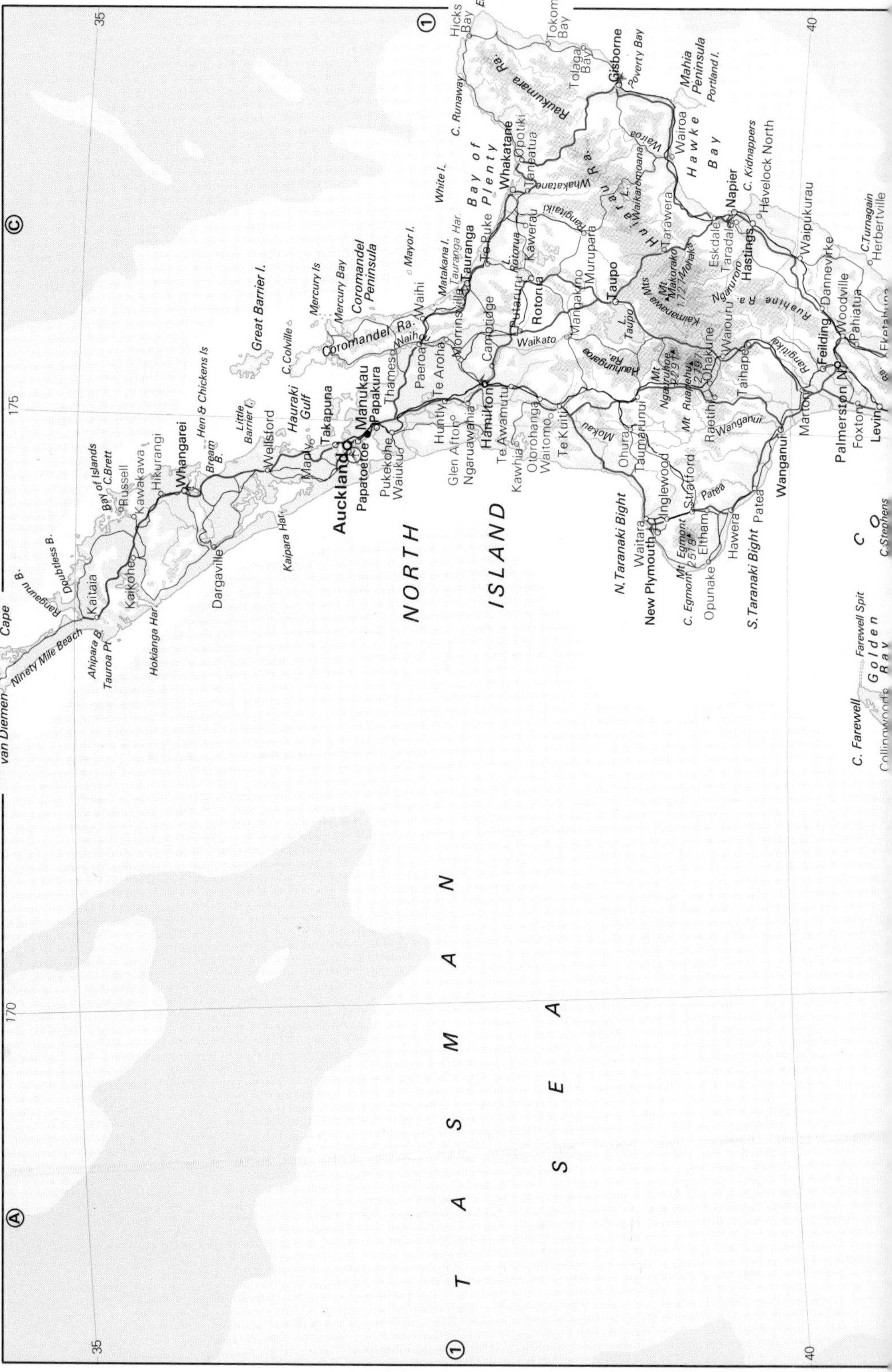

TASMAN SEA

NORTH ISLAND

Three Kings Is
C. Maria van Diemen
North Cape
Ninety Mile Beach
Rangaunu B.
Doubtless B.
Kaitaia
Ahipara B.
Tauroa Pt
Kaikohe
Hokianga Har
Bay of Islands
C.Brett
Russell
Kawakawa
Hikurangi
Whangarei
Bream B.
Hen & Chickens Is
Dargaville
Kaipara Har
Wellsford
Little Barrier I.
Great Barrier I.
Hauraki Gulf
C.Colville
Mercury Is
Mercury Bay
Coromandel Peninsula
Coromandel Ra.
Takapuna
Auckland
Manukau
Papatoetoe
Papakura
Pukekohe
Waiuku
Thames
Paeroa
Waihi
Te Aroha
Huntly
Glen Afton
Ngaruawahia
Hamilton
Te Awamutu
Cambridge
Morrinsville
Matakana I.
Tauranga Har.
Tauranga
Mayor I.
Te Puke
Bay of Plenty
White I.
Whakatane
Opotiki
Rotorua
L. Rotorua
Putaruru
Kawerau
Waikato
Mangakino
Murupara
Taupo
L. Taupo
Kawhia
Otorohanga
Waitomo
Te Kuiti
Mokau
Ohura
Taumarunui
Hauhungaroa Ra.
Mt Ngauruhoe 2291
Mt Ruapehu 2797
Ohakune
Raetihi
Waiouru
Taihape
Kaimanawa Mts
Mt Makorako 1727
Wanganui
Marton
Feilding
Palmerston N.
Foxton
Levin
Woodville
Pahiatua
Dannevirke
Waipukurau
Hastings
Napier
Taradale
Eskdale
Havelock North
C. Kidnappers
Hawke Bay
Wairoa
Mahia Peninsula
Portland I.
Gisborne
Poverty Bay
Tolaga Bay
Tokomaru Bay
Hicks Bay
East C.
C. Runaway
Raukumara Ra.
Huiarau Ra.
Ruahine Ra.
Rangitikei
N.Taranaki Bight
S.Taranaki Bight
Waitara
New Plymouth
Inglewood
Stratford
Mt Egmont 2518
C. Egmont
Eltham
Opunake
Hawera
Patea
C. Farewell
Farewell Spit
Golden Bay
C.Stephens
C.Turnagain
Herbertville

35 170 175 40

SOUTH ISLAND

PACIFIC OCEAN

SOUTHERN ALPS

Canterbury Plains

Canterbury Bight

Pegasus Bay

Foveaux Strait

Stewart Island

Fiordland Nat. Park

Wellington
Lower Hutt
Martinborough
L. Wairarapa
Mt Ross 983
Palliser Bay
C. Palliser
C. Campbell
Blenheim
Awatere
Picton
Nelson
Richmond
Richmond Ra.
Wairau
Kaikoura Ra.
Tapuaenuku 2885
Kaikoura
Kaikoura Pen.
Clarence
Cheviot
Waiau
Hurunui
Hanmer Springs
Mt Travers 2338
L. Rotoiti
L. Rotoroa
Spenser Mts
Lewis Pass
Culverden
Waipara
Kaiapoi
Rangiora
Christchurch
Lyttelton
Banks Peninsula
Akaroa
Lincoln
L. Ellesmere
Hornby
Waimakariri
Puketeraki Ra.
Victoria Ra.
Murchison
Motueka
Mt Owen 1826
Karamea
Karamea Bight
Seddonville
Westport
C. Foulwind
Buller
Reefton
Grey
L. Brunner
L. Sumner
Arthurs Pass
L. Coleridge
Rakaia
Runanga
Greymouth
Hokitika
Ross
Methven
Ashburton
Rangitata
Temuka
Timaru
Geraldine
Fairlie
L. Tekapo
Hermitage
Mt Cook 3764
Mt Sefton 3157
L. Pukaki
Lake Pukaki
L. Benmore
L. Aviemore
Omarama
Kurow
Waitaki
Waimate
Oamaru
Hampden
Palmerston
Waikouaiti
Port Chalmers
Otago Peninsula
Dunedin
Ranfurly
Taieri
Mosgiel
Milton
Lawrence
Balclutha
Kaitangata
Owaka
Clutha
Hawkdun Ra.
L. Ohau
L. Hawea
Dunstan Mts
Clyde
Alexandra
Roxburgh
Heriot
Tapanui
Mataura
Gore
Edendale
Invercargill
Bluff
Riversdale
Lumsden
Kingston
Cromwell
Wanaka
L. Wanaka
Young Ra.
Pollux 2542
Mt Aspiring 3027
Arrowtown
Queenstown
L. Wakatipu
Abut Hd
Franz Josef Gl.
Jackson Hd
Cascade Pt
Awarua Pt
Homer Tunnel
Mt Pyramid 2326
Milford Sd
Te Anau
L. Te Anau
Manapouri
L. Manapouri
Mt Ward 1718
Waiau
Oreti
Winton
Ohai
L. Hauroko
Tuatapere
Te Waewae Bay
Riverton
Cameron Mts
Caswell Sd
George Sd
Secretary I.
Doubtful Sd
Breaksea Sd
Resolution I.
Dusky Sd
Puysegur Pt
Solander I.
Codfish I.
Oban
Paterson Inlet
Shelter Pt
Mt Allen 730
Port Pegasus

45
170
175

1:40M 0 400 800 1200 1600 km
0 400 800 mls

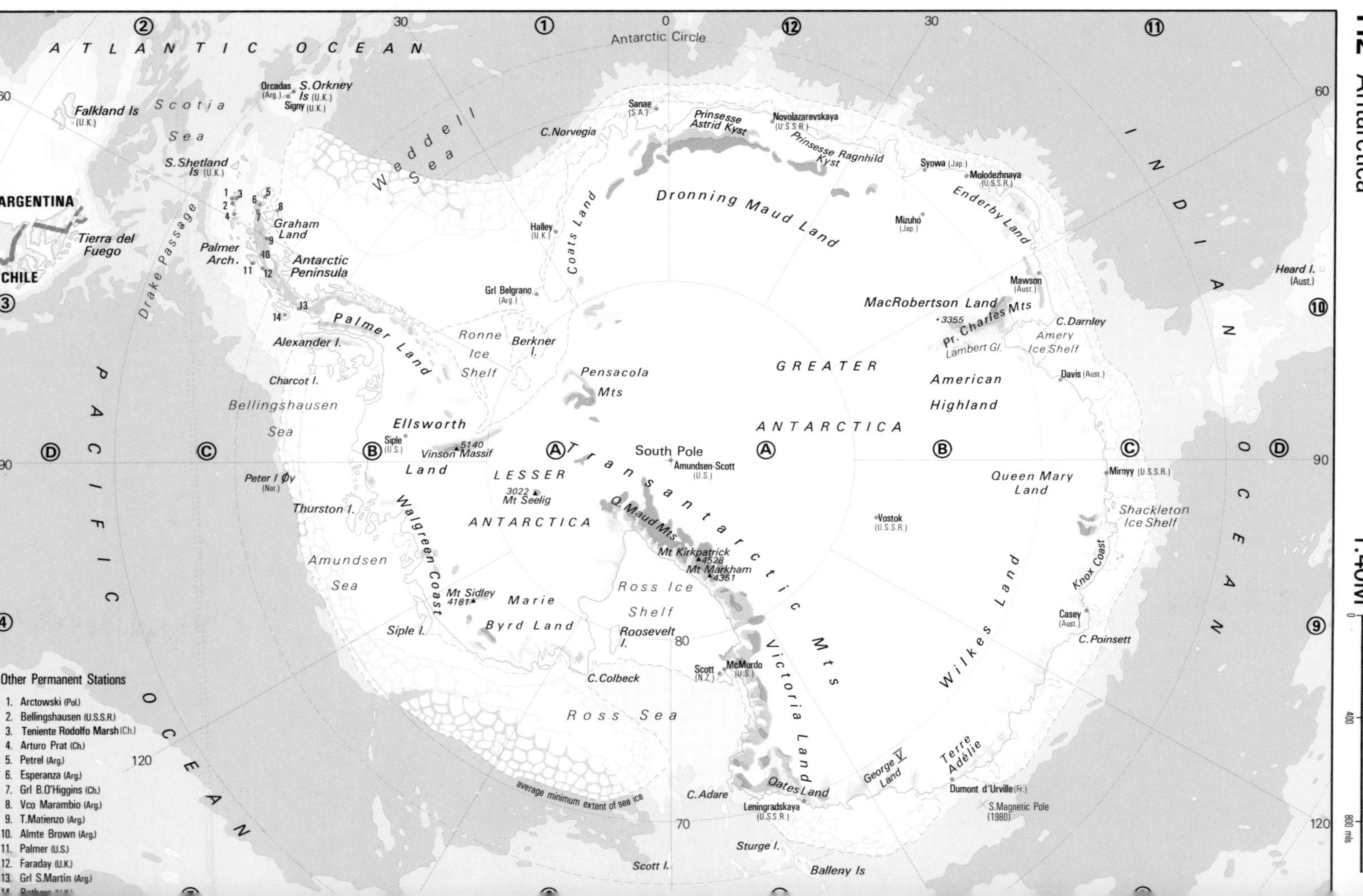

Index

In the index, the first number refers to the page, and the following letter and number to the section of the map in which the index entry can be found. For example, Paris 48C2 means that Paris can be found on page 48 where column C and row 2 meet.

Abbreviations used in the index

Afghan	Afghanistan	Hung	Hungary	Pol	Poland	Arch	Archipelago
Alb	Albania	Ind	Indonesia	Port	Portugal	B	Bay
Alg	Algeria	Irish Rep	Ireland	Rom	Romania	C	Cape
Ant	Antarctica	N Ire	Ireland, Northern	S Arabia	Saudi Arabia	Chan	Channel
Arg	Argentina	Leb	Lebanon	Scot	Scotland	Gl	Glacier
Aust	Australia	Lib	Liberia	Sen	Senegal	I(s)	Island(s)
Bang	Bangladesh	Liech	Liechtenstein	S Africa	South Africa	Lg	Lagoon
Belg	Belgium	Lux	Luxembourg	S Yemen	South Yemen	L	Lake
Bol	Bolivia	Madag	Madagascar	Switz	Switzerland	Mt(s)	Mountain(s)
Bulg	Bulgaria	Malay	Malaysia	Tanz	Tanzania	O	Ocean
Camb	Cambodia	Maur	Mauritania	Thai	Thailand	P	Pass
Can	Canada	Mor	Morocco	Turk	Turkey	Pass	Passage
CAR	Central African Republic	Mozam	Mozambique	USSR	Union of Soviet Socialist Republics	Pen	Peninsula
Czech	Czechoslovakia	Neth	Netherlands			Plat	Plateau
Den	Denmark	NZ	New Zealand	USA	United States of America	Pt	Point
Dom Rep	Dominican Republic	Nic	Nicaragua	U Volta	Upper Volta	Res	Reservoir
E Germ	East Germany	Nig	Nigeria	Urug	Uruguay	R	River
El Sal	El Salvador	Nor	Norway	Ven	Venezuela	S	Sea
Eng	England	Pak	Pakistan	Viet	Vietnam	Sd	Sound
Eq Guinea	Equatorial Guinea	PNG	Papua New Guinea	W Germ	West Germany	Str	Strait
Eth	Ethiopia	Par	Paraguay	Yugos	Yugoslavia	V	Valley
Fin	Finland	Phil	Philippines	Zim	Zimbabwe		

A

Aachen *W Germ* **57B2**
Aalst *Belg* **46C1**
Äänekoski *Fin* **38K6**
Aarau *Switz* **47C1**
Aare, R *Switz* **47B1**
Aba *China* **72A3**
Aba *Nig* **97C4**
Aba *Zaïre* **99D2**
Abādān *Iran* **91A3**
Abādeh *Iran* **90B3**
Abadla *Alg* **96B1**
Abaeté *Brazil* **35B1**
Abaeté, R *Brazil* **35B1**
Abaetetuba *Brazil* **31B2**
Abagnar Qi *China* **72D1**
Abakaliki *Nig* **97C4**
Abakan *USSR* **63B2**
Abala *Niger* **97C3**
Abalessa *Alg* **96C2**
Abancay *Peru* **32C6**
Abarqū *Iran* **90B3**
Abashiri *Japan* **74E2**
Abashiri-wan, B *Japan* **74E2**
Abau *PNG* **71F4**
Abaya, L *Eth* **99D2**
Abbai, R *Eth* **99D1**
Abbe, L *Eth* **99E1**
Abbeville *France* **48C1**
Abbeville, Louisiana *USA* **19B4**
Abbeville, S Carolina *USA* **17B1**
Abbeyfeale *Irish Rep* **45B2**
Abbiategrasso *Italy* **47C2**
Abbotsford *Can* **20B1**
Abbottabad *Pak* **84C2**
Abdulino *USSR* **61H3**
Abéché *Chad* **98C1**
Åbenrå *Den* **39F7**
Abeokuta *Nig* **97C4**
Abera *Eth* **99D2**
Aberaeron *Wales* **43B3**
Aberdeen, Maryland *USA* **15C3**
Aberdeen *S Africa* **100B4**
Aberdeen *Scot* **44C3**
Aberdeen, S Dakota *USA* **8D2**
Aberdeen, Washington *USA* **8A2**
Aberdeen L *Can* **4J3**
Aberfeldy *Scot* **44C3**
Abergavenny *Wales* **43C4**
Aberystwyth *Wales* **43B3**
Abhā *S Arabia* **81C4**
Abhar *Iran* **90A2**
Abidjan *Ivory Coast* **97B4**
Abilene, Kansas *USA* **18A2**
Abilene, Texas *USA* **9D3**
Abingdon *Eng* **43D4**
Abitibi, R *Can* **7B4**
Abitibi,L *Can* **7C5**
Abkhazskaya, Republic *USSR* **61F5**
Abohar *India* **84C2**
Abomey *Benin* **97C4**
Abong Mbang *Cam* **98B2**
Aborlan *Phil* **79A4**
Abou Deïa *Chad* **98B1**
Abqaiq *S Arabia* **91A4**
Abrantes *Port* **50A2**
Abri *Sudan* **95C2**
Abrolhos, Is *Aust* **106A3**
Absaroka Range, Mts *USA* **8B2**
Abū al Abyad, I *UAE* **91B5**
Abū 'Ali, I *S Arabia* **91A4**
Abū Dhabi *UAE* **91B5**
Abu Hamed *Sudan* **95C3**
Abunã *Brazil* **33D5**
Abunã, R *Bol* **32D6**
Abú Sukhayr *Iraq* **93D3**
Abut Head, C *NZ* **111B2**
Abu 'Urug, Well *Sudan* **95C3**
Abuye Meda, Mt *Eth* **99D1**
Abu Zabad *Sudan* **99C1**
Abwong *Sudan* **99D2**
Åby *Den* **56B1**
Aby 'Aweigîla, Well *Egypt* **94B3**
Abyei *Sudan* **99C2**
Acambaro *Mexico* **24B2**
Acaponeta *Mexico* **24B2**
Acapulco *Mexico* **24B3**
Acaraú *Brazil* **31D2**
Acarigua *Ven* **32D2**
Acatlán *Mexico* **24C3**
Acatzingo *Mexico* **23B2**
Accra *Ghana* **97B4**
Achalpur *India* **85D4**
Achao *Chile* **29B4**
Achensee, L *Austria* **47D1**
Achern *W Germ* **46E2**
Achill, I *Irish Rep* **41A3**
Achinsk *USSR* **63B2**
Acireale *Italy* **53C3**
Acklins, I *Caribbean* **26C2**
Acobamba *Peru* **32C6**
Aconcagua, Mt *Chile* **29B2**
Acopiara *Brazil* **31D3**
Açores, Is *Atlantic O* **88B4**
Acqui *Italy* **47C2**
Acraman,L *Aust* **108A2**
Acre, State *Brazil* **32C5**
Acton *USA* **22C3**
Actopan *Mexico* **23B1**
Ada *USA* **19A3**
Adaja, R *Spain* **50B1**
Adam *Oman* **91C5**
Adama *Eth* **99D2**
Adamantina *Brazil* **35A2**
Adamaoua, Region *Nig/Cam* **98B2**
Adamello, Mt *Italy* **47D1**
Adams *USA* **16C1**
Adam's Bridge *India/Sri Lanka* **87B3**
Adams L *Can* **13D2**
Adams,Mt *USA* **8A2**
Adam's Peak, Mt *Sri Lanka* **87C3**
'Adan *S Yemen* **81C4**
Adana *Turk* **92C2**
Adapazari *Turk* **60D5**
Adare,C *Ant* **112B7**
Adavale *Aust* **108B1**
Adda, R *Italy* **47C2**
Ad Dahna', Region *S Arabia* **91A4**
Ad Damman *S Arabia* **91B4**
Ad Dibdibah, Region *S Arabia* **91A4**
Ad Dilam *S Arabia* **91A5**
Ad Dir'iyah *S Arabia* **91A5**
Addis Ababa *Eth* **99D2**
Ad Dīwanīyah *Iraq* **93D3**
Ad Dīī' *S Yemen* **81C4**
Ad Duwayd *S Arabia* **93D3**
Adelaide *Aust* **106C4**
Adelaide Pen *Can* **4J3**
Adelanto *USA* **22D3**
Aden,G of *Yemen/Somalia* **81C4**
Aderbissinat *Niger* **97C3**
Adhra *Syria* **94C2**
Adi, I *Indon* **71E4**
Adige, R *Italy* **52B1**
Adigrat *Eth* **99D1**
Adilābād *India* **85D5**
Adin *USA* **20B2**
Adirondack Mts *USA* **15D2**
Adi Ugai *Eth* **95C3**
Adıyaman *Turk* **93C2**
Adjud *Rom* **54C1**
Admiralty I *USA* **4E4**
Admiralty Inlet, B *Can* **6B2**
Ādoni *India* **87B1**
Adour, R *France* **48B3**
Adrar, Region *Maur* **96A2**
Adrar, Mts *Alg* **96C2**
Adrar Soutouf, Region *Mor* **96A2**

Adré *Chad* **98C1**
Adri *Libya* **95A2**
Adria *Italy* **47E2**
Adrian, Michigan *USA* **14B2**
Adriatic S *Italy/Yugos* **52B2**
Aduwa *Eth* **99D1**
Adzopé *Ivory Coast* **97B4**
Aegean, S *Greece* **55B3**
Afghanistan, Republic *Asia* **80E2**
Afgooye *Somalia* **99E2**
Afikpo *Nig* **97C4**
Åfjord *Nor* **38G6**
Aflou *Alg* **96C1**
Afmadu *Somalia* **99E2**
Afollé, Region *Maur* **97A3**
Afula *Israel* **94B2**
Afyon *Turk* **92B2**
Agadem *Niger* **95A3**
Agadez *Niger* **97C3**
Agadir *Mor* **96B1**
Agar *India* **85D4**
Agartala *India* **86C2**
Agassiz *Can* **20B1**
Agboville *Ivory Coast* **97B4**
Agdam *USSR* **93E1**
Agematsu *Japan* **75B1**
Agen *France* **48C3**
Agha Jārī *Iran* **90A3**
Agno, R *Italy* **47D2**
Agordo *Italy* **47E1**
Agout, R *France* **48C3**
Āgra *India* **85D3**
Ağri *Turk* **93D2**
Agri, R *Italy* **53C2**
Agrigento *Italy* **53B3**
Agrínion *Greece* **55B3**
Agrio, R *Chile* **34A3**
Agropoli *Italy* **53B2**
Agryz *USSR* **61H2**
Agto *Greenland* **6E3**
Aguadilla *Puerto Rico* **27D3**
Agua Prieta *Mexico* **24B1**
Aguascalientes *Mexico* **24B2**
Aguascalientes, State *Mexico* **23A1**
Aguas Formosas *Brazil* **35C1**
Agueda *Port* **50A1**
Aguelhok *Mali* **96C3**
Agüenit, Well *Mor* **96A2**
Aguilas *Spain* **50B2**
Aguililla *Mexico* **23A2**
Agulhas,C *S Africa* **100B4**
Agusan, R *Phil* **79C4**
Ahar *Iran* **93E2**
Ahipara B *NZ* **110B1**
Ahmadābād *India* **85C4**
Ahmadnagar *India* **87A1**
Ahmar, Mts *Eth* **99E2**
Ahr, R *W Germ* **46D1**
Ahrgebirge, Region *W Germ* **46D1**
Ahuacatlán *Mexico* **23A1**
Ahualulco *Mexico* **23A1**
Åhus *Sweden* **39G7**
Āhuvān *Iran* **90B2**
Ahvāz *Iran* **90A3**
Aiajuela *Costa Rica* **26A4**
Aigle *Switz* **47B1**
Aiguille d'Arves, Mt *France* **47B2**
Aiguille de la Grand Sassière, Mt *France* **47B2**
Aikawa *Japan* **75B1**
Aiken *USA* **17B1**
Ailao Shan, Upland *China* **73A5**
Aimorés *Brazil* **35C1**
Ain Beni Mathar *Mor* **96B1**
Ain Dalla, Well *Egypt* **95B2**
Aïn el Hadjel *Alg* **51C2**
Aïn Galakka *Chad* **95A3**
Aïn Sefra *Alg* **96B1**
'Ain Sukhna *Egypt* **92B4**
Aioi *Japan* **75A2**
Aioun Abd el Malek, Well *Maur* **96B2**
Aïoun El Atrouss *Maur* **97B3**
Aiquile *Bol* **30C2**
Aïr, Desert Region *Niger* **97C3**
Airdrie *Can* **13E2**
Aire *France* **46B1**
Aire, R *Eng* **42D3**
Aire, R *France* **46C2**
Airforce I *Can* **6C3**
Airolo *Switz* **47C1**
Aishihik *Can* **4E3**
Aishihik L *Can* **12G2**
Aisne, Department *France* **46B2**
Aisne, R *France* **49C2**
Aitape *PNG* **71F4**
Aiviekste, R *USSR* **58D1**
Aixa Zuogi *China* **72B2**
Aix-en-Provence *France* **49D3**
Aix-les-Bains *France* **47A2**
Aiyar Res *India* **86B2**
Aíyion *Greece* **55B3**
Aíyna, I *Greece* **55B3**
Āīzawl *India* **86C2**
Aizeb, R *Namibia* **100A3**
Aizu-Wakamatsu *Japan* **74E3**
Ajaccio *Corse* **52A2**
Ajalpan *Mexico* **23B2**
Ajdabiyah *Libya* **95B1**
Ajigasawa *Japan* **74E2**
Ajlūn *Jordan* **94B2**
Ajman *UAE* **91C4**
Ajmer *India* **85C3**
Ajo *USA* **9B3**
Ajtos *Bulg* **54C2**
Ajuchitan *Mexico* **23A2**
Ak, R *Turk* **55C3**
Akaishi-sanchi, Mts *Japan* **75B1**
Akalkot *India* **87B1**
Akaroa *NZ* **111B2**
Akashi *Japan* **75A2**
Akbulak *USSR* **61J3**
Akçakale *Turk* **93C2**
Akchar, Watercourse *Maur* **96A2**
Ak Dağ, Mt *Turk* **55C3**
Aketi *Zaïre* **98C2**
Akhalkalaki *USSR* **93D1**
Akhalsikhe *USSR* **93D1**
Akharnái *Greece* **55B3**
Akhiok *USA* **12D3**
Akhisar *Turk* **92A2**
Akhiste *USSR* **58D1**
Akhmîm *Egypt* **95C2**
Akhtubinsk *USSR* **61G4**
Akhtyrka *USSR* **60D4**
Aki *Japan* **75A2**
Akimiski I *Can* **7B4**
Akita *Japan* **74E3**
Akjoujt *Maur* **96A3**
'Akko *Israel* **94B2**
Aklavik *USA* **4E3**
Aklé Aouana, Desert Region *Maur* **97B3**
Akobo *Sudan* **99D2**
Akobo, R *Sudan* **99D2**
Akoha *Afghan* **84B1**
Akola *India* **85D4**
Akot *India* **85D4**
Akpatok I *Can* **6D3**
Ákra Kafirévs, C *Greece* **55B3**
Ákra Maléa, C *Greece* **55B3**
Akranes *Iceland* **38A2**
Ákra Sídheros, C *Greece* **55C3**
Ákra Spátha, C *Greece* **55B3**
Ákra Taínaron, C *Greece* **55B3**
Akron *USA* **10B2**
Akrotiri B *Cyprus* **94A1**
Aksai Chin, Mts *China* **84D1**
Aksaray *Turk* **92B2**
Aksay *USSR* **61H3**
Aksayquin Hu, L *China* **84D1**
Akşehir *Turk* **92B2**
Akseki *Turk* **92B2**
Aksenovo Zilovskoye *USSR* **63D2**
Aksha *USSR* **68D1**
Aksu *China* **82C1**
Aktogay *USSR* **65J5**
Aktumsyk *USSR* **61J4**
Aktyubinsk *USSR* **65G4**
Akureyri *Iceland* **38B1**
Akzhal *USSR* **65K5**
Alabama, State *USA* **11B3**
Alabama, R *USA* **11B3**
Alabaster *USA* **17A1**
Ala Dağlari, Mts *Turk* **92C2**
Alagir *USSR* **61F5**
Alagna *Italy* **47B2**
Alagoas, State *Brazil* **31D3**
Alagoinhas *Brazil* **31D4**
Alagón *Spain* **51B1**
Al Ahmadi *Kuwait* **93E4**
Alajuela *Costa Rica* **25D3**
Alakanuk *USA* **12B2**
Alakurtti *USSR* **38L5**
Al Amārah *Iraq* **93E3**
Alameda *USA* **21A2**
Alamo *Mexico* **23B1**
Alamogordo *USA* **9C3**
Alamosa *USA* **9C3**
Åland, I *Fin* **39H6**
Alanya *Turk* **92B2**
Alapaha, R *USA* **17B1**
Alapayevsk *USSR* **65H4**
Alaşehir *Turk* **92A2**
Ala Shan, Mts *China* **68C3**
Alaska, State *USA* **4C3**
Alaska,G of *USA* **4D4**
Alaska Pen *USA* **12C3**
Alaska Range, Mts *USA* **4C3**
Alassio *Italy* **52A2**
Alatna, R *USA* **12D1**
Alatyr *USSR* **61G3**
Alawoona *Aust* **108B2**
Al'Ayn *UAE* **91C5**
Alayskiy Khrebet, Mts *USSR* **82B2**
Alba *Italy* **49D3**
Al Bāb *Syria* **92C2**
Albacete *Spain* **51B2**
Alba de Tormes *Spain* **50A1**
Al Badi *Iraq* **93D2**
Alba Iulia *Rom* **54B1**
Albania, Republic *Europe* **54A2**
Albany *Aust* **106A4**
Albany, Georgia *USA* **17B1**
Albany, New York *USA* **15D2**
Albany, Oregon *USA* **8A2**
Albany, R *Can* **7B4**
Albardón *Arg* **34B2**
Al Batinah, Region *Oman* **91C5**
Albatross B *Aust* **71F5**
Al Baydā *Libya* **95B1**
Albemarle Sd *USA* **11C3**
Alberche, R *Spain* **50B1**
Alberga *Aust* **108A1**
Albert *France* **46B1**
Alberta, Province *Can* **5G4**
Albert,L *Uganda/Zaïre* **99D2**
Albert Lea *USA* **10A2**
Albert Nile, R *Uganda* **99D2**
Albertville *France* **49D2**
Albi *France* **48C3**
Albia *USA* **18B1**
Albina *Suriname* **33G2**
Albion, Michigan *USA* **14B2**
Albion, New York *USA* **15C2**
Al Bi'r *S Arabia* **92C4**
Al Biyadh, Region *S Arabia* **91A5**
Alborán, I *Spain* **50B2**
Ålborg *Den* **39G7**
Al Brayqah *Libya* **95A1**
Al Bū Kamāl *Syria* **93D3**
Albula, R *Switz* **47C1**
Albuquerque *USA* **9C3**
Al Buraymi *Oman* **91C5**
Al Burdī *Libya* **95B1**
Albury *Aust* **107D4**
Al Buşayyah *Iraq* **93E3**
Alcalá de Henares *Spain* **50B1**
Alcamo *Italy* **53B3**
Alcaniz *Spain* **51B1**
Alcântara *Brazil* **31C2**
Alcaraz *Spain* **50B2**
Alcázar de San Juan *Spain* **50B2**
Alcira *Spain* **51B2**
Alcobaça *Brazil* **35D1**
Alcolea de Pinar *Spain* **50B1**
Alcoy *Spain* **51B2**
Alcudia *Spain* **51C2**
Aldabra, Is *Indian O* **89J8**
Aldan *USSR* **63E2**
Aldanskoye Nagor'ye, Upland *USSR* **63E2**
Aldeburgh *Eng* **43E3**
Alderney, I *UK* **48B2**
Aldershot *Eng* **43D4**
Aleg *Maur* **97A3**
Alegrete *Brazil* **30E4**
Alejandro Roca *Arg* **34C2**
Alejandro Selkirk, I *Chile* **30H6**
Aleksandrovsk Sakhalinskiy *USSR* **63G2**
Alekseyevka *USSR* **65J4**
Aleksin *USSR* **60E3**
Älem *Sweden* **58B1**
Além Paraíba *Brazil* **35C2**
Alençon *France* **49C2**
Alenuihaha Chan *Hawaiian Is* **21C4**
Alert *Can* **6D1**
Alès *France* **49C3**
Alessandria *Italy* **52A2**
Ålesund *Nor* **64B3**
Aleutian Range, Mts *USA* **12C3**
Alexander Arch *USA* **4E4**
Alexander Bay *S Africa* **100A3**
Alexander City *USA* **17A1**
Alexander I *Ant* **112C3**
Alexandra *NZ* **111A3**
Alexandra,C *South Georgia* **29G8**
Alexandra Fjord *Can* **6C2**
Alexandria *Egypt* **95B1**
Alexandria, Louisiana *USA* **11A3**
Alexandria, Minnesota *USA* **10A2**
Alexandria, Virginia *USA* **10C3**
Alexandroúpolis *Greece* **55C2**
Alexis Creek *Can* **13C2**
Aley *Leb* **94B2**
Aleysk *USSR* **65K4**
Al Fallūjah *Iraq* **93D3**
Alfaro *Spain* **51B1**
Alfatar *Bulg* **54C2**
Al Fāw *Iraq* **93E3**
Alfonsas *Brazil* **35B2**
Alfiós, R *Greece* **55B3**
Alfonsine *Italy* **47D2**
Alfonzo Cláudio *Brazil* **35C2**
Alfredo Chaves *Brazil* **35C2**
Alga *USSR* **61J4**
Algarrobo del Águila *Arg* **34B3**
Algeciras *Spain* **50A2**
Alger *Alg* **96C1**
Algeria, Republic *Africa* **96B2**
Alghero *Sardegna* **53A2**

Algonquin Park *Can* **15C1**
Al Hadd *Oman* **91C5**
Al Hadithah *Iraq* **93D3**
Al Hadithah *S Arabia* **92C3**
Al Hadr *Iraq* **93D2**
Al Hajar al Gharbī, Mts *Oman* **91C5**
Al Hajar ash Sharqī, Mts *Oman* **91C5**
Al Hamad, Desert Region *Jordan/S Arabia* **93C3**
Al Haniyah, Desert Region *Iraq* **93E4**
Al Harīq *S Arabia* **91A5**
Al Harrah, Desert Region *S Arabia* **93C3**
Al Harūj al Aswad, Upland *Libya* **95A2**
Al Hasa, Region *S Arabia* **91A4**
Al Hasakah *Syria* **93D2**
Al Hawjā' *S Arabia* **93C4**
Al Hayy *Iraq* **93E3**
Al Hījānah *Syria* **94C2**
Al Hillah *Iraq* **93D3**
Al Hillah *S Arabia* **91A5**
Al Hoceima *Mor* **96B1**
Al Hufūf *S Arabia* **91A4**
Al Humrah, Region *UAE* **91B5**
Al Huwatsah *Oman* **91C5**
Alīābad *Iran* **90A2**
Aliabad *Iran* **91C4**
Aliákmon, R *Greece* **55B2**
Alī al Gharbī *Iraq* **93E3**
Alībāg *India* **87A1**
Alicante *Spain* **51B2**
Alice *USA* **9D4**
Alice Springs *Aust* **106C3**
Alicudi, I *Italy* **53B3**
Aligarh *India* **84D3**
Aligūdarz *Iran* **90A3**
Ali-Khel *Afghan* **84B2**
Alimniá, I *Greece* **55C3**
Alīpur Duār *India* **86B1**
Aliquippa *USA* **14B2**
Alisal *USA* **22B2**
Al' Īsawiyah *S Arabia* **93C3**
Aliwal North *S Africa* **100B4**
Al Jaghbūb *Libya* **95B2**
Al Jālamīd *S Arabia* **93D3**
Al Jawf *Libya* **95B2**
Al Jawf *S Arabia* **93C4**
Al Jazīrah, Desert Region *Syria/Iraq* **93D2**
Aljezur *Port* **50A2**
Al Jubayl *S Arabia* **91A4**
Al Kāmil *Oman* **91C5**
Al Khābūr, R *Syria* **93D2**
Al Khābūrah *Oman* **91C5**
Al Khālis *Iraq* **93D3**
Al Khasab *Oman* **91C4**
Al Khawr *Qatar* **91B4**
Al Khums *Libya* **95A1**
Al Kidan, Region *S Arabia* **91B5**
Al Kiswah *Syria* **94C2**
Alkmaar *Neth* **56A2**
Al Kufrah Oasis *Libya* **95B2**
Al Kūt *Iraq* **93E3**
Al Lādhiqīyah *Syria* **92C2**
Allahābād *India* **86A1**
Al Lajāh, Mt *Syria* **94C2**
Allakaket *USA* **12D1**
Allanmyo *Burma* **76B2**
'Allaqi, Watercourse *Egypt* **95C2**
Allatoona L *USA* **17B1**
Allegheny, R *USA* **15C2**
Allegheny Mts *USA* **10C3**
Allendale *USA* **17B1**
Allen,Mt *NZ* **111A3**
Allentown *USA* **15C2**
Alleppey *India* **87B3**
Aller, R *France* **49C2**
Allgäu, Mts *W Germ* **47D1**
Alliance *USA* **8C2**
Al Līth *S Arabia* **81C3**
Al Liwā, Region *UAE* **91B5**
Allora *Aust* **109D1**
Alma, Michigan *USA* **14B2**
Alma Ata *USSR* **82B1**
Almada *Port* **50A2**
Almagan, I *Pacific O* **71F2**
Al Manāmah *Bahrain* **91B4**
Al Ma'nīyah *Iraq* **93D3**
Almanor,L *USA* **21A1**
Almansa *Spain* **51B2**
Alma Peak, Mt *Can* **13B1**
Al Māriyyah *UAE* **91B5**
Al Marj *Libya* **95B1**
Almazán *Spain* **50B1**
Almenara *Brazil* **35C1**
Almeria *Spain* **50B2**
Al'met'yevsk *USSR* **61H3**
Älmhult *Sweden* **56C1**
Al Miqdādīyah *Iraq* **93E3**
Almirante Brown, Base *Ant* **112C3**
Almirante Latorre *Chile* **34A1**
Almirós *Greece* **55B3**
Al Mish'ab *A Arabia* **91A4**
Almodôvar *Port* **50A2**
Almora *India* **84D3**
Al Mubarraz *S Arabia* **91A4**
Al Mudawwara *Jordan* **92C4**
Al Mudaybi *Oman* **91C5**
Al Muharraq *Bahrain* **91B4**
Al Mukallā *S Yemen* **81C4**
Al Mukhā *Yemen* **81C4**
Al Musayyib *Iraq* **93D3**
Alness *Scot* **44B3**
Al Nu'mānīyah *Iraq* **93E3**
Alnwick *Eng* **42D2**
Alor, I *Indon* **71D4**
Alor Setar *Malay* **77C4**
Alotau *PNG* **107E2**
Aloysius,Mt *Aust* **106B3**
Alpachiri *Arg* **34C3**
Alpena *USA* **14B1**
Alpes du Valais, Mts *Switz* **47B2**
Alpi Dolomitiche, Mts *Italy* **52B1**
Alpi Graie, Mts *Italy* **47B2**
Alpine, Texas *USA* **9C3**
Alpi Orobie, Mts *Italy* **47C1**
Alpi Pennine, Mts *Italy* **47B2**
Alpi Retiche, Mts *Switz* **47C1**
Alpi Venoste, Mts *Italy* **47D1**
Alps, Mts *Europe* **52A1**
Al Qaddāhiyah *Libya* **95A1**
Al Qadmūs *Syria* **94C1**
Al Qā'im *Iraq* **93D3**
Al Qalībah *S Arabia* **93C4**
Al Qāmishlī *Syria* **93D2**
Al Qaryah Ash Sharqiyah *Libya* **95A1**
Al Qaryatayn *Syria* **92C3**
Al Qātif *S Arabia* **91A4**
Al Qatrūn *Libya* **95A2**
Al Qayşāmah *S Arabia* **91A4**
Al Quatayfah *Syria* **94C2**
Al Qunayţirah *Syria* **92C3**
Al Qunfidhah *S Arabia* **81C4**
Al Qurnah *Iraq* **93E3**
Al Quşayr *Syria* **94C1**
Al Qutayfah *Syria* **92C3**
Als, I *Den* **56B1**
Alsace, Region *France* **49D2**
Alsfeld *W Germ* **57B2**
Alston *Eng* **42C2**
Alta *Nor* **38J5**
Alta Gracia *Arg* **29D2**
Altagracia de Orituco *Ven* **27D5**
Altai, Mts *Mongolia* **68A2**
Altamaha, R *USA* **17B1**
Altamira *Brazil* **33G4**
Altamira *Mexico* **23B1**
Altamura *Italy* **53C2**
Altanbulag *Mongolia* **68C1**
Altape *PNG* **71F4**
Altata *Mexico* **24B2**
Altay *China* **63A3**
Altay *Mongolia* **63B3**
Altay, Mts *USSR* **63A2**
Altdorf *Switz* **47C1**
Altenkirchen *W Germ* **46D1**
Altiplanicie del Payún, Plat *Arg* **34B3**
Altkirch *France* **47B1**
Alto Molócue *Mozam* **101C2**
Alton *USA* **10A3**
Altoona *USA* **15C2**
Alto Pencoso, Mts *Arg* **34B2**
Alto Sucuriú *Brazil* **35A1**
Altotonga *Mexico* **23B2**
Altoyac de Alvarez *Mexico* **23A2**
Altun Shan, Mts *China* **82C2**
Alturas *USA* **20B2**
Altus *USA* **9D3**
Al'Ubaylah *S Arabia* **91B5**
Alula *Somalia* **99F1**
Al Urayq, Desert Region *S Arabia* **93C4**
Al'Uruq al Mu'taridah, Region *S Arabia* **91B5**
Alva *USA* **9D2**
Alvarado *Mexico* **23B2**
Alvarado *USA* **19A3**
Älvdalen *Sweden* **39G6**
Alvin *USA* **19A4**
Alvsbyn *Sweden* **38J5**
Al Wajh *S Arabia* **80B3**
Alwar *India* **85D3**
Al Widyān, Desert Region *Iraq/S Arabia* **93D3**
Alxa Yougi *China* **72A2**
Alyat *USSR* **93E2**
Alytus *USSR* **39J8**
Alzey *W Germ* **46E2**
Amacuzac, R *Mexico* **23B2**
Amadi *Sudan* **99D2**
Amādīyah *Iraq* **93D2**
Amadjuak L *Can* **6C3**
Amakusa-shotō, I *Japan* **74B4**
Åmål *Sweden* **39G7**
Amalat, R *USSR* **63D2**
Amaliás *Greece* **55B3**
Amalner *India* **85D4**
Amami, I *Japan* **69E4**
Amami gunto, Arch *Japan* **69E4**
Amanzimtoti *S Africa* **100C4**
Amapá *Brazil* **33G3**
Amapá, State *Brazil* **33G3**
Amarillo *USA* **9C3**
Amasya *Turk* **60E5**
Amatitan *Mexico* **23A1**
Amazonas *Brazil* **33G4**
Amazonas, State *Brazil* **32D4**
Amazonas, R *Brazil* **28C3**
Ambāla *India* **84D2**
Ambalangoda *Sri Lanka* **87C3**
Ambalavao *Madag* **101D3**
Ambam *Cam* **98B2**
Ambanja *Madag* **101D2**
Ambarchik *USSR* **1C7**
Ambato *Ecuador* **32B4**
Ambato-Boeny *Madag* **101D2**
Ambatolampy *Madag* **101D2**
Ambatondrazaka *Madag* **101D2**
Amberg *W Germ* **57C3**
Ambergris Cay, I *Belize* **25D3**
Ambikāpur *India* **86A2**
Ambilobe *Madag* **101D2**
Amboasary *Madag* **101D3**
Ambodifototra *Madag* **101D2**
Ambohimahasoa *Madag* **101D3**
Ambon *Indon* **71D4**
Ambositra *Madag* **101D3**
Ambovombe *Madag* **101D3**
Ambriz *Angola* **98B3**
Am Dam *Chad* **98C1**
Amderma *USSR* **64H3**
Ameca *Mexico* **24B2**
Amecacameca *Mexico* **23B2**
Ameghino *Arg* **34C2**
Ameland, I *Neth* **56B2**
Amenia *USA* **16C2**
American Highland, Upland *Ant* **112B10**
American Samoa, Is *Pacific O* **105H4**
Americus *USA* **17B1**
Amersfoort *S Africa* **101G1**
Amery Ice Shelf *Ant* **112C10**
Amfilokhía *Greece* **55B3**
Amfissa *Greece* **55B3**
Amga *USSR* **63F1**
Amgal, R *USSR* **63F1**
Amgu *USSR* **69F2**
Amgun', R *USSR* **69F1**
Amhara, Region *Eth* **99D1**
Amherst *Can* **7D5**
Amherst, Massachusetts *USA* **16C1**
Amhūr *India* **87B2**
Amiens *France* **48C2**
Amino *Japan* **75B1**
Amioune *Leb* **94B1**
Amirante Is *Indian O* **89K8**
Amlekhgan *Nepal* **86B1**
Amman *Jordan* **92C3**
Ämmänsaario *Fin* **38K6**
Ammersfoort *Neth* **56B2**
Amoda'ya, R *USSR* **80E1**
Amol *Iran* **90B2**
Amos *Can* **7C5**
Ampanihy *Madag* **101D3**
Amparo *Brazil* **35B2**
Amposta *Spain* **51C1**
Amrāvati *India* **85D4**
Amreli *India* **85C4**
Amritsar *India* **84C2**
Amsterdam *Neth* **56A2**
Amsterdam *S Africa* **101H1**
Amsterdam *USA* **15D2**
Am Timan *Chad* **98C1**
Amu Darya, R *USSR* **88L3**
Amund Ringes I *Can* **6A2**
Amundsen G *Can* **4F2**
Amundsen S *Ant* **112B4**
Amundsen-Scott, Base *Ant* **80E**
Amuntai *Indon* **78D3**
Amur, R *USSR* **63E2**
Anaco *Ven* **33E2**
Anaconda *USA* **8B2**
Anacortes *USA* **20B1**
Anáfi, I *Greece* **55C3**
'Ānah *Iraq* **93D3**
Anaheim *USA* **21B3**
Anaimalai Hills *India* **87B2**
Anakapalle *India* **83C4**
Anaktuvuk P *USA* **12E1**
Analalaya *Madag* **101D2**
Anamur *Turk* **92B2**
Anan *Japan* **75A2**
Anantapur *India* **87B2**
Anantnag *India* **84D2**
Anápolis *Brazil* **31B5**
Anār *Iran* **90C3**
Anārak *Iran* **90B3**
Anatahan, I *Pacific O* **71F2**
Añatuya *Arg* **30D4**
Anbyŏn *N Korea* **74B3**
Ancapa Is *USA* **22C4**
Anchorage *USA* **4D3**
Ancohuma, Mt *Bol* **30C2**
Ancón *Peru* **32B6**
Ancona *Italy* **52B2**
Ancram *USA* **16C1**
Ancud *Chile* **29B4**
Anda *China* **69E2**
Andacollo *Arg* **34A3**
Andado *Aust* **108A1**
Andahuaylas *Peru* **32C6**
Andalsnes *Nor* **38F6**

Andalucia, Region *Spain* **50A2**
Andalusia *USA* **17A1**
Andaman Is *Burma* **83D4**
Andaman S *Burma* **83D4**
Andamooka *Aust* **108A2**
Andenes *Nor* **38H5**
Andermatt *Switz* **47C1**
Andernach *W Germ* **57B2**
Anderson, Indiana *USA* **14A2**
Anderson, Missouri *USA* **18B2**
Anderson, S Carolina *USA* **17B1**
Anderson, R *Can* **4F3**
Andhra Pradesh, State *India* **87B1**
Andikíthira, I *Greece* **55B3**
Andizhan *USSR* **65J5**
Andkhui *Afghan* **65H6**
Andong *S Korea* **74B3**
Andorra, Principality *SW Europe* **51C1**
Andorra-La-Vella *Andorra* **51C1**
Andover *Eng* **43D4**
Andradina *Brazil* **35A2**
Andreafsky *USA* **12B2**
Andreas,C *Cyprus* **92B2**
Andria *Italy* **53C2**
Andros, I *Bahamas* **11C4**
Ándros, I *Greece* **55B3**
Androth, I *India* **87A2**
Andújar *Spain* **50B2**
Andulo *Angola* **100A2**
Anécho *Togo* **97C4**
Anéfis *Mali* **97C3**
Añelo *Arg* **34B3**
Angarsk *USSR* **63C2**
Ånge *Sweden* **38H6**
Angel de la Guarda, I *Mexico* **24A2**
Angeles *Phil* **79B2**
Angelholm *Sweden* **39G7**
Angellala Creek, R *Aust* **109C1**
Angels Camp *USA* **22B1**
Angemuk, Mt *Indon* **71E4**
Angers *France* **48B2**
Angkor, Hist Site *Camb* **76C3**
Anglesey, I *Wales* **41C3**
Angleton *USA* **19A4**
Angmagssalik *Greenland* **6G3**
Angoche *Mozam* **101D2**
Angol *Chile* **29B3**
Angola, Indiana *USA* **14B2**
Angola, Republic *Africa* **100A2**
Angola Basin *Atlantic O* **103H6**
Angoon *USA* **12H3**
Angoulême *France* **48C2**
Angra do Heroismo *Açores* **96A1**
Angra dos Reis *Brazil* **35C2**
Anguil *Arg* **34C3**
Anguilla, I *Caribbean* **27E3**
Anguilla Cays, Is *Caribbean* **26B2**
Angul *India* **86B2**
Angumu *Zaïre* **99C3**
Anholt, I *Den* **56C1**
Anhua *China* **73C4**
Anhui, Province *China* **72D3**
Aniak *USA* **12C2**
Anicuns *Brazil* **35B1**
Anizy-le-Château *France* **46B2**
Anjak *USA* **4C3**
Anjou, Republic *France* **48B2**
Anjouan, I *Comoros* **101D2**
Anjozorobe *Madag* **101D2**
Anju *N Korea* **74B3**
Ankang *China* **72B3**
Ankara *Turk* **92B2**
Ankaratra, Mt *Madag* **101D2**
Ankazoabo *Madag* **101D3**
Ankazobe *Madag* **101D2**
Anklam *E Germ* **56C2**
An Loc *Viet* **76D3**
Anlong *China* **73B4**
Anlu *China* **73C3**
Anna *USA* **18C2**
'Annaba *Alg* **96C1**
An Nabk *S Arabia* **92C3**
An Nabk *Syria* **92C3**
Anna Creek *Aust* **108A1**
An Najaf *Iraq* **93D3**
Annan *Scot* **42C2**
Annapolis *USA* **15C3**
Annapurna, Mt *Nepal* **86A1**
Ann Arbor *USA* **14B2**
An Nāsirah *Syria* **94C1**
An Nāsirīyah *Iraq* **93E3**
Annecy *France* **47B2**
Annemasse *France* **47B1**
An Nhon *Viet* **76D3**
Anning *China* **73A5**
Anniston *USA* **17A1**
Annonay *France* **49C2**
Annotto Bay *Jamaica* **27J1**
Anqing *China* **73D3**
Ansai *China* **72B2**
Ansbach *W Germ* **57C3**
Anse d'Hainault *Haiti* **26C3**
Anshan *China* **72E1**
Anshun *China* **73B4**
Ansongo *Mali* **97C3**
Ansted *USA* **14B3**
Antakya *Turk* **92C2**
Antalaha *Madag* **101E2**
Antalya *Turk* **92B2**
Antalya Körfezi, B *Turk* **92B2**
Antananarivo *Madag* **101D2**
Antarctic Circle *Ant* **112C1**
Antarctic Pen *Ant* **112C3**
Antequera *Spain* **50B2**
Anti-Atlas, Mts *Mor* **96B2**
Anticosti I *Can* **7D5**
Antigua, I *Caribbean* **27E3**
Antioch *USA* **21A2**
Antlers *USA* **19A3**
Antofagasta *Chile* **30B3**
Antrim, County *N Ire* **45C1**
Antrim *N Ire* **45C1**
Antrim Hills *N Ire* **45C1**
Antseranana *Madag* **101D2**
Antsirabe *Madag* **101D2**
Antsohiny *Madag* **101D2**
An Tuc *Viet* **76D3**
Antwerpen *Belg* **46C1**
An Uaimh *Irish Rep* **45C2**
Anupgarh *India* **84C3**
Anuradhapura *Sri Lanka* **87C3**
Anvik *USA* **4B3**
Anxi *China* **63B3**
Anyang *China* **72C2**
A'nyêmaqên Shan, Upland *China* **72A3**
Anza, R *Italy* **47C2**
Anzac *Can* **13E1**
Anzhero-Sudzhensk *USSR* **65K4**
Anzio *Italy* **53B2**
Aomori *Japan* **74E2**
Aosta *Italy* **52A1**
Aoukar, Desert Region *Maur* **97B3**
Aoulef *Alg* **96C2**
Aozou *Chad* **95A2**
Apa, R *Brazil/Par* **30E3**
Apalachee B *USA* **11B4**
Apalachicola *USA* **17B2**
Apalachicola B *USA* **17A2**
Apan *Mexico* **23B2**
Apaporis, R *Colombia* **32C3**
Aparecida do Taboado *Brazil* **35A2**
Aparri *Phil* **79B2**
Apatin *Yugos* **54A1**
Apatzingan *Mexico* **24B3**
Apeldoorn *Neth* **56B2**
Apiai *Brazil* **35B2**
Apoera *Surinam* **33F2**
Apollo Bay *Aust* **108B3**
Apo,Mt, Mt *Phil* **79C4**
Apopka,L *USA* **17B2**
Aporé, R *Brazil* **30F2**
Apostle Is *USA* **10A2**
Apostle L *USA* **10A2**
Apozol *Mexico* **23A1**
Appalachian Mts *USA* **11B3**
Appennino Abruzzese, Mts *Italy* **52B2**
Appennino Ligure, Mts *Italy* **52A2**
Appennino Lucano, Mts *Italy* **53C2**
Appennino Napoletano, Mts *Italy* **53B2**
Appennino Tosco-Emilliano, Mts *Italy* **52B2**
Appennino Tosco-Emilliano, Mts *Italy* **52B2**
Appennino Umbro-Marchigiano, Mts *Italy* **52B2**
Appenzell *Switz* **47C1**
Appleby *Eng* **42C2**
Appleton, Wisconsin *USA* **14A2**
Apucarana *Brazil* **30F3**
Apulco *Mexico* **23B1**
Apure, R *Ven* **32D2**
Apurimac, R *Peru* **32C6**
'Aqaba *Jordan* **92C4**
'Aqaba,G of *Egypt/S Arabia* **92B4**
'Aqdā *Iran* **90B3**
Aquidauana *Brazil* **30E3**
Aquila *Mexico* **23A2**
Ara *India* **86A1**
Arab *USA* **17A1**
Arabian, S *Asia/Arabian Pen* **81D4**
Aracajú *Brazil* **31D4**
Aracati *Brazil* **31D2**
Araçatuba *Brazil* **30F3**
Aracena *Spain* **50A2**
Araçuai *Brazil* **31C5**
Arad *Israel* **94B3**
Arad *Rom* **60B4**
Arada *Chad* **98C1**
'Arādah *UAE* **91B5**
Arafura S *Indon/Aust* **106C1**
Aragarças *Brazil* **30F2**
Aragón, Region *Spain* **51B1**
Aragon, R *Spain* **50B1**
Araguaia, R *Brazil* **33G6**
Araguaína *Brazil* **31B3**
Araguari *Brazil* **31B5**
Araguari, R *Brazil* **35B1**
Arai *Japan* **75B1**
Arak *Alg* **96C2**
Arāk *Iran* **90A3**
Arakan Yoma, Mts *Burma* **76A2**
Arakkonam *India* **87B2**
Araks, R *USSR* **93E2**
Aral S *USSR* **62D3**
Aral'sk *USSR* **80E1**
Aral'skoye More, S *USSR* **65G5**
Aran, I *Irish Rep* **40B2**
Aran, Is *Irish Rep* **41B3**
Aranda de Duero *Spain* **50B1**
Arandas *Mexico* **23A1**
Aranjuez *Spain* **50B1**
Arao *Japan* **75A2**
Araouane *Mali* **97B3**
Arapey, R *Urug* **29E2**
Arapiraca *Brazil* **31D4**
Araporgas *Brazil* **35A2**
Ararangua *Brazil* **30G4**
Araraquara *Brazil* **31B6**
Araras *Brazil* **35B2**
Ararat *Aust* **107D4**
Ararat *USSR* **93D2**
Aras, R *Turk* **93D1**
Arato *Japan* **75C1**
Arauca, R *Ven* **32D2**
Arauco *Chile* **34A3**
Arauea *Colombia* **32C2**
Arāvalli Range, Mts *India* **85C4**
Araxá *Brazil* **31B5**
Arba Minch *Eth* **99D2**
Arbatax *Sardegna* **53A3**
Arbīl *Iraq* **93D2**
Arbois *France* **47A1**
Arbrå *Sweden* **39H6**
Arbroath *Scot* **44C3**
Arc *France* **47A1**
Arc, R *France* **47B2**
Arcachon *France* **48B3**
Arcadia *USA* **17B2**
Arcata *USA* **20B2**
Arcelia *Mexico* **23A2**
Archipiélago de Camaguey, Arch *Cuba* **26B2**
Archipiélago de la Reina Adelaida, Arch *Chile* **29B6**
Archipiélago de las Chones, Arch *Chile* **29B4**
Archipiélago de las Perlas, Arch *Panama* **32B2**
Arcos *Brazil* **35B2**
Arcos de la Frontera *Spain* **50A2**
Arctic Circle **1C1**
Arctic Red *Can* **4E3**
Arctic Red R *Can* **4E3**
Arctic Village *USA* **4D3**
Arctowski, Base *Ant* **112C2**
Arda, R *Bulg* **54C2**
Ardabīl *Iran* **65F6**
Ardahan *Turk* **93D1**
Ardal *Nor* **39F6**
Ardar des Iforas, Upland *Alg/Mali* **96C2**
Ardee *Irish Rep* **45C2**
Ardekān *Iran* **90B3**
Ardennes, Department *France* **46C2**
Ardennes, Region *Belg* **57A2**
Ardestan *Iran* **90B3**
Ardh es Suwwan, Desert Region *Jordan* **92C3**
Ardila, R *Port* **50A2**
Ardlethan *Aust* **109C2**
Ardmore *USA* **9D3**
Ardnamurchan, Pt *Scot* **44A3**
Ardres *France* **46A1**
Ardrishaig *Scot* **44B3**
Ardrossan *Scot* **42B2**
Arecibo *Puerto Rico* **27D3**
Areia Branca *Brazil* **31D2**
Arena,Pt *USA* **21A2**
Arendal *Nor* **39F7**
Arequipa *Peru* **30B2**
Arezzo *Italy* **52B2**
Argenta *Italy* **52B2**
Argentan *France* **49C2**
Argenteuil *France* **46B2**
Argentina, Republic *S America* **28C7**
Argentine Basin *Atlantic O* **103F7**
Argenton-sur-Creuse *France* **48C2**
Argeşul, R *Rom* **54C2**
Arghardab, R *Afghan* **84B2**
Argolikós Kólpos, G *Greece* **55B3**
Argonne, Region *France* **46C2**
Árgos *Greece* **55B3**
Argostólion *Greece* **55B3**
Arguello,Pt *USA* **22B3**

Argyle,L *Aust* 106B2
Århus *Den* 56C1
Ariamsvlei *Namibia* 100A3
Arian zón, R *Spain* 50B1
Arias *Arg* 34C2
Aribinda *Upper Volta* 97B3
Arica *Chile* 30B2
Arifwala *Pak* 84C2
Arima *Trinidad* 27L1
Arinos *Brazil* 35B1
Arinos, R *Brazil* 33F6
Ario de Rosales *Mexico* 23A2
Aripo,Mt *Trinidad* 27L1
Aripuana *Brazil* 33E5
Aripuaná, R *Brazil* 33E5
Arisaig *Scot* 44B3
Ariskere *India* 87B2
Aristazabal I *Can* 13B2
Arizona *Arg* 34B3
Arizona, State *USA* 9B3
Årjäng *Sweden* 39G7
Arkadak *USSR* 61F3
Arkadelphia *USA* 19B3
Arkalya *USSR* 65H4
Arkansas, State *USA* 11A3
Arkansas, R *USA* 11A3
Arkansas City *USA* 18A2
Arkhangel'sk *USSR* 64F3
Arklow *Irish Rep* 41B3
Arlberg P *Austria* 47D1
Arles *France* 49C3
Arlington, Texas *USA* 19A3
Arlington, Virginia *USA* 15C3
Arlington, Washington *USA* 20B1
Arlit *Niger* 97C3
Arlon *Belg* 57B3
Armagh, County *N Ire* 45C1
Armagh *N Ire* 45C1
Armagós, I *Greece* 55C3
Armavir *USSR* 61F5
Armena *Mexico* 23A2
Armenia *Colombia* 32B3
Armidale *Aust* 107E4
Armstrong *Can* 13D2
Armyanskaya SSR, Republic *USSR* 65F5
Arnaud, R *Can* 7C3
Arnauti, C *Cyprus* 92B2
Arnhem *Neth* 56B2
Arnhem,C *Aust* 106C2
Arnhem Land *Aust* 106C2
Arnold *USA* 22B1
Arnprior *Can* 15C1
Arnsberg *W Germ* 46E1
Aroab *Namibia* 100A3
Arona *Italy* 47C2
Aropuk L *USA* 12B2
Arosa *Switz* 52A1
Arquipélago dos Bijagós, Arch *Guinea-Bissau* 97A3
Ar Ramādī *Iraq* 93D3
Arran, I *Scot* 42B2
Ar Raqqah *Syria* 93C2
Arras *France* 49C1
Arrecife *Canary Is* 96A2
Arrecifes *Arg* 34C2
Arriaga *Mexico* 23A1
Ar Rifā't *Iraq* 93E3
Ar Rihāb, Desert Region *Iraq* 93E3
Arrochar *Scot* 44B3
Arrowtown *NZ* 111A2
Arroyo Seco *Mexico* 23B1
Ar Ru'ays *Qatar* 91B4
Ar Rustaq *Oman* 91C5
Ar Rutbah *Iraq* 93D3
Arsiero *Italy* 47D2
Arsizio *Italy* 49D2
Arsk *USSR* 61G2
Árta *Greece* 55B3
Arteaga *Mexico* 23A2
Artemovsk *USSR* 63B2
Artemovskiy *USSR* 63D2
Artesia *USA* 9C3
Arthurs P *NZ* 111B2
Artic Bay *Can* 6B2
Artigas *Urug* 29E2
Artillery L *Can* 4H3
Artois, Region *France* 48C1
Arturo Prat, Base *Ant* 112C2
Artvin *Turk* 93D1
Aru *Zaïre* 99D2
Aruanã *Brazil* 33G6
Aruba, I *Caribbean* 27C4
Arun, R *Nepal* 86B1
Arunāchal Pradesh, Union Territory *India* 86C1
Aruppukkottai *India* 87B3
Arusha *Tanz* 99D3
Aruwimi, R *Zaïre* 98C2
Arvayheer *Mongolia* 68C2
Arve, R *France* 47B2
Arvida *Can* 7C5
Arvidsjaur *Sweden* 38H5
Arvika *Sweden* 39G7
Arvin *USA* 21B2
Arwad, I *Syria* 94B1
Arzamas *USSR* 61F2
Asadabad *Afghan* 84C2
Asahi, R *Japan* 75A2
Asahi dake, Mt *Japan* 74E2
Asahikawa *Japan* 74E2
Asansol *India* 86B2
Asawanwah, Well *Libya* 95A2
Asbest *USSR* 61K2
Asbury Park *USA* 15D2
Ascension, I *Atlantic O* 103H5
Aschaffenburg *W Germ* 57B3
Aschersleben *E Germ* 56C2
Ascoli Piceno *Italy* 52B2
Ascona *Switz* 47C1
Asedjirad, Upland *Alg* 96C2
Åsele *Sweden* 38H6
Aselle *Eth* 99D2
Asenovgrad *Bulg* 54B2
Asfeld *France* 46C2
Asha *USSR* 61J2
Ashburn *USA* 17B1
Ashburton *NZ* 111B2
Ashburton, R *Aust* 106A3
Ashdod *Israel* 92B3
Ashdown *USA* 19B3
Asheville *USA* 11B3
Ashford *Aust* 109D1
Ashford *Eng* 43E4
Ashikaga *Japan* 74D3
Ashizuri-misaki, Pt *Japan* 75A2
Ashkhabad *USSR* 65G6
Ashland, Kentucky *USA* 10B3
Ashland, Nebraska *USA* 18A1
Ashland, Ohio *USA* 14B2
Ashland, Oregon *USA* 8A2
Ashley *Aust* 109C1
Ashokan Res *USA* 16B2
Ashqelon *Israel* 94B3
Ash Shabakh *Iraq* 93D3
Ash Sha'm *UAE* 91C4
Ash Sharqāt *Iraq* 93D2
Ash Shatrah *Iraq* 93E3
Ash Shihr *S Yemen* 81C4
Ash Shumlul *S Arabia* 91A4
Ashtabula *USA* 14B2
Ashuanipi L *Can* 7D4
Asi, R *Syria* 92C3
Asiago *Italy* 47D2
Asinara, I *Medit S* 53A2
Asino *USSR* 65K4
Aşkale *Turk* 93D2
Askersund *Sweden* 39G7
Asmar *Afghan* 84C1
Asmara *Eth* 95C3
Aso *Japan* 75A2
Asosa *Eth* 99D1
Aspiring,Mt *NZ* 111A2
Assab *Eth* 99E1
As Sabkhah *Syria* 93C2
As Salamiyah *S Arabia* 91A5
As Salamīyah *Syria* 92C2
As Salman *Iraq* 93D3
Assam, State *India* 86C1
As Samāwah *Iraq* 93E3
As Şanām, Region *S Arabia* 91B5
As Sanamayn *Syria* 94C2
Assen *Neth* 56B2
Assens *Den* 56B1
As Sidrah *Libya* 95A1
Assiniboia *Can* 5H5
Assiniboine,Mt *Can* 5G4
Assis *Brazil* 30F3
As Sukhnah *Syria* 93C3
As Summan, Region *S Arabia* 91A5
Assumption, I *Seychelles* 99E3
As Suwaydā' *Syria* 92C3
As Suwayrah *Iraq* 93D3
Astara *USSR* 93E2
Asti *Italy* 52A2
Astipálaia, I *Greece* 55C3
Astorga *Spain* 50A1
Astoria *USA* 8A2
Astrakhan' *USSR* 61G4
Asturias, Region *Spain* 50A1
Asunción *Par* 30E4
Aswa, R *Uganda* 99D2
Aswân *Egypt* 80B3
Aswân High Dam *Egypt* 95C2
Asyût *Egypt* 95C2
As Zilaf *Syria* 92C3
Atakpamé *Togo* 97C4
Atambua *Indon* 71D4
Atangmik *Greenland* 6E3
Atar *Maur* 96A2
Atasu *USSR* 65J5
Atbara *Sudan* 95C3
Atbasar *USSR* 65H4
Atchafalaya B *USA* 11A4
Atchison *USA* 10A3
Atco *USA* 16B3
Atenguillo *Mexico* 23A1
Atessa *Italy* 52B2
Ath *Belg* 46B1
Athabasca *Can* 13E2
Athabasca, R *Can* 5G4
Athabasca L *Can* 5H4
Athenry *Irish Rep* 45B2
Athens, Georgia *USA* 11B3
Athens, Ohio *USA* 14B3
Athens, Texas *USA* 19A3
Athínai *Greece* 55B3
Athlone *Irish Rep* 41B3
Athol *USA* 16C1
Áthos, Mt *Greece* 55B2
Athy *Irish Rep* 45C2
Ati *Chad* 98B1
Atikoken *Can* 7A5
Atkarsk *USSR* 61F3
Atkins *USA* 18B2
Atlacomulco *Mexico* 23B2
Atlanta, Georgia *USA* 11B3
Atlanta, Michigan *USA* 14B2
Atlantic *USA* 18A1
Atlantic City *USA* 10C3
Atlantic Highlands *USA* 16B2
Atlantic Indian Basin *Atlantic O* 103H8
Atlantic Indian Ridge *Atlantic O* 103H7
Atlas Saharien, Mts *Alg* 96C1
Atlin *Can* 4E4
Atlin L *Can* 4E4
'Atlit *Israel* 94B2
Atlixco *Mexico* 23B2
Atmore *USA* 11B3
Atofinandrahana *Madag* 101D3
Atognak I *USA* 12D3
Atoka *USA* 19A3
Atotonilco *Mexico* 23A1
Atoyac, R *Mexico* 23B2
Atrato, R *Colombia* 32B2
Attaf, Region *UAE* 91D5
At Tā'if *S Arabia* 81C3
At Tall *Syria* 94C2
Attalla *USA* 17A1
Attauapiskat *Can* 7B4
Attauapiskat, R *Can* 7B4
At Taysīyah, Desert Region *S Arabia* 93D3
Attica, Indiana *USA* 14A2
Attigny *France* 46C2
Attleboro, Massachusetts *USA* 15D2
Attopeu *Laos* 76D3
At Tubayq, Upland *S Arabia* 92C4
Atuel, R *Arg* 34B3
Atvidaberg *Sweden* 39H7
Atwater *USA* 22B2
Aubagne *France* 49D3
Aube, Department *France* 46C2
Aubenas *France* 49C3
Auburn, Alabama *USA* 17A1
Auburn, California *USA* 21A2
Auburn, Indiana *USA* 14A2
Auburn, Nebraska *USA* 18A1
Auburn, New York *USA* 15C2
Auburn, Washington *USA* 20B1
Auch *France* 48C3
Auckland *NZ* 110B1
Auckland Is *NZ* 105G6
Aude, R *France* 48C3
Auden *Can* 7B4
Audincourt *France* 47B1
Augathella *Aust* 109C1
Augsburg *W Germ* 57C3
Augusta *Aust* 106A4
Augusta, Georgia *USA* 11B3
Augusta, Kansas *USA* 18A2
Augusta, Maine *USA* 10D2
Augustine I *USA* 12D3
Augustow *Pol* 58C2
Augustus,Mt *Aust* 106A3
Aumale *France* 46A2
Auraiya *India* 85D3
Aurangābād *India* 85D5
Aurès, Mts *Alg* 96C1
Aurillac *France* 48C3
Aurora, Colorado *USA* 8C3
Aurora, Illinois *USA* 10B2
Aurora, Indiana *USA* 14B3
Aurora, Mississippi *USA* 18B2
Aus *Namibia* 100A3
Au Sable *USA* 14B2
Ausert, Well *Mor* 96A2
Austin, Minnesota *USA* 10A2
Austin, Nevada *USA* 21B2
Austin, Texas *USA* 9D3
Australian Alps, Mts *Aust* 107D4
Austria, Fed Republic *Europe* 37E4
Authie, R *France* 46A1
Autlán *Mexico* 24B3
Autun *France* 49C2
Auvergne, Region *France* 49C2
Auxerre *France* 49C2
Auxi-le-Château *France* 46B1
Avallon *France* 49C2
Avalon *USA* 22C4
Avalon Pen *Can* 7E5
Avaré *Brazil* 35B2
Avaz *Iran* 90D3
Avedat, Hist Site *Israel* 94B3
Aveíro *Brazil* 33F4
Aveiro *Port* 50A1
Avellaneda *Arg* 29E2

Avellino *Italy* **53B2**
Avesnes-sur-Helpe *France* **46B1**
Avesta *Sweden* **39H6**
Avezzano *Italy* **52B2**
Aviemore *Scot* **44C3**
Aviemore,L *NZ* **111B2**
Avigliana *Italy* **47B2**
Avignon *France* **49C3**
Avila *Spain* **50B1**
Aviles *Spain* **50A1**
Avisio, R *Italy* **47D1**
Avoca, R *Aust* **108B3**
Avon, County *Eng* **43C4**
Avon, R, Dorset *Eng* **43D4**
Avon, R, Warwick *Eng* **43D3**
Avonmouth *Wales* **43C4**
Avon Park *USA* **17B2**
Avre, R *France* **46B2**
Avtovac *Yugos* **54A2**
A'waj, R *Syria* **94C2**
Awaji-shima, B *Japan* **74D4**
Awarem *Eth* **99E2**
Awarua Pt *NZ* **111A2**
Awash *Eth* **99E2**
Awash, R *Eth* **99E2**
Awa-shima, I *Japan* **75B1**
Awatere, R *NZ* **111B2**
Awbārī *Libya* **95A2**
Aweil *Sudan* **98C2**
Awjilan *Libya* **95B2**
Axel Heiburg I *Can* **6A2**
Axminster *Eng* **43C4**
Ayabe *Japan* **75B1**
Ayacucho *Arg* **29E3**
Ayacucho *Peru* **32C6**
Ayaguz *USSR* **65K5**
Ayakkum Hu, L *China* **82C2**
Ayamonte *Spain* **50A2**
Ayan *USSR* **63F2**
Ayauiri *Peru* **32C6**
Aydin *Turk* **92A2**
Áyios Evstrátios, I *Greece* **55C3**
Aylesbury *Eng* **43D4**
Aylmer,Mt *Can* **13D2**
'Ayn al Fījah *Syria* **94C2**
Ayn Zālah *Iraq* **93D2**
Ayn Zuwayyah, Well *Libya* **95B2**
Ayod *Sudan* **99D2**
Ayr *Aust* **107D2**
Ayr *Scot* **42B2**
Ayr, R *Scot* **42B2**
Ayre,Pt of *Eng* **42B2**
Aytthaya *Thai* **76C3**
Ayutla *Mexico* **23A1**
Ayvacik *Turk* **55C3**
Ayvalik *Turk* **55C3**
Āzamgarh *India* **86A1**
Azaouad, Desert Region *Mali* **97B3**
Azare *Nig* **97D3**
A'Zāz *Syria* **92C2**
Azeffal, Watercourse *Maur* **96A2**
Azerbaydzhanskaya SSR, Republic *USSR* **65F5**
Azogues *Ecuador* **32B4**
Azoum, R *Chad* **98C1**
Azovskoye More, S *USSR* **60E4**
Azrou *Mor* **96B1**
Azucena *Arg* **34D3**
Azuero,Pen de *Panama* **32A2**
Azúl *Arg* **29E3**
Az-Zabdānı *Syria* **94C2**
Az Zāhirah, Mts *Oman* **91C5**
Az Zubayr *Iraq* **93E3**

B

Ba'abda *Leb* **94B2**
Ba'albek *Leb* **92C3**
Ba'al Hazor, Mt *Israel* **94B3**
Baardheere *Somalia* **99E2**
Babadag *Rom* **54C2**
Babaeski *Turk* **92A1**
Babahoyo *Ecuador* **32B4**
Bāb al Mandab, Str *Djibouti/S Yemen* **81C4**
Babar, I *Indon* **71D4**
Babati *Tanz* **99D3**
Babayevo *USSR* **60E2**
Baberton *USA* **14B2**
Babine, R *Can* **13B1**
Babine L *Can* **5F4**
Bābol *Iran* **90B2**
Babuyan Chan *Phil* **79B2**
Babuyan Is *Phil* **79B2**
Bacabal *Brazil* **31C2**
Bacan, I *Indon* **71D4**
Bačau *Rom* **60C4**
Bac Can *Viet* **76D1**
Baccchus Marsh *Aust* **108B3**
Bachu *China* **82B2**
Back, R *Can* **4J3**
Backbone Ranges, Mts *Can* **12J2**
Bac Ninh *Viet* **76D1**
Bacolod *Phil* **79B3**
Baco,Mt *Phil* **79B3**
Badagara *India* **87B2**
Badain Jaran Shamo, Desert *China* **72A1**
Badajoz *Spain* **50A2**
Badalona *Spain* **51C1**
Badanah *S Arabia* **93D3**
Bad Bergzabern *W Germ* **46D2**
Bad Ems *W Germ* **46D1**
Baden *Switz* **47C1**
Baden-Baden *W Germ* **57B3**
Baden-Württemberg, State *W Germ* **57B3**
Badgastein *Austria* **57C3**
Badger *USA* **22C2**
Bad-Godesberg *W Germ* **57B2**
Bad Hersfeld *W Germ* **57B2**
Bad Honnef *W Germ* **46D1**
Badin *Pak* **85B4**
Bad Ischl *Austria* **52B1**
Badiyat ash Sham, Desert Region *Jordan/Iraq* **93C3**
Bad-Kreuznach *W Germ* **57B3**
Bad Nevenahr-Ahrweiler *W Germ* **46D1**
Bad Ragaz *Switz* **47C1**
Bad Tolz *W Germ* **57C3**
Badulla *Sri Lanka* **87C3**
Baena *Spain* **50B2**
Bafatá *Guinea-Bissau* **97A3**
Baffin B *Greenland/Can* **6C2**
Baffin I *Can* **6C2**
Bafia *Cam* **98B2**
Bafing, R *Mali* **97A3**
Bafoulabé *Mali* **97A3**
Bafoussam *Cam* **98B2**
Bāfq *Iran* **90C3**
Bafra Burun, Pt *Turk* **60E5**
Bāft *Iran* **91C4**
Bafwasende *Zaïre* **98C2**
Bagaha *India* **86A1**
Bāgalkot *India* **87B1**
Bagamoyo *Tanz* **99D3**
Bagé *Brazil* **29F2**
Baghdād *Iraq* **93D3**
Bagherhat *Bang* **86B2**
Bāghīn *Iran* **91C3**
Baghlan *Afghan* **84B1**
Bagnoa *Ivory Coast* **97B4**
Bagnols-sur-Cèze *France* **49C3**
Bagoé, R *Mali* **97B3**
Baguio *Phil* **79B2**
Bāhādurābād *India* **86B1**
Bahamas,The, Is *Caribbean* **11C4**
Baharampur *India* **86B2**
Bahar Dar *Eth* **99D1**
Baharîya Oasis *Egypt* **92A4**
Bahawahpur, Province *Pak* **85C3**
Bahawalpur *Pak* **84C3**
Bahawathagar *Pak* **85C3**
Bahia, State *Brazil* **31C4**
Bahía Blanca *Arg* **29D3**
Bahia Blanca, B *Arg* **29D3**
Bahia Concepción, B *Chile* **34A3**
Bahia da Ilha Grande, B *Brazil* **35C2**
Bahia de Banderas, B *Mexico* **24B2**
Bahia de Campeche, B *Mexico* **24C2**
Bahia de la Ascension, B *Mexico* **25D3**
Bahia de Petacalco, B *Mexico* **24B3**
Bahia de Rio de Oro, B *Mor* **96A2**
Bahia de Sepetiba, B *Brazil* **35C2**
Bahía Grande, B *Arg* **29C6**
Bahia Kino *Mexico* **9B4**
Bahia Magdalena, B *Mexico* **24A2**
Bahia Sebastia Vizcaino, B *Mexico* **24A2**
Bahraich *India* **86A1**
Bahrain, Sheikdom *Arabian Pen* **80D3**
Bahr al Milh, L *Iraq* **93D3**
Bahr Aouk, R *Chad/CAR* **98C2**
Bahr el Arab, Watercourse *Sudan* **98C2**
Bahr el Ghazal, R *Sudan* **99D2**
Bahr el Ghazal, Watercourse *Chad* **98B1**
Baia de Maputo, B *Mozam* **101H1**
Baia de Marajó, B *Brazil* **31B2**
Baiá de Pemba, B *Mozam* **101D2**
Baia de São Marcos, B *Brazil* **31C2**
Baia de Setúbal, B *Port* **50A2**
Baia de Todos os Santos, B *Brazil* **31D4**
Baia dos Tigres *Angola* **100A2**
Baia Mare *Rom* **60B4**
Baïbokoum *Chad* **98B2**
Baicheng *China* **69E2**
Baie Antongila, B *Madag* **101E2**
Baie-Comeau *Can* **7D5**
Baie de Bombetoka, B *Madag* **101D2**
Baie de Mahajamba, B *Madag* **101D2**
Baie de St Augustin, B *Madag* **101D3**
Baie de St Georges, B *Leb* **94B2**
Baie des Chaleurs, B *Can* **10D2**
Baie-du-Poste *Can* **7C4**
Baihe *China* **72B3**
Bai He, R *China* **72C3**
Ba'ījī *Iraq* **93D3**
Baikunthpur *India* **86A2**
Băilesti *Rom* **54B2**
Bailleul *France* **46B1**
Baima *China* **72A3**
Bainbridge *USA* **17B1**
Baird Inlet *USA* **12B2**
Baird Mts *USA* **4B3**
Bairin Youqi *China* **72D1**
Bairin Zuoqi *China* **72D1**
Bairnsdale *Aust* **107D4**
Bais *Phil* **79B4**
Baja *Hung* **54A1**
Baja California, State *Mexico* **9B3**
Baja California, Pen *Mexico* **24A1**
Bakal *USSR* **61J2**
Bakala *CAR* **98C2**
Bakel *Sen* **97A3**
Baker, Montana *USA* **8C2**
Baker, Oregon *USA* **8B2**
Baker Foreland, Pt *Can* **6A3**
Baker L *Can* **4J3**
Baker Lake *Can* **4J3**
Baker,Mt *USA* **8A2**
Bakersfield *USA* **9B3**
Bakharden *USSR* **90C2**
Bakhardok *USSR* **90C2**
Bakhmach *USSR* **60D3**
Bakkaflói, B *Iceland* **38C1**
Bako *Eth* **99D2**
Bakouma *CAR* **98C2**
Baku *USSR* **65F5**
Balâ *Turk* **92B2**
Balabac, I *Phil* **79A4**
Balabac, Str *Malay* **70C3**
Balaikarangan *Indon* **78C2**
Balaklava *Aust* **108A2**
Balakovo *USSR* **61G3**
Balāngīr *India* **86A2**
Balashov *USSR* **61F3**
Balasore *India* **86B2**
Balât *Egypt* **80A3**
Balaton, L *Hung* **52C1**
Balbniggan *Irish Rep* **45C2**
Balcarce *Arg* **29E3**
Balchik *Bulg* **54C2**
Balclutha *NZ* **111B3**
Bald Knob *USA* **18B2**
Baldwin *USA* **17B1**
Baldy Peak, Mt *USA* **9C3**
Baleh, R *Malay* **78C2**
Baler *Phil* **79B2**
Balezino *USSR* **61H2**
Bali, I *Indon* **106A1**
Balıkesir *Turk* **92A2**
Balīkh, R *Syria* **93C2**
Balikpapan *Indon* **78D3**
Balintang Chan *Phil* **79B2**
Bali S *Indon* **78C4**
Baliza *Brazil* **35A1**
Balkh *Afghan* **84B1**
Balkhash *USSR* **65J5**
Ballachulish *Scot* **44B3**
Ballaghaderreen *Irish Rep* **45B2**
Ballantrae *Scot* **42B2**
Ballantyne Str *Can* **4G2**
Ballapur *India* **87B2**
Ballarat *Aust* **107D4**
Ballater *Scot* **44C3**
Balleny Is *Ant* **112C7**
Ballia *India* **86A1**
Ballina *Aust* **109D1**
Ballina *Irish Rep* **41B3**
Ballinasloe *Irish Rep* **45B2**
Ballinrobe *Irish Rep* **45B2**
Ballycastle *Irish Rep* **45B1**
Ballycastle *N Ire* **45C1**
Ballymena *N Ire* **45C1**
Ballymoney *N Ire* **45C1**
Ballyshannon *Irish Rep* **45B1**
Ballyvaghan *Irish Rep* **45B2**
Balmoral *Aust* **108B3**
Balnearia *Arg* **34C2**
Balombo *Angola* **100A2**
Balonn, R *Aust* **109C1**
Balotra *India* **85C3**
Balrāmpur *India* **86A1**
Balranald *Aust* **107D4**
Balsas *Brazil* **31B3**
Balsas *Mexico* **23B2**
Balsas, R *Mexico* **24B3**
Balta *USSR* **60C4**
Baltic S *N Europe* **39H7**
Baltîm *Egypt* **92B3**
Baltimore *Irish Rep* **45B3**
Baltimore *USA* **10C3**

Baluchistan, Region *Pak* **84B3**
Bālurghāt *India* **86B1**
Balykshi *USSR* **61H4**
Bam *Iran* **91C4**
Bama *Nig* **98B1**
Bamako *Mali* **97B3**
Bambari *CAR* **98C2**
Bamberg *USA* **17B1**
Bamberg *W Germ* **57C3**
Bambili *Zaïre* **98C2**
Bambui *Brazil* **35B2**
Bamenda *Cam* **98B2**
Bamfield *Can* **13C3**
Bamingui, R *CAR* **98B2**
Bamingui Bangoran, National Park *CAR* **98B2**
Bamiyan *Afghan* **84B2**
Bampur *Iran* **91D4**
Bampur, R *Iran* **91D4**
Banalia *Zaïre* **98C2**
Banamba *Mali* **97B3**
Ban Aranyaprathet *Thai* **76C3**
Ban Ban *Laos* **76C2**
Ban Betong *Thai* **77C4**
Banbridge *N Ire* **45C1**
Banbury *Eng* **43D3**
Banchory *Scot* **44C3**
Banco Chinchorro, Is *Mexico* **25D3**
Bancroft *Can* **15C1**
Bānda *India* **86A1**
Banda Aceh *Indon* **70A3**
Bandama, R *Ivory Coast* **97B4**
Bandar Abbās *Iran* **91C4**
Bandar Anzalī *Iran* **90A2**
Bandar-e Daylam *Iran* **91B4**
Bandar-e Lengheh *Iran* **91B4**
Bandar-e Māqām *Iran* **91B4**
Bandar-e Rig *Iran* **91B4**
Bandar-e Torkoman *Iran* **90B2**
Bandar Khomeynī *Iran* **91A3**
Bandar Seri Begawan *Brunei* **78C2**
Banda S *Indon* **71D4**
Band Bont *Iran* **91C4**
Bandeira, Mt *Brazil* **35C2**
Bandiagara *Mali* **97B3**
Bandirma *Turk* **60C5**
Bandon *Irish Rep* **45B3**
Bandundu *Zaïre* **98B3**
Bandung *Indon* **78B4**
Banes *Cuba* **25E2**
Banff *Can* **13D2**
Banff *Scot* **44C3**
Banff, R *Can* **5G4**
Banff Nat Pk *Can* **13D2**
Bangalore *India* **87B2**
Bangassou *CAR* **98C2**
Banggi, I *Malay* **70C3**
Bang Hieng, R *Laos* **76D2**
Bangka, I *Indon* **78B3**
Bangko *Indon* **78A3**
Bangkok *Thai* **76C3**
Bangladesh, Republic *Asia* **82C3**
Bangong Co, L *China* **84D2**
Bangor, Maine *USA* **10D2**
Bangor *N Ire* **45D1**
Bangor, Pennsylvania *USA* **16B2**
Bangor *Wales* **42B3**
Bangsalsembera *Indon* **78D3**
Bang Saphan Yai *Thai* **76B3**
Bangued *Phil* **79B2**
Bangui *CAR* **98B2**
Bangweulu, L *Zambia* **100C2**
Ban Hat Yai *Thai* **77C4**
Ban Hin Heup *Laos* **76C2**
Ban Houei Sai *Laos* **76C1**
Ban Hua Hin *Thai* **76B3**
Bani, R *Mali* **97B3**
Bani Bangou *Niger* **97C3**
Banī Walīd *Libya* **95A1**
Bāniyās *Syria* **92C2**
Baniyas *Syria* **94B2**
Banja Luka *Yugos* **52C2**
Banjarmasin *Indon* **78C3**
Banjul *The Gambia* **97A3**
Ban Kantang *Thai* **77B4**
Ban Khemmarat *Laos* **76D2**
Ban Khok Kloi *Thai* **77B4**
Banks I *Aust* **71F5**
Banks I, British Columbia *Can* **5E4**
Banks I, Northwest Territories *Can* **4F2**
Banks L *USA* **20C1**
Banks Pen *NZ* **111B2**
Banks Str *Aust* **109C4**
Bankura *India* **86B2**
Ban Mae Sariang *Thai* **76B2**
Ban Mae Sot *Thai* **76B2**
Ban Me Thuot *Viet* **76D3**
Bann, R *N Ire* **45C1**
Ban Na San *Thai* **77B4**
Bannu *Pak* **84C2**
Baños Maule *Chile* **34A3**
Ban Pak Neun *Laos* **76C2**
Ban Pak Phanang *Thai* **77C4**
Ban Ru Kroy *Camb* **76D3**
Ban Sai Yok *Thai* **76B3**
Ban Sattahip *Thai* **76C3**
Banská Bystrica *Czech* **59B3**
Bānswāra *India* **85C4**
Ban Tha Kham *Thai* **77B4**
Ban Thateng *Laos* **76D2**
Ban Tha Tum *Thai* **76C2**
Bantry *Irish Rep* **41B3**
Bantry, B *Irish Rep* **41A3**
Ban Ya Soup *Viet* **76D3**
Banyuwangi *Indon* **78C4**
Baofeng *China* **72C3**
Bao Ha *Viet* **76C1**
Baoji *China* **72B3**
Bao Loc *Viet* **76D3**
Baoshan *China* **68B4**
Baotou *China* **72C1**
Bāpatla *India* **87C1**
Bapaume *France* **46B1**
Ba'Qūbah *Iraq* **93D3**
Baquerizo Morena *Ecuador* **32J7**
Bar *Yugos* **54A2**
Bara *Sudan* **99D1**
Baraawe *Somalia* **99E2**
Barabai *Indon* **78D3**
Bāra Banki *India* **86A1**
Barabinsk *USSR* **65J4**
Barabinskaya Step, Steppe *USSR* **65J4**
Baracaldo *Spain* **50B1**
Baracoa *Cuba* **26C2**
Baradá, R *Syria* **94C2**
Baradine *Aust* **109C2**
Bārāmati *India* **87A1**
Baramula *Pak* **84C2**
Bārān *India* **85D3**
Barangas *Phil* **79B3**
Baranof I *USA* **4E4**
Baranovichi *USSR* **60C3**
Baratta *Aust* **108A2**
Barauni *India* **86B1**
Barbacena *Brazil* **31C6**
Barbados, I *Caribbean* **27F4**
Barbastro *Spain* **51C1**
Barberton *S Africa* **101H1**
Barbezieux *France* **48B2**
Barbòsa *Colombia* **32C2**
Barbuda, I *Caribbean* **27E3**
Barcaldine *Aust* **107D3**
Barcellona *Italy* **53C3**
Barcelona *Spain* **51C1**
Barcelona *Ven* **33E1**
Barcoo, R *Aust* **107D3**
Barda del Medio *Arg* **34B3**
Bardai *Chad* **95A2**
Bardas Blancas *Arg* **29C3**
Barddhamān *India* **86B2**
Bardejov *Czech* **59C3**
Bardi *Italy* **47C2**
Bardonecchia *Italy* **47B2**
Bardsey, I *Wales* **43B3**
Bareilly *India* **84D3**
Barentsøya, I *Barents S* **64D2**
Barentu *Eth* **95C3**
Bargarh *India* **86A2**
Barge *Italy* **47B2**
Barguzin *USSR* **63D2**
Barguzin, R *USSR* **63D2**
Barhi *India* **86B2**
Bari *Italy* **53C2**
Barika *Alg* **51D2**
Barinas *Ven* **32C2**
Baripāda *India* **86B2**
Bari Sādri *India* **85C4**
Barisal *Bang* **86C2**
Barito, R *Indon* **78C3**
Barjuj, Watercourse *Libya* **95A2**
Barkam *China* **73A3**
Barkley,L *USA* **18C2**
Barkley Sd *Can* **13B3**
Barkly East *S Africa* **100B4**
Barkly Tableland, Mts *Aust* **106C2**
Bar-le-Duc *France* **46C2**
Barlee,L *Aust* **106A3**
Barlee Range, Mts *Aust* **106A3**
Barletta *Italy* **53C2**
Barmer *India* **85C3**
Barmera *Aust* **108B2**
Barmouth *Wales* **43B3**
Barnard Castle *Eng* **42D2**
Barnaul *USSR* **65K4**
Barnegat *USA* **16B3**
Barnegat B *USA* **16B3**
Barnes Icecap *Can* **6C2**
Barnesville, Georgia *USA* **17B1**
Barnesville, Ohio *USA* **14B3**
Barnsley *Eng* **42D3**
Barnstaple *Eng* **43B4**
Baro *Nig* **97C4**
Barpeta *India* **86C1**
Barquisimeto *Ven* **32D1**
Barra *Brazil* **31C4**
Barra, I *Scot* **44A3**
Barraba *Aust* **109D2**
Barra de Navidad *Mexico* **23A2**
Barra de Piraí *Brazil* **35C2**
Barra do Garças *Brazil* **35A1**
Barragem do Castelo do Bode, Res *Port* **50A2**
Barragem do Maranhão *Port* **50A2**
Barra Head, Pt *Scot* **44A3**
Barra Mansa *Brazil* **31C6**
Barranca *Peru* **32B6**
Barrancabermeja *Colombia* **32C2**
Barrancas *Ven* **33E2**
Barranqueras *Arg* **30E4**
Barranquilla *Colombia* **32C1**
Barra,Sound of, Chan *Scot* **44A3**
Barre *USA* **16C1**
Barreal *Arg* **34B2**
Barreiras *Brazil* **31C4**
Barreiro *Port* **50A2**
Barreiros *Brazil* **31D3**
Barren,C *Aust* **107D5**
Barren Is *USA* **12D3**
Barretos *Brazil* **31B6**
Barrhead *Can* **13E2**
Barrie *Can* **14C2**
Barrière *Can* **13C2**
Barrier Range, Mts *Aust* **108B2**
Barrington,Mt *Aust* **107E4**
Barrouaillie *St Vincent* **27N2**
Barrow *USA* **4C2**
Barrow, R *Irish Rep* **45C2**
Barrow Creek *Aust* **106C3**
Barrow I *Aust* **106A3**
Barrow-in-Furness *Eng* **42C2**
Barrow,Pt *USA* **4C2**
Barrow Str *Can* **6A2**
Barry's Bay *Can* **15C1**
Barsi *India* **87B1**
Barstow *USA* **9B3**
Bar-sur-Aube *France* **49C2**
Bartica *Guyana* **33F2**
Bartın *Turk* **92B1**
Bartle Frere,Mt *Aust* **107D2**
Bartlesville *USA* **9D3**
Bartolomeu Dias *Mozam* **101C3**
Bartoszyce *Pol* **58C2**
Barung, I *Indon* **78C4**
Barwāh *India* **85D4**
Barwāni *India* **85C4**
Barwon, R *Aust* **109C1**
Barysh *USSR* **61G3**
Basankusu *Zaïre* **98B2**
Basavilbas *Arg* **34D2**
Basco *Phil* **79B1**
Basel *Switz* **52A1**
Basento, R *Italy* **53C2**
Bashaw *Can* **13E2**
Bashi Chan *Phil* **79B1**
Bashkirskaya ASSR, Republic *USSR* **61H3**
Basilan, I *Phil* **79B4**
Basildon *Eng* **43E4**
Basingstoke *Eng* **43D4**
Basin Region *USA* **8B2**
Basra *Iraq* **93E3**
Bas-Rhin, Department *France* **46D2**
Bassac, R *Camb* **76D3**
Bassano *Can* **13E2**
Bassano *Italy* **52B1**
Bassano del Grappa *Italy* **47D2**
Bassari *Togo* **97C4**
Bassas da India, I *Mozam Chan* **101C3**
Bassein *Burma* **76A2**
Basse Terre *Guadeloupe* **27E3**
Bassila *Benin* **97C4**
Bass Lake *USA* **22C2**
Bass Str *Aust* **107D4**
Båstad *Sweden* **39G7**
Bastak *Iran* **91B4**
Basti *India* **86A1**
Bastia *Corse* **52A2**
Bastogne *Belg* **57B3**
Bastrop, Louisiana *USA* **19B3**
Bastrop, Texas *USA* **19A3**
Bata *Eq Guinea* **98A2**
Batakan *Indon* **78C3**
Batala *India* **84D2**
Batang *China* **68B3**
Batangafo *CAR* **98B2**
Batan Is *Phil* **79B1**
Batatais *Brazil* **35B2**
Batavia *USA* **15C2**
Batemans Bay *Aust* **109D3**
Batesburg *USA* **17B1**
Batesville, Arkansas *USA* **18B2**
Batesville, Mississippi *USA* **19C3**
Bath *Eng* **43C4**
Bath, New York *USA* **15C2**
Batha, R *Chad* **98B1**
Bathurst *Aust* **107D4**
Bathurst *Can* **7D5**
Bathurst,C *Can* **4F2**
Bathurst I *Aust* **106C2**
Bathurst I *Can* **4H2**
Bathurst Inlet, B *Can* **4H3**
Bātlāq-e-Gavkhūnī, Salt Flat *Iran* **90B3**
Batlow *Aust* **109C3**
Batman *Turk* **93D2**
Batna *Alg* **96C1**
Baton Rouge *USA* **11A3**
Batroun *Leb* **94B1**
Battambang *Camb* **76C3**
Batticaloa *Sri Lanka* **87C3**
Battle, R *Can* **13F2**
Battle Creek *USA* **10B2**

Battle Harbour *Can* **7E4**
Battle Mountain *USA* **20C2**
Batukelau *Indon* **78D2**
Batumi *USSR* **65F5**
Batu Pahat *Malay* **77C5**
Baturaja *Indon* **78A3**
Bat Yam *Israel* **94B2**
Baubau *Indon* **71D4**
Bauchi *Nig* **97C3**
Bauges, Mts *France* **47B2**
Bauld,C *Can* **7E4**
Baumes-les-Dames *France* **47B1**
Baunt *USSR* **63D2**
Bauru *Brazil* **31B6**
Baus *Brazil* **35A1**
Bautzen *E Germ* **57C2**
Baween, I *Indon* **78C4**
Bawîti *Egypt* **95B2**
Bawku *Ghana* **97B3**
Bawlake *Burma* **76B2**
Bawlen *Aust* **108A2**
Baxley *USA* **17B1**
Bayamo *Cuba* **25E2**
Bayan *Indon* **78D4**
Bayandalay *Mongolia* **72A1**
Bayandzürh *Mongolia* **68C2**
Bayan Har Shan, Mts *China* **68B3**
Bayan Mod *China* **72A1**
Bayan Obo *China* **72B1**
Bayard, P *France* **47A2**
Bayard,Mt *Can* **12J3**
Baybay *Phil* **79B3**
Bayburt *Turk* **93D1**
Bay City, Michigan *USA* **10B2**
Bay City, Texas *USA* **19A4**
Bay Dağlari *Turk* **92B2**
Baydaratskaya Guba, B *USSR* **64H3**
Baydhabo *Somalia* **99E2**
Bayeaux *France* **48B2**
Bayerische Alpen, Mts *W Germ* **47D1**
Bayern, State *W Germ* **57C3**
Bāyir *Jordan* **92C3**
Baykalskiy Khrebet, Mts *USSR* **68C1**
Baykit *USSR* **63B1**
Baylik Shan, Mts *China/Mongolia* **63B3**
Baymak *USSR* **61J3**
Bayombang *Phil* **79B2**
Bayonne *France* **48B3**
Bayreuth *W Germ* **57C3**
Bay St Louis *USA* **19C3**
Bay Shore *USA* **15D2**
Bays,L of *Can* **15C1**
Baytik Shan, Mts *China* **68A2**
Baytown *USA* **19B4**
Baza *Spain* **50B2**
Bazaliya *USSR* **59D3**
Bazas *France* **48B3**
Bazhong *China* **73B3**
Bazmān *Iran* **91D4**
Bcharre *Leb* **94C1**
Beach Haven *USA* **16B3**
Beachy Head *Eng* **43E4**
Beacon *USA* **16C2**
Bealanana *Madag* **101D2**
Beardstown *USA* **18B1**
Bear Valley *USA* **22B1**
Beatrice *USA* **8D2**
Beatrice, Oilfield *N Sea* **44C2**
Beatton, R *Can* **13C1**
Beatton River *Can* **5F4**
Beauchene Is *Falkland Is* **29E6**
Beaudesert *Aust* **109D1**
Beaufort S *Can* **1B5**
Beaufort West *S Africa* **100B4**
Beauharnois *Can* **15D1**
Beauly *Scot* **44B3**
Beaumont, California *USA* **21B3**
Beaumont, Texas *USA* **11A3**
Beaune *France* **49C2**
Beauvais *France* **48C2**
Beauval *Can* **13F1**
Beaver, Alaska *USA* **12E1**
Beaver, R, Saskatchewan *Can* **13F2**
Beaver Creek *Can* **4D3**
Beaver Creek *USA* **12E1**
Beaver Dam, Kentucky *USA* **18C2**
Beaverhill L *Can* **13E2**
Beaver I *USA* **14A1**
Beaver L *USA* **18B2**
Beaverlodge *Can* **13D1**
Beawar *India* **85C3**
Beazley *Arg* **34B2**
Bebedouro *Brazil* **35B2**
Beccles *Eng* **43E3**
Bečej *Yugos* **54B1**
Béchar *Alg* **96B1**
Becharof L *USA* **12C3**
Beckley *USA* **11B3**
Bedford, County *Eng* **43D3**
Bedford *Eng* **43D3**
Bedford, Indiana *USA* **14A3**
Bedford Pt *Grenada* **27M2**
Beechey, Pt *USA* **4D2**
Beechworth *Aust* **109C3**
Beenleigh *Aust* **109D1**
Beersheba *Israel* **92B3**
Beér Sheva, R *Israel* **94B3**
Beeville *USA* **9D4**
Befale *Zaïre* **98C2**
Befandriana *Madag* **101D2**
Bega *Aust* **109C3**
Behbehān *Iran* **91B3**
Behm Canal, Sd *USA* **12H3**
Behshahr *Iran* **90B2**
Behsud *Afghan* **84B2**
Bei'an *China* **69E2**
Beihai *China* **73B5**
Beijing *China* **72D2**
Beiliu *China* **76E1**
Beipan Jiang, R *China* **73B4**
Beipiao *China* **72E1**
Beirut *Leb* **92C3**
Bei Shan, Mts *China* **68B2**
Beit ed Dīne *Leb* **94B2**
Beit Jala *Israel* **94B3**
Beja *Port* **50A2**
Beja *Tunisia* **96C1**
Bejaïa *Alg* **96C1**
Béjar *Spain* **50A1**
Bejestān *Iran* **90C3**
Békéscsaba *Hung* **59C3**
Bekily *Madag* **101D3**
Bela *India* **86A1**
Bela *Pak* **85B3**
Belaga *Malay* **78C2**
Bel Air *USA* **16A3**
Belamoalli *India* **87B1**
Belang *Indon* **71D3**
Belangpidie *Indon* **70A3**
Belau, Republic *Pacific O* **71E3**
Belau, I *Pacific O* **104E3**
Bela Vista *Mozam* **101C3**
Belawan *Indon* **70A3**
Belaya, R *USSR* **61J2**
Belcher Chan *Can* **6A2**
Belcher Is *Can* **7C4**
Belchiragh *Afghan* **84B1**
Belebey *USSR* **61H3**
Belém *Brazil* **31B2**
Belén *Colombia* **32B3**
Belén *Urug* **34D2**
Belen *USA* **9C3**
Belet Uen *Somalia* **99E2**
Belfast *N Ire* **45D1**
Belfast *S Africa* **101H1**
Belfast Lough, Estuary *N Ire* **45D1**
Belfodio *Eth* **99D1**
Belford *Eng* **42D2**
Belfort *France* **49D2**
Belgaum *India* **87A1**
Belgium, Kingdom *N W Europe* **56A2**
Belgorod *USSR* **60E3**
Belgorod Dnestrovskiy *USSR* **60D4**
Bel Hedan *Libya* **95A2**
Belinyu *Indon* **78B3**
Belitung, I *Indon* **78B3**
Belize *Belize* **25D3**
Belize, Republic *C America* **25D3**
Bellac *France* **48C2**
Bella Coola *Can* **5F4**
Bellagio *Italy* **47C2**
Bellaire *USA* **19A4**
Bellano *Italy* **47C1**
Bellary *India* **87B1**
Bellata *Aust* **109C1**
Belledonne, Mts *France* **47B2**
Belle Fourche *USA* **8C2**
Bellegarde *France* **49D2**
Belle Glade *USA* **17B2**
Belle I *Can* **7E4**
Belle-Ile, I *France* **48B2**
Belle Isle,Str of *Can* **7E4**
Belleville *Can* **7C5**
Belleville, Kansas *USA* **18A2**
Bellevue, Washington *USA* **20B1**
Bellin *Can* **7C3**
Bellingen *Aust* **109D2**
Bellingham *USA* **8A2**
Bellingshausen, Base *Ant* **112C2**
Bellingshausen S *Ant* **112C3**
Bellinzona *Switz* **52A1**
Bello *Colombia* **32B2**
Bellona Reefs *Nouvelle Calédonie* **107E3**
Bellota *USA* **22B1**
Bellows Falls *USA* **15D2**
Bell Pen *Can* **6B3**
Belluno *Italy* **52B1**
Bell Ville *Arg* **29D2**
Belmonte *Brazil* **31D5**
Belmopan *Belize* **25D3**
Belmullet *Irish Rep* **45B1**
Belogorsk *USSR* **69E1**
Beloha *Madag* **101D3**
Belo Horizonte *Brazil* **31C5**
Beloit, Wisconsin *USA* **10B2**
Belomorsk *USSR* **64E3**
Beloretsk *USSR* **61J3**
Belorusskaya SSR, Republic *USSR* **60C3**
Belo-Tsiribihina *Madag* **101D2**
Beloye More, S *USSR* **64E3**
Beloye Ozero, L *USSR* **60E1**
Belozersk *USSR* **60E1**
Belpre *USA* **14B3**
Beltana *Aust* **108A2**
Belton *USA* **19A3**
Bel'tsy *USSR* **59D3**
Belvidere, New Jersey *USA* **16B2**
Bembe *Angola* **98B3**
Bembéréke *Benin* **97C3**
Bemidji *USA* **10A2**
Bena *Nor* **39G6**
Bena Dibele *Zaïre* **98C3**
Benalla *Aust* **108C3**
Ben Attow, Mt *Scot* **44B3**
Benavente *Spain* **50A1**
Benbecula, I *Scot* **44A3**
Bencubbin *Aust* **106A4**
Bend *USA* **8A2**
Ben Dearg, Mt *Scot* **44B3**
Bender Beyla *Somalia* **99F2**
Bendery *USSR* **60C4**
Bendigo *Aust* **107D4**
Benešov *Czech* **57C3**
Benevento *Italy* **53B2**
Bengal,B of *Asia* **83C4**
Ben Gardane *Tunisia* **96D1**
Bengbu *China* **72D3**
Benghāzī *Libya* **95B1**
Bengkalis *Indon* **78A2**
Bengkulu *Indon* **78A3**
Benguela *Angola* **100A2**
Benha *Egypt* **92B3**
Ben Hope, Mt *Scot* **44B2**
Beni *Zaïre* **99C2**
Béni, R *Bol* **32D6**
Beni Abbes *Alg* **96B1**
Benicarló *Spain* **51C1**
Benidji *USA* **7A5**
Benidorm *Spain* **51B2**
Beni Mansour *Alg* **51C2**
Beni Mazar *Egypt* **95C2**
Beni Mellal *Mor* **96B1**
Benin, Republic *Africa* **97C4**
Benin City *Nig* **97C4**
Beni Suef *Egypt* **95C2**
Ben Kilbreck, Mt *Scot* **44B2**
Ben Lawers, Mt *UK* **44B3**
Ben Lomond, Mt *Aust* **109C4**
Ben Macdui, Mt *Scot* **44C3**
Ben More Assynt, Mt *Scot* **44B2**
Benmore,L *NZ* **111B2**
Ben Nevis, Mt *Scot* **44B3**
Bennington *USA* **15D2**
Bennt Jbail *Leb* **94B2**
Bénoué, R *Cam* **98B2**
Benson, Arizona *USA* **9B3**
Bentiu *Sudan* **99C2**
Benton, Arkansas *USA* **19B3**
Benton, Kentucky *USA* **18C2**
Benton Harbor *USA* **14A2**
Benue, R *Nig* **97C4**
Benwee Hd, C *Irish Rep* **45B1**
Ben Wyvis, Mt *Scot* **44B3**
Benxi *China* **72E1**
Beograd *Yugos* **54B2**
Beohāri *India* **86A2**
Beppu *Japan* **74C4**
Berat *Alb* **55A2**
Berber *Sudan* **95C3**
Berbera *Somalia* **99E1**
Berbérati *CAR* **98B2**
Berck *France* **46A1**
Berdichev *USSR* **60C4**
Berdyansk *USSR* **60E4**
Berekum *Ghana* **97B4**
Berenda *USA* **22B2**
Berens, R *Can* **5J4**
Berens River *Can* **5J4**
Beresford *Aust* **108A1**
Berettyóújfalu *Hung* **59C3**
Bereza *USSR* **58D2**
Berezhany *USSR* **59C3**
Berezniki *USSR* **65G4**
Berezovka *USSR* **60D4**
Berezovo *USSR* **64H3**
Bergama *Turk* **92A2**
Bergamo *Italy* **52A1**
Bergen *Nor* **39F6**
Bergen op Zoom *Neth* **46C1**
Bergerac *France* **48C3**
Bergisch-Gladbach *W Germ* **46D1**
Bering Gl *USA* **12F2**
Bering Str *USSR/USA* **1C6**
Berīzak *Iran* **91C4**
Berja *Spain* **50B2**
Berkeley *USA* **8A3**
Berkner I *Ant* **112B2**
Berkovitsa *Bulg* **54B2**
Berkshire, County *Eng* **43D4**
Berkshire Hills *USA* **16C1**
Berland, R *Can* **13D2**
Berlin *E Germ* **56C2**
Berlin, New Hampshire *USA* **15D2**
Bermejo *Bol* **30D3**
Bermejo, R *Arg* **30D4**
Bermuda, I *Atlantic O* **3M5**
Bern *Switz* **52A1**
Bernardsville *USA* **16B2**
Bernasconi *Arg* **34C3**
Bernburg *E Germ* **56C2**

Berner Orberland, Mts *Switz* **47B1**
Bernier B *Can* **6B2**
Berounka, R *Czech* **57C3**
Berri *Aust* **108B2**
Berriane *Alg* **96C1**
Berry, Region *France* **48C2**
Berryessa,L *USA* **22A1**
Berry Is *Bahamas* **11C4**
Bertoua *Cam* **98B2**
Bertraghboy B *Irish Rep* **45B2**
Berwick *USA* **15C2**
Berwick-upon-Tweed *Eng* **42C2**
Berwyn, Mts *Wales* **43C3**
Besalampy *Madag* **101D2**
Besançon *France* **49D2**
Beskidy Zachodnie, Mts *Pol* **59C3**
Besni *Turk* **93C2**
Besor, R *Israel* **94B3**
Bessemer *USA* **11B3**
Betafo *Madag* **101D2**
Betanzos *Spain* **50A1**
Bet Guvrin *Israel* **94B3**
Bethal *S Africa* **101G1**
Bethanie *Namibia* **100A3**
Bethany, Missouri *USA* **18B1**
Bethany, Oklahoma *USA* **18A2**
Bethel, Alaska *USA* **4B3**
Bethel, Connecticut *USA* **16C2**
Bethel Park *USA* **14B2**
Bethesda *USA* **15C3**
Bethlehem *Israel* **94B3**
Bethlehem *S Africa* **101G1**
Bethlehem *USA* **15C2**
Bethune *France* **48C1**
Betioky *Madag* **101D3**
Betoota *Aust* **108B1**
Betou *Congo* **98B2**
Betpak Dala, Steppe *USSR* **82A1**
Betroka *Madag* **101D3**
Betsiamites *Can* **7D5**
Bettiah *India* **86A1**
Bettles *USA* **12D1**
Béttola *Italy* **47C2**
Bētul *India* **85D4**
Betwa, R *India* **85D3**
Betzdorf *W Germ* **46D1**
Beverley,L *USA* **12C3**
Beverly *USA* **16D1**
Beverly Hills *USA* **21B3**
Beyla *Guinea* **97B4**
Beypore *India* **87B2**
Beyşehir *Turk* **92B2**
Beysehir Gölü, L *Turk* **92B2**
Beyt Shean *Israel* **94B2**
Bezau *Austria* **47C1**
Bezhetsk *USSR* **60E2**
Béziers *France* **49C3**
Bezmein *USSR* **90C2**
Beznosova *USSR* **63C2**
Bhadgaon *Nepal* **86B1**
Bhadrāchalam *India* **87C1**
Bhadrakh *India* **86B2**
Bhadra Res *India* **87B2**
Bhadrāvati *India* **87B2**
Bhag *Pak* **84B3**
Bhāgalpur *India* **86B1**
Bhakkar *Pak* **84C2**
Bhamo *Burma* **82D3**
Bhandāra *India* **85D4**
Bharatpur *India* **85D3**
Bharūch *India* **85C4**
Bhātiāpāra Ghat *Bang* **86B2**
Bhatinda *India* **84C2**
Bhatkal *India* **87A2**
Bhātpāra *India* **86B2**
Bhāvnagar *India* **85C4**
Bhera *Pak* **84C2**
Bheri, R *Nepal* **86A1**
Bhilai *India* **86A2**
Bhīlwāra *India* **85C3**
Bhimavaram *India* **87C1**
Bhind *India* **85D3**
Bhiwāni *India* **84D3**
Bhongir *India* **87B1**
Bhopāl *India* **85D4**
Bhubaneshwar *India* **86B2**
Bhuj *India* **85B4**
Bhusāwal *India* **85D4**
Bhutan, Kingdom *Asia* **82C3**
Biak, I *Indon* **71E4**
Biala Podlaska *Pol* **58C2**
Bialograd *Pol* **58B2**
Bialystok *Pol* **58C2**
Biargtangar, C *Iceland* **38A1**
Biārjmand *Iran* **90C2**
Biarritz *France* **48B3**
Biasca *Switz* **47C1**
Biba *Egypt* **92B4**
Bibai *Japan* **74E2**
Bibala *Angola* **100A2**
Biberach *W Germ* **57B3**
Bibiani *Ghana* **97B4**
Bicaz *Rom* **54C1**
Bida *Nig* **97C4**
Bīdar *India* **87B1**
Bidbid *Oman* **91C5**
Bideford *Eng* **43B4**
Bideford B *Eng* **43B4**
Bidon 5 *Alg* **96C2**
Bié *Angola* **100A2**
Biebrza *Pol* **58C2**
Biel *Switz* **52A1**
Bielawa *Pol* **59B2**
Bielefeld *W Germ* **56B2**
Bieler See, L *Switz* **47B1**
Biella *Italy* **52A1**
Bielsk Podlaski *Pol* **58C2**
Bien Hoa *Viet* **76D3**
Biferno, R *Italy* **53B2**
Biga *Turk* **92A1**
Bigadiç *Turk* **55C3**
Big Black, R *USA* **19C3**
Big Blue, R *USA* **18A1**
Big Cypress Swamp *USA* **17B2**
Big Delta *USA* **4D3**
Bigent *W Germ* **49D2**
Biggar *Can* **13F2**
Biggar Kindersley *Can* **5H4**
Biggenden *Aust* **109D1**
Bigger,Mt *Can* **12G3**
Bighorn, R *USA* **8C2**
Bight of Bangkok, B *Thai* **76C3**
Bight of Benin, B *W Africa* **97C4**
Bight of Biafra, B *Cam* **97C4**
Big I *Can* **6C3**
Bignasco *Switz* **47C1**
Bignona *Sen* **97A3**
Big Pine *USA* **21B2**
Big Pine Key *USA* **17B2**
Big Pine Mt *USA* **22C3**
Big Rapids *USA* **14A2**
Big River *Can* **5H4**
Big Spring *USA* **9C3**
Big Trout L *Can* **7A4**
Big Trout Lake *Can* **7B4**
Bihać *Yugos* **52C2**
Bihār *India* **86B1**
Bihar, State *India* **86B2**
Biharamulo *Tanz* **99D3**
Bihor, Mt *Rom* **60B4**
Bijāpur *India* **87B1**
Bījāpur *India* **87C1**
Bījār *Iran* **90A2**
Bijauri *Nepal* **86A1**
Bijeljina *Yugos* **54A2**
Bijie *China* **73B4**
Bijnor *India* **84D3**
Bijnot *Pak* **84C3**
Bikāner *India* **84C3**
Bikfaya *Leb* **94B2**
Bikin *USSR* **69F2**
Bikoro *Zaïre* **98B3**
Bilara *India* **85C3**
Bilaspur *India* **84D2**
Bilāspur *India* **86A2**
Bilauktaung Range, Mts *Thai* **76B3**
Bilbao *Spain* **50B1**
Bilé, R *Czech* **59B3**
Bileća *Yugos* **54A2**
Bilecik *Turk* **92B1**
Bili, R *Zaïre* **98C2**
Biliran, I *Phil* **79B3**
Billings *USA* **8C2**
Bilma *Niger* **95A3**
Biloxi *USA* **11B3**
Biltine *Chad* **98C1**
Bina-Etawa *India* **85D4**
Binalbagan *Phil* **79B3**
Bindura *Zim* **101C2**
Binga *Zim* **100B2**
Binga, Mt *Zim* **101C2**
Bingara *Aust* **109D1**
Bingen *W Germ* **57B3**
Binghamton *USA* **10C2**
Bingkor *Malay* **78D1**
Bingöl *Turk* **93D2**
Binhai *China* **72D3**
Bintan, I *Indon* **78A2**
Bintuhan *Indon* **78A3**
Bintulu *Malay* **78C2**
Bió Bió, R *Chile* **29B3**
Bioko, I *Atlantic O* **102J4**
Bīr *India* **87B1**
Bîr Abu Husein, Well *Egypt* **95B2**
Bi'r al Harash, Well *Libya* **95B2**
Birao *CAR* **98C1**
Biratnagar *Nepal* **86B1**
Birch Creek *USA* **12E1**
Birchip *Aust* **108B3**
Birch Mts *Can* **5G4**
Bird *Can* **7A4**
Birdsville *Aust* **106C3**
Birdum *Aust* **106C2**
Birganj *Nepal* **86A1**
Bîr Gifgâfa, Well *Egypt* **94A3**
Bîr Hasana, Well *Egypt* **94A3**
Birigui *Brazil* **35A2**
Birjand *Iran* **90C3**
Birkat Qarun, L *Egypt* **92B4**
Birkenfeld *W Germ* **46D2**
Birkenhead *Eng* **42C3**
Bîrlad *Rom* **60C4**
Bir Lahfân, Well *Egypt* **94A3**
Birmingham *Eng* **43C3**
Birmingham *USA* **11B3**
Bîr Misâha, Well *Egypt* **95B2**
Bir Moghrein *Maur* **96A2**
Birnin Kebbi *Nig* **97C3**
Birni N'Konni *Nig* **97C3**
Birobidzhan *USSR* **69F2**
Birr *Irish Rep* **45C2**
Bir Rabalou *Alg* **51C2**
Birrie, R *Aust* **109C1**
Birsay *Scot* **44C2**
Birsk *USSR* **61J2**
Bîr Tarfâwi, Well *Egypt* **95B2**
Biryusa *USSR* **63B2**
Birzai *USSR* **39J7**
Bir Zreigat, Well *Maur* **96B2**
Biscay,B of *Spain/ France* **48A2**
Biscayne B *USA* **17B2**
Bischwiller *France* **46D2**
Bishan *China* **73B4**
Bishop *USA* **8B3**
Bishop Auckland *Eng* **42D2**
Bishop's Stortford *Eng* **43E4**
Bishrāmpur *India* **86A2**
Biskra *Alg* **96C1**
Bislig *Phil* **79C4**
Bismarck *USA* **8C2**
Bīsotūn *Iran* **90A3**
Bissau *Guinea-Bissau* **97A3**
Bissett *Can* **10A1**
Bistcho L *Can* **5G4**
Bistrita, R *Rom* **54C1**
Bitam *Gabon* **98B2**
Bitburg *W Germ* **57B3**
Bitche *France* **46D2**
Bitlis *Turk* **93D2**
Bitola *Yugos* **55B2**
Bitterfeld *E Germ* **56C2**
Bitterfontein *S Africa* **100A4**
Bitter Lakes *Egypt* **92B3**
Bitteroot Range, Mts *USA* **8B2**
Biwa-ko, L *Japan* **74D3**
Biyo Kaboba *Eth* **99E1**
Biysk *USSR* **65K4**
Bizerte *Tunisia* **96C1**
Bj bou Arréridj *Alg* **51C2**
Bjelovar *Yugos* **52C1**
Bj Flye Ste Marie *Alg* **96B2**
Bjørnøya, I *Barents S* **64C2**
Black, R *USA* **12F1**
Black, R *USA* **18B2**
Blackall *Aust* **107D3**
Blackburn *Eng* **42C3**
Blackburn,Mt *USA* **4D3**
Black Diamond *Can* **13E2**
Black Hills *USA* **5H5**
Black Isle, Pen *Scot* **44B3**
Blackman's *Barbados* **27R3**
Black Mts *Wales* **43C4**
Blackpool *Eng* **43C3**
Black River *Jamaica* **27H1**
Black Rock Desert *USA* **8B2**
Black S *USSR/Europe* **65E5**
Blacksod B *Irish Rep* **45A1**
Black Sugarloaf, Mt *Aust* **109D2**
Black Volta, R *Ghana* **97B3**
Blackwater, R *Irish Rep* **41B3**
Blackwell *USA* **18A2**
Blagoevgrad *Bulg* **54B2**
Blagoveshchensk *USSR* **63E2**
Blaine *USA* **20B1**
Blair Atholl *Scot* **44C3**
Blairgowrie *Scot* **44C3**
Blakely *USA* **17B1**
Blanche,L *Aust* **108A1**
Blanco, R *Arg* **34A2**
Blanco, R *Arg* **34B1**
Blanco,C *USA* **8A2**
Blanc Sablon *Can* **7E4**
Blandford Forum *Eng* **43C4**
Blangy-sur-Bresle *France* **46A2**
Blankenberge *Belg* **46B1**
Blantyre *Malawi* **101C2**
Blaye *France* **48B2**
Blayney *Aust* **109C2**
Blenheim *NZ* **111B2**
Blida *Alg* **96C1**
Blind River *Can* **14B1**
Blinman *Aust* **108A2**
Blitar *Indon* **78C4**
Block I *USA* **15D2**
Block Island Sd *USA* **16D2**
Bloemfontein *S Africa* **101G1**
Bloemhof *S Africa* **101G1**
Bloemhof Dam, Res *S Africa* **101G1**
Blommesteinmeer, L *Surinam* **33F3**
Blonduós *Iceland* **38A1**
Bloody Foreland, C *Irish Rep* **45B1**
Bloomfield, Indiana *USA* **14A3**
Bloomfield, Iowa *USA* **18B1**
Bloomington, Illinois *USA* **10B2**
Bloomington, Indiana *USA* **14A3**
Bloomsburg *USA* **16A2**
Blora *Indon* **78C4**
Blosseville Kyst, Mts *Greenland* **6H3**
Bludenz *Austria* **57B3**
Bluefield *USA* **11B3**

Bluefields *Nic* **32A1**
Blue Mountain Peak, Mt *Jamaica* **26B3**
Blue Mt *USA* **16A2**
Blue Mts *Aust* **109D2**
Blue Mts *Jamaica* **27J1**
Blue Mts *USA* **8A2**
Blue Nile, R *Sudan* **99D1**
Bluenose L *Can* **4G3**
Blue Ridge Mts *USA* **11B3**
Blue River *Can* **13D2**
Blue Stack, Mt *Irish Rep* **45B1**
Bluff *NZ* **111A3**
Bluff Knoll, Mt *Aust* **106A4**
Blumenau *Brazil* **30G4**
Blundez *Austria* **49D2**
Bly *USA* **20B2**
Blying Sd *USA* **12E3**
Blyth *Eng* **42D2**
Blythe *USA* **9B3**
Blytheville *USA* **11B3**
Bo *Sierra Leone* **97A4**
Boac *Phil* **79B3**
Boading *China* **72D2**
Boardman *USA* **14B2**
Boatou *China* **63C3**
Boa Vista *Brazil* **33E3**
Boa Vista, I *Cape Verde* **97A4**
Bobai *China* **76E1**
Bóbbio *Italy* **47C2**
Bobo Dioulasso *U Volta* **97B3**
Bobruysk *USSR* **60C3**
Boca Chica Key, I *USA* **17B2**
Bõca do Acre *Brazil* **32D5**
Bocaiúva *Brazil* **35C1**
Bocaranga *CAR* **98B2**
Boca Raton *USA* **17B2**
Bochnia *Pol* **59C3**
Bocholt *W Germ* **56B2**
Bochum *W Germ* **46D1**
Bocoio *Angola* **100A2**
Boda *CAR* **98B2**
Bodaybo *USSR* **63D2**
Bodega Head, Pt *USA* **21A2**
Bodélé, Region *Chad* **95A3**
Boden *Sweden* **38J5**
Bodensee, L *Switz/W Germ* **47C1**
Bodhan *India* **87B1**
Bodināyakkanūr *India* **87B2**
Bodmin *Eng* **43B4**
Bodmin Moor, Upland *Eng* **43B4**
Bodø *Nor* **38G5**
Bodorodskoye *USSR* **63G2**
Bodrum *Turk* **55C3**
Boende *Zaïre* **98C3**
Boffa *Guinea* **97A3**
Bogale *Burma* **76B2**
Bogalusa *USA* **19C3**
Bogan, R *Aust* **109C2**
Bogandé *U Volta* **97B3**
Bogarnes *Iceland* **6H3**
Boğazlıyan *Turk* **92C2**
Bogdanovich *USSR* **61K2**
Bogda Shan, Mt *China* **68A2**
Bogenfels *Namibia* **100A3**
Boggabilla *Aust* **109D1**
Boggabri *Aust* **109C2**
Boggeragh Mts *Irish Rep* **45B2**
Bogo *Phil* **79B3**
Bogong,Mt *Aust* **109C3**
Bogor *Indon* **78B4**
Bogorodskoye *USSR* **61H2**
Bogotá *Colombia* **32C3**
Bogotol *USSR* **63A2**
Bogra *Bang* **86B2**
Bo Hai, B *China* **72D2**
Bohain-en-Vermandois *France* **46B2**
Bohai Wan, B *China* **72D2**
Böhmer-Wald, Upland *W Germ* **57C3**
Bohol, I *Phil* **79B4**
Bohol S *Phil* **79B4**
Bois, R *Brazil* **35A1**
Bois Blanc I *USA* **14B1**
Boise *USA* **8B2**
Bojador,C *Mor* **96A2**
Bojeador,C *Phil* **79B2**
Bojnūrd *Iran* **90C2**
Boké *Guinea* **97A3**
Bokhara, R *Aust* **109C1**
Boknafjord, Inlet *Nor* **39F7**
Boko *Congo* **98B3**
Bokor *Camb* **76C3**
Bokungu *Zaïre* **98C3**
Bol *Chad* **98B1**
Bolaãnos *Mexico* **23A1**
Bolama *Guinea-Bissau* **97A3**
Bolanos, R *Mexico* **23A1**
Bolbec *France* **48C2**
Bole *Ghana* **97B4**
Boleslawiec *Pol* **59B2**
Bolgatanga *Ghana* **97B3**
Bolgrad *USSR* **60C4**
Bolívar *Arg* **34C3**
Bolivar, Missouri *USA* **18B2**
Bolivar, Tennessee *USA* **18C2**
Bolivia, Republic *S America* **30C2**
Bollnas *Sweden* **38H6**
Bollon *Aust* **109C1**
Bollvar, Mt *Ven* **32C2**
Bologna *Italy* **52B2**
Bologoye *USSR* **60D2**
Bolon *USSR* **69F2**
Bol'shoy Irgiz, R *USSR* **61G3**
Bol'shoy Kamen *USSR* **74C2**
Bol'shoy Kavkaz, Mts *USSR* **65F5**
Bol'shoy Uzen, R *USSR* **61G4**
Bolson de Mapimi, Desert *Mexico* **9C4**
Bolton *Eng* **43C3**
Bolu *Turk* **92B1**
Bolungarvik *Iceland* **38A1**
Bolvadin *Turk* **92B2**
Bolzano *Italy* **52B1**
Boma *Zaïre* **98B3**
Bombala *Aust* **107D4**
Bombay *India* **87A1**
Bombo *Uganda* **99D2**
Bom Despacho *Brazil* **35B1**
Bomdila *India* **86C1**
Bomi Hills *Lib* **97A4**
Bom Jesus da Lapa *Brazil* **31C4**
Bomnak *USSR* **63E2**
Bomokandi, R *Zaïre* **99C2**
Bomu, R *CAR/Zaïre* **98C2**
Bonaire, I *Caribbean* **27D4**
Bona,Mt *USA* **12F2**
Bonanza *Nic* **25D3**
Bonavista *Can* **7E5**
Bon Bon *Aust* **108A2**
Bondo *Zaïre* **98C2**
Bondoukou *Ivory Coast* **97B4**
Bonfim *Guyana* **33E3**
Bongandanga *Zaïre* **98C2**
Bongor *Chad* **98B1**
Bonham *USA* **19A3**
Bonifacio *Corse* **53A2**
Bonifacio,Str of, Chan *Medit S* **52A2**
Bonita Springs *USA* **17B2**
Bonn *W Germ* **57B2**
Bonners Ferry *USA* **20C1**
Bonnet Plume, R *Can* **12H1**
Bonnyville *Can* **13E2**
Bonthe *Sierra Leone* **97A4**
Booaaso *Somalia* **99E1**
Booligal *Aust* **108B2**
Boonah *Aust* **109D1**
Boonville *USA* **15C2**
Boorowa *Aust* **109C2**
Boothia,G of *Can* **6A2**
Boothia Pen *Can* **6A2**
Booué *Gabon* **98B3**
Bopeechee *Aust* **108A1**
Bor *Sudan* **99D2**
Bor *Turk* **92B2**
Bor *Yugos* **54B2**
Borah Peak, Mt *USA* **8B2**
Borås *Sweden* **39G7**
Borāzjān *Iran* **91B4**
Borda,C *Aust* **108A3**
Bordeaux *France* **48B3**
Borden I *Can* **4G2**
Borden Pen *Can* **6B2**
Bordentown *USA* **16B2**
Borders, Region *Scot* **42C2**
Bordertown *Aust* **108B3**
Bordi Omar Dris *Alg* **96C2**
Borens River *Can* **8D1**
Borgå *Fin* **39K6**
Borgarnes *Iceland* **38A2**
Borger *USA* **9C3**
Borgholm *Sweden* **39H7**
Borgosia *Italy* **47C2**
Borgo Valsugana *Italy* **47D1**
Borislav *USSR* **59C3**
Borisoglebsk *USSR* **61F3**
Borisov *USSR* **60C3**
Borisovka *USSR* **60E3**
Borkou, Region *Chad* **95A3**
Borlänge *Sweden* **39H6**
Bormida *Italy* **47C2**
Bormio *Italy* **47D1**
Borneo, I *Malaysia/Indon* **67F5**
Bornholm, I *Den* **39H7**
Bornova *Turk* **55C3**
Boro, R *Sudan* **98C2**
Boromo *U Volta* **97B3**
Borovichi *USSR* **60D2**
Borroloola *Aust* **106C2**
Borsa *Rom* **54B1**
Borūjed *Iran* **90A3**
Borūjen *Iran* **90B3**
Bory Tucholskie, Region *Pol* **58B2**
Borzya *USSR* **63D2**
Bose *China* **73B5**
Boshof *S Africa* **101G1**
Bosna, R *Yugos* **54A2**
Bōsō-hantō, B *Japan* **75C1**
Bosquet *Alg* **51C2**
Bossangoa *CAR* **98B2**
Bossèmbélé *CAR* **98B2**
Bossier City *USA* **19B3**
Bosten Hu, L *China* **65K5**
Boston *Eng* **43D3**
Boston *USA* **10C2**
Boston Mts *USA* **11A3**
Botād *India* **85C4**
Botevgrad *Bulg* **54B2**
Bothaville *S Africa* **101G1**
Bothnia,G of *Sweden/Fin* **64C3**
Botletli, R *Botswana* **100B3**
Botosani *Rom* **60C4**
Botswana, Republic *Africa* **100B3**
Botte Donato, Mt *Italy* **53C3**
Bottrop *W Germ* **46D1**
Botucatu *Brazil* **35B2**
Botwood *Can* **7E5**
Bouaflé *Ivory Coast* **97B4**
Bouaké *Ivory Coast* **89D7**
Bouar *CAR* **98B2**
Bouârfa *Mor* **96B1**
Bouca *CAR* **98B2**
Boufarik *Alg* **51C2**
Bougouni *Mali* **97B3**
Bouillon *France* **46C2**
Bou Izakarn *Mor* **96B2**
Boulay-Moselle *France* **46D2**
Boulder, Colorado *USA* **8C2**
Boulder City *USA* **9B3**
Boulder Creek *USA* **22A2**
Boulogne *France* **48C1**
Boumba, R *CAR* **98B2**
Bouna *Ivory Coast* **97B4**
Boundary Peak, Mt *USA* **8B3**
Boundiali *Ivory Coast* **97B4**
Bourail *Nouvelle Calédonie* **107F3**
Bourem *Mali* **97B3**
Bourg *France* **49D2**
Bourg de Péage *France* **49D2**
Bourges *France* **48C2**
Bourg-Madame *France* **48C3**
Bourgogne, Region *France* **49C2**
Bourg-St-Maurice *France* **47B2**
Bourke *Aust* **108C2**
Bournemouth *Eng* **43D4**
Bou Saâda *Alg* **96C1**
Bousso *Chad* **98B1**
Boutilmit *Maur* **97A3**
Bouvet I *Atlantic O* **103J7**
Bovril *Arg* **34D2**
Bow, R *Can* **13E2**
Bowen *Aust* **107D2**
Bowie, Texas *USA* **19A3**
Bow Island *Can* **13E2**
Bowling Green, Kentucky *USA* **11B3**
Bowling Green, Missouri *USA* **18B2**
Bowling Green, Ohio *USA* **14B2**
Bowling Green, Virginia *USA* **15C3**
Bowmanville *Can* **15C2**
Bowral *Aust* **109D2**
Bowron, R *Can* **13C2**
Bo Xian *China* **72D3**
Boxing *China* **72D2**
Boyabat *Turk* **92B1**
Boyali *CAR* **98B2**
Boyd *Can* **5J4**
Boyertown *USA* **16B2**
Boyle *Can* **13E2**
Boyle *Irish Rep* **41B3**
Boyne, R *Irish Rep* **45C2**
Boynoton Beach *USA* **17B2**
Boyoma Falls *Zaïre* **98C2**
Bozcaada, I *Turk* **55C3**
Boz Dağlari, Mts *Turk* **55C3**
Bozeman *USA* **8B2**
Bozene *Zaïre* **98B2**
Bozoum *CAR* **98B2**
Bra *Italy* **47B2**
Brač, I *Yugos* **52C2**
Bracebridge *Can* **15C1**
Brach *Libya* **95A2**
Bräcke *Sweden* **38H6**
Bradenton *USA* **17B2**
Bradford *Eng* **42D3**
Brae *Scot* **44E1**
Braemar *Scot* **44C3**
Braga *Port* **50A1**
Bragado *Arg* **34C3**
Bragana *Port* **50A1**
Bragança *Brazil* **31B2**
Bragança Paulista *Brazil* **35B2**
Brahman-Baria *Bang* **86C2**
Brāhmani, R *India* **86B2**
Brahmaputra, R *India* **86C1**
Braie Verte *Can* **7E5**
Brăila *Rom* **60C4**
Brainerd *USA* **10A2**
Brakna, Region *Maur* **97A3**
Bralorne *Can* **5F4**
Brampton *Can* **14C2**
Branco, R *Brazil* **33E3**
Brandberg, Mt *Namibia* **100A3**
Brandenburg *E Germ* **56C2**
Brandfort *S Africa* **101G1**
Brandon *Can* **8D2**
Brandvlei *S Africa* **100B4**
Brandys nad Lebem *Czech* **57C2**
Braniewo *Pol* **58B2**
Brantford *Can* **10B2**

Branxholme *Aust* **108B3**
Bras D'Or L *Can* **7D5**
Brasíla de Minas *Brazil* **35C1**
Brasiléia *Brazil* **32D6**
Brasilia *Brazil* **31B5**
Brasov *Rom* **54C1**
Brassay Range, Mts *Malay* **78D1**
Bratislava *Czech* **59B3**
Bratsk *USSR* **63C2**
Brattleboro *USA* **15D2**
Braunschweig *W Germ* **56C2**
Brava, I *Cape Verde* **97A4**
Brawley *USA* **9B3**
Bray *Irish Rep* **45C2**
Bray I *Can* **6C3**
Brazeau, R *Can* **13D2**
Brazeau,Mt *Can* **13D2**
Brazil, Republic *S America* **28D4**
Brazil Basin *Atlantic O* **103G5**
Brazos, R *USA* **9D3**
Brazzaville *Congo* **98B3**
Brdy, Upland *Czech* **57C3**
Breaksea Sd *NZ* **111A3**
Bream B *NZ* **110B1**
Brebes *Indon* **78B4**
Brechin *Scot* **44C3**
Brecht *Belg* **46C1**
Břeclav *Czech* **59B3**
Brecon *Wales* **43C4**
Brecon Beacons, Mts *Wales* **43C4**
Brecon Beacons Nat Pk *Wales* **43B3**
Breda *Neth* **56A2**
Bredasdorp *S Africa* **100B4**
Bredbyn *Sweden* **38H6**
Bredy *USSR* **61J3**
Breezewood *USA* **15C2**
Bregenz *Austria* **47C1**
Bregenzer Ache, R *Austria* **47C1**
Breiðafjörður, B *Iceland* **38A1**
Brembo, R *Italy* **47C2**
Bremen *USA* **17A1**
Bremen *W Germ* **56B2**
Bremerhaven *W Germ* **56B2**
Bremerton *USA* **20B1**
Brenham *USA* **19A3**
Brenner, P *Austria/Italy* **57C3**
Breno *Italy* **47D2**
Brenta, R *Italy* **47D2**
Brentwood *USA* **22B2**
Brescia *Italy* **52B1**
Bressanone *Italy* **47D1**
Bressay, I *Scot* **44D1**
Bressuire *France* **48B2**
Brest *France* **48B2**
Brest *USSR* **58C2**
Bretagne, Region *France* **48B2**
Breteuil *France* **46B2**
Breton Woods *USA* **16B2**
Brett,C *NZ* **110B1**
Brewarrina *Aust* **109C1**
Brewster, New York *USA* **16C2**
Brewster, Washington *USA* **20C1**
Breyten *S Africa* **101G1**
Brezhnev *USSR* **61H2**
Brežice *Yugos* **52C1**
Bria *CAR* **98C2**
Briancon *France* **49D3**
Briare *France* **49C2**
Bridgeport, California *USA* **21B2**
Bridgeport, Connecticut *USA* **15D2**
Bridgeport, Texas *USA* **19A3**
Bridgeport Res *USA* **22C1**
Bridgeton *USA* **16B3**
Bridgetown *Barbados* **27F4**
Bridgewater *Can* **7D5**
Bridgewater *USA* **16D2**
Bridgwater *Eng* **43C4**
Bridgwater B *Eng* **43C4**
Bridlington *Eng* **42D2**
Bridport *Aust* **109C4**
Brienzer See, L *Switz* **47B1**
Briey *France* **46C2**
Brig *Switz* **52A1**
Brigham City *USA* **8B2**
Bright *Aust* **109C3**
Brighton *Eng* **43D4**
Brilon *W Germ* **46E1**
Brindisi *Italy* **55A2**
Brinkley *USA* **19B3**
Brisbane *Aust* **107E3**
Bristol, Connecticut *USA* **15D2**
Bristol *Eng* **43C4**
Bristol, Pennsylvania *USA* **15D2**
Bristol, Rhode Island *USA* **16D2**
Bristol, Tennessee *USA* **11B3**
Bristol B *USA* **12B3**
Bristol Chan *Eng/Wales* **43B4**
British, Mts *USA* **4D3**
British Columbia, Province *Can* **5F4**
British Empire Range, Mts *Can* **6B1**
Brits *S Africa* **101G1**
Britstown *S Africa* **100B4**
Brive *France* **48C2**
Brno *Czech* **59B3**
Broad, R *USA* **17B1**
Broadback, R *Can* **7C4**
Broad Bay, Inlet *Scot* **44A2**
Broadford *Scot* **44B3**
Brochet *Can* **5H4**
Brock I *Can* **4G2**
Brockport *USA* **15C2**
Brockton *USA* **16D1**
Brockville *Can* **15C2**
Brodeur Pen *Can* **6B2**
Brodick *Scot* **42B2**
Brodnica *Pol* **58B2**
Brody *USSR* **60C3**
Broken Bow, Oklahoma *USA* **19B3**
Broken Bow L *USA* **19B3**
Broken Hill *Aust* **107D4**
Broni *Italy* **47C2**
Brønnøysund *Nor* **38G5**
Bronx, Borough, New York *USA* **16C2**
Brooke's Point *Phil* **79A4**
Brookfield, Missouri *USA* **18B2**
Brookhaven *USA* **11A3**
Brookings, Oregon *USA* **20B2**
Brookings, South Dakota *USA* **8D2**
Brookline *USA* **16D1**
Brooklyn, Borough, New York *USA* **16C2**
Brooks *Can* **5G4**
Brooks,L *USA* **12C3**
Brooks Mt *USA* **12A1**
Brooks Range, Mts *USA* **4C3**
Brooksville *USA* **17B2**
Brooloo *Aust* **109D1**
Broome *Aust* **106B2**
Brora *Scot* **44C2**
Brothers *USA* **20B2**
Broulkou *Chad* **95A3**
Browning *USA* **13E3**
Brownsville *USA* **9D4**
Brownwood *USA* **9D3**
Bruay-en-Artois *France* **46B1**
Bruce,Mt *Aust* **106A3**
Bruce Pen *Can* **14B1**
Bruck an der Mur *Austria* **59B3**
Brugge *Belg* **46B1**
Brühl *W Germ* **46D1**
Brunei, Sultanate *S E Asia* **78C2**
Brunico *Italy* **52B1**
Brunner,L *NZ* **111B2**
Brunswick, Georgia *USA* **11B3**
Brunswick, Mississippi *USA* **18B2**
Brunswick,Pen de *Chile* **29B6**
Bruny I *Aust* **109C4**
Brusenets *USSR* **61F1**
Brus Laguna *Honduras* **26A3**
Bruxelles *Belg* **56A2**
Bryan *USA* **9D3**
Bryan,Mt *Aust* **108A2**
Bryansk *USSR* **60D3**
Bryant *USA* **19B3**
Brzeg *Pol* **59B2**
Būbīyan, I *Kuwait/Iraq* **93E4**
Bubu, R *Tanz* **99D3**
Bucaramanga *Colombia* **32C2**
Buchan, Oilfield *N Sea* **44D3**
Buchanan *Lib* **97A4**
Buchan Deep *N Sea* **44D3**
Buchan G *Can* **6C2**
Buchan Ness, Pen *Scot* **40C2**
Buchans *Can* **7E5**
Buchardo *Arg* **34C2**
Buchs *Switz* **47C1**
Buckingham *Eng* **43D3**
Buckland *USA* **12B1**
Buckland, R *USA* **12B1**
Buckleboo *Aust* **108A2**
Buco Zau *Congo* **98B3**
Bucureşti *Rom* **54C2**
Budapest *Hung* **59B3**
Budaun *India* **84D3**
Bude *Eng* **43B4**
Bude *USA* **19B3**
Budennovsk *USSR* **61F5**
Budva *Yugos* **54A2**
Buéa *Cam* **98A2**
Buellton *USA* **22B3**
Buena Esperanza *Arg* **34B2**
Buenaventura *Colombia* **32B3**
Buenavista *Mexico* **23A2**
Buenos Aires *Arg* **29E2**
Buenos Aires, State *Arg* **29D3**
Buffalo, Mississipi *USA* **18B2**
Buffalo, New York *USA* **10C2**
Buffalo, South Dakota *USA* **8C2**
Buffalo, Texas *USA* **19A3**
Buffalo, Wyoming *USA* **8C2**
Buffalo, R *S Africa* **101H1**
Buffalo L, Alberta *Can* **13E2**
Buffalo L, Northwest Territories *Can* **5G3**
Buffalo Narrows *Can* **5H4**
Buford *USA* **17B1**
Buftea *Rom* **54C2**
Bug, R *USSR/Pol* **59C2**
Buga *Colombia* **32B3**
Bugdayli *USSR* **90B2**
Bugulma *USSR* **61H3**
Buguruslan *USSR* **61H3**
Buhayrat al Asad, Res *Syria* **93C2**
Builth Wells *Wales* **41C3**
Buin *Chile* **34A2**
Bujumbura *Burundi* **99C3**
Bukama *Zaïre* **98C3**
Bukavu *Zaïre* **99C3**
Bukhara *USSR* **80E2**
Bukit Batubrok, Mt *Indon* **78C2**
Bukittinggi *Indon* **70B4**
Bukoba *Tanz* **99D3**
Buku Gandadiwata, Mt *Indon* **78D3**
Bula *Indon* **71E4**
Bulan *Phil* **79B3**
Bulandshahr *India* **84D3**
Bulawayo *Zim* **100B3**
Buldan *Turk* **55C3**
Buldāna *India* **85D4**
Bulgan *Mongolia* **68C2**
Bulgaria, Republic *Europe* **54B2**
Bulle *Switz* **47B1**
Buller, R *NZ* **111B2**
Buller,Mt *Aust* **109C3**
Bullfinch *Aust* **106A4**
Bulloo, R *Aust* **108B1**
Bulloo Downs *Aust* **108B1**
Bulloo L *Aust* **108B1**
Bull Shoals Res *USA* **18B2**
Bulnes *Chile* **34A3**
Bulolo *PNG* **71F4**
Bultfontein *S Africa* **101G1**
Bumpa *Zaïre* **98C2**
Bumphal Dam *Thai* **76B2**
Buna *Kenya* **99D2**
Bunbury *Aust* **106A4**
Buncrana *Irish Rep* **45C1**
Bundaberg *Aust* **107E3**
Bundarra *Aust* **109D2**
Būndi *India* **85D3**
Bundoran *Irish Rep* **45B1**
Bungil, R *Aust* **109C1**
Bungo *Angola* **98B3**
Bungo-suidō, Str *Japan* **75A2**
Bunguran, I *Ind* **70B3**
Bunia *Zaïre* **99D2**
Bunker *USA* **18B2**
Bunkie *USA* **19B3**
Bunnell *USA* **17B2**
Buntok *Indon* **78C3**
Buol *Indon* **71D3**
Burāg *Syria* **94C2**
Buram *Sudan* **98C1**
Burauen *Phil* **79B3**
Buraydah *S Arabia* **80C3**
Burbank *USA* **21B3**
Burcher *Aust* **109C2**
Burco *Somalia* **99E2**
Burdur *Turk* **92B2**
Bureinskiy Khrebet, Mts *USSR* **63F3**
Burg *E Germ* **56C2**
Burgas *Bulg* **54C2**
Burgaw *USA* **17C1**
Burgdorf *Switz* **47B1**
Burgersdorp *S Africa* **100B4**
Burgin *USSR* **65K5**
Burgos *Spain* **50B1**
Burgsvik *Sweden* **58B1**
Burhaniye *Turk* **55C3**
Burhānpur *India* **85D4**
Burias, I *Phil* **79B3**
Buriram *Thai* **76C2**
Buritis *Brazil* **35B1**
Burke Chan *Can* **13B2**
Burketown *Aust* **106C2**
Burks Falls *Can* **15C1**
Burley *USA* **8B2**
Burlington, Iowa *USA* **10A2**
Burlington, New Jersey *USA* **16B2**
Burlington, Vermont *USA* **10C2**
Burlington, Washington *USA* **20B1**
Burma, Republic *Asia* **83D3**
Burney *USA* **20B2**
Burnham *USA* **16A2**
Burnie *Aust* **107D5**
Burnley *Eng* **42C3**
Burns *USA* **20C2**
Burns Lake *Can* **5F4**
Burqin *China* **82C1**
Burra *Aust* **108A2**
Burragorang,L *Aust* **109D2**
Burray, I *Scot* **44C2**
Burren Junction *Aust* **109C2**

Burrinjuck Res *Aust* **109C2**
Bursa *Turk* **60C5**
Bur Safâga *Egypt* **80B3**
Burton *USA* **14B2**
Burton upon Trent *Eng* **43D3**
Burtrask *Sweden* **38J6**
Burtundy *Aust* **108B2**
Buru *Indon* **71D4**
Burundi, Republic *Africa* **99C3**
Burung *Indon* **78A2**
Buryatskaya ASSR, Republic *USSR* **63D2**
Burye *Eth* **99D1**
Burynshik *USSR* **61H4**
Bury St Edmunds *Eng* **43E3**
Būshehr *Iran* **91B4**
Busira, R *Zaïre* **98B3**
Buskozdroj *Pol* **58C2**
Busrā ash Shām *Syria* **94C2**
Busselton *Aust* **106A4**
Busto *Italy* **49D2**
Busto Arsizio *Italy* **52A1**
Busuanga, I *Phil* **79A3**
Buta *Zaïre* **98C2**
Buta Ranquil *Arg* **34B3**
Butare *Rwanda* **99C3**
Bute, I *Scot* **42B2**
Butha Qi *China* **69E2**
Butler *USA* **14C2**
Butte *USA* **8B2**
Butterworth *Malay* **77C4**
Butt of Lewis, C *Scot* **40B2**
Button Is *Can* **6D3**
Butuan *Phil* **79C4**
Butung, I *Indon* **71D4**
Buturlinovka *USSR* **61F3**
Butwal *Nepal* **86A1**
Buulo Barde *Somalia* **99E2**
Buur Hakaba *Somalia* **99E2**
Buy *USSR* **61F2**
Buyant Ovvo *Mongolia* **72B1**
Buynaksk *USSR* **61G5**
Buyr Nuur, L *Mongolia* **63D3**
Büyük Ağri, Mt *Turk* **93D2**
Büyük Menderes, R *Turk* **92A2**
Buzău *Rom* **54C1**
Buzau, R *Rom* **54C1**
Buzuluk *USSR* **61H3**
Buzzards B *USA* **16D2**
Byala *Bulg* **54C2**
Byala Slatina *Bulg* **54B2**
Byam Martin, Chan *Can* **4H2**
Byam Martin I *Can* **4H2**
Bydgoszcz *Pol* **58B2**
Bygland *Nor* **39F7**
Bylot I *Can* **6C2**
Byrock *Aust* **109C2**
Byron *USA* **22B2**
Byron,C *Aust* **109D1**
Bytom *Pol* **59B2**

C

Caacupé *Par* **30E4**
Caála *Angola* **100A2**
Caamano Sd *Can* **13B2**
Caazapá *Par* **30E4**
Cabanatuan *Phil* **79B2**
Cabedelo *Brazil* **31E3**
Cabeza del Buey *Spain* **50A2**
Cabildo *Arg* **34C3**
Cabildo *Chile* **34A2**
Cabimas *Ven* **32C1**
Cabinda *Angola* **98B3**
Cabinda, Province *Angola* **98B3**
Cabo Beata *Dom Rep* **27C3**
Cabo Binibeca, C *Spain* **51C2**
Cabo Carbonara, C *Sardegna* **53A3**
Cabo Carranza, C *Chile* **34A3**
Cabo Carvoeiro, C *Port* **50A2**
Cabo Colnett, C *Mexico* **9B3**
Cabo Corrientes, C *Colombia* **32B2**
Cabo Corrientes, C *Mexico* **24B2**
Cabo Cruz, C *Cuba* **26B3**
Cabo de Ajo, C *Spain* **50B1**
Cabo de Caballeria, C *Spain* **51C1**
Cabo de Creus, C *Spain* **51C1**
Cabo de Gata, C *Spain* **50B2**
Cabo de Hornos, C *Chile* **29C7**
Cabo de la Nao, C *Spain* **51C2**
Cabo de Peñas, C *Spain* **50A1**
Cabo de Roca, C *Port* **50A2**
Cabo de Salinas, C *Spain* **51C2**
Cabo de São Tomé, C *Brazil* **35C2**
Cabo de São Vicente, C *Port* **50A2**
Cabo de Sines, C *Port* **50A2**
Cabo de Tortosa, C *Spain* **51C1**
Cabo Dos Bahias, C *Arg* **29C4**
Cabo Espichel, C *Port* **50A2**
Cabo Falso, C *Mexico* **9B4**
Cabo Ferrat, C *Alg* **51B2**
Cabo Finisterre, C *Spain* **50A1**
Cabo Formentor, C *Spain* **51C1**
Cabo Frio *Brazil* **35C2**
Cabo Frio, C *Brazil* **35C2**
Cabo Gracias à Dios *Honduras* **26A4**
Cabo Maguarinho, C *Brazil* **31B2**
Cabo Negro, C *Mor* **50A2**
Cabonga,Résr *Can* **10C2**
Caboolture *Aust* **109D1**
Cabo Orange, C *Brazil* **33G3**
Cabo Punta Banda, C *Mexico* **21B3**
Cabora Bassa Dam *Mozam* **101C2**
Caborca *Mexico* **24A1**
Cabo Rojo, C *Mexico* **24C2**
Cabos *Mexico* **23B1**
Cabo San Diego, C *Arg* **29C6**
Cabo San Lorenzo, C *Ecuador* **32A4**
Cabo Teulada, C *Sardegna* **53A3**
Cabo Trafalgar, C *Spain* **50A2**
Cabo Tres Forcas, C *Mor* **50B2**
Cabo Tres Puntas, C *Arg* **29C5**
Cabot Str *Can* **7D5**
Cabra *Spain* **50B2**
Cabreira, Mt *Port* **50A1**
Cabrera, I *Spain* **51C2**
Cabrero *Chile* **34A3**
Cabriel, R *Spain* **51B2**
Cacahuamilpa *Mexico* **23B2**
Čačak *Yugos* **54B2**
C A Carillo *Mexico* **23B2**
Cáceres *Brazil* **30E2**
Caceres *Spain* **50A2**
Cache, R *USA* **18B2**
Cache Creek *Can* **13C2**
Cachi *Arg* **30C4**
Cachimbo *Brazil* **33G5**
Cachoeira *Brazil* **31D4**
Cachoeira Alta *Brazil* **35A1**
Cachoeira de Paulo Alfonso, Waterfall *Brazil* **31D3**
Cachoeira do Sul *Brazil* **29F2**
Cachoeiro de Itapemirim *Brazil* **31C6**
Cachuma,L *USA* **22C3**
Cacolo *Angola* **100A2**
Caconda *Angola* **100A2**
Caçu *Brazil* **35A1**
Caculuvar, R *Angola* **100A2**
Čadca *Czech* **59B3**
Cader Idris, Mts *Wales* **43C3**
Cadillac *USA* **10B2**
Cadiz *Phil* **79B3**
Cadiz *Spain* **50A2**
Caen *France* **48B2**
Caernarfon *Wales* **42B3**
Caernarfon B *Wales* **43B3**
Caesarea, Hist Site *Israel* **94B2**
Caetité *Brazil* **31C4**
Cafayate *Arg* **30C4**
Caga Tepe *Turk* **92B2**
Cagayan, R *Phil* **79B2**
Cagayan de Oro *Phil* **79B4**
Cagayan Is *Phil* **79B4**
Cagayan Sulu, I *Phil* **79A4**
Cagliari *Sardegna* **53A3**
Caguas *Puerto Rico* **27D3**
Caha Mts *Irish Rep* **45B3**
Cahersiveen *Irish Rep* **45A3**
Cahir *Irish Rep* **45C2**
Cahone Pt *Irish Rep* **45C2**
Cahors *France* **48C3**
Caia *Mozam* **101C2**
Caianda *Angola* **100B2**
Caiapó, R *Brazil* **35A1**
Caiapõnia *Brazil* **35A1**
Caicó *Brazil* **31D3**
Caicos Is *Caribbean* **26C2**
Caicos Pass *Bahamas* **11C4**
Cairn Mt *USA* **12C2**
Cairngorms, Mts *Scot* **44C3**
Cairns *Aust* **107D2**
Cairo *Egypt* **92B3**
Cairo *USA* **11B3**
Caiwarro *Aust* **108B1**
Cajabamba *Peru* **32B5**
Cajamarca *Peru* **32B5**
Calabozo *Ven* **27D5**
Calafat *Rom* **54B2**
Calafate *Arg* **29B6**
Calagua Is *Phil* **79B3**
Calahorra *Spain* **51B1**
Calais *France* **48C1**
Calama *Chile* **30C3**
Calamar *Colombia* **32C3**
Calamian Group, Is *Phil* **79A3**
Calang *Indon* **70A3**
Calanscio Sand Sea *Libya* **95B2**
Calapan *Phil* **79B3**
Calarasi *Rom* **54C2**
Calatayud *Spain* **51B1**
Calaveras Res *USA* **22B2**
Calbayog *Phil* **79B3**
Calcasieu L *USA* **19B4**
Calcutta *India* **86B2**
Caldas da Rainha *Port* **50A2**
Caldas Novas *Brazil* **31B5**
Caldera *Chile* **30B4**
Caldwell *USA* **8B2**
Caleta Olivia *Arg* **29C5**
Calexico *USA* **9B3**
Calgary *Can* **5G4**
Calhoun *USA* **17B1**
Calhoun Falls *USA* **17B1**
Cali *Colombia* **32B3**
Calicut *India* **87B2**
Caliente, Nevada *USA* **8B3**
California, State *USA* **8A3**
California Aqueduct *USA* **22C3**
Calimera,Pt *India* **87B2**
Calingasta *Arg* **34B2**
Calistoga *USA* **22A1**
Callabonna, R *Aust* **108B1**
Callabonna,L *Aust* **108A1**
Callander *Can* **15C1**
Callander *Scot* **44B3**
Callanna *Aust* **108A1**
Callao *Peru* **32B6**
Calling L *Can* **13E1**
Calnali *Mexico* **23B1**
Caloosahatchee, R *USA* **17B2**
Caloundra *Aust* **109D1**
Calpulalpan *Mexico* **23B2**
Caltanissetta *Italy* **53B3**
Caluango *Angola* **98B3**
Calulo *Angola* **100A2**
Caluquembe *Angola* **100A2**
Calvert I *Can* **13B2**
Calvi *Corse* **52A2**
Calvillo *Mexico* **23A1**
Calvinia *S Africa* **100A4**
Camagüey *Cuba* **25E2**
Camagüey,Arch de, Is *Cuba* **25E2**
Camaná *Peru* **30B2**
Camargo *Bol* **30C3**
Camarillo *USA* **22C3**
Camarones *Arg* **29C4**
Camas *USA* **20B1**
Camaxilo *Angola* **98B3**
Cambatela *Angola* **98B3**
Cambodia, Republic *S E ASia* **76C3**
Camborne *Eng* **43B4**
Cambrai *France* **49C1**
Cambrian Mts *Wales* **43C3**
Cambridge *Can* **14B2**
Cambridge, County *Eng* **43D3**
Cambridge *Eng* **43E3**
Cambridge *Jamaica* **27H1**
Cambridge, Maryland *USA* **15C3**
Cambridge, Massachussets *USA* **15D2**
Cambridge *NZ* **110C1**
Cambridge, Ohio *USA* **14B2**
Cambridge Bay *Can* **4H3**
Cam Burun, Pt *Turk* **60E5**
Camden, Arkansas *USA* **11A3**
Camden *Aust* **109D2**
Camden, New Jersey *USA* **15D3**
Camden, South Carolina *USA* **17B1**
Cameron, Missouri *USA* **18B2**
Cameron, Texas *USA* **19A3**
Cameron I *Can* **4H2**
Cameron Mts *NZ* **111A3**
Cameroon, Federal Republic *Africa* **98A2**
Cameroun, Mt *Cam* **98A2**
Cametá *Brazil* **31B2**
Camiguin, I *Phil* **79B4**
Camiling *Phil* **79B2**
Camilla *USA* **17B1**
Camino *USA* **22B1**
Camiri *Bol* **30D3**
Camocim *Brazil* **31C2**
Camooweal *Aust* **106C2**
Campana *Arg* **34D2**
Campana, I *Chile* **29A5**
Campania I *Can* **13B2**
Campbell,C *NZ* **111B2**
Campbell I *Can* **13B2**
Campbell I *NZ* **105G6**
Campbell,Mt *Can* **4E3**
Campbellpore *Pak* **84C2**
Campbell River *Can* **5F5**
Campbellton *Can* **7D5**
Campbelltown *Aust* **109D2**
Campbeltown *Scot* **42B2**
Campeche *Mexico* **25C3**
Camperdown *Aust* **108B3**

Campina Grande *Brazil* 31D3
Campinas *Brazil* 31B6
Campina Verde *Brazil* 35B1
Campo *Cam* 98A2
Campobasso *Italy* 53B2
Campo Belo *Brazil* 35B2
Campo Florido *Brazil* 35B1
Campo Gallo *Arg* 30D4
Campo Grande *Brazil* 30F3
Campo Maior *Brazil* 31C2
Campo Mourão *Brazil* 30F3
Campos *Brazil* 35C2
Campos Altos *Brazil* 35B1
Campo Tures *Italy* 47D1
Cam Ranh *Viet* 76D3
Camrose *Can* 5G4
Camucuio *Angola* 100A2
Canaan *Tobago* 27K1
Canaan *USA* 16C1
Canacupa *Angola* 100A2
Canada, Dominion *N America* 2F3
Cañada de Gomez *Arg* 29D2
Canadian, R *USA* 9C3
Canakkale *Turk* 60C5
Canalejas *Arg* 34B3
Canal Flats *Can* 13D2
Cananea *Mexico* 24A1
Canary Basin *Atlantic O* 102G3
Canas *Mexico* 23A2
Canatlán *Mexico* 24B2
Canaveral,C *USA* 11B4
Canavieiras *Brazil* 31D5
Canberra *Aust* 107D4
Canby, California *USA* 20B2
Candala *Somalia* 99F1
Çandarli Körfezi, B *Turk* 55C3
Candlewood,L *USA* 16C2
Canelones *Urug* 29E2
Caney *USA* 18A2
Cangamba *Angola* 100A2
Cangombe *Angola* 100B2
Cangzhou *China* 72D2
Caniapiscau, R *Can* 7D4
Caniapiscau,L *Can* 7D4
Canicatti *Italy* 53B3
Canindé *Brazil* 31D2
Çankırı *Turk* 92B1
Canmore *Can* 13D2
Canna, I *Scot* 44A3
Cannanore *India* 87B2
Cannes *France* 49D3
Cann River *Aust* 109C3
Canõas *Brazil* 30F4
Canoe L *Can* 13F1
Canon City *USA* 9C3
Canopus *Aust* 108B2
Canora *Can* 5H4
Canowindra *Aust* 109C2
Cansore Pt *Irish Rep* 45C2
Canterbury *Eng* 43E4
Canterbury Bight, B *NZ* 111B2
Canterbury Plains *NZ* 111B2
Can Tho *Viet* 77D4
Canton, Mississippi *USA* 19C3
Canton, Missouri *USA* 18B1
Canton, Ohio *USA* 10B2
Cantwell *USA* 12E2
Canyon City *USA* 20C2
Canyon Range, Mts *Can* 12J2
Canyonville *USA* 20B2
Canzar *Angola* 98C3
Cao Bang *Viet* 76D1
Capanema *Brazil* 31B2
Capão Bonito *Brazil* 35B2
Capbreton *France* 48B3
Cap Corrientes, C *Mexico* 24B2
Cap Corse, C *Corse* 52A2
Cap d'Ambre, C *Madag* 101D2
Cap de la Hague, C *France* 48B2
Cap-de-la-Madeleine *Can* 15D1
Cap de Nouvelle-France, C *Can* 6C3
Capdepera *Spain* 51C2
Cap de Tancitiario, C *Mexico* 23A2
Cape Barren I *Aust* 109C4
Cape Basin *Atlantic O* 103J6
Cape Breton I *Can* 7E5
Cape Coast *Ghana* 97B4
Cape Cod B *USA* 15D2
Cape Dorset *Can* 6C3
Cape Fear, R *USA* 17C1
Cape Girardeau *USA* 18C2
Cape Henrietta Maria *Can* 6B3
Cape Johnston Depth *Pacific O* 104E3
Capelinha *Brazil* 35C1
Cape Lisburne *USA* 4B3
Capelongo *Angola* 100A2
Cape May *USA* 15D3
Cape Mendocino *USA* 5F5
Capenda Camulemba *Angola* 98B3
Cape Perry *Can* 4F2
Cape Province *S Africa* 100B4
Cape Tatnam *Can* 7A4
Cape Town *S Africa* 100A4
Cape Verde, Is *Atlantic O* 102G4
Cape Verde Basin *Atlantic O* 102G4
Cape Yakataga *USA* 12F3
Cape York Pen *Aust* 107D2
Cap Gris Nez, C *France* 46A1
Cap-Haitien *Haiti* 26C3
Capim, R *Brazil* 31B2
Cap Moule à Chique, C *St Lucia* 27P2
Capo Isola de Correnti C *Italy* 53C3
Capo Rizzuto, C *Italy* 53C3
Capo Santa Maria di Leuca, C *Italy* 55A3
Capo San Vito *Italy* 53B3
Capo Spartivento, C *Italy* 53C3
Cap Pt *St Lucia* 27P2
Capri, I *Italy* 53B2
Caprivi Strip, Region *Namibia* 100B2
Cap Rosso, C *Corse* 52A2
Cap Vert, C *Sen* 97A3
Caquetá, R *Colombia* 32C4
Caracal *Rom* 54B2
Caracaraí *Brazil* 33E3
Caracas *Ven* 32D1
Caraguatatuba *Brazil* 35B2
Carahue *Chile* 29B3
Caraí *Brazil* 35C1
Carandaí *Brazil* 35C2
Carangola *Brazil* 31C6
Caransebeş *Rom* 54B1
Carappee Hill, Mt *Aust* 108A2
Caratasca *Honduras* 26A3
Caratinga *Brazil* 35C1
Caravaca *Spain* 51B2
Caravelas *Brazil* 35D1
Carbondale, Illinois *USA* 18C2
Carbonia *Sardegna* 53A3
Carborear *Can* 7E5
Carcaion *Can* 5G4
Carcar Mts *Somalia* 99E1
Carcassonne *France* 48C3
Carcross *Can* 4E3
Cardel *Mexico* 23B2
Cardenas *Cuba* 25D2
Cárdenas *Mexico* 23B1
Cardiff *Wales* 43C4
Cardigan *Wales* 43B3
Cardigan B *Wales* 43B3
Cardston *Can* 13E2
Carei *Rom* 54B1
Careiro *Brazil* 33F4
Carén *Chile* 34A2
Carey *USA* 14B2
Carhaix-Plouguer *France* 48B2
Carhué *Arg* 29D3
Cariacica *Brazil* 31C6
Caribou *Can* 5J4
Caribou Mts, Alberta *Can* 5G4
Caribou Mts, British Columbia *Can* 5F4
Carigara *Phil* 79B3
Carignan *France* 46C2
Caripito *Ven* 33E1
Carleton Place *Can* 15C1
Carletonville *S Africa* 101G1
Carlinville *USA* 18C2
Carlisle *Eng* 42C2
Carlisle *USA* 15C2
Carlos *Arg* 34C3
Carlos Chagas *Brazil* 35C1
Carlow, County *Irish Rep* 45C2
Carlow *Irish Rep* 45C2
Carlsbad, California *USA* 21B3
Carlsbad, New Mexico *USA* 9C3
Carlyle *Can* 5H5
Carmacks *Can* 12G2
Carmagnola *Italy* 47B2
Carmarthen *Wales* 43B4
Carmarthen B *Wales* 43B4
Carmel, California *USA* 22B2
Carmel, New York *USA* 16C2
Carmel,Mt *Israel* 94B2
Carmelo *Urug* 34D2
Carmel Valley *USA* 22B2
Carmen, I *Mexico* 9B4
Carmen de Patagones *Arg* 29D4
Carmi *USA* 18C2
Carmichael *USA* 21A2
Carmo do Paranaiba *Brazil* 35B1
Carmona *Spain* 50A2
Carnarvon *Aust* 106A3
Carnarvon *S Africa* 100B4
Carncacá *Brazil* 35D1
Carndonagh *Irish Rep* 45C1
Carnegi,L *Aust* 106B3
Carnot *CAR* 98B2
Carnot,C *Aust* 108A2
Carol City *USA* 17B2
Carolina *Brazil* 31B3
Carolina *S Africa* 101H1
Carolina Beach *USA* 17C1
Caroline Is *Pacific O* 104F3
Carpathians, Mts *E Europe* 60B4
Carpatii Orientali, Mts *Rom* 59D3
Carpentaria,G of *Aust* 106C2
Carpenter Ridge *Indian O* 83C5
Carpentras *France* 49D3
Carpi *Italy* 52B2
Carpinteria *USA* 22C3
Carrabelle *USA* 17B2
Carrara *Italy* 52B2
Carrauntoohill, Mt *Irish Rep* 41B3
Carrickmacross *Irish Rep* 45C2
Carrick on Shannon *Irish Rep* 45B2
Carrick-on-Suir *Irish Rep* 45C2
Carrieton *Aust* 108A2
Carrington *USA* 8D2
Carrión, R *Spain* 50B1
Carroll *USA* 10A2
Carrollton, Georgia *USA* 17A1
Carrollton, Kentucky *USA* 14A3
Carrollton, Missouri *USA* 18B2
Carruthersville *USA* 18C2
Carsamba *Turk* 60E5
Carsamba, R *Turk* 92B2
Carson City *USA* 8B3
Carsonville *USA* 14B2
Cartagena *Colombia* 26B4
Cartagena *Spain* 51B2
Cartago *Colombia* 32B3
Cartago *Costa Rica* 25D4
Carterton *NZ* 111C2
Carthage, Missouri *USA* 18B2
Carthage, New York *USA* 15C2
Carthage, Texas *USA* 19B3
Cartier I *Timor S* 106B2
Cartwright *Can* 7E4
Caruaru *Brazil* 31D3
Carúpano *Ven* 33E1
Carvin *France* 46B1
Casablanca *Chile* 34A2
Casablanca *Mor* 96B1
Casa Branca *Brazil* 35B2
Casa Grande *USA* 9B3
Casale Monferrato *Italy* 52A1
Casalmaggiore *Italy* 47D2
Casares *Arg* 34C3
Cascade Mts *Can/USA* 13C3
Cascade Pt *NZ* 111A2
Cascade Range, Mts *USA* 8A2
Cascavel *Brazil* 30F3
Caserta *Italy* 53B2
Casey, Base *Ant* 112C9
Cashel *Irish Rep* 45C2
Casilda *Arg* 34C2
Casino *Aust* 107E3
Casma *Peru* 32B5
Caspe *Spain* 51B1
Casper *USA* 8C2
Caspian S *USSR* 65G6
Cass *USA* 14C3
Cassamba *Angola* 100B2
Cassel *France* 46B1
Cassiar *Can* 12J3
Cassiar Mts *Can* 4E3
Cassilândia *Brazil* 35A1
Cassino *Italy* 53B2
Castaic *USA* 22C3
Castaño, R *Arg* 34B2
Castelfranco *Italy* 47D2
Castellane *France* 49D3
Castelli *Arg* 34D3
Castellon de la Plana *Spain* 51B2
Castelo *Brazil* 31C3
Castelo Branco *Port* 50A2
Castelsarrasin *France* 48C3
Castelvetrano *Italy* 53B3
Casterton *Aust* 108B3
Castilla La Nueva, Region *Spain* 50B2
Castilla La Vieja, Region *Spain* 50B1
Castlebar *Irish Rep* 41B3
Castlebay *Scot* 44A3
Castle Douglas *Scot* 42C2
Castlegar *Can* 20C1
Castleisland *Irish Rep* 45B2
Castlemain *Aust* 108B3
Castlerea *Irish Rep* 45B2
Castlereagh *Aust* 109C2
Castres-sur-l'Agout *France* 48C3
Castries *St Lucia* 27E4
Castro *Arg* 29B4
Castro *Brazil* 30F3
Castro Alves *Brazil* 31D4
Castrovillari *Italy* 53C3
Castroville *USA* 22B2

Caswell Sd *NZ* 111A2
Cat, I *Bahamas* 25E2
Catabalogan *Phil* 79B3
Catacaos *Peru* 32A5
Cataguases *Brazil* 35C2
Catahoula L *USA* 19B3
Catalão *Brazil* 35B1
Cataluña, Region *Spain* 51C1
Catamarca *Arg* 30C4
Catamarca, State *Arg* 30C4
Catandica *Mozam* 101C2
Catanduanes, I *Phil* 79B3
Catanduva *Brazil* 31B6
Catania *Italy* 53C3
Catanzaro *Italy* 53C3
Catarman *Phil* 79B3
Catastrophe,C *Aust* 108A2
Catatumbo, R *Ven* 26C5
Catawissa *USA* 16A2
Catemaco *Mexico* 23B2
Cater *Corse* 49D3
Cateraggio *Corse* 52A2
Catete *Angola* 98B3
Catio *Guinea-Bissau* 97A3
Cat Lake *Can* 7A4
Catlegar *Can* 13D3
Cato, I *Aust* 107E3
Catoche,C *Mexico* 25D2
Catoctin Mt *USA* 16A3
Catonsville *USA* 15C3
Catrilo *Arg* 34C3
Catskill *USA* 15D2
Catskill Mts *USA* 15D2
Cauca, R *Colombia* 32C2
Caucaia *Brazil* 31D2
Caucasia *Colombia* 32B2
Caudry *France* 46B1
Caungula *Angola* 98B3
Cauquenes *Chile* 29B3
Cauvery, R *India* 87B2
Cavaillon *France* 49D3
Cavalese *italy* 47D1
Cavally, R *Lib* 97B4
Cavan, County *Irish Rep* 45C2
Cavan *Irish Rep* 45C2
Cavite *Phil* 79B3
Caxias *Brazil* 31C2
Caxias *Brazil* 32C4
Caxias do Sul *Brazil* 30F4
Caxito *Angola* 98B3
Cayce *USA* 17B1
Çayeli *Turk* 93D1
Cayenne *French Guiana* 33G3
Cayeux-sur-Mer *France* 46A1
Cayman Brac, I *Caribbean* 25E3
Cayman Is *Caribbean* 26A3
Cayman Trench *Caribbean* 26A3
Caynabo *Somalia* 99E2
Cayo Romana, I *Cuba* 25E2
Cayos Miskitos, Is *Nic* 25D3
Cay Sal, I *Caribbean* 26A2
Cazombo *Angola* 100B2
Ceara, State *Brazil* 31C3
Cebu *Phil* 79B3
Cebu, I *Phil* 79B3
Cecilton *USA* 16B3
Cecina *Italy* 52B2
Cedar City *USA* 8B3
Cedar Creek Res *USA* 19A3
Cedar L *Can* 5J4
Cedar Rapids *USA* 10A2
Cedartown *USA* 17A1
Cedros, I *Mexico* 24A2
Ceduna *Aust* 106C4
Ceelbuur *Somalia* 99E2
Ceerigaabo *Somalia* 99E1
Cefalù *Italy* 53B3
Cegléd *Hung* 59B3
Cela *Angola* 100A2
Celaya *Mexico* 24B2
Celebes S *S E Asia* 70C3
Celina *USA* 14B2
Celje *Yugos* 52C1
Celle *W Germ* 56C2
Cendrawasih, Pen *Indon* 71E4
Ceno, R *Italy* 47C2
Center *USA* 19B3
Center Moriches *USA* 16C2
Center Point *USA* 17A1
Cento *Italy* 47D2
Central, Region *Scot* 44B3
Central African Republic *Africa* 98B2
Central Falls *USA* 16D2
Centralia, Illinois *USA* 18C2
Centralia, Washington *USA* 8A2
Central Point *USA* 20B2
Central Range, Mts *PNG* 71F4
Centreville, Maryland *USA* 16A3
Cepu *Indon* 78C4
Ceram Sea *Indonesia* 71D4
Cereales *Arg* 34C3
Ceres *Brazil* 31B5
Ceres *S Africa* 100A4
Ceres *USA* 22B2
Cergy-Pontoise *France* 48C2
Cerignola *Italy* 53C2
Cernavodă *Rom* 60C5
Cerralvo, I *Mexico* 9C4
Cerritos *Mexico* 23A1
Cerro Aconcagua, Mt *Arg* 34B2
Cerro Azul *Mexico* 23B1
Cerro Campanario, Mt *Chile* 34A3
Cerro Champaqui, Mt *Arg* 34C2
Cerro Cuachaia, Mt *Mexico* 23A2
Cerro de Astillero *Mexico* 23B1
Cerro de Olivares, Mt *Arg* 34B2
Cerro de Pasco *Peru* 32B6
Cerro de Punta, Mt *Puerto Rico* 27D3
Cerro El Cantado, Mt *Mexico* 23A2
Cerro El Nevado, Mt *Arg* 34B3
Cerro Grande, Mts *Mexico* 23A2
Cerro Juncal, Mt *Arg/ Chile* 34A2
Cerro la Ardilla, Mts *Mexico* 23A1
Cerro las Tortolas, Mt *Chile* 34B1
Cerro Laurel, Mt *Mexico* 23A2
Cerro Mercedario, Mt *Arg* 34A2
Cerro Mora, Mt *Chile* 34A3
Cerron, Mt *Ven* 27C4
Cerro Payún, Mt *Arg* 34B3
Cerro Penón del Rosario, Mt *Mexico* 23B2
Cerro Sosneado, Mt *Arg* 34B2
Cerro Teotepec, Mt *Mexico* 23A2
Cerro Tupungato, Mt *Arg* 34B2
Cerro Yucuyacau, Mt *Mexico* 23B2
Cervo, R *Italy* 47C2
Cesena *Italy* 52B2
Cēsis *USSR* 60B2
České Budějovice *Czech* 57C3
České Zemé, Region *Czech* 57C3
Českomoravská Vysočina, U *Czech* 59B3
Çeşme *Turk* 55C3
Cessnock *Aust* 107E4
Cetina, R *Yugos* 52C2
Ceuta *N W Africa* 96B1
Ceyham *Turk* 92C2
Ceyhan, R *Turk* 92C2
Ceylanpınar *Turk* 93C2
Chaa-Khol *USSR* 63B2
Chaâteaudun *France* 48C2
Chablais, Region *France* 47B1
Chacabuco *Arg* 34C2
Chachapoyas *Peru* 32B5
Chacharramendi *Arg* 34B3
Chachran *Pak* 84C3
Chaco, State *Arg* 30D4
Chad, Republic *Africa* 98B1
Chad, L *C Africa* 98B1
Chadileuvu, R *Arg* 34B3
Chadron *USA* 8C2
Chaffee *USA* 18C2
Chagai *Pak* 85A3
Chagda *USSR* 63F2
Chaghcharan *Afghan* 84B2
Chagos Arch *Indian O* 104B4
Chaguanas *Trinidad* 27L1
Chāh Bahār *Iran* 91D4
Chai Badan *Thai* 76C2
Chaine des Cardamomes, Mts *Camb* 76C3
Chaine des Mitumba, Mts *Zaïre* 98C4
Chaiyaphum *Thai* 76C2
Chajari *Arg* 34D2
Chakwal *Pak* 84C2
Chala *Peru* 30B2
Chalabesa *Zambia* 100C2
Chalap Dalam, Mts *Afghan* 84A2
Chaling *China* 73C4
Chālisgaon *India* 85C4
Chalkyitsik *USA* 12F1
Challerange *France* 46C2
Châlons sur Marne *France* 46C2
Chalon sur Saône *France* 49C2
Cham *W Germ* 57C3
Chaman *Pak* 84B2
Chamba *India* 84D2
Chambal, R *India* 85D3
Chambersburg *USA* 15C3
Chambéry *France* 49D2
Chambly *France* 46B2
Chambor Kalat *Pak* 85A3
Chamgordan *Iran* 90B3
Chamical *Arg* 34B2
Chamonix *France* 47B2
Champa *India* 86A2
Champagne, Region *France* 49C2
Champagne Castle, Mt *Lesotho* 101G1
Champagnole *France* 47A1
Champaign *USA* 10B2
Champassak *Laos* 76D3
Champlain,L *USA* 10C2
Chāmrājnagar *India* 87B2
Chañaral *Chile* 30B4
Chanco *Chile* 34A3
Chandalar *USA* 4D3
Chandalar, R *USA* 4D3
Chandīgarh *India* 84D2
Chandpur *Bang* 86C2
Chandrapur *India* 85D5
Chānf *Iran* 91D4
Changara *Mozam* 101C2
Changbai *China* 74B2
Changchun *China* 69E2
Changde *China* 73C4
Chang-hua *Taiwan* 68E4
Changjiang *China* 76D2
Chang Jiang, R *China* 73D3
Changjin *N Korea* 74B2
Changsha *China* 73C4
Changshu *China* 72E3
Changtu *China* 74A2
Changwu *China* 72B2
Changyŏn *N Korea* 74B3
Changzhi *China* 72C2
Changzhou *China* 73E3
Channel Is *UK* 48B2
Channel Is *USA* 9B3
Channel Port-aux-Basques *Can* 7E5
Chanthaburi *Thai* 76C3
Chantilly *France* 46B2
Chanute *USA* 18A2
Chaoàn *China* 73D5
Chao'an *China* 73D5
Chao Hu, L *China* 73D3
Chao Phraya, R *Thai* 76C3
Chaoyang *China* 72E1
Chapada Diamantina, Mts *Brazil* 31C4
Chapadinha *Brazil* 31C2
Chapala *Mexico* 23A1
Chapala,Lac de, L *Mexico* 23A1
Chapayevo *USSR* 61H3
Chapecó *Brazil* 30F4
Chapeltown *Jamaica* 27H1
Chapleau *Can* 7B5
Chaplygin *USSR* 61E3
Charcot I *Ant* 112C3
Chardzhou *USSR* 80E2
Charente, R *France* 48C2
Chari, R *Chad* 98B1
Chari Baguirmi, Region *Chad* 98B1
Charikar *Afghan* 84B1
Chariton, R *USA* 18B1
Charity *Guyana* 33F2
Charkhāri *India* 85D3
Charleroi *Belg* 46C1
Charleston, Illinois *USA* 18C2
Charleston, Missouri *USA* 18C2
Charleston, S Carolina *USA* 11C3
Charleston, W Virginia *USA* 10B3
Charlesville *Zaïre* 98C3
Charleville *Aust* 107D3
Charleville-Mézières *France* 49C2
Charlevoix *USA* 14A1
Charlotte, Michigan *USA* 14B2
Charlotte, N Carolina *USA* 11B3
Charlotte Harbor, B *USA* 17B2
Charlottesville *USA* 10C3
Charlottetown *Can* 7D5
Charlotteville *Tobago* 27K1
Charlton *Aust* 108B3
Charlton I *Can* 10C1
Charsadda *Pak* 84C2
Charters Towers *Aust* 107D3
Chartres *France* 48C2
Chascomús *Arg* 29E3
Chase *Can* 13D2
Châteaubriant *France* 48B2
Châteaudun *France* 48C2
Châteaulin *France* 48B2
Châteauroux *France* 48C2
Chäteau-Salins *France* 46D2
Cháteau-Thierry *France* 49C2
Châtelet *Belg* 46C1
Châtellerault *France* 48C2
Chatham *Eng* 43E4
Chatham, New Brunswick *Can* 7D5
Chatham, New York *USA* 16C1
Chatham, Ontario *Can* 14B2
Chatham Sd *Can* 13A2
Chatham Str *USA* 12H3
Châtillon *France* 49C2
Châtillon *Italy* 47B2
Chatsworth *USA* 16B3
Chattahoochee *USA* 17B1
Chattahoochee, R *USA* 17A1

Chattanooga *USA* **11B3**
Chauk *Burma* **76A1**
Chaumont *France* **49D2**
Chauny *France* **46B2**
Chau Phu *Viet* **77D3**
Chaves *Port* **50A1**
Chazaouet *Alg* **50B2**
Chazón *Arg* **34C2**
Chcontá *Colombia* **32C2**
Cheb *Czech* **57C2**
Cheboksary *USSR* **65F4**
Cheboygan *USA* **10B2**
Chech'on *S Korea* **74B3**
Chechro *Pak* **85C3**
Checotah *USA* **18A2**
Cheduba, I *Burma* **76A2**
Cheepie *Aust* **108B1**
Chegga *Maur* **96B2**
Chegutu *Zim* **100C2**
Chehalis *USA* **20B1**
Cheju *S Korea* **74B4**
Cheju do, I *S Korea* **74B4**
Cheju-haehyŏp, Str *S Korea* **74B4**
Chekunda *USSR* **63F2**
Chelan,L *USA* **20B1**
Cheleken *USSR* **90B2**
Chelforo *Arg* **34B3**
Chelkar *USSR* **80D1**
Chelm *Pol* **59C2**
Chelmno *Pol* **58B2**
Chelmsford *Eng* **43E4**
Cheltenham *Eng* **43C4**
Chelyabinsk *USSR* **65H4**
Chemba *Mozam* **101C2**
Chenab, R *India/Pak* **84D2**
Chenachen *Alg* **96B2**
Cheney *USA* **20C1**
Cheney Res *USA* **18A2**
Chengda *China* **72D1**
Chengdu *China* **73A3**
Chengshan Jiao, Pt *China* **72E2**
Chenxi *China* **73C4**
Chen Xian *China* **73C4**
Cheo Xian *China* **73D3**
Chepén *Peru* **32B5**
Chepes *Arg* **34B2**
Cher, R *France* **48C2**
Cheran *Mexico* **23A2**
Cheraw *USA* **17C1**
Cherbourg *France* **48B2**
Cherchell *Alg* **96C1**
Cheremkhovo *USSR* **63C2**
Cherepovets *USSR* **60E2**
Cherkassy *USSR* **60D4**
Cherkessk *USSR* **61F5**
Chernigov *USSR* **60D3**
Chernobyl *USSR* **60D2**
Chernovtsy *USSR* **60C4**
Chernushka *USSR* **61J2**
Chernyakhovsk *USSR* **60B3**
Chernyye Zemli, Region *USSR* **61G4**
Cherokees,L o'the *USA* **18A2**
Cherquenco *Chile* **34A3**
Cherrapunji *India* **86C1**
Cherven' *USSR* **60C3**
Chervonograd *USSR* **59C2**
Chesapeake, B *USA* **10C3**
Cheshire, County *Eng* **42C3**
Cheshire *USA* **16C1**
Chëshskaya Guba, B *USSR* **64F3**
Chester, California *USA* **21A1**
Chester *Eng* **42C3**
Chester, Illinois *USA* **18C2**
Chester, Massachusets *USA* **16C1**
Chester, Pennsylvania *USA* **15C3**
Chester, S Carolina *USA* **17B1**
Chester, R *USA* **16A3**
Chesterfield *Eng* **42D3**
Chesterfield Inlet *Can* **6A3**
Chestertown *USA* **16A3**
Chetumal *Mexico* **25D3**
Chetwynd *Can* **13C1**
Chevak *USA* **12A2**
Cheviot *NZ* **111B2**
Cheviots, Hills *Eng/Scot* **40C2**
Chewelah *USA* **13D3**
Cheyenne *USA* **8C2**
Chhapra *India* **86A1**
Chhātak *Bang* **86C1**
Chhatarpur *India* **85D4**
Chhindwāra *India* **85D4**
Chhuka *Bhutan* **86B1**
Chia'i *Taiwan* **73E5**
Chiange *Angola* **100A2**
Chiang Kham *Thai* **76C2**
Chiang Mai *Thai* **76B2**
Chiavenna *Italy* **47C1**
Chiba *Japan* **74E3**
Chībāsa *India* **86B2**
Chibia *Angola* **100A2**
Chibougamou *Can* **7C4**
Chiburi-jima, I *Japan* **75A1**
Chibuto *Mozam* **101C3**
Chicago *USA* **10B2**
Chicago Heights *USA* **14A2**
Chichagof I *USA* **12G3**
Chichester *Eng* **43D4**
Chichibu *Japan* **75B1**
Chichi-jima, I *Japan* **69G4**
Chickamauga L *USA* **11B3**
Chickasawhay, R *USA* **19C3**
Chickasha *USA* **9D3**
Chicken *USA* **12F2**
Chiclayo *Peru* **32A5**
Chico *USA* **8A3**
Chico, R *Arg* **29C4**
Chicoa *Mozam* **101C2**
Chicopee *USA* **15D2**
Chicoutimi *Can* **7C5**
Chicualacuala *Mozam* **101C3**
Chidambaram *India* **87B2**
Chidley,C *Can* **6D3**
Chiefland *USA* **17B2**
Chiehn *Lib* **97B4**
Chiengi *Zambia* **99C3**
Chieri *Italy* **47B2**
Chiers, R *France* **46C2**
Chiesa *Italy* **47C1**
Chiese, R *Italy* **47D2**
Chieti *Italy* **52B2**
Chifeng *China* **72D1**
Chiginigak,Mt *USA* **12C3**
Chigmit Mts *USA* **4C3**
Chignahuapán *Mexico* **23B2**
Chignik *USA* **12C3**
Chihuahua *Mexico* **24B2**
Chik Ballāpur *India* **87B2**
Chikmagalūr *India* **87B2**
Chikuminuk L *USA* **12C2**
Chikwawa *Malawi* **101C2**
Chi-kyaw *Burma* **76A1**
Chilakalūrupet *India* **87C1**
Chilapa *Mexico* **23B2**
Chilaw *Sri Lanka* **87B3**
Chile, Republic **28B6**
Chilecito, Mendoza *Arg* **34B2**
Chililabombwe *Zambia* **100B2**
Chilka, L *India* **86B2**
Chilko, R *Can* **13C2**
Chilko L *Can* **5F4**
Chilkotin, R *Can* **13C2**
Chillán *Chile* **34A3**
Chillar *Arg* **34D3**
Chillicothe, Missouri *USA* **18B2**
Chillicothe, Ohio *USA* **14B3**
Chilliwack *Can* **13C3**
Chilmari *India* **86B1**
Chilongozi *Zambia* **101C2**
Chiloquin *USA* **20B2**
Chilpancingo *Mexico* **24C3**
Chiltern Hills, Upland *Eng* **43D4**
Chilton *USA* **14A2**
Chilumba *Malawi* **101C2**
Chi-lung *Taiwan* **69E4**
Chilwa, L *Malawi* **101C2**
Chimay *Belg* **46C1**
Chimbay *USSR* **65G5**
Chimborazo, Mt *Ecuador* **32B4**
Chimbote *Peru* **32B5**
Chimkent *USSR* **65H5**
Chimoio *Mozam* **101C2**
China, Republic *Asia* **67E3**
Chinandega *Nic* **25D3**
Chincha Alta *Peru* **32B6**
Chinchilla *Aust* **109D1**
Chinde *Mozam* **101C2**
Chindwin, R *Burma* **86C2**
Chingola *Zambia* **100B2**
Chinguar *Angola* **100A2**
Chinguetti *Maur* **96A2**
Chinhae *S Korea* **74B3**
Chinhoyi *Zim* **100C2**
Chiniak,C *USA* **12D3**
Chiniot *Pak* **84C2**
Chinju *S Korea* **74B3**
Chinko, R *CAR* **98C2**
Chino *Japan* **75B1**
Chinsali *Zambia* **101C2**
Chioggia *Italy* **52B1**
Chipata *Zambia* **101C2**
Chipinge *Zim* **101C3**
Chiplūn *India* **87A1**
Chippenham *Eng* **43C4**
Chippewa Falls *USA* **10A2**
Chipuriro *Zim* **100C2**
Chira, R *Peru* **32A4**
Chīrāla *India* **87C1**
Chiredzi *Zim* **101C3**
Chirfa *Niger* **95A2**
Chiriqui, Mt *Panama* **32A2**
Chirpan *Bulg* **54C2**
Chirrípo Grande, Mt *Costa Rica* **32A2**
Chirundu *Zim* **100B2**
Chisamba *Zambia* **100B2**
Chishui He, R *China* **73B4**
Chisone, R *Italy* **47B2**
Chita *USSR* **68D1**
Chitado *Angola* **100A2**
Chitembo *Angola* **100A2**
Chitina *USA* **12F2**
Chitina, R *USA* **12F2**
Chitradurga *India* **87B2**
Chitral *Pak* **84C1**
Chitré *Panama* **32A2**
Chittagong *Bang* **86C2**
Chittaurgarh *India* **85C4**
Chittoor *India* **87B2**
Chiume *Angola* **100B2**
Chiusa *Italy* **47D1**
Chivasso *Italy* **47B2**
Chivilcoy *Arg* **29D2**
Chivu *Zim* **100C2**
Chizu *Japan* **75A1**
Choele Choel *Arg* **29C3**
Choique *Arg* **34C3**
Choix *Mexico* **24B2**
Chojnice *Pol* **58B2**
Choke, Mts *Eth* **99D1**
Cholet *France* **48B2**
Cholula *Mexico* **23B2**
Choma *Zambia* **100B2**
Chomo Yummo, Mt *China/India* **86B1**
Chomutov *Czech* **57C2**
Chona, R *USSR* **63C1**
Ch'ŏnan *S Korea* **74B3**
Chon Buri *Thai* **76C3**
Chone *Ecuador* **32A4**
Ch'ŏngjin *N Korea* **74B2**
Chongju *N Korea* **74B3**
Ch'ŏngju *S Korea* **74B3**
Chongoroi *Angola* **100A2**
Chongqing *China* **73B4**
Chŏngŭp *S Korea* **74B3**
Chŏnju *S Korea* **74B3**
Chooyu, Mt *China/Nepal* **86B1**
Chortkov *USSR* **59D3**
Ch'ŏrwŏn *N Korea* **74B3**
Chorzow *Pol* **59B2**
Choshi *Japan* **74E3**
Chos-Malal *Arg* **34A3**
Choszczno *Pol* **58B2**
Chotanāgpur, Region *India* **86A2**
Chott Melrhir *Alg* **96C1**
Chowchilla *USA* **22B2**
Choybalsan *Mongolia* **63D3**
Chrantrey Inlet, B *Can* **6A3**
Chraykovskiy *USSR* **61H2**
Christchurch *NZ* **111B2**
Christiana *S Africa* **101G1**
Christian,C *Can* **6D2**
Christian Sd *USA* **12H3**
Christianshab *Greenland* **6E3**
Christmas I *Indian O* **104D4**
Christopol *USSR* **61G2**
Chu *USSR* **65J5**
Chu, R *USSR* **65J5**
Chubut, State *Arg* **29C4**
Chubut, R *Arg* **29C4**
Chudovo *USSR* **60D2**
Chudskoye Ozer, L *USSR* **64D4**
Chugach Mts *USA* **4D3**
Chugiak *USA* **12E2**
Chūgoku-sanchi, Mts *Japan* **75A1**
Chuí *Brazil* **29F2**
Chuillán *Chile* **29B3**
Chukai *Malay* **77C5**
Chu Lai *Viet* **76D2**
Chula Vista *USA* **21B3**
Chulitna *USA* **12E2**
Chulman *USSR* **63E2**
Chulucanas *Peru* **32A5**
Chulumani *Bol* **30C2**
Chulym *USSR* **65K4**
Chulym, R *USSR* **63A2**
Chuma, R *USSR* **63B2**
Chumar *India* **84D2**
Chumikan *USSR* **63F2**
Chumphon *Thai* **77B3**
Ch'unch'ŏn *S Korea* **74B3**
Chunchura *India* **86B2**
Ch'ungju *S Korea* **74B3**
Chunya *Tanz* **99D3**
Chunya, R *USSR* **63C1**
Chupara Pt *Trinidad* **27L1**
Chuquicamata *Chile* **30C3**
Chur *Switz* **52A1**
Churāchāndpur *India* **86C2**
Churchill *Can* **7A4**
Churchill, R, Labrador *Can* **7D4**
Churchill, R, Manitoba *Can* **7A4**
Churchill,C *Can* **7A4**
Churchill Falls *Can* **7D4**
Churchill L *Can* **5H4**
Chūru *India* **84C3**
Churumuco *Mexico* **23A2**
Chusovoy *USSR* **61J2**
Chuvashkaya ASSR, Republic *USSR* **61G2**
Chuxiong *China* **68B4**
Chu Yang Sin, Mt *Viet* **76D3**
Cianjur *Indon* **78B4**
Ciano d'Enza *Italy* **47D2**
Cianorte *Brazil* **35A2**
Ciechanow *Pol* **58C2**
Ciego de Avila *Cuba* **25E2**
Ciénaga *Colombia* **32C1**
Cienfuegos *Cuba* **25D2**
Cieszyn *Pol* **59B3**
Cieza *Spain* **51B2**
Cihanbeyli *Turk* **92B2**
Cihuatlán *Mexico* **23A2**
Cijulang *Indon* **78B4**
Cilacap *Indon* **78B4**
Cîmpina *Rom* **54C1**
Cinca, R *Spain* **51C1**
Činčer, Mt *Yugos* **52C2**
Cincinnati *USA* **10B3**
Cindrelu, Mt *Rom* **54B1**
Cine, R *Turk* **55C3**

Ciney *Belg* **46C1**
Cipolletti *Arg* **34B3**
Circle, Alaska *USA* **4D3**
Circleville *USA* **14B3**
Cirebon *Indon* **78B4**
Cirencester *Eng* **43D4**
Citadella *Italy* **47D2**
Citlaltepetl, Mt *Mexico* **24C3**
Citrusdal *S Africa* **100A4**
Citta del Vaticano *Italy* **52B2**
Città di Castello *Italy* **52B2**
Ciudad Acuña *Mexico* **24B2**
Ciudad Altamirano *Mexico* **23A2**
Ciudad Bolivar *Ven* **33E2**
Ciudad Camargo *Mexico* **24B2**
Ciudad del Carmen *Mexico* **25C3**
Ciudad del Maiz *Mexico* **23B1**
Ciudadela *Spain* **51C1**
Ciudad Guayana *Ven* **33E2**
Ciudad Guzman *Mexico* **24B3**
Ciudad Hidalgo *Mexico* **23A2**
Ciudad Juárez *Mexico* **24B1**
Ciudad Lerdo *Mexico* **9C4**
Ciudad Madero *Mexico* **24C2**
Ciudad Mendoza *Mexico* **23B2**
Ciudad Obregon *Mexico* **24B2**
Ciudad Ojeda *Ven* **27C4**
Ciudad Piar *Ven* **33E2**
Ciudad Real *Spain* **50B2**
Ciudad Rodrigo *Spain* **50A1**
Ciudad Valles *Mexico* **24C2**
Ciudad Victoria *Mexico* **24C2**
Civitavecchia *Italy* **52B2**
Cizre *Turk* **93D2**
Clacton-on-Sea *Eng* **43E4**
Claire,L *Can* **5G4**
Clairton *USA* **14C2**
Clairvaux *France* **47A1**
Clanton *USA* **17A1**
Clanwilliam *S Africa* **100A4**
Clara *Irish Rep* **45C2**
Claraz *Arg* **34D3**
Clare, County *Irish Rep* **45B2**
Clare *USA* **14B2**
Clare, I *Irish Rep* **45A2**
Claremont *USA* **15D2**
Claremore *USA* **18A2**
Claremorris *Irish Rep* **45B2**
Clarence, R *Aust* **109D1**
Clarence, R *NZ* **111B2**
Clarence Str *Aust* **106C2**
Clarence Str *USA* **12H3**
Clarendon *USA* **19B3**
Clarenville *Can* **7E5**
Claresholm *Can* **5G4**
Clarinda *USA* **18A1**
Clarion, Pennsylvania *USA* **15C2**
Clarión, I *Mexico* **24A3**
Clarion, R *USA* **15C2**
Clarion Fracture Zone *Pacific O* **105J3**
Clark Hill Res *USA* **11B3**
Clark,Pt *Can* **14B2**
Clarksburg *USA* **14B3**
Clarksdale *USA* **11A3**
Clarks Point *USA* **12C3**
Clarkston *USA* **20C1**
Clarksville, Arkansas *USA* **18B2**
Claro, R *Brazil* **35A1**
Claromecó *Arg* **29D3**
Clay Center *USA* **18A2**
Claymore, Oilfield *N Sea* **44D2**
Clayoquot Sd *Can* **13B3**
Clayton, New Mexico *USA* **9C3**
Clayton, New York *USA* **15C2**
Clear, C *Irish Rep* **41B3**
Cleare,C *USA* **12E3**
Clear Hills, Mts *Can* **13D1**
Clear L *USA* **21A2**
Clear Lake Res *USA* **20B2**
Clearwater *Can* **13D2**
Clearwater *USA* **11B4**
Clearwater, R *Can* **13E1**
Clearwater L *Can* **13C2**
Cleburne *USA* **9D3**
Clements *USA* **22B1**
Cleopatra Needle, Mt *Phil* **79A3**
Clermont *Aust* **107D3**
Clermont *France* **46B2**
Clermont-en-Argonne *France* **46C2**
Clermont-Ferrand *France* **49C2**
Clervaux *W Germ* **46D1**
Cles *Italy* **47D1**
Cleve *Aust* **108A2**
Cleveland, County *Eng* **42D2**
Cleveland, Mississippi *USA* **19B3**
Cleveland, Ohio *USA* **10B2**
Cleveland, Tennessee *USA* **11B3**
Cleveland, Texas *USA* **19A3**
Clew, B *Irish Rep* **41B3**
Clifden *Irish Rep* **45A2**
Clifton *Aust* **109D1**
Clifton, New Jersey *USA* **16B2**
Clifton Hills *Aust* **108A1**
Climax *Can* **13F3**
Clinton, Arkansas *USA* **18B2**
Clinton *Can* **5F4**
Clinton, Connecticut *USA* **16C2**
Clinton, Massachusetts *USA* **16D1**
Clinton, Mississippi *USA* **19B3**
Clinton, Missouri *USA* **18B2**
Clinton, New Jersey *USA* **16B2**
Clinton-Colden L *Can* **4H3**
Clipperton I *Pacific O* **24B3**
Cliza *Bol* **30C2**
Clonakilty *Irish Rep* **45B3**
Cloncurry *Aust* **107D3**
Clones *Irish Rep* **45C1**
Clonmel *Irish Rep* **45C2**
Cloquet *USA* **10A2**
Cloudy Mt *USA* **12C2**
Clovis, California *USA* **22C2**
Clovis, New Mexico *USA* **9C3**
Cluj *Rom* **60B4**
Cluj-Napoca *Rom* **54B1**
Cluses *France* **47B1**
Clusone *Italy* **47C2**
Clutha, R *NZ* **111A3**
Clwyd, County *Wales* **43C3**
Clyde *Can* **6D2**
Clyde *NZ* **111A3**
Clyde, R *Scot* **42B2**
Coahuayana *Mexico* **23A2**
Coalcomán *Mexico* **23A2**
Coaldale *Can* **13E2**
Coaldale *USA* **21B2**
Coalinga *USA* **21A2**
Coari, R *Brazil* **33E5**
Coastal Plain *USA* **17A1**
Coast Mts *Can* **4E4**
Coast Ranges, Mts *USA* **8A2**
Coatbridge *Scot* **42B2**
Coatepec *Mexico* **23B2**
Coatesville *USA* **16B3**
Coaticook *Can* **15D1**
Coats I *Can* **6B3**
Coats Land, Region *Ant* **112B1**
Coatzacoalcos *Mexico* **25C3**
Cobalt *Can* **7C5**
Cobán *Guatemala* **25C3**
Cobar *Aust* **107D4**
Cobargo *Aust* **109C3**
Cobh *Irish Rep* **45B3**
Cobija *Bol* **32D6**
Cobleskill *USA* **16B1**
Cobo de Palos, C *Spain* **51B2**
Cobourg *Can* **7C5**
Cobourg Pen *Aust* **106C2**
Coburg *W Germ* **57C2**
Coca *Ecuador* **32B4**
Coca *USA* **17B2**
Cochabamba *Bol* **30C2**
Cochem *W Germ* **46D1**
Cochin *India* **87B3**
Cochrane, Alberta *Can* **13E2**
Cochrane, Ontario *Can* **7B5**
Cockburn *Aust* **108B2**
Cockeysville *USA* **16A3**
Cockpit Country,The *Jamaica* **27H1**
Coco, R *Honduras/Nic* **25D3**
Cocobeach *Gabon* **98A2**
Cocos B *Trinidad* **27L1**
Cocos Is *Indian O* **104C4**
Cocula *Mexico* **23A1**
Cod,C *USA* **10C2**
Codfish I *NZ* **111A3**
Cod I *Can* **7D4**
Codigoro *Italy* **47E2**
Codó *Brazil* **31C2**
Codogno *Italy* **47C2**
Cody *USA* **8C2**
Coesfeld *W Germ* **56B2**
Coeur d'Alene *USA* **8B2**
Coffeyville *USA* **9D3**
Coffin B *Aust* **108A2**
Coff's Harbour *Aust* **109D2**
Cofre de Perote, Mt *Mexico* **23B2**
Cognac *France* **48B2**
Cohoes *USA* **15D2**
Cohuna *Aust* **108B3**
Coihaique *Chile* **29B5**
Coimbatore *India* **87B2**
Coimbra *Port* **50A1**
Cojimies *Ecuador* **32A3**
Colac *Aust* **107D4**
Colatina *Brazil* **31C5**
Colbeck,C *Ant* **112B6**
Colchester *Eng* **43E4**
Colchester *USA* **16C2**
Col de la Faucille *France* **47B1**
Cold L *Can* **13E2**
Col du Grand St Bernard, P *Switz/Italy* **52A1**
Col du Lautaret, P *France* **47B2**
Col du Mont Cenis, P *Italy/France* **52A1**
Coldwater *USA* **14B2**
Coleen, R *USA* **12F1**
Coleman, Michigan *USA* **14B2**
Colenso *S Africa* **101G1**
Coleraine *N Ire* **45C1**
Coleridge,L *NZ* **111B2**
Colesberg *S Africa* **100B4**
Coleville *USA* **22C1**
Colfax, California *USA* **21A2**
Colfax, Louisiana *USA* **19B3**
Colfax, Washington *USA* **20C1**
Colima *Mexico* **24B3**
Colima, State *Mexico* **23A2**
Colina *Chile* **34A2**
Coll, I *Scot* **44A3**
Collarenebri *Aust* **109C1**
Colle de Tende, P *Italy/France* **52A2**
College *USA* **12E2**
College Park, Georgia *USA* **17B1**
College Park, Washington *USA* **16A3**
College Station *USA* **19A3**
Collie *Aust* **106A4**
Collier B *Aust* **106B2**
Collines de L'Artois, Mts *France* **46A1**
Collines De Thiérache *France* **46B2**
Collingwood *Can* **14B2**
Collingwood *NZ* **110B2**
Collins, Mississippi *USA* **19C3**
Collinson Pen *Can* **4H2**
Collinsville *Aust* **107D3**
Collinsville, Illinois *USA* **18C2**
Collinsville, Oklahoma *USA* **18A2**
Collipulli *Chile* **34A3**
Colmar *France* **49D2**
Colômbia *Brazil* **35B2**
Colombia, Republic *S America* **32B3**
Colombia *USA* **15C3**
Colombo *Sri Lanka* **87B3**
Colon *Cuba* **25D2**
Colón *Panama* **32B2**
Colonia *Urug* **29E2**
Colonia del Sacramento *Urug* **34D2**
Colonia 25 de Mayo *Arg* **34B3**
Colonia Las Heras *Arg* **29C5**
Colonsay, I *Scot* **44A3**
Colontlán *Mexico* **23A1**
Coloradito *Ven* **27E5**
Colorado, State *USA* **8C3**
Colorado, R, Arizona *USA* **9B3**
Colorado, R, Buenos Aires *Arg* **29D3**
Colorado, R, Texas *USA* **9D3**
Colorado Plat *USA* **9B3**
Colorado Springs *USA* **8C3**
Colton *USA* **22D3**
Columbia, Maryland *USA* **16A3**
Columbia, Mississippi *USA* **19C3**
Columbia, Missouri *USA* **10A3**
Columbia, Pennsylvania *USA* **15C2**
Columbia, S Carolina *USA* **11B3**
Columbia, Tennessee *USA* **11B3**
Columbia, R *Can* **13D2**
Columbia, R *USA* **8A2**
Columbia,Mt *Can* **5G4**
Columbia Plat *USA* **20C1**
Columbus, Georgia *USA* **11B3**
Columbus, Indiana *USA* **14A3**
Columbus, Mississippi *USA* **11B3**
Columbus, Nebraska *USA* **8D2**
Columbus, Ohio *USA* **10B2**
Columbus, Texas *USA* **19A4**
Colville *USA* **20C1**
Colville, R *USA* **4C3**
Colville,C *NZ* **110C1**
Colville L *Can* **4F3**
Colwyn Bay *Wales* **42C3**
Comacchio *Italy* **47E2**
Comanche Res *USA* **22B1**
Comayagua *Honduras* **25D3**
Combarbalá *Chile* **34A2**

Comeragh, Mts *Irish Rep* **45C2**
Comilla *Bang* **86C2**
Comitán *Mexico* **25C3**
Commercy *France* **46C2**
Committees B *Can* **6B3**
Como *Italy* **52A1**
Comodoro Rivadavia *Arg* **29C5**
Comonfort *Mexico* **23A1**
Comorin,C *India* **87B3**
Comoros, Is *Indian O* **101D2**
Compiègne *France* **49C2**
Compostela *Mexico* **23A1**
Comte Salas *Arg* **34B2**
Cona *China* **86C1**
Conakry *Guinea* **97A4**
Concarán *Arg* **34B2**
Concarneau *France* **48B2**
Conceiçao da Barra *Brazil* **35D1**
Conceição do Araguaia *Brazil* **31B3**
Conceiçao do Mato Dentro *Brazil* **35C1**
Concepción *Chile* **29B3**
Concepción *Par* **30E3**
Concepción, R *Arg* **29E2**
Concepcion del Oro *Mexico* **24B2**
Concepcion del Uruguay *Arg* **34D2**
Conception,Pt *USA* **9A3**
Conchas *Brazil* **35B2**
Conchos, R *Mexico* **9C4**
Concord, California *USA* **21A2**
Concord, New Hampshire *USA* **10C2**
Concordia *Arg* **29E2**
Concordia *USA* **8D3**
Concrete *USA* **20B1**
Condamine *Aust* **109D1**
Condobolin *Aust* **107D4**
Condon *USA* **20B1**
Condroz, Mts *Belg* **46C1**
Conecuh, R *USA* **17A1**
Conegliano *Italy* **47E2**
Congo, Republic *Africa* **89F8**
Congo, R *Congo* **89F8**
Coniston *Can* **14B1**
Connaught, Region *Irish Rep* **45B2**
Conneaut *USA* **14B2**
Connecticut, State *USA* **10C2**
Connecticut, R *USA* **15D2**
Connellsville *USA* **15C2**
Connemara,Mts of *Irish Rep* **45B2**
Connersville *USA* **14A3**
Conoble *Aust* **108B2**
Conroe *USA* **19A3**
Conselheiro Lafaiete *Brazil* **35C2**
Con Son, Is *Viet* **77D4**
Constanta *Rom* **60C5**
Constantine *Alg* **96C1**
Constantine,C *USA* **12C3**
Constitución *Chile* **29B3**
Consul *Can* **13F3**
Contarina *Italy* **47E2**
Contas, R *Brazil* **31C4**
Contreras *Mexico* **23B2**
Contuoyto L *Can* **4H3**
Conway, Arkansas *USA* **11A3**
Conway, New Hampshire *USA* **15D2**
Conway, South Carolina *USA* **17C1**
Conway,L *Aust* **108A1**
Conwy *Wales* **42C3**
Coober Pedy *Aust* **106C3**
Cook, Str *NZ* **110B2**
Cook,C *Can* **13B2**
Cook Inlet, B *USA* **4C3**
Cook Is *Pacific O* **105H4**
Cook,Mt *NZ* **111B2**
Cooktown *Aust* **107D2**
Coolabah *Aust* **109C2**
Cooladdi *Aust* **108C1**
Coolah *Aust* **109C2**
Coolamon *Aust* **109C2**
Coolgardie *Aust* **106B4**
Cooma *Aust* **109C3**
Coonabarabran *Aust* **109C2**
Coonambie *Aust* **109C2**
Coonbah *Aust* **108B2**
Coondambo *Aust* **108A2**
Coondapoor *India* **87A2**
Coongoola *Aust* **108C1**
Coonoor *India* **87B2**
Cooper Basin *Aust* **108B1**
Cooper Creek *Aust* **106C3**
Cooper Creek, R *Aust* **108B1**
Coorong,The *Aust* **108A3**
Cooroy *Aust* **109D1**
Coos B *USA* **20B2**
Coos Bay *USA* **20B2**
Cootamundra *Aust* **107D4**
Cootehill *Irish Rep* **45C1**
Copala *Mexico* **23B2**
Copalillo *Mexico* **23B2**
Copiapó *Chile* **30B4**
Copparo *Italy* **47D2**
Copper, R *USA* **12F2**
Copper Centre *USA* **4D3**
Copper Cliff *Can* **14B1**
Coppermine *Can* **4G3**
Coppermine, R *Can* **4G3**
Coquimbo *Chile* **30B4**
Corabia *Rom* **54B2**
Coral Gables *USA* **17B2**
Coral Harbour *Can* **6B3**
Coral S *Aust/PNG* **107D2**
Coral Sea Basin *Pacific O* **104F4**
Coral Sea Island Territories *Aust* **107E2**
Corangamite,L *Aust* **108B3**
Corantijn, R *Surinam/Guyana* **33F3**
Corbeil-Essonnes *France* **46B2**
Corcubíon *Spain* **50A1**
Cordele *USA* **11B3**
Cordillera Cantabrica, Mts *Spain* **50A1**
Cordillera Central, Mts *Dom Rep* **26C3**
Cordillera Central, Mts *Phil* **79B2**
Cordillera de Ansita, Mts *Arg* **34B2**
Cordillera de los Andes, Mts *Peru* **32B5**
Cordillera del Toro, Mt *Arg* **30C4**
Cordillera de Mérida *Ven* **32C2**
Cordillera de Viento, Mts *Arg* **34A3**
Cordillera Isabelia, Mts *Nicaragua* **25D3**
Cordillera Occidental, Mts *Colombia* **32B3**
Cordillera Oriental, Mts *Colombia* **32B3**
Cordillo Downs *Aust* **108B1**
Córdoba *Arg* **29D2**
Córdoba *Mexico* **24C3**
Córdoba *Spain* **50B2**
Córdoba, State *Arg* **29D2**
Cordova *USA* **4D3**
Coricudgy,Mt *Aust* **109D2**
Corigliano Calabro *Italy* **53C3**
Corinth, Mississippi *USA* **11B3**
Corinto *Brazil* **31C5**
Cork, County *Irish Rep* **45B2**
Cork *Irish Rep* **41B3**
Çorlu *Turk* **92A1**
Cornel Fabriciano *Brazil* **31C5**
Cornelio Procópio *Brazil* **35A2**
Corner Brook *Can* **7E5**
Corner Inlet, B *Aust* **109C3**
Corning *USA* **15C2**
Cornwall *Can* **7C5**
Cornwall, County *Eng* **43B4**
Cornwall,C *Eng* **43B4**
Cornwall I *Can* **4H2**
Cornwallis I *Can* **6A2**
Coro *Ven* **32D1**
Coroatá *Brazil* **31C2**
Coroico *Bol* **30C2**
Coromandel *Brazil* **35B1**
Coromandel Coast *India* **87C2**
Coromandel Pen *NZ* **110C1**
Coromandel Range, Mts *NZ* **110C1**
Corona, California *USA* **22D4**
Coronation *Can* **13E2**
Coronation G *Can* **4G3**
Coronda *Arg* **34C2**
Coronel *Chile* **29B3**
Coronel Brandsen *Arg* **34D3**
Coronel Dorrego *Arg* **34C3**
Coronel Fabriciano *Brazil* **35C1**
Coronel Oviedo *Par* **30E4**
Coronel Pringles *Arg* **29D3**
Coronel Suárez *Arg* **34C3**
Coronel Vidal *Arg* **34D3**
Coropuna, Mt *Peru* **30B2**
Corowa *Aust* **109C3**
Corps *France* **49D3**
Corpus Christi *USA* **9D4**
Corpus Christi,L *USA* **9D4**
Corregidor, I *Phil* **79B3**
Corrente, R, Mato Grosso *Brazil* **35A1**
Corrientes *Arg* **30E4**
Corrientes, State *Arg* **30E4**
Corrigan *USA* **19B3**
Corrigin *Aust* **106A4**
Corringe Is *Aust* **107E2**
Corryong *Aust* **109C3**
Corse, I *Medit S* **52A2**
Corsewall, Pt *Scot* **42B2**
Corsicana *USA* **9D3**
Corte *Corse* **52A2**
Cortez *USA* **9C3**
Cortina d'Ampezzo *Italy* **52B1**
Cortland *USA* **15C2**
Coruca de Catalan *Mexico* **23A2**
Çoruh, R *Turk* **93D1**
Çorum *Turk* **60E5**
Corumbá *Brazil* **30E2**
Corumba, R *Brazil* **35B1**
Corumbaiba *Brazil* **35B1**
Corvallis *USA* **20B2**
Corvo, I *Açores* **96A1**
Corwen *Wales* **43C3**
Coscomatopec *Mexico* **23B2**
Cosenza *Italy* **53C3**
Cosmoledo, Is *Seychelles* **101D1**
Cosquín *Arg* **34C2**
Costa Blanca, Region *Spain* **51B2**
Costa Brava, Region *Spain* **51C1**
Costa de la Luz, Region *Spain* **50B2**
Costa del Sol, Region *Spain* **50B2**
Costa Mesa *USA* **22D4**
Costa Rica, Republic *C America* **25D3**
Cotabato *Phil* **79B4**
Cotagaita *Bol* **30C3**
Côte d'Azur, Region *France* **49D3**
Côtes de Meuse, Mts *France* **46C2**
Cotonou *Benin* **97C4**
Cotopaxi, Mt *Ecuador* **32B4**
Cotswold Hills, Upland *Eng* **43C4**
Cottage Grove *USA* **20B2**
Cottbus *E Germ* **56C2**
Couedic,C du *Aust* **108A3**
Couer d'Alene L *USA* **20C1**
Coulommiers *France* **46B2**
Coulonge, R *Can* **15C1**
Coulterville *USA* **22B2**
Council *USA* **4B3**
Council Bluffs *USA* **8D2**
Courmayeur *Italy* **47B2**
Courtenay *Can* **13B3**
Coutances *France* **48B2**
Coventry *Eng* **43D3**
Covilhã *Spain* **50A1**
Covington, Georgia *USA* **17B1**
Covington, Louisiana *USA* **19B3**
Cowal,L *Aust* **109C2**
Cowangie *Aust* **108B3**
Cowansville *Can* **15D1**
Coward Springs *Aust* **108A1**
Cowell *Aust* **108A2**
Cowes *Aust* **108C3**
Cowichan L *Can* **20B1**
Cowiltz, R *USA* **20B1**
Cowra *Aust* **109C2**
Coxim *Brazil* **30F2**
Coxsackie *USA* **16C1**
Cox's Bazar *Bang* **86C2**
Coyote *USA* **22B2**
Coyuca de Benitez *Mexico* **23A2**
Cradock *S Africa* **100B4**
Craig *USA* **8C2**
Crailsheim *W Germ* **57C3**
Craiova *Rom* **54B2**
Cranberry L *USA* **15D2**
Cranbrook *Can* **5G5**
Crane, Oregon *USA* **20C2**
Cranston *USA* **16D2**
Crater L *USA* **20B2**
Crater Lake Nat Pk *USA* **20B2**
Crateus *Brazil* **31C3**
Crato *Brazil* **31D3**
Crawfordsville *USA* **14A2**
Crawfordville *USA* **17B1**
Crawley *Eng* **43D4**
Cree L *Can* **5H4**
Creil *France* **46B2**
Crema *Italy* **47C2**
Cremona *Italy* **52B1**
Crépy-en-Valois *France* **46B2**
Cres, I *Yugos* **52B2**
Crescent City *USA* **20B2**
Crespo *Arg* **34C2**
Creston *Can* **13D3**
Creston *USA* **18B1**
Crestview *USA* **17A1**
Creswick *Aust* **108B3**
Crêt de la Neige, Mt *France* **47A1**
Crete *USA* **18A1**
Crete,S of *Greece* **55B3**
Creuse, R *France* **48C2**
Crewe *Eng* **43C3**
Crianlarich *Scot* **44B3**
Criciuma *Brazil* **30G4**
Crieff *Scot* **44C3**
Crillon,Mt *USA* **12G3**
Cristalina *Brazil* **35B1**
Croatia, Region *Yugos* **52C1**
Crocker Range, Mts *Malay* **78D1**
Crockett *USA* **19A3**
Croker I *Aust* **106C2**
Cromarty *Scot* **44C3**
Cromer *Eng* **43E3**
Cromwell *NZ* **111A3**
Crooked, I *Bahamas* **11C4**

Crooked, R *Can* 13C2
Crookston *USA* 8D2
Crookwell *Aust* 109C2
Croppa Creek *Aust* 109D1
Crossett *USA* 11A3
Cross Sd *USA* 12G3
Crotone *Italy* 53C3
Crowley *USA* 19B3
Crown Pt *Tobago* 27K1
Crows Nest *Aust* 109D1
Croydon *Aust* 107D2
Croydon *Eng* 43D4
Crozet Basin *Indian O* 104B5
Crozier Chan *Can* 4F2
Cruz Alta *Brazil* 30F4
Cruz,C *Cuba* 25E3
Cruz del Eje *Arg* 29D2
Cruzeiro *Brazil* 35C2
Cruzeiro do Sul *Brazil* 32C5
Crysdale,Mt *Can* 13C1
Crystal Brook *Aust* 108A2
Crystal City, Missouri *USA* 18B2
Crystal Falls *USA* 14A1
Cuamba *Mozam* 101C2
Cuando, R *Angola* 100B2
Cuangar *Angola* 100A2
Cuarto, R *Arg* 34C2
Cuauhtémoc *Mexico* 24B2
Cuautla *Mexico* 23B2
Cuba, Republic *Caribbean* 25D2
Cubango, R *Angola* 100A2
Cuchi *Angola* 100A2
Cuchi, R *Angola* 100A2
Cuchillo Có *Arg* 34C3
Cucui *Brazil* 32D3
Cúcuta *Colombia* 32C2
Cuddalore *India* 87B2
Cuddapah *India* 87B2
Cue *Aust* 106A3
Cuenca *Ecuador* 32B4
Cuenca *Spain* 51B1
Cuernavaca *Mexico* 24C3
Cuero *USA* 19A4
Cuiabá *Brazil* 30E2
Cuiabá, R *Brazil* 30E2
Cuicatlan *Mexico* 23B2
Cuieté, R *Brazil* 35C1
Cuillin Hills, Mts *Scot* 44A3
Cuilo, R *Angola* 98B3
Cuito, R *Angola* 100A2
Cuito Cunavale *Angola* 100A2
Cuitzeo *Mexico* 23A2
Cu Lao Hon, I *Viet* 77D3
Culcairn *Aust* 109C3
Culgoa, R *Aust* 109C1
Culiacán *Mexico* 24B2
Culion, I *Phil* 79A3
Cullman *USA* 17A1
Culoz *France* 47A2
Culpeper *USA* 15C3
Culpepper, I *Ecuador* 32J7
Culter Ridge *USA* 17B2
Culverden *NZ* 111B2
Cumaná *Ven* 33E1
Cumberland, Maryland *USA* 10C3
Cumberland, R *USA* 11B3
Cumberland Pen *Can* 6D3
Cumbernauld Sd *Can* 6D3
Cumbria *Eng* 42C2
Cummings *USA* 21A2
Cummins *Aust* 108A2
Cumnock *Scot* 42B2
Cunco *Chile* 34A3
Cunene, R *Angola/ Namibia* 100A2
Cuneo *Italy* 52A2
Cunnamulla *Aust* 107D3
Cupar *Scot* 44C3
Čuprija *Yugos* 54B2
Curaçao, I *Caribbean* 27D4
Curacautin *Chile* 34A3
Curaco, R *Arg* 34B3
Curanilahue *Chile* 34A3
Curepto *Chile* 34A3
Curicó *Chile* 29B2
Curitiba *Brazil* 30G4
Curnamona *Aust* 108A2
Curoca, R *Angola* 100A2
Curvelo *Brazil* 31C5
Cushing *USA* 18A2
Cutbank, R *Can* 13D2
Cuthbert *USA* 17B1
Cutral-Có *Arg* 34B3
Cuttack *India* 86B2
Cuvelai *Angola* 100A2
Cuxhaven *W Germ* 56B2
Cuyahoga Falls *USA* 14B2
Cuyo Is *Phil* 79B3
Cuzco *Peru* 32C6
Cyangugu *Zaïre* 99C3
Cypress Hills, Mts *Can* 13F3
Cyprus, Republic *Medit S* 92B3
Cyrus Field B *Can* 6D3
Czechoslovakia, Republic *Europe* 59B3
Częstochowa *Pol* 59B2

D

Da, R *Viet* 76C1
Da'an *China* 69E2
Dab'a *Jordan* 94C3
Dabajuro *Ven* 27C4
Dabaro *Somalia* 99E2
Daba Shan, Mts *China* 73B3
Dabat *Eth* 99D1
Dabhoi *India* 85C4
Dabie Shan, U *China* 73C3
Dabola *Guinea* 97A3
Dabou *Ivory Coast* 97B4
Dabrowa Gorn *Pol* 59B2
Dachau *W Germ* 57C3
Dachstein, Mt *Austria* 52B1
Dada He, R *China* 73A3
Dade City *USA* 17B2
Dadhar *Pak* 84B3
Dadu *Pak* 85B3
Dadu He, R *China* 68C3
Daet *Phil* 79B3
Dafang *China* 73B4
Daga, R *Burma* 76B2
Dagabur *Eth* 99E2
Dagana *Sen* 97A3
Dagestanskaya ASSR, Republic *USSR* 65F5
Dagupan *Phil* 79B2
Dahab *Egypt* 92B4
Da Hinggan Ling, Mts *China* 63E3
Dahlonega *USA* 17B1
Dāhod *India* 85C4
Dahra *Libya* 95A2
Dahra, Region *Alg* 51C2
Dailekh *Nepal* 86A1
Daireaux *Arg* 34C3
Daitō, Is *Pacific Oc* 69F4
Dajarra *Aust* 106C3
Dakar *Sen* 97A3
Dakhla *Mor* 96A2
Dakhla Oasis *Egypt* 95B2
Dakoro *Niger* 97C3
Dakovica *Yugos* 54B2
Dakovo *Yugos* 54A1
Dala *Angola* 100B2
Dalaba *Guinea* 97A3
Dalai Nur, L *China* 72D1
Dalandzadgad *Mongolia* 68C2
Dalanganem Is *Phil* 79B3
Dalanjargalan *Mongolia* 68C2
Da Lat *Viet* 76D3
Dalby *Aust* 107E3
Dalen *Nor* 39F7
Dales,The, Upland *Eng* 42C2
Daleville *USA* 17A1
Dalhart *USA* 9C3
Dalhousie,C *Can* 4E2
Dallas *USA* 9D3
Dalles,The *USA* 20B1
Dall I *USA* 5E4
Dalli Rajhara *India* 86A2
Dallol, R *Niger* 97C3
Dallol Bosso, R *Niger* 97C3
Dalmatia, Region *Yugos* 52C2
Dal'nerechensk *USSR* 69F2
Daloa *Ivory Coast* 97B4
Dalou Shan, Mts *China* 73B4
Dāltenganj *India* 86A2
Dalton, Georgia *USA* 17B1
Dalton, Massachusetts *USA* 16C1
Daly, R *Aust* 106C2
Daly City *USA* 21A2
Daly Waters *Aust* 106C2
Damaguete *Phil* 79B4
Damān *India* 85C4
Damanhûr *Egypt* 92B3
Damar, I *Indon* 71D4
Damara *CAR* 98B2
Damascus *Syria* 92C3
Damascus *USA* 16A3
Damaturu *Nig* 97D3
Damavand *Iran* 90B2
Damba *Angola* 98B3
Dambulla *Sri Lanka* 87C3
Damghan *Iran* 90B2
Damoh *India* 85D4
Damot *Eth* 99E2
Damour *Leb* 94B2
Dampier *Aust* 106A3
Danā *Jordan* 94B3
Dana,Mt *USA* 22C2
Danané *Lib* 97B4
Da Nang *Viet* 76D2
Danao *Phil* 79B3
Danau Tobu, L *Indon* 70A3
Danau Tuwuti, L *Indon* 71D4
Danbu *China* 73A3
Danbury *USA* 15D2
Dandeldhura *Nepal* 86A1
Dandeli *India* 87A1
Dandenong *Aust* 108C3
Dandong *China* 74A2
Danger Pt *S Africa* 100A4
Dangila *Eth* 99D1
Danguard Jenson Land, Region *Can* 6D1
Daniels Harbour *Can* 7E4
Dannebrogs Øy, I *Greenland* 6G3
Dannevirke *NZ* 110C2
Dantewāra *India* 87C1
Danville, Illinois *USA* 10B2
Danville, Kentucky *USA* 11B3
Danville, Pennsylvania *USA* 16A2
Danville, Virginia *USA* 11C3
Dao Xian *China* 73C4
Daozhen *China* 73B4
Dapiak,Mt *Phil* 79B4
Dapitan *Phil* 79B4
Da Qaidam *China* 68B3
Dar'a *Syria* 94C2
Dārāb *Iran* 91B4
Daraj *Libya* 95A1
Dārān *Iran* 90B3
Dar'ā Salkhad *Syria* 92C3
Darbhanga *India* 86B1
Dardanelle *USA* 22C1
Dardanelle,L *USA* 18B2
Dar es Salaam *Tanz* 99D3
Dargaville *NZ* 110B1
Darien *USA* 17B1
Dārjiling *India* 86B1
Darling, R *Aust* 107D4
Darling Downs *Aust* 109C1
Darling Pen *Can* 6C1
Darlington *Aust* 108B2
Darlington *Eng* 42D2
Darlington *USA* 17C1
Darmstadt *W Germ* 57B3
Darnah *Libya* 95B1
Darnick *Aust* 108B2
Darnley B *Can* 4F3
Darnley,C *Ant* 112C10
Daroca *Spain* 51B1
Dar Rounga, Region *CAR* 98C2
Dart, R *Eng* 43C4
Dartmoor, Moorland *Eng* 41C3
Dartmoor Nat Pk *Eng* 43C4
Dartmouth *Can* 7D5
Dartmouth *Eng* 43C4
Daru *PNG* 107D1
Daruvar *Yugos* 52C1
Darwin *Aust* 106C2
Daryacheh-ye Bakhtegan, L *Iran* 91B4
Daryacheh-ye Mahārlū L *Iran* 91B4
Daryācheh-ye Namak, Salt Flat *Iran* 90B3
Daryacheh-ye-Sistan, Salt Lake *Iran/ Afghan* 90D3
Daryacheh-ye Tashk, L *Iran* 91B4
Daryācheh-ye Urumīyeh, L *Iran* 65F6
Dārzīn *Iran* 91C4
Das, I *UAE* 91B4
Dashennonglia, Mt *China* 73C3
Dasht *Iran* 90C2
Dasht-e-Kavir, Salt Desert *Iran* 90B3
Dasht-e Lut, Salt Desert *Iran* 90C3
Dasht-e Naomid, Desert Region *Iran* 90D3
Datia *India* 85D3
Datong *China* 72A2
Datong *China* 72C1
Datong He, R *China* 72A2
Datu Piang *Phil* 79B4
Daugava, R *USSR* 39K7
Daugavpils *USSR* 60C2
Dauguard Jensen Land *Greenland* 6D1
Daulatabad *Afghan* 84A1
Daulpur *India* 85D3
Daun *W Germ* 46D1
Daund *India* 87A1
Dauphin *Can* 5H4
Dauphin *USA* 16A2
Dauphiné, Region *France* 49D2
Daura *Nig* 97C3
Dausa *India* 85D3
Dāvangere *India* 87B2
Davao *Phil* 79C4
Davao G *Phil* 79C4
Davenport, California *USA* 22A2
Davenport, Iowa *USA* 10A2
David *Panama* 32A2
Davidson Mts *USA* 4D3
Davis *USA* 21A2
Davis, Base *Ant* 112C10
Davis Inlet *Can* 7D4
Davis Str *Greenland/ Can* 6E3
Davlekanovo *USSR* 61J3
Davos *Switz* 47C1
Dawa, R *Eth* 99E2
Dawan *China* 73A4
Dawat Yar *Afghan* 84B2
Dawḥat Salwah, B *Qatar/S Arabia* 91B4
Dawna Range, Mts *Burma* 76B2
Dawson *Can* 4E3
Dawson, Georgia *USA* 17B1
Dawson, R *Aust* 107D3
Dawson Creek *Can* 5F4
Dawson,Mt *Can* 13D2
Dawson Range, Mts *Can* 12G2
Dawu *China* 73A3
Dawu *China* 73C3
Dax *France* 48B3

Daxian *China* **73B3**
Daxin *China* **73B5**
Daxue Shan, Mts *China* **73A3**
Dayong *China* **73C4**
Dayr'Ali *Syria* **94C2**
Dayr'Atīyah *Syria* **94C1**
Dayr az Zawr *Syria* **93D2**
Dayton, Ohio *USA* **10B3**
Dayton, Texas *USA* **19B4**
Dayton, Washington *USA* **20C1**
Daytona Beach *USA* **11B4**
Dayu *China* **73C4**
Dayu *Indon* **78D3**
Da Yunhe, R *China* **72D2**
Dayville *USA* **20C2**
Dazhu *China* **73B3**
De Aar *S Africa* **100B4**
Deadman's Cay *Bahamas* **26C2**
Dead S *Israel/Jordan* **92C3**
Deal *Eng* **46A1**
Dealesville *S Africa* **101G1**
Dean, R *Can* **13B2**
Dean Chan *Can* **13B2**
Deán Funes *Arg* **34C2**
Dearborn *USA* **14B2**
Dease Arm, B *Can* **4F3**
Dease Lake *Can* **4E4**
Death V *USA* **9B3**
Deauville *France* **48C2**
Debakala *Ivory Coast* **97B4**
Debauch Mt *USA* **12B2**
Débé *Trinidad* **27L1**
Debica *Pol* **59C2**
Deblin *Pol* **58C2**
Débo,L *Mali* **97B3**
Debra Birhan *Eth* **99D2**
Debra Markos *Eth* **99D1**
Debra Tabor *Eth* **99D1**
Debrecen *Hung* **59C3**
Decatur, Alabama *USA* **11B3**
Decatur, Georgia *USA* **17B1**
Decatur, Illinois *USA* **10B3**
Decatur, Indiana *USA* **14B2**
Decazeville *France* **48C3**
Dechang *China* **73A4**
Dedza *Malawi* **101C2**
Dee, R, Dumfries and Galloway *Scot* **42B2**
Dee, R *Eng/Wales* **42C3**
Dee, R, Grampian *Scot* **44C3**
Deep River *Can* **15C1**
Deep River *USA* **16C2**
Deepwater *Aust* **109D1**
Deer Lake *Can* **7E5**
Deer Lodge *USA* **8B2**
Defferrari *Arg* **34D3**
De Funiak Springs *USA* **17A1**
Dêgê *China* **68B3**
De Grey, R *Aust* **106A3**
Deh Bīd *Iran* **91B3**
Dehi *Afghan* **84B1**
Dehibat *Tunisia* **96D1**
Dehiwala-Mt Lavinia *Sri Lanka* **87B3**
Dehlorān *Iran* **90A3**
Dehra Dūn *India* **84D2**
Dehri *India* **86A2**
Deim Zubeir *Sudan* **98C2**
Deir Abu Sa'id *Jordan* **94B2**
Deir el Ahmar *Leb* **94C1**
Dej *Rom* **60B4**
De Kalb, Texas *USA* **19B3**
De Kastri *USSR* **63G2**
Dekese *Zaïre* **98C3**
Dekoa *CAR* **98B2**
Delano *USA* **9B3**
Delaware, State *USA* **10C3**
Delaware *USA* **14B2**
Delaware, R *USA* **15C2**
Delaware B *USA* **10C3**
Delegate *Aust* **109C3**
Delemont *Switz* **47B1**
Delgado, C *Mozam* **101D2**
Delhi *India* **84D3**
Delhi, New York *USA* **15D2**
Delice *Turk* **92B1**
Delicias *Mexico* **24B2**
Delījān *Iran* **90B3**
Delle *France* **47B1**
Del Mar *USA* **22D4**
Delmenhorst *W Germ* **39F8**
De Long, Mts *USA* **4B3**
Deloraine *Aust* **109C4**
Deloraine *Can* **5H5**
Delray Beach *USA* **17B2**
Del Rio *USA* **9C4**
Delta *USA* **8B3**
Delta, R *USA* **12E2**
Delta Junction *USA* **12E2**
Dembidollo *Eth* **99D2**
Demer, R *Belg* **46C1**
Deming *USA* **9C3**
Demirköy *Turk* **54C2**
Denain *France* **49C1**
Denau *USSR* **82A2**
Denbigh *Wales* **42C3**
Denbigh,C *USA* **12B2**
Dendang *Indon* **78B3**
Dendermond *Belg* **46C1**
Dendi, Mt *Eth* **99D2**
Dèndre, R *Belg* **46B1**
Dengkou *China* **72B1**
Deng Xian *China* **72C3**
Denham,Mt *Jamaica* **27H1**
Den Helder *Neth* **56A2**
Denia *Spain* **51C2**
Deniliquin *Aust* **107D4**
Denio *USA* **20C2**
Denison, Texas *USA* **9D3**
Denison,Mt *USA* **12D3**
Denizli *Turk* **92A2**
Denmark, Kingdom *Europe* **39F7**
Denmark Str *Greenland/Iceland* **1C1**
Dennery *St Lucia* **27P2**
Denpasar *Indon* **78D4**
Denton, Maryland *USA* **16B3**
Denton, Texas *USA* **9D3**
D'Entrecasteaux Is *PNG* **107E1**
Dents du Midi, Mt *Switz* **47B1**
Denver *USA* **8C3**
Déo, R *Cam* **98B2**
Deoghar *India* **86B2**
Deolāli *India* **85C5**
Deosai Plain *India* **84D1**
Dépression du Mourdi *Chad* **95B3**
De Queen *USA* **19B3**
Dera *Pak* **84C3**
Dera Bugti *Pak* **84B3**
Dera Ismail Khan *Pak* **84C2**
Derby *Aust* **106B2**
Derby, Connecticut *USA* **16C2**
Derby, County *Eng* **43D3**
Derby *Eng* **43D3**
Derby, Kansas *USA* **18A2**
Dergachi *USSR* **60E3**
De Ridder *USA* **19B3**
Derna *Libya* **95B1**
Derudeb *Sudan* **95C3**
Derwent Bridge *Aust* **109C4**
Desaguadero *Arg* **34B2**
Desaguadero, R *Arg* **34B2**
Désaguadero, R *Bol* **30C2**
Descanso *Mexico* **21B3**
Deschutes, R *USA* **20B2**
Deseado *Arg* **29C5**
Deseado, R *Arg* **29C5**
Desenzano *Italy* **47D2**
Deserta Grande, I *Medeira* **96A1**
Desierto de Atacama, Desert *Chile* **30C4**
Desloge *USA* **18B2**
Des Moines, Iowa *USA* **10A2**
Desna, R *USSR* **60D3**
Desolación, I *Chile* **29B6**
Des Plaines *USA* **14A2**
Dessau *E Germ* **56C2**
Dessye *Eth* **99D1**
Destruction Bay *Can* **12G2**
Desvres *France* **46A1**
Deta *Rom* **54B1**
Dete *Zim* **100B2**
Detroit *USA* **10B2**
Det Udom *Thai* **76D3**
Deva *Rom* **54B1**
Deventer *Neth* **56B2**
Deveron, R *Scot* **44C3**
Devikot *India* **85C3**
Devil Postpile Nat Mon *USA* **22C2**
Devils Gate, P *USA* **22C1**
Devils Lake *USA* **8D2**
Devils Paw, Mt *Can* **12H3**
Devizes *Eng* **43D4**
Devli *India* **85D3**
Devoll, R *Alb* **55B2**
Devon, County *Eng* **43B4**
Devon I *Can* **6A2**
Devonport *Aust* **107D5**
Dewangiri *Bhutan* **86C1**
Dewās *India* **85D4**
Dewetsdorp *S Africa* **101G1**
Dewey Res *USA* **11B3**
De Witt *USA* **19B3**
Dexter, Missouri *USA* **18C2**
Deyang *China* **73A3**
Deyhuk *Iran* **90C3**
Dezfūl *Iran* **90A3**
Dezhou *China* **72D2**
Dezh Shāhpūr *Iran* **90A2**
Dhahran *S Arabia* **91B4**
Dhākā *Bang* **86C2**
Dhamavaram *India* **87B2**
Dhamtari *India* **86A2**
Dhanbād *India* **86B2**
Dhangarhi *Nepal* **86A1**
Dhankuta *Nepal* **86B1**
Dhār *India* **85D4**
Dharmapuri *India* **87B2**
Dharmsāla *India* **84D2**
Dhar Oualata, Desert Region *Maur* **97B3**
Dhaulagiri, Mt *Nepal* **86A1**
Dhenkānāi *India* **86B2**
Dhibah *Jordan* **94B3**
Dhíkti Óri, Mt *Greece* **55C3**
Dhomokós *Greece* **55B3**
Dhone *India* **87B1**
Dhoraji *India* **85C4**
Dhrāngadhra *India* **85C4**
Dhuburi *India* **86B1**
Dhule *India* **85C4**
Diablo,Mt *USA* **22B2**
Diablo Range, Mts *USA* **21A2**
Diamante *Arg* **34C2**
Diamante, R *Arg* **34B2**
Diamantina *Brazil* **31C5**
Diamantina, R *Aust* **107D3**
Diamond Harbours *India* **86B2**
Diamond Springs *USA* **22B1**
Dibā *UAE* **91C4**
Dibaya *Zaïre* **98C3**
Dibrugarh *India* **86C1**
Dickinson *USA* **8C2**
Dickson *USSR* **1B10**
Dickson City *USA* **15C2**
Dicle, R *Turk* **93D2**
Didsbury *Can* **13E2**
Dīdwāna *India* **85C3**
Diebougou *U Volta* **97B3**
Diekirch *Lux* **46D2**
Diéma *Mali* **97B3**
Dien Bien Phu *Viet* **76C1**
Diepholz *W Germ* **56B2**
Dieppe *France* **48C2**
Diest *Belg* **46C1**
Dieuze *France* **46D2**
Digby *Can* **7D5**
Digne *France* **49D3**
Digoin *France* **49C2**
Digos *Phil* **79C4**
Digul, R *Indon* **71E4**
Dihang, R *India* **86C1**
Dijon *France* **49C2**
Dik *Chad* **98B2**
Dikhil *Djibouti* **99E1**
Diksmuide *Belg* **46B1**
Dilaram *Afghan* **82A2**
Dili *Indon* **106B1**
Di Linh *Viet* **76D3**
Dillenburg *W Germ* **46E1**
Dilling *Sudan* **99C1**
Dillingham *USA* **12C3**
Dillon *USA* **8B2**
Dillsburg *USA* **16A2**
Dilolo *Zaïre* **100B2**
Dimbelenge *Zaïre* **98C3**
Dimbokro *Ivory Coast* **97B4**
Dimitrovgrad *Bulg* **54C2**
Dimitrovgrad *USSR* **61G3**
Dimona *Israel* **94B3**
Dimpāpur *India* **86C1**
Dinagat, I *Phil* **79C3**
Dinajpur *India* **86B1**
Dinan *France* **48B2**
Dinant *Belg* **46C1**
Dinar *Turk* **92B2**
Dinder, R *Sudan* **99D1**
Dindigul *India* **87B2**
Dingbian *China* **72B2**
Dinggyê *China* **86B1**
Dingle *Irish Rep* **41A3**
Dingle, B *Irish Rep* **41A3**
Dinguiraye *Guinea* **97A3**
Dingwall *Scot* **44B3**
Dingxi *China* **72A2**
Ding Xian *China* **72D2**
Dinh Lap *Viet* **76D1**
Dinuba *USA* **22C2**
Diouloulou *Sen* **97A3**
Diphu *India* **86C1**
Diredawa *Eth* **99E2**
Dirk Hartog, I *Aust* **106A3**
Dirkou *Niger* **95A3**
Dirranbandi *Aust* **109C1**
Dirri *Somalia* **99E2**
Disappointment,C *South Georgia* **29G8**
Disappointment,C *USA* **20B1**
Disappointment,L *Aust* **106B3**
Discovery B *Aust* **108B3**
Discovery Tablemount *Atlantic O* **103J7**
Disentis Muster *Switz* **47C1**
Disko *Greenland* **6E3**
Disko Bugt, B *Greenland* **6E3**
Diskorjord *Greenland* **6E3**
Disna, R *USSR* **58D1**
Distrito Federal, Federal District *Brazil* **35B1**
Diu *India* **85C4**
Diuat Mts *Phil* **79C4**
Divinópolis *Brazil* **31C6**
Divnoye *USSR* **61F4**
Divriği *Turk* **93C2**
Dixon, California *USA* **22B1**
Dixon Entrance, Sd *Can/USA* **5E4**
Dixonville *Can* **13D1**
Diyālā, R *Iraq* **93E3**
Diyarbakir *Turk* **65F6**
Diz, R *Iran* **90A3**
Dja, R *Cam* **98B2**
Djadi, R *Alg* **96C1**
Djado,Plat du *Niger* **95A2**
Djambala *Congo* **98B3**
Djanet *Alg* **96C2**
Djebel Bouhalla, Mt *Mor* **50A2**
Djelfa *Alg* **96C1**
Djéma *CAR* **98C2**

Djenné *Mali* **97B3**
Djibo *Upper Volta* **97B3**
Djibouti *Djibouti* **99E1**
Djibouti, Republic *E Africa* **99E1**
Djolu *Zaïre* **98C2**
Djougou *Benin* **97C4**
Djugu *Zaïre* **99D2**
Djúpivogur *Iceland* **38C2**
Djurdjura, Mts *Alg* **51C2**
Dmitrov *USSR* **60E2**
Dnepr, R *USSR* **60D4**
Dneprodzerzhinsk *USSR* **60D4**
Dnepropetrovsk *USSR* **60E4**
Dneprovskaya Nizmennost', Region *USSR* **60C3**
Dnestr, R *USSR* **60B4**
Dno *USSR* **60D2**
Doba *Chad* **98B2**
Dobele *USSR* **58C1**
Doblas *Arg* **34C3**
Dobo *Indon* **71E4**
Doboj *Yugos* **54A2**
Dobrush *USSR* **60D3**
Doce, R *Brazil* **31C5**
Doctor R P Peña *Arg* **30D3**
Dod *India* **87B2**
Doda Betta, Mt *India* **87B2**
Dodge City *USA* **9C3**
Dodoma *Tanz* **99D3**
Dōgo, I *Japan* **75A1**
Dogondoutchi *Niger* **97C3**
Doğubayazit *Turk* **93D2**
Doha *Qatar* **91B4**
Dolbeau *Can* **7C5**
Dôle *France* **49D2**
Dolgellau *Wales* **43C3**
Dolo *Eth* **99E2**
Dolomitche, Mts *Italy* **47D1**
Dolores *Arg* **29E3**
Dolores *Urug* **34D2**
Dolores Hidalgo *Mexico* **23A1**
Dolphin and Union Str *Can* **4G3**
Dolphin,C *Falkland Is* **29E6**
Dom, Mt *Indon* **71E4**
Dombarovskiy *USSR* **65G4**
Dombas *Nor* **38F6**
Dombasle-sur-Meurthe *France* **46D2**
Dombóvár *Hung* **54A1**
Domfront *France* **48B2**
Dominica, I *Caribbean* **27E3**
Dominican Republic *Caribbean* **27C3**
Dominion,C *Can* **6C3**
Domino *Can* **7E4**
Domna *USSR* **68D1**
Domodossola *Italy* **52A1**
Dompu *Indon* **78D4**
Domuyo, Mt *Arg* **29B3**
Domville,Mt *Aust* **109D1**
Dom-yanskoya *USSR* **65H4**
Don, R *Scot* **44C3**
Don, R *USSR* **61F4**
Donaghadee *N Ire* **45C1**
Donau, R *W Germ* **57C3**
Donauwörth *W Germ* **57C3**
Don Benito *Spain* **50A2**
Doncaster *Eng* **42D3**
Dondo *Angola* **98B3**
Dondo *Mozam* **101C2**
Dondra Head, C *Sri Lanka* **87C3**
Donegal, County *Irish Rep* **45B1**
Donegal *Irish Rep* **40B3**
Donegal, B *Irish Rep* **40B3**
Donegal, Mts *Irish Rep* **45B1**
Donetsk *USSR* **60E4**
Dong'an *China* **73C4**
Dongara *Aust* **106A3**
Dongchuan *China* **73A4**
Dongfang *China* **76D2**
Dongfeng *China* **74B2**
Donggala *Indon* **70C4**
Donggi Cona, L *China* **68B3**
Donggou *China* **74A3**
Donghai Dao, I *China* **73C5**
Dong He, R *China* **72A1**
Dong Hoi *Viet* **76D2**
Dong Jiang, R *China* **73C5**
Dongola *Sudan* **95C3**
Dongshan *China* **73D5**
Dongsha Qundao, I *China* **68D4**
Dongsheng *China* **72C2**
Dongtai *China* **72E3**
Dongting Hu, L *China* **73C4**
Dongxing *China* **73B5**
Dongzhi *China* **73D3**
Doniphan *USA* **18B2**
Donji Vakuf *Yugos* **52C2**
Dönna, I *Nor* **38G5**
Donner, P *USA* **21A2**
Donnersberg, Mt *W Germ* **46D2**
Donnybrook *S Africa* **101G1**
Don Pedro Res *USA* **22B2**
Doonerak,Mt *USA* **12D1**
Dopolong *Phil* **79B4**
Do Qu, R *China* **73A3**
Dora Baltea, R *Italy* **47B2**
Dorbirn *Austria* **49D2**
Dorchester *Eng* **43C4**
Dorchester,C *Can* **6C3**
Dordogne, R *France* **48C2**
Dordrecht *Neth* **56A2**
Dore, L *Can* **13F2**
Dore Lake *Can* **13F2**
Dori *Upper Volta* **97B3**
Dormans *France* **46B2**
Dornbirn *Austria* **57B3**
Dornoch *Scot* **44B3**
Dornoch Firth, Estuary *Scot* **44B3**
Dorotea *Sweden* **38H6**
Dorrigo *Aust* **109D2**
Dorris *USA* **20B2**
Dorset, County *Eng* **43C4**
Dorsten *W Germ* **46D1**
Dortmund *W Germ* **56B2**
Doruma *Zaïre* **98C2**
Dosatuy *USSR* **63D2**
Doshi *Afghan* **84B1**
Dos Palos *USA* **22B2**
Dosso *Niger* **97C3**
Dossor *USSR* **65G5**
Dothan *USA* **11B3**
Douai *France* **49C1**
Douala *Cam* **98A2**
Double Island Pt *Aust* **109D1**
Doubs, R *France* **49D2**
Doubtful Sd *NZ* **111A3**
Douentza *Mali* **97B3**
Douglas, Arizona *USA* **9C3**
Douglas *Eng* **42B2**
Douglas, Georgia *USA* **17B1**
Douglas, Wyoming *USA* **8C2**
Douglas,C *USA* **12A1**
Douglas Chan *Can* **13B2**
Douglas,Mt *USA* **12D3**
Doullens *France* **46B1**
Doun, County *N Ire* **45C1**
Dourados *Brazil* **30F3**
Douro, R *Port* **50A1**
Dover, Delaware *USA* **15C3**
Dover *Eng* **43E4**
Dover, New Hampshire *USA* **15D2**
Dover, New Jersey *USA* **16B2**
Dover, Ohio *USA* **14B2**
Dover, R *Eng* **43D3**
Dover,Str of *UK/France* **41D3**
Downington *USA* **16B3**
Downpatrick *N Ire* **42B2**
Downton,Mt *Can* **13C2**
Doylestown *USA* **16B2**
Dōzen, I *Japan* **75A1**
Dr'aa, R *Mor* **96A2**
Dracena *Brazil* **35A2**
Dracut *USA* **16D1**
Draguignan *France* **49D3**
Drakensberg, Mts *S Africa* **101C3**
Drakensberg, Mt *S Africa* **101G1**
Drake Pass *Pacific/Atlantic O* **103E7**
Dráma *Greece* **55B2**
Drammen *Nor* **39G7**
Drangajökull *Iceland* **38A1**
Drava, R *Yugos* **52C1**
Drayton Valley *Can* **13D2**
Dreaux *France* **49C2**
Dresden *E Germ* **57C2**
Dreux *France* **48C2**
Drewsey *USA* **20C2**
Drin, R *Alb* **54B2**
Drina, R *Yugos* **54A2**
Drissa, R *USSR* **58D1**
Drogheda *Irish Rep* **45C2**
Drogobych *USSR* **59C3**
Dronning Maud Land, Region *Ant* **112B12**
Dr P.P. Pená *Par* **30D3**
Drumheller *Can* **5G4**
Drummond I *USA* **14B1**
Drummondville *Can* **15D1**
Druskininksi *USSR* **58C2**
Dry B *USA* **12G3**
Dryden *Can* **7A5**
Dry Harbour Mts *Jamaica* **27H1**
Duang, I *Burma* **76B3**
Dubai *UAE* **91C4**
Dubawnt, R *Can* **5H3**
Dubawnt L *Can* **4H3**
Dubbo *Aust* **107D4**
Dublin, County *Irish Rep* **45C2**
Dublin *Irish Rep* **45C2**
Dublin *USA* **17B1**
Dubna *USSR* **60E2**
Dubno *USSR* **60C3**
Du Bois *USA* **15C2**
Dubose,Mt *Can* **13B2**
Dubrovica *USSR* **58D2**
Dubrovnik *Yugos* **54A2**
Dubuque *USA* **10A2**
Dudelange *Lux* **46D2**
Dudinka *USSR* **1C10**
Dudley *Eng* **43C3**
Duekoué *Ivory Coast* **97B4**
Duero, R *Spain* **50B1**
Dufftown *Scot* **44C3**
Dugi Otok, I *Yugos* **52B2**
Duisburg *W Germ* **56B2**
Dūkan *Iraq* **93E3**
Duk Faiwil *Sudan* **99D2**
Dukhān *Qatar* **91B4**
Dukou *China* **73A4**
Dulan *China* **68B3**
Dulce, R *Arg* **34C2**
Dulit Range, Mts *Malay* **78C2**
Dullabchara *India* **86C2**
Duluth *USA* **10A2**
Dūmā *Syria* **94C2**
Dumai *Indon* **78A2**
Dumaran, I *Phil* **79A3**
Dumas *USA* **9C3**
Dumayr *Syria* **94C2**
Dumbarton *Scot* **42B2**
Dumfries *Scot* **42C2**
Dumfries and Galloway, Region *Scot* **42B2**
Dumka *India* **86B2**
Dumoine,L *Can* **15C1**
Dumont d'Urville, Base *Ant* **112C8**
Dumyat *Egypt* **95C1**
Dunărea, R *Rom* **54C2**
Dunary Head, Pt *Irish Rep* **45C2**
Dunav, R *Bulg* **54B2**
Dunayevtsy *USSR* **59D3**
Duncan *Can* **13C3**
Duncannon *USA* **16A2**
Duncansby Head, Pt *Scot* **44C2**
Dundalk *Irish Rep* **45C1**
Dundalk *USA* **16A3**
Dundalk B *Irish Rep* **45C2**
Dundas *Greenland* **6D2**
Dundas Pen *Can* **4G2**
Dundas Str *Aust* **71E5**
Dundee *S Africa* **101H1**
Dundee *Scot* **44C3**
Dundoo *Aust* **108B1**
Dundrum, B *N Ire* **42B2**
Dunedin *NZ* **111B3**
Dunedin *USA* **17B2**
Dunedoo *Aust* **109C2**
Dunfermline *Scot* **44C3**
Dungarpur *India* **85C4**
Dungarvan *Irish Rep* **45C2**
Dungeness *Eng* **43E4**
Dungog *Aust* **109D2**
Dungu *Zaïre* **99C2**
Dungunab *Sudan* **95C2**
Dunhuang *China* **68B2**
Dunkerque *France* **46B1**
Dunkirk *USA* **10C2**
Dunkur *Eth* **99D1**
Dunkwa *Ghana* **97B4**
Dun Laoghaire *Irish Rep* **41B3**
Dunmanway *Irish Rep* **45B3**
Dunmore Town *Bahamas* **26B1**
Dunnet Head, Pt *Scot* **44C2**
Duns *Scot* **42C2**
Dunsmuir *USA* **20B2**
Dunstan Mts *NZ* **111A2**
Dun-sur-Meuse *France* **46C2**
Duolun *China* **72D1**
Duque de Braganca *Angola* **98B3**
Du Quoin *USA* **18C2**
Dura *Israel* **94B3**
Durance, R *France* **49D3**
Durango *Mexico* **24B2**
Durango *Spain* **50B1**
Durango *USA* **9C3**
Durano *Urug* **29E2**
Durant *USA* **9D3**
Duraykīsh *Syria* **94C1**
Durban *S Africa* **101H1**
Duren *W Germ* **46D1**
Durg *India* **86A2**
Durgapur *India* **86B2**
Durham, County *Eng* **42D2**
Durham *Eng* **42D2**
Durham, N Carolina *USA* **11C3**
Durham, New Hampshire *USA* **16D1**
Durham Downs *Aust* **108B1**
Durmitor, Mt *Yugos* **54A2**
Durness *Scot* **44B2**
Durrës *Alb* **55A2**
Durrie *Aust* **108B1**
Dursey, I *Irish Rep* **45A3**
Dursunbey *Turk* **55C3**
D'Urville I *NZ* **110B2**
Dushak *USSR* **90D2**
Dushan *China* **73B4**
Dushanbe *USSR* **82A2**
Dusky Sd *NZ* **111A3**
Düsseldorf *W Germ* **56B2**
Duyun *China* **73B4**
Düzce *Turk* **92B1**
Dvina, R *USSR* **60C2**
Dwārka *India* **85B4**
Dyer,C *Can* **6D3**
Dyersburg *USA* **11B3**
Dyfed, County *Wales* **43B3**
Dykh Tau Dağlari, Mt *USSR* **61F5**
Dynevor Downs *Aust* **108B1**
Dzag *Mongolia* **68B2**
Dzamin Uüd *USSR* **63C3**
Dzaoudzi *Mayotte* **101D2**

Dzarnïn Uüd *Mongolia* 68C2
Dzavhan Gol, R *Mongolia* 68B2
Dzehezkazgan *USSR* 80E1
Dzerzhinsk *USSR* 61F2
Dzhalinda *USSR* 63E2
Dzhambul *USSR* 65J5
Dzhankoy *USSR* 60D4
Dzhezkazgan *USSR* 65H4
Dzhilikul' *USSR* 84B1
Dzhungarskiy Alatau, Mts *USSR* 65J5
Dzierzoniow *Pol* 59B2
Dzungaria, Basin *China* 82C1

E

Eabamet L *Can* 7B4
Eagle, Alaska *USA* 12F2
Eagle L, California *USA* 20B2
Eagle Mountain L *USA* 19A3
Eagle Pass *USA* 9C4
Eagle Plain *Can* 4E3
Eagle River *USA* 12E2
Earlimart *USA* 21B2
Easley *USA* 17B1
East Aurora *USA* 15C2
Eastbourne *Eng* 43E4
East Chicago *USA* 14A2
East China Sea *China/Japan* 69E3
Eastern Ghats, Mts *India* 83B4
East Falkland, I *Falkland Is* 29E6
East Fork, R *USA* 12E1
Eastgate *USA* 21B2
East Germany, Republic *Europe* 56C2
Easthampton *USA* 16C1
East Hampton *USA* 16C2
East Lake *USA* 14A2
East Liverpool *USA* 14B2
East London *S Africa* 100B4
Eastmain *Can* 7C4
Eastmain, R *Can* 7C4
Eastman *USA* 17B1
Easton, Maryland *USA* 15C3
Easton, Pennsylvania *USA* 15C2
East Orange *USA* 16B2
East Pacific Ridge *Pacific O* 105L4
East Point *USA* 17B1
East Retford *Eng* 42D3
East St Louis *USA* 11A3
East Siberian S *USSR* 1B7
East Sussex, County *Eng* 43E4
Eatonton *USA* 17B1
Eau Claire *USA* 10A2
Eauripik, I *Pacific O* 71F3
Ebano *Mexico* 23B1
Ebebiyin *Eq Guinea* 98B2
Eberswalde *E Germ* 56C2
Ebian *China* 73A4
Ebinur, L *China* 65K5
Eboli *Italy* 53C2
Ebolowa *Cam* 98B2
Ebro, R *Spain* 51B1
Eceabat *Turk* 92A1
Eching *China* 72D2
Echo *USA* 20C1
Echo Bay *Can* 4G3
Echternach *Lux* 46D2
Echuca *Aust* 108B3
Ecija *Spain* 50A2
Eclipse Sd *Can* 6B2
Ecuador, Republic *S America* 32B4
Eday, I *Scot* 44C2
Edd *Eth* 99E1
Ed Da'ein *Sudan* 98C1
Ed Damer *Sudan* 95C3
Ed Debba *Sudan* 95C3
Eddrachillis, B *Scot* 44B2
Ed Dueim *Sudan* 99D1
Eddystone Pt *Aust* 109C4
Edea *Cam* 98A2
Eden *Aust* 109C3
Eden, R *Eng* 42C2
Edenburg *S Africa* 101G1
Edendale *NZ* 111A3
Edenkoben *W Germ* 46E2
Eder, R *W Germ* 46E1
Edgell I *Can* 6D3
Edgeøya, I *Barents S* 64D2
Edgewood *USA* 16A3
Edh Dhahiriya *Israel* 94B3
Edhessa *Greece* 55B2
Edinburgh *Scot* 44C3
Edirne *Turk* 60C5
Edisto, R *USA* 17B1
Edith Cavell,Mt *Can* 13D2
Edmonds *USA* 20B1
Edmonton *Can* 5G4
Edmundston *Can* 7D5
Edna *USA* 19A4
Edna Bay *USA* 12H3
Edolo *Italy* 52B1
Edom, Region *Jordan* 94B3
Edremit *Turk* 92A2
Edremit Körfezi, B *Turk* 55C3
Edrengiyn Nuruu, Mts *Mongolia* 68B2
Edson *Can* 5G4
Eduardo Castex *Arg* 34C3
Eduni,Mt *Can* 12J2
Edward, R *Aust* 108B3
Edward,L *Zaïre/Uganda* 99C3
Edwards Creek *Aust* 108A1
Edwards Plat *USA* 9C3
Edwardsville *USA* 18C2
Edziza,Mt *Can* 12H3
Eek *USA* 12B2
Eeklo *Belg* 46B1
Effingham *USA* 10B3
Egedesminde *Greenland* 6E3
Egegik *USA* 12C3
Eger *Hung* 59C3
Egersund *Nor* 39F7
Egg Harbor City *USA* 16B3
Eglinton I *Can* 4G2
Egmont,C *NZ* 110B1
Egmont,Mt *NZ* 110B1
Eğridir Gölü, L *Turk* 92B2
Egypt, Republic *Africa* 95B2
Eibar *Spain* 50B1
Eibeuf *France* 49C2
Eifel, Region *W Germ* 46D1
Eigg, I *Scot* 44A3
Eight Degree Chan *Indian O* 83B5
Eighty Mile Beach *Aust* 106B2
Eildon,L *Aust* 108C3
Eindhoven *Neth* 56B2
Einsiedeln *Switz* 47C1
Ein Yahav *Israel* 94B3
Eisenach *E Germ* 57C2
Eisenerz *Austria* 57C3
Eitorf *W Germ* 46D1
Ejin qi *China* 72A1
Ejutla *Mexico* 23B2
Eketahuna *NZ* 110C2
Ekibastuz *USSR* 65J4
Ekimchan *USSR* 63F2
Ek Mahalla el Kubra *Egypt* 92B3
Eksjo *Sweden* 39H7
Ekwen, R *Can* 10B1
El'Alamein *Egypt* 92A3
El'Arîsh *Egypt* 92B3
El Asnam *Alg* 96C1
Elat *Israel* 92B4
El'Atrun Oasis *Sudan* 95B3
Elazig *Turk* 93C2
El Azraq *Jordan* 92C3
Elba, I *Italy* 52B2
El Balyana *Egypt* 95C2
El Banco *Colombia* 32C2
Elbasan *Alb* 55B2
El Baúl *Ven* 27D5
Elbe, R *E Germ/W Germ* 57C2
El Bega'a, R *Leb* 94C1
Elberta *USA* 14A2
Elbert,Mt *USA* 8C3
Elberton *USA* 17B1
Elbistan *Turk* 92C2
Elblag *Pol* 58B2
El Bolson *Arg* 29B4
Elbrus, Mt *USSR* 61F5
El Cajon *USA* 21B3
El Campo *USA* 19A4
Elche *Spain* 51B2
Elda *Spain* 51B2
El Diviso *Colombia* 32B3
El Djouf, Desert Region *Maur* 96B2
Eldon *USA* 18B2
El Dorado, Arkansas *USA* 11A3
Eldorado *Brazil* 35B2
El Dorado, Kansas *USA* 9D3
El Dorado *Mexico* 24B2
El Dorado *Ven* 33E2
Eldoret *Kenya* 99D2
Eleanor,L *USA* 22C1
El Eglab, Region *Alg* 96B2
El Escorial *Spain* 50B1
Eleşkirt *Turk* 93D2
Eleuthera, I *Bahamas* 11C4
El Faiyûm *Egypt* 92B4
El Farsia, Well *Mor* 96B2
El Fasher *Sudan* 98C1
El Fashn *Egypt* 92B4
El Ferrol del Caudillo *Spain* 50A1
El Fula *Sudan* 99C1
El Gassi *Alg* 96C1
El Geteina *Sudan* 99D1
El Gezīra, Region *Sudan* 99D1
El Ghor, V *Israel/Jordan* 94B3
Elgin, Illinois *USA* 10B2
Elgin *Scot* 44C3
El Gîza *Egypt* 92B3
El Golea *Alg* 96C1
Elgon,Mt *Uganda/Kenya* 99D2
El Goran *Eth* 99E2
El Grullo *Mexico* 23A2
El Guettara, Well *Mali* 96B2
El Hamurre *Somalia* 99E2
El Haricha, Desert Region *Mali* 96B2
El Harra *Egypt* 92A4
El Harrach *Alg* 51C2
El Hawata *Sudan* 99D1
El Higo *Mexico* 23B1
El Huecu *Arg* 34A3
El'Igma, Desert Region *Egypt* 92B4
Elim *USA* 12B2
Elira,C *Can* 4H2
Elisenvaara *Fin* 39K6
Elista *USSR* 61F4
Elizabeth *Aust* 106C4
Elizabeth *USA* 15D2
Elizabeth City *USA* 11C3
Elizabethtown, N Carolina *USA* 17C1
Elizabethtown, Pennsylvania *USA* 16A2
El Jadida *Mor* 96B1
El Jafr *Jordan* 92C3
El Jebelein *Sudan* 99D1
El Jem *Tunisia* 96D1
Elk *Pol* 58C2
Elk, R, Maryland *USA* 16B3
Elk, R, W Virginia *USA* 14B3
El Kamlin *Sudan* 95C3
El Kef *Tunisia* 96C1
Elk Grove *USA* 22B1
El Khârga *Egypt* 80B3
El Khârga Oasis *Egypt* 80B3
Elkhart *USA* 14A2
El Khenachich, Desert Region *Mali* 96B2
Elkhovo *Bulg* 54C2
Elkins *USA* 14C3
Elko *USA* 8B2
Elkton *USA* 16B3
El Kuntilla *Egypt* 92B3
El Lagowa *Sudan* 99C1
Ellef Ringnes I *Can* 4H2
Ellensburg *USA* 8A2
Ellenville *USA* 16B2
Ellesmere I *Can* 6B2
Ellesmere,L *NZ* 111B2
Ellicott City *USA* 16A3
Elliot *S Africa* 100B4
Elliot Lake *Can* 7B5
El Lisan, Pen *Jordan* 94B3
Ellsworth Land, Region *Ant* 112B3
El Maghra, L *Egypt* 95B1
El Mansûra *Egypt* 92B3
Elmer *USA* 16B3
El Merelé, Desert Region *Maur* 96B3
El Milagro *Arg* 34B2
El Mīna *Leb* 94B1
El Minya *Egypt* 92B4
Elmira, California *USA* 22B1
Elmira, New York *USA* 10C2
El Mreitl, Well *Maur* 96B2
Elmsborn *W Germ* 56B2
El Muglad *Sudan* 98C1
El Mzereb, Well *Mali* 96B2
El Nido *Phil* 79A3
El Obeid *Sudan* 99D1
El Oro *Mexico* 23A2
El Oued *Alg* 96C1
El Paso *USA* 9C3
El Porta *USA* 21A2
El Portal *USA* 22C2
El Puerto del Sta Maria *Spain* 50A2
El Quseima *Egypt* 94B3
El Reno *USA* 9D3
Elsa *Can* 4E3
El Salvador, Republic *C America* 25D3
Elsinore L *USA* 22D4
El Sosneade *Arg* 34B3
Elsterwerde *E Germ* 57C2
El Teleno, Mt *Spain* 50A1
Eltham *NZ* 110B1
El Tigre *Ven* 33E2
El Tîh, Desert Region *Egypt* 92B4
El Tio *Arg* 34C2
Eltopia *USA* 20C1
El Tûr *Egypt* 92B4
Elūru *India* 87C1
Elvas *Port* 50A2
Elvira *Brazil* 32C5
El Volcán *Chile* 34A2
Elwood *USA* 14A2
Ely *Eng* 43E3
Ely, Minnesota *USA* 10A2
Ely, Nevada *USA* 8B3
Elyria *USA* 14B2
Emāmrūd *Iran* 90B2
Emām Sāheb *Afghan* 84B1
Eman, R *Sweden* 58B1
Emba *USSR* 61J4
Emba, R *USSR* 61J4
Embalse Cerros Colorados, L *Arg* 29C3
Embalse de Alarcón, Res *Spain* 51B2
Embalse de Alcántarà, Res *Spain* 50A2
Embalse de Almendra, Res *Spain* 50A1
Embalse de Garcia de Sola, Res *Spain* 50A2
Embalse de Guri, L *Ven* 33E2

Embalse de Mequinenza, Res *Spain* **51B1**
Embalse de Ricobayo, Res *Spain* **50A1**
Embalse de Rio Negro Res *Urug* **29E2**
Embalse El Chocón, L *Arg* **29C3**
Embalse Florentine Ameghino, L *Arg* **29C4**
Embalse Gabriel y Galan, Res *Spain* **50A1**
Embarcación *Arg* **30D3**
Embarras Portage *Can* **5G4**
Embrun *France* **47B2**
Embu *Kenya* **99D3**
Emden *W Germ* **56B2**
Emei *China* **73A4**
Emerald *Aust* **107D3**
Emeri *Can* **7D4**
Emerson *Can* **5J5**
Emigrant P *USA* **21B1**
Emi Koussi, Mt *Chad* **95A3**
Emilo Mitre *Arg* **34B3**
Emirdağ *Turk* **92B2**
Emmaus *USA* **16B2**
Emmen *Neth* **56B2**
Emmett *USA* **20C2**
Emmitsburg *USA* **16A3**
Emmonak *USA* **12B2**
Emory Peak, Mt *USA* **9C4**
Empalme *Mexico* **24A2**
Empangeni *S Africa* **101H1**
Empedrado *Arg* **30E4**
Emperor Seamount Chain *Pacific O* **105G1**
Emporia, Kansas *USA* **18A2**
Ems, R *W Germ* **56B2**
Enard, B *Scot* **44B2**
Encarnacion *Mexico* **23A1**
Encarnación *Par* **30E4**
Enchi *Ghana* **97B4**
Encinitas *USA* **22D4**
Encruzilhada *Brazil* **35C1**
Ende *Indon* **106B1**
Enderby *Can* **13D2**
Enderby Land, Region *Ant* **112C11**
Endicott *USA* **15C2**
Endicott Mts *USA* **12D1**
Engadin, Mts *Switz* **47D1**
Engaño,C *Phil* **79B2**
En Gedi *Israel* **94B3**
Engelberg *Switz* **47C1**
Engel's *USSR* **61G3**
Enggano, I *Indon* **78A4**
England, Country *UK* **41C3**
Englee *Can* **7E4**
English Channel *Eng/France* **41C3**
Enji, Well *Maur* **97B3**
Enkoping *Sweden* **39H7**
Enna *Italy* **53B3**
En Nahud *Sudan* **99C1**
Ennedi, Region *Chad* **95B3**
Enngonia *Aust* **109C1**
Ennis *Irish Rep* **41B3**
Ennis, Texas *USA* **19A3**
Enniscorthy *Irish Rep* **45C2**
Enniskillen *N Ire* **45C1**
Ennistimon *Irish Rep* **45B2**
Enn Nâqoûra *Leb* **94B2**
Enns, R *Austria* **57C3**
Enschede *Neth* **39F8**
Ensenada *Mexico* **24A1**
Enshi *China* **73B3**
Entebbe *Uganda* **99D2**
Enterprise, Alabama *USA* **17A1**
Enterprise, Oregon *USA* **20C1**
Enugu *Nig* **97C4**
Enzan *Japan* **75B1**
Epernay *France* **49C2**
Ephrata, Pennsylvania *USA* **16A2**
Ephrata, Washington *USA* **20C1**
Épinal *France* **49D2**
Epte, R *France* **46A2**
Epukiro *Namibia* **100A3**
Epu pel *Arg* **34C3**
Eqlid *Iran* **90B3**
Equator **89D7**
Equatorial Guinea, Republic *Africa* **98A2**
Erba *Italy* **47C2**
Erbeskopf, Mt *W Germ* **46D2**
Ercilla *Chile* **34A3**
Erciş *Turk* **93D2**
Erciyas Daglari, Mt *Turk* **92C2**
Erdaobaihe *China* **74B2**
Erdene *Mongolia* **72C1**
Erdenet *Mongolia* **68C2**
Erdi, Region *Chad* **95B3**
Erechim *Brazil* **30F4**
Ereğlī *Turk* **92B1**
Ereğli *Turk* **92B2**
Erenhot *China* **68D2**
Eresma, R *Spain* **50B1**
Erft, R *W Germ* **46D1**
Erfurt *E Germ* **57C2**
Ergani *Turk* **93C2**
Erg Chech, Desert Region *Alg* **96B2**
Erg du Djourab, Desert *Chad* **95A3**
Erg Du Ténéré, Desert Region *Niger* **97D3**
Ergene, R *Turk* **92A1**
Erg Iguidi, Region *Alg* **96B2**
Ergli *USSR* **58D1**
Erguig, R *Chad* **98B1**
Ergun' *USSR* **63D2**
Ergun, R *USSR* **68D1**
Ergun Zuoqi *China* **63E2**
Eriba *Sudan* **95C3**
Erie *USA* **10C2**
Erie,L *USA/Can* **10B2**
Erin Port *Eng* **42B2**
Eriskay, I *Scot* **44A3**
Erkelenz *W Germ* **46D1**
Erlangen *W Germ* **57C3**
Erling,L *USA* **19B3**
Ermelo *S Africa* **101G1**
Ernākulam *India* **87B3**
Erode *India* **87B2**
Eromanga *Aust* **108B1**
Er Rachidia *Mor* **96B1**
Er Rahad *Sudan* **99D1**
Errego *Mozam* **101C2**
Errigal, Mt *Irish Rep* **40B2**
Erris Head, Pt *Irish Rep* **41A3**
Er Roseires *Sudan* **99D1**
Er Rummān *Jordan* **94B2**
Erzgebirge, Upland *E Germ* **57C2**
Erzincan *Turk* **93C2**
Erzurum *Turk* **65F6**
Esara, R *Spain* **48C3**
Esbjerg *Den* **56B1**
Escalón *Mexico* **9C4**
Escanaba *USA* **10B2**
Escárcega *Mexico* **25C3**
Esch *Luxembourg* **46C2**
Escondido *USA* **21B3**
Escuinapa *Mexico* **24B2**
Escuintla *Guatemala* **25C3**
Eséka *Cam* **98B2**
Esera, R *Spain* **51C1**
Eşfahān *Iran* **90B3**
Eshowe *S Africa* **101H1**
Eskdale *NZ* **110C1**
Eskifjörður *Iceland* **38C1**
Eskilstuna *Sweden* **39H7**
Eskimo L *Can* **4E3**
Eskimo Point *Can* **7A3**
Eskisehir *Turk* **92B2**
Esla, R *Spain* **50A1**
Esmeralda, I *Chile* **29A5**
Esmeraldas *Ecuador* **32B3**
Esmerelda *Cuba* **26B2**
Espalion *France* **49C3**
Espanola *Can* **14B1**
Española, I *Ecuador* **32J7**
Esperance *Aust* **106B4**
Esperanza *Arg* **34C2**
Esperanza, Base *Ant* **112C2**
Espírito Santo, State *Brazil* **35C1**
Espungabera *Mozam* **101C3**
Esquel *Arg* **29B4**
Esquimalt *Can* **20B1**
Esquina *Arg* **34D2**
Es Samra *Jordan* **94C2**
Essaourira *Mor* **96B1**
Essen *W Germ* **56B2**
Essequibo, R *Guyana* **33F3**
Essex, County *Eng* **43E4**
Essexville *USA* **14B2**
Esslingen *W Germ* **57B3**
Essonne *France* **46B2**
Estância *Brazil* **31D4**
Estcourt *S Africa* **101G1**
Este *Italy* **47D2**
Esternay *France* **46B2**
Esteros *Par* **30D3**
Estevan *Can* **5H5**
Estill *USA* **17B1**
Estonskaya SSR, Republic *USSR* **60B2**
Estrecho de Magallanes, Str *Chile* **29B6**
Estremoz *Port* **50A2**
Esztergom *Hung* **59B3**
Etadunna *Aust* **108A1**
Etam *France* **46C2**
Etampes *France* **48C2**
Etamunbanie,L *Aust* **108A1**
Etaples *France* **46A1**
Etāwah *India* **85D3**
Ethiopia, Republic *Africa* **99D2**
Etla *Mexico* **23B2**
Etna, Mt *Italy* **53B3**
Etolin I *USA* **12H3**
Etolin Str *USA* **12A2**
Eton *Can* **6C2**
Etosha Nat Pk *Namibia* **100A2**
Etosha Pan, Salt L *Namibia* **100A2**
Etowah, R *USA* **17B1**
Ettelbruck *Lux* **46D2**
Euabalong *Aust* **109C2**
Euclid *USA* **14B2**
Eucumbene,L *Aust* **109C3**
Eudunda *Aust* **108A2**
Eufala L *USA* **19A2**
Eufaula *USA* **17A1**
Eugene *USA* **8A2**
Eulo *Aust* **108C1**
Eunice, Louisiana *USA* **19B3**
Eupen *W Germ* **46D1**
Euphrates, R *Iraq* **93D3**
Eupora *USA* **19C3**
Eure, R *France* **48C2**
Eureka, California *USA* **20B2**
Eureka *Can* **6B1**
Eureka, Nevada *USA* **8B3**
Eureka, Sd *Can* **6B2**
Euroa *Aust* **108C3**
Eurombah, R *Aust* **109C1**
Europa, I *Mozam Chan* **101D3**
Euskirchen *W Germ* **57B2**
Eutsuk L *Can* **13B2**
Evansburg *Can* **13D2**
Evans,C *Can* **6B1**
Evans,L *Can* **7C4**
Evans Str *Can* **6B3**
Evanston, Illinois *USA* **14A2**
Evanston, Wyoming *USA* **8B2**
Evansville, Indiana *USA* **11B3**
Evaton *S Africa* **101G1**
Everard,L *Aust* **106C4**
Everest,Mt *Nepal/China* **82C3**
Everett, Washington *USA* **8A2**
Everett,Mt *USA* **16C1**
Everglades,The, Swamp *USA* **11B4**
Evesham *Eng* **43D3**
Evinayong *Eq Guinea* **98B2**
Evje *Nor* **39F7**
Evolène *Switz* **47B1**
Évora *Port* **50A2**
Évreux *France* **48C2**
Évvoia, I *Greece* **55B3**
Ewo *Congo* **98B3**
Excelisor Mt *USA* **22C1**
Excelsior Springs *USA* **18B2**
Exeter, California *USA* **21B2**
Exeter *Eng* **43C4**
Exeter, New Hampshire *USA* **15D2**
Exmoor Nat Pk *Eng* **43C4**
Exmouth *Eng* **43C4**
Extremadura, Region *Spain* **50A2**
Exuma Sd *Bahamas* **25E2**
Eyasi, L *Tanz* **99D3**
Eyemouth *Scot* **42C2**
Eyl *Somalia* **99E2**
Eyre *Aust* **106B4**
Eyre Creek, R *Aust* **106C3**
Eyre,L *Aust* **106C3**
Eyre Pen *Aust* **106C4**
Eyte, I *Phil* **79B3**
Ezatlan *Mexico* **23A1**
Ezine *Turk* **55C3**

F

Faber L *Can* **4G3**
Fåborg *Den* **39G7**
Fabriano *Italy* **52B2**
Fachi *Niger* **95A3**
Fada *Chad* **95B3**
Fada N'Gourma *U Volta* **97C3**
Faenza *Italy* **52B2**
Faeringehavn *Greenland* **6E3**
Faeroerne, Is *N Atlantic* **36C2**
Fafa, R *CAR* **98B2**
Fafan, R *Eth* **99E2**
Făgăras *Rom* **54B1**
Fagnes, Region *Belg* **46C1**
Faguibine,L, L *Mali* **97B3**
Fahud *Oman* **91C5**
Faiol, I *Açores* **96A1**
Fairbanks *USA* **4D3**
Fairbault *USA* **7A5**
Fairborn *USA* **14B3**
Fairbury *USA* **8D2**
Fairfax *USA* **16A3**
Fairfield, California *USA* **21A2**
Fairfield, Connecticut *USA* **16C2**
Fairfield, Ohio *USA* **14B3**
Fair Head, Pt *N Ire* **45C1**
Fair Isle, I *Scot* **40C2**
Fairlie *NZ* **111B2**
Fairmont, W Virginia *USA* **14B3**
Fairview *Can* **13D1**
Fairweather,Mt *USA* **4E4**
Fais, I *Pacific O* **71F3**
Faisalabad *Pak* **84C2**
Faith *USA* **8C2**
Faither,The, Pen *Scot* **44D1**
Faizabad *Afghan* **84C1**
Faizābād *India* **86A1**
Fakenham *Eng* **43E3**
Faköping *Sweden* **39G7**
Falam *Burma* **86C2**
Falcon Res *USA/Mexico* **24C2**
Falémé, R *Mali/Sen* **97A3**

Falkenberg *Sweden* 39G7
Falkirk *Scot* 42C2
Falkland Is, Dependency *S Atlantic* 29D6
Falkland Sd *Falkland Is* 29E6
Fallbrook *USA* 22D4
Fallon *USA* 8B3
Fall River *USA* 15D2
Falls City *USA* 18A1
Falmouth *Eng* 43B4
Falmouth *Jamaica* 27H1
Falmouth, Massachusetts *USA* 16D2
False B *S Africa* 100A4
Falso,C *Mexico* 24A2
Falster, I *Den* 56C2
Fălticeni *Rom* 54C1
Falun *Sweden* 39H6
Famagusta *Cyprus* 92B2
Famenne, Region *Belg* 46C1
Fang *Thai* 76B2
Fangak *Sudan* 99D2
Fang liao *Taiwan* 73E5
Fano *Italy* 52B2
Faraday, Base *Ant* 112C3
Faradje *Zaïre* 99C2
Farafangana *Madag* 101D3
Farafra Oasis *Egypt* 95B2
Farah *Afghan* 80E2
Farallon de Medinilla, I *Pacific O* 71F2
Faranah *Guinea* 97A3
Faraulep, I *Pacific O* 71F3
Fareham *Eng* 43D4
Farewell,C *NZ* 107G5
Farewell Spit, Pt *NZ* 110B2
Fargo *USA* 8D2
Fari'a, R *Israel* 94B2
Faribault *USA* 10A2
Faridpur *Bang* 86B2
Farīmān *Iran* 90C2
Farmington, Missouri *USA* 18B2
Farmington, New Mexico *USA* 9C3
Farmington Res *USA* 22B2
Farne Deep *N Sea* 42D2
Farnham,Mt *Can* 13D2
Faro *Can* 12H2
Faro *Port* 50A2
Fåro, I *Sweden* 39H7
Farquhar, Is *Indian O* 89K9
Farrar, R *Scot* 44B3
Farrell *USA* 14B2
Fársala *Greece* 55B3
Fasā *Iran* 91B4
Fastnet Rock *Irish Rep* 45B3
Fastov *USSR* 60C3
Fatehpur *India* 86A1
Father *Can* 13D1
Fatima du Sul *Brazil* 30F2
Fauresmith *S Africa* 101G1
Faverges *France* 47B2
Fawn, R *Can* 7B4
Fax, R *Sweden* 38H6
Faxaflói, B *Iceland* 38A2
Faya *Chad* 95A3
Fayetteville, Arkansas *USA* 11A3
Fayetteville, N Carolina *USA* 11C3
Faylakah, I *Kuwait* 93E4
Fāzilka *India* 84C2
Fdérik *Maur* 96A2
Fear,C *USA* 11C3
Feather Middle Fork, R *USA* 21A2
Fécamp *France* 48C2
Federación *Arg* 34D2
Federal *Arg* 34D2
Federated States of Micronesia, Is *Pacific O* 71F3
Fehmarn, I *W Germ* 56C2
Feijó *Brazil* 32C5
Feilai Xai Bei Jiang, R *China* 73C5
Feilding *NZ* 110C2
Feira *Zambia* 100C2
Feira de Santan *Brazil* 31D4
Feke *Turk* 92C2
Feldkirch *Austria* 57B3
Feliciano, R *Arg* 34D2
Felixstowe *Eng* 41D3
Feltre *Italy* 47D1
Femund, L *Nor* 38G6
Fengcheng *China* 74A2
Fengdu *China* 73B4
Fenging *China* 72D1
Fengjie *China* 73B3
Feng Xian *China* 72B3
Fengzhen *China* 72C1
Fen He, R *China* 72C2
Fenoarivo Atsinanana *Madag* 101D2
Feodosiya *USSR* 60E5
Ferdow *Iran* 90C3
Fère-Champenoise *France* 46B2
Fergana *USSR* 82B2
Fermanagh, County *N Ire* 45C1
Fermoy *Irish Rep* 45B2
Fern, Mt *Austria* 47D1
Fernandina, I *Ecuador* 32J7
Fernandina Beach *USA* 17B1
Fernando de Noronha, I *Atlantic O* 103G5
Fernandópolis *Brazil* 35A2
Ferndale *USA* 20B1
Fernley *USA* 21B2
Ferrara *Italy* 52B2
Ferreñafe *Peru* 32B5
Ferriday *USA* 19B3
Fès *Mor* 96B1
Festus *USA* 18B2
Feteşti *Rom* 54C2
Fethiye *Turk* 92A2
Fetisovo *USSR* 61H5
Fetlar, I *Scot* 44D1
Feyzabad *Afghan* 65J6
Fianarantsoa *Madag* 101D3
Fiche *Eth* 99D2
Ficksburg *S Africa* 101G1
Fidenza *Italy* 47D2
Fier *Alb* 55A2
Fiera Di Primeiro *Italy* 47D1
Fife, Region *Scot* 44C3
Fife Ness, Pen *Scot* 44C3
Figeac *France* 48C3
Figueira da Foz *Port* 50A1
Figueras *Spain* 51C1
Figuig *Mor* 96B1
Fiji, Is *Pacific O* 105G4
Filadelfia *Par* 30D3
Filiaşi *Rom* 54B2
Filiatrá *Greece* 55B3
Filicudi, I *Italy* 53B3
Fillmore, California *USA* 21B3
Findhorn, R *Scot* 44B3
Findlay *USA* 10B2
Findlay,Mt *Can* 13D2
Finger Lakes *USA* 15C2
Fingoè *Mozam* 101C2
Finike *Turk* 92B2
Finke, R *Aust* 106C3
Finke Flood Flats *Aust* 108A1
Finland, Republic *N Europe* 64D3
Finland,G of *N Europe* 39J7
Finlay, R *Can* 5F4
Finlay Forks *Can* 5F4
Finley *Aust* 108C3
Finnsnes *Nor* 38H5
Finschhafen *PNG* 71F4
Finsteraarhorn, Mt *Switz* 47C1
Finsterwalde *E Germ* 56C2
Fintona *N Ire* 45C1
Fiordland Nat Pk *NZ* 111A3
Fiq *Syria* 94B2
Firat, R *Turk* 93C2
Firebaugh *USA* 22B2
Firenze *Italy* 52B2
Firmat *Arg* 34C2
Firozābād *India* 85D3
Firozpur *India* 84C2
Firspång *Sweden* 39H7
Firth of Clyde, Estuary *Scot* 42B2
Firth of Forth, Estuary *Scot* 44C3
Firth of Lorn, Estuary *Scot* 44A3
Firth of Tay, Estuary *Scot* 40C2
Firūzābād *Iran* 91B4
Fish, R *Namibia* 100A3
Fish Camp *USA* 22C2
Fishers I *USA* 16C2
Fisher Str *Can* 6B3
Fishguard *Wales* 43B4
Fiskenaesset *Greenland* 6E3
Fismes *France* 46B2
Fitchburg *USA* 15D2
Fitful Head, Pt *Scot* 44D2
Fitzgerald *USA* 17B1
Fitzroy, R *Aust* 106B2
Fitzroy Crossing *Aust* 106B2
Fitzwilliam I *Can* 14B1
Fizi *Zaïre* 99C3
Flagstaff *USA* 9B3
Flamborough Head, C *Eng* 42D2
Flaming Gorge Res *USA* 8C2
Flannan Isles, Is *Scot* 44A2
Flat, R *Can* 12J2
Flathead, R *USA* 13E3
Flathead L *USA* 8B2
Flat River *USA* 18B2
Flattery,C *USA* 8A2
Fleetwood *Eng* 42C3
Flekkefjord *Nor* 39F7
Fleming Deep *Pacific Oc* 69G4
Flemington *USA* 16B2
Flensburg *W Germ* 56B2
Fleurier *Switz* 47B1
Flinders, I *Aust* 106C4
Flinders, I *Aust* 107D4
Flinders, R *Aust* 107D2
Flinders Range, Mts *Aust* 106C4
Flin Flon *Can* 5H4
Flint *USA* 10B2
Flint *Wales* 42C3
Flint, R *USA* 11B3
Flixecourt *France* 46B1
Florala *USA* 17A1
Florence, Alabama *USA* 11B3
Florence, Kansas *USA* 18A2
Florence, Oregon *USA* 20B2
Florence, S Carolina *USA* 11C3
Florencia *Colombia* 32B3
Florenville *Belg* 46C2
Flores *Guatemala* 25D3
Flores, I *Açores* 96A1
Flores, I *Indon* 106B1
Flores, R *Arg* 34D3
Flores S *Indon* 70C4
Floriano *Brazil* 31C3
Florianópolis *Brazil* 30G4
Florida, State *USA* 25D2
Florida *Urug* 29E2
Florida B *USA* 17B2
Florida City *USA* 17B2
Florida Is *Solomon Is* 107E1
Florida Keys, Is *USA* 11B4
Florida,Strs of *USA* 11B4
Flórina *Greece* 55B2
Florø *Nor* 38F6
Fluchthorn, Mt *Austria* 47D1
Focsani *Rom* 54C1
Foggia *Italy* 53C2
Fogo, I *Cape Verde* 97A4
Foix *France* 48C3
Foley I *Can* 6C3
Foligno *Italy* 52B2
Folkestone *Eng* 43E4
Folkston *USA* 17B1
Follonica *Italy* 52B2
Folsom *USA* 22B1
Folsom L, L *USA* 22B1
Fond-du-Lac *Can* 5H4
Fond du Lac *USA* 10B2
Fontainebleau *France* 48C2
Fontenac *USA* 18B2
Fontenay-le-Comte *France* 48B2
Fonyód *Hung* 52C1
Foraker,Mt *USA* 12D2
Forbach *France* 46D2
Forbes *Aust* 109C2
Forcados *Nig* 97C4
Forde *Nor* 38F6
Fords Bridge *Aust* 108C1
Fordyce *USA* 19B3
Forécarian *Guinea* 97A4
Forel,Mt *Greenland* 6G3
Forest *Can* 14B2
Forest Park *USA* 17B1
Forestville *USA* 22A1
Forfar *Scot* 44C3
Forges-les-Eaux *France* 46A2
Forks *USA* 20B1
Forlì *Italy* 52B2
Formentera, I *Spain* 51C2
Formia *Italy* 53B2
Formigas, I *Açores* 96A1
Formosa *Arg* 30E4
Formosa *Brazil* 31B5
Formosa, State *Arg* 30D3
Formosa Str *Taiwan/China* 73D5
Fornovo di Taro *Italy* 47D2
Forres *Scot* 44C3
Forrest *Aust* 106B4
Forrest City *USA* 11A3
Forsayth *Aust* 107D2
Forssa *Fin* 39J6
Forster *Aust* 109D2
Forsyth, Missouri *USA* 18B2
Fort Abbas *Pak* 84C3
Fort Albany *Can* 7B4
Fortaleza *Brazil* 31D2
Fort Augustus *Scot* 44B3
Fort Beaufort *S Africa* 100B4
Fort Bragg *USA* 21A2
Fort Collins *USA* 8C2
Fort Coulogne *Can* 15C1
Fort de France *Martinique* 27E4
Fort Deposit *USA* 17A1
Fort Dodge *USA* 10A2
Fortescue, R *Aust* 106A3
Fort Frances *Can* 7A5
Fort Franklin *Can* 4F3
Fort George *Can* 7C4
Fort Good Hope *Can* 4F3
Fort Grey *Aust* 108B1
Forth, R *Scot* 44B3
Fort Hope *Can* 7B4
Fortin Uno *Arg* 34B3
Fort Laird *Can* 4F3
Fort Lallemand *Alg* 96C1
Fort Lauderdale *USA* 11B4
Fort Liard *Can* 4F3
Fort Mackay *Can* 5G4
Fort Macleod *Can* 5G5
Fort McMurray *Can* 5G4
Fort McPherson *Can* 4E3
Fort Madison *USA* 18B2
Fort Morgan *USA* 8C2
Fort Myers *USA* 11B4
Fort Nelson *Can* 5F4
Fort Norman *Can* 4F3
Fort Payne *USA* 17A1
Fort Peck Res *USA* 8C2
Fort Pierce *USA* 11B4
Fort Providence *Can* 4G3
Fort Resolution *Can* 5G3
Fort Rousset *Congo* 98B3

Fort Rupert Can 7C4
Fort St James Can 5F4
Fort St John Can 13C1
Fort Saskatchewan Can 13E2
Fort Scott USA 18B2
Fort Selkirk Can 4E3
Fort Severn Can 7B4
Fort Shevchenko USSR 61H5
Fort Simpson Can 4F3
Fort Smith Can 5G3
Fort Smith USA 11A3
Fort Stockton USA 9C3
Fortuna, California USA 20B2
Fort Vermillion Can 5G4
Fort Walton Beach USA 17A1
Fort Wayne USA 10B2
Fort William Scot 44B3
Fort Worth USA 9D3
Fortymile, R USA 12F2
Fort Yukon USA 12E1
Foshan China 73C5
Fossano Italy 47B2
Foster,Mt USA 12G3
Fougamou Gabon 98B3
Fougères France 48B2
Foulness I Eng 43E4
Foulwind,C NZ 111B2
Foumban Cam 98B2
Fourmies France 49C1
Foúrnoi, I Greece 55C3
Fouta Djallon, Mts Guinea 97A3
Foveaux, Str NZ 111B3
Fowey Eng 43B4
Fox Creek Can 13D2
Foxe Basin, G Can 6B3
Foxe Chan Can 6B3
Foxe Pen Can 6C3
Foxton NZ 110C2
Fox Valley Can 13F2
Foynes Irish Rep 45B2
Foz do Cuene Angola 100A2
Foz do Iquaçu Brazil 30F4
Frackville USA 16A2
Fraga Arg 34B2
Framingham USA 16D1
Franca Brazil 31B6
France, Republic Europe 49C2
Frances Can 10A2
Frances, R Can 12J2
France Ville Gabon 98B3
Franche Comté, Region France 49D2
Francistown Botswana 100B3
Francois L Can 13B2
Frankfort, Indiana USA 14A2
Frankfort, Kentucky USA 11B3
Frankfort S Africa 101G1
Frankfurt W Germ 57B2
Frankfurt am Main W Germ 46E1
Frankfurt-an-der-Oder E Germ 56C2
Fränkischer Alb, Upland W Germ 57C3
Franklin, Indiana USA 14A3
Franklin, Louisiana USA 19B4
Franklin, Massachusetts USA 16D1
Franklin, New Jersey USA 16B2
Franklin, Pennsylvania USA 14C2
Franklin, Region Can 4G2
Franklin B Can 4F2
Franklin D Roosevelt, L USA 20C1
Franklin Mts Can 4F3
Franklin Str Can 4J2
Frankovsk USSR 64D5
Franz Josef Glacier NZ 111B2
Fraser, R Can 5F5
Fraserburgh Scot 44C3
Fraser I Aust 109D1
Fraser L Can 13B2
Frasne France 47B1
Frauenfield Switz 47C1
Fray Bentos Urug 34D2
Frazerburgh Scot 40C2
Frederica USA 16B3
Fredericia Den 56B1
Frederick, Maryland USA 15C3
Fredericksburg, Virginia USA 15C3
Frederick Sd USA 12H3
Fredericktown USA 18B2
Fredericton Can 7D5
Frederikshab Greenland 6E3
Frederikshavn Den 39G7
Fredonia USA 15C2
Fredrikstad Nor 39G7
Freehold USA 16B2
Freeport Bahamas 26B1
Freeport, Texas USA 19A4
Freetown Sierra Leone 97A4
Freiburg W Germ 57B3
Freistadt Austria 57C3
Fremantle Aust 106A4
Fremont, California USA 22B2
Fremont, Nebraska USA 18A1
Fremont, Ohio USA 14B2
French Guiana, Dependency S America 33G3
Frenchmans Cap, Mt Aust 109C4
French Polynesia, Is Pacific O 105J4
Fresnillo Mexico 24B2
Fresno USA 8B3
Fresno, R USA 22C2
Fretigney France 47A1
Frévent France 46B1
Freycinet Pen Aust 109C4
Fria Guinea 97A3
Friant USA 22C2
Friant Dam USA 22C2
Fribourg Switz 52A1
Friedrichshafen W Germ 57B3
Frobisher B Can 6D3
Frobisher Bay Can 6D3
Frobisher L Can 5H4
Frolovo USSR 61F4
Frome Eng 43C4
Frome, R Aust 108A1
Frome, R Eng 43C4
Frome,L Aust 106C4
Frontera Mexico 25C3
Front Royal USA 15C3
Frosinone Italy 53B2
Frunze USSR 82B1
Fuchuan China 73C5
Fuding China 73E4
Fuerte, R Mexico 24B2
Fuerte Olimpo Par 30E3
Fuerteventura, I Canary Is 96A2
Fugu China 72C2
Fuhai China 68A2
Fujairah UAE 91C4
Fuji Japan 75B1
Fujian, Province China 73D4
Fujin China 69F2
Fujinomiya Japan 75B1
Fuji-san, Mt Japan 74D3
Fujisawa Japan 75B1
Fuji-Yoshida Japan 75B1
Fukang China 63A3
Fukuchiyima Japan 74C3
Fukui Japan 74D3
Fukuoka Japan 74C4
Fukushima Japan 74E3
Fukuyama Japan 74C4
Fulda W Germ 57B2
Fulda, R W Germ 57B2
Fuling China 73B4
Fullarton Trinidad 27L1
Fullerton USA 22D4
Fulton, Kentucky USA 18C2
Fulton, New York USA 15C2
Fumay France 46C1
Funabashi Japan 75C1
Funchal Medeira 96A1
Fundão Brazil 35C1
Fundy,B of Can 7D5
Funhalouro Mozam 101C3
Funing China 72D3
Funing China 73B5
Funtua Nig 97C3
Fuqing China 73D4
Furancungo Mozam 101C2
Fürg Iran 91C4
Furka, P Switz 47C1
Furneaux Group, Is Aust 107D5
Fürstenwalde E Germ 56C2
Fürth W Germ 57C3
Furukawa Japan 74D3
Fury and Hecla St Can 6B3
Fushun, Liaoning China 74A2
Fushun, Sichuan China 73A4
Fusong China 74B2
Füssen W Germ 57C3
Fu Xian China 72E2
Fuxin China 72E1
Fuyang China 72D3
Fuyuan, Liaoning China 72E1
Fuyuan, Yunnan China 73A4
Fuyun China 68A2
Fuzhou China 73D4
Fyn, I Den 56C1

G

Gaalkacyo Somalia 99E2
Gabbs USA 21B2
Gabela Angola 100A2
Gabe's Tunisia 96D1
Gabilan Range, Mts USA 22B2
Gabon, Republic Africa 98B3
Gaborone Botswana 100B3
Gabrovo Bulg 54C2
Gach Sārān Iran 91B3
Gadsden, Alabama USA 17A1
Gads L Can 10A1
Gaeta Italy 53B2
Gaferut, I Pacific O 71F3
Gafsa Tunisia 96C1
Gagarin USSR 60D2
Gagnon Can 7D4
Gagra USSR 61F5
Gaibanda India 86B1
Gaimán Arg 29C4
Gainesville, Florida USA 17B2
Gainesville, Georgia USA 17B1
Gainesville, Texas USA 19A3
Gainsborough Eng 42D3
Gairdner,L Aust 108A2
Gairloch Scot 44B3
Gaithersburg USA 16A3
Gajendragarh India 87B1
Ga Jiang, R China 73D4
Galadi Eth 99E2
Galana, R Kenya 99D3
Galapagos Is Pacific O 103D5
Galashiels Scot 42C2
Galaţi Rom 54C1
Galena, Alaska USA 4C3
Galena, Kansas USA 18B2
Galeota Pt Trinidad 27L1
Galera Pt Trinidad 27L1
Galesburg USA 10A2
Galeton USA 15C2
Galich USSR 61F2
Galicia, Region Spain 50A1
Galina Pt Jamaica 27J1
Gallabat Sudan 99D1
Gallarate Italy 47C2
Galle Sri Lanka 87C3
Gállego, R Spain 51B1
Gallipoli Italy 55A2
Gällivare Sweden 38J5
Galloway, District 42B2
Galloway,Mull of, C Scot 42B2
Gallup USA 8C3
Galt USA 22B1
Galveston USA 25C2
Galveston B USA 11A4
Galvez Arg 34C2
Galvi Corse 49D3
Galway, County Irish Rep 45B2
Galway Irish Rep 41B3
Galway, B Irish Rep 41B3
Gamba China 86B1
Gambaga Ghana 97B3
Gambell USA 4A3
Gambia, R The Gambia/Sen 97A3
Gambia,The, Republic Africa 97A3
Gamboma Congo 98B3
Gambos Angola 100A2
Gampola Sri Lanka 87C3
Ganale Dorya, R Eth 99E2
Gananoque Can 15C2
Ganda Angola 100A2
Gandajika Zaïre 98C3
Gandava Pak 84B3
Gander Can 7E5
Gāndhīdhām India 85C4
Gāndhīnagar India 85C4
Gāndhi Sāgar, L India 85D4
Gandia Spain 51B2
Ganga, R India 86B2
Ganganar India 85C3
Gangaw Burma 86C2
Gangca China 72A2
Gangdise Shan, Mts China 82C2
Gangtok India 86B1
Gangu China 72B3
Gannett Peak, Mt USA 8C2
Ganquan China 72B2
Gantheaume, C Aust 108A3
Gantseviohi USSR 39K8
Ganzhou China 73D4
Gao Mali 97C3
Gaolan China 72A2
Gaoping China 72C2
Gaoua U Volta 97B3
Gaoual Guinea 97A3
Gaoyou Hu, L China 72D3
Gaozhou China 73C5
Gap France 49D3
Gapan Phil 79B2
Gar China 84D2
Garah Aust 109C1
Garanhuns Brazil 31D3
Garberville USA 21A1
Garça Brazil 35B2
Garcias Brazil 35A2
Garda Italy 47D2
Garden City USA 9C3
Garden Pen USA 14A1
Gardey Arg 34D3
Gardez Afghan 84B2
Gardiners I USA 16C2
Gardner USA 16D1
Gardone Italy 47D2
Gardula Eth 99D2
Gargano Italy 47D2
Garhākota India 85D4
Gari USSR 61K2
Garies S Africa 100A4
Garissa Kenya 99D3
Garland USA 19A3

Garmisch-Partenkirchen *W Germ* 57C3
Garmsar *Iran* 90B2
Garnett *USA* 18A2
Garnett Peak, Mt *USA* 8B2
Garonne, R *France* 48C3
Garry, R *Scot* 44B3
Garut *Indon* 78B4
Garwa *India* 86A2
Gary *USA* 14A2
Garyarsa *China* 82C2
Gary L *Can* 4H3
Garza-Little Elm, Res *USA* 19A3
Gasan Kuli *USSR* 90B2
Gascogne, Region *France* 48B3
Gasconade, R *USA* 18B2
Gascoyne, R *Aust* 106A3
Gashaka *Nig* 98B2
Gashua *Nig* 97D3
Gaspé *Can* 10D2
Gaspé,C *Can* 10D2
Gaspé Pen *Can* 10D2
Gata,C *Cyprus* 94A1
Gatchina *USSR* 60C2
Gateshead *Eng* 42D2
Gatesville *USA* 19A3
Gatineau *Can* 15C1
Gatineau, R *Can* 15C1
Gatton *Aust* 109D1
Gauháti *India* 86C1
Gauja, R *USSR* 58C1
Gauri Phanta *India* 86A1
Gaviota *USA* 22B3
Gävle *Sweden* 39H6
Gawler Ranges, Mts *Aust* 108A2
Gaxun Nur, L *China* 72A1
Gaya *India* 86A2
Gaya *Niger* 97C3
Gaylord *USA* 14B1
Gayndah *Aust* 109D1
Gayny *USSR* 61H1
Gaysin *USSR* 60C4
Gaza *Israel* 92B3
Gaziantep *Turk* 92C2
Gbaringa *Lib* 97B4
Gdańsk *Pol* 58B2
Gdansk *Sweden* 88F2
Gdańsk,G of *Pol* 58B2
Gdov *USSR* 39K7
Gdynia *Pol* 58B2
Gebel Halâl, Mt *Egypt* 94A3
Gebel Hamata, Mt *Egypt* 95C2
Gebel Katherina, Mt *Egypt* 92B4
Gebel Libni, Mt *Egypt* 94A3
Gebel Maghâra, Mt *Egypt* 94A3
Gedaref *Sudan* 99D1
Gediz, R *Turk* 55C3
Gedser *Den* 56C2
Geel *Belg* 46C1
Geelong *Aust* 108B3
Geeveston *Aust* 109C4
Geidam *Nig* 97D3
Geilenkirchen *W Germ* 46D1
Geita *Tanz* 99D3
Gejiu *China* 73A5
Gela *Italy* 53B3
Geldern *W Germ* 46D1
Gelibolu *Turk* 55C2
Gelidonya Burun *Turk* 92B2
Gelsenkirchen *W Germ* 46D1
Gelting *W Germ* 39F8
Gemas *Malay* 77C5
Gembloux *Belg* 46C1
Gemena *Zaïre* 98B2
Gemerek *Turk* 92C2
Gemlik *Turk* 92A1
Gemona *Italy* 52B1
Gemsbok, Nat Pk *Botswana* 100B3
Geneina *Sudan* 98C1
General Acha *Arg* 34C3
General Alvear, Buenos Aires *Arg* 34C3
General Alvear, Mendoza *Arg* 34B2
General Arenales *Arg* 34C2
General Belgrano *Arg* 34D3
General Belgrano, Base *Ant* 112B2
General Bernardo O'Higgins, Base *Ant* 112C2
General Conesa, Buenos Aires *Arg* 34D3
General Eugenio A Garay *Par* 30D3
General Guido *Arg* 34D3
General La Madrid *Arg* 34C3
General Levalle *Arg* 34C2
General Manuel Belgrano, Mt *Arg* 30C4
General Paz, Buenos Aires *Arg* 34D3
General Pico *Arg* 34C3
General Pinto *Arg* 34C2
General Pirán *Arg* 34D3
General Roca *Arg* 29C3
General Santos *Phil* 79C4
General Viamonte *Arg* 34C3
General Villegas *Arg* 34C3
Genesee, R *USA* 15C2
Geneseo *USA* 15C2
Geneva, Nebraska *USA* 18A1
Geneva, New York *USA* 15C2
Genève *Switz* 52A1
Genil, R *Spain* 50B2
Genoa *Aust* 109C3
Genova *Italy* 52A2
Genovesa, I *Ecuador* 32J7
Gent *Belg* 46B1
Genteng *Indon* 78B4
Genthin *E Germ* 56C2
Geokchay *USSR* 93E1
George *S Africa* 100B4
George, R *Can* 7D4
George,L *Aust* 109C2
George,L, Florida *USA* 17B2
George,L, New York *USA* 15D2
George Sd *NZ* 111A2
George Town *Aust* 109C4
Georgetown, Delaware *USA* 15C3
Georgetown *Guyana* 33F2
Georgetown, Kentucky *USA* 14B3
George Town *Malay* 77C4
Georgetown *St Vincent* 27N2
Georgetown, S Carolina *USA* 17C1
Georgetown, Texas *USA* 19A3
Georgetown *The Gambia* 97A3
George V Land, Region *Ant* 112C8
Georgia, State *USA* 17B1
Georgian B *Can* 14B1
Georgia,Str of *Can* 13C3
Georgina, R *Aust* 106C3
Georgiu-Dezh *USSR* 60E3
Georgiyevsk *USSR* 61F5
Gera *E Germ* 57C2
Geraardsbergen *Belg* 46B1
Geraldine *NZ* 111B2
Geraldton *Aust* 106A3
Geraldton *Can* 10B2
Gerar, R *Israel* 94B3
Gerdine,Mt *USA* 4C3
Gerdova Peak, Mt *USA* 12E2
Gerik *Malay* 77C4
Gerlachovsky, Mt *Pol* 60B4
Germanson Lodge *Can* 13C1
Germiston *S Africa* 101G1
Gerolstein *W Germ* 46D1
Gerona *Spain* 51C1
Geseke *W Germ* 46E1
Gestro, R *Eth* 99E2
Getafe *Spain* 50B1
Gettysburg, Pennsylvania *USA* 16A3
Gevaş *Turk* 93D2
Gevgeliija *Yugos* 55B2
Gex *France* 47B1
Ghabāghib *Syria* 94C2
Ghadamis *Libya* 96C1
Ghaem Shahr *Iran* 90B2
Ghāghara, R *India* 86A1
Ghana, Republic *Africa* 97B4
Ghanzi *Botswana* 100B3
Ghardaïa *Alg* 96C1
Gharyan *Libya* 95A1
Ghāt *Libya* 95A2
Ghāziābād *India* 84D3
Ghazi Khan *Pak* 84C3
Ghazni *Afghan* 84B2
Gheorgheni *Rom* 54C1
Gheorghiu G Dei *Rom* 54C1
Ghudamis *Alg* 88E4
Ghurian *Afghan* 90D3
Gialo *Libya* 95B2
Giamame *Somalia* 99E2
Giarre *Italy* 53C3
Gibeon *Namibia* 100A3
Gibraltar, Colony *SW Europe* 50A2
Gibraltar,Str of *Spain/Africa* 50A2
Gibson Desert *Aust* 106B3
Gibsons *Can* 20B1
Giddalūr *India* 87B1
Giessen *W Germ* 57B2
Gifford *USA* 17B2
Gifu *Japan* 74D3
Gigha, I *Scot* 42B2
Giglio, I *Italy* 52B2
Gijón *Spain* 50A1
Gilbert, R *Aust* 107D2
Gilbert,Mt *Can* 13C2
Gilé *Mozam* 101C2
Gilead, Region *Jordan* 94B2
Gilf Kebir Plat *Egypt* 95B2
Gilgandra *Aust* 109C2
Gilgit *Pak* 84C1
Gilgit, R *Pak* 84C1
Gilgunnia *Aust* 108C2
Gillam *Can* 7A4
Gilles, L *Aust* 108A2
Gill I *Can* 13B2
Gills Rock *USA* 14A1
Gilman *USA* 14A2
Gilroy *USA* 22B2
Gimli *Can* 8D1
Gingindlovu *S Africa* 101H1
Gingoog *Phil* 79C4
Ginir *Eth* 99E2
Gióna, Mt *Greece* 55B3
Gippsland, Mts *Aust* 109C3
Girard *USA* 14B2
Girardot *Colombia* 32C3
Girdle Ness, Pen *Scot* 44C3
Giresun *Turk* 93C1
Gir Hills *India* 85C4
Giri, R *Zaïre* 98B2
Girīdīh *India* 86B2
Gironde, R *France* 48B2
Girvan *Scot* 42B2
Gisborne *NZ* 111C2
Gisors *France* 46A2
Gitega *Burundi* 99C3
Giurgiu *Rom* 54C2
Givet *Belg* 46C1
Gizycko *Pol* 58C2
Gjirokastër *Alb* 55B2
Gjoatlaven *Can* 4J3
Gjøvik *Nor* 39G6
Glace Bay *Can* 7D5
Glacier Bay Nat Mon *USA* 12G3
Glacier Nat Pk, USA/Can *USA* 13E3
Glacier Peak, Mt *USA* 20B1
Glacier Str *Can* 6B2
Gladstone, Queensland *Aust* 107E3
Gladstone, S Aust *Aust* 108A2
Gladstone, Tasmania *Aust* 109C4
Gladstone *USA* 14A1
Glama, Mt *Iceland* 38A1
Glåma, R *Nor* 39G6
Glan, R *W Germ* 46D2
Glarner, Mts *Switz* 47C1
Glarus *Switz* 47C1
Glasco *USA* 18A2
Glasgow, Montana *USA* 8C2
Glasgow *Scot* 42B2
Glassboro *USA* 16B3
Glastonbury *Eng* 43C4
Glazov *USSR* 61H2
Gleisdorf *Austria* 59B3
Glen Afton *NZ* 110C1
Glen Burnie *USA* 16A3
Glencoe *S Africa* 101H1
Glendale, Arizona *USA* 9B3
Glendale, California *USA* 22C3
Glenhallen *USA* 12E2
Glen Innes *Aust* 109D1
Glenmorgan *Aust* 109C1
Glenreagh *Aust* 109D2
Glen Rock *USA* 16A3
Glen Rose *USA* 19A3
Glenrothes *UK* 44C3
Glens Falls *USA* 15D2
Glenties *Irish Rep* 45B1
Glenwood, Arkansas *USA* 19B3
Glenwood Springs *USA* 8C3
Glittertind, Mt *Nor* 39F6
Gliwice *Pol* 59B2
Globe *USA* 9B3
Głogów *Pol* 58B2
Glomfjord *Nor* 38G5
Gloucester *Aust* 109D2
Gloucester *Eng* 43C4
Gloucester *USA* 16D1
Glubokoye *USSR* 58D1
Glukhov *USSR* 60D3
Gmünd *Austria* 59B3
Gmunden *Austria* 57C3
Gniezno *Pol* 58B2
Goabeg *Namibia* 100A3
Goa, Daman and Diu, Union Territory *India* 87A1
Goālpāra *India* 86C1
Goba *Eth* 99D2
Gobabis *Namibia* 100A3
Gobernador Crespo *Arg* 34C2
Gobernador Duval *Arg* 34B3
Gobi, Desert *China/Mongolia* 72B1
Gobo *Japan* 75B2
Godag *India* 87B1
Godāvari, R *India* 87C1
Goderich *Can* 14B2
Godhavn *Greenland* 6E3
Godhra *India* 85C4
Godoy Cruz *Arg* 34B2
Gods L *Can* 7A4
Godthab *Greenland* 6E3
Goiandira *Brazil* 35B1
Goianésia *Brazil* 35B1
Goiânia *Brazil* 35B1
Goiás *Brazil* 35A1
Goiás, State *Brazil* 31B4
Goio-Erê *Brazil* 35A2
Gojab, R *Eth* 99D2
Gökçeada, I *Turk* 55C2
Göksun *Turk* 92C2
Gol, R *USSR* 63C3
Golāghāt *India* 86C1
Gölbaşi *Turk* 93C2

Golconda *USA* **20C2**
Gold Beach *USA* **20B2**
Gold Coast *Aust* **109D1**
Golden *Can* **13D2**
Golden B *NZ* **110B2**
Goldendale *USA* **20B1**
Golden Gate, Chan *USA* **22A2**
Golden Meadow *USA* **19B4**
Goldfield *USA* **21B2**
Gold River *Can* **13B3**
Goleniów *Pol* **56C2**
Goleta *USA* **22C3**
Golfe d'Ajaccio, G *Corse* **52A2**
Golfe de Gabes, G *Tunisia* **96D1**
Golfe de St Florent, G *Corse* **52A2**
Golfe de St-Malo, B *France* **48B2**
Golfe du Lion, G *France* **49C3**
Golfo Corcovado, G *Chile* **29B4**
Golfo de Almeira, G *Spain* **50B2**
Golfo de Ancud, G *Chile* **29B4**
Golfo de Batabano, G *Cuba* **25D2**
Golfo de Cadiz, G *Spain* **50A2**
Golfo de Cagliari, G *Sardegna* **53A3**
Golfo de California, G *Mexico* **24A1**
Golfo de Chiriqui, G *Panama* **25D4**
Golfo de Fonseca *Honduras* **25D3**
Golfo de Guacanayabo, G *Cuba* **26B2**
Golfo de Guayaquil, G *Ecuador* **32A4**
Golfo del Darien, G *Colombia/Panama* **26B5**
Golfo de los Mosquitos, G *Panama* **32A2**
Golfo del Papagaya, G *Nic* **25D3**
Golfo de Mazarrón, G *Spain* **51B2**
Golfo de Nicoya, G *Costa Rica* **25D4**
Golfo de Oristano, G *Sardegna* **53A3**
Golfo de Panamá, G *Panama* **25E4**
Golfo de Papagayo, G *Costa Rica* **25D3**
Golfo de Paria, G *Ven* **27E4**
Golfo de Penas, G *Chile* **29B5**
Golfo de St Florent *Corse* **49D3**
Golfo de San Jorge, G *Spain* **51C1**
Golfo de Tehuantepec G *Mexico* **24C3**
Golfo de Torugas, G *Colombia* **32B3**
Golfo de Uraba, G *Colombia* **32B2**
Golfo de Valencia, G *Spain* **51C2**
Golfo de Venezuela, G *Ven* **27C4**
Golfo di Genova, G *Italy* **52A2**
Golfo di Policastro, G *Italy* **53C3**
Golfo di Squillace, G *Italy* **53C3**
Golfo di Taranto, G *Italy* **53C2**
Golfo di Venezia, G *Italy* **52B1**
Golfo Dulce, G *Costa Rica* **25D4**
Golfo San Jorge, G *Arg* **29C5**
Golfo San Matías, G *Arg* **29D4**
Golmud *China* **68B3**
Golocha *Eth* **99E2**
Golovin B *USA* **12B2**
Golovnino *USSR* **74F2**
Goma *Zaïre* **99C3**
Gombe *Nig* **97D3**
Gomel *USSR* **60D3**
Gomera, I *Canary Is* **96A2**
Gómez Palacio *Mexico* **24B2**
Gonam, R *USSR* **63E2**
Gonbad-e Kāvūs *Iran* **90C2**
Gonda *India* **86A1**
Gondal *India* **85C4**
Gondar *Eth* **99D1**
Gönen *Turk* **92A1**
Gonen, R *Turk* **55C3**
Gongga Shan, Mt *China* **73A4**
Gonghe *China* **72A2**
Gongola, R *Nig* **97D3**
Gonzales, California *USA* **22B2**
Gonzales, Texas *USA* **19A4**
Gonzalez Chaves *Arg* **34C3**
Good Hope Mt *Can* **13C2**
Goodland *USA* **8C2**
Goodnews Bay *USA* **12B3**
Goodooga, R *Aust* **109C1**
Goole *Eng* **42D3**
Goolgowi *Aust* **108C2**
Goolwa *Aust* **108A3**
Goomalling *Aust* **106A4**
Goombalie *Aust* **108C2**
Goomer *Aust* **109D1**
Goomeri *Aust* **109D1**
Goondiwindi *Aust* **109D1**
Goose Bay *Can* **7E4**
Goose Creek *USA* **17C1**
Goose L *USA* **20B2**
Gooty *India* **87B1**
Gora Munku Sardyk, Mt *USSR* **63C2**
Goražde *Yugos* **54A2**
Gordon *USA* **4D3**
Gordon L *Can* **13E1**
Gordonsville *USA* **15C3**
Goré *Chad* **98B2**
Gore *Eth* **99D2**
Gore *NZ* **111A3**
Gore Topko, Mt *USSR* **63F2**
Gorey *Irish Rep* **45C2**
Gorgān *Iran* **90B2**
Goris *USSR* **93E2**
Gorizia *Italy* **52B1**
Gor'kiy *USSR* **65F4**
Gor'kovskoye Vodokhranilishche, Res *USSR* **61F2**
Gorlitz *E Germ* **57C2**
Gorlovka *USSR* **60E4**
Gorman *USA* **22C3**
Gorna Orjahovica *Bulg* **54C2**
Gorno-Altaysk *USSR* **68A1**
Gornozavodsk *USSR* **69G2**
Gorodets *USSR* **61F2**
Gorodok, Ukrainskaya S.S.R. *USSR* **59C3**
Gorodok, Ukrainskaya S.S.R. *USSR* **59D3**
Goroka *PNG* **71F4**
Gorokhpur *India* **86A1**
Gorongosa *Mozam* **101C2**
Gorontalo *Indon* **71D3**
Goro Yurma, Mt *USSR* **61K2**
Gort *Irish Rep* **45B2**
Goryachinsk *USSR* **63C2**
Goryn', R *USSR* **59D3**
Góry Świetokrzyskie, Upland *Pol* **59C2**
Gory Tel'pos-iz', Mt *USSR* **64G3**
Gorzow Wielkopolski *Pol* **39H8**
Goshogawara *Japan* **74E2**
Gospić *Yugos* **52C2**
Gostivar *Yugos* **54B2**
Gostynin *Pol* **58B2**
Göteborg *Sweden* **39G7**
Gotel, Mts *Nig* **98B2**
Gotland, I *Sweden* **39H7**
Gotō-retto, I *Japan* **74B4**
Gotska Sandön, I *Sweden* **39H7**
Gōtsu *Japan* **74C3**
Gottwaldov *Czech* **59B3**
Goudoumaria *Niger* **98B1**
Gough I *Atlantic O* **103H7**
Goulburn *Aust* **109C2**
Goumbou *Mali* **97B3**
Goundam *Mali* **97B3**
Gouré *Niger* **98B1**
Gourma Rharous *Mali* **97B3**
Gournay-en-Bray *France* **46A2**
Gouro *Chad* **95A3**
Gove Pen *Aust* **71E5**
Goverla, Mt *USSR* **60B4**
Governador Valadares *Brazil* **35C1**
Govind Ballabh Paht Sāgar, L *India* **86A2**
Gowanda *USA* **15C2**
Gowārān *Afghan* **84B3**
Goya *Arg* **30E4**
Goz-Beída *Chad* **98C1**
Gozo, I *Medit S* **53B3**
Goz Regeb *Sudan* **95C3**
Graaff-Reinet *S Africa* **100B4**
Gracefield *Can* **15C1**
Grafton *Aust* **109D1**
Grafton, N Dakota *USA* **8D2**
Grafton, W Virginia *USA* **14B3**
Graham, I *Can* **5E4**
Graham, R *Can* **13C1**
Graham L *Can* **13E1**
Grahamstown *S Africa* **100B4**
Grajaú *Brazil* **31B3**
Grajewo *Pol* **58C2**
Grámmos, Mt *Greece/Alb* **55B2**
Grampian, Region *Scot* **44C3**
Grampian, Mts *Scot* **44B3**
Granada *Colombia* **32C3**
Granada *Nic* **25D3**
Granada *Spain* **50B2**
Granby *Can* **15D1**
Gran Canaria, I *Canary Is* **96A2**
Gran Chaco, Region *Arg* **30D4**
Grand, R, Michigan *USA* **14A2**
Grand, R, Missouri *USA* **18B1**
Grand B *Dominica* **27Q2**
Grand Bahama, I *Bahamas* **11C4**
Grand Bank *Can* **7E5**
Grand Banks *Atlantic O* **102F2**
Grand Bassam *Ivory Coast* **97B4**
Grand Canyon *USA* **9B3**
Grand Cayman, I *Caribbean* **26A3**
Grand Centre *Can* **13E2**
Grand Coulee *USA* **20C1**
Grande, R *Arg* **34B3**
Grande, R, Bahia *Brazil* **31C4**
Grande, R, Minas Gerais/São Paulo *Brazil* **35B1**
Grande Cache *Can* **13D2**
Grande Chartreuse, Region *France* **47A2**
Grande Comore, I *Comoros* **101D2**
Grande Prairie *Can* **13D1**
Grande Prairie *USA* **19A3**
Grand Erg de Bilma, Desert *Niger* **95A3**
Grand erg Occidental, Mts *Alg* **96B2**
Grand erg Oriental, Mts *Alg* **96C2**
Grande Rivière de la Baleine, R *Can* **7C4**
Grande Ronde, R *USA* **20C1**
Grand Falls, New Brunswick *Can* **7D5**
Grand Falls, Newfoundland *Can* **7E5**
Grand Forks *Can* **20C1**
Grand Forks *USA* **8D2**
Grand Gorge *USA* **16B1**
Grand Haven *USA* **14A2**
Grand Isle *USA* **19C3**
Grand L *USA* **19B4**
Grand Mère *Can* **15D1**
Grāndola *Port* **50A2**
Grand Rapids *Can* **5J4**
Grand Rapids, Michigan *USA* **14A2**
Grand Rapids, Minnesota *USA* **10A2**
Grand St Bernard, P *Italy/Switz* **47B2**
Grand Teton, Mt *USA* **8B2**
Grand Teton Nat Pk *USA* **8B2**
Grandvilliers *France* **46A2**
Grangeburg *USA* **25D1**
Granollérs *Spain* **51C1**
Gran Paradiso, Mt *Italy* **52A1**
Gran Pilastro, Mt *Austria/Italy* **47D1**
Grantham *Eng* **43D3**
Grant,Mt *USA* **21B2**
Grantown-on-Spey *Scot* **44C3**
Grants *USA* **9C3**
Grants Pass *USA* **20B2**
Granville *France* **48B2**
Granville L *Can* **5H4**
Grão Mogol *Brazil* **35C1**
Grasse *France* **49D3**
Grass Valley *USA* **21A2**
Gravelbourg *Can* **5H5**
Gravelines *France* **46B1**
Gravelotte *S Africa* **100C3**
Gravenhurst *Can* **15C2**
Gravesend *Aust* **109D1**
Gravina I *USA* **12H3**
Grayling *USA* **12B2**
Grays Harbor, B *USA* **20B1**
Grayson *USA* **14B3**
Grayville *USA* **18C2**
Graz *Austria* **59B3**
Great, R *Jamaica* **27H1**
Great Abaco, I *Bahamas* **11C4**
Great Australian Bight, G *Aust* **106B4**
Great B, New Jersey *USA* **16B3**
Great Bahama Bank *Bahamas* **25E2**
Great Barrier I *NZ* **110C1**
Great Barrier Reef, Is *Aust* **107D2**
Great Barrington *USA* **16C1**
Great Bear L *Can* **4F3**
Great Bend *USA* **9D2**
Great Dividing Range, Mts *Aust* **107D3**
Great Driffield *Eng* **42D2**
Great Egg Harbor, B *USA* **16B3**
Greater Antarctic, Region *Ant* **112B10**

Greater Antilles, Is *Caribbean* **26B2**
Greater London, Metropolitan County *Eng* **43D4**
Greater Manchester, Metropolitan County *Eng* **43C3**
Great Exuma, I *Bahamas* **25E2**
Great Falls *USA* **8B2**
Great Glen, V *Scot* **44B3**
Great Himalayan Range, Mts *Asia* **86B1**
Great Inagua, I *Bahamas* **11C4**
Great Karroo, Mts *S Africa* **100B4**
Great L *Aust* **109C4**
Great Namaland, Region *Namibia* **100A3**
Great Ormes Head, C *Wales* **42C3**
Great Ragged, I *Bahamas* **11C4**
Great Ruaha, R *Tanz* **99D3**
Great Sacandaga L *USA* **15D2**
Great Salt L *USA* **8B2**
Great Sand Sea *Libya/Egypt* **95B2**
Great Sandy Desert *Aust* **106B3**
Great Sandy Desert *USA* **8A2**
Great Slave L *Can* **4G3**
Great South B *USA* **16C2**
Great Victoria Desert *Aust* **106B3**
Great Wall *China* **72B2**
Great Yarmouth *Eng* **43E3**
Greco,C *Cyprus* **94B1**
Greece, Republic *Europe* **55B3**
Greece *USA* **15C2**
Greeley *USA* **8C2**
Greely Fjord *Can* **6B1**
Green B *USA* **14A1**
Green Bay *USA* **14A2**
Greencastle, Indiana *USA* **14A3**
Greenfield, Massachusetts *USA* **16C1**
Greenfield, Wisconsin *USA* **14A2**
Green Lake *Can* **13F2**
Greenland, Dependency *N Atlantic* **6F2**
Greenland Basin *Greenland S* **102H1**
Greenland S *Greenland* **1B1**
Greenock *Scot* **42B2**
Greenport *USA* **16C2**
Greensboro, Maryland *USA* **16B3**
Greensboro, N Carolina *USA* **11C3**
Greensburg, Pennsylvania *USA* **15C2**
Greenstone, Pt *Scot* **44B3**
Greenup *USA* **18C2**
Greenville, Alabama *USA* **17A1**
Greenville *Lib* **97B4**
Greenville, Mississippi *USA* **19B3**
Greenville, N Hampshire *USA* **16D1**
Greenville, Ohio *USA* **14B2**
Greenville, S Carolina *USA* **17B1**
Greenville, Texas *USA* **19A3**
Greenwich *Eng* **43E4**
Greenwich *USA* **16C2**
Greenwood, Delaware *USA* **16B3**
Greenwood, Mississippi *USA* **19B3**
Greenwood, S Carolina *USA* **17B1**
Greers Ferry L *USA* **18B2**
Gregory,L *Aust* **108A1**
Gregory Range, Mts *Aust* **107D2**
Greifswald *E Germ* **56C2**
Gremikha *USSR* **64F3**
Grenå *Den* **56C1**
Grenada *USA* **19C3**
Grenada, I *Caribbean* **27E4**
Grenadines,The, Is *Caribbean* **27E4**
Grenfell *Aust* **109C2**
Grenoble *France* **49D2**
Grenville *Grenada* **27M2**
Grenville,C *Aust* **107D2**
Gresham *USA* **20B1**
Gresik, Jawa *Indon* **78C4**
Gresik, Sumatera *Indon* **78A3**
Gretna *USA* **19B4**
Grey, R *NZ* **111B2**
Grey Hunter Pk, Mt *Can* **12G2**
Grey Is *Can* **7E4**
Greylock,Mt *USA* **16C1**
Greymouth *NZ* **111B2**
Grey Range, Mts *Aust* **107D3**
Greystones *Irish Rep* **45C2**
Greytown *S Africa* **101H1**
Griekwastad *S Africa* **101F1**
Griffin *USA* **17B1**
Griffith *Aust* **108C2**
Grim,C *Aust* **107D5**
Grimsby *Can* **15C2**
Grimsby *Eng* **42D3**
Grimsey, I *Iceland* **38B1**
Grimshaw *Can* **13D1**
Grimstad *Nor* **39F7**
Grindelwald *Switz* **47C1**
Grinnell Pen *Can* **6A2**
Grise Fjord *Can* **6B2**
Griva *USSR* **61H1**
Grobina *USSR* **39J7**
Grodno *USSR* **58C2**
Gromati, R *India* **86A1**
Groningen *Neth* **56B2**
Groote Eylandt, I *Aust* **106C2**
Grootfontein *Namibia* **100A2**
Grootvloer, Salt L *S Africa* **100B3**
Gros Islet *St Lucia* **27P2**
Grosser Feldberg, Mt *W Germ* **46E1**
Grosseto *Italy* **52B2**
Gross-Gerau *W Germ* **46E2**
Grossglockner, Mt *Austria* **57C3**
Gross Venediger, Mt *Austria* **47E1**
Grosvenor,L *USA* **12C3**
Groveland *USA* **22B2**
Grover City *USA* **21A2**
Groveton *USA* **15D2**
Groznyy *USSR* **61G5**
Grudziadz *Pol* **58B2**
Grünau *Namibia* **100A3**
Grutness *Scot* **44D2**
Gruzinskaya SSR, Republic *USSR* **65F5**
Gryazi *USSR* **61F3**
Gryazovets *USSR* **61E2**
Grytviken *South Georgia* **29G8**
Gt Blasket, I *Irish Rep* **45A2**
Guaçuí *Brazil* **35C2**
Guadalajara *Mexico* **23A1**
Guadalajara *Spain* **50B1**
Guadalcanal, I *Solomon Is* **107E1**
Guadalimar, R *Spain* **50B2**
Guadalope, R *Spain* **51B1**
Guadalqivir, R *Spain* **50B2**
Guadalupe *Mexico* **24B2**
Guadalupe, I *Mexico* **3G6**
Guadeloupe, I *Caribbean* **27E3**
Guadian, R *Spain* **50B2**
Guadiana, R *Port* **50A2**
Guadix *Spain* **50B2**
Guajará Mirim *Brazil* **32D6**
Guajira,Pen de *Colombia* **32C1**
Gualaceo *Ecuador* **32B4**
Gualeguay *Arg* **34D2**
Gualeguaychú *Arg* **34D2**
Guam, I *Pacific O* **71F2**
Guamini *Arg* **34C3**
Gua Musang *Malay* **77C5**
Guanajuato *Mexico* **23A1**
Guanajuato, State *Mexico* **23A1**
Guanare *Ven* **32D2**
Guane *Cuba* **25D2**
Guangdong, Province *China* **73C5**
Guanghan *China* **73A3**
Guanghua *China* **72C3**
Guangmao Shan, Mt *China* **73A4**
Guangnan *China* **73B5**
Guangyuan *China* **72B3**
Guangze *China* **73D4**
Guangzhou *China* **67F3**
Guanhães *Brazil* **35C1**
Guania, R *Colombia* **32D3**
Guanipa, R *Ven* **27E5**
Guantánamo *Cuba* **26B2**
Guanting Shuiku, Res *China* **72D1**
Guanxi, Province *China* **73B5**
Guan Xian *China* **73A3**
Guapa *Colombia* **32B2**
Guaporé, R *Brazil/Bol* **33E6**
Guaquí *Bol* **30C2**
Guaranda *Ecuador* **32B4**
Guarapuava *Brazil* **30F4**
Guaratinguetá *Brazil* **35B2**
Guarda *Port* **50A1**
Guardafui,C *Somalia* **99F1**
Guarda Mor *Brazil* **35B1**
Guasave *Mexico* **9C4**
Guastalla *Italy* **47D2**
Guatemala *Guatemala* **25C3**
Guatemala, Republic *C America* **25C3**
Guatraché *Arg* **34C3**
Guavrare, R *Colombia* **32C3**
Guaxupé *Brazil* **35B2**
Guayaguayare *Trinidad* **27L1**
Guayaquil *Ecuador* **32A4**
Guaymas *Mexico* **24A2**
Guayquiraro, R *Arg* **34D2**
Guba *Eth* **99D2**
Guba *Zaïre* **100B2**
Guban, Region *Somalia* **99E2**
Gubat *Phil* **79B3**
Gubin *Pol* **56C2**
Güdür *India* **87B2**
Guelpho *Can* **14B2**
Guelta Zemmur *Mor* **96A2**
Guenabacoa *Cuba* **26A2**
Guéréda *Chad* **98C1**
Guéret *France* **48C2**
Guernsey, I *UK* **48B2**
Guerrero, State *Mexico* **23A2**
Gughe, Mt *Eth* **99D2**
Gugigu *China* **63E2**
Guguan, I *Pacific O* **71F2**
Guiargambone *Aust* **109C2**
Guidong *China* **73C4**
Guiglo *Ivory Coast* **97B4**
Gui Jiang, R *China* **73C5**
Guildford *Eng* **43D4**
Guilin *China* **73C4**
Guillestre *France* **47B2**
Guinan *China* **72A2**
Guinea, Republic *Africa* **97A3**
Guinea Basin *Atlantic O* **102H4**
Guinea-Bissau, Republic *Africa* **97A3**
Guinea,G of *W Africa* **97C4**
Güines *Cuba* **26A2**
Guir, Well *Mali* **97B3**
Guiranwala *Pak* **84C2**
Güiria *Ven* **33E1**
Guise *France* **46B2**
Guiuan *Phil* **79C3**
Gui Xian *China* **73B5**
Guiyang *China* **73B4**
Guizhou, Province *China* **73B4**
Gujarāt, State *India* **85C4**
Gujrat *Pak* **84C2**
Gulbarga *India* **87B1**
Gulbene *USSR* **58D1**
Guledagudda *India* **87B1**
Gulf,The *S W Asia* **80D3**
Gulgong *Aust* **109C2**
Gulin *China* **73B4**
Gulkana *USA* **12E2**
Gulkana, R *USA* **12E2**
Gull L *Can* **13E2**
Gull Lake *Can* **13F2**
Gulu *Uganda* **99D2**
Guluguba *Aust* **109C1**
Gumel *Nig* **97C3**
Gummersbach *W Germ* **46D1**
Gumpla *India* **86A2**
Gümüşhane *Turk* **93C1**
Guna *India* **85D4**
Guna, Mt *Eth* **99D1**
Gundagai *Aust* **109C3**
Gungu *Zaïre* **98B3**
Gunnedah *Aust* **109D2**
Guntakal *India* **87B1**
Guntersville *USA* **17A1**
Guntersville L *USA* **17A1**
Guntūr *India* **87C1**
Gunung Batu Putch, Mt *Malay* **77C5**
Gunung Besar, Mt *Indon* **78D3**
Gunung Bulu, Mt *Indon* **78D2**
Gunung Gedang, Mt *Indon* **78A3**
Gunung Lawit, Mt *Malay* **78C2**
Gunung Lawu, Mt *Indon* **78C4**
Gunung Menyapa, Mt *Indon* **78D2**
Gunung Niapa, Mt *Indon* **78D2**
Gunung Patah, Mt *Indon* **78A3**
Gunung Raung, Mt *Indon* **78C4**
Gunung Resag, Mt *Indon* **78A3**
Gunung Sarempaka, Mt *Indon* **78D3**
Gunung Sumbing, Mt *Indon* **78C4**
Gunung Tahan, Mt *Malay* **77C5**
Gunung Talakmau, Mt *Indon* **78A2**
Gunza *Angola* **100A2**
Guoyang *China* **72D3**
Gurdāspur *India* **84D2**
Gurgaon *India* **84D3**
Gurkha *Nepal* **86A1**
Gürün *Turk* **92C2**
Gurupi, R *Brazil* **31B2**
Gurvan Sayhan Uul, Upland *Mongolia* **72A1**
Gur'yev *USSR* **61H4**
Gurzinskaya, Republic *USSR* **65F5**
Gusau *Nig* **97C3**
Gusev *USSR* **58C2**
Gushan *China* **74A3**

Gus'khrustalnyy *USSR* 61F2
Gustavus *USA* 12G3
Gustine *USA* 22B2
Guston *USA* 11B3
Gütersloh *W Germ* 56B2
Guthrie, Kentucky *USA* 18C2
Guthrie, Oklahoma *USA* 18A2
Gutiérrez Zamora *Mexico* 23B1
Guyana, Republic *S America* 33F3
Guyana Basin *Atlantic O* 102F4
Guyang *China* 72C1
Guyenne, Region *France* 48B3
Guymon *USA* 9C3
Guyra *Aust* 109D2
Guyuan *China* 72B2
Gwabegar *Aust* 109C2
Gwalior *India* 85D3
Gwanda *Zim* 100B3
Gwane *Zaïre* 98C2
Gwardar *Pak* 82A3
Gweebarra B *Irish Rep* 45B1
Gwelo *Zim* 89G9
Gwent, County *Wales* 43C4
Gweru *Zim* 100B2
Gwydir, R *Aust* 109C1
Gwynedd *Wales* 43C3
Gyangzê *China* 86B1
Gyaring Hu, L *China* 68B3
Gydanskiy Poluostrov, Pen *USSR* 64J2
Gyirong *China* 86B1
Gyldenløues *Greenland* 6F3
Gympie *Aust* 109D1
Gyöngyös *Hung* 59B3
Györ *Hung* 59B3

H

Haapajärvi *Fin* 38K6
Haapsalu *USSR* 60B2
Haarlem *Neth* 56A2
Haarstrang, Region *W Germ* 46D1
Habana *Cuba* 25D2
Habiganj *Bang* 86C2
Hachijō-jima, I *Japan* 74D4
Hachiman *Japan* 75B1
Hachinohe *Japan* 74E2
Hachioji *Japan* 75B1
Hackettstown *USA* 16B2
Hack,Mt, Mt *Aust* 108A2
Haddington *Scot* 42C2
Haddon Corner *Aust* 108B1
Haddon Downs *Aust* 108B1
Hadejia *Nig* 97D3
Hadejia, R *Nig* 97C3
Hadera *Israel* 94B2
Haderslev *Den* 56B1
Hadiboh *Socotra* 81D4
Hadley B *Can* 4H2
Hadong *Vietnam* 73B5
Hadramawt, Region *S Yemen* 81C4
Hadsund *Den* 56C1
Haeju *N Korea* 74B3
Hafar al Bātin *S Arabia* 91A4
Haffners Bjerg, Mt *Greenland* 6D2
Hafizabad *Pak* 84C2
Hāflong *India* 86C1
Hafnafjörður *Iceland* 38A2
Hagemeister, I *USA* 12B3
Hagen *W Germ* 56B2
Hagerstown *USA* 15C3
Hagi *Japan* 75A2
Ha Giang *Vietnam* 73A5
Hagondange *France* 46D2
Hags Hd, C *Irish Rep* 45B2
Haguenan *France* 46D2
Hagunia, Well *Mor* 96A2
Haha-jima, I *Japan* 69G4
Hah Xil Hu, L *China* 68B3
Haicheng *China* 74A2
Hai Duong *Viet* 76D1
Haifa *Israel* 94B2
Haifa,B of *Israel* 94B2
Hai He, R *China* 72D2
Haikang *China* 73C5
Haikou *China* 76E1
Ha'il *S Arabia* 80C3
Hailākāndi *India* 86C2
Hailar *China* 63D3
Hailong *China* 74B2
Hailun *China* 69E2
Hailuoto, I *Fin* 38J5
Hainan, I *China* 76D2
Haines *USA* 12G3
Haines Junction *Can* 12G2
Hainfeld *Austria* 59B3
Haiphong *Vietnam* 73B5
Haiti, Republic *Caribbean* 26C3
Haiya *Sudan* 95C3
Haiyan *China* 72A2
Haiyuan *China* 72B2
Haizhou Wan, B *China* 72D3
Hajdúböszörmény *Hung* 59C3
Hajiki-saki, Pt *Japan* 75B1
Haka *Burma* 86C2
Hakalau *Hawaiian Is* 21C4
Hakkâri *Turk* 93D2
Hakodate *Japan* 74E2
Hakui *Japan* 75B1
Haku-san, Mt *Japan* 75B1
Ḩalab *Syria* 92C2
Halabja *Iraq* 93E3
Halaib *Sudan* 95C2
Halba *Leb* 94C1
Halberstadt *E Germ* 56C2
Halcon,Mt *Phil* 79B3
Halden *Nor* 39G7
Haldia *India* 86B2
Haldwāni *India* 84D3
Halfway, R *Can* 13C1
Halifax *Can* 7D5
Halifax *Eng* 42D3
Hall Basin, Sd *Can* 6D1
Hall Beach *Can* 6B3
Halle *Belg* 46C1
Halle *E Germ* 56C2
Halley, Base *Ant* 112B1
Hallingdal, R *Nor* 39F6
Hall Pen *Can* 6D3
Hall's Creek *Aust* 106B2
Halmahera, I *Indon* 71D3
Halmstad *Sweden* 39G7
Haltern *W Germ* 56B2
Haltia, Mt *Nor* 38J5
Haltwhistle *Eng* 42C2
Halul, I *Qatar* 91B4
Haluza, Hist Site *Israel* 94B3
Hamada *Japan* 75A2
Hamada de Tinrhert, Desert Region *Alg* 96C2
Hamada du Dra, Upland *Alg* 96B2
Hamadān *Iran* 90A3
Hamada Tounassine, Region *Alg* 96B2
Ḩamāh *Syria* 92C2
Hamamatsu *Japan* 75B2
Hamar *Nor* 39G6
Hambantota *Sri Lanka* 87C3
Hamburg, Arkansas *USA* 19B3
Hamburg, Iowa *USA* 18A1
Hamburg, Pennsylvania *USA* 16B2
Hamburg *W Germ* 56B2
Hamden *USA* 16C2
Hämeeninna *Fin* 39J6
Hamersley Range, Mts *Aust* 106A3
Hamgyong Sanmaek, Mts *N Korea* 74B2
Hamhŭng *N Korea* 74B2
Hami *China* 68B2
Hamīdīyah *Syria* 94B1
Hamilton *Aust* 108B3
Hamilton *Can* 14C2
Hamilton *NZ* 110C1
Hamilton, Ohio *USA* 14B3
Hamilton *Scot* 42B2
Hamilton Inlet, B *Can* 7E4
Hamilton,Mt *USA* 22B2
Hamina *Fin* 38K6
Hamirpur *India* 86A1
Hamm *W Germ* 56B2
Hammādāh al Hamra, Upland *Libya* 95A2
Hammerdal *Sweden* 38H6
Hammerfest *Nor* 38J4
Hammond, Illinois *USA* 14A2
Hammond, Louisiana *USA* 19B3
Hammonton *USA* 16B3
Hampden *NZ* 111B3
Hampshire, County *Eng* 43D4
Hampton, Arkansas *USA* 19B3
Hāmūn-e Jaz Mūrīan, L *Iran* 91C4
Hamun-i-Lora, Salt L *Pak* 84B3
Hana *Hawaiian Is* 21C4
Hanalei *Hawaiian Is* 21C4
Hanamaki *Japan* 74E3
Hancheng *China* 72C2
Hanchuan *China* 73C3
Hancock, Maryland *USA* 15C3
Hancock, Michigan *USA* 10B2
Handa *Japan* 75B2
Handan *China* 72C2
Handeni *Tanz* 99D3
Hanggin Qi *China* 72B2
Hangö *Fin* 39J7
Hangzhou *China* 73E3
Hangzhou Wan, B *China* 73E3
Hanmer Springs *NZ* 111B2
Hanna *Can* 13E2
Hannibal *USA* 18B2
Hannover *W Germ* 56B2
Hanöbukten, B *Sweden* 39G7
Hanoi *Viet* 76D1
Hanover *USA* 16A3
Hanover, I *Chile* 29B6
Han Shui *China* 72B3
Han Shui, R *China* 73C3
Hānsi *India* 85D3
Hantay *Mongolia* 68C2
Hanzhong *China* 72B3
Hāora *India* 86B2
Haparanda *Sweden* 38J5
Hāpoli *India* 86C1
Haql *S Arabia* 92C4
Haradh *S Arabia* 91A5
Hara Fanna *Eth* 99E2
Haramachi *Japan* 75C1
Harar *Eth* 99E2
Harare *Zim* 101C2
Harazé *Chad* 98C1
Harbor Beach *USA* 14B2
Harda *India* 85D4
Hardangerfjord, Inlet *Nor* 39F6
Hardt, Region *W Germ* 46D2
Hardwicke B *Aust* 108A2
Hardy *USA* 18B2
Hargeysa *Somalia* 99E2
Har Hakippa, Mt *Israel* 94B3
Harhu, L *China* 68B3
Hari, R *Indon* 78A3
Harima-nada, B *Japan* 75A2
Harlingen *Neth* 56B2
Harlingen *USA* 9D4
Harlow *Eng* 43E4
Har Meron, Mt *Israel* 94B2
Harney Basin *USA* 20C2
Harney L *USA* 20C2
Härnösand *Sweden* 38H6
Har Nuur, L *Mongolia* 63B3
Harper *Lib* 97B4
Harper,Mt *USA* 12F2
Harpers Ferry *USA* 15C3
Har Ramon, Mt *Israel* 94B3
Harricanaw, R *Can* 7C4
Harrington *USA* 16B3
Harrington Harbour *Can* 7E4
Harris, District *Scot* 44A3
Harrisburg, Illinois *USA* 18C2
Harrisburg, Pennsylvania *USA* 16A2
Harrismith *S Africa* 101G1
Harrison *USA* 18B2
Harrisonburg *USA* 15C3
Harrison,C *Can* 7E4
Harrison L *Can* 13C3
Harrisonville *USA* 18B2
Harris,Sound of, Chan *Scot* 44A3
Harrisville *USA* 14B2
Harrogate *Eng* 42D3
Har Saggi, Mt *Israel* 94B3
Harstad *Nor* 38H5
Hart, R *Can* 12G2
Hårteigen, Mt *Nor* 39F6
Hartford, Connecticut *USA* 16C2
Hartford, Michigan *USA* 14A2
Hartkjølen, Mt *Nor* 38G6
Hart,L *Aust* 108A2
Hartland Pt *Eng* 43B4
Hartlepool *Eng* 42D2
Hartshorne *USA* 19A3
Hartwell Res *USA* 17B1
Hartz, R *S Africa* 101F1
Har Us Nuur, L *Mongolia* 68B2
Harwich *Eng* 43E4
Haryāna, State *India* 84D3
Hāsā *Jordan* 94B3
Hāsbaiya *Leb* 94B2
Haselmere *Eng* 43D4
Hashimoto *Japan* 75B2
Hashtpar *Iran* 90A2
Hashtrūd *Iran* 90A2
Hassan *India* 87B2
Hasselt *Belg* 56B2
Hassi Inifel *Alg* 96C2
Hassi Mdakane, Well *Alg* 96B2
Hassi Messaoud *Alg* 96C1
Hastings *Aust* 108C3
Hastings *Eng* 43E4
Hastings, Nebraska *USA* 8D2
Hastings *NZ* 110C1
Hatfield *Aust* 108B2
Hatham Inlet *USA* 12B1
Hāthras *India* 85D3
Ha Tinh *Viet* 76D2
Hattah *Aust* 108B2
Hatteras,C *USA* 11C3
Hattiesburg *USA* 19C3
Hatvan *Hung* 59B3
Hau Bon *Viet* 76D3
Haud, Region *Eth* 99E2
Haugesund *Nor* 39F7
Hauhungaroa Range, Mts *NZ* 110C1
Haultain, R *Can* 13F1
Hauraki G *NZ* 110B1
Hauroko,L *NZ* 111A3
Hausstock, Mt *Switz* 47C1
Haut Atlas, Mts *Mor* 96B1
Haute Kotto, Region *CAR* 98C2
Hautes Fagnes, Mts *Belg* 46C1
Hautmont *Belg* 46B1
Hauts Plateaux, Mts *Alg* 96B1
Hauzdar *Iran* 90D3

Havana *USA* **18B1**
Havankulam *Sri Lanka* **87B3**
Havelock North *NZ* **110C1**
Haverfordwest *West* **43B4**
Haverhill *USA* **16D1**
Hāveri *India* **87B2**
Haverstraw *USA* **16C2**
Havlíčkův Brod *Czech* **59B3**
Havre *USA* **8C2**
Havre de Grace *USA* **16A3**
Havre-St-Pierre *Can* **7D4**
Havsa *Turk* **54C2**
Hawaii, I *Hawaiian Is* **21C4**
Hawaii Volcanoes Nat Pk *Hawaiian Is* **21C4**
Hawea,L *NZ* **111A2**
Hawera *NZ* **110B1**
Hawick *Scot* **42C2**
Hawkdun Range, Mts *NZ* **111A2**
Hawke B *NZ* **110C1**
Hawke,C *Aust* **109D2**
Hawker *Aust* **108A2**
Hawng Luk *Burma* **76B1**
Hawr al Habbaniyah, L *Iraq* **93D3**
Hawr al Hammár, L *Iraq* **93E3**
Hawthorne *USA* **21B2**
Hay *Aust* **108B2**
Hay, R *Can* **5G3**
Hayange *France* **46D2**
Haycock *USA* **4B3**
Hayes, R *Can* **7A4**
Hayes Halvø, Region *Greenland* **6D2**
Hayes,Mt *USA* **12E2**
Hay River *Can* **5G3**
Haysville *USA* **18A2**
Hayward, California *USA* **22A2**
Hazārībāg *India* **86B2**
Hazebrouck *France* **46B1**
Hazelhurst *USA* **19B3**
Hazel Str *Can* **4G2**
Hazelton *Can* **5F4**
Hazelton Mts *Can* **13B1**
Hazen L *Can* **6C1**
Hazeva *Israel* **94B3**
Hazleton *USA* **16B2**
Healdsburg *USA* **22A1**
Healesville *Aust* **108C3**
Healy *USA* **12E2**
Heard I *Indian O* **104B6**
Hearne *USA* **19A3**
Hearst *Can* **10B2**
Hebei, Province *China* **72D2**
Hebel *Aust* **109C1**
Hebi *China* **72C2**
Hebian *China* **72C2**
Hebron *Can* **7D4**
Hebron *Israel* **94B3**
Hebron, Nebraska *USA* **18A1**
Hecate, Str *Can* **5E4**
Heceta I *USA* **12H3**
Hechi *China* **73B5**
Hecla and Griper B *Can* **4G2**
Hector,Mt *NZ* **111C2**
Hede *Sweden* **38G6**
Hedemora *Sweden* **39H6**
He Devil Mt *USA* **20C1**
Heerenveen *Neth* **56B2**
Heerlen *Neth* **46C1**
Hefei *China* **73D3**
Hefeng *China* **73B4**
Hegang *China* **69F2**
Hegura-jima, I *Japan* **75B1**
Heidan, R *Jordan* **94B3**
Heide *W Germ* **56B2**
Heidelberg, Transvaal *S Africa* **101G1**
Heidelberg *W Germ* **57B3**
Heihe *China* **63E2**
Heilbron *S Africa* **101G1**
Heilbronn *W Germ* **57B3**
Heiligenstadt *E Germ* **56C2**
Heinola *Fin* **38K6**
Hejiang *China* **73B4**
Hekla, Mt *Iceland* **6J3**
Hekou *Viet* **76C1**
Hekou Yaozou Zizhixian *China* **73A5**
Helan *China* **72B2**
Helan Shan, Mt *China* **72B2**
Helena, Arkansas *USA* **19B3**
Helena, Montana *USA* **8B2**
Helendale *USA* **22D3**
Helen Reef, I *Pacific O* **71E3**
Helensburgh *Scot* **44B3**
Helleh, R *Iran* **91B4**
Hellin *Spain* **51B2**
Hells Canyon, R *USA* **20C1**
Hellweg, Region *W Germ* **46D1**
Helm *USA* **22B2**
Helmand, R *Afghan* **80E2**
Helmeringhausen *Namibia* **100A3**
Helmond *Neth* **46C1**
Helmsdale *Scot* **44C2**
Helong *China* **74B2**
Helsingborg *Sweden* **39G7**
Helsingør *Den* **56C1**
Helsinki *Fin* **38J6**
Helston *Eng* **43B4**
Helwân *Egypt* **92B4**
Hempstead *USA* **19A3**
Hemse *Sweden* **39H7**
Henan *China* **72A3**
Henan, Province *China* **72C3**
Hen and Chicken Is *NZ* **110B1**
Henderson, Kentucky *USA* **14A3**
Henderson, Nevada *USA* **9B3**
Henderson, Texas *USA* **19B3**
Heng-ch'un *Taiwan* **73E5**
Hengduan Shan, Mts *China* **68B4**
Hengelo *Neth* **56B2**
Hengshan *China* **72B2**
Hengshui *China* **72D2**
Heng Xian *China* **76D1**
Hengyang *China* **73C4**
Henhoaha *Nicobar Is* **77A4**
Henley-on-Thames *Eng* **43D4**
Henlopen,C *USA* **16B3**
Henrietta Maria,C *Can* **7B4**
Henryetta *USA* **18A2**
Henry Kater Pen *Can* **6D3**
Hentiyn Nuruu, Mts *Mongolia* **68C2**
Henzada *Burma* **76B2**
Hepu *China* **73B5**
Herat *Afghan* **80E2**
Herbert *Can* **5H4**
Herbertville *NZ* **110C2**
Herborn *W Germ* **46E1**
Heredia *Costa Rica* **26A4**
Hereford *Eng* **43C3**
Hereford & Worcester County *Eng* **43C3**
Herentals *Belg* **46C1**
Héricourt *France* **47B1**
Herington *USA* **18A2**
Heriot *NZ* **111A3**
Herisau *Switz* **47C1**
Herkimer *USA* **15D2**
Herma Ness, Pen *Scot* **44D1**
Hermidale *Aust* **109C2**
Hermitage *NZ* **111B2**
Hermosillo *Mexico* **24A2**
Herndon, Pennsylvania *USA* **16A2**
Herndon, California *USA* **22C2**
Herne *W Germ* **46D1**
Herning *Den* **56B1**
Herowābad *Iran* **90A2**
Herrera del Duque *Spain* **50A2**
Hershey *USA* **16A2**
Hertford, County *Eng* **43D4**
Herzliyya *Israel* **94B2**
Hesbaye, Region *Belg* **46C1**
Hesdin *France* **46B1**
Heshui *China* **72B2**
Hesperia *USA* **22D3**
Hess, R *Can* **12H2**
Hessen, State *W Germ* **57B2**
Hetch Hetchy Res *USA* **22C2**
Hexham *Eng* **42C2**
He Xian *China* **73C5**
Heyuan *China* **73C5**
Heywood *Aust* **108B3**
Heze *China* **72D2**
Hialeah *USA* **17B2**
Hibbing *USA* **10A2**
Hicks Bay *NZ* **110C1**
Hicks,Pt *Aust* **109C3**
Hidalgo, State *Mexico* **23B1**
Hidalgo del Parral *Mexico* **24B2**
Hidrolândia *Brazil* **35B1**
Hierro, I *Canary Is* **96A2**
Higashine *Japan* **75C1**
Higashi-suidō, Str *Japan* **74B4**
High Desert *USA* **20B2**
High Island *USA* **19B4**
Highland, Region *Scot* **44B3**
Highland *USA* **22D3**
Highland Peak, Mt *USA* **22C1**
Highlands Falls *USA* **16B2**
High Point *USA* **11B3**
High Prairie *Can* **13D1**
High River *Can* **5G4**
High Springs *USA* **17B2**
Hightstown *USA* **16B2**
High Wycombe *Eng* **43D4**
Hiiumaa, I *USSR* **39J7**
Hijaz, Region *S Arabia* **80B3**
Hikigawa *Japan* **75B2**
Hikone *Japan* **75B1**
Hikurangi *NZ* **110B1**
Hildago *Mexico* **9C4**
Hildago del Parral *Mexico* **9C4**
Hildesheim *W Germ* **56B2**
Hillaby,Mt *Barbados* **27R3**
Hillerød *Den* **56C1**
Hillsboro, Ohio *USA* **14B3**
Hillsboro, Oregon *USA* **20B1**
Hillsboro, Texas *USA* **19A3**
Hillston *Aust* **108C2**
Hillswick *Scot* **44D1**
Hilo *Hawaiian Is* **21C4**
Hilvan *Turk* **93C2**
Hilversum *Neth* **56B2**
Himachal Pradesh, State *India* **84D2**
Himalaya, Mts *Asia* **82B3**
Himatnagar *India* **85C4**
Himeji *Japan* **74C4**
Himi *Japan* **74D3**
Himş *Syria* **92C3**
Hinchinbrook Entrance *USA* **12E2**
Hinchinbrook I *USA* **12E2**
Hindaun *India* **85D3**
Hindu Kush, Mts *Afghan* **84B1**
Hindupur *India* **87B2**
Hines Creek *Can* **13D1**
Hinganghāt *India* **85D4**
Hinggan Ling, Upland *China* **69E2**
Hingol, R *Pak* **85B3**
Hingoli *India* **85D5**
Hinnøya, I *Nor* **38H5**
Hinsdale *USA* **16C1**
Hinton *Can* **13D2**
Hipolito Itrogoyen *Arg* **34B2**
Hirakud Res *India* **86A2**
Hirfanli Baraji, Res *Turk* **92B2**
Hirihar *India* **87B2**
Hirosaki *Japan* **74E2**
Hiroshima *Japan* **74C4**
Hirson *France* **46C2**
Hirşova *Rom* **54C2**
Hirtshals *Den* **56B1**
Hisār *India* **84D3**
Hispaniola, I *Caribbean* **26C3**
Hisyah *Syria* **94C1**
Hīt *Iraq* **93D3**
Hitachi *Japan* **74E3**
Hitachi-Ota *Japan* **75C1**
Hitchin *Eng* **43D4**
Hitra, I *Nor* **38F6**
Hiuchi-nada, B *Japan* **75A2**
Hiwasa *Japan* **75A2**
Hjørring *Den* **56B1**
Hka, R *Burma* **76B1**
Ho *Ghana* **97C4**
Hoa Binh *Viet* **76D1**
Hoa Da *Viet* **76D3**
Hobart *Aust* **109C4**
Hobbs *USA* **9C3**
Hobro *Den* **56B1**
Hobson L *Can* **13C2**
Hobyo *Somalia* **99E2**
Hochkonig, Mt *Austria* **57C3**
Hódmezó'hely *Hung* **54B1**
Hodonin *Czech* **59B3**
Hoeryong *N Korea* **74B2**
Hof *W Germ* **57C2**
Hofsjökull, Mts *Iceland* **38B2**
Hōfu *Japan* **74C4**
Hoggar, Upland *Alg* **96C2**
Hohe Acht, Mt *W Germ* **46D1**
Hohhot *China* **72C1**
Höhn *Iceland* **6J3**
Hoh Sai Hu, L *China* **68B3**
Hoh Xil Shan, Mts *China* **82C2**
Hoima *Uganda* **99D2**
Hojāi *India* **86C1**
Hojo *Japan* **75A2**
Hokianga Harbour, B *NZ* **110B1**
Hokitika *NZ* **111B2**
Hokkaidō *Japan* **74E2**
Hokmābād *Iran* **90C2**
Holbrook *Aust* **109C3**
Holbrook *USA* **9B3**
Holdenville *USA* **19A2**
Hole Narsipur *India* **87B2**
Holetown *Barbados* **27R3**
Holguín *Cuba* **26B2**
Holitika *NZ* **111B2**
Holitna, R *USA* **12C2**
Hollabrunn *Austria* **59B3**
Holland *USA* **14A2**
Hollister *USA* **22B2**
Holly Springs *USA* **19C3**
Hollywood, California *USA* **22C3**
Hollywood, Florida *USA* **17B2**
Holman Island *Can* **4G2**
Holmsund *Sweden* **38J6**
Holon *Israel* **94B2**
Holstebro *Den* **56B1**
Holsteinborg *Greenland* **6E3**
Holt *USA* **14B2**
Holton *USA* **18A2**
Holy Cross *USA* **12C2**
Holyhead *Wales* **42B3**
Holy I *Eng* **42D2**
Holy I *Wales* **43B3**
Holyoke, Massachusetts *USA* **16C1**
Homalin *Burma* **86C2**
Home B *Can* **6D3**
Homer, Alaska *USA* **12D3**
Homer, Louisiana *USA* **19B3**
Homer Tunnel *NZ* **111A2**

Homerville *USA* 17B1
Homestead *USA* 17B2
Homewood *USA* 17A1
Homnābād *India* 87B1
Homoine *Mozam* 101C3
Hondo, R *Mexico* 25D3
Honduras, Republic *C America* 25D3
Honduras,G of *Honduras* 25D3
Hønefoss *Nor* 39G6
Honesdale *USA* 15C2
Honey L *USA* 21A1
Hong, R *Viet* 76C1
Hon Gai *Viet* 76D1
Hongguo *China* 73A4
Hong Hu, L *China* 73C4
Honghui *China* 72B2
Hongjiang *China* 73C4
Hong Kong, Colony *S E Asia* 73C5
Hongor *Mongolia* 68D2
Hongshui He, R *China* 73B5
Hongyuan *China* 72A3
Hongze Hu, L *China* 72D3
Honiara *Solomon Is* 107E1
Hon Khoai, I *Camb* 77C4
Hon Lan, I *Viet* 76D3
Honnigsvåg *Nor* 38K4
Honolulu *Hawaiian Is* 21C4
Hon Panjang, I *Viet* 77C4
Honshu, I *Japan* 74D3
Hood,Mt *USA* 20B1
Hood River *USA* 20B1
Hook Head, C *Irish Rep* 45C2
Hoonah *USA* 12G3
Hooper Bay *USA* 12A2
Hoopstad *S Africa* 101G1
Hoorn *Neth* 56A2
Hoover Dam *USA* 9B3
Hope, Alaska *USA* 12E2
Hope, Arkansas *USA* 19B3
Hope *Can* 13C3
Hopedale *Can* 7D4
Hopen, I *Barents S* 64D2
Hopes Advance,C *Can* 6D3
Hopetoun *Aust* 108B3
Hopetown *S Africa* 100B3
Hopkinsville *USA* 18C2
Hoquiam *USA* 20B1
Horasan *Turk* 93D1
Hordiyo *Somalia* 99F1
Horgen *Switz* 47C1
Horizon Depth *Pacific O* 105H5
Hormuz,Str of *Oman/Iran* 91C4
Horn *Austria* 59B3
Horn, C *Iceland* 6H3
Hornavan, L *Sweden* 38H5
Hornbeck *USA* 19B3
Hornbrook *USA* 20B2
Hornby *NZ* 111B2
Hornepayne *Can* 7B5
Horn Mts *Can* 4F3
Hornsea *Eng* 42D3
Horn Uul, Mt *Mongolia* 72B1
Horqueta *Par* 30E3
Horseheads *USA* 15C2
Horsens *Den* 56C1
Horseshoe Bay *Can* 20B1
Horsham *Aust* 108B3
Horsham *Eng* 43D4
Horten *Nor* 39G7
Horton, R *Can* 4F3
Hose Mts *Malay* 78C2
Hoshangābād *India* 85D4
Hoshiārpur *India* 84D2
Hospet *India* 87B1
Hoste, I *Chile* 29C7
Hotan *China* 82B2
Hot Springs, Arkansas *USA* 19B3
Hot Springs, S. Dakota *USA* 8C2
Hottah *Can* 4G3
Houdan *France* 46A2
Houma *China* 72C2
Houma *USA* 19B4
Housatonic, R *USA* 16C2
Houston *Can* 13B2
Houston, Mississippi *USA* 19C3
Houston, Texas *USA* 19A4
Houtman, Is *Aust* 106A3
Hovd *Mongolia* 68B2
Hövsgol Nuur, L *Mongolia* 68C1
Howard City *USA* 14A2
Howard P *USA* 12C1
Howe,C *Aust* 109C3
Howick *S Africa* 101H1
Hoy, I *Scot* 44C2
Høyanger *Nor* 39F6
Hradeç-Králové *Czech* 59B2
Hranice *Czech* 59B3
Hron, R *Czech* 59B3
Hsin-chu *Taiwan* 73E5
Hsüeh Shan, Mt *Taiwan* 73E5
Huachi *China* 72B2
Huacho *Peru* 32B6
Huade *China* 72C1
Huaibei *China* 72D3
Huaibin *China* 72D3
Huai He, R *China* 72D3
Huaihua *China* 73C4
Huaiji *China* 73C5
Huainan *China* 72D3
Hua-lien *Taiwan* 69E4
Huallaga, R *Peru* 32B5
Huallanca *Peru* 32B5
Huamachuco *Peru* 32B5
Huambo *Angola* 100A2
Huanay *Bol* 30C2
Huancabamba *Peru* 32B5
Huancavelica *Peru* 32B6
Huancayo *Peru* 32B6
Huangchuan *China* 73D3
Huang He, R *China* 72D2
Huangling *China* 72B2
Huangliu *China* 76D2
Huangpi *China* 73C3
Huangshi *China* 73D3
Huanguelén *Arg* 34C3
Huangyan *China* 73E4
Huanren *China* 74B2
Huānuco *Peru* 32B5
Huanuni *Bol* 30C2
Huan Xian *China* 72B2
Huaráz *Peru* 32B5
Huarmey *Peru* 32B6
Huascarán, Mt *Peru* 32B5
Huasco *Chile* 30B4
Huatusco *Mexico* 23B2
Huauchinango *Mexico* 23B1
Huautla *Mexico* 23B2
Hua Xian *China* 72C2
Huayapan, R *Mexico* 24B2
Hubei, Province *China* 73C3
Hubli *India* 87B1
Hucal *Arg* 34C3
Huch'ang *N Korea* 74B2
Huddersfield *Eng* 42D3
Hudiksvall *Sweden* 39H6
Hudson, Florida *USA* 17B2
Hudson, Michigan *USA* 14B2
Hudson, New York *USA* 16C1
Hudson, R *USA* 16C1
Hudson B *Can* 7B4
Hudson Bay *Can* 5H4
Hudson's Hope *Can* 13C1
Hudson Str *Can* 6C3
Hue *Viet* 76D2
Huejutla *Mexico* 23B1
Huelva *Spain* 50A2
Hueramo *Mexico* 23A2
Húercal Overa *Spain* 51B2
Huesca *Spain* 51B1
Huexotla, Hist Site *Mexico* 23B2
Hughenden *Aust* 107D3
Hughes *USA* 12D1
Hugli, R *India* 86B2
Hugo *USA* 19A3
Hui'an *China* 73D4
Huiarau Range, Mts *NZ* 110C1
Hŭich'ŏn *N Korea* 74B2
Huifa He, R *China* 74B2
Huila, Mt *Colombia* 32B3
Huilai *China* 73D5
Huili *China* 73A4
Huinan *China* 74B2
Huinca Renancó *Arg* 34C2
Huixtla *Mexico* 25C3
Huize *China* 73A4
Huizhou *China* 73C5
Hujuápan de Léon *Mexico* 23B2
Hulin *China* 69F2
Hull *Can* 15C1
Hull *Eng* 42D3
Hultsfred *Sweden* 58B1
Hulun Nur, L *China* 63D3
Huma *China* 69E1
Humaita *Brazil* 33E5
Humansdorp *S Africa* 100B4
Humber, R *Eng* 42D3
Humberside, County *Eng* 42D3
Humboldt *Can* 5H4
Humboldt, R *USA* 20C2
Humboldt B *USA* 20B2
Humboldt Gletscher, Gl *Greenland* 6D2
Humboldt L *USA* 21B2
Humeburn *Aust* 108C1
Hume,L *Aust* 109C3
Humpata *Angola* 100A2
Humphreys *USA* 22C2
Húnaflói, B *Iceland* 38A1
Hunan, Province *China* 73C4
Hunchun *China* 74C2
Hundred Mile House *Can* 13C2
Hunedoara *Rom* 54B1
Hungary, Republic *Europe* 59B3
Hungerford *Aust* 108B1
Hŭngnam *N Korea* 74B3
Hunjiang *China* 74B2
Hunsrück, Mts *W Germ* 46D2
Hunter, R *Aust* 109D2
Hunter I *Can* 13B2
Hunter Is *Aust* 109C4
Hunter,Mt *USA* 12D2
Huntingburg *USA* 14A3
Huntingdon *Eng* 43D3
Huntingdon, Indiana *USA* 14A2
Huntington *USA* 14B3
Huntington Beach *USA* 22C4
Huntington L *USA* 22C2
Huntly *NZ* 110C1
Huntly *Scot* 44C3
Hunt,Mt *Can* 12J2
Hunt Pen *Aust* 108A1
Huntsville, Alabama *USA* 17A1
Huntsville *Can* 15C1
Huntsville, Texas *USA* 19A3
Huong Khe *Viet* 76D2
Huon Peninsula, Pen *PNG* 71F4
Huonville *Anst* 109C4
Hurd,C *Can* 14B1
Hurghada *Egypt* 80B3
Huron, S. Dakota *USA* 8D2
Huron,L *USA/Can* 14B1
Hurtado *Chile* 34A2
Hurunui, R *NZ* 111B2
Husavik *Iceland* 38B1
Huşi *Rom* 54C1
Huskvarna *Sweden* 39G7
Huslia *USA* 12C1
Husn *Jordan* 94B2
Husum *W Germ* 56B2
Hutton,Mt *Aust* 109C1
Hutuo He, R *China* 72D2
Huy *Belg* 46C1
Huzhu *China* 72A2
Hvar, I *Yugos* 52C2
Hwange *Zim* 100B2
Hwange Nat Pk *Zim* 100B2
Hyannis *USA* 15D2
Hyaryas Nuur, L *Mongolia* 68B2
Hydaburg *Can* 5E4
Hyde Park *USA* 16C2
Hyderābād *India* 87B1
Hyderabad *Pak* 85B3
Hyères *France* 49D3
Hyland, R *Can* 12J2
Hyndman Peak, Mt *USA* 8B2
Hyrynsalmi *Fin* 38K6
Hythe *Can* 13D1
Hyūga *Japan* 74C4
Hyvikää *Fin* 39J6

I

Iaçu *Brazil* 31C4
Ialomiţa, R *Rom* 54C2
Iaşi *Rom* 54C1
Ibadan *Nig* 97C4
Ibagué *Colombia* 32B3
Ibar, R *Yugos* 54B2
Ibarra *Ecuador* 32B3
Ibiá *Brazil* 35B1
Ibicui, R *Brazil* 30E4
Ibicuy *Arg* 34D2
Ibiza *Spain* 51C2
Ibiza, I *Spain* 51C2
Ibo *Mozam* 101D2
Ibotirama *Brazil* 31C4
'Ibrī *Oman* 91C5
Ica *Peru* 32B6
Icá, R *Brazil* 32D4
Icana *Brazil* 32D3
Iceland, Republic *N Atlantic O* 38A1
Ice Mt *Can* 13C2
Ichalkaranji *India* 87A1
Ichihara *Japan* 74E3
Ichinomiya *Japan* 75B1
Ichinoseki *Japan* 74E3
Icy B *USA* 12F3
Icy C *USA* 4B2
Ida, R *USSR* 63B2
Idabell *USA* 19B3
Idaho Falls *USA* 8B2
Idanha *USA* 20B2
Idar Oberstein *W Germ* 46D2
Idehan Marzūg, Desert *Libya* 95A2
Idehan Ubari, Desert *Libya* 95A2
Idelés *Alg* 96C2
Iderlym Gol, R *Mongolia* 68B2
Idfu *Egypt* 95C2
Ídhi Óros, Mt *Greece* 55B3
Ídhra, I *Greece* 55B3
Idiofa *Zaïre* 98B3
Iditarod, R *USA* 12C2
Idlib *Syria* 92C2
Idritsa *USSR* 39K7
Idutywa *S Africa* 100B4
Ierápetra *Greece* 55C3
Itakara *Tanz* 99D3
Ifalik, I *Pacific* 71F3
Ifanadiana *Madag* 101D3
Ife *Nig* 97C4
Iférouane *Niger* 97C3
Igan *Malay* 78C2
Igaranava *Brazil* 35B2
Igdir *Iran* 93E2
Iggesund *Sweden* 39H6
Iglesia *Arg* 34B2
Iglesias *Sardegna* 53A3
Igloolik *Can* 6B3
Ignace *Can* 10A2

Igoumenítsa *Greece* 55B3
Igra *USSR* 61H2
Iguala *Mexico* 23B2
Iguape *Brazil* 31B6
Iguape *Brazil* 35B2
Iguatama *Brazil* 35B2
Iguatu *Brazil* 31D3
Iguéla *Gabon* 98A3
Ihosy *Madag* 101D3
Iida *Japan* 74D3
Iide-san, Mt *Japan* 75B1
Iisalmi *Fin* 38K6
Iizuka *Japan* 75A2
Ijebu Ode *Nig* 97C4
Ijsselmeer, S *Neth* 56B2
Ikaría, I *Greece* 55C3
Ikeda *Japan* 74E2
Ikela *Zaïre* 98C3
Ikhtiman *Bulg* 54B2
Ikolik,C *USA* 12D3
Ikopa, R *Madag* 101D2
Ilagan *Phil* 79B2
Ilām *Iran* 90A3
Ilanz *Switz* 47C1
Île à la Crosse *Can* 13F1
Île à la Crosse,L *Can* 13F1
Ilebo *Zaire* 89G8
Île de Jerba, I *Tunisia* 96D1
Ile de Noirmoutier, I *France* 48B2
Ile de Ré, I *France* 48B2
Île des Pins, I *Nouvelle Calédonie* 107F3
Ile d'Ouessant, I *France* 48A2
Ile d'Yeu, I *France* 48B2
Ilek, R *USSR* 61J3
Îles Bélèp *Nouvelle Calédonie* 107F2
Îles Chesterfield *Nouvelle Calédonie* 107E2
Iles d'Hyìeres, Is *France* 49D3
Ilfracombe *Eng* 43B4
Ilgaz Dağları, Mts *Turk* 92B1
Ilha Bazaruto, I *Mozam* 101C3
Ilha De Maracá, I *Brazil* 33G3
Ilha de Marajó, I *Brazil* 33G4
Ilha de São Sebastião, I *Brazil* 35B2
Ilha do Bananal, Region *Brazil* 33G6
Ilha Grande, I *Brazil* 35C2
Ilha Santo Amaro, I *Brazil* 35B2
Ilhas Selvegens, I *Atlantic O* 96A1
Ilhéus *Brazil* 31D4
Iliamna L *USA* 12C3
Iliamna V *USA* 12D2
Iligan *Phil* 79B4
Il'inskiy *USSR* 63G3
Iliodhrómia, I *Greece* 55B3
Illana B *Phil* 79B4
Illapel *Chile* 34A2
Illapel, R *Chile* 34A2
Illéla *Niger* 97C3
Iller, R *W Germ* 47D1
Illiamna L *USA* 4C4
Illinois, State *USA* 10A2
Illinois, R *USA* 18B2
Illizi *Alg* 96C2
Ilo *Peru* 30B2
Iloilo *Phil* 79B3
Ilomantsi *Fin* 38L6
Ilorin *Nig* 97C4
Imabari *Japan* 75A2
Imalchi *Japan* 75B1
Imatra *Fin* 60C1
Imbituba *Brazil* 30G4
Imi *Eth* 99E2
Imlay *USA* 20C2
Immenstadt *W Germ* 47D1
Imola *Italy* 52B2
Imperatriz *Brazil* 31B3
Imperia *Italy* 52A2
Impfondo *Congo* 98B2
Imphāl *India* 86C2
Imst *Austria* 47D1
Imuruk L *USA* 12B1
Ina *Japan* 75B1
In Afahleleh, Well *Alg* 96C2
Inamba-jima, I *Japan* 75B2
In Amenas *Alg* 96C2
Inari *Fin* 38K5
Inarijärvi, L *Fin* 38K5
Inawashiro-ko, L *Japan* 75C1
In Belbel *Alg* 96C2
Ince Burun, Pt *Turk* 60E5
Incekum Burun, Pt *Turk* 92B2
Inch'ŏn *S Korea* 74B3
In Dagouber, Well *Mali* 96B2
Indaia, R *Brazil* 35B1
Indals, R *Sweden* 38H6
Independence, California *USA* 21B2
Independence, Kansas *USA* 18A2
Independence, Missouri *USA* 18B2
Inderagiri, R *Indon* 78A3
Inderborskiy *USSR* 61H4
India, Federal Republic *Asia* 83B3
Indiana, State *USA* 14A2
Indiana *USA* 15C2
Indian-Antarctic Ridge *Indian O* 104C6
Indianapolis *USA* 14A3
Indian Harbour *Can* 7E4
Indian O 104B4
Indianola, Iowa *USA* 18B1
Indianola, Mississippi *USA* 19B3
Indianópolis *Brazil* 35B1
Indo China, Region *S E Asia* 76D2
Indonesia, Republic *S E Asia* 70C4
Indore *India* 85D4
Indramayu *Indon* 78B4
Indre, R *France* 48C2
Indus, R *Pak* 85B3
Inebdu *Turk* 60D5
In Ebeggi, Well *Alg* 96C2
In Ecker *Alg* 96C2
Inegöl *Turk* 92A1
In Ezzane *Alg* 96D2
Ingal *Niger* 97C3
Ingersoll *Can* 14B2
Ingham *Aust* 107D2
Inglefield Land, Region *Can* 6D2
Inglewood *NZ* 110B1
Inglewood, Queensland *Aust* 109D1
Inglewood *USA* 22C4
Inglewood, Victoria *Aust* 108B3
Ingólfshöfði, I *Iceland* 38B2
Ingolstadt *W Germ* 57C3
Ingrāj Bāzār *India* 86B2
In-Guezzam, Well *Alg* 96C3
Inhambane *Mozam* 101C3
Inharrime *Mozam* 101C3
Inhumas *Brazil* 35B1
Inirida, R *Colombia* 32D3
Inishbofin, I *Irish Rep* 45A2
Inishkea, I *Irish Rep* 45A1
Inishmaan, I *Irish Rep* 45B2
Inishmore, I *Irish Rep* 45B2
Inishmurray, I *Irish Rep* 45B1
Inishowen, District *Irish Rep* 45C1
Inishshark, I *Irish Rep* 45A2
Inishturk, I *Irish Rep* 45A2
Injune *Aust* 109C1
Inklin *Can* 12H3
Inklin, R *Can* 12H3
Inland L *USA* 12C1
Inn, R *Austria* 47D1
Innamincka *Aust* 108B1
Inner Mongolia, Autonomous Region *China* 68C2
Innisfail *Aust* 107D2
Innoko, R *USA* 12C2
Innsbruck *Austria* 57C3
Inongo *Zaïre* 98B3
Inowrocław *Pol* 58B2
In Salah *Alg* 96C2
Interlaken *Switz* 47B1
Intexpec *Mexico* 24C3
Intra *Italy* 47C2
Intu *Indon* 78D3
Inubo-saki, C *Japan* 75C1
Inukjuac *Can* 7C4
Inuvik *Can* 4E3
Inveraray *Scot* 44B3
Invercargill *NZ* 111A3
Inverell *Aust* 109D1
Invermere *Can* 13D2
Inverness *Scot* 44B3
Inverurie *Scot* 44C3
Investigator Str *Aust* 108A3
Inya *USSR* 68A1
Inyanga *Zim* 101C2
Inyokern *USA* 21B2
Inzia, R *Zaïre* 98B3
Ioánnina *Greece* 55B3
Iola *USA* 18A2
Iona, I *Scot* 44A3
Iôna Nat Pk *Angola* 100A2
Ione *USA* 20C1
Ionian S *Italy/Greece* 55A3
Ioníoi Nísoi, Is *Greece* 55B3
Íos, I *Greece* 55C3
Iowa, R *USA* 10A2
Iowa City *USA* 10A2
Ipameri *Brazil* 35B1
Ipanema *Brazil* 35C1
Ipatovo *USSR* 61F4
Ipiales *Colombia* 32B3
Ipoh *Malay* 77C5
Iporá *Brazil* 30F2
Ipsala *Turk* 55C2
Ipswich *Aust* 109D1
Ipswich *Eng* 43E3
Ipswich *USA* 16D1
Iquique *Chile* 30B3
Iquitos *Peru* 32C4
Iráklion *Greece* 55C3
Iran, Republic *S W Asia* 80D2
Irānshahr *Iran* 91D4
Irapuato *Mexico* 23A1
Iraq, Republic *S W Asia* 93D3
Irā Wan, Watercourse *Libya* 95A2
Irbid *Jordan* 94B2
Irbit *USSR* 61K2
Ireland, Republic *NW Europe* 36C3
Ireng, R *Guyana* 33F3
Iri *S Korea* 74B3
Irian Jaya, Province *Indon* 71E4
Iriba *Chad* 95B3
Iriga *Phil* 79B3
Iringa *Tanz* 99D3
Iriomote, I *Japan* 69E4
Iriri, R *Brazil* 33G5
Irish S *Eng/Irish Rep* 42B3
Irkillik, R *USA* 12D1
Irkutsk *USSR* 63C2
Irlysh *USSR* 65J4
Iron Knob *Aust* 108A2
Iron Mountain *USA* 14A1
Iron Range *Aust* 107D2
Iron River *USA* 14A1
Irontown *USA* 14B3
Ironwood *USA* 10A2
Iroquois Falls *Can* 10B2
Iro-zaki, C *Japan* 75B2
Irrawaddy,Mouths of the *Burma* 76A2
Irtysh, R *USSR* 65H4
Irun *Spain* 51B1
Irvine *Scot* 42B2
Irving *USA* 19A3
Isabela *Phil* 79B4
Isabela, I *Ecuador* 32J7
Isachsen *Can* 4H2
Isachsen,C *Can* 4H2
Ísafjörður *Iceland* 6H3
Isahaya *Japan* 74C4
Isangi *Zaïre* 98C2
Isar, R *W Germ* 47D1
Isarco, R *Italy* 47D1
Isbister *Scot* 44D1
Ischgl *Austria* 47D1
Ischia, I *Italy* 53B2
Ise *Japan* 75B2
Iseo *Italy* 47D2
Iserlohn *W Germ* 46D1
Isernia *Italy* 53B2
Ise-wan, B *Japan* 75B2
Ishigaki, I *Japan* 69E4
Ishikari, R *Japan* 74E2
Ishikari-wan, B *Japan* 74E2
Ishim *USSR* 65H4
Ishim, R *USSR* 65H4
Ishinomaki *Japan* 74E3
Ishioka *Japan* 75C1
Ishkashim *Afghan* 84C1
Ishpeming *USA* 14A1
Isil'kul *USSR* 65J4
Isiolo *Kenya* 99D2
Isiro *Zaïre* 98C2
Iskenderun *Turk* 92C2
Iskenferun Körfezi, B *Turk* 92C2
İskilip *Turk* 92B1
Iskitim *USSR* 65K4
Iskur, R *Bulg* 54B2
Iskut, R *Can/USA* 12H3
Isla *Mexico* 23B2
Isla Bermejo, I *Arg* 34C3
Isla Blanquilla *Ven* 27E4
Isla Coiba, I *Panama* 32A2
Isla de Cedros, I *Mexico* 9B4
Isla de Chiloé, I *Chile* 29B4
Isla de Cozumel, I *Mexico* 25D2
Isla de la Gonâve *Cuba* 26C3
Isla de la Juventud, I *Cuba* 26A2
Isla de las Lechiguanas, I *Arg* 34D2
Isla del Coco, I *Costa Rica* 3K8
Isla del Maiz, I *Caribbean* 25D3
Isla de Lobos, I *Mexico* 23B1
Isla de los Estados, I *Arg* 29D6
Isla de Marajó, I *Brazil* 28E2
Isla de Pascua, I *Pacific O* 105L5
Isla de Providencia, I *Caribbean* 26A4
Isla de San Andres, I *Caribbean* 26A4
Isla de Santa Catarina, I *Brazil* 30G4
Isla du Diable, I *French Guiana* 33G2
Isla Fernando de Noronha, I *Brazil* 31E2
Isla Grande de Tierra del Fuego, I *Arg/Chile* 29C6
Isla la Tortuga, I *Ven* 27D4
Islamabad *Pak* 84C2
Isla Magdalena, I *Mexico* 24A2
Isla Margarita *Ven* 27E4
Isla Mocha *Chile* 34A3
Islamorada *USA* 17B2
Island L *Can* 10A1
Island Lg *Aust* 108A2
Islands,B of *NZ* 110B1

Isla Puná, I *Ecuador* **32A4**
Isla San Ambrosia, I *Pacific O* **103D6**
Isla San Felix, I *Pacific O* **103D6**
Isla Santa Margarita, I *Mexico* **24A2**
Isla Santa Maria, I *Chile* **34A3**
Islas Baleares, Is *Spain* **51C2**
Islas Canarias, Is *Atlantic O* **96A2**
Islas Columbretes, Is *Spain* **51C2**
Islas de la Bahia, Is *Honduras* **25D3**
Islas del Maíz, Is *Caribbean* **26A4**
Islas de Margarita, Is *Ven* **33E1**
Islas Diego Ramírez, Is *Chile* **29C7**
Islas Galapagos, Is *Pacific O* **32J7**
Islas Juan Fernández *Chile* **30H6**
Islas los Roques, Is *Ven* **32D1**
Islas Revilla Gigedo, Is *Pacific O* **105L3**
Islas Wollaston, Is *Chile* **29C7**
Isla Tidra, I *Maur* **97A3**
Isla Wellington, I *Chile* **29B5**
Isle, R *France* **48C2**
Isle Amsterdam, I *Indian O* **104B5**
Isle of Wight, I *Eng* **43D4**
Isle Royale, I *USA* **10B2**
Isle St Paul, I *Indian O* **104B5**
Îsles Crozet, I *Indian O* **104A6**
Îsles de la Société *Pacific O* **105J4**
Îsles Gambier, Is *Pacific O* **105K5**
Isles Glorieuses, Is *Madag* **101D2**
Îsles Kerguelen, Is *Indian O* **104B6**
Îsles Marquises, Is *Pacific O* **105K4**
Îsles Tuamotu, Is *Pacific O* **105J4**
Îsles Tubai, Is *Pacific O* **105J5**
Isleton *USA* **22B1**
Ismâ'ilîya *Egypt* **92B3**
Isoanala *Madag* **101D3**
Isoka *Zambia* **101C2**
Isola Egadi, I *Italy* **53B3**
Isola Ponziane, I *Italy* **52B2**
Isole Lipari, Is *Italy* **53B3**
Isoles Tremiti, Is *Italy* **52C2**
Isosaki *Japan* **75B1**
İsparta *Turk* **92B2**
Israel, Republic *S W Asia* **94B2**
Isser, R *Alg* **51C2**
Issoire *France* **48C2**
Issoudun *France* **49C2**
İstanbul *Turk* **92A1**
Istiáia *Greece* **55B3**
Istmo de Tehuantepec Isthmus *Mexico* **25C3**
Istokpoga,L *USA* **17B2**
Istra, Pen *Yugos* **52B1**
Istranca Dağlari, Upland *Turk* **54C2**
Itaberai *Brazil* **35B1**
Itabira *Brazil* **35C1**
Itabirito *Brazil* **35C2**
Itabuna *Brazil* **31D4**
Itacoatiara *Brazil* **33F4**
Itagui *Colombia* **32B2**
Itaituba *Brazil* **33F4**
Itajaí *Brazil* **30G4**
Itajuba *Brazil* **35B2**
Italy, Repubic *Europe* **52B2**
Itamaraju *Brazil* **35D1**
Itamarandiba *Brazil* **35C1**
Itambacuri *Brazil* **35C1**
Itambé, Mt *Brazil* **35C1**
Itānagar *India* **86C1**
Itanhaém *Brazil* **35B2**
Itanhém *Brazil* **35C1**
Itanhém, R *Brazil* **35C1**
Itaobím *Brazil* **35C1**
Itapecerica *Brazil* **35B2**
Itaperuna *Brazil* **35C2**
Itapetinga *Brazil* **31C5**
Itapetininga *Brazil* **35B2**
Itapeva *Brazil* **35B2**
Itapipoca *Brazil* **31D2**
Itapuranga *Brazil* **35B1**
Itaqui *Brazil* **30E4**
Itarantim *Brazil* **35C1**
Itararé *Brazil* **35B2**
Itararé, R *Brazil* **35B2**
Itaúna *Brazil* **35C2**
Iténez, R *Brazil/Bol* **33E6**
Ithaca *USA* **15C2**
Itimbiri, R *Zaïre* **98C2**
Itinga *Brazil* **35C1**
Itivdleg *Greenland* **6E3**
Ito *Japan* **75B2**
Itoigawa *Japan* **74D3**
Itonomas, R *Bol* **33E6**
Itu *Brazil* **35B2**
Itumbiara *Brazil* **35B1**
Iturama *Brazil* **35A1**
Iturbe *Arg* **30C3**
Iturutaba *Brazil* **35B1**
Itzehoe *W Germ* **56B2**
Iurga *USSR* **65K4**
Ivacevichi *USSR* **58D2**
Ivai, R *Brazil* **35A2**
Ivalo *Fin* **38K5**
Ivangrad *Yugos* **54A2**
Ivanhoe *Aust* **108B2**
Ivano *USSR* **64D5**
Ivano-Frankovsk *USSR* **59C3**
Ivanovo *USSR* **61F2**
Ivdel' *USSR* **65H3**
Ivindo, R *Gabon* **98B2**
Ivohibe *Madag* **101D3**
Ivongo Soanierana *Madag* **101D2**
Ivory Coast, Republic *Africa* **97B4**
Ivrea *Italy* **52A1**
Ivujivik *Can* **6C3**
Iwaki *Japan* **74E3**
Iwakuni *Japan* **74C4**
Iwanai *Japan* **74E2**
Iwo *Nig* **97C4**
Iwo Jima, I *Japan* **69G4**
Ixmiquilpa *Mexico* **23B1**
Ixtapa *Mexico* **23A2**
Ixtlán *Mexico* **23A1**
Iyo *Japan* **75A2**
Iyo-nada, B *Japan* **75A2**
Izhevsk *USSR* **65G4**
Izhma *USSR* **64G3**
Izkī *Oman* **91C5**
Izmail *USSR* **60C4**
İzmir *Turk* **92A2**
Izmir Körfezi, B *Turk* **55C3**
İzmit *Turk* **92A1**
İznik *Turk* **92A1**
Iznik Golü, L *Turk* **55C2**
Izra' *Syria* **94C2**
Izúcar de Matamoros *Mexico* **23B2**
Izumi-sano *Japan* **75B2**
Izumo *Japan* **75A1**
Izu-shotō, Is *Japan* **74D4**

J

Jabal al Akhdar, Mts *Libya* **95B1**
Jabal al 'Arab *Syria* **94C2**
Jabal as Sawdā, Mts *Libya* **95A2**
Jabal az Ẕannah *UAE* **91B5**
Jabal Halīmah, Mt *Syria/Leb* **94C1**
Jabalpur *India* **83B3**
Jablonec nad Nisou *Czech* **59B2**
Jaboatão *Brazil* **31D3**
Jaboticabal *Brazil* **35B2**
Jaca *Spain* **51B1**
Jacala *Mexico* **23B1**
Jacareacanga *Brazil* **33F5**
Jacarei *Brazil* **35B2**
Jacarezinho *Brazil* **30F3**
Jáchal *Arg* **29C2**
Jacinto *Brazil* **35C1**
Jackfish L *Can* **13F2**
Jackson *Aust* **109C1**
Jackson, California *USA* **22B1**
Jackson, Michigan *USA* **14B2**
Jackson, Mississippi *USA* **19B3**
Jackson, Missouri *USA* **18C2**
Jackson, Ohio *USA* **14B3**
Jackson, Tennessee *USA* **11B3**
Jackson,C *NZ* **111B2**
Jackson Head, Pt *NZ* **111A2**
Jacksonville, Arkansas *USA* **19B3**
Jacksonville, Florida *USA* **17B1**
Jacksonville, Illinois *USA* **18B2**
Jacksonville, N Carolina *USA* **17C1**
Jacksonville, Texas *USA* **19A3**
Jacksonville Beach *USA* **17B1**
Jacmel *Haiti* **26C3**
Jacobabad *Pak* **84B3**
Jacobina *Brazil* **31C4**
Jacona *Mexico* **23A2**
Jaén *Peru* **32B5**
Jaén *Spain* **50B2**
Jaffa,C *Aust* **108A3**
Jaffna *Sri Lanka* **87B3**
Jagannathganj Ghat *Bang* **86B2**
Jagdalpur *India* **87C1**
Jagin, R *Iran* **91C4**
Jagtial *India* **87B1**
Jaguarão, R *Brazil* **29F2**
Jaguarialva *Brazil* **35B2**
Jahrom *Iran* **91B4**
Jāina *India* **85D5**
Jainca *China* **72A2**
Jaipur *India* **85D3**
Jaisalmer *India* **85C3**
Jajarm *Iran* **90C2**
Jajce *Yugos* **52C2**
Jakarta *Indon* **78B4**
Jakobshavn *Greenland* **6E3**
Jakobstad *Fin* **38J6**
Jalaca *Mexico* **23B2**
Jalai-Kut *Afghan* **84B2**
Jalapa *Mexico* **23B2**
Jales *Brazil* **35A2**
Jaleswar *Nepal* **86B1**
Jalgaon *India* **85D4**
Jalingo *Nig* **97D4**
Jalón, R *Spain* **51B1**
Jalo Oasis *Libya* **95B2**
Jālor *India* **85C3**
Jalostotitlan *Mexico* **23A1**
Jalpāiguri *India* **86B1**
Jalpan *Mexico* **23B1**
Jama *Ecuador* **32A4**
Jamaica, I *Caribbean* **26B3**
Jamaica Chan *Caribbean* **26B3**
Jamalpur *Bang* **86B2**
Jambi *Indon* **78A3**
Jambussar *India* **85C4**
James B *Can* **7B4**
Jameston *USA* **5J5**
Jamestown *Aust* **108A2**
Jamestown, N. Dakota *USA* **8D2**
Jamestown, New York *USA* **15C2**
Jamestown, Rhode Island *USA* **16D2**
Jamiltepec *Mexico* **23B2**
Jamkhandi *India* **87B1**
Jammu *India* **84C2**
Jammu and Kashmir, State *India* **84D2**
Jamnagar *India* **85B4**
Jampur *Pak* **84C3**
Jämsä *Fin* **38K6**
Jamshedpur *India* **86B2**
Janakpur *Nepal* **86B1**
Janaúba *Brazil* **35C1**
Jandaq *Iran* **90B3**
Jandowae *Aust* **109D1**
Jan Mayen, I *Norwegian S* **1B1**
Januária *Brazil* **35C1**
Jaora *India* **85D4**
Japan, Empire *E Asia* **51**
Japan,S of *S E Asia* **74C3**
Japan Trench *Pacific O* **104F2**
Japurá, R *Brazil* **32D4**
Jarābulus *Syria* **93C2**
Jaraguá *Brazil* **35B1**
Jarama, R *Spain* **50B1**
Jarash *Jordan* **94B2**
Jardim *Brazil* **30E3**
Jardin, R *Spain* **51B2**
Jardines de la Reina, Is *Cuba* **26B2**
Jari, R *Brazil* **33G3**
Jaria Jhānjail *Bang* **86C1**
Jarny *France* **46C2**
Jarocin *Pol* **58B2**
Jaroslaw *Pol* **59C2**
Järpen *Sweden* **38G6**
Jartai *China* **72B2**
Jasdan *India* **85C4**
Jasikan *Ghana* **97C4**
Jāsk *Iran* **91C4**
Jaslo *Pol* **59C3**
Jason Is *Falkland Is* **29D6**
Jasper, Arkansas *USA* **18B2**
Jasper *Can* **13D2**
Jasper, Florida *USA* **17B1**
Jasper, Indiana *USA* **14A3**
Jasper, Texas *USA* **19B3**
Jasper Nat Pk *Can* **13D2**
Jastrowie *Pol* **58B2**
Jatai *Brazil* **35A1**
Játiva *Spain* **51B2**
Jatobá *Brazil* **31B2**
Jau *Brazil* **35B2**
Jauja *Peru* **32B6**
Jaunpur *India* **86A1**
Javadi Hills *India* **87B2**
Java S *Indon* **70B4**
Java Trench *Indon* **106A2**
Jawa, I *Indon* **78B4**
Jayapura *Indon* **71F4**
Jayrūd *Syria* **94C2**
Jbel Ouarkziz, Mts *Mor* **96B2**
Jbel Sarhro, Mt *Mor* **96B1**
Jeanerette *USA* **19B4**
Jebba *Nig* **97C4**
Jebel 'Abd al 'Azīz, Mt *Syria* **93D2**
Jebel Abyad *Sudan* **95B3**
Jebel Akhdar, Mt *Oman* **91C5**
Jebel al Lawz, Mt *S Arabia* **92C4**
Jebel ash Shaykh, Mt *Syria* **94B2**
Jebel Asoteriba, Mt *Sudan* **95C2**
Jebel Ed Dabab, Mt *Jordan* **94B3**
Jebel el Ata'ita, Mt *Jordan* **94B3**

Jebel esh Sharqi, Mts *Leb/Syria* **92C3**
Jebel Ithrīyat, Mt *Jordan* **94C3**
Jebel Ja'lan, Mt *Oman* **91C5**
Jebel Liban, Mts *Leb* **94B2**
Jebel Ma'lūlā, Mt *Syria* **94C2**
Jebel Marra, Mt *Sudan* **98C1**
Jebel Mudeisisat, Mt *Jordan* **94C3**
Jebel Oda, Mt *Sudan* **95C2**
Jebel Qasr ed Deir, Mt *Jordan* **94B3**
Jebel Um ed Daraj, Mt *Jordan* **94B2**
Jebel Uweinat, Mt *Sudan* **95B2**
Jedburgh *Scot* **42C2**
Jedrzejów *Pol* **59C2**
Jefferson, Texas *USA* **19B3**
Jefferson City *USA* **11A3**
Jefferson,Mt *USA* **8B3**
Jeffersonville *USA* **14A3**
Jekabpils *USSR* **60C2**
Jelena Gora *Pol* **59B2**
Jelgava *USSR* **60B2**
Jember *Indon* **78C4**
Jena *E Germ* **57C2**
Jenaja, I *Indon* **78B2**
Jenbach *Austria* **47D1**
Jenin *Israel* **94B2**
Jennings *USA* **19B3**
Jenseniky, Upland *Czech* **59B2**
Jensen Nunatakker, Mt *Greenland* **6F3**
Jens Munk, I *Can* **6B3**
Jeparit *Aust* **108B3**
Jequié *Brazil* **31D4**
Jequital, R *Brazil* **35C1**
Jequitinhonha *Brazil* **35C1**
Jequitinhonha, R *Brazil* **31C5**
Jerez de la Frontera *Spain* **50A2**
Jerez de los Caballeros *Spain* **50A2**
Jericho *Israel* **94B3**
Jerilderie *Aust* **108C3**
Jersey, I *UK* **48B2**
Jersey City *USA* **10C2**
Jersey Shore *USA* **15C2**
Jerseyville *USA* **18B2**
Jerusalem *Israel* **92C3**
Jervis B *Aust* **109D3**
Jervis Inlet, Sd *Can* **13C2**
Jesenice *Yugos* **52B1**
Jessore *Bang* **86B2**
Jesup *USA* **11B3**
Jesus Maria *Arg* **34C2**
Jewett City *USA* **16D2**
Jezerce, Mt *Alb* **54A2**
Jezioro Mamry, L *Pol* **58C2**
Jezioro Śniardwy, L *Pol* **58C2**
Jezzine *Leb* **94B2**
Jhābua *India* **85C4**
Jhālāwār *India* **85D4**
Jhang Maghiana *Pak* **84C2**
Jhānsi *India* **85D3**
Jhārsuguda *India* **86A2**
Jhelum *Pak* **84C2**
Jhelum, R *Pak* **84C2**
J H Kerr L *USA* **11C3**
Jhunjhunūn *India* **84D3**
Jiamusi *China* **69F2**
Ji'an, Jiangxi *China* **73C4**
Ji'an, Jilin *China* **74B2**
Jiande *China* **73D4**
Jiang'an *China* **73B4**
Jiangbiancun *China* **73D4**
Jiangcheng *China* **73A5**
Jiang Jiang, R *China* **73B3**
Jiangmen *China* **73C5**
Jiangsu, Province *China* **72D3**
Jiangxi, Province *China* **73C4**
Jiangyou *China* **73A3**
Jianping *China* **72D1**
Jianshui *China* **73A5**
Jian Xi, R *China* **73D4**
Jianyang *China* **73D4**
Jiaonan *China* **72E2**
Jiao Xian *China* **72E2**
Jiaozhou Wan, B *China* **72E2**
Jiaozuo *China* **72C2**
Jiaxiang *China* **73E3**
Jiayuguan *China* **68B3**
Jiddah *S Arabia* **81B3**
Jieshou *China* **72D3**
Jiexiu *China* **72C2**
Jigzhi *China* **72A3**
Jihlava *Czech* **59B3**
Jilib *Somalia* **99E2**
Jilin *China* **69E2**
Jiloca, R *Spain* **51B1**
Jiménez, Coahuila *Mexico* **9C4**
Jimma *Eth* **99D2**
Jinan *China* **72D2**
Jind *India* **84D3**
Jingbian *China* **72B2**
Jingdezhen *China* **73D4**
Jinghong *China* **76C1**
Jingmen *China* **73C3**
Jingning *China* **72B2**
Jing Xiang *China* **73B4**
Jinhua *China* **73D4**
Jining, Nei Monggol *China* **72C1**
Jining, Shandong *China* **72D2**
Jinja *Uganda* **99D2**
Jinping *China* **76C1**
Jinsha Jiang, R *China* **73A4**
Jinshi *China* **73C4**
Jinxi *China* **72E1**
Jin Xian *China* **72E2**
Jinzhou *China* **72E1**
Jiparaná, R *Brazil* **33E5**
Jipijapa *Ecuador* **32A4**
Jiquilpan *Mexico* **23A2**
Jīroft *Iran* **91C4**
Jishou *China* **73B4**
Jisr ash Shughūr *Syria* **92C2**
Jiu, R *Rom* **54B2**
Jiujiang *China* **73D4**
Jiulong *China* **73A4**
Jiulong Jiang, R *China* **73D4**
Jixi *China* **69F2**
Jiza *Jordan* **94B3**
Jīzan *S Arabia* **81C4**
Joal *Sen* **97A3**
João Monlevade *Brazil* **35C1**
João Pessoa *Brazil* **31E3**
João Pirheiro *Brazil* **35B1**
Jocoli *Arg* **34B2**
Jodhpur *India* **85C3**
Joensuu *Fin* **38K6**
Joeuf *France* **46C2**
Joffre,Mt *Can* **13D2**
Jogbani *India* **86B1**
Jog Falls *India* **87A2**
Johannesburg *S Africa* **101G1**
Johannesburg *USA* **21B2**
Johan Pen *Can* **6C2**
John, R *USA* **12D1**
John Day *USA* **20C2**
John Day, R *USA* **20B1**
John O'Groats *Scot* **44C2**
John Redmond Res *USA* **18A2**
Johnson City, Tennessee *USA* **11B3**
Johnston *USA* **17B1**
Johnston Pt *St Vincent* **27N2**
Johnstown, Pennsylvania *USA* **15C2**
Johor Bharu *Malay* **77C5**
Joigny *France* **49C2**
Joinville *Brazil* **30G4**
Jok, R *USSR* **61H3**
Jokkmokk *Sweden* **38H5**
Jolfa *Iran* **93E2**
Joliet *USA* **10B2**
Joliette *Can* **7C5**
Jolo *Phil* **79B4**
Jolo, I *Phil* **79B4**
Joma, Mt *China* **82D2**
Jonava *USSR* **58C1**
Jonê *China* **72A3**
Jonesboro, Arkansas *USA* **11A3**
Jonesboro, Louisiana *USA* **19B3**
Jones Sd *Can* **6B2**
Joniśkis *USSR* **58C1**
Jönköping *Sweden* **39G7**
Joplin *USA* **11A3**
Jordan, Kingdom *S W Asia* **92C3**
Jordan, R *Israel* **94B2**
Jordan Valley *USA* **20C2**
Jorhāt *India* **86C1**
Jörn *Sweden* **38J5**
Jorong *Indon* **78C3**
Jørpeland *Nor* **39F7**
Jose Pañganiban *Phil* **79B3**
Joseph Bonaparte G *Aust* **106B2**
Jotunheimen, Mt *Nor* **64B3**
Jouai'ya *Leb* **94B2**
Jounié *Leb* **94B2**
Jowal *India* **86C1**
Jowhar *Somalia* **99E2**
Joy,Mt *Can* **12H2**
Juan de Fuca,Str of *USA/Can* **5F5**
Juan de Nova, I *Mozam Chan* **101D2**
Juárez *Arg* **34D3**
Juàzeiro *Brazil* **31C3**
Juazeiro do Norte *Brazil* **31D3**
Juba *Sudan* **99D2**
Juba, R *Somalia* **99E2**
Jubail *Leb* **94B1**
Jubbah *S Arabia* **93D3**
Jucar, R *Spain* **51B2**
Juchatengo *Mexico* **23B2**
Juchipila, R *Mexico* **23A1**
Juchitlan *Mexico* **23A1**
Judenburg *Austria* **57C3**
Juilaca *Peru* **30B2**
Juiling Shan, Hills *China* **73C4**
Juiz de Fora *Brazil* **31C6**
Jujuy, State *Arg* **30C3**
Juli *Peru* **30C2**
Julianatop, Mt *Surinam* **33F3**
Julianehab *Greenland* **6F3**
Jülich *W Germ* **46D1**
Jullundur *India* **84D2**
Jumla *Nepal* **86A1**
Jum Suwwāna, Mt *Jordan* **94B3**
Jūnāgadh *India* **85C4**
Junan *China* **72D2**
Junction City *USA* **9D3**
Jundiaí *Brazil* **31B6**
Juneau *USA* **4E4**
Junee *Aust* **107D4**
June Lake *USA* **22C2**
Jungfrau, Mt *Switz* **52A1**
Juniata, R *USA* **16A2**
Junín *Arg* **29D2**
Junlian *China* **73A4**
Juquiá *Brazil* **31B6**
Jur, R *Sudan* **99C2**
Jura, I *Scot* **42B2**
Jura, Mts *France* **49D2**
Jura,Sound of, Chan *Scot* **44B3**
Jurf ed Darāwīsh *Jordan* **94B3**
Jūrmala *USSR* **60B2**
Juruá, R *Brazil* **32D4**
Juruena, R *Brazil* **33F6**
Jūsīyah *Syria* **94C1**
Justo Daract *Arg* **34B2**
Jutai, R *Brazil* **32D4**
Juticalpa *Honduras* **25D3**
Jūymand *Iran* **90C3**
Jylland, Pen *Den* **56B1**
Jyväskyla *Fin* **38K6**

K

K2, Mt *China/India* **82B2**
Kaakhka *USSR* **90C2**
Kaapmuiden *S Africa* **101H1**
Kabaena, I *Indon* **71D4**
Kabala *Sierra Leone* **97A4**
Kabale *Rwanda* **99D3**
Kabalo *Zaïre* **98C3**
Kabambare *Zaïre* **98C3**
Kabarole *Uganda* **99D2**
Kabinda *Zaïre* **98C3**
Kabir Kuh, Mts *Iran* **90A3**
Kabompo *Zambia* **100B2**
Kabompo, R *Zambia* **100B2**
Kabongo *Zaïre* **98C3**
Kabul *Afghan* **84B2**
Kachchh,G of *India* **85B4**
Kachkanar *USSR* **61J2**
Kachug *USSR* **63C2**
Kadan *Burma* **76B3**
Kadapongan, I *Indon* **78D3**
Kadi *India* **85C4**
Kadina *Aust* **108A2**
Kadınhanı *Turk* **92B2**
Kadiri *India* **87B2**
Kadiyevka *USSR* **60E4**
Kadoma *Zim* **100B2**
Kadugli *Sudan* **99C1**
Kaduna *Nig* **97C3**
Kaduna, R *Nig* **97C3**
Kadūr *India* **87B2**
Kaédi *Maur* **97A3**
Kaena Pt *Hawaiian Is* **21C4**
Kaesŏng *N Korea* **74B3**
Kafanchan *Nig* **97C4**
Kaffrine *Sen* **97A3**
Kafrūn Bashūr *Syria* **94C1**
Kafue *Zambia* **100B2**
Kafue, R *Zambia* **100B2**
Kafue Nat Pk *Zambia* **100B2**
Kaga *Japan* **74D3**
Kagan *USSR* **65H6**
Kağizman *Turk* **93D1**
Kagoshima *Japan* **74C4**
Kāhak *Iran* **90C2**
Kahama *Tanz* **99D3**
Kahan *Pak* **84B3**
Kahayan, R *Indon* **78C3**
Kahemba *Zaïre* **98B3**
Kahler Asten, Mt *W Germ* **46E1**
Kahnūj *Iran* **91C4**
Kahoka *USA* **18B1**
Kahoolawe, I *Hawaiian Is* **21C4**
Kahramanmaraş *Turk* **92C2**
Kahuku Pt *Hawaiian Is* **21C4**
Kaiapoi *NZ* **111B2**
Kaieteur Fall *Guyana* **33F2**
Kaifeng *China* **72C3**
Kaikohe *NZ* **110B1**
Kaikoura *NZ* **111B2**
Kaikoura Pen *NZ* **111B2**
Kaikoura Range, Mts *NZ* **111B2**
Kaili *China* **73B4**
Kailua *Hawaiian Is* **21C4**
Kaimana *Indon* **71E4**
Kainan *Japan* **75B2**
Kainji Res *Nig* **97C3**
Kaipara Harbour, B *NZ* **110B1**
Kaiping *China* **73C5**
Kairouan *Tunisia* **96D1**
Kaiser Peak, Mt *USA* **22C2**
Kaiserslautern *W Germ* **57B3**
Kaishantun *China* **74B2**
Kaisiadorys *USSR* **58D2**
Kaitaia *NZ* **110B1**

Kaitangata *NZ* 111A3
Kaithal *India* 84D3
Kaiwi Chan *Hawaiian Is* 21C4
Kai Xian *China* 73B3
Kaiyuan, Liaoning *China* 73A5
Kaiyuan, Yunnan *China* 74A2
Kaiyuh Mts *USA* 12C2
Kajaani *Fin* 38K6
Kajaki *Afghan* 84B2
Kajiado *Kenya* 99D3
Kajrān *Afghan* 84B2
Kaka *Sudan* 99D1
Kakamega *Kenya* 99D2
Kake *Japan* 75A2
Kake *USA* 12H3
Kakhonak *USA* 12D3
Kakhovskoye Vodokhranilishche, Res *USSR* 65E5
Kākī *Iran* 91B4
Kākināda *India* 87C1
Kakogawa *Japan* 75A2
Kaktovik *USA* 4D2
Kakuda *Japan* 75C1
Kalabáka *Greece* 55B3
Kalabakan *Malay* 78D1
Kalabo *Zambia* 100B2
Kalach *USSR* 61F3
Kalach-na-Donu *USSR* 61F4
Kaladan, R *Burma* 86C2
Ka Lae, C *Hawaiian Is* 21C4
Kalahari Desert *Botswana* 100B3
Kalajoki *Fin* 38J6
Kalakan *USSR* 63D2
Kalakepen *Indon* 70A3
Kalam *Pak* 84C1
Kalámai *Greece* 55B3
Kalamazoo *USA* 10B2
Kalat *Pak* 84B3
Kalecik *Turk* 92B1
Kalembau, I *Indon* 78D3
Kalémié *Zaïre* 99C3
Kalevala *USSR* 38L5
Kalewa *Burma* 86C2
Kalgin I *USA* 12D2
Kalgoorlie *Aust* 106B4
Kalianda *Indon* 78B4
Kalibo *Phil* 79B3
Kalima *Zaïre* 98C3
Kalimantan, Province *Indon* 78C3
Kálimnos, I *Greece* 55C3
Kālimpang *India* 86B1
Kalinin *USSR* 60E2
Kaliningrad *USSR* 60B3
Kalinkovichi *USSR* 60C3
Kalispell *USA* 8B2
Kalisz *Pol* 58B2
Kaliua *Tanz* 99D3
Kalix, R *Sweden* 38J5
Kalkfeld *Namibia* 100A3
Kalkrand *Namibia* 100A3
Kallakoopah, R *Aust* 108A1
Kallávesi, L *Fin* 38K6
Kallonis Kólpos, B *Greece* 55C3
Kalmar *Sweden* 39H7
Kalmytskaya ASSR, Republic *USSR* 61G4
Kalomo *Zambia* 100B2
Kalona *USA* 18B1
Kalone Peak, Mt *Can* 13B2
Kalpeni, I *India* 87A2
Kālpi *India* 85D3
Kalskag *USA* 12B2
Kaltag *USA* 12C2
Kaluga *USSR* 60E3
Kalundborg *Den* 39G7
Kalush *USSR* 59C3
Kalyandurg *India* 87B2
Kalyazin *USSR* 60E2
Kama, R *USSR* 61H1
Kamaishi *Japan* 74E3
Kamalia *Pak* 84C2
Kamanawa Mts *NZ* 110C1
Kamanjab *Namibia* 100A2
Kamat, Mt *India* 84D2
Kamban *India* 87B3
Kambarka *USSR* 61H2
Kambia *Sierra Leone* 97A4
Kamenets Podolskiy *USSR* 59D3
Kamenka *USSR* 61F3
Kamen-na-Obi *USSR* 65K4
Kamensk-Ural'skiy *USSR* 61K2
Kamilukuak L *Can* 5H3
Kamina *Zaïre* 98C3
Kaminak L *Can* 7A3
Kaminoyama *Japan* 75C1
Kamloops *Can* 5F4
Kamo *USSR* 93E1
Kamogawa *Japan* 75C1
Kampala *Uganda* 99D2
Kampar *Malay* 77C5
Kampar, R *Indon* 78A2
Kampen *Neth* 56B2
Kamphaeng Phet *Thai* 76B2
Kampot *Camb* 77C3
Kamsaptar *Iran* 91D4
Kamskoye Vodokhranilishche, Res *USSR* 61J2
Kāmthi *India* 85D4
Kamyshin *USSR* 61G3
Kamyshlov *USSR* 61K2
Kanaaupscow, R *Can* 7C4
Kananga *Zaïre* 98C3
Kanash *USSR* 61G2
Kanayama *Japan* 75B1
Kanazawa *Japan* 74D3
Kanbisha *USA* 4C3
Kānchipuram *India* 87B2
Kandahar *Afghan* 84B2
Kandalaksha *USSR* 64E3
Kandalakshskaya Guba B *USSR* 38L5
Kandi *Benin* 97C3
Kandos *Aust* 109C2
Kandy *Sri Lanka* 87C3
Kane *USA* 15C2
Kane Basin, B *Can* 6C1
Kanem, Desert Region *Chad* 98B1
Kangaba *Mali* 97B3
Kangal *Turk* 92C2
Kangâmiut *Greenland* 6E3
Kangān *Iran* 91B4
Kangar *Malay* 77C4
Kangaroo I *Aust* 106C4
Kanga'tsiaq *Greenland* 6E3
Kangavar *Iran* 90A3
Kangbao *China* 72C1
Kangchenjunga, Mt *Nepal* 82C3
Kangding *China* 73A4
Kangerdlugssuaq, B *Greenland* 6G3
Kangerdlugssvatsaiq, B *Greenland* 6G3
Kangetet *Kenya* 99D2
Kanggye *N Korea* 74B2
Kangiqsualujjuaq *Can* 7D4
Kangiqsujuaq *Can* 6C3
Kangnŭng *S Korea* 74B3
Kango *Gabon* 98B2
Kangto, Mt *China* 68B4
Kang Xian *China* 72B3
Kanh Hung *Viet* 77D4
Kaniama *Zaïre* 98C3
Kani Giri *India* 87B1
Kanin Nos, Pt *USSR* 64F3
Kankaanpää *Fin* 39J6
Kankakee *USA* 14A2
Kankakee, R *USA* 14A2
Kankan *Guinea* 97B3
Kānker *India* 86A2
Kanniyākuman *India* 87B3
Kano *Nig* 97C3
Kanoya *Japan* 74C4
Kānpur *India* 86A1
Kansas, State *USA* 9D3
Kansas, R *USA* 18A2
Kansas City *USA* 10A3
Kanshi *China* 73D5
Kansk *USSR* 63B2
Kantchari *U Volta* 97C3
Kanthi *India* 86B2
Kantishna *USA* 12D2
Kantishna, R *USA* 12D2
Kanye *Botswana* 100B3
Kao-hsiung *Taiwan* 68D4
Kaoka Veld, Plain *Namibia* 100A2
Kaolack *Sen* 97A3
Kaoma *Zambia* 100B2
Kapaau *Hawaiian Is* 21C4
Kapanga *Zaïre* 98C3
Kap Cort Adelaer, C *Greenland* 6F3
Kap Dalton, C *Greenland* 6H3
Kapellskär *Sweden* 39H7
Kap Farvel, C *Greenland* 6F3
Kap Gustav Holm, C *Greenland* 6G3
Kapiri *Zambia* 100B2
Kapit *Malay* 78C2
Kaplan *USA* 19B3
Kaplice *Czech* 57C3
Kapoe *Thai* 77B4
Kapona *Zaïre* 99C3
Kaposvár *Hung* 52C1
Kap Parry, C *Can* 6C2
Kap Ravn, C *Greenland* 6H3
Kapsukas *USSR* 60B3
Kapuas, R *Indon* 78B3
Kapunda *Aust* 108A2
Kapurthala *India* 84D2
Kapuskasing *Can* 7B5
Kaputar, Mt *Aust* 109D2
Kapydzhik, Mt *USSR* 93E2
Kap York, C *Greenland* 6D2
Karabük *Turk* 92B1
Karacabey *Turk* 55C2
Karachi *Pak* 85B4
Karād *India* 87A1
Kara Daglari, Mt *Turk* 60E5
Karadeniz Boğazi, Sd *Turk* 60C5
Karaftit *USSR* 68D1
Karaganda *USSR* 65J5
Karagayly *USSR* 65J5
Kāraikāl *India* 87B2
Karaj *Iran* 90B2
Karak *Jordan* 92C3
Kara Kalpakskaya, Republic *USSR* 65G5
Karakax He, R *China* 84D1
Karakelong, I *Indon* 71D3
Karakoram, Mts *India* 84D1
Karakoram, P *India/China* 84D1
Karakoro, R *Maur/Sen* 97A3
Karakumy, Desert *USSR* 65G6
Karama *Jordan* 94B3
Karaman *Turk* 92B2
Karamay *China* 65K5
Karamea *NZ* 111B2
Karamea Bight, B *NZ* 111B2
Kāranja *India* 85D4
Karapınar *Turk* 92B2
Kara S *USSR* 64H2
Karasburg *Namibia* 100A3
Karasjok *Nor* 38K5
Karasuk *USSR* 65J4
Karataş *Turk* 92C2
Kara Tau, Mts *USSR* 65H5
Karathuri *Burma* 76B3
Karatsu *Japan* 74B4
Karāz *Iran* 91B4
Karbalā' *Iraq* 93D3
Karcag *Hung* 59C3
Kardhítsa *Greece* 55B3
Karel'skaya ASSR, Republic *USSR* 64E3
Karesvando *Sweden* 38J5
Karet, Desert Region *Maur* 96B2
Kargasok *USSR* 65K4
Kari *Nig* 97D3
Kariba *Zim* 100B2
Kariba, L *Zim/Zambia* 100B2
Kariba Dam *Zim/Zambia* 100B2
Karima *Sudan* 95C3
Karimata, I *Indon* 78B3
Karimganj *Bang* 86C2
Karīmnagar *India* 87B1
Karin *Somalia* 99E1
Karis *Fin* 39J6
Karishimbe, Mt *Zaïre* 99C3
Káristos *Greece* 55B3
Kārkal *India* 87A2
Karkar, I *PNG* 71F4
Karkheh, R *Iran* 90A3
Karkinitskiy Zaliv, B *USSR* 60D4
Karlik Shan, Mt *China* 63B3
Karlino *Pol* 58B2
Karl Marx Stadt *E Germ* 57C2
Karlobag *Yugos* 52C2
Karlovac *Yugos* 52C1
Karlovo *Bulg* 54B2
Karlovy Vary *Czech* 57C2
Karlshamn *Sweden* 39G7
Karlskoga *Sweden* 39G7
Karlskrona *Sweden* 39H7
Karlsruhe *W Germ* 57B3
Karlstad *Sweden* 39G7
Karluk *USA* 12D3
Karnafuli Res *Bang* 86C2
Karnal *India* 84D3
Karnataka, State *India* 87A1
Karnobat *Bulg* 54C2
Karoi *Zim* 100B2
Karonga *Malawi* 99D3
Karora *Sudan* 95C3
Karossa *Indon* 78D3
Kárpathos, I *Greece* 55C3
Karrats Fjord *Greenland* 6E2
Kars *Turk* 93D1
Karsakpay *USSR* 65H4
Kārsava *USSR* 58D1
Karshi *USSR* 80E2
Karstula *Fin* 38J6
Kartaba *Leb* 94B1
Kartal *Turk* 54C2
Kartaly *USSR* 61K3
Kārūn, R *Iran* 90A3
Karwa *India* 86A1
Kārwār *India* 87A2
Karymskoye *USSR* 68D1
Kasai, R *Zaïre* 98B3
Kasaji *Zaïre* 100B2
Kasama *Zambia* 101C2
Kasanga *Tanz* 99D3
Kāsaragod *India* 87A2
Kasba L *Can* 5H3
Kasempa *Zambia* 100B2
Kasenga *Zaïre* 100B2
Kasese *Uganda* 99D2
Kāshān *Iran* 90B3
Kashegelok *USA* 12C2
Kashi *China* 82B2
Kāshipur *India* 84D3
Kashiwazaki *Japan* 74D3
Kashmar *Iran* 90C2
Kashmir, State *India* 66D3
Kasimov *USSR* 61F3
Kaskaskia, R *USA* 18C2
Kasko *Fin* 38J6
Kasli *USSR* 61K2
Kaslo *Can* 5G5
Kasonga *Zaïre* 98C3
Kasongo-Lunda *Zaïre* 98B3
Kásos, I *Greece* 55C3
Kaspiyskiy *USSR* 61G4
Kassala *Sudan* 95C3
Kassel *W Germ* 56B2
Kasserine *Tunisia* 96C1
Kassinga *Angola* 100A2

Kastamonou *Turk* 92B1
Kastélli *Greece* 55B3
Kastellorizon, I *Greece* 92A2
Kastoría *Greece* 55B2
Kástron *Greece* 55C3
Kasugai *Japan* 74D3
Kasumi *Japan* 75A1
Kasungu *Malawi* 101C2
Kasur *Pak* 84C2
Kataba *Zambia* 100B2
Katako-kombe *Zaïre* 98C3
Katalla *USA* 4D3
Katangli *USSR* 63G2
Katanning *Aust* 106A4
Kateríni *Greece* 55B2
Kates Needle, Mt *Can/USA* 5E4
Katha *Burma* 82D3
Katherine *Aust* 106C2
Kāthiāwār, Pen *India* 85C4
Kathmandu *Nepal* 86B1
Kathua *India* 84D2
Katihār *India* 86B1
Katima Mulilo *Namibia* 100B2
Katmai,Mt *USA* 4C4
Katmai Nat Mon *USA* 12D3
Katni *India* 86A2
Katoomba *Aust* 109D2
Katowice *Pol* 59B2
Katrineholm *Sweden* 39H7
Katsina *Nig* 97C3
Katsina Ala *Nig* 97C4
Katsuta *Japan* 75C1
Katsuura *Japan* 75C1
Katsuy *Japan* 75B1
Kattakurgan *USSR* 65H6
Kattegat, Str *Denmark/Sweden* 39G7
Kauai, I *Hawaiian Is* 21C4
Kauai Chan *Hawaiian Is* 21C4
Kaulakahi Chan *Hawaiian Is* 21C4
Kaunakaki *Hawaiian Is* 21C4
Kaunas *USSR* 60B3
Kaura Namoda *Nig* 97C3
Kautokeino *Nor* 38J5
Kavadarci *Yugos* 55B2
Kavajë *Alb* 55A2
Kavali *India* 87B2
Kavállа *Greece* 55B2
Kāvda *India* 85B4
Kawagoe *Japan* 75B1
Kawaguchi *Japan* 75B1
Kawakawa *NZ* 110B1
Kawambwa *Zambia* 99C3
Kawardha *India* 86A2
Kawartha Lakes *Can* 15C2
Kawasaki *Japan* 74D3
Kawerau *NZ* 110C1
Kawhia *NZ* 110B1
Kaya *U Volta* 97B3
Kayak I *USA* 12F3
Kayan, R *Indon* 78D2
Kāyankulam *India* 87B3
Kayes *Mali* 97A3
Kayseri *Turk* 92C2
Kazach'ye *USSR* 1B8
Kazakh *USSR* 93E1
Kazakhskaya SSR, Republic *USSR* 65G5
Kazan' *USSR* 61G2
Kazanlŭk *Bulg* 54C2
Kazan Retto, Is *Japan* 69G4
Kāzerūn *Iran* 91B4
Kazhim *USSR* 61H1
Kazi Magomed *USSR* 93E1
Kazincbarcika *Hung* 59C3
Kéa, I *Greece* 55B3
Kealaikahiki Chan *Hawaiian Is* 21C4
Kearney *USA* 8D2
Keban Baraji, Res *Turk* 93C2
Kébémer *Sen* 97A3
Kebili *Tunisia* 96C1
Kebīr, R *Syria/Leb* 94C1
Kebrekaise, Mt *Sweden* 38H5
Kecskemet *Hung* 59B3
Kedainiai *USSR* 58C1
Kédougou *Sen* 97A3
Keele, R *Can* 12J2
Keele Pk, Mt *Can* 12H2
Keeler *USA* 21B2
Keene, New Hampshire *USA* 15D2
Keetmanshoop *Namibia* 100A3
Keewanee *USA* 18C1
Keewatin, Region *Can* 6A3
Kefallinía, I *Greece* 55B3
Kefar Sava *Israel* 94B2
Keffi *Nig* 97C4
Keflavik *Iceland* 38A2
Keg River *Can* 5G4
Kehsi Mansam *Burma* 76B1
Keith *Aust* 108B3
Keith *Scot* 44C3
Keith Arm, B *Can* 4F3
Kekertuk *Can* 6D3
Kekri *India* 85D3
Kelang *Malay* 77C5
Kelantan, R *Malay* 77C4
Kelif *USSR* 84B1
Kelkit, R *Turk* 92C1
Kellé *Congo* 98B3
Kellet,C *Can* 4F2
Kellogg *USA* 20C1
Kelloselka *Fin* 64D3
Kells *Irish Rep* 45C2
Kells Range, Hills *Scot* 42B2
Kelme *USSR* 58C1
Kelowna *Can* 5G5
Kelsey Bay *Can* 5F4
Kelso *Scot* 42C2
Kelso *USA* 20B1
Kem' *USSR* 64E3
Kem', R *USSR* 38L6
Ke Macina *Mali* 97B3
Kemano *Can* 13B2
Kemerovo *USSR* 65K4
Kemi *Fin* 38J5
Kemi, R *Fin* 38K5
Kemijärvi *Fin* 38K5
Kempen, Region *Belg* 46C1
Kemps Bay *Bahamas* 26B2
Kempsey *Aust* 109D2
Kempten *W Germ* 57C3
Kenai *USA* 12D2
Kenai Mts *USA* 12D3
Kenai Pen *USA* 12D2
Kenamuke Swamp *Sudan* 99D2
Kendal *Eng* 42C2
Kendall *Aust* 109D2
Kendari *Indon* 71D4
Kendawangan *Indon* 78C3
Kendrāpāra *India* 86B2
Kendrick *USA* 20C1
Kenema *Sierra Leone* 97A4
Kenge *Zaïre* 98B3
Kengtung *Burma* 76B1
Kenhardt *S Africa* 100B3
Kéniéba *Mali* 97A3
Kenitra *Mor* 96B1
Kenmare *Irish Rep* 45B3
Kenmare, R *Irish Rep* 45B3
Kenner *USA* 19B4
Kennett *USA* 18C2
Kennett Square *USA* 16B3
Kennewick *USA* 20C1
Kenny Dam *Can* 5F4
Kenora *Can* 7A5
Kenosha *USA* 10B2
Kent, County *Eng* 43E4
Kent, Washington *USA* 20B1
Kentland *USA* 14A2
Kenton *USA* 14B2
Kent Pen *Can* 4H3
Kentucky, State *USA* 11B3
Kentucky L *USA* 11B3
Kentwood, Louisiana *USA* 19B3
Kentwood, Michigan *USA* 14A2
Kenya, Republic *Africa* 99D2
Kenya,Mt *Kenya* 99D3
Keokuk *USA* 18B1
Keonchi *India* 86A2
Keonjhargarh *India* 86B2
Kepaluan Tanimbar, Arch *Indon* 71E4
Keplavik *Iceland* 6H3
Kepno *Pol* 59B2
Kepulauan Anambas, Arch *Indon* 78B2
Kepulauan Aru, Arch *Indon* 71E4
Kepulauan Badas, Is *Indon* 78B2
Kepulauan Banda, Arch *Indon* 71E4
Kepulauan Banggai, I *Indon* 71D4
Kepulauan Bunguran Seletan, Arch *Indon* 78B2
Kepulauan Kai, Arch *Indon* 71E4
Kepulauan Leti, I *Indon* 71D4
Kepulauan Lingga, Is *Indon* 78A3
Kepulauan Mentawi, Arch *Indon* 70A4
Kepulauan Riau, Arch *Indon* 78A2
Kepulauan Sabalana, Arch *Indon* 78D4
Kepulauan Sangihe, Arch *Indon* 71D3
Kepulauan Sula, I *Indon* 71D4
Kepulauan Talaud, Arch *Indon* 71D3
Kepulauan Tambelan, Is *Indon* 78B2
Kepulauan Tanimbar, I *Indon* 71E4
Kepulauan Togian, I *Indon* 71D4
Kepulauan Tukambesi, Is *Indon* 71D4
Kerala, State *India* 87B2
Kerang *Aust* 108B3
Kerava *Fin* 39K6
Kerch' *USSR* 60E4
Kerema *PNG* 71F4
Keremeps *Can* 20C1
Keren *Eth* 95C3
Kerguelen Ridge *Indian O* 104B6
Kericho *Kenya* 99D3
Kerinci, Mt *Indon* 70B4
Kerio, R *Kenya* 99D2
Kerki *USSR* 80E2
Kérkira *Greece* 55A3
Kérkira, I *Greece* 55A3
Kerman *Iran* 91C3
Kerman *USA* 22B2
Kermānshāh *Iran* 90A3
Kerme Körfezi, B *Turk* 55C3
Kern, R *USA* 21B2
Kerrobert *Can* 13F2
Kerry, County *Irish Rep* 45B2
Kershaw *USA* 17B1
Kertamulia *Indon* 78B3
Kerulen, R *Mongolia* 63D3
Kerzaz *Alg* 96B2
Keşan *Turk* 55C2
Kesennuma *Japan* 74E3
Kestenga *USSR* 38L5
Keswick *Eng* 42C2
Kéta *Ghana* 97C4
Ketapang *Indon* 78C3
Ketchikan *USA* 5E4
Ketia *Niger* 97C3
Keti Bandar *Pak* 85B4
Ketrzyn *Pol* 58C2
Kettering *Eng* 43D3
Kettering *USA* 14B3
Kettle, R *Can* 20C1
Kettle River Range, Mts *USA* 20C1
Kettlestone B *Can* 7C3
Kevir-i Namak, Salt Flat *Iran* 90C3
Kewaunee *USA* 14A2
Key Harbour *Can* 14B1
Key Largo *USA* 17B2
Key West *USA* 11B4
Kezhma *USSR* 63C2
K'félegháza *Hung* 54A1
Kgun L *USA* 12B2
Khabab *Syria* 94C2
Khabarovsk *USSR* 62H3
Khairpur *Pak* 85B3
Khairpur, Region *Pak* 85B3
Khakhea *Botswana* 100B3
Khálki, I *Greece* 55C3
Khalkidhíki, Pen *Greece* 55B2
Khalkís *Greece* 55B3
Khalturin *USSR* 61G2
Khambhāt,G of *India* 85C4
Khāmgaon *India* 85D4
Kham Keut *Laos* 76C2
Khammam *India* 87C1
Khamseh, Mts *Iran* 90A2
Khan, R *Laos* 76C2
Khanabad *Afghan* 84B1
Khānaqīn *Iraq* 93E3
Khandwa *India* 85D4
Khanewal *Pak* 84C2
Khan ez Zabib *Jordan* 94C3
Khanh Hung *Viet* 77D4
Khaniá *Greece* 55B3
Khanpur *Pak* 84C3
Khanty-Mansiysk *USSR* 65H3
Khan Yunis *Egypt* 94B3
Khapalu *India* 84D1
Khapcheranga *USSR* 68C2
Kharabali *USSR* 61G4
Kharagpur *India* 86B2
Khāran *Iran* 91C4
Kharan *Pak* 84B3
Kharānaq *Iran* 90B3
Khārg, Is *Iran* 91B4
Khârga Oasis *Egypt* 95C2
Khargon *India* 85D4
Khar'Kov *USSR* 60E4
Kharmanli *Bulg* 54C2
Kharovsk *USSR* 61F2
Khartoum *Sudan* 95C3
Khartoum North *Sudan* 95C3
Khasan *USSR* 74C2
Khashm el Girba *Sudan* 95C3
Khasi-Jaintīa Hills *India* 86C1
Khaskovo *Bulg* 54C2
Khatanga *USSR* 1B9
Khawsa *Burma* 76B3
Khe Bo *Viet* 76C2
Khed Brahma *India* 85C4
Khemis *Alg* 51C2
Kherrata *Alg* 51D2
Kherson *USSR* 60D4
Khilok *USSR* 63D2
Khíos *Greece* 55C3
Khíos, I *Greece* 55C3
Khmel'nitskiy *USSR* 60C4
Khodorov *USSR* 59C3
Kholm *Afghan* 84B1
Khong *Laos* 76D3
Khonj *Iran* 91B4
Khor *USSR* 69F2
Khoramshahr *Iran* 91A3
Khōr Duwayhin, B *UAE* 91B5
Khorog *USSR* 84C1
Khorramābad *Iran* 90A3
Khosf *Iran* 90C3
Khost *Pak* 84B2
Khotin *USSR* 60C4
Khotol, Mt *USA* 12C2
Khoyniku *USSR* 60C3

Khrebet Dzhugdzhur, Mts *USSR* **63F2**
Khrebet Kopet Dag, Mts *USSR* **90C2**
Khrebet Pay-khoy, Mts *USSR* **64H3**
Khrebet Tarbagatay, Mts *USSR* **82C1**
Khrebet Tukuringra, Mts *USSR* **63E2**
Khulna *Bang* **86B2**
Khunjerab, P *China/ India* **84D1**
Khunsar *Iran* **90B3**
Khurays *S Arabia* **91A4**
Khurda *India* **86B2**
Khurja *India* **84D3**
Khushab *Pak* **84C2**
Khushnīyah *Syria* **94B2**
Khust *USSR* **59C3**
Khuwei *Sudan* **99C1**
Khuzdar *Pak* **85B3**
Khvāf *Iran* **90D3**
Khvalynsk *USSR* **61G3**
Khvor *Iran* **90C3**
Khvormūj *Iran* **91B4**
Khvoy *Iran* **93D2**
Khwaja Muhammad, Mts *Afghan* **84C1**
Khyber P *Afghan/Pak* **84C2**
Kiambi *Zaïre* **99C3**
Kiamichi, R *USA* **19A3**
Kiana *USA* **12B1**
Kibangou *Congo* **98B3**
Kibaya *Tanz* **99D3**
Kibombo *Zaïre* **98C3**
Kibondo *Tanz* **99D3**
Kibungu *Rwanda* **99D3**
Kičevo *Yugos* **55B2**
Kicking Horse P *Can* **5G4**
Kidal *Mali* **97C3**
Kidderminster *Eng* **43C3**
Kidira *Sen* **97A3**
Kidnappers,C *NZ* **110C1**
Kiel *W Germ* **56C2**
Kielce *Pol* **59C2**
Kieler Bucht, B *W Germ* **56C2**
Kifab *USSR* **80E2**
Kiffa *Maur* **97A3**
Kigali *Rwanda* **89H8**
Kigluaik Mts *USA* **12A2**
Kigoma *Tanz* **99C3**
Kii-sanchi, Mts *Japan* **75B2**
Kii-suido, B *Japan* **74C4**
Kikinda *Yugos* **54B1**
Kikládhes, Is *Greece* **55B3**
Kikori *PNG* **71F4**
Kikwit *Zaïre* **98B3**
Kilauea Crater, Mt *Hawaiian Is* **21C4**
Kilbuck Mts *USA* **4C3**
Kilchu *N Korea* **74B2**
Kilcoy *Aust* **109D1**
Kildare, County *Irish Rep* **45C2**
Kildare *Irish Rep* **45C2**
Kilgore *USA* **19B3**
Kilifi *Kenya* **99D3**
Kilimanjaro, Mt *Tanz* **99D3**
Kilindoni *Tanz* **99D3**
Kilis *Turk* **92C2**
Kilkee *Irish Rep* **45B2**
Kilkenny, County *Irish Rep* **45C2**
Kilkenny *Irish Rep* **45C2**
Kilkieran B *Irish Rep* **45B2**
Kilkís *Greece* **55B2**
Killala B *Irish Rep* **45B1**
Killaloe *Irish Rep* **45B2**
Killarney *Aust* **109D1**
Killarney *Irish Rep* **41B3**
Killeen *USA* **19A3**
Killik, R *USA* **12D1**
Killin *Scot* **44B3**
Killíni, Mt *Greece* **55B3**
Killybegs *Irish Rep* **45B1**
Kilmarnock *Scot* **42B2**
Kil'mez *USSR* **61H2**
Kilosa *Tanz* **99D3**
Kilrush *Irish Rep* **41B3**
Kilwa *Zaïre* **99C3**
Kilwa Kisiwani *Tanz* **99D3**
Kilwa Kivinje *Tanz* **99D3**
Kimba *Aust* **108A2**
Kimball,Mt *USA* **12F2**
Kimberley *Can* **13D3**
Kimberley *S Africa* **101F1**
Kimberley Plat *Aust* **106B2**
Kimch'aek *N Korea* **74B2**
Kimch'ŏn *S Korea* **74B3**
Kími *Greece* **55B3**
Kimry *USSR* **60E2**
Kinabalu, Mt *Malay* **70C3**
Kinabatangan, R *Malay* **78D1**
Kincardine *Can* **14B2**
Kincolith *Can* **13B1**
Kinder *USA* **19B3**
Kindersley *Can* **13F2**
Kindia *Guinea* **97A3**
Kindu *Zaïre* **98C3**
Kinel' *USSR* **61H3**
Kineshma *USSR* **61F2**
Kingaroy *Aust* **109D1**
King City *USA* **21A2**
Kingcome Inlet *Can* **5F4**
King George Is *Can* **7C4**
King I *Aust* **107D4**
King I *Can* **13B2**
Kingisepp *USSR* **60B2**
King Leopold Range, Mts *Aust* **106B2**
Kingman *USA* **9B3**
Kingombe *Zaïre* **98C3**
Kingoonya *Aust* **108A2**
Kingsburg *USA* **22C2**
Kings Canyon Nat Pk *USA* **21B2**
Kingscote *Aust* **108A3**
King Sd *Aust* **106B2**
Kingsford *USA* **14A1**
Kingsland *USA* **17B1**
King's Lynn *Eng* **43E3**
Kings Park *USA* **16C2**
Kings Peak, Mt *USA* **8B2**
Kingston *Aust* **107C4**
Kingston *Can* **7C5**
Kingston *Jamaica* **25E3**
Kingston, New York *USA* **15D2**
Kingston *NZ* **111A3**
Kingstown *St Vincent* **27E4**
Kingsville *USA* **9D4**
Kingussie *Scot* **44B3**
King William I *Can* **4J3**
King William's Town *S Africa* **100B4**
Kinkala *Congo* **98B3**
Kinna *Sweden* **39G7**
Kinnairds Head, Pt *Scot* **44D3**
Kinomoto *Japan* **75B1**
Kinross *Scot* **44C3**
Kinsale *Irish Rep* **45B3**
Kinshasa *Zaïre* **98B3**
Kintap *Indon* **78D3**
Kintyre, Pen *Scot* **42B2**
Kinuso *Can* **13D1**
Kinyeti, Mt *Sudan* **99D2**
Kiparissía *Greece* **55B3**
Kiparissiakós Kólpos, G *Greece* **55B3**
Kipawa,L *Can* **15C1**
Kipili *Tanz* **99D3**
Kipnuk *USA* **12B3**
Kippure, Mt *Irish Rep* **45C2**
Kipushi *Zaïre* **100B2**
Kirensk *USSR* **63C2**
Kirgizskaya SSR, Republic *USSR* **65J5**
Kirgizskiy Khrebet, Mts *USSR* **82B1**
Kiri *Zaïre* **98B3**
Kiribati, Is *Pacific O* **105G4**
Kırıkkale *Turk* **92B2**
Kirishi *USSR* **60D2**
Kirithar Range, Mts *Pak* **85B3**
Kirkağaç *Turk* **55C3**
Kirk Bulāg Dāgh, Mt *Iran* **90A2**
Kirkby *Eng* **42C2**
Kirkcaldy *Scot* **44C3**
Kirkcudbright *Scot* **42B2**
Kirkenes *Nor* **38K5**
Kirkland Lake *Can* **7B5**
Kirkpatrick,Mt *Ant* **80E**
Kirksville *USA* **10A2**
Kirkūk *Iraq* **93D2**
Kirkwall *Scot* **44C2**
Kirkwood *USA* **18B2**
Kirov *USSR* **60D3**
Kirov *USSR* **61G2**
Kirovabad *USSR* **65F5**
Kirovakan *USSR* **93D1**
Kirovgrad *USSR* **61J2**
Kirovograd *USSR* **60D4**
Kirovsk *USSR* **64E3**
Kirs *USSR* **61H2**
Kirşehir *Turk* **92B2**
Kiruna *Sweden* **56C2**
Kiryū *Japan* **75B1**
Kisangani *Zaïre* **98C2**
Kisarazu *Japan* **75B1**
Kishanganj *India* **86B1**
Kishangarh *India* **85C3**
Kishinev *USSR* **60C4**
Kishiwada *Japan* **75B2**
Kisii *Kenya* **99D3**
Kisiju *Tanz* **99D3**
Kiskunhalas *Hung* **59B3**
Kislovodsk *USSR* **65F5**
Kismaayo *Somalia* **99E3**
Kiso-sammyaku, Mts *Japan* **75B1**
Kissidougou *Guinea* **97A4**
Kissimmee,L *USA* **17B2**
Kisumu *Kenya* **99D3**
Kisvárda *Hung* **59C3**
Kita *Mali* **97B3**
Kitab *USSR* **65H6**
Kitakata *Japan* **75C1**
Kita-Kyūshū *Japan* **74C4**
Kitale *Kenya* **99D2**
Kitalo, I *Japan* **69G4**
Kitami *Japan* **74E2**
Kitchener *Can* **7B5**
Kitgum *Uganda* **99D2**
Kíthira, I *Greece* **55B3**
Kíthnos, I *Greece* **55B3**
Kiti,C *Cyprus* **94A1**
Kitimat *Can* **5F4**
Kitnen, R *Fin* **38K5**
Kitsuki *Japan* **75A2**
Kittanning *USA* **15C2**
Kittilä *Fin* **38J5**
Kitunda *Tanz* **99D3**
Kitwanga *Can* **13B1**
Kitwe *Zambia* **100B2**
Kitzbühel *Austria* **57C3**
Kitzbühler Alpen, Mts *Austria* **47E1**
Kitzingen *W Germ* **57C3**
Kiumbi *Zaïre* **98C3**
Kivalina *USA* **12B1**
Kivercy *USSR* **59D2**
Kivu,L *Zaïre/Rwanda* **99C3**
Kiwalik *USA* **4B3**
Kiyev *USSR* **60D3**
Kizel *USSR* **61J2**
Kizil, R *Turk* **92C2**
Kizyl-Arvat *USSR* **80D2**
Kizyl-Atrek *USSR* **90B2**
Kladno *Czech* **57C2**
Klagenfurt *Austria* **57C3**
Klaipēda *USSR* **60B2**
Klamath *USA* **8A2**
Klamath, R *USA* **20B2**
Klamath Falls *USA* **8A2**
Klamath Mts *USA* **20B2**
Klatovy *Czech* **57C3**
Klawak *USA* **12H3**
Kleiat *Leb* **94B1**
Klerksdorp *S Africa* **101G1**
Klin *USSR* **60E2**
Klintehamn *Sweden* **58B1**
Klintsy *USSR* **60D3**
Ključ *Yugos* **52C2**
Kłodzko *Pol* **59B2**
Klondike, R *USA/Can* **12G2**
Klondike Plat *USA/ Can* **4D3**
Klosterneuburg *Austria* **59B3**
Kluane, R *Can* **12G2**
Kluane L *Can* **12G2**
Kluane Nat Pk *Can* **12G2**
Kluczbork *Pol* **59B2**
Klukwan *USA* **12G3**
Klutina L *USA* **12E2**
Knight I *USA* **12E2**
Knighton *Wales* **43C3**
Knin *Yugos* **52C2**
Knob,C *Aust* **106A4**
Knokke-Heist *Belg* **46B1**
Knox Coast *Ant* **112C9**
Knoxville, Tennessee *USA* **11B3**
Knud Ramsussens Land, Region *Greenland* **6H3**
Koba *Indon* **78B3**
Kobbermirebugt *Greenland* **6F3**
Kobe *Japan* **74D4**
København *Den* **56C1**
Koblenz *W Germ* **57B2**
Kobrin *USSR* **60B3**
Kobroör, I *Indon* **71E4**
Kobuk, R *USA* **12C1**
Kočani *Yugos* **54B2**
Ko Chang, I *Thai* **76C3**
Koch Bihār *India* **86B1**
Kochel *W Germ* **47D1**
Koch I *Can* **6C3**
Kōchi *Japan* **74C4**
Kodiak *USA* **12D3**
Kodiak I *USA* **12D3**
Kodikkarai *India* **87B2**
Kodok *Sudan* **99D2**
Koes *Namibia* **100A3**
Koffiefontein *S Africa* **101G1**
Koforidua *Ghana* **97B4**
Kōfu *Japan* **74D3**
Koga *Japan* **75B1**
Køge *Den* **39G7**
Kohat *Pak* **84C2**
Koh-i-Baba, Mts *Afghan* **84B2**
Koh-i-Hisar, Mts *Afghan* **84B1**
Koh-i-Khurd, Mt *Afghan* **84B2**
Kohīma *India* **86C1**
Koh-i-Mazar, Mt *Afghan* **84B1**
Kohlu *Pak* **84B3**
Kohtla Järve *USSR* **60C2**
Koide *Japan* **75B1**
Koidern *Can* **12F2**
Koihoa, Is *Nicobar Is* **77A4**
Kōje-do, I *S Korea* **74B4**
Kokchetav *USSR* **65H4**
Kokemaki, L *Fin* **39J6**
Kokkola *Fin* **38J6**
Kokoda *PNG* **107D1**
Kokomo *USA* **14A2**
Kokonau *Indon* **71E4**
Kokpekty *USSR* **65K5**
Koksoak, R *Can* **7D4**
Kokstad *S Africa* **100B4**
Ko Kut, I *Thai* **76C3**
Kola *USSR* **38L5**
Kolaka *Indon* **71D4**
Ko Lanta, I *Thai* **77B4**
Kolār *India* **87B2**
Kolār Gold Fields *India* **87B2**
Kolda *Sen* **97A3**
Kolding *Den* **39F7**
Kolhāpur *India* **87A1**
Koliganek *USA* **12C3**

Kolín *Czech* 59B2
Köln *W Germ* 57B2
Kolo *Pol* 58B2
Kolobrzeg *Pol* 58B2
Kolokani *Mali* 97B3
Kolomna *USSR* 60E2
Kolomyya *USSR* 60C4
Kolpashevo *USSR* 65K4
Kolpekty *USSR* 68A2
Kólpos Merabéllou, B *Greece* 55C3
Kólpos Singitikós, G *Greece* 55B2
Kólpos Strimonikós, G *Greece* 55B2
Kólpos Toronaíos, G *Greece* 55B2
Kol'skiy Poluostrov, Pen *USSR* 38L5
Kolvereid *Nor* 38G6
Kolwezi *Zaïre* 100B2
Kolyma, R *USSR* 1C7
Kom, Mt *Bulg/Yugos* 54B2
Koma *Eth* 99D2
Komaduga Gana, R *Nig* 97D3
Komárno *Czech* 59B3
Komati, R *S Africa* 101H1
Komatsu *Japan* 74D3
Komatsushima *Japan* 75A2
Komi, Republic *USSR* 64G3
Komodo, I *Indon* 70C4
Komoran, I *Indon* 71E4
Komoro *Japan* 75B1
Komotiní *Greece* 55C2
Kompong Cham *Camb* 76D3
Kompong Chhnang, Mts *Camb* 76C3
Kompong Som *Camb* 77C3
Kompong Thom *Camb* 76C3
Kompong Trabek *Camb* 76D3
Komsomol'sk na Amure *USSR* 63F2
Konda, R *USSR* 65H4
Kondoa *Tanz* 99D3
Kondukür *India* 87B1
Kong Christian IX Land, Region *Greenland* 6G3
Kong Frederik VI Kyst, Mts *Greenland* 6F3
Kong Karls Land, Is *Barents S* 64C2
Kongkemul, Mt *Indon* 78D2
Kongolo *Zaïre* 98C3
Kongsberg *Den* 39F7
Kongsvinger *Nor* 39G6
Konin *Pol* 58B2
Konjic *Yugos* 54A2
Konosha *USSR* 61F1
Konosu *Japan* 75B1
Konotop *USSR* 60D3
Konsk *USSR* 63B2
Końskie *Pol* 59C2
Konstanz *W Germ* 49D2
Kontagora *Nig* 97C3
Kontum *Viet* 76D3
Konya *Turk* 92B2
Kootenay, R *Can* 13D3
Kopargaon *India* 85C5
Kópasker *Iceland* 6J3
Kópavogur *Iceland* 38A2
Koper *Yugos* 52B1
Kopet Dag, Mts *Iran/USSR* 80D2
Kopeysk *USSR* 61K2
Ko Phangan, I *Thai* 77C4
Ko Phuket, I *Thai* 77B4
Köping *Sweden* 39H7
Koppal *India* 87B1
Koprivnica *Yugos* 52C1
Korangi *Pak* 85B4
Koraput *India* 87C1
Korba *India* 86A2
Korbach *W Germ* 57B2
Korbuk, R *USA* 4B3
Korçë *Alb* 55B2
Korčula, I *Yugos* 52C2
Korea B *China/Korea* 72E2
Korea Str *S Korea/Japan* 74B4
Korec *USSR* 59D2
Körğlu Tepesi, Mt *Turk* 92B1
Korhogo *Ivory Coast* 97B4
Kori Creek *India* 85B4
Korinthiakós Kólpos, G *Greece* 55B3
Kórinthos *Greece* 55B3
Kōriyama *Japan* 74E3
Korkino *USSR* 61K3
Korkuteli *Turk* 92B2
Korla *China* 82C1
Kornat, I *Yugos* 52C2
Köroğlu Tepesi, Mt *Turk* 60D5
Korogwe *Tanz* 99D3
Koroit *Aust* 108B3
Koror, Palau Is *Pacific O* 71E3
Körös, R *Hung* 59C3
Korosten *USSR* 60C3
Koro Toro *Chad* 95A3
Korovin, I *USA* 12B3
Korsakov *USSR* 69G2
Korsør *Den* 39G7
Kortrijk *Belg* 56A2
Kós, I *Greece* 55C3
Ko Samui, I *Thai* 77C4
Koscierzyna *Pol* 58B2
Kosciusko, Mt *Aust* 107D4
Kosciusko I *USA* 12H3
Koshikijima-retto, I *Japan* 74B4
Košice *Czech* 59C3
Kosong *N Korea* 74B3
Kosovska Mitrovica *Yugos* 54B2
Kossou, L *Ivory Coast* 97B4
Koster *S Africa* 101G1
Kosti *Sudan* 99D1
Kostopol' *USSR* 59D2
Kostroma *USSR* 61F2
Kostrzyn *Pol* 56C2
Koszalin *Pol* 39H8
Kota *India* 85D3
Kotaagung *Indon* 78A4
Kotabaharu *Indon* 78C3
Kotabaru *Indon* 78D3
Kota Bharu *Malay* 77C4
Kotabum *Indon* 78A3
Kot Addu *Pak* 84C2
Kota Kinabulu *Malay* 78D1
Kotapad *India* 87C1
Kotel'nich *USSR* 61G2
Kotel'nikovo *USSR* 61F4
Kotka *Fin* 39K6
Kotlas *USSR* 64F3
Kotlik *USA* 12B2
Kotor *Yugos* 54A2
Kotovsk *USSR* 60C4
Kotri *Pak* 85B3
Kottagūdem *India* 87C1
Kottayam *India* 87B3
Kotto, R *CAR* 98C2
Kottūru *India* 87B2
Kotzebue *USA* 12B1
Kotzebue Sd *USA* 4B3
Kouande *Benin* 97C3
Kouango *CAR* 98C2
Koudougou *U Volta* 97B3
Koulamoutou *Gabon* 98B3
Koulikoro *Mali* 97B3
Koupéla *U Volta* 97B3
Kourou *French Guiana* 33G2
Kouroussa *Guinea* 97B3
Kousséri *Cam* 98B1
Kouvola *Fin* 39K6
Kovel *USSR* 60B3
Kovrov *USSR* 61F2
Kovylkino *USSR* 61F3
Kovzha, R *USSR* 60E1
Ko Way, I *Thai* 77C4
Kowloon *Hong Kong* 73C5
Kowt-e-Ashrow *Afghan* 84B2
Köycegğiz *Turk* 92A2
Koydor *USSR* 38L5
Koyna Res *India* 87A1
Koyuk *USA* 12B2
Koyuk, R *USA* 12B1
Koyukuk *USA* 12C2
Koyukuk, R *USA* 12C1
Kozan *Turk* 92C2
Kozańi *Greece* 55B2
Koz'modemyansk *USSR* 61G2
Koztroma *USSR* 61F2
Kōzu-shima, I *Japan* 75B2
Kragerø *Nor* 39F7
Kragujevac *Yugos* 54B2
Kra,Isthmus of *Burma/Malay* 77B3
Krak des Chevaliers, Hist Site *Syria* 94C1
Kraków *Pol* 59B2
Kraljevo *Yugos* 54B2
Kramatorsk *USSR* 60E4
Kramfors *Sweden* 38H6
Kranj *Yugos* 52B1
Krapotkin *USSR* 61F4
Krasavino *USSR* 61G1
Krashnokamsk *USSR* 61J2
Krasino *USSR* 64G2
Kraśnik *Pol* 59C2
Krasnoarmeysk *USSR* 61G3
Krasnodar *USSR* 60E5
Krasnotur'insk *USSR* 61K2
Krasnoufimsk *USSR* 61J2
Krasnousol'-skiy *USSR* 61J3
Krasnovishersk *USSR* 65G3
Krasnovodsk *USSR* 65G5
Krasnoyarsk *USSR* 63B2
Krasnystaw *Pol* 59C2
Krasnyy Kut *USSR* 61G3
Krasnyy Luch *USSR* 60E4
Krasnyy Yar *USSR* 61G4
Kratie *Camb* 76D3
Kraulshavn *Greenland* 6E2
Krefeld *W Germ* 56B2
Kremenchug *USSR* 60D4
Kremenchugskoye Vodokhranilische, Res *USSR* 60D4
Kremenets *USSR* 59D2
Kribi *Cam* 98A2
Krichev *USSR* 60D3
Krimml *Austria* 47E1
Krinstinestad *Fin* 38J6
Krishna, R *India* 87B1
Krishnagiri *India* 87B2
Krishnangar *India* 86B2
Kristiansand *Nor* 39F7
Kristianstad *Sweden* 39G7
Kristiansund *Nor* 64B3
Kristinehamn *Sweden* 39G7
Kríti, I *Greece* 55B3
Krivoy Rog *USSR* 60D4
Krk, I *Yugos* 52B1
Kronpris Frederik Bjerge, Mts *Greenland* 6G3
Kronshtadt *USSR* 39K7
Kroonstad *S Africa* 101G1
Kropotkin *USSR* 65F5
Krugersdorp *S Africa* 101G1
Krui *Indon* 78A4
Kruje *Alb* 55A2
Krupki *USSR* 58D2
Krusenstern,C *USA* 12B1
Kruševac *Yugos* 54B2
Krustpils *USSR* 39K7
Kruzof I *USA* 12G3
Krym, Pen *USSR* 65E5
Krym, R *USSR* 60D5
Krymsk *USSR* 60E5
Krzyz *Pol* 58B2
Ksar El Boukhari *Alg* 96C1
Ksar el Kebir *Mor* 96B1
Kuala *Indon* 70A3
Kuala Dungun *Malay* 77C5
Kuala Kerai *Malay* 77C4
Kuala Kubu Baharu *Malay* 77C5
Kuala Lipis *Malay* 77C5
Kuala Lumpur *Malay* 77C5
Kuala Trengganu *Malay* 77C4
Kuamut *Malay* 78D1
Kuandian *China* 74A2
Kuantan *Malay* 77C5
Kuba *USSR* 93E1
Kubar *PNG* 71F4
Kuching *Malay* 78C2
Kudat *Malay* 70C3
Kudus *Indon* 78C4
Kudymkar *USSR* 61H2
Kufstein *Austria* 57C3
Kuh Duren, Upland *Iran* 90C3
Kūh e Bazmān, Mt *Iran* 91C4
Kūh-e Dinar, Mt *Iran* 90B3
Kūh-e-Hazār Masjed, Mts *Iran* 90C2
Kūh-e Jebāl Barez, Mts *Iran* 91C4
Kūh-e Karkas, Mts *Iran* 90B3
Kuh-e Laleh Zar, Mt *Iran* 91C4
Kūh-e Sahand, Mt *Iran* 90A2
Kuh e Taftān, Mt *Iran* 91D4
Kūhhaye Sabalan, Mts *Iran* 90A2
Kūhjā-ye Zāgros, Mts *Iran* 90A3
Kuhmo *Fin* 38K6
Kūhpāyeh *Iran* 90B3
Kūhpāyeh, Mt *Iran* 90C3
Kūh ye Bashākerd, Mts *Iran* 91C4
Kūh ye Sabalan, Mt *Iran* 90A2
Kuibis *Namibia* 100A3
Kuigillingok *USA* 4B4
Kuiu I *USA* 12H3
Kuji *Japan* 74E2
Kuju-san, Mt *Japan* 75A2
Kukaklek L *USA* 12C3
Kukës *Alb* 54B2
Kukup *Malay* 77C5
Kül, R *Iran* 91C4
Kula *Turk* 55C3
Kulakshi *USSR* 61J4
Kulal,Mt *Kenya* 99D2
Kulata *Bulg* 55B2
Kuldīga *USSR* 60B2
Kul'sary *USSR* 61H4
Kulu *India* 84D2
Kulu *Turk* 92B2
Kulunda *USSR* 65J4
Kulwin *Aust* 108B2
Kuma, R *USSR* 61G5
Kumagaya *Japan* 75B1
Kumai *Indon* 78C3
Kumamoto *Japan* 74C4
Kumano *Japan* 75B2
Kumanovo *Yugos* 54B2
Kumara *China* 63E2
Kumasi *Ghana* 97B4
Kumba *Cam* 98A2
Kumbakonam *India* 87B2
Kumertau *USSR* 61J3
Kūmhwa *S Korea* 74B3
Kumla *Sweden* 39H7
Kumta *India* 87A2
Kümüx *China* 82C1
Kunar, R *Afghan* 84C2
Kunda *USSR* 39K7
Kundla *India* 85C4
Kunduz *Afghan* 84B1
Kunene, R *Angola* 89F9
Kungsbacka *Sweden* 39G7
Kungur *USSR* 61J2
Kunhing *Burma* 76B1
Kunlun Shan, Mts *China* 82B2
Kunming *China* 73A4
Kunsan *S Korea* 74B3
Kuopio *Fin* 38K6

Kupa, R *Yugos* 52C1
Kupang *Indon* 106B2
Kupiano *PNG* 107D2
Kupreanof I *USA* 12H3
Kupyansk *USSR* 60E4
Kuqa *China* 82C1
Kurabe *Japan* 75B1
Kurashiki *Japan* 74C4
Kurayoshi *Japan* 75A1
Kurdistan, Region *Iran* 90A2
Kŭrdzhali *Bulg* 54C2
Kure *Japan* 74C4
Kureyka, R *USSR* 63A1
Kurgan *USSR* 65H4
Kurikka *Fin* 38J6
Kurnool *India* 87B1
Kuroiso *Japan* 75C1
Kurow *NZ* 111B2
Kurri Kurri *Aust* 109D2
Kursk *USSR* 60E3
Kurskiy Zaliv, Lg *USSR* 58C1
Kuruktag, R *China* 68A2
Kuruman *S Africa* 100B3
Kurume *Japan* 74C4
Kurunegala *Sri Lanka* 87C3
Kurunktag, R *China* 65K5
Kusa *USSR* 61J2
Kuşadasi Körfezi, B *Turk* 55C3
Kus Golü, L *Turk* 55C2
Kushimoto *Japan* 74D4
Kushiro *Japan* 74E2
Kushtia *Bang* 86B2
Kushum, R *USSR* 61H3
Kushra *Afgan* 80E2
Kushva *USSR* 65G4
Kuskokwim, R *USA* 12B2
Kuskokwim B *USA* 12B3
Kuskokwim Mts *USA* 12C2
Kusma *Nepal* 86A1
Kussharo-ko, L *Japan* 74E2
Kustanay *USSR* 65H4
Kütahya *Turk* 92A2
Kutai, R *Indon* 78D3
Kutná Hora *Czech* 59B3
Kutno *Pol* 58B2
Kutu *Zaïre* 98B3
Kutubdia I *Bang* 86C2
Kutum *Sudan* 98C1
Kuujjuaq *Can* 7D4
Kuusamo *Fin* 38K5
Kuvandyk *USSR* 61J3
Kuwait *Kuwait* 93E4
Kuwait, Sheikdom *S W Asia* 80C3
Kuwana *Japan* 75B1
Kuybyshev *USSR* 65G4
Kuybyshev *USSR* 65J4
Kuybyshevskoye Vodokhranilishche, Res *USSR* 61G3
Kuytun *USSR* 63C2
Kuzey Anadolu Daglari Mts *Turk* 60E5
Kuznetsk *USSR* 61G3
Kvaenangen, Sd *Nor* 38J4
Kvichak *USA* 12C3
Kvichak, R *USA* 12C3
Kvichak B *USA* 12C3
Kvigtind, Mt *Nor* 38G5
Kvikkjokk *Sweden* 38H5
Kwale *Kenya* 99D3
Kwangju *S Korea* 74B3
Kwango, R *Zaïre* 98B3
Kwekwe *Zim* 100B2
Kwethluk *USA* 12B2
Kwethluk, R *USA* 12B2
Kwidzyn *Pol* 58B2
Kwoka, Mt *Indon* 71E4
Kyabram *Aust* 108C3
Kyaikkami *Burma* 76B2
Kyaikto *Burma* 76B2
Kyakhta *USSR* 68C1
Kyancutta *Aust* 108A2
Kyaukme *Burma* 76B1
Kyauk-padaung *Burma* 76B1
Kyaukpyu *Burma* 76A2
Kyle of Lochalsh *Scot* 40B2
Kyll, R *W Germ* 46D1
Kyneton *Aust* 108B3
Kyoga, L *Uganda* 99D2
Kyogle *Aust* 109D1
Kyŏngju *S Korea* 74B3
Kyoto *Japan* 74D3
Kyshtym *USSR* 65H4
Kyūshū, I *Japan* 74C4
Kyushu-Palau Ridge *Pacific O* 104E3
Kyustendil *Bulg* 54B2
Kyzyl *USSR* 68B1
Kyzylkum, Desert *USSR* 65H5
Kzyl Orda *USSR* 65H5

L

Laas Caanood *Somalia* 99E2
Laasphe *W Germ* 46E1
Laas Qoray *Somalia* 99E1
La Asunción *Ven* 33E1
La Barca *Mexico* 23A1
Labé *Guinea* 97A3
Labe, R *Czech* 59B2
Labelle *Can* 15D1
La Belle *USA* 17B2
Laberge,L *Can* 12G2
Labi *Brunei* 78D1
la Biche,L *Can* 13E2
Labinsk *USSR* 61F5
Laboué *Leb* 94C1
Laboulaye *Arg* 34C2
Labrador, Region *Can* 7D4
Labrador City *Can* 7D4
Labrador S *Greenland/Can* 7E4
Lábrea *Brazil* 33E5
Labuan, I *Malay* 78D1
Labuhan *Indon* 78B4
Labutta *Burma* 76A2
Labytnangi *USSR* 65H3
La Capelle *France* 46B2
La Carlota *Arg* 34C2
La Carlota *Phil* 79B3
Lac Belot, L *Can* 12J1
Lac Bienville, L *Can* 7C4
Laccadive Is *India* 83B4
Lac d'Annecy, L *France* 47B2
Lac de Gras, L *Can* 4G3
Lac de Joux, L *Switz* 47B1
Lac de Neuchâtel, L *Switz* 47B1
Lac de Patzcuaro, L *Mexico* 23A2
Lac de Sayula, L *Mexico* 23A2
Lac des Bois, L *Can* 4F3
Lac du Bourget, L *France* 47A2
La Ceiba *Honduras* 25D3
Lacepede B *Aust* 108A3
La Châtre *France* 48C2
La-Chaux-de-Fonds *Switz* 47B1
Lachish, Hist Site *Israel* 94B3
Lachlan, R *Aust* 107D4
La Chorrera *Panama* 32B2
Lachute *Can* 15D1
Lac Joseph, L *Can* 7D4
Lackawanna *USA* 15C2
Lac la Biche *Can* 5G4
Lac la Martre, L *Can* 4G3
Lac la Ronge, L *Can* 5H4
Lac L'eau Claire *Can* 7C4
Lac Léman, L *Switz/ France* 52A1
Lac Manouane *Can* 7C4
Lac Manouane, L *Can* 10C1
Lac Megantic *Can* 15D1
Lac Mistassini, L *Can* 7C4
Lacombe *Can* 13E2
Laconia *USA* 15D2
La Coruña *Spain* 50A1
La Crosse *USA* 10A2
La Cruces *USA* 9C3
Lac Seul, L *Can* 7A4
La Cygne *USA* 18B2
Ladākh Range *India* 84D2
Lādnūn *India* 85C3
Ladong *China* 73B5
Ladozhskoye Ozero, L *USSR* 60D1
Lady Ann Str *Can* 6B2
Lady Barron *Aust* 109C4
Ladybrand *S Africa* 101G1
Ladysmith *Can* 13C3
Ladysmith *S Africa* 101G1
Lae *PNG* 71F4
Laem Ngop *Thai* 76C3
Laesø, I *Den* 56C1
Lafayette, Indiana *USA* 10B2
Lafayette, Louisiana *USA* 11A3
La Fère *France* 46B2
La-Ferté-sous-Jouarre *France* 46B2
Lafia *Nig* 97C4
Lafiagi *Nig* 97C4
La Flèche *France* 48B2
La Galite, I *Tunisia* 96C1
Lagan, R *Sweden* 56C1
Lagarto *Brazil* 31D4
Laghouat *Alg* 96C1
Lagoa de Araruama *Brazil* 35C2
Lagoa dos Patos, Lg *Brazil* 29F2
Lagoa Feia *Brazil* 35C2
Lago Agrio *Ecuador* 32B4
Lagoa Juparanã, L *Brazil* 35C1
Lagoa mar Chiguita, L *Arg* 29D2
Lagoa Mirim, L *Urug/ Brazil* 29F2
Lago Argentino, L *Arg* 29B6
Lago Buenos Aries, L *Arg* 29B5
Lago Cochrane, L *Chile/Arg* 29B5
Lago Colhué Huapi, L *Arg* 29C5
Lago de Chapala, L *Mexico* 24B2
Lago de Chiriqui, L *Panama* 32A2
Lago de Cuitzeo, L *Mexico* 23A2
Lago de la Laja, L *Chile* 29B3
Lago del Coghinas, L *Sardegna* 53A2
Lago de Maracaibo, L *Ven* 32C2
Lago de Nicaragua, L *Nic* 25D3
Lago de Perlas, L *Nic* 32A1
Lago di Bolsena, L *Italy* 52B2
Lago di Bracciano, L *Italy* 52B2
Lago di Como, L *Italy* 52A1
Lago d'Idro, L *Italy* 47D2
Lago di Garda, L *Italy* 52B1
Lago di Lecco, L *Italy* 47C2
Lago di Lugano, L *Italy* 47C2
Lago d'Iseo, L *Italy* 47D2
Lago d'Orta, L *Italy* 47C2
Lago General Carrera, L *Chile* 29B5
Lago Maggiore, L *Italy* 52A1
Lago Musters, L *Arg* 29C5
Lagon *France* 48B3
Lago Nahuel Haupi, L *Arg* 29B4
Lago O'Higgins, L *Chile* 29B5
Lago Omodeo, L *Sardegna* 53A2
Lago Poopó, L *Bol* 30C2
Lago Ranco, L *Chile* 29B4
Lago Rogaguado, L *Bol* 32D6
Lagos *Nig* 97C4
Lagos *Port* 50A2
Lago San Martin, L *Chile/Arg* 29B5
Lagos de Moreno *Mexico* 24B2
Lago Titicaca *Bol/ Peru* 30C2
Lago Viedma, L *Arg* 29B5
La Grande *USA* 8B2
La Grande Rivière, R *Can* 7C4
Lagrange *Aust* 106B2
La Grange, Georgia *USA* 11B3
La Grange, Kentucky *USA* 14A3
La Grange, Texas *USA* 19A4
La Gran Sabana, Mts *Ven* 33E2
La Grave *France* 47B2
Lagronño *Spain* 48B3
Laguna Aluminé, L *Arg* 34A3
Laguna Beach *USA* 21B3
Laguna Colorada Grande, L *Arg* 34C3
Laguna de Bay, Lg *Phil* 79B3
Laguna de Caratasca, Lg *Honduras* 25D3
Laguna de Chiriqui, L *Panama* 25D4
Laguna de Managua, L *Nicaragua* 25D3
Laguna de Nicaragua, L *Nicaragua* 25D3
Laguna de Perlas, Lg *Nic* 26A4
Laguna de Pueblo Viejo, L *Mexico* 23B1
Laguna de Tamiahua, Lg *Mexico* 24C2
Laguna de Términos, Lg *Mexico* 25C3
Laguna de Yuriria, L *Mexico* 23A1
Laguna le Altamira *Mexico* 23B1
Laguna Madre, Lg *Mexico* 24C2
Laguna Mar Chiquita, L *Arg* 34C2
Laguna Nahuel Huapi, L *Arg* 29B4
Laguna Paiva *Arg* 34C2
Laguna Ranco *Chile* 29B4
Laguna Seca *Mexico* 9C4
Laguna Tortugas, L *Mexico* 23B1
Lahad Datu *Malay* 70C3
Lahat *Indon* 78A3
Lahia *Fin* 38J6
Lāhījān *Iran* 90B2
Lahn, R *W Germ* 46D1
Lahnstein *W Germ* 46D1
Lahore *Pak* 84C2
Lahti *Fin* 39K6
La Huerta *Mexico* 23A2
Lai *Chad* 98B2
Laibin *China* 73B5
Lai Chau *Viet* 76C1
Laingsburg *S Africa* 100B4
Lairg *Scot* 44B2
Lais *Indon* 78A3
Lais *Phil* 79C4
Laiyang *China* 72E2
Laizhou Wan, B *China* 72D2
Laja, R *Chile* 34A3
Lajes *Brazil* 30F4
La Jolla *USA* 22D4
La Junta *USA* 9C3
Lake Cargelligo *Aust* 109C2
Lake Charles *USA* 11A3
Lake City, Florida *USA* 17B1

Lake City, S Carolina *USA* **17C1**
Lake District, Region *Eng* **42C2**
Lake Elsinore *USA* **22D4**
Lake Eyre Basin *Aust* **106C3**
Lakefield *Can* **15C2**
Lake Harbour *Can* **6D3**
Lake Hughes *USA* **22C3**
Lakehurst *USA* **16B2**
Lake Jackson *USA* **19A4**
Lake la Biche *Can* **13E2**
Lakeland *USA* **17B2**
Lake of the Woods *Can* **7A5**
Lake Oswego *USA* **20B1**
Lakeport *USA* **21A2**
Lake Providence *USA* **19B3**
Lake Pukaki *NZ* **111B2**
Lakes Entrance *Aust* **109C3**
Lakeshore *USA* **22C2**
Lake Stewart *Aust* **108B1**
Lake Traverse *Can* **15C1**
Lakeview *USA* **8A2**
Lakeview Mt *Can* **20B1**
Lake Village *USA* **19B3**
Lake Wales *USA* **17B2**
Lakewood, California *USA* **22C4**
Lakewood, New Jersey *USA* **16B2**
Lakewood, Ohio *USA* **14B2**
Lake Worth *USA* **17B2**
Lakhīmpur *India* **86A1**
Lakhpat *India* **85B4**
Lakki *Pak* **84C2**
Lakonikós Kólpos, G *Greece* **55B3**
Lakota *Ivory Coast* **97B4**
Laksefjord, Inlet *Nor* **38K4**
Lakselv *Nor* **38K4**
La Laguna *Arg* **34C2**
La Libertad *Ecuador* **32A4**
La Ligua *Chile* **34A2**
La Linea *Spain* **50A2**
Lalitpur *India* **85D4**
La Loche *Can* **5H4**
la Loche,L *Can* **13F1**
La Louviète *Belg* **46C1**
La Luz *Nic* **26A4**
La Malbaie *Can* **7C5**
La Malinche, Mt *Mexico* **23B2**
La Mancha, Region *Spain* **50B2**
Lamar, Colorado *USA* **9C3**
Lamar, Missouri *USA* **18B2**
La Marque *USA* **19A4**
Lambaréné *Gabon* **98B3**
Lambayeque *Peru* **32A5**
Lambert Gl *Ant* **112B10**
Lambertville *USA* **16B2**
Lamblon,C *Can* **4F2**
Lambro, R *Italy* **47C2**
Lam Chi, R *Thai* **76C2**
Lamego *Port* **50A1**
La Meije, Mt *France* **47B2**
La Merced *Peru* **32B6**
La Mesa *USA* **21B3**
Lamía *Greece* **55B3**
Lammermuir Hills *Scot* **42C2**
Lammhult *Sweden* **39G7**
Lamon B *Phil* **79B3**
Lamoni *USA* **18B1**
Lamotrek, I *Pacific O* **71F3**
Lampeter *Wales* **43B3**
Lamu *Kenya* **99E3**
Lana *Italy* **47D1**
Lanai, I *Hawaiian Is* **21C4**
Lanai City *Hawaiian Is* **21C4**
Lanark *Scot* **42C2**
Lanbi, I *Burma* **76B3**
Lancang, R *China* **76C1**
Lancashire, County *Eng* **42C3**
Lancaster, California *USA* **21B3**
Lancaster *Eng* **42C2**
Lancaster, Mississippi *USA* **18B1**
Lancaster, New Hampshire *USA* **15D2**
Lancaster, Ohio *USA* **14B3**
Lancaster, Pennsylvania *USA* **10C3**
Lancaster, S Carolina *USA* **17B1**
Lancaster Sd *Can* **6B2**
Landak, R *Indon* **78B3**
Landan *W Germ* **46E2**
Landeck *Austria* **57C3**
Lander *USA* **8C2**
Landeta *Arg* **34C2**
Landsberg *W Germ* **57C3**
Lands End, C *Can* **4F2**
Land's End, Pt *Eng* **43B4**
Landshut *W Germ* **57C3**
Làndskrona *Sweden* **39G7**
Lanett *USA* **17A1**
Langenhagen *W Germ* **56B2**
Langenthal *Switz* **47B1**
Langholm *Scot* **42C2**
Langjökull, Mts *Iceland* **38A2**
Langkawi, I *Malay* **77B4**
Langley *Can* **13C3**
Langlo, R *Aust* **108C1**
Langnau *Switz* **47B1**
Langres *France* **49D2**
langsa *Indon* **70A3**
Lang Shan, Mts *China* **68C2**
Lang Son *Viet* **76D1**
Languedoc, Region *France* **48C3**
Lanin, Mt *Arg* **29B3**
Lanoa,L, L *Phil* **79B4**
Lansdale *USA* **16B2**
Lansdowne House *Can* **7B4**
Lansford *USA* **16B2**
Lansing *USA* **10B2**
Lanslebourg *France* **47B2**
Lanzarote, I *Canary Is* **96A2**
Lanzhou *China* **72A2**
Lanzo Torinese *Italy* **47B2**
Laoag *Phil* **79B2**
Lao Cai *Viet* **76C1**
Laoha He, R *China* **72D1**
Laois, County *Irish Rep* **45C2**
Laon *France* **46B2**
La Oroya *Peru* **32B6**
Laos, Republic *S E Asia* **76C2**
Lapalisse *France* **49C2**
La Palma *Panama* **32B2**
La Palma, I *Canary Is* **96A2**
La Pampa, State *Arg* **34B3**
La Paragua *Ven* **33E2**
La Paz *Arg* **29E2**
La Paz *Arg* **34B2**
La Paz *Bol* **30C2**
La Paz *Mexico* **24A2**
La Perouse, Str *USSR/Japan* **69G2**
La Piedad *Mexico* **23A1**
La Pine *USA* **20B2**
Laplace *USA* **19B3**
la Placita *Mexico* **23A2**
La Plata *Arg* **29E2**
La Plonge,L *Can* **13F1**
La Porte *USA* **14A2**
Lappeenranta *Fin* **39K6**
Lappland, Region *Sweden/Fin* **38H5**
Laprida *Arg* **34C3**
Laptev S *USSR* **1B8**
Lapua *Fin* **38J6**
Lapu-Lapu *Phil* **79B3**
La Purisma *Mexico* **9B4**
Laqiya Arba'in, Well *Sudan* **95B2**
La Quiaca *Arg* **30C3**
L'Aquila *Italy* **52B2**
Lār *Iran* **91B4**
Larache *Mor* **96B1**
Laramie *USA* **8C2**
Laramie Range, Mts *USA* **8C2**
Larca *Spain* **50B2**
Laredo *USA* **9D4**
Larestan, Region *Iran* **91B4**
L'Argentière *France* **47B2**
Largo *USA* **17B2**
Largs *Scot* **42B2**
Lārī *Iran* **90A2**
La Rioja *Arg* **30C4**
La Rioja, State *Arg* **30C4**
Lárisa *Greece* **55B3**
Larkana *Pak* **85B3**
Larnaca *Cyprus* **92B3**
Larnaca B *Cyprus* **94A1**
Larne *N Ire* **45D1**
La Robla *Spain* **50A1**
La Roche-en-Ardenne *Belg* **46C1**
La Rochelle *France* **48B2**
La Roche-sur-Foron *France* **47B1**
La Roche-sur-Yon *France* **48B2**
La Roda *Spain* **51B2**
La Romana *Dom Rep* **27D3**
La Ronge *Can* **5H4**
La Ronge,L *Can* **5H4**
Larvik *Nor* **39F7**
Lar'yak *USSR* **65J3**
La Sagra, Mt *Spain* **50B2**
La Salle *Can* **15D1**
La Salle *USA* **18C1**
La Sarre *Can* **7C5**
Las Avispas *Arg* **34C1**
Las Cabras *Chile* **34A2**
Lascombe *Can* **5G4**
Las Cruces *USA* **9C3**
La Selle, Mt *Haiti* **26C3**
Lasengmia *China* **72B2**
La Serena *Chile* **30B4**
Las Flores *Arg* **29E3**
Lashio *Burma* **76B1**
La Sila, Mts *Italy* **53C3**
Lāsjerd *Iran* **90B2**
Las Lajas *Chile* **34A3**
Las Marismas, Marshland *Spain* **50A2**
Las Palmas de Gran Canaria *Canary Is* **96A2**
La Spezia *Italy* **52A2**
Las Plumas *Arg* **29C4**
Las Rosas *Arg* **34C2**
Lassen Peak, Mt *USA* **20B2**
Lassen Volcanic Nat Pk *USA* **20B2**
las Tinai *Mexico* **23B2**
Lastoursville *Gabon* **98B3**
Lastovo, I *Yugos* **52C2**
Las Tres Marias, Is *Mexico* **24B2**
Las Varillas *Arg* **34C2**
Las Vegas *USA* **9C3**
Latina *Italy* **53B2**
La Toma *Arg* **34B2**
La Tortuga, I *Ven* **32D1**
La Trinidad *Phil* **79B2**
Latrobe *Aust* **109C4**
Latrun *Israel* **94B3**
La Tuque *Can* **7C5**
Lātūr *India* **87B1**
Latviyskaya SSR, Republic *USSR* **60B2**
Launceston *Aust* **107D5**
Launceston *Eng* **43B4**
La Unión *Chile* **29B4**
La Union *El Salvador* **25D3**
La Union *Mexico* **23A2**
La Unión *Peru* **32B5**
Laura *Aust* **107D2**
Laurel, Delaware *USA* **15C3**
Laurel, Maryland *USA* **16A3**
Laurel, Mississippi *USA* **11B3**
Laurens *USA* **17B1**
Laurinburg *USA* **17C1**
Lausanne *Switz* **52A1**
Laut, I *Indon* **78D3**
Lautaro, Mt *Chile* **29B5**
Lauterecken *W Germ* **46D2**
Laval *Can* **15D1**
Laval *France* **48B2**
Laveaga Peak, Mt *USA* **22B2**
Laveno *Italy* **47C2**
Lavras *Brazil* **31B6**
Lavrentiya *USSR* **4A3**
Lavumisa *Swaziland* **101H1**
Lawas *Malay* **78D1**
Lawksawk *Burma* **76B1**
Lawrence, Kansas *USA* **18A2**
Lawrence, Massachusetts *USA* **15D2**
Lawrence *NZ* **111A3**
Lawrenceville, Illinois *USA* **14A3**
Lawton *USA* **9D3**
Layla *S Arabia* **91A5**
Laylo *Sudan* **99D2**
La'youn *Mor* **96A2**
Lázaro Cárdenas *Mexico* **23A2**
Laz Daua *Somalia* **99E1**
Lazi *Phil* **79B4**
Lead *USA* **8C2**
Leader *Can* **13F2**
Leavenworth *USA* **18A2**
Leba *Pol* **58B2**
Lebanon, Missouri *USA* **18B2**
Lebanon, Oregon *USA* **20B2**
Lebanon, Pennsylvania *USA* **15C2**
Lebanon, Republic *S W Asia* **92C3**
Lebombo, Mts *Mozam/S Africa/ Swaziland* **101C3**
Lebork *Pol* **58B2**
Le Bourg-d'Oisans *France* **47A2**
Le Brassus *Switz* **47B1**
Lebu *Chile* **29B3**
Le Buet, Mt *France* **47B1**
Le Cateau *France* **46B1**
Lecce *Italy* **55A2**
Lecco *Italy* **52A1**
Lech, R *Austria* **47D1**
Lechtaler Alpen, Mts *Austria* **47D1**
Le Creusot *France* **49C2**
Ledbury *Eng* **43C3**
Leduc *Can* **13E2**
Lee *USA* **16C1**
Lee, R *Irish Rep* **45B3**
Leeds *Eng* **41C3**
Leek *Eng* **43C3**
Leer *W Germ* **56B2**
Leesburg, Florida *USA* **17B2**
Leesburg, Virginia *USA* **16A3**
Leesville *USA* **19B3**
Leeton *Aust* **109C2**
Leeuwarden *Neth* **56B2**
Leeuwin,C *Aust* **106A4**
Lee Vining *USA* **22C2**
Leeward Is *Caribbean* **27E3**
Lefkara *Cyprus* **94A1**
Legazpi *Phil* **79B3**
Legnago *Italy* **47D2**
Legnica *Pol* **59B2**
Leguan Inlet *Guyana* **33F2**
Leguizamo *Colombia* **32C4**
Leh *India* **84D2**
Le Harve *France* **48C2**
Lehigh, R *USA* **16B2**
Lehighton *USA* **16B2**
Leiah *Pak* **84C2**
Leibnitz *Austria* **59B3**
Leicester, County *Eng* **43D3**
Leicester *Eng* **43D3**
Leichhardt, R *Aust* **107C2**
Leiden *Neth* **56A2**
Leie, R *Belg* **46B1**

Leigh Creek *Aust* **106C4**
Leighton Buzzard *Eng* **43D4**
Leine, R *W Germ* **56B2**
Leinster, Region *Irish Rep* **45C2**
Leipzig *E Germ* **57C2**
Leiria *Port* **50A2**
Leirvik *Nor* **39F7**
Leitrim, County *Irish Rep* **45B1**
Leiyang *China* **73C4**
Leizhou Bandao, Pen *China* **73B5**
Leizhou Wan, B *China* **73C5**
Lek, R *Neth* **56A2**
Lekemti *Eth* **99D2**
Leland *USA* **19B3**
Lelija, Mt *Yugos* **54A2**
Le Locle *France* **47B1**
Le Mans *France* **48C2**
Lemicux Is *Can* **6D3**
Lemmon *USA* **8C2**
Lemoore *USA* **21B2**
Lempdes *France* **49C2**
Lemro, R *Burma* **86C2**
Le Murge, Region *Italy* **52C2**
Lena, R *USSR* **63C2**
Lendery *USSR* **38L6**
Lengshujiang *China* **73C4**
Leninabad *USSR* **82A1**
Leninakan *USSR* **65F5**
Leningrad *USSR* **60D2**
Leningradskaya, Base *Ant* **112B7**
Leninogorsk, Tatar ASSR *USSR* **61H3**
Leninogorsk *USSR* **68A1**
Leninsk-Kuznetskiy *USSR* **65K4**
Leninskoye *USSR* **69F2**
Lenkoran' *USSR* **65F6**
Lenne, R *W Germ* **46E1**
Lenox *USA* **16C1**
Lens *France* **46B1**
Lensk *USSR* **63D1**
Lentini *Italy* **53B3**
Lenya, R *Burma* **76B3**
Leoben *Austria* **52B1**
Leominster *Eng* **43C3**
Leominster *USA* **16D1**
Leon *Mexico* **24B2**
León *Nic* **25D3**
Leon, Region *Spain* **50A1**
León *Spain* **50A1**
Leonardville *Namibia* **100A3**
Leonora *Aust* **106B3**
Leopoldina *Brazil* **35C2**
Lepel *USSR* **60C3**
Leper *Belg* **46B1**
Leping *China* **73D4**
Le Puy *France* **49C2**
Léré *Chad* **98B2**
Leribe *Lesotho* **101G1**
Lerici *Italy* **47C2**
Lérida *Spain* **51C1**
Lerma, R *Mexico* **23A1**
Lermoos *Austria* **47D1**
Léros, I *Greece* **55C3**
Lerwick *Scot* **40C1**
Les Andelys *France* **46A2**
Les Cayes *Haiti* **26C3**
Les Ecrins, Mt *France* **47B2**
Leshan *China* **73A4**
Leskovac *Yugos* **54B2**
Les Landes, Region *France* **48B3**
Leslie *S Africa* **101G1**
Lesnoy *USSR* **61H2**
Lesosibirsk *USSR* **63B2**
Lesotho, Kingdom *S Africa* **101G1**
Lesozavodsk *USSR* **69F2**
Les Sables-d'Olonne *France* **48B2**
Lesser Antarctica, Region *Ant* **80E**
Lesser Antilles, Is *Caribbean* **27D4**
Lesser Slave L *Can* **13E1**
Lésvos, I *Greece* **55C3**
Leszno *Pol* **58B2**
Letha Range, Mts *Burma* **86C2**
Lethbridge *Can* **5G5**
Lethem *Guyana* **33F3**
Letichev *USSR* **59D3**
Let Oktyobr'ya *USSR* **63D2**
Letong *Indon* **78B2**
Le Touquet-Paris-Plage *France* **46A1**
Letpadan *Burma* **76B2**
Le Tréport *France* **48C1**
Leuk *Switz* **47B1**
Leuven *Belg* **57A2**
Levádhia *Greece* **55B3**
Levanger *Nor* **38G6**
Levanna, Mt *Italy* **47B2**
Lévèque,C *Aust* **71D5**
Leverkusen *W Germ* **46D1**
Levice *Czech* **59B3**
Levico *Italy* **47D1**
Levin *NZ* **110C2**
Lévis *Can* **7C5**
Levittown *USA* **15D2**
Lévka Óri, Mt *Greece* **55B3**
Levkás *Greece* **55B3**
Levkás, I *Greece* **55B3**
Lévque,C *Aust* **106B2**
Levski *Bulg* **54C2**
Lewes *Eng* **43E4**
Lewis, I *Scot* **40B2**
Lewisburg *USA* **16A2**
Lewis P *NZ* **111B2**
Lewis Range, Mts *USA* **8B2**
Lewiston, Idaho *USA* **8B2**
Lewiston, Maine *USA* **10C2**
Lewistown, Montana *USA* **8C2**
Lewistown, Pennsylvania *USA* **15C2**
Lewisville *USA* **19B3**
Lexington, Kentucky *USA* **11B3**
Lexington, Missouri *USA* **18B2**
Lexington Park *USA* **15C3**
Leyte G *Phil* **79C3**
Lezhe *Alb* **54A2**
Lhasa *China* **82D3**
Lhazê *China* **86B1**
Lhokseumawe *Indon* **70A3**
Lhozhag *China* **86C1**
Lhunze *China* **68B4**
Lianga *Phil* **79C4**
Liangdang *China* **72B3**
Lianjiang *China* **73C5**
Lianping *China* **73C5**
Lian Xian *China* **73C5**
Lianyungang *China* **72D3**
Liaoding Bandao, Pen *China* **72E1**
Liaodong Wan, B *China* **72E1**
Liao He, R *China* **72E1**
Liaoning, Province *China* **72E1**
Liaoyang *China* **72E1**
Liaoyuan *China* **72E1**
Liaoyuang *China* **74B2**
Liard, R *Can* **4F3**
Liard River *Can* **4F4**
Liart *France* **46C2**
Libenge *Zaïre* **98B2**
Liberal *USA* **9C3**
Liberec *Czech* **57C2**
Liberia, Republic *Africa* **97A4**
Liberty, Missouri *USA* **18B2**
Liberty, New York *USA* **15D2**
Liberty, Texas *USA* **19B3**
Libourne *France* **48B3**
libres *Mexico* **23B2**
Libreville *Gabon* **98A2**
Libya, Republic *Africa* **95A2**
Libyan Desert *Libya* **95B2**
Libyan Plat *Egypt* **95B1**
Licata *Italy* **53B3**
Lichfield *Eng* **43D3**
Lichinga *Mozam* **101C2**
Lichtenburg *S Africa* **101G1**
Licking, R *USA* **14B3**
Lick Observatory *USA* **22B2**
Lida *USSR* **60C3**
Lidköping *Sweden* **39G7**
Lido di Ostia *Italy* **53B2**
Liechtenstein, Principality *Europe* **52A1**
Liège *Belg* **57B2**
Lielupe, R *USSR* **58C1**
Lienart *Zaïre* **98C2**
Lienz *Austria* **57C3**
Liepāja *USSR* **60B2**
Lier *Belg* **46C1**
Liestal *Switz* **47B1**
Liévre, R *Can* **15C1**
Liezen *Austria* **57C3**
Liffey, R *Irish Rep* **45C2**
Lifford *Irish Rep* **45C1**
Lifu, I *Nouvelle Calédonie* **107F3**
Lightning Ridge *Aust* **109C1**
Ligny-en-Barrois *France* **46C2**
Ligonha, R *Mozam* **101C2**
Liguria, Region *Italy* **47C2**
Ligurian, S *Italy* **52A2**
Lihue *Hawaiian Is* **21C4**
Likasi *Zaïre* **100B2**
Lille *France* **49C1**
Lillehammer *Nor* **39G6**
Lillers *France* **46B1**
Lillestøm *Nor* **39G7**
Lillooet *Can* **13C2**
Lillooet, R *Can* **13C2**
Lilongwe *Malawi* **101C2**
Liloy *Phil* **79B4**
Lim, R *Yugos* **54A2**
Lima *Peru* **32B6**
Lima *Spain* **50A1**
Lima *USA* **10B2**
Limassol *Cyprus* **92B3**
Limavady *N Ire* **45C1**
Limay, R *Arg* **34B3**
Limay Mahuida *Arg* **34B3**
Limbe *Malawi* **101C2**
Limburg *W Gem* **57B2**
Limeira *Brazil* **31B6**
Limerick, County *Irish Rep* **45B2**
Limerick *Irish Rep* **41B3**
Limfjorden, L *Den* **56B1**
Limmen Bight, B *Aust* **106C2**
Límnos, I *Greece* **55C3**
Limoeiro *Brazil* **31D3**
Limoges *France* **48C2**
Limón *Costa Rica* **25D4**
Limon *USA* **8C3**
Limousin, Region *France* **48C2**
Linapacan Str *Phil* **79A3**
Linares *Chile* **29B3**
Linares *Mexico* **9D4**
Linares *Spain* **50B2**
Lincang *China* **68B4**
Lincoln *Arg* **29D2**
Lincoln, California *USA* **18A1**
Lincoln, County *Eng* **42D3**
Lincoln *Eng* **42D3**
Lincoln, Illinois *USA* **18C1**
Lincoln, Nebraska *USA* **8D2**
Lincoln, New Hampshire *USA* **15D2**
Lincoln *NZ* **111B2**
Lincoln, S *Greenland* **80A**
Lincoln City *USA* **20B2**
Lincoln Park *USA* **14B2**
L'Incudina, Mt *Corse* **52A2**
Lindau *W Germ* **57B3**
Linden *Guyana* **33F2**
Lindesnes, C *Nor* **39F7**
Lindi *Tanz* **99D3**
Lindi, R *Zaïre* **98C2**
Lindley *S Africa* **101G1**
Lindos *Greece* **55C3**
Lindsay *Can* **15C2**
Line Is *Pacific O* **105J3**
Linfen *China* **72C2**
Lingao *China* **76D2**
Lingayen *Phil* **79B2**
Lingen *W Germ* **56B2**
Lingling *China* **73C4**
Lingshan *China* **73B5**
Lingshi *China* **72C2**
Linguère *Sen* **97A3**
Linhai, Rhejiang *China* **73E4**
Linhares *Brazil* **31D5**
Linhe *China* **72B1**
Linjiang *China* **74B2**
Linköping *Sweden* **39H7**
Linqing *China* **72D2**
Lins *Brazil* **35B2**
Lintao *China* **72A2**
Linthal *Switz* **47C1**
Linxi *China* **68D2**
Linxia *China* **72A2**
Linz *Austria* **57C3**
Lipa *Phil* **79B3**
Lipari, I *Italy* **53B3**
Lipetsk *USSR* **61E3**
Lipova *Rom* **54B1**
Lippe, R *W Germ* **56B2**
Lippstadt *W Germ* **46E1**
Lira *Uganda* **99D2**
Liranga *Congo* **98B3**
Lisala *Zaïre* **98C2**
Lisboa *Port* **50A2**
Lisburn *N Ire* **45C1**
Liscannor B *Irish Rep* **45B2**
Lishui *China* **73D4**
Li Shui, R *China* **73C4**
Lisichansk *USSR* **60E4**
Lisieux *France* **48C2**
L'Isle-Adam *France* **46B2**
L'Isle-sur-le-Doubs *France* **47B1**
Lismore *Aust* **107E3**
Listowel *Irish Rep* **45B2**
Litang *China* **73B5**
Lītanī, R *Leb* **94B2**
Litani, R *Suriname* **33G3**
Litchfield *USA* **18C2**
Lithgow *Aust* **107E4**
Lititz *USA* **16A2**
Litovko *USSR* **69F2**
Litovskaya SSR, Republic *USSR* **60B2**
Little, R *USA* **19A3**
Little Abaco, I *Bahamas* **11C4**
Little Barrier I *NZ* **110C1**
Little Bow, R *Can* **13E2**
Little Cayman, I *Caribbean* **25D3**
Little Egg Harbor, B *USA* **16B3**
Little Inagua, I *Caribbean* **26C2**
Little Nicobar, I *Nicobar Is* **77A4**
Little Rock *USA* **11A3**
Littlerock *USA* **22D3**
Little Smoky *Can* **13D2**
Little Smoky, R *Can* **13D2**
Littlestown *USA* **16A3**
Littleton, New Hampshire *USA* **15D2**
Liuhe *China* **74B2**
Liuzhou *China* **73B5**
Livanátais *Greece* **55B3**
Līvāni *USSR* **58D1**
Livengood *USA* **12E1**
Live Oak *USA* **17B1**
Livermore *USA* **21A2**
Liverpool *Can* **7D5**
Liverpool *Eng* **42C3**
Liverpool B *Can* **4E2**

Liverpool B *Eng* 42C3
Liverpool,C *Can* 6C2
Liverpool Range, Mts *Aust* 109D2
Livingston, Montana *USA* 8B2
Livingston, Texas *USA* 19B3
Livingston *UK* 44C4
Livingston,L *USA* 19A3
Livno *Yugos* 52C2
Livny *USSR* 60E3
Livonia *USA* 14B2
Livorno *Italy* 52B2
Liwale *Tanz* 99D3
Ljubljana *Yugos* 52B1
Ljungan, R *Sweden* 38G6
Ljungby *Sweden* 39G7
Ljusdal *Sweden* 39H6
Ljusnan, R *Sweden* 38H6
Llandeilo *Wales* 43C4
Llandovery *Wales* 43C4
Llandrindod Wells *Wales* 43C3
Llandudno *Wales* 42C3
Llanelli *Wales* 43B4
Llangollen *Wales* 43C3
Llano Estacado, Plat *USA* 9C3
Llanos, Region *Colombia/Ven* 24D2
Llanos de Chiquitos, Region *Bol* 30D2
Llerena *Spain* 50A2
Lleyn, Pen *Wales* 43B3
Llimsk *USSR* 63C2
Llin *USSR* 63C2
Llorin *Nigeria* 89E7
Lloydminster *Can* 5H4
Llullaillaco, Mt *Chile/Arg* 30C3
Loa, R *Chile* 30C3
Loan *France* 49C2
Loange, R *Zaïre* 98B3
Lobatse *Botswana* 100B3
Lobaye, R *CAR* 98B2
Loberia *Arg* 34D3
Lobito *Angola* 100A2
Lobos *Arg* 34D3
Locano *Italy* 47B2
Locarno *Switz* 47C1
Loch Awe, L *Scot* 44B3
Lochboisdale *Scot* 44A3
Loch Bracadale, Inlet *Scot* 44A3
Loch Broom, Estuary *Scot* 44B3
Loch Doon, L *Scot* 42B2
Loch Earn, L *Scot* 44B3
Loch Eriboll, Inlet *Scot* 44B2
Loch Ericht, L *Scot* 44B3
Loches *France* 48C2
Loch Etive, Inlet *Scot* 44B3
Loch Ewe, Inlet *Scot* 44B3
Loch Fyne, Inlet *Scot* 44B3
Loch Hourn, Inlet *Scot* 44B3
Lochinver *Scot* 44B2
Loch Katrine, L *Scot* 44B3
Loch Leven, L *Scot* 44C3
Loch Linnhe, Inlet *Scot* 44B3
Loch Lochy, L *Scot* 44B3
Loch Lomond, L *Scot* 44B3
Loch Long, Inlet *Scot* 44B3
Lochmaddy *Scot* 44A3
Loch Maree, L *Scot* 44B3
Loch Morar, L *Scot* 44B3
Lochnagar, Mt *Scot* 44C3
Loch Ness, L *Scot* 44B3
Loch Rannoch, L *Scot* 44B3
Loch Roag, Inlet *Scot* 44A2
Loch Sheil, L *Scot* 44B3
Loch Shin, L *Scot* 44B2
Loch Snizort, Inlet *Scot* 44A3
Loch Sunart, Inlet *Scot* 44B3
Loch Tay, L *Scot* 44B3
Loch Torridon, Inlet *Scot* 44B3
Lock *Aust* 108A2
Lockerbie *Scot* 42C2
Lock Haven *USA* 15C2
Lockport *USA* 15C2
Loc Ninh *Viet* 76D3
Locri *Italy* 53C3
Lod *Israel* 94B3
Loddon, R *Aust* 108B3
Lodeynoye Pole *USSR* 60D1
Lodhran *Pak* 84C3
Lodi *Italy* 52A1
Lodi *USA* 21A2
Lodja *Zaïre* 98C3
Lods *France* 47B1
Lodwar *Kenya* 99D2
Łódź *Pol* 58B2
Lofoten, Is *Nor* 38G5
Logan, Utah *USA* 8B2
Logan,Mt *Can* 4D3
Logansport, Indiana *USA* 14A2
Logansport, Louisiana *USA* 19B3
Logroño *Spain* 50B1
Lohārdaga *India* 86A2
Lohja *Fin* 39J6
Loikaw *Burma* 76B2
Loimaa *Fin* 39J6
Loir, R *France* 48C2
Loire, R *France* 49C2
Loja *Ecuador* 32B4
Loja *Spain* 50B2
Lokan Tekojärvi, Res *Fin* 38K5
Lokeren *Belg* 46B1
Lokitaung *Kenya* 99D2
Loknya *USSR* 58D1
Lokolo, R *Zaïre* 98C3
Lokoro, R *Zaïre* 98C3
Loks Land, I *Can* 6D3
Lolland, I *Den* 56C2
Lom *Bulg* 54B2
Lomami, R *Zaïre* 98C3
Loma Mts *Sierra Leone/Guinea* 97A4
Lombardia, Region *Italy* 47C2
Lomblen, I *Indon* 71D4
Lombok, I *Indon* 78D4
Lomé *Togo* 97C4
Lomela *Zaïre* 98C3
Lomela, R *Zaïre* 98C3
Lomonosov *USSR* 60C2
Lomont, Region *France* 47B1
Lompoc *USA* 21A3
Łomza *Pol* 58C2
Lonāvale *India* 87A1
Loncoche *Chile* 29B3
London *Can* 7B5
London *Eng* 43D4
Londonderry, County *N Ire* 45C1
Londonderry *N Ire* 45C1
Londonderry, I *Chile* 29B7
Londonderry,C *Aust* 106B2
Londres *Arg* 30C4
Londrina *Brazil* 30F3
Lone Pine *USA* 21B2
Long, I *Bahamas* 11C4
Long, I *PNG* 71F4
Long Akah *Malay* 78C2
Longarone *Italy* 47E1
Longavi, Mt *Chile* 34A3
Long B *Jamaica* 27H2
Long B *USA* 17C1
Long Beach, California *USA* 9B3
Long Beach, New York *USA* 15D2
Long Branch *USA* 15D2
Longchuan *China* 73D5
Long Creek *USA* 20C2
Longford *Aust* 109C4
Longford, County *Irish Rep* 45C2
Longford *Irish Rep* 45C2
Long Forties, Region *N Sea* 44D3
Longhua *China* 72D1
Long I *Can* 7C4
Long I *USA* 10C2
Long Island Sd *USA* 16C2
Longlac *Can* 7B4
Longlin *China* 73B5
Longmont *USA* 8C2
Longnawan *Indon* 78D2
Longquimay *Chile* 29B3
Longreach *Aust* 107D3
Longshou Shan, Upland *China* 72A2
Longtown *Eng* 42C2
Longueuil *Can* 15D1
Longuimay *Chile* 34A3
Longuyon *France* 46C2
Longview, Texas *USA* 11A3
Longview, Washington *USA* 8A2
Longwy *France* 46C2
Longxi *China* 72A3
Long Xuyen *Viet* 77D3
Longyan *China* 73D4
Longzhou *China* 73B5
Lonigo *Italy* 47D2
Lons-le-Saunier *France* 49D2
Lookout,C *USA* 11C3
Loolmalasin, Mt *Tanz* 99D3
Loon, R *Can* 13D1
Loop Hd, C *Irish Rep* 45B2
Lop Buri *Thai* 76C3
Lopez, C *Gabon* 98A3
Lop Nur, L *China* 68B2
Lora del Rio *Spain* 50A2
Lorain *USA* 10B2
Loralai *Pak* 84B2
Lordegān *Iran* 90B3
Lord Howe, I *Aust* 107E4
Lord Howe Rise *Pacific O* 105G5
Lord Mayor B *Can* 6A3
Lordsburg *USA* 9C3
Lorena *Brazil* 35B2
Loreo *Italy* 47E2
Loreto *Mexico* 23A1
Lorient *France* 48B2
Lorne *Aust* 108B3
Lörrach *W Germ* 57B3
Lorraine, Region *France* 49D2
Los Alamos *USA* 9C3
Los Andes *Chile* 34A2
Los Angeles *Chile* 29B3
Los Angeles *USA* 9B3
Los Banos *USA* 21A2
Los Cerrillos *Arg* 34B2
Los Gatos *USA* 21A2
Lošinj, I *Yugos* 52B2
Los Lagos *Chile* 29B3
Los Mochis *Mexico* 24B2
Los Olivos *USA* 22B3
Los Sauces *Chile* 34A3
Lossiemouth *Scot* 44C3
Los Testigos, Is *Ven* 27E4
Los Vilos *Chile* 29B2
Lot, R *France* 48C3
Lota *Chile* 34A3
Lothian, Region *Scot* 42C2
Lotikipi Plain *Sudan/Kenya* 99D2
Loto *Zaïre* 98C3
Lötschberg Tunnel *Switz* 47B1
Lotta, R *Fin/USSR* 38K5
Loudéac *France* 48B2
Louga *Sen* 97A3
Lough Allen, L *Irish Rep* 41B3
Lough Boderg, L *Irish Rep* 45C2
Loughborough *Eng* 43D3
Lough Bowna, L *Irish Rep* 45C2
Lough Carlingford, L *N Ire* 45C1
Lough Conn, L *Irish Rep* 41B3
Lough Corrib, L *Irish Rep* 41B3
Lough Derg, L *Irish Rep* 41B3
Lough Derravaragh, L *Irish Rep* 45C2
Loughead I *Can* 4H2
Lough Ennell, L *Irish Rep* 45C2
Lough Erne, L *N Ire* 41B3
Lough Foyle, Estuary *N Ire/Irish Rep* 40B2
Lough Neagh, L *N Ire* 40B3
Lough Oughter, L *Irish Rep* 45C1
Loughrea *Irish Rep* 45B2
Lough Ree, L *Irish Rep* 45C2
Lough Sheelin, L *Irish Rep* 45C2
Lough Strangford, L *Irish Rep* 42B2
Lough Swilly, Estuary *Irish Rep* 45C1
Louisa *USA* 14B3
Louisa Reef, I *S E Asia* 70C3
Louise,L *USA* 12E2
Louisiade Arch *Solomon Is* 107E2
Louisiana, State *USA* 11A3
Louisville, Georgia *USA* 17B1
Louisville, Kentucky *USA* 11B3
Loukhi *USSR* 38L5
Lourdes *France* 48B3
Louth *Aust* 108C2
Louth, County *Irish Rep* 45C2
Louth *Eng* 42D3
Louviers *France* 48C2
Lovat, R *USSR* 60D2
Lovech *Bulg* 54B2
Lovelock *USA* 21B1
Lóvere *Italy* 52B1
Lovington *USA* 9C3
Lovozero *USSR* 38L5
Low,C *Can* 6B3
Lowell, Massachusetts *USA* 10C2
Lowell, Oregon *USA* 20B2
Lowell *USA* 16D1
Lower Hutt *NZ* 111B2
Lower Seal,L *Can* 7C4
Lowestoft *Eng* 43E3
Łowicz *Pol* 58B2
Loxton *Aust* 108B2
Loyd George,Mt *Can* 5F4
Loznica *Yugos* 54A2
loz Reyes *Mexico* 23A2
Lozva, R *USSR* 65H3
Luacano *Angola* 100B2
Luachimo *Angola* 98C3
Lualaba, R *Zaïre* 98C3
Luampa *Zambia* 100B2
Luân *Angola* 100B2
Lu'an *China* 73D3
Luanda *Angola* 98B3
Luando, R *Angola* 100A2
Luanginga, R *Angola* 100B2
Luang Namtha *Laos* 76C1
Luang Prabang *Laos* 76C2
Luangue, R *Angola* 98B3
Luangwa, R *Zambia* 100C2
Luan He, R *China* 72D1
Luanping *China* 72D1
Luanshya *Zambia* 100B2
Luapula, R *Zaïre* 100B2
Luarca *Spain* 50A1
Lubalo *Angola* 98B3
L'uban *USSR* 58D2
Lubang Is *Phil* 79B3
Lubango *Angola* 100A2
Lubbock *USA* 9C3
Lübeck *W Germ* 56C2

Lubefu *Zaïre* 98C3
Lubefu, R *Zaïre* 98C3
Lubero *Zaïre* 99C3
Lubilash, R *Zaïre* 98C3
Lublin *Pol* 59C2
Lubny *USSR* 60D3
Lubok Antu *Malay* 78C2
Lubudi *Zaïre* 98C3
Lubudi, R *Zaïre* 98C3
Lubuklinggau *Indon* 78A3
Lubumbashi *Zaïre* 100B2
Lubutu *Zaïre* 98C3
Lucban *Phil* 79B3
Lucca *Italy* 52B2
Luce, B *Scot* 42B2
Lucedale *USA* 19C3
Lucena *Phil* 79B3
Lucenec *Czech* 59B3
Luchuan *China* 73C5
Luckenwalde *E Germ* 56C2
Luckhoff *S Africa* 101F1
Lucknow *India* 86A1
Lucusse *Angola* 100B2
Lüda *China* 72E2
Lüdenscheid *W Germ* 46D1
Lüderitz *Namibia* 100A3
Ludhiana *India* 84D2
Ludington *USA* 14A2
Ludlow *Eng* 43C3
Ludogorie, Upland *Bulg* 54C2
Ludowici *USA* 17B1
Luduş *Rom* 54B1
Ludvika *Sweden* 39H6
Ludwigsburg *W Germ* 57B3
Ludwigshafen *W Germ* 57B3
Ludwigslust *E Germ* 56C2
Luebo *Zaïre* 98C3
Luema, R *Zaïre* 98C3
Luembe, R *Angola* 98C3
Luena *Angola* 100A2
Luene, R *Angola* 100B2
Lüeyang *China* 72B3
Lufeng *China* 73D5
Lufkin *USA* 11A3
Luga *USSR* 60C2
Luga, R *USSR* 60C2
Lugano *Switz* 52A1
Lugela *Mozam* 101C2
Lugenda, R *Mozam* 101C2
Lugo *Spain* 50A1
Lugoj *Rom* 54B1
Luhuo *China* 72A3
Lui, R *Angola* 98B3
Luiana *Angola* 100B2
Luiana, R *Angola* 100B2
Luino *Italy* 47C2
Luionga, R *Zaïre* 98B2
Luipan Shan, Upland *China* 72B2
Luishia *Zaïre* 100B2
Luixi *China* 68B4
Luiza *Zaïre* 98C3
Luján *Arg* 34B2
Luján *Arg* 34D2
Lujiang *China* 73D3
Lukenie, R *Zaïre* 98B3
Luki *USSR* 64E4
Lukolela *Zaïre* 98B3
Łuków *Pol* 58C2
Lukuga, R *Zaïre* 98C3
Lukulu *Zambia* 100B2
Lule, R *Sweden* 38J5
Luleå *Sweden* 38J5
Lüleburgaz *Turk* 54C2
Lüliang Shan, Mts *China* 72C2
Luling *USA* 19A4
Lulonga, R *Zaïre* 98C2
Lumbala *Angola* 100B2
Lumberton *USA* 11C3
Lumbis *Indon* 78D1
Lumding *India* 86C1
Lumeje *Angola* 100B2
Lumsden *NZ* 111A3
Lund *Sweden* 39G7
Lundazi *Zambia* 101C2
Lundi, R *Zim* 100C3
Lundy, I *Eng* 43B4
Lüneburg *W Germ* 56C2
Lunéville *France* 46D2
Lunga, R *Zambia* 100B2
Lunglei *India* 86C2
Lungue Bungo, R *Angola* 100A2
Luninec *USSR* 58D2
Luobomo *Congo* 98B3
Luocheng *China* 73B5
Luoding *China* 73C5
Luohe *China* 72C3
Luo He, R, Henan *China* 72C3
Luo He, R, Shaanxi *China* 72B2
Luoxiao Shan, Hills *China* 73C4
Luoyang *China* 72C3
Luozi *Zaïre* 98B3
Lupane *Zim* 100B2
Lupilichi *Mozam* 101C2
Luque *Par* 30E4
Lurgan *N Ire* 45C1
Lurio, R *Mozam* 101C2
Luristan, Region *Iran* 90A3
Lusaka *Zambia* 100B2
Lusambo *Zaïre* 98C3
Lushnjë *Alb* 55A2
Lushoto *Tanz* 99D3
Lushui *China* 68B4
Lüshun *China* 72E2
Luton *Eng* 43D4
Lutsk *USSR* 60C3
Luuq *Somalia* 99E2
Luvua, R *Zaïre* 99C3
Luwegu, R *Tanz* 99D3
Luwingu *Zambia* 100C2
Luwuk *Indon* 71D4
Luxembourg, Grand Duchy *N W Europe* 46D2
Luxembourg *Lux* 49D2
Luxi *China* 73A5
Luxor *Egypt* 95C2
Luza *USSR* 61G1
Luza, R *USSR* 61G1
Luzern *Switz* 52A1
Luzhai *China* 73B5
Luzhi *China* 73B4
Luzhou *China* 73B4
Luziânia *Brazil* 35B1
Luzon, I *Phil* 79B2
Luzon Str *Phil* 79B1
L'vov *USSR* 59C3
Lybster *Scot* 44C2
Lycksele *Sweden* 38H6
Lydenburg *S Africa* 100B3
Lyell,Mt *USA* 8B3
Lykens *USA* 16A2
Lyme B *Eng* 43C4
Lyme Regis *Eng* 43C4
Lynchburg *USA* 11C3
Lyndhurst *Aust* 108A2
Lynn *USA* 15D2
Lynn Canal, Sd *USA* 12G3
Lynn Haven *USA* 17A1
Lynn Lake *Can* 5H4
Lynx L *Can* 5H3
Lyon *France* 49C2
Lyon Canal, Sd *USA* 12G3
Lyons, Georgia *USA* 17B1
Lyons, R *Aust* 106A3
Lys, R *Italy* 47B2
Lys'va *USSR* 61J2
Lyttelton *NZ* 111B2
Lytton *Can* 13C2
Lytton *USA* 22A1
Lyubeshov *USSR* 58D2
Lyublino *USSR* 60E2

M

Ma, R *Viet* 76C1
Ma'agan *Jordan* 94B2
Ma'alot Tarshīha *Israel* 94B2
Ma'an *Jordan* 92C3
Ma'anshan *China* 73D3
Ma'arrat an Nu'mān *Syria* 92C2
Maas, R *Neth* 46C1
Maaseik *Belg* 46C1
Maasin *Phil* 79B3
Maastricht *Belg* 57B2
Mabalane *Mozam* 101C3
Mabaruma *Guyana* 33F2
Mablethorpe *Eng* 42E3
Mabote *Mozam* 101C3
Mabrita *USSR* 58C2
M'adel *USSR* 58D2
Macaé *Brazil* 35C2
McAlester *USA* 9D3
McAllen *USA* 9D4
Macaloge *Mozam* 101C2
Macapá *Brazil* 33G3
Macarani *Brazil* 35C1
Macas *Ecuador* 32B4
Macaú *Brazil* 31D3
Macau, Dependency *China* 73C5
M'Bari, R *CAR* 98C2
McBride *Can* 13C2
McCarthy *USA* 12F2
McCauley I *Can* 13A2
Macclesfield *Eng* 42C3
McClintock B *Can* 6B1
McClintock Chan *Can* 4H2
McClure *USA* 16A2
McClure,L *USA* 22B2
McClure Str *Can* 4G2
McComb *USA* 19B3
McCook *USA* 8C2
Macculloch,C *Can* 6C2
McCusker,Mt *Can* 13C1
McDame *Can* 4F4
McDermitt *USA* 20C2
Macdonald, R *Can* 13E2
Macdonnell Ranges, Mts *Aust* 106C3
Macedo de Cavaleiros *Port* 50A1
Maceió *Brazil* 31D3
Macenta *Guinea* 97B4
Macerata *Italy* 52B2
Macfarlane,L *Aust* 108A2
McGehee *USA* 19B3
MacGillycuddys Reeks Mts *Irish Rep* 45B3
McGrath *USA* 4C3
Machado *Brazil* 35B2
Machaíla *Mozam* 101C3
Machakos *Kenya* 99D3
Machala *Ecuador* 32B4
Machaze *Mozam* 101C3
Mācherla *India* 87B1
Machgharab *Leb* 94B2
Machilīpatnam *India* 87C1
Machiques *Ven* 32C1
Machu-Picchu, Hist Site *Peru* 32C6
Macia *Mozam* 101C3
MacIntyre, R *Aust* 109C1
Mackay *Aust* 107D3
Mackay,L *Aust* 106B3
McKeesport *USA* 14C2
Mackenzie *Can* 13C1
Mackenzie, R *Can* 4F3
Mackenzie, Region *Can* 4F3
Mackenzie B *Can* 4E3
Mackenzie King I *Can* 4G2
Mackenzie Mts *Can* 4E3
Mackinac,Str of *USA* 14B1
Mackinaw City *USA* 14B1
McKinley,Mt *USA* 12D2
McKinney *USA* 19A3
Mackinson Inlet, B *Can* 6C2
Macksville *Aust* 109D2
Mclaoughlin,Mt *USA* 20B2
Maclean *Aust* 109D1
Maclear *S Africa* 100B4
McLennan *Can* 5G4
McLeod, R *Can* 13D2
McLeod B *Can* 4G3
McLeod,L *Aust* 106A3
McLeod Lake *Can* 13C1
Macmillan, R *Can* 4E3
Macmillan P *Can* 12H2
McMinnville, Oregon *USA* 20B1
McMurdo, Base *Ant* 112B7
McNaughton L *Can* 13D2
Macomb *USA* 18B1
Macomer *Sardegna* 53A2
Macomia *Mozam* 101C2
Mâcon *France* 49C2
Macon, Georgia *USA* 11B3
Macon, Missouri *USA* 18B2
Macondo *Angola* 100B2
McPherson *USA* 18A2
Macquarie, Is *Aust* 104F6
Macquarie, R *Aust* 109C2
Macquarie Harbour, B *Aust* 109C4
Macquarie,L *Aust* 109D2
McRae *USA* 17B1
MacRobertsn Land, Region *Ant* 112B11
Macroom *Irish Rep* 45B3
M'Sila *Alg* 96C1
McTavish Arm, B *Can* 4G3
Macumba, R *Aust* 108A1
Macunaga *Italy* 47C2
McVicar Arm, B *Can* 4F3
M'yaróvár *Hung* 59B3
Mādabā *Jordan* 94B3
Madadi, Well *Chad* 95A3
Madagascar, I *Indian O* 89J10
Madama *Niger* 95A2
Madang *PNG* 71F4
Madaoua *Niger* 97C3
Madaripur *Bang* 86C2
Madau *USSR* 90B2
Madawaska, R *Can* 15C1
Madeira, I *Atlantic O* 96A1
Madeira, R *Brazil* 33E5
Madera *Mexico* 24B2
Madera *USA* 21A2
Madgaon *India* 87A1
Madhubani *India* 86B1
Madhya Pradesh, State *India* 86A2
Madikeri *India* 87B2
Madimba *Zaïre* 98B3
Madingo Kayes *Congo* 98B3
Madingou *Congo* 98B3
Madison, Indiana *USA* 10B3
Madison, Wisconsin *USA* 10B2
Madisonville, Kentucky *USA* 18C2
Madisonville, Texas *USA* 19A3
Madiun *Indon* 78C4
Mado Gashi *Kenya* 99D2
Madonna Di Campiglio *Italy* 47D1
Madras *India* 87C2
Madras *USA* 20B2
Madre de Dios, I *Chile* 29A6
Madre de Dios, R *Bol* 32D6
Madrid *Spain* 50B1
Madridejos *Spain* 50B2
Madura, I *Indon* 78C4
Madurai *India* 87B3
Maebashi *Japan* 75B1
Mae Khlong, R *Thai* 76B3
Mae Nam Lunang, R *Thai* 77B4
Mae Nam Mun, R *Thai* 76C2
Mae Nam Ping, R *Thai* 76B2
Maevatanana *Madag* 101D2
Mafeteng *Lesotho* 101G1
Maffra *Aust* 109C3
Mafia, I *Tanz* 99D3
Mafikeng *S Africa* 101G1
Mafra *Brazil* 30G4
Mafraq *Jordan* 92C3
Magangué *Colombia* 32C2
Magdalena *Arg* 34D3
Magdalena *Mexico* 9B3

Magdalena *Mexico* **24A1**
Magdalena, R *Colombia* **26C4**
Magdalena,Mt *Malay* **78D1**
Magdalen Is *Can* **7D5**
Magdeburg *E Germ* **56C2**
Magé *Brazil* **31C6**
Magelang *Indon* **78C4**
Maggia, R *Switz* **47C1**
Maghâgha *Egypt* **92B4**
Magherafelt *N Ire* **45C1**
Maglie *Italy* **55A2**
Magnitogorsk *USSR* **61J3**
Magnolia *USA* **19B3**
Magoé *Mozam* **101C2**
Magog *Can* **15D1**
Magosal *Mexico* **23B1**
Magrath *Can* **13E2**
Maguse River *Can* **7A3**
Magwe *Burma* **76B1**
Mahābād *Iran* **90A2**
Mahabharat Range, Mts *Nepal* **86B1**
Mahād *India* **87A1**
Mahadeo Hills *India* **85D4**
Mahajanga *Madag* **101D2**
Mahalapye *Botswana* **100B3**
Mahānadi, R *India* **86A2**
Mahanoro *Madag* **101D2**
Mahanoy City *USA* **16A2**
Maharashtra, State *India* **87A1**
Māhāsamund *India* **86A2**
Maha Sarakham *Thai* **76C2**
Mahavavy, R *Madag* **101D2**
Mahbūbnagar *India* **87B1**
Mahdia *Tunisia* **96D1**
Mahe *India* **87B2**
Mahekar *India* **85D4**
Mahéli, I *Comoros* **101D2**
Mahendragarh *India* **86A2**
Mahenge *Tanz* **99D3**
Mahesāna *India* **85C4**
Mahia Pen *NZ* **110C1**
Mahoba *India* **85D3**
Mahón *Spain* **51C2**
Mahony L *Can* **12J1**
Mahrés *Tunisia* **96D1**
Mahuva *India* **85C4**
Maicao *Colombia* **32C1**
Maîche *France* **47B1**
Maidstone *Eng* **43E4**
Maiduguri *Nig* **98B1**
Maihar *India* **86A2**
Maijdi *Bang* **86C2**
Mail Kyun, I *Burma* **76B3**
Maimana *Afghan* **84A1**
Main Chan *Can* **14B1**
Mai-Ndombe, L *Zaïre* **98B3**
Maine, State *USA* **10D2**
Maine, Region *France* **48B2**
Mainland, I *Scot* **44C2**
Mainpuri *India* **85D3**
Maintenon *France* **46A2**
Maintirano *Madag* **101D2**
Mainz *W Germ* **57B2**
Maio, I *Cape Verde* **97A4**
Maipó, Mt *Arg/Chile* **29C2**
Maipú *Arg* **34D3**
Maiquetía *Ven* **32D1**
Maira, R *Italy* **47B2**
Mairābāri *India* **86C1**
Maiskhal I *Bang* **86C2**
Maitland, New South Wales *Aust* **107E4**
Maitland, S Australia *Aust* **108A2**
Maizuru *Japan* **74D3**
Majene *Indon* **70C4**
Majes, R *Peru* **30B2**
Maji *Eth* **99D2**
Majia He, R *China* **72D2**
Makale *Eth* **99D1**
Makale *Indon* **70C4**
Makalu, Mt *China/Nepal* **86B1**
Makarska *Yugos* **52C2**
Makaryev *USSR* **61F2**
Makassar Str *Indon* **78D3**
Makat *USSR* **61H4**
Makeni *Sierra Leone* **97A4**
Makeyevka *USSR* **60E4**
Makgadikgadi, Salt Pan *Botswana* **100B3**
Makhachkala *USSR* **61G5**
Makindu *Kenya* **99D3**
Makkovik *Can* **7E4**
Makó *Hung* **59C3**
Makokou *Gabon* **98B2**
Makorako,Mt *NZ* **110C1**
Makoua *Congo* **98B2**
Makrāna *India* **85C3**
Makran Coast Range, Mts *Pak* **85A3**
Maktar *Tunisia* **96C1**
Mākū *Iran* **93D2**
Makumbi *Zaïre* **98C3**
Makurazaki *Japan* **74C4**
Makurdi *Nig* **97C4**
Malabang *Phil* **79B4**
Malabar Coast *India* **87A2**
Malabo *Bioko* **89E7**
Malacca,Str of *S E Asia* **77C5**
Málaga *Colombia* **32C2**
Malaga *Spain* **50B2**
Malaimbandy *Madag* **101D3**
Malaita, I *Solomon Is* **107F1**
Malakal *Sudan* **99D2**
Malakand *Pak* **84C2**
Malang *Indon* **78C4**
Malange *Angola* **98B3**
Malanville *Benin* **97C3**
Mälaren, L *Sweden* **39H7**
Malargüe *Arg* **34B3**
Malaspina Gl *USA* **12F3**
Malatya *Turk* **93C2**
Malawi, Republic *Africa* **101C2**
Malaybalay *Phil* **79C4**
Malāyer *Iran* **90A3**
Malaysia, Federation *S E Asia* **70B3**
Malazgirt *Turk* **93D2**
Malbork *Pol* **58B2**
Malchin *E Germ* **56C2**
Malden *USA* **18C2**
Maldives Is *Indian O* **83B5**
Maldives Ridge *Indian O* **104B4**
Maldonado *Urug* **29F2**
Male *Italy* **47D1**
Malegaon *India* **85C4**
Malé Karpaty, Upland *Czech* **59B3**
Malema *Mozam* **101C2**
Mālestān *Afghan* **84B2**
Maleuz *USSR* **61J3**
Malgomaj, L *Sweden* **38H5**
Malha, Well *Sudan* **95B3**
Malheur L *USA* **20C2**
Mali, Republic *Africa* **97B3**
Malinau *Indon* **78D1**
Malindi *Kenya* **99E3**
Malin Head, Pt *Irish Rep* **40B2**
Malkala Range, Mts *India* **86A2**
Malkāpur *India* **85D4**
Malkara *Turk* **55C2**
Malko Tŭrnovo *Bulg* **54C2**
Mallaig *Scot* **44B3**
Mallawi *Egypt* **95C2**
Málles Venosta *Italy* **47D1**
Mallorca, I *Spain* **51C2**
Mallow *Irish Rep* **45B2**
Malm *Nor* **38G6**
Malmberget *Sweden* **38J5**
Malmédy *W Germ* **46D1**
Malmesbury *Eng* **43C4**
Malmesbury *S Africa* **100A4**
Malmö *Sweden* **39G7**
Malmyzh *USSR* **61G2**
Malolos *Phil* **79B3**
Malone *USA* **15D2**
Maloti Mts *Lesotho* **101G1**
Måløy *Nor* **38F6**
Malpelo, I *Colombia* **28A2**
Malpo, R *Chile* **34A2**
Mālpura *India* **85D3**
Malta, Montana *USA* **8C2**
Malta, Chan *Malta/Italy* **53B3**
Malta, I *Medit S* **53B3**
Maltahöhe *Namibia* **100A3**
Malton *Eng* **42D2**
Malung *Sweden* **39G6**
Mālvan *India* **87A1**
Malvern *USA* **19B3**
Malwa Plat *India* **85D4**
Malyy Kavkaz, Mts *USSR* **65F5**
Malyy Uzen', R *USSR* **H006**
Mama *USSR* **63D2**
Mamadysh *USSR* **61H2**
Mambasa *Zaïre* **99C2**
Mamberamo, R *Indon* **71E4**
Mambéré, R *CAR* **98B2**
Mamfé *Cam* **98A2**
Mamoré, R *Bol* **33D6**
Mamou *Guinea* **97A3**
Mampikony *Madag* **101D2**
Mampong *Ghana* **97B4**
Mamshit, Hist Site *Israel* **94B3**
Mamuno *Botswana* **100B3**
Man *Ivory Coast* **97B4**
Mana *Hawaiian Is* **21C4**
Manabo *Madag* **101D3**
Manacapuru *Brazil* **33E4**
Manacor *Spain* **51C2**
Manado *Indon* **71D3**
Managua *Nic* **25D3**
Manakara *Madag* **101D3**
Mananara *Madag* **101D2**
Mananjary *Madag* **101D3**
Manapouri *NZ* **111A3**
Manapouri,L *NZ* **111A3**
Manas *Bhutan* **86C1**
Manas *China* **82C1**
Manas Hu, L *China* **65K5**
Manaslu, Mt *Nepal* **86A1**
Manasquan *USA* **16B2**
Manaus *Brazil* **33F4**
Manavgat *Turk* **92B2**
Manbij *Syria* **93C2**
Man,Calf of, I *Eng* **42B2**
Mancheral *India* **87B1**
Manchester, Connecticut *USA* **15D2**
Manchester *Eng* **42C3**
Manchester, New Hampshire *USA* **10C2**
Manchester, Pennsylvania *USA* **16A2**
Manchuria, Hist Region *China* **69E2**
Mand, R *Iran* **91B4**
Manda *Tanz* **101C2**
Mandaguari *Brazil* **35A2**
Mandal *Nor* **39F7**
Mandalay *Burma* **76B1**
Mandalgovĭ *Mongolia* **68C2**
Mandal Ovoo *Mongolia* **72A1**
Mandalya Körfezi, B *Turk* **55C3**
Mandan *USA* **8C2**
Mandelona *USA* **14A2**
Mandera *Eth* **99E2**
Mandeville *Jamaica* **26B3**
Mandidzudzure *Zim* **100C2**
Mandimba *Mozam* **101C2**
Mandla *India* **86A2**
Mandritsara *Madag* **101D2**
Mandsaur *India* **85D4**
Manduria *Italy* **53C2**
Māndvi *India* **85B4**
Mandya *India* **87B2**
Manevichi *USSR* **58D2**
Manfield *Eng* **42D3**
Manfredonia *Italy* **53C2**
Manga, Desert Region *Niger* **98B1**
Mangakino *NZ* **110C1**
Mangalia *Rom* **54C2**
Mangalmé *Chad* **98B1**
Mangalore *India* **87A2**
Manggar *Indon* **78B3**
Mangnia *China* **68B3**
Mangoche *Malawi* **101C2**
Mangoky, R *Madag* **101D3**
Mangole, I *Indon* **71D4**
Māngral *India* **85B4**
Mangui *China* **63E2**
Manhattan *USA* **8D3**
Manhuacu *Brazil* **31C6**
Mania, R *Madag* **101D2**
Manica *Mozam* **101C2**
Manicouagan, R *Can* **7D5**
Manicouagan Res *Can* **7D4**
Manifah *S Arabia* **91A4**
Manila *Phil* **79B3**
Manilla *Aust* **109D2**
Maninian *Ivory Coast* **97B3**
Manipur, State *India* **86C2**
Manipur, R *Burma* **86C2**
Manisa *Turk* **92A2**
Man,Isle of *Irish Sea* **41C3**
Manistee *USA* **14A2**
Manistee, R *USA* **14A2**
Manistique *USA* **14A1**
Manitoba, Province *Can* **5H4**
Manitoba,L *Can* **5J4**
Manito L *Can* **13F2**
Manitou Is *USA* **14A1**
Manitoulin, I *Can* **7B5**
Manitowoc *USA* **14A2**
Maniwaki *Can* **15C1**
Manizales *Colombia* **32B2**
Manja *Madag* **101D3**
Manjimup *Aust* **106A4**
Mānjra, R *India* **87B1**
Mankato *USA* **10A2**
Mankono *Ivory Coast* **97B4**
Manley Hot Springs *USA* **12D2**
Manly *NZ* **110B1**
Manmād *India* **85C4**
Manna *Indon* **78A3**
Mannahill *Aust* **108A2**
Mannar *Sri Lanka* **87B3**
Mannār,G of *India* **87B3**
Mannārgudi *India* **87B2**
Mannheim *W Germ* **57B3**
Manning *Can* **13D1**
Manning *USA* **17B1**
Mannum *Aust* **108A2**
Mano *Sierra Leone* **97A4**
Manokwari *Indon* **71E4**
Manono *Zaïre* **98C3**
Manoron *Burma* **76B3**
Mano-wan, B *Japan* **75B1**
Manp'o *N Korea* **74B2**
Mānsa *India* **84D3**
Mansa *Zambia* **100B2**
Mansel I *Can* **6B3**
Mansfield, Arkansas *USA* **19B2**
Mansfield *Aust* **108C3**
Mansfield, Louisiana *USA* **19B3**
Mansfield, Massachusetts *USA* **16D1**
Mansfield, Ohio *USA* **10B2**
Mansfield, Pennsylvania *USA* **15C2**
Mansyu Deep *Pacific O* **71E2**
Manta *Ecuador* **32A4**
Mantalingajan,Mt *Phil* **79A4**
Mantaro, R *Peru* **32B6**
Manteca *USA* **22B2**
Mantes *France* **48C2**
Mantova *Italy* **52B1**
Mantta *Fin* **38J6**
Manturovo *USSR* **61F2**
Manuel Ribas *Brazil* **35A2**
Manukan *Phil* **79B4**
Manukau *NZ* **110B1**
Manus, I *Pacific O* **71F4**

Manzanares *Spain* 50B2
Manzanillo *Cuba* 25E2
Manzanillo *Mexico* 24B3
Manzhouli *USSR* 63D3
Manzil *Jordan* 94C3
Manzini *Swaziland* 101C3
Mao *Chad* 98B1
Maomao Shan, Mt *China* 72A2
Maoming *China* 73C5
Mapai *Mozam* 101C3
Mapia, Is *Pacific O* 71E3
Maple Creek *Can* 5H5
Maputo *Mozam* 101H1
Maputo, R *Mozam* 101H1
Maqu *China* 72A3
Maquan He, R *China* 86B1
Maquela do Zombo *Angola* 98B3
Maquinchao *Arg* 29C4
Marabá *Brazil* 31B3
Maracaibo *Ven* 32C1
Maracay *Ven* 32D1
Marādah *Libya* 95A2
Maradi *Niger* 97C3
Marāgheh *Iran* 90A2
Maralal *Kenya* 99D2
Maramasike, I *Solomon Is* 107F1
Maramba *Zambia* 100B2
Marand *Iran* 90A2
Maranhõa, State *Brazil* 31B2
Maranoa, R *Aust* 109C1
Marañón, R *Peru* 32B4
Marathon *Can* 7B5
Marathon, Florida *USA* 17B2
Maratua, I *Indon* 78D2
Maravatio *Mexico* 23A2
Marawi *Phil* 79B4
Marayes *Arg* 34B2
Marbella *Spain* 50B2
Marble Bar *Aust* 106A3
Marblehall *S Africa* 100B3
Marblehead *USA* 16D1
Marburg *W Germ* 57B2
Marche *Belg* 57B2
Marchean *Spain* 50A2
Marche-en-Famenne *Belg* 46C1
Marchena, I *Ecuador* 32J7
Marco *USA* 17B2
Marcos Juárez *Arg* 34C2
Marcus Baker,Mt *USA* 12E2
Marcy,Mt *USA* 15D2
Mardan *Pak* 84C2
Mar del Plata *Arg* 29E3
Mardin *Turk* 93D2
Mareb, R *Eth* 99D1
Margaretville *USA* 16B1
Margate *Eng* 43E4
Marghita *Rom* 54B1
Maria I *Aust* 109C4
Mariana, Is *Pacific O* 104F3
Mariana Lake *Can* 13E1
Marianas Trench *Pacific O* 104F3
Mariāni *India* 86C1
Marianna, Arkansas *USA* 19B3
Marianna, Florida *USA* 17A1
Maria Van Diemen,C *NZ* 7G4
Mariazell *Austria* 59B3
Maribor *Yugos* 52C1
Maridi *Sudan* 99C2
Marie Byrd Land, Region *Ant* 112B5
Marie Galante, I *Caribbean* 27E3
Mariehamn *Fin* 39H6
Mariembourg *Belg* 46C1
Marienburg *Surinam* 33G2
Mariental *Namibia* 100A3
Mariestad *Sweden* 39G7
Marietta, Georgia *USA* 17B1
Marietta, Ohio *USA* 14B3
Marietta, Oklahoma *USA* 19A3
Marigot *Dominica* 27Q2
Marilia *Brazil* 31B6
Marimba *Angola* 98B3
Marinduque, I *Phil* 79B3
Marinette *USA* 10B2
Maringá *Brazil* 30F3
Maringa, R *Zaïre* 98C2
Marion, Arkansas *USA* 18B2
Marion, Illinois *USA* 18C2
Marion, Indiana *USA* 10B2
Marion, Ohio *USA* 10B2
Marion, S Carolina *USA* 17C1
Marion,L *USA* 11B3
Marion Reef *Aust* 107E2
Mariposa *USA* 21B2
Mariposa, R *USA* 22B2
Mariposa Res *USA* 22B2
Marista, R *Bulg* 60C5
Mariyskaya ASSR, Republic *USSR* 61G2
Marjayoun *Leb* 94B2
Marjina Gorki *USSR* 58D2
Marka *Jordan* 94B3
Marka *Somalia* 99E2
Markaryd *Sweden* 56C1
Market Drayton *Eng* 43C3
Market Harborough *Eng* 43D3
Markham,Mt *Ant* 80E
Markleeville *USA* 22C1
Marlboro, Massachusetts *USA* 16D1
Marlborough *Aust* 107D3
Marle *France* 46B2
Marlin *USA* 19A3
Marmande *France* 48C3
Marmara Adi, I *Turk* 55C2
Marmara,S of *Turk* 92A1
Marmaris *Turk* 55C3
Marmet *USA* 14B3
Marmolada, Mt *Italy* 52B1
Marmot B *USA* 12D3
Marnay *France* 47A1
Marne, Department *France* 46B2
Marne, R *France* 46B2
Maro *Chad* 98B2
Maroantsetra *Madag* 101D2
Marondera *Zim* 101C2
Maroni, R *French Guiana* 33G3
Maroochydore *Aust* 109D1
Maroua *Cam* 98B1
Marovoay *Madag* 101D2
Marquesas Keys, Is *USA* 11B4
Marquette *USA* 10B2
Marquise *France* 46A1
Marra, R *Aust* 109C2
Marracuene *Mozam* 101H1
Marrakech *Mor* 96B1
Marree *Aust* 106C3
Marrero *USA* 19B4
Marromeu *Mozam* 101C2
Marrupa *Mozam* 101C2
Marsa Alam *Egypt* 95C2
Marsabit *Kenya* 99D2
Marsala *Italy* 53B3
Marseille *France* 49D3
Marshall, Alaska *USA* 12B2
Marshall, Illinois *USA* 14A3
Marshall, Michigan *USA* 14B2
Marshall, Missouri *USA* 18B2
Marshall, Texas *USA* 11A3
Marshall Is *Pacific O* 105G3
Marshfield, Missouri *USA* 18B2
Marsh Harbour *Bahamas* 26B1
Marsh I *USA* 19B4
Marsh L *Can* 12H2
Martaban,G of *Burma* 76B2
Martapura *Indon* 78A3
Martapura *Indon* 78C3
Martha's Vineyard, I *USA* 15D2
Martigny *Switz* 49D2
Martin *Czech* 59B3
Martinborough *NZ* 111C2
Martín de Loyola *Arg* 34B3
Martínez de la Torre *Mexico* 23B1
Martinique, I *Caribbean* 27E4
Martin,L *USA* 17A1
Martinsburg *USA* 15C3
Martins Ferry *USA* 14B2
Martin Vaz, I *Atlantic O* 103G6
Martiques *France* 49D3
Marton *NZ* 110C2
Martos *Spain* 50B2
Marudi *Malay* 78D1
Maruf *Afghan* 84B2
Marugame *Japan* 75A2
Mārwār *India* 85C3
Mary *USSR* 65H6
Maryborough, Queensland *Aust* 107E3
Maryborough, Victoria *Aust* 108B3
Mary Henry,Mt *Can* 5F4
Maryland, State *USA* 10C3
Maryport *Eng* 42C2
Marysville, California *USA* 21A2
Marysville, Kansas *USA* 18A2
Marysville, Washington *USA* 20B1
Maryville, Iowa *USA* 10A2
Maryville, Missouri *USA* 18B1
Marzuq *Libya* 95A2
Mas'adah *Syria* 94B2
Masai Steppe, Upland *Tanz* 99D3
Masaka *Uganda* 99D3
Masally *USSR* 93E2
Masan *S Korea* 74B3
Masasi *Tanz* 101C2
Masaya *Nic* 25D3
Masbate *Phil* 79B3
Masbate, I *Phil* 79B3
Mascara *Alg* 96C1
Mascota *Mexico* 23A1
Mascote *Brazil* 35D1
Maseru *Lesotho* 101G1
Mashad *Iran* 66C3
Mashaki *Afghan* 84B2
Mashhad *Iran* 90C2
Masi-Manimba *Zaïre* 98B3
Masindi *Uganda* 99D2
Masisi *Zaïre* 99C3
Masjed Soleyman *Iran* 90A3
Masoala, C *Madag* 101E2
Mason City *USA* 10A2
Masqat *Oman* 91C5
Mass, R *Neth* 56B2
Massa *Italy* 52B2
Massachusetts, State *USA* 10C2
Massachusetts B *USA* 15D2
Massakori *Chad* 98B1
Massangena *Mozam* 101C3
Massawa *Eth* 95C3
Massena *USA* 15D2
Massénya *Chad* 98B1
Massey *Can* 14B1
Massif Central, Mts *France* 49C2
Massif de l'Adamaoua Mts *Cam* 98B2
Massif de la Hotte, Mts *Haiti* 26C3
Massif de l'Isalo, Upland *Madag* 101D3
Massif des Bongo, Upland *CAR* 98C2
Massif du Pelvoux, Mts *France* 49D2
Massif du Tsaratanana Mt *Madag* 101D2
Massillon *USA* 14B2
Massina, Region *Mali* 97B3
Massinga *Mozam* 101C3
Massingir *Mozam* 101C3
Masteksay *USSR* 61H4
Masterton *NZ* 111C2
Masuda *Japan* 74C4
Maşyāf *Syria* 92C2
Matadi *Zaïre* 98B3
Matagalpa *Nic* 25D3
Matagami *Can* 7C4
Matagorda B *USA* 9D4
Matakana I *NZ* 110C1
Matala *Angola* 100A2
Matale *Sri Lanka* 87C3
Matam *Sen* 97A3
Matameye *Niger* 97C3
Matamoros *Mexico* 24C2
Ma'tan as Sarra, Well *Libya* 95B2
Matane *Can* 7D5
Matanó *Spain* 51C1
Matanzas *Cuba* 25D2
Mataquito, R *Chile* 34A2
Matara *Sri Lanka* 87C3
Mataram *Indon* 106A1
Matarani *Peru* 30B2
Mataura *NZ* 111A3
Matehuala *Mexico* 24B2
Matelot *Trinidad* 27L1
Matera *Italy* 53C2
Mátészalka *Hung* 59C3
Mathura *India* 85D3
Mati *Phil* 79C4
Matisiri, I *Indon* 78D3
Matlock *Eng* 43D3
Mato Grosso *Brazil* 33F6
Mato Grosso, State *Brazil* 33F6
Mato Grosso do Sul, State *Brazil* 30E2
Matola *Mozam* 101H1
Matrah *Oman* 91C5
Matrûh *Egypt* 92A3
Matsue *Japan* 74C3
Matsumae *Japan* 74E2
Matsumoto *Japan* 74D3
Matsusaka *Japan* 74D4
Matsuyama *Japan* 74C4
Mattagami, R *Can* 7B5
Mattawa *Can* 15C1
Matterhorn, Mt *Switz/Italy* 52A1
Matthew Town *Bahamas* 26C2
Mattituck *USA* 16C2
Mattoon *USA* 18C2
Matun *Afghan* 84B2
Matura B *Trinidad* 27L1
Maturin *Ven* 33E2
Mau *India* 86A1
Maúa *Mozam* 101C2
Maubeuge *France* 49C1
Maude *Aust* 108B2
Maud Seamount *Atlantic O* 103J8
Maui, I *Hawaiian Is* 21C4
Maule, R *Chile* 34A3
Maumee *USA* 14B2
Maumee, R *USA* 14B2
Maun *Botswana* 100B2
Mauna Kea, Mt *Hawaiian Is* 21C4
Mauna Loa, Mt *Hawaiian Is* 21C4
Maunoir, L *Can* 4F3
Maunoir,L *Can* 4F3
Mauriac *France* 48C2
Mauritania, Republic *Africa* 96A2
Mavinga *Angola* 100B2
Mawlaik *Burma* 86C2
Mawson, Base *Ant* 112C10
Maya, I *Indon* 78B3
Maya, R *USSR* 63F2
Mayādīn *Syria* 93D2

Mayaguana, I *Bahamas* **11C4**
Mayagüez *Puerto Rico* **27D3**
Mayahi *Niger* **97C3**
Mayama *Congo* **98B3**
Mayamey *Iran* **90C2**
Maybole *Scot* **42B2**
May,C *USA* **10C3**
Maydena *Aust* **109C4**
Mayen *W Germ* **46D1**
Mayenne *France* **48B2**
Mayerthorpe *Can* **13D2**
Mayfield *USA* **18C2**
Maykop *USSR* **61E5**
Maymaneh *Afghan* **65H6**
Maymyo *Burma* **76B1**
Mayo *Can* **4E3**
Mayo, County *Irish Rep* **45B2**
Mayo *USA* **16A3**
Mayo,Mts of *Irish Rep* **45B1**
Mayon, Mt *Phil* **79B3**
Mayor, Mt *Spain* **51C2**
Mayor Buratovich *Arg* **34C3**
Mayor I *NZ* **110C1**
Mayor P Lagerenza *Par* **30D2**
Mayotte, I *Indian O* **101D2**
May Pen *Jamaica* **27H2**
May Point,C *USA* **16B3**
Mayrhofen *Austria* **47D1**
Mays Landing *USA* **16B3**
Maysville *USA* **14B3**
Mayumba *Gabon* **98B3**
Mazabuka *Zambia* **100B2**
Mazaffarnagar *India* **84D3**
Mazar *China* **84D1**
Mazār *Jordan* **94B3**
Mazara del Vallo *Italy* **53B3**
Mazar-i-Sharif *Afghan* **84B1**
Mazatlán *Mexico* **24B2**
Mazeikiai *USSR* **60B2**
Mazra *Jordan* **94B3**
Mbabane *Swaziland* **101C3**
Mbaïki *CAR* **98B2**
Mbala *Zambia* **99D3**
Mbalabala *Zim* **100B3**
Mbale *Uganda* **99D2**
Mbalmayo *Cam* **98B2**
Mbam, R *Cam* **98B2**
Mbamba Bay *Tanz* **101C2**
Mbandaka *Zaïre* **98B2**
Mbanza Congo *Angola* **98B3**
Mbanza-Ngungu *Zaïre* **98B3**
Mbarara *Uganda* **99D3**
Mbènza *Congo* **98B2**
Mbére, R *Cam* **98B2**
Mbeya *Tanz* **99D3**
Mbinda *Congo* **98B3**
Mbout *Maur* **97A3**
Mbuji-Mayi *Zaïre* **98C3**
Mbulu *Tanz* **99D3**
Mcherrah, Region *Alg* **96B2**
Mchinji *Malawi* **101C2**
Mdrak *Viet* **76D3**
Mead,L *USA* **9B3**
Meadow Lake *Can* **5H4**
Meadville *USA* **14B2**
Mealy Mts *Can* **7E4**
Meandarra *Aust* **109C1**
Meander River *Can* **5G4**
Meath, County *Irish Rep* **45C2**
Meaux *France* **49C2**
Mechanicville *USA* **16C1**
Mechelen *Belg* **56A2**
Mecheria *Alg* **96B1**
Mecklenburger Bucht, B *E Germ* **56C2**
Meconta *Mozam* **101C2**
Mecuburi *Mozam* **101C2**
Mecufi *Mozam* **101D2**
Mecula *Mozam* **101C2**
Medan *Indon* **70A3**
Medanos *Arg* **34C3**
Médanos *Arg* **34D2**
Medecine Hat *Can* **13E2**
Medellín *Colombia* **32B2**
Medenine *Tunisia* **96D1**
Medford *USA* **8A2**
Medgidia *Rom* **54C2**
Media Agua *Arg* **34B2**
Mediaş *Rom* **54B1**
Medical Lake *USA* **20C1**
Medicine Hat *Can* **5G5**
Medina *Brazil* **35C1**
Medina *S Arabia* **80B3**
Medinaceli *Spain* **50B1**
Medina del Campo *Spain* **50B1**
Medina de Rio Seco *Spain* **50A1**
Medinīpur *India* **86B2**
Mediterranean S *Europe* **88E4**
Medley *Can* **13F2**
Mednogorsk *USSR* **61J3**
Mêdog *China* **86D1**
Medouneu *Gabon* **98B2**
Medvedista, R *USSR* **61F3**
Medvezh'yegorsk *USSR* **64E3**
Meekatharra *Aust* **106A3**
Meerut *India* **84D3**
Mega *Eth* **99D2**
Megalópolis *Greece* **55B3**
Mégara *Greece* **55B3**
Meghālaya, State *India* **86C1**
Meghna, R *Bang* **86C2**
Megido, Hist Site *Israel* **94B2**
Mehran, R *Iran* **91B4**
Mehriz *Iran* **90B3**
Meia Ponte, R *Brazil* **35B1**
Meiganga *Cam* **98B2**
Meiktila *Burma* **76B1**
Meiringen *Switz* **47C1**
Meishan *China* **73A4**
Meissen *E Germ* **57C2**
Mei Xian *China* **73D5**
Meizhou *China* **73D5**
Mejillones *Chile* **30B3**
Mekambo *Gabon* **98B2**
Meknès *Mor* **96B1**
Mekong, R *Camb* **76D3**
Mekrou, R *Benin* **97C3**
Melaka *Malay* **77C5**
Melanesia, Region *Pacific O* **104F4**
Melawi, R *Indon* **78C3**
Melbourne *Aust* **107D4**
Melbourne *USA* **11B4**
Melchor Muźguiz *Mexico* **9C4**
Melfi *Chad* **98B1**
Melfort *Can* **5H4**
Melilla *N W Africa* **96B1**
Melimoyu, Mt *Chile* **29B4**
Melincué *Arg* **34C2**
Melipilla *Chile* **34A2**
Melitopol' *USSR* **60E4**
Meliville Bugt, B *Greenland* **6D2**
Melmoth *S Africa* **101H1**
Melo *Arg* **34C2**
Melo *Urug* **29F2**
Melones Res *USA* **22B2**
Melozitna, R *USA* **12D1**
Mels *Switz* **47C1**
Melton Mowbry *Eng* **43D3**
Melun *France* **49C2**
Melville *Can* **5H4**
Melville,C *Dominica* **27Q2**
Melville Hills, Mts *Can* **4F3**
Melville I *Aust* **106C2**
Melville I *Can* **4G2**
Melville,L *Can* **7E4**
Melville Pen *Can* **6B3**
Melvin,L *Irish Rep* **45B1**
Memba *Mozam* **101D2**
Memboro *Indon* **106A1**
Memmingen *W Germ* **57C3**
Mempawan *Indon* **78B2**
Memphis, Tennessee *USA* **11B3**
Mena *USA* **19B3**
Menai Str *Wales* **43B3**
Ménaka *Mali* **97C3**
Menasha *USA* **14A2**
Mendawai, R *Indon* **78C3**
Mende *France* **49C3**
Mendebo, Mts *Eth* **99D2**
Mendip Hills, Upland *Eng* **43C4**
Mendocino,C *USA* **20B2**
Mendocino Seascarp *Pacific O* **105J2**
Mendota, California *USA* **22B2**
Mendoza *Arg* **29C2**
Mendoza, State *Arg* **29C3**
Menemen *Turk* **55C3**
Menen *Belg* **46B1**
Mengcheng *China* **72D3**
Menggala *Indon* **78B3**
Menghai *China* **76B1**
Mengla *China* **73A5**
Menglian *China* **76B1**
Mengzi *China* **73A5**
Menindee *Aust* **107D4**
Menindee L *Aust* **108B2**
Meningie *Aust* **108A3**
Menominee *USA* **14A1**
Menomonee Falls *USA* **14A2**
Menongue *Angola* **100A2**
Menorca, I *Spain* **51C1**
Mentasta Mts *USA* **12F2**
Mentok *Indon* **78B3**
Mentor *USA* **14B2**
Ménu *France* **46B2**
Menyuan *China* **72A2**
Menzelinsk *USSR* **61H2**
Meppen *W Germ* **56B2**
Merah *Indon* **78D2**
Meramec, R *USA* **18B2**
Merano *Italy* **52B1**
Merauke *Indon* **71F4**
Merced *USA* **8A3**
Merced, R *USA* **22B2**
Mercedario, Mt *Chile* **29B2**
Mercedes *Arg* **29C2**
Mercedes, Buenos Aires *Arg* **29E2**
Mercedes, Corrientes *Arg* **30E4**
Mercedes *Urug* **29E2**
Mercury B *NZ* **110C1**
Mercury Is *NZ* **110C1**
Mercy B *Can* **4F2**
Mercy,C *Can* **6D3**
Meregh *Somalia* **99E2**
Mergui *Burma* **76B3**
Mergui Arch *Burma* **76B3**
Mérida *Mexico* **25D2**
Mérida *Spain* **50A2**
Mérida *Ven* **32C2**
Meridian *USA* **11B3**
Merimbula *Aust* **109C3**
Meringur *Aust* **108B2**
Merowe *Sudan* **95C3**
Merredin *Aust* **106A4**
Merrick, Mt *Scot* **42B2**
Merrillville *USA* **14A2**
Merritt *Can* **13C2**
Merritt Island *USA* **17B2**
Merriwa *Aust* **109D2**
Mersa Fatma *Eth* **99E1**
Mers el Kebir *Alg* **51B2**
Mersey, R *Eng* **42C3**
Merseyside, Metropolitan County *Eng* **42C3**
Mersin *Turk* **92B2**
Mersing *Malay* **77C5**
Merta *India* **85C3**
Merthyr Tydfil *Wales* **43C4**
Mertola *Port* **50A2**
Meru, Mt *Tanz* **99D3**
Merzifon *Turk* **60E5**
Merzig *W Germ* **46D2**
Mesa *USA* **9B3**
Meschede *W Germ* **40E1**
Mescit Dağ, Mt *Turk* **93D1**
Meshik *USA* **12C3**
Meshra Er Req *Sudan* **99C2**
Mesocco *Switz* **47C1**
Mesolóngion *Greece* **55B3**
Mesquite, Texas *USA* **19A3**
Messalo, R *Mozam* **101C2**
Messina *Italy* **53C3**
Messina *S Africa* **100B3**
Messíni *Greece* **55B3**
Messiniakós Kólpos, G *Greece* **55B3**
Mesta, R *Bulg* **54B2**
Mestre *Italy* **52B1**
Meta, R *Colombia* **32C3**
Meta, R *USSR* **60D2**
Meta, R *Ven* **32D2**
Meta Incognito Pen *Can* **6C3**
Metairie *USA* **19B4**
Metaline Falls *USA* **20C1**
Metán *Arg* **30D4**
Metangula *Mozam* **101C2**
Metaponto *Italy* **53C2**
Methil *Scot* **44C3**
Methuen *USA* **16D1**
Methven *NZ* **111B2**
Metlakatla *USA* **12H3**
Metropolis *USA* **18C2**
Mettūr *India* **87B2**
Metz *France* **49D2**
Meulaboh *Indon* **70A3**
Meulan *France* **46A2**
Meuse, Department *France* **46C2**
Meuse, R *France* **49D2**
Mexia *USA* **19A3**
Mexicali *Mexico* **24A1**
Mexico, Federal Republic *Central America* **24B2**
México *Mexico* **24C3**
México, State *Mexico* **23A2**
Mexico *USA* **18B2**
Mexico,G of *C America* **24C2**
Mezada, Hist Site *Israel* **94B3**
Mezcala *Mexico* **23B2**
Mezen' *USSR* **64F3**
Mezhdusharskiy, I *USSR* **64G3**
Mhow *India* **85D4**
Miahuatlán *Mexico* **23B2**
Miami, Florida *USA* **11B4**
Miami, Oklahoma *USA* **18B2**
Miami Beach *USA* **11B4**
Miandowāb *Iran* **90A2**
Miandrivazo *Madag* **101D2**
Mīāneh *Iran* **90A2**
Mianwali *Pak* **84C2**
Mianyang *China* **73A3**
Mianyang *China* **73C3**
Mianzhu *China* **73A3**
Miaodao Qundao, Arch *China* **72E2**
Miao Ling, Upland *China* **73B4**
Miass *USSR* **61K3**
Michalovce *Czech* **59C3**
Miches *Dom Rep* **27D3**
Michigan, State *USA* **10B2**
Michigan City *USA* **14A2**
Michigan,L *USA* **10B2**
Michipicoten I *Can* **7B5**
Michoacan, State *Mexico* **23A2**
Michunnsk *USSR* **65F4**
Michurin *Bulg* **54C2**
Michurinsk *USSR* **61F3**
Micronesia, Region *Pacific O* **104F3**
Midai, I *Indon* **78B2**
Mid Atlantic Ridge *Atlantic O* **102F4**
Middelburg *Neth* **46B1**

Middle Alkali L *USA* **20B2**
Middleboro *USA* **16D2**
Middleburg, Cape Province *S Africa* **100B4**
Middleburg, Pennsylvania *USA* **16A2**
Middleburg, Transvaal *S Africa* **101G1**
Middleburgh *USA* **16B1**
Middlebury *USA* **15D2**
Middlesboro *USA* **11B3**
Middlesbrough *Eng* **42D2**
Middletown, Connecticut *USA* **16C2**
Middletown, Delaware *USA* **16B3**
Middletown, New York *USA* **15D2**
Middletown, Ohio *USA* **14B3**
Middletown, Pennsylvania *USA* **16A2**
Midelt *Mor* **96B1**
Mid Glamorgan, County *Wales* **43C4**
Mid Indian Basin *Indian O* **104B4**
Mid Indian Ridge *Indian O* **104B4**
Midland *Can* **7C5**
Midland, Michigan *USA* **14B2**
Midland, Texas *USA* **9C3**
Midongy Atsimo *Madag* **101D3**
Mid Pacific Mts *Pacific O* **105G2**
Midvale *USA* **20C2**
Midway Is *Pacific O* **105H2**
Midwest City *USA* **18A2**
Midyat *Turk* **93D2**
Midžor, Mt *Yugos* **54B2**
Mielec *Pol* **59B2**
Miercurea-Ciuc *Rom* **54C1**
Mieres *Spain* **50A1**
Mifflintown *USA* **16A2**
Mihara *Japan* **75A2**
Mijun Shuiku, Res *China* **72D1**
Mikhayiovka *USSR* **65F4**
Mikhaylovgrad *Bulg* **54B2**
Mikhaylovka *USSR* **61F3**
Mikhaylovskiy *USSR* **65J4**
Mikkeli *Fin* **38K6**
Míkonos, I *Greece* **55C3**
Mikulov *Czech* **59B3**
Mikumi *Tanz* **99D3**
Mikuni-sammyaku, Mts *Japan* **74D3**
Mikura-jima, I *Japan* **75B2**
Milagro *Ecuador* **32B4**
Milana *Alg* **51C2**
Milange *Mozam* **101C2**
Milano *Italy* **52A1**
Milas *Turk* **92A2**
Mildura *Aust* **107D4**
Mile *China* **73A5**
Mileh Tharthār, L *Iraq* **93D3**
Miles *Aust* **107E3**
Miles City *USA* **8C2**
Milford, Connecticut *USA* **16C2**
Milford, Delaware *USA* **15C3**
Milford, Massachusetts *USA* **15D2**
Milford, Nebraska *USA* **18A1**
Milford, Pennsylvania *USA* **16B2**
Milford Haven *Wales* **43B4**
Milford Haven, Sd *Wales* **43B4**
Milford L *USA* **18A2**
Milford Sd *NZ* **111A2**
Milk River *Can* **13E2**
Millau *France* **49C3**
Millbrook *USA* **16C2**
Milledgeville *USA* **17B1**
Miller,Mt *USA* **12F2**
Millerovo *USSR* **61F4**
Millersburg *USA* **16A2**
Millers Creek *Aust* **108A1**
Millers Falls *USA* **16C1**
Millerton *USA* **16C2**
Millerton L *USA* **22C2**
Millicent *Aust* **108B3**
Millmerran *Aust* **109D1**
Milltown Malbay *Irish Rep* **45B2**
Mill Valley *USA* **22A2**
Millville *USA* **15D3**
Milne Land, I *Greenland* **6H2**
Milolii *Hawaiian Is* **21C4**
Mílos, I *Greece* **55B3**
Milparinka *Aust* **107D3**
Milroy *USA* **16A2**
Milton *NZ* **111A3**
Milton, Pennsylvania *USA* **16A2**
Milwaukee *USA* **10B2**
Mina, R *Alg* **51C2**
Mīnā' al Ahmadī *Kuwait* **93E4**
Mīnāb *Iran* **91C4**
Minamata *Japan* **74C4**
Minas *Indon* **78A2**
Minas *Urug* **29E2**
Minas Gerais, State *Brazil* **31B5**
Minas Novas *Brazil* **35C1**
Minatitlan *Mexico* **25C3**
Minbu *Burma* **76A1**
Minbya *Burma* **76A1**
Mincha *Chile* **34A2**
Minch,Little, Sd *Scot* **44A3**
Minch,North, Sd *Scot* **44A2**
Minch,The, Sd *Scot* **40B2**
Minchumina,L *USA* **12D2**
Mincio, R *Italy* **47D2**
Mindanao, I *Phil* **79B4**
Minden, Louisiana *USA* **19B3**
Minden *W Germ* **56B2**
Mindona L *Aust* **108B2**
Mindoro, I *Phil* **79B3**
Mindoro Str *Phil* **79B3**
Mine Hd, C *Irish Rep* **45C3**
Minehead *Eng* **43C4**
Mineiros *Brazil* **30F2**
Mineola *USA* **19A3**
Mineral de Monte *Mexico* **23B1**
Minersville *USA* **16A2**
Mingary *Aust* **108B2**
Minhe *China* **72A2**
Minicoy, I *India* **87A3**
Min Jiang, R, Fujian *China* **73D4**
Min Jiang, R, Sichuan *China* **73A4**
Minkler *USA* **22C2**
Minlaton *Aust* **108A2**
Minle *China* **72A2**
Minna *Nig* **97C4**
Minneapolis *USA* **10A2**
Minnedosa *Can* **5J4**
Minnesota, State *USA* **10A2**
Miño, R *Spain* **50A1**
Minot *USA* **8C2**
Minqin *China* **72A2**
Min Shan, Upland *China* **72A3**
Minsk *USSR* **60C3**
Minsk Mazowiecki *Pol* **58C2**
Minto *USA* **12E2**
Minto Inlet, B *Can* **4G2**
Minto,L *Can* **7C4**
Minusinsk *USSR* **63B2**
Min Xian *China* **72A3**
Miquelon *Can* **7E5**
Mirage L *USA* **22D3**
Miraj *India* **87A1**
Miramar *Arg* **29E3**
Miram Shah *Pak* **84B2**
Miranda de Ebro *Spain* **50B1**
Mirandola *Italy* **47D2**
Mir Bachchen Kūt *Afghan* **84B2**
Miri *Malay* **78D1**
Mirik,C *Maur* **96A3**
Mirnoye *USSR* **63A1**
Mirnyy *USSR* **63D1**
Mirnyy, Base *Ant* **112C9**
Mirpur *Pak* **84C2**
Mirpur Khas *Pak* **85B3**
Mirtoan S *Greece* **55B3**
Miryang *S Korea* **74B3**
Mirzāpur *India* **86A1**
Misantla *Mexico* **23B2**
Misgar *Pak* **84C1**
Mishawaka *USA* **14A2**
Misheguk Mt *USA* **12B1**
Mi-shima, I *Japan* **75A2**
Misima, I *Solomon Is* **107E2**
Misiones, State *Arg* **30F4**
Miskolc *Hung* **59C3**
Mismīyah *Syria* **94C2**
Misoöl, I *Indon* **71E4**
Misrātah *Libya* **95A1**
Missinaibi, R *Can* **7B5**
Mission City *Can* **20B1**
Mississauga *Can* **15C2**
Mississippi, State *USA* **11A3**
Mississippi, R *USA* **11A3**
Mississippi Delta *USA* **19C3**
Missoula *USA* **8B2**
Missour *Mor* **96B1**
Missouri, State *USA* **11A3**
Missouri, R *USA* **10A2**
Mistassini,L *Can* **10C1**
Misti, Mt *Peru* **30B2**
Mitchell *Aust* **109C1**
Mitchell *USA* **8D2**
Mitchell, R *Aust* **107D2**
Mitchell,Mt *USA* **11B3**
Mitchelstown *Irish Rep* **45B2**
Mithankot *Pak* **84C3**
Mitilíni *Greece* **55C3**
Mitla *Mexico* **23B2**
Mitu *Colombia* **32C3**
Mitumbar, Mts *Zaïre* **99C3**
Mitwaba *Zaïre* **98C3**
Mitzic *Gabon* **98B2**
Miura *Japan* **75B1**
Mi Xian *China* **72C3**
Miyake, I *Japan* **69F3**
Miyake-jima, I *Japan* **75B2**
Miyako, I *Japan* **69E4**
Miyakonojō *Japan* **74C4**
Miyazaki *Japan* **74C4**
Miyazu *Japan* **75B1**
Miyoshi *Japan* **74C4**
Miyun *China* **72D1**
Mizan Teferi *Eth* **99D2**
Mizdah *Libya* **95A1**
Mizen Hd, C *Irish Rep* **45B3**
Mizil *Rom* **54C1**
Mizo Hills *India* **86C2**
Mizoram, Union Territory *India* **86C2**
Mizpe Ramon *Israel* **94B3**
Mizuho, Base *Ant* **112B11**
Mizusawa *Japan* **74E3**
Mjolby *Sweden* **39H7**
Mkushi *Zambia* **100B2**
Mkuzi *S Africa* **101H1**
Mladá Boleslav *Czech* **57C2**
Mława *Pol* **58C2**
Mljet, I *Yugos* **52C2**
Mmabatho *S Africa* **100B3**
Mnadi *India* **84D2**
Moa, R *Sierra Leone* **97A4**
Moab, Region *Jordan* **94B3**
Moab *USA* **9C3**
Moanda *Congo* **98B3**
Moanda *Gabon* **98B3**
Moba *Zaïre* **99C3**
Mobara *Japan* **75C1**
Mobaye *CAR* **98C2**
Mobayi *Zaire* **98C2**
Moberly *USA* **10A3**
Mobile *USA* **11B3**
Mobile B *USA* **11B3**
Mobridge *USA* **8C2**
Moçambique *Mozam* **101D2**
Moc Chau *Viet* **76C1**
Mochudi *Botswana* **100B3**
Mocimboa da Praia *Mozam* **101D2**
Mocoa *Colombia* **32B3**
Mococa *Brazil* **35B2**
Mocoreta, R *Arg* **34D2**
Moctezuma, R *Mexico* **23B1**
Mocuba *Mozam* **101C2**
Modane *France* **47B2**
Modder, R *S Africa* **101G1**
Modena *Italy* **52B2**
Moder, R *France* **46D2**
Modesto *USA* **8A3**
Modesto Res *USA* **22B2**
Modica *Italy* **53B3**
Mödling *Austria* **59B3**
Moe *Aust* **107D4**
Moesa, R *Switz* **47C1**
Moffat *Scot* **42C2**
Moga *India* **84D2**
Mogi das Cruzes *Brazil* **35B2**
Mogilev *USSR* **60C3**
Mogilev Podolskiy *USSR* **60C4**
Mogi-Mirim *Brazil* **35B2**
Mogincual *Mozam* **101D2**
Mogliano *Italy* **47E2**
Mogna *Arg* **34B2**
Mogocha *USSR* **68D1**
Mogochin *USSR* **65K4**
Moguer *Spain* **50A2**
Mohaka, R *NZ* **110C1**
Mohanganj *Bang* **86C2**
Mohawk, R *USA* **15D2**
Mohoro *Tanz* **99D3**
Mointy *USSR* **65J5**
Mo i Rana *Nor* **38G5**
Moissac *France* **48C3**
Mojave *USA* **21B2**
Mojave, R *USA* **22D3**
Mojave Desert *USA* **9B3**
Mojokerto *Indon* **78C4**
Mokama *India* **86B1**
Mokau, R *NZ* **110B1**
Mokelumne Aqueduct *USA* **22B1**
Mokelumne Hill *USA* **22B1**
Mokelumne North Fork, R *USA* **22B1**
Mokhotlong *Lesotho* **101G1**
Moknine *Tunisia* **96D1**
Mokokchūng *India* **86C1**
Mokolo *Cam* **98B1**
Mokp'o *S Korea* **74B4**
Moksha, R *USSR* **61F3**
Molango *Mexico* **23B1**
Moláoi *Greece* **55B3**
Moldavskaya SSR, Republic *USSR* **60C4**
Molde *Nor* **38F6**
Moldoveanu, Mt *Rom* **54B1**
Molepolole *Botswana* **100B3**
Molfetta *Italy* **53C2**
Molina *Chile* **34A3**
Mollendo *Peru* **30B2**
Molodechno *USSR* **60C3**
Molodezhnaya, Base *Ant* **112C11**
Molokai, I *Hawaiian Is* **21C4**
Moloma, R *USSR* **61G2**
Molong *Aust* **109C2**
Molopo, R *Botswana* **100B3**
Molounddu *Cam* **98B2**
Molson L *Can* **8D1**
Molucca, S *Indon* **71D4**
Moluccas, Is *Indon* **71D4**
Moma *Mozam* **101C2**
Mombaca *Brazil* **31C3**
Mombasa *Kenya* **99D3**
Mompono *Zaïre* **98C2**
Mon, I *Den* **56C2**

Monach, Is *Scot* **44A3**
Monaco, Principality *Europe* **49D3**
Monadhliath, Mts *Scot* **44B3**
Monaghan, County *Irish Rep* **45C1**
Monaghan *Irish Rep* **45C1**
Mona Pass *Caribbean* **27D3**
Monarch Mt *Can* **13B2**
Monashee Mts *Can* **5G4**
Monastereven *Irish Rep* **41B3**
Moncalieri *Italy* **47B2**
Monção *Brazil* **31B2**
Monchegorsk *USSR* **38L5**
Mönchen-gladbach *W Germ* **56B2**
Monclova *Mexico* **24B2**
Moncton *Can* **7D5**
Monctova *Mexico* **9C4**
Mondego, R *Port* **50A1**
Mondovi *Italy* **52A2**
Moneague *Jamaica* **27H1**
Monessen *USA* **14C2**
Monett *USA* **18B2**
Monfalcone *Italy* **52B1**
Monforte de Lemos *Spain* **50A1**
Monga *Zaïre* **98C2**
Mongala, R *Zaïre* **98C2**
Mongalla *Sudan* **99D2**
Mong Cai *Viet* **76D1**
Mongo *Chad* **98B1**
Mongolia, Republic *Asia* **68B2**
Mongu *Zambia* **100B2**
Mönhhaan *Mongolia* **63D3**
Monitor Range, Mts *USA* **21B2**
Monkoto *Zaïre* **98C3**
Monmouth *Eng* **43C4**
Monmouth *USA* **18B1**
Monmouth,Mt *Can* **13C2**
Mono, R *Togo* **97C4**
Mono L *USA* **21B2**
Monopoli *Italy* **53C2**
Monreal del Campo *Spain* **51B1**
Monroe, Louisiana *USA* **19B3**
Monroe, Michigan *USA* **14B2**
Monroe, Washington *USA* **20B1**
Monroe City *USA* **18B2**
Monrovia *Lib* **97A4**
Monrovia *USA* **20D3**
Mons *Belg* **56A2**
Monselice *Italy* **47D2**
Monson *USA* **16C1**
Mönsterås *Sweden* **58B1**
Montagne d'Ambre, Mt *Madag* **101D2**
Montagnes des Ouled Naïl, Mts *Alg* **96C1**
Montague I *USA* **12E3**
Mont Aigoual, Mt *France* **49C3**
Montaigu *France* **48B2**
Montallo, Mt *Italy* **53C3**
Montana, State *USA* **8B2**
Montañas de León, Mts *Spain* **50A1**
Montargis *France* **49C2**
Montauban *France* **48C3**
Montauk *USA* **15D2**
Montauk Pt *USA* **15D2**
Montbéliard *France* **49D2**
Mont Blanc, Mt *France/Italy* **52A1**
Montceau les Mines *France* **49C2**
Montceny, Mt *Spain* **51C1**
Mont Cinto, Mt *Corse* **49D3**
Montcornet *France* **46C2**
Mont-de-Marsin *France* **48B3**
Montdidier *France* **48C2**
Monteagudo *Bol* **30D2**
Monte Alegre *Brazil* **33G4**
Monte Amiata, Mt *Italy* **52B2**
Monte Baldo, Mt *Italy* **47D2**
Montebello *Can* **15C1**
Monte Bello Is *Aust* **106A3**
Montebelluna *Italy* **47E2**
Monte Carlo *France* **49D3**
Monte Carmelo *Brazil* **35B1**
Monte Caseros *Arg* **34D2**
Monte Cimone, Mt *Italy* **52B2**
Monte Cinto, Mt *Corse* **52A2**
Monte Coman *Arg* **34B2**
Monte Corno, Mt *Italy* **52B2**
Montecristi *Dom Rep* **27C3**
Montecristo, I *Italy* **52B2**
Monte Escobedo *Mexico* **23A1**
Monte Gargano, Mt *Italy* **53C2**
Montego Bay *Jamaica* **26B3**
Monte Grappa, Mt *Italy* **47D2**
Monte Lesima, Mt *Italy* **47C2**
Montélimar *France* **49C3**
Monte Miletto, Mt *Italy* **53B2**
Montemo-o-Novo *Port* **50A2**
Montemorelos *Mexico* **24C2**
Montená *Colombia* **26B5**
Montenegro, Region *Yugos* **54A2**
Monte Pascoal, Mt *Brazil* **35D1**
Monte Patria *Chile* **34A2**
Monte Pollino, Mt *Italy* **53C3**
Montepuez *Mozam* **101C2**
Monterey, California *USA* **8A3**
Monterey, Virginia *USA* **15C3**
Monterey B *USA* **8A3**
Montería *Colombia* **32B2**
Montero *Bol* **30D2**
Monte Rosa, Mt *Italy/Switz* **47B2**
Monterrey *Mexico* **24B2**
Montes Claros *Brazil* **31C5**
Montes de Toledo, Mts *Spain* **50B2**
Montevideo *Urug* **29E2**
Monte Viso, Mt *Italy* **52A2**
Mont Gimie, Mt *St Lucia* **27P2**
Montgomery, Alabama *USA* **11B3**
Mont Gréboun *Niger* **96C2**
Montherme *France* **46C2**
Monthey *Switz* **47B1**
Monticello, Arkansas *USA* **19B3**
Monticello, New York *USA* **16B2**
Monticello, Utah *USA* **9C3**
Monti del Gennargentu, Mt *Sardegna* **53A2**
Monti Lessini, Mts *Italy* **47D2**
Monti Nebrodi, Mts *Italy* **53B3**
Mont-Laurier *Can* **7C5**
Montluçon *France* **48C2**
Montmagny *Can* **7C5**
Montmédy *France* **46C2**
Mont Mézenc, Mt *France* **49C3**
Montmirail *France* **46B2**
Montoro *Spain* **50B2**
Mont Pelat, Mt *France* **49D3**
Montpelier, Ohio *USA* **14B2**
Montpelier, Vermont *USA* **10C2**
Montpellier *France* **49C3**
Montréal *Can* **7C5**
Montreuil *France* **48C1**
Montreux *Switz* **52A1**
Mont Risoux, Mt *France* **47B1**
Montrose, Colorado *USA* **8C3**
Montrose *Scot* **40C2**
Mont-St-Michel *France* **48B2**
Monts des Ksour, Mts *Alg* **96B1**
Monts des Ouled Neil, Mts *Alg* **51C3**
Monts du Hodna, Mts *Alg* **51C2**
Montserrat, I *Caribbean* **27E3**
Monument Mt *USA* **12B1**
Monument V *USA* **9B3**
Monveda *Zaïre* **98C2**
Monywa *Burma* **76B1**
Monza *Italy* **52A1**
Monze *Zambia* **100B2**
Mooi, R *S Africa* **101H1**
Mool River *S Africa* **101G1**
Moomba *Aust* **108B1**
Moonbi Range, Mts *Aust* **109D2**
Moonda L *Aust* **108B1**
Moonie *Aust* **109D1**
Moonie, R *Aust* **109C1**
Moonta *Aust* **108A2**
Moora *Aust* **106A4**
Moore,L *Aust* **106A3**
Moorfoot Hills *Scot* **42C2**
Moorhead *USA* **8D2**
Moorpark *USA* **22C3**
Moose, R *Can* **7B4**
Moose Jaw *Can* **5H4**
Moosomin *Can* **5H4**
Moosonee *Can* **7B4**
Moosup *USA* **16D2**
Mopeia *Mozam* **101C2**
Mopti *Mali* **97B3**
Moquegua *Peru* **30B2**
Mora *Sweden* **39G6**
Morada *Brazil* **31D3**
Morādābād *India* **84D3**
Morada Nova de Minas, L *Brazil* **35B1**
Morafenobe *Madag* **101D2**
Moramanga *Madag* **101D2**
Morant Bay *Jamaica* **27J2**
Morant Pt *Jamaica* **27J2**
Moratuwa *Sri Lanka* **87B3**
Morava, R *Austria/Czech* **59B3**
Morava, R *Yugos* **54B2**
Moraveh Tappeh *Iran* **90C2**
Moray Firth, Estuary *Scot* **40C2**
Morbegno *Italy* **47C1**
Morbi *India* **85C4**
Mor Dağ, Mt *Turk* **93D2**
Morden *Can* **5J5**
Mordovskaya ASSR, Republic *USSR* **61F3**
Morecambe *Eng* **42C2**
Morecambe B *Eng* **42C2**
Moree *Aust* **107D3**
Morehead *USA* **14B3**
Mörel *Switz* **47C1**
Morelia *Mexico* **24B3**
Morelos, State *Mexico* **23B2**
Morena *India* **85D3**
Moresby I *Can* **5E4**
Moreton I *Aust* **109D1**
Moreuil *France* **46B2**
Morez *France* **47B1**
Morgan City *USA* **19B4**
Morgan Hill *USA* **22B2**
Morgantown *USA* **14C3**
Morgenzon *S Africa* **101G1**
Morges *Switz* **47B1**
Morhange *France* **46D2**
Mori *Japan* **74E2**
Moriatio *Tobago* **27K1**
Morice L *Can* **13B2**
Morinville *Can* **13E2**
Morioka *Japan* **74E3**
Morisset *Aust* **109D2**
Morkoka, R *USSR* **63D1**
Morlaix *France* **48B2**
Morne Diablotin, Mt *Dominica* **27Q2**
Mornington, I *Aust* **106C2**
Moro *Pak* **85B3**
Morocco, Kingdom *Africa* **96B2**
Moro G *Phil* **79B4**
Morogoro *Tanz* **99D3**
Moroleon *Mexico* **23A1**
Morombe *Madag* **101D3**
Morón *Cuba* **26B2**
Morondava *Madag* **101D3**
Moron de la Frontera *Spain* **50A2**
Moroni *Comoros* **101D2**
Morotai, I *Indon* **71D3**
Moroto *Uganda* **99D2**
Morozovsk *USSR* **61F4**
Morpeth *Eng* **42D2**
Morrilton *USA* **19B2**
Morrinhos *Brazil* **35B1**
Morrinsville *NZ* **110C1**
Morristown, New Jersey *USA* **16B2**
Morristown, New York *USA* **15C2**
Morrisville, Pennsylvania *USA* **16B2**
Morro Bay *USA* **21A2**
Morro de Papanoa *Mexico* **23A2**
Morro de Petatlán *Mexico* **23A2**
Morrumbala *Mozam* **101C2**
Morrumbene *Mozam* **101C3**
Morshansk *USSR* **61F3**
Mortara *Italy* **47C2**
Morteros *Arg* **34C2**
Mortes, R, Mato Grosso *Brazil* **33G6**
Mortes, R, Minas Gerais *Brazil* **35C2**
Mortlake *Aust* **108B3**
Moruga *Trinidad* **27L1**
Moruya *Aust* **109D3**
Morven *Aust* **109C1**
Morvern, Pen *Scot* **44B3**
Morwell *Aust* **109C3**
Moscos Is *Burma* **76B3**
Moscow, Idaho *USA* **20C1**
Mosel, R *W Germ* **56B2**
Moselle, Department *France* **46D2**
Moselle, R *France* **46D2**
Moses Lake *USA* **20C1**
Mosgiel *NZ* **111B3**
Moshi *Tanz* **99D3**
Mosjøen *Nor* **38G5**
Moskal'vo *USSR* **63G2**
Moskva *USSR* **64E4**
Mosquito, R *Brazil* **35C1**
Moss *Nor* **39G7**
Mossaka *Congo* **98B3**
Mossel Bay *S Africa* **100B4**
Mossendjo *Congo* **98B3**
Mossgiel *Aust* **108B2**
Mossoró *Brazil* **31D3**
Most *Czech* **57C2**
Mostaganem *Alg* **96C1**
Mostar *Yugos* **54A2**
Mosty *USSR* **58C2**
Mosul *Iraq* **93D2**
Motala *Sweden* **39H7**
Motherwell *Scot* **42C2**
Motihāri *India* **86A1**
Motilla del Palancar *Spain* **51B2**
Motril *Spain* **50B2**
Motueka *NZ* **111B2**
Motueka, R *NZ* **111B2**

Moudon *Switz* **47B1**
Mouila *Gabon* **98B3**
Moulamein *Aust* **108B2**
Mould Bay *Can* **4G2**
Moulins *France* **49C2**
Moulmein *Burma* **76B2**
Moulouya, R *Mor* **96B1**
Moultrie *USA* **17B1**
Moultrie,L *USA* **17C1**
Mound City, Illinois *USA* **18C2**
Mound City, Missouri *USA* **18A1**
Moundou *Chad* **98B2**
Moundsville *USA* **14B3**
Mountain, R *Can* **12J1**
Mountain Brook *USA* **17A1**
Mountain Grove *USA* **18B2**
Mountain Home, Arkansas *USA* **18B2**
Mountain View *USA* **22A2**
Mountain Village *USA* **12B2**
Mount Airy, Maryland *USA* **16A3**
Mount Carmel *USA* **16A2**
Mount Dutton *Aust* **108A1**
Mount Eba *Aust* **108A2**
Mount Gambier *Aust* **108B3**
Mount Holly *USA* **16B3**
Mount Holly Springs *USA* **16A2**
Mount Hope *Aust* **108A2**
Mount Isa *Aust* **106C3**
Mount Lofty Range, Mts *Aust* **108A2**
Mount McKinley Nat Pk *USA* **12D2**
Mount Magnet *Aust* **106A3**
Mount Manara *Aust* **108B2**
Mount Morgan *Aust* **107E3**
Mount Pleasant, Texas *USA* **19B3**
Mount Rainier Nat Pk *USA* **20B1**
Mounts B *Eng* **43B4**
Mount Shasta *USA* **20B2**
Mount Vernon, Illinois *USA* **11B3**
Mount Vernon, Kentucky *USA* **19A3**
Mount Vernon, Washington *USA* **20B1**
Mourne Mts *N Ire* **45C1**
Moussoro *Chad* **98B1**
Mouth of the Indus *Pak* **85B4**
Mouths of the Ganga *India/Bang* **86B2**
Mouths of the Mekong *Viet* **77D4**
Mouths of the Niger *Nigeria* **97C4**
Moutier *Switz* **47B1**
Moûtiers *France* **47B2**
Mouydir, Mts *Alg* **96C2**
Mouyondzi *Congo* **98B3**
Mouzon *France* **46C2**
Moyahua *Mexico* **23A1**
Moyale *Kenya* **99D2**
Moyamba *Sierra Leone* **97A4**
Moyen Atlas, Mts *Mor* **96B1**
Moyeni *Lesotho* **100B4**
Moyo *Uganda* **99D2**
Moyobamba *Peru* **32B5**
Moyu *China* **84D1**
Mozambique, Republic *Africa* **101C3**
Mozambique Chan *Mozam/Madag* **101C3**
Mozhga *USSR* **61H2**
Mozyr *USSR* **60C3**
Mpanda *Tanz* **99D3**
Mpika *Zambia* **101C2**
Mporokosa *Zambia* **99D3**
Mposhi *Zambia* **100B2**
Mpulungu *Zambia* **99D3**
Mpwapwa *Tanz* **99D3**
Mtsensk *USSR* **60E3**
Mtubatuba *S Africa* **101H1**
Mtwara *Tanz* **101D2**
Muang Chainat *Thai* **76C2**
Muang Chiang Rai *Thai* **76C2**
Muang Kalasin *Thai* **76C2**
Muang Khon Kaen *Thai* **76C2**
Muang Lampang *Thai* **76B2**
Muang Lamphun *Thai* **76B2**
Muang Loei *Thai* **76C2**
Muang Lom Sak *Thai* **76C2**
Muang Nakhon Phanom *Thai* **76C2**
Muang Nakhon Sawan *Thai* **76B2**
Muang Nan *Thai* **76C2**
Muang Phayao *Thai* **76C2**
Muang Phetchabun *Thai* **76C2**
Muang Phichit *Thai* **76C2**
Muang Phitsanulok *Thai* **76C2**
Muang Phrae *Thai* **76C2**
Muang Roi Et *Thai* **76C2**
Muang Sakon Nakhon *Thai* **76C2**
Muang Samut Prakan *Thai* **76C3**
Muang Uthai Thani *Thai* **76C2**
Muang Yasothon *Thai* **76C2**
Muar *Malay* **77C5**
Muara *Brunei* **78C2**
Muara *Indon* **70B4**
Muaralakitan *Indon* **78A3**
Muaratebo *Indon* **78A3**
Muaratewah *Indon* **78C3**
Muarenim *Indon* **78A3**
Muaungmaya *Burma* **76A2**
Mubende *Uganda* **99D2**
Muchinga, Mts *Zambia* **100C2**
Muck, I *Scot* **44A3**
Muckadilla *Aust* **109C1**
Mucuri *Brazil* **35D1**
Mucuri, R *Brazil* **35C1**
Mucusso *Angola* **100B2**
Mudanjiang *China* **69E2**
Mudgee *Aust* **109C2**
Mudon *Burma* **76B2**
Mueda *Mozam* **101C2**
Mueo *Nouvelle Calédonie* **107F3**
Mufulira *Zambia* **100B2**
Mufu Shan, Hills *China* **73C4**
Mugadzhary, Mts *USSR* **61J4**
Mughayra *S Arabia* **93C4**
Muğla *Turk* **92A2**
Mugodzhary, Mts *USSR* **65G5**
Muguaping *China* **73A3**
Muhaywir *Iraq* **93D3**
Mühldorf *W Germ* **57C3**
Muhlhausen *E Germ* **57C2**
Muhos *Fin* **38K6**
Mui Bai Bung, C *Camb* **77C4**
Muine Bheag *Irish Rep* **45C2**
Mujimbeji *Zambia* **100B2**
Mukachevo *USSR* **59C3**
Mukah *Malay* **78C2**
Muko-jima, I *Japan* **69G4**
Muktinath *Nepal* **86A1**
Mukur *Afghan* **84B2**
Mulberry *USA* **18B2**
Mulchatna, R *USA* **12C2**
Mulchén *Chile* **34A3**
Mulde, R *E Germ* **56C2**
Mulgrave I *Aust* **71F5**
Mulhacén, Mt *Spain* **50B2**
Mülheim *W Germ* **46D1**
Mulhouse *France* **49D2**
Muli *China* **73A4**
Mull, I *Scot* **44B3**
Mullaitvu *Sri Lanka* **87C3**
Mullaley *Aust* **109C2**
Mullewa *Aust* **106A3**
Mullica, R *USA* **16B3**
Mullingar *Irish Rep* **45C2**
Mull of Kintyre, Pt *Scot* **42B2**
Mull of Oa, C *Scot* **45C1**
Mullumbimby *Aust* **109D1**
Mulobezi *Zambia* **100B2**
Multan *Pak* **84C2**
Mumbwa *Zambia* **100B2**
Mumra *USSR* **61G4**
Muna, I *Indon* **71D4**
München *W Germ* **57C3**
Muncie *USA* **14A2**
Muncy *USA* **15C2**
Münden *W Germ* **56B2**
Mundubbera *Aust* **109D1**
Mungallala *Aust* **109C1**
Mungallala, R *Aust* **109C1**
Mungbere *Zaïre* **99C2**
Mungeli *India* **86A2**
Munger *India* **86B1**
Mungindi *Aust* **109C1**
Munising *USA* **14A1**
Muñoz Gomero,Pen *Chile* **29B6**
Munster, Region *Irish Rep* **45B2**
Münster *Switz* **47C1**
Münster *W Germ* **56B2**
Muntii Apuseni, Mts *Rom* **54B1**
Muntii Călimanilor, Mts *Rom* **54B1**
Muntii Carpaţii Meridionali, Mts *Rom* **54B1**
Muntii Rodnei, Mts *Rom* **54B1**
Muntii Zarandului, Mts *Rom* **54B1**
Munzur Silsilesi, Mts *Turk* **93C2**
Muomio *Fin* **64D3**
Muong Khoua *Laos* **76C1**
Muong Man *Viet* **76D3**
Muong Nong *Laos* **76D2**
Muong Ou Neua *Laos* **76C1**
Muong Sai *Laos* **76C1**
Muong Sen *Viet* **76C2**
Muong Sing *Laos* **76C1**
Muong Son *Laos* **76C1**
Muonio *Fin* **38J5**
Muonio, R *Sweden/Fin* **38J5**
Muqdisho *Somalia* **99E2**
Mur, R *Austria* **52B1**
Murakami *Japan* **74D3**
Murallón, Mt *Chile/Arg* **29B5**
Murashi *USSR* **61G2**
Murat, R *Turk* **93D2**
Muravera *Sardegna* **53A3**
Murayama *Japan* **75C1**
Murcheh Khvort *Iran* **90B3**
Murchison *NZ* **111B2**
Murchison, R *Aust* **106A3**
Murcia, Region *Spain* **51B2**
Murcia *Spain* **51B2**
Mureş, R *Rom* **54B1**
Muresui, R *Rom* **54B1**
Murg, R *W Germ* **46E2**
Murgab, R *USSR* **65H6**
Murgha Kibzai *Pak* **84B2**
Murgon *Aust* **109D1**
Muri *India* **86B2**
Muriaé *Brazil* **35C2**
Muriege *Angola* **98C3**
Murmansk *USSR* **64E3**
Murom *USSR* **61F2**
Muroran *Japan* **74E2**
Muros *Spain* **50A1**
Muroto *Japan* **74C4**
Muroto-zaki, C *Japan* **75A2**
Murphy, Idaho *USA* **20C2**
Murphys *USA* **22B1**
Murray, Kentucky *USA* **18C2**
Murray, R *Aust* **108B2**
Murray, R *Can* **13C2**
Murray Bridge *Aust* **108A3**
Murray,L *PNG* **71F4**
Murray,L *USA* **17B1**
Murray Seacarp *Pacific O* **105J2**
Murrumbidgee, R *Aust* **108B2**
Murrumburrah *Aust* **109C2**
Murrurundi *Aust* **109D2**
Murten *Switz* **47B1**
Murtoa *Aust* **108B3**
Murupara *NZ* **110C1**
Murwāra *India* **86A2**
Murwillimbah *Aust* **109D1**
Muş *Turk* **93D2**
Musala, Mt *Bulg* **54B2**
Musan *N Korea* **74B2**
Musandam, Pen *Oman* **91C4**
Muscat, Region *Oman* **91C5**
Musgrave Range, Mts *Aust* **106C3**
Mushie *Zaïre* **98B3**
Muskegon *USA* **14A2**
Muskegon, R *USA* **14A2**
Muskogee *USA* **18A2**
Muskoka,L *Can* **15C2**
Musmar *Sudan* **95C3**
Musoma *Tanz* **99D3**
Musselshell, R *USA* **8C2**
Mussende *Angola* **100A2**
Mussidan *France* **48C2**
Mustafa-Kemalpasa *Turk* **55C2**
Mustang *Nepal* **86A1**
Muswelibrook *Aust* **109D2**
Mut *Egypt* **95B2**
Mutarara *Mozam* **101C2**
Mutari *Zim* **101C2**
Mutoko *Zim* **101C2**
Mutsamudu *Comoros* **101D2**
Mutshatsha *Zaïre* **100B2**
Mutsu *Japan* **74E2**
Mutsu-wan, B *Japan* **74E2**
Mutton, I *Irish Rep* **45B2**
Mu Us Shamo, Desert *China* **72B2**
Muxima *Angola* **98B3**
Muya *USSR* **63D2**
Muyezerskiy *USSR* **38L6**
Muyinga *Burundi* **99D3**
Muyumba *Zaïre* **98C3**
Muyun Kum, Desert *USSR* **82A1**
Muzaffarābad *Pak* **84C2**
Muzaffargarh *Pak* **84C2**
Muzaffarpur *India* **86B1**
Muzhi *USSR* **64H3**
Muztag, Mt *China* **82C2**
Muztagata, Mt *China* **82B2**
Mvuma *Zim* **100C2**
Mwanza *Tanz* **99D3**
Mwanza *Zaïre* **98C3**
Mweka *Zaïre* **98C3**
Mwene Ditu *Zaïre* **98C3**
Mwenezi *Zim* **100C3**
Mwenga *Zaïre* **99C3**
Mweru, L *Zambia* **99C3**
Mwinilunga *Zambia* **100B2**
Myanaung *Burma* **83D4**
Myingyan *Burma* **86D2**
Myingyao *Burma* **76B1**
Myinmoletkat, Mt *Burma* **76B3**
Myitkyina *Burma* **82D3**
Myitta *Burma* **76B3**
Mymensingh *Bang* **86C2**
Myojin, I *Japan* **69F3**
Myrdal *Nor* **39F6**
Myrdalsjökur, Mts *Iceland* **38B2**
Myrtle Beach *USA* **17C1**
Myrtle Creek *USA* **20B2**
Mysen *Nor* **39G7**
Mysiloborz *Pol* **56C2**

Myc Kanin Nos, C *USSR* **64F3**
Myślenice *Pol* **59B3**
Mys Lopatka, C *USSR* **69H1**
Mysore *India* **87B2**
Mys Sarych, C *USSR* **60D5**
Mystic *USA* **16D2**
Mys Tyub-Karagan, Pt *USSR* **61H5**
Mys Yelizavety, C *USSR* **63G2**
Mys Zhelaniya, C *USSR* **64H2**
My Tho *Viet* **77D3**
Mytle Point *USA* **20B2**
Mzimba *Malawi* **101C2**
Mzuzú *Malawi* **101C2**

N

Naalehu *Hawaiian Is* **21C4**
Naantali *Fin* **39J6**
Naas *Irish Rep* **45C2**
Nabari *Japan* **75B2**
Nabesna, R *USA* **12F2**
Nabeul *Tunisia* **96D1**
Nablus *Israel* **94B2**
Nacala *Mozam* **101D2**
Naches *USA* **20B1**
Nachingwea *Tanz* **101C2**
Nacogdoches *USA* **19B3**
Nacondam, I *Indian O* **76A3**
Nacozari *Mexico* **24B1**
Nadiād *India* **85C4**
Nador *Mor* **50B2**
Nadūshan *Iran* **90B3**
Nadvornaya *USSR* **59C3**
Naestved *Den* **56C1**
Nafoora *Libya* **95B2**
Nagahama *Japan* **75A2**
Naga Hills *Burma* **82D3**
Nagai *Japan* **75B1**
Nāgāland, State *India* **86C1**
Nagano *Japan* **74D3**
Nagaoka *Japan* **74D3**
Nāgappattinam *India* **87B2**
Nagar Parkar *Pak* **85C4**
Nagasaki *Japan* **74B4**
Nagashima *Japan* **75B2**
Nagato *Japan* **75A2**
Nāgaur *India* **85C3**
Nāgercoil *India* **87B3**
Nagha Kalat *Pak* **85B3**
Nagīna *India* **84D3**
Nagoya *Japan* **74D3**
Nāgpur *India* **85D4**
Nagqu *China* **82D2**
Nagykanizsa *Hung* **59B3**
Nagykörös *Hung* **59B3**
Naha *Japan* **69E4**
Nahaimo *Can* **8A2**
Nāhan *India* **84D2**
Nahanni Butte *Can* **4F3**
Nahariya *Israel* **94B2**
Nahāvand *Iran* **90A3**
Nahe, R *W Germ* **46D2**
Nahpu *China* **72D2**
Naimen Qi *China* **72E1**
Nain *Can* **7D4**
Nā'īn *Iran* **90B3**
Naini Tai *India* **84D3**
Nairn *Scot* **44C3**
Nairobi *Kenya* **99D3**
Najafābād *Iran* **90B3**
Najin *N Korea* **74C2**
Nakama *Japan* **75A2**
Nakaminato *Japan* **74E3**
Nakamura *Japan* **75A2**
Nakano *Japan* **75B1**
Nakano-shima, I *Japan* **75A1**
Nakatsu *Japan* **74C4**
Nakatsu-gawa *Japan* **75B1**
Nakfa *Eth* **95C3**
Nakhichevan *USSR* **93E2**
Nakhl *Egypt* **92B4**
Nakhodka *USSR* **74C2**
Nakhon Pathom *Thai* **76C3**
Nakhon Ratchasima *Thai* **76C3**
Nakhon Si Thammarat *Thai* **77C4**
Nakina *Can* **12H3**
Nakina, Ontario *Can* **7B4**
Naknek *USA* **12C3**
Naknek L *USA* **12C3**
Nakrek *USA* **4C4**
Nakskov *Den* **39G8**
Nakuru *Kenya* **99D3**
Nakusp *Can* **13D2**
Nal'chik *USSR* **61F5**
Nalgonda *India* **87B1**
Nallamala Range, Mts *India* **87B1**
Nālūt *Libya* **95A1**
Namaacha *Mozam* **101H1**
Namak, L *Iran* **65G6**
Namakzar-e Shadad, Salt Flat *Iran* **90C3**
Namangan *USSR* **65J5**
Namapa *Mozam* **101C2**
Namaqualand, Region *S Africa* **100A4**
Nambour *Aust* **109D1**
Nambucca Heads *Aust* **109D2**
Nam Can *Viet* **77D4**
Namcha Barwa, Mt *China* **82D3**
Nam Co, L *China* **82D2**
Nam Dinh *Viet* **76D1**
Nametil *Mozam* **101C2**
Namhae-do, I *S Korea* **74B4**
Namib Desert *Namibia* **100A2**
Namibe *Angola* **100A2**
Namibia, Dependency *Africa* **100A3**
Namlea *Indon* **71D4**
Namoi, R *Aust* **109C2**
Nampa *Can* **13D1**
Nampa *USA* **20C2**
Nampala *Mali* **97B3**
Nam Phong *Thai* **76C2**
Namp'o *N Korea* **74B3**
Nampula *Mozam* **101C2**
Namsos *Nor* **38G6**
Namton *Burma* **76B1**
Namtu *Burma* **86D2**
Namu *Can* **13B2**
Namuno *Mozam* **101C2**
Namur *Belg* **46C1**
Namutoni *Namibia* **100A2**
Namwŏn *S Korea* **74B3**
Nanaimo *Can* **13C3**
Nanam *N Korea* **74B2**
Nanango *Aust* **109D1**
Nanao *Japan* **74D3**
Nanatsu-jima, I *Japan* **75B1**
Nanbu *China* **73B3**
Nanchang *China* **73D4**
Nanchong *China* **73B3**
Nancy *France* **49D2**
Nānded *India* **87B1**
Nandewar Range, Mts *Aust* **109D2**
Nandurbar *India* **85C4**
Nandyāl *India* **87B1**
Nanga Eboko *Cam* **98B2**
Nanga Parbat, Mt *Pak* **84C1**
Nangapinoh *Indon* **78C3**
Nangatayap *Indon* **78C3**
Nangnim Sanmaek, Mts *N Korea* **74B2**
Nang Xian *China* **86C1**
Nangzhou *China* **67F3**
Nanjangūd *India* **87B2**
Nanjing *China* **72D3**
Nankoku *Japan* **75A2**
Nan Ling, Region *China* **73C4**
Nanliu, R *China* **76D1**
Nanning *China* **73B5**
Nanortalik *Greenland* **6F3**
Nanpan Jiang, R *China* **73A5**
Nānpāra *India* **86A1**
Nanping *China* **73D4**
Nanoon Sd *Can* **6A1**
Nansio *Tanz* **99D3**
Nantes *France* **48B2**
Nanton *Can* **13E2**
Nantong *China* **72E3**
Nantucket, I *USA* **10C2**
Nanuque *Brazil* **35C1**
Nanyang *China* **72C3**
Nanyang Hu, L *China* **72D2**
Nanyuki *Kenya* **99D2**
Naoetsu *Japan* **74D3**
Naokot *Pak* **85B4**
Napa *USA* **22A1**
Napaiskak *USA* **12B2**
Napanee *Can* **15C2**
Napas *USSR* **65K4**
Napassoq *Greenland* **6E3**
Nape *Laos* **76D2**
Napier *NZ* **110C1**
Naples, Florida *USA* **17B2**
Naples, Texas *USA* **19B3**
Napo *China* **73B5**
Napo, R *Peru/Ecuador* **32C4**
Napoli *Italy* **53B2**
Naqadeh *Iran* **90A2**
Naqb Ishtar *Jordan* **92C4**
Nara *Japan* **75B2**
Nara *Mali* **97B3**
Naracoorte *Aust* **107D4**
Naranjos *Mexico* **23B1**
Narasarāopet *India* **87C1**
Narathiwat *Thai* **77C4**
Narayanganj *Bang* **86C2**
Nārāyenpet *India* **87B1**
Narbonne *France* **49C3**
Narendranagar *India* **84D2**
Nares Str *Can* **6C2**
Narew, R *Pol* **58C2**
Narita *Japan* **75C1**
Narmada, R *India* **85C4**
Nārnaul *India* **84D3**
Naro Fominsk *USSR* **60E2**
Narok *Kenya* **99D3**
Narowal *Pak* **84C2**
Narrabri *Aust* **107D4**
Narran, L *Aust* **109C1**
Narran, R *Aust* **109C1**
Narrandera *Aust* **109C2**
Narrogin *Aust* **106A4**
Narromine *Aust* **109C2**
Narsimhapur *India* **85D4**
Narsīpatnam *India* **87C1**
Narssalik *Greenland* **6F3**
Narssaq *Greenland* **6F3**
Narssarssuaq *Greenland* **6F3**
Narugo *Japan* **75C1**
Naruto *Japan* **75A2**
Narva *USSR* **60C2**
Narvik *Nor* **38H5**
Narwāna *India* **84D3**
Nar'yan Mar *USSR* **64G3**
Narylico *Aust* **108B1**
Naryn *USSR* **65J5**
Nasarawa *Nig* **97C4**
Nasca Ridge *Pacific O* **103D5**
Nashua *USA* **16D1**
Nashville, Arkansas *USA* **19B3**
Nashville, Tennessee *USA* **11B3**
Našice *Yugos* **54A1**
Nāsik *India* **85D4**
Nasir *Sudan* **99D2**
Nass, R *Can* **13B1**
Nassau *Bahamas* **26B1**
Nassau *USA* **16C1**
Nasser,L *Egypt* **95C2**
Nässjö *Sweden* **39G7**
Nastapoka Is *Can* **7C4**
Nata *Botswana* **100B3**
Natal *Brazil* **31D3**
Natal *Indon* **70A3**
Natal, Province *S Africa* **101H1**
Natanz *Iran* **90B3**
Natashquan *Can* **7D4**
Natashquan, R *Can* **7D4**
Natchez *USA* **19B3**
Natchitoches *USA* **19B3**
Nathalia *Aust* **108C3**
Nathorsts Land, Region *Greenland* **6H2**
Nation, R *Can* **13C1**
National City *USA* **21B3**
Natori *Japan* **75C1**
Natovl'a *USSR* **58D2**
Natron, L *Tanz* **99D3**
Naturaliste,C *Aust* **106A4**
Nauders *Austria* **47D1**
Nauen *E Germ* **56C2**
Naugatuck *USA* **16C2**
Naumburg *E Germ* **57C2**
Naur *Jordan* **94B3**
Nauru, I *Pacific O* **105G4**
Naushki *USSR* **63C2**
Nautla *Mexico* **23B1**
Navajo Res *USA* **9C3**
Navalmoral de la Mata *Spain* **50A2**
Navarino, I *Chile* **29C7**
Navarra, Province *Spain* **51B1**
Navarro *Arg* **34D3**
Navasota *USA* **19A3**
Navasota, R *USA* **19A3**
Navia, R *Spain* **50A1**
Navidad *Chile* **34A2**
Navlakhi *India* **85C4**
Navlya *USSR* **60D3**
Navojoa *Mexico* **24B2**
Návpaktos *Greece* **55B3**
Návplion *Greece* **55B3**
Navsāri *India* **85C4**
Nawá *Syria* **94C2**
Nawāda *India* **86B2**
Nawah *Afghan* **84B2**
Nawrabshah *Pak* **85B3**
Naxi *China* **73B4**
Náxos, I *Greece* **55C3**
Nayar *Mexico* **23A1**
Nay Band *Iran* **90C3**
Nāy Band *Iran* **91B4**
Nayoro *Japan* **74E2**
Nazareth *Israel* **94B2**
Nazay *France* **48B2**
Nazca *Peru* **32C6**
Nazilli *Turk* **92A2**
Nazimovo *USSR* **63B2**
Nazko, R *Can* **13C2**
Nazwa *Oman* **91C5**
Nazyvayevsk *USSR* **65J4**
Ndalatando *Angola* **98B3**
Ndélé *CAR* **98C2**
Ndendé *Gabon* **98B3**
N'Djamena *Chad* **98B1**
Ndjolé *Gabon* **98B3**
Ndola *Zambia* **100B2**
Neabul *Aust* **109C1**
Neales, R *Aust* **108A1**
Neápolis *Greece* **55B3**
Neath *Wales* **43C4**
Nebine, R *Aust* **109C1**
Nebit Dag *USSR* **65G6**
Nebraska, State *USA* **8C2**
Nebraska City *USA* **18A1**
Nechako, R *Can* **13C2**
Neches, R *USA* **19A3**
Necochea *Arg* **34D3**
Nêdong *China* **86C1**
Needles *USA* **9B3**
Neenah *USA* **14A2**
Neepawa *Can* **5J4**
Neerpelt *Belg* **46C1**
Neftelensk *USSR* **63C2**
Negelli *Eth* **99D2**
Negev, Desert *Israel* **94B3**
Negolu, Mt *Rom* **60B4**
Negombo *Sri Lanka* **87B3**
Negrais,C *Burma* **76A2**
Negritos *Peru* **32A4**
Negro, R, Amazonas *Brazil* **33E4**
Negro, R *Arg* **29C4**
Negro, R *Urug* **34D2**

Negros, I *Phil* **79B4**
Negru Voda *Rom* **54C2**
Nehbāndan *Iran* **90D3**
Neijiang *China* **73B4**
Nei Monggol, Autononous Region *China* **72B1**
Neiva *Colombia* **32B3**
Nejo *Eth* **99D2**
Nelidovo *USSR* **60D2**
Nellore *India* **87B2**
Nel'ma *USSR* **69F2**
Nelson *Can* **13D3**
Nelson *NZ* **111B2**
Nelson, R *Can* **7A4**
Nelson,C *Aust* **108B3**
Nelson I *USA* **12B2**
Néma *Maur* **97B3**
Nemagt Uul, Mt *Mongolia* **72A1**
Neman, R *USSR* **58C1**
Neman, R *USSR* **58D2**
Nemira, Mt *Rom* **54C1**
Nemuro *Japan* **74F2**
Nen, R *China* **63E3**
Nenagh *Irish Rep* **41B3**
Nenana *USA* **12E2**
Nenana, R *USA* **12E2**
Nene, R *Eng* **43D3**
Nenjiang *China* **69E2**
Neodesha *USA* **18A2**
Neosho *USA* **18B2**
Nepa *USSR* **63C2**
Nepal, Kingdom *Asia* **82C3**
Nepalganj *Nepal* **86A1**
Nephin, Mt *Irish Rep* **45B1**
Neqarot, R *Israel* **94B3**
Nequén, State *Arg* **34A3**
Nerchinsk *USSR* **68D1**
Neretva, R *Yugos* **52C2**
Nero Deep *Pacific O* **71F2**
Neskaupstaður *Iceland* **38C1**
Nesle *France* **46B2**
Nesleyville *Can* **7E5**
Néstos, R *Greece* **54B2**
Netanya *Israel* **94B2**
Netcong *USA* **16B2**
Netherlands, Kingdom *Europe* **56B2**
Netherlands Antilles, Is *Caribbean* **3M7**
Netrakona *Bang* **86C2**
Nettilling L *Can* **6C3**
Neubrandenburg *E Germ* **56C2**
Neuchâtel *Switz* **47B1**
Neufchâteau *Belg* **46C2**
Neufchâtel *France* **48C2**
Neufchâtel-en-Bray *France* **46A2**
Neumünster *W Germ* **56B2**
Neunkirchen *Austria* **52C1**
Neunkirchen *W Germ* **46D2**
Neuquén *Arg* **34B3**
Neuquén, State *Arg* **29B4**
Neuquén, R *Arg* **34B3**
Neuruppin *E Germ* **56C2**
Neuss *W Germ* **46D1**
Neustadt *W Germ* **46E2**
Neustadt *W Germ* **56C2**
Neustrelitz *E Germ* **56C2**
Neuwied *W Germ* **46D1**
Nevada, State *USA* **8B3**
Nevada *USA* **18B2**
Nevada de Chillán, Mts *Chile/Arg* **34A3**
Nevada de Collima *Mexico* **23A2**
Nevada de Toluca, Mt *Mexico* **23B2**
Nevatim *Israel* **94B3**
Nevel *USSR* **60C2**
Nevers *France* **49C2**
Nevertire *Aust* **109C2**
Nevis, I *Caribbean* **27E3**
Nevis, R *USSR* **58D2**
Nevşehir *Turk* **92B2**
Nev'yansk *USSR* **61K2**
Newala *Tanz* **101C2**
New Albany, Indiana *USA* **14A3**
New Albany, Mississippi *USA* **19C3**
New Amsterdam *Guyana* **33F2**
New Angledool *Aust* **109C1**
Newark, Delaware *USA* **15C3**
Newark, New Jersey *USA* **10C2**
Newark, Ohio *USA* **14B2**
Newark-upon-Trent *Eng* **43D3**
New Bedford *USA* **15D2**
New Bella Bella *Can* **13B2**
Newberg *USA* **20B1**
New Bern *USA* **11C3**
Newberry *USA* **17B1**
New Bight *Bahamas* **26B2**
New Boston *USA* **14B3**
New Braunfels *USA* **9D4**
New Britain *USA* **16C2**
New Brunswick, Province *Can* **7D5**
New Brunswick *USA* **16B2**
Newburgh *USA* **16B2**
Newbury *Eng* **43D4**
Newburyport *USA* **16D1**
New Canaan *USA* **16C2**
Newcastle *Aust* **109D2**
New Castle, Indiana *USA* **14A3**
Newcastle *N Ire* **42B2**
New Castle, Pennsylvania *USA* **14B2**
Newcastle *S Africa* **101G1**
Newcastle, Wyoming *USA* **8C2**
Newcastle upon Tyne *Eng* **42D2**
Newcastle Waters *Aust* **106C2**
Newcastle West *Irish Rep* **45B2**
New Delhi *India* **84D3**
New England Range, Mts *Aust* **109D2**
Newenham,C *USA* **12B3**
New Forest,The *Eng* **43D4**
Newfoundland, Province *Can* **7D4**
Newfoundland, I *Can* **7E5**
Newfoundland Basin *Atlantic O* **102F2**
New Franklin *USA* **18B2**
New Galloway *Scot* **42B2**
New Georgia, I *Solomon Is* **107E1**
New Glasgow *Can* **7D5**
New Guinea *SE Asia* **71F4**
Newhalen *USA* **12D3**
Newhall *USA* **22C3**
New Hampshire, State *USA* **10C2**
New Hanover *S Africa* **101H1**
Newhaven *Eng* **43E4**
New Haven *USA* **15D2**
New Hazelton *Can* **13B1**
New Iberia *USA* **19B3**
New Jersey, State *USA* **10C2**
New Liskeard *Can* **7C5**
New London *USA* **16C2**
Newman *Aust* **106A3**
Newman *USA* **22B2**
Newmarket *Eng* **43E3**
Newmarket *Irish Rep* **45B2**
New Market *USA* **15C3**
New Mexico, State *USA* **9C3**
New Milford, Connecticut *USA* **16C2**
Newnan *USA* **17B1**
New Norfolk *Aust* **109C4**
New Orleans *USA* **11A3**
New Paltz *USA* **16B2**
New Philadelphia *USA* **14B2**
New Plymouth *NZ* **110B1**
Newport, Arkansas *USA* **18B2**
Newport *Eng* **43D4**
Newport, Kentucky *USA* **14B3**
Newport, Oregon *USA* **20B2**
Newport, Pennsylvania *USA* **16A2**
Newport, Rhode Island *USA* **15D2**
Newport, Vermont *USA* **15D2**
Newport *Wales* **43C4**
Newport, Washington *USA* **20C1**
Newport Beach *USA* **22D4**
Newport News *USA* **11C3**
New Providence, I *Caribbean* **26B1**
Newquay *Eng* **43B4**
New Quebec Crater *Can* **6C3**
New Ross *Irish Rep* **45C2**
Newry *N Ire* **45C1**
New Smyrna Beach *USA* **17B2**
New South Wales, State *Aust* **107D4**
New Stuyahok *USA* **12C3**
Newton, Kansas *USA* **18A2**
Newton, Massachusetts *USA* **16D1**
Newton, Mississippi *USA* **19C3**
Newton, New York *USA* **16B2**
Newton Abbot *Eng* **43C4**
Newton Stewart *N Ire* **45C1**
Newton Stewart *Scot* **42B2**
Newtown *Wales* **43C3**
Newtownards *N Ire* **42B2**
Newville *USA* **16A2**
New Westminster *Can* **5F5**
New York, State *USA* **10C2**
New York *USA* **10C2**
New Zealand, Dominion *SW Pacific O* **110**
New Zealand Plat *Pacific O* **105G6**
Neya *USSR* **61F2**
Neyrīz *Iran* **91B4**
Neyshābūr *Iran* **90C2**
Nezeto *Angola* **98B3**
Nezhin *USSR* **60D3**
Ngabé *Congo* **98B3**
Ngami, L *Botswana* **100B3**
Ngaruawahia *NZ* **110C1**
Ngaruroro, R *NZ* **110C1**
Ngauruhoe,Mt *NZ* **110C1**
Ngo *Congo* **98B3**
Ngoc Linh, Mt *Viet* **76D2**
Ngoko, R *Cam* **98B2**
Ngoring Hu, L *China* **68B3**
Ngorongoro Crater *Tanz* **99D3**
N'Gounié, R *Gabon* **98B3**
Nguigmi *Niger* **98B1**
Ngulu, I *Pacific O* **71E3**
Nguru *Nig* **97D3**
Nha Trang *Viet* **76D3**
Nhill *Aust* **108B3**
Nhlangano *Swaziland* **101H1**
Nhommarath *Laos* **76D2**
Nhulunbuy *Aust* **106C2**
Niafounké *Mali* **97B3**
Niagara *USA* **14A1**
Niagara Falls *Can* **15C2**
Niagara Falls *USA* **15C2**
Niah *Malay* **70C3**
Niakaramandougou *Ivory Coast* **97B4**
Niamey *Niger* **97C3**
Niangara *Zaïre* **99C2**
Nia Nia *Zaïre* **98C2**
Nias, I *Indon* **70A3**
Nicaragua, Republic *C America* **25D3**
Nicastro *Italy* **53C3**
Nice *France* **49D3**
Nicholl's Town *Bahamas* **26B1**
Nicobar Is *Indian O* **83D5**
Nicosia *Cyprus* **92B2**
Nicoya,Pen de *Costa Rica* **25D3**
Nidzica *Pol* **58C2**
Niederbronn *France* **46D2**
Niedersachsen, State *W Germ* **56B2**
Niemba *Zaïre* **99C3**
Nienburg *W Germ* **56B2**
Niers, R *W Germ* **46D1**
Niete,Mt *Lib* **97B4**
Nieuw Amsterdam *Surinam* **33F2**
Nieuw Nickerie *Surinam* **33F2**
Nieuwpoort *Belg* **46B1**
Niğde *Turk* **92B2**
Niger, Republic *Africa* **97C3**
Niger, R *Nig* **97C4**
Nigeria, Federal Republic *Africa* **97C4**
Nigríta *Greece* **55B2**
Nihommatsu *Japan* **75C1**
Niigata *Japan* **74D3**
Niihama *Japan* **74C4**
Nii-jima, I *Japan* **75B2**
Niimi *Japan* **75A2**
Niitsu *Japan* **74D3**
Nijil *Jordan* **94B3**
Nijmegen *Neth* **56B2**
Nikel' *USSR* **64E3**
Nikki *Benin* **97C3**
Nikko *Japan* **74D3**
Nikolayev *USSR* **60D4**
Nikolayevsk *USSR* **61G4**
Nikolayevsk-na-Amure *USSR* **63G2**
Nikol'sk, RSFSR *USSR* **61G2**
Nikol'sk *USSR* **61G3**
Nikopol *USSR* **60D4**
Niksar *Turk* **92C1**
Nīkshahr *Iran* **91D4**
Nikšić *Yugos* **54A2**
Nila, I *Indon* **71D4**
Nile, R *N E Africa* **80B3**
Niles *USA* **14A2**
Nilgiri Hills *India* **87B2**
Nimach *India* **85C4**
Nimbe *Cam* **98A2**
Nîmes *France* **49C3**
Nimmitabel *Aust* **109C3**
Nimule *Sudan* **99D2**
Nine Degree Chan *Indian O* **83B5**
Ninety-East Ridge *Indian O* **104C4**
Ninety Mile Beach *Aust* **109C3**
Ningde *China* **73D4**
Ningdu *China* **73D4**
Ningjing Shan, Mts *China* **68B3**
Ningming *China* **76D1**
Ningnan *China* **73A4**
Ningxia, Province *China* **72B2**
Ning Xian *China* **72B2**
Ninh Binh *Vietnam* **73B5**
Ninigo Is *PNG* **107D1**
Ninilchik *USA* **12D2**
Niobrara, R *USA* **8D2**
Nioki *Zaïre* **98B3**
Nioro du Sahel *Mali* **97B3**
Niort *France* **48B2**
Nipawin *Can* **5H4**
Nipigon *Can* **7B5**
Nipigon,L *Can* **7B5**
Nipissing, R *Can* **7B5**
Nipissing,L *Can* **14B1**
Nirmal *India* **87B1**
Nirmāli *India* **86B1**

Niš *Yugos* **54B2**
Nisāb *S Yemen* **81C4**
Nishino-shima, I *Japan* **69F4**
Nishino-shima, I *Japan* **75A1**
Nishiwaki *Japan* **75A2**
Nisling, R *Can* **12G2**
Nisutlin, R *Can* **12H2**
Nitchequon *Can* **7C4**
Niterói *Brazil* **31C6**
Nith, R *Scot* **42C2**
Nitra *Czech* **59B3**
Nitro *USA* **14B3**
Niut, Mt *Malay* **78C2**
Nivelles *Belg* **46C1**
Nivernais, Region *France* **49C2**
Nivskiy *USSR* **38L5**
Nizāmābād *India* **87B1**
Nizana, Hist Site *Israel* **94B3**
Nizhniye Sergi *USSR* **61J2**
Nizhniy Lomov *USSR* **61F3**
Nizhniy Tagil *USSR* **65G4**
Nizhnyaya Tunguska, R *USSR* **63B1**
Nizip *Turk* **93C2**
Nizmennost *USSR* **60D4**
Njoko, R *Zambia* **100B2**
Njombe *Tanz* **99D3**
Nkambé *Cam* **98B2**
Nkhata Bay *Malawi* **101C2**
Nkongsamba *Cam* **98B2**
N'Konni *Niger* **97C3**
Noakhali *Bang* **86C2**
Noatak *USA* **12B1**
Noatak, R *USA* **12C1**
Nobeoka *Japan* **74C4**
Noce, R *Italy* **47D1**
Nochistlán *Mexico* **23A1**
Nochixtlán *Mexico* **23B2**
Nocona *USA* **19A3**
Nogales, Sonora *Mexico* **24A1**
Nogales *USA* **9B3**
Nogales, Veracruz *Mexico* **23B2**
Nogara *Italy* **47D2**
Nogata *Japan* **75A2**
Noginsk *USSR* **60E2**
Nogoyá *Arg* **34D2**
Nogoyá, R *Arg* **34D2**
Nohar *India* **84C3**
Nojima-zaki, C *Japan* **75B2**
Nola *CAR* **98B2**
Nolinsk *USSR* **61G2**
Nomans Land, I *USA* **16D2**
Nome *USA* **12A2**
Nomeny *France* **46D2**
Nomgon *Mongolia* **72B1**
Nonachol L *Can* **5H3**
Nong Khai *Thai* **76C2**
Nongoma *S Africa* **101H1**
Noorvik *USA* **12B1**
Nootka Sd *Can* **13B3**
Noqui *Angola* **98B3**
Noranda *Can* **7C5**
Nord, Department *France* **46B1**
Nordaustlandet, I *Barents S* **64D2**
Nordegg *Can* **13D2**
Nordfjord, Inlet *Nor* **38F6**
Nordfriesische, Is *W Germ* **39F8**
Nordhausen *E Germ* **56C2**
Nordhrein Westfalen, State *W Germ* **56B2**
Nordkapp, C *Nor* **38J4**
Nordre *Greenland* **6E3**
Nord Stronfjället, Mt *Sweden* **38H5**
Nordvik *USSR* **1B9**
Nore, R *Irish Rep* **45C2**
Norfolk, County *Eng* **43E3**
Norfolk, Nebraska *USA* **8D2**
Norfolk, Virginia *USA* **11C3**
Norfolk I *Aust* **107F3**
Norfolk L *USA* **18B2**
Norfolk Ridge *Pacific O* **105G5**
Noril'sk *USSR* **1C10**
Normal *USA* **18C1**
Norman *USA* **19A2**
Normandie, Region *France* **48B2**
Normanton *Aust* **107D2**
Norman Wells *Can* **12J1**
Norne *USA* **4B3**
Norristown *USA* **15C2**
Norrköping *Sweden* **39H7**
Norrsundet *Sweden* **39H6**
Norrtälje *Sweden* **39H7**
Norseman *Aust* **106B4**
Norsk *USSR* **63F2**
North, S *N W Europe* **102J2**
Northallerton *Eng* **42D2**
Northam *Aust* **106A4**
North American Basin *Atlantic O* **102E3**
Northampton *Aust* **106A3**
Northampton, County *Eng* **43D3**
Northampton *Eng* **43D3**
Northampton *USA* **15D2**
North Arm, B *Can* **4G3**
North Augusta *USA* **17B1**
North Aulatsvik, I *Can* **6D4**
North Battleford *Can* **13F2**
North Bay *Can* **7C5**
North Bend *USA* **20B2**
North Berwick *Scot* **44C3**
North,C *Can* **7D5**
North C *NZ* **7G4**
North Carolina, State *USA* **11B3**
North Cascade Nat Pk *USA* **20B1**
North Chan *Can* **14B1**
North Chan *Ire/Scot* **42B2**
North Dakota, State *USA* **8C2**
North Downs *Eng* **43E4**
North East *USA* **14C2**
North East Atlantic Basin *Atlantic O* **102H2**
Northeast C *USA* **4B3**
Northern Ireland *UK* **40B3**
Northern Range, Mts *Trinidad* **27L1**
Northern Territory *Aust* **106C2**
North Esk, R *Scot* **44C3**
Northfield, Massachusetts *USA* **16C1**
North Fork, R *USA* **12D2**
North I *NZ* **110B1**
North Korea, Republic *S E Asia* **74B3**
North Little Rock *USA* **19B3**
North Magnetic Pole *Can* **1B4**
North Miami *USA* **17B2**
North Miami Beach *USA* **17B2**
North Platte *USA* **8C2**
North Platte, R *USA* **8C2**
North Pt *Barbados* **27R3**
North Pt *USA* **14B1**
North Rona, I *Scot* **40B2**
North Ronaldsay, I *Scot* **44C2**
North Saskatchewan, R *Can* **13F2**
North Sea *N W Europe* **40D2**
North Slope, Region *USA* **4D3**
North Stradbroke, I *Aust* **109D1**
North Taranaki Bight, B *NZ* **110B1**
North Truchas Peak, Mt *USA* **9C3**
North Uist, I *Scot* **44A3**
Northumberland, County *Eng* **42C2**
Northumberland Is *Aust* **107E3**
Northumberland Str *Can* **7D5**
North Vancouver *Can* **20B1**
North Walsham *Eng* **43E3**
Northway *USA* **12F2**
North West C *Aust* **106A3**
North West Frontier, Province *Pak* **84C2**
North West River *Can* **7D4**
North West Territories *Can* **4F3**
North York Moors Nat Pk *Eng* **42D2**
Norton B *USA* **12B2**
Norton Sd *USA* **12B2**
Norvegia,C *Ant* **112B1**
Norwalk, Connecticut *USA* **16C2**
Norwalk, Ohio *USA* **14B2**
Norway, Kingdom *Europe* **39F6**
Norway House *Can* **5J4**
Norwegian B *Can* **6A2**
Norwegian Basin *Norewegian S* **102H1**
Norwegian S *N W Europe* **64A3**
Norwich, Connecticut *USA* **16C2**
Norwich *Eng* **43E3**
Norwood, Massachusetts *USA* **16D1**
Norwood, Ohio *USA* **14B3**
Nos Emine, C *Bulg* **54C2**
Noshiro *Japan* **74D2**
Nos Kaliakra, C *Bulg* **54C2**
Noss, I *Scot* **44D1**
Nostrābād *Iran* **91D4**
Nosy Barren, I *Madag* **101D2**
Nosy Bé, I *Madag* **101D2**
Nosy Boraha, I *Madag* **101E2**
Nosy Varika *Madag* **101D3**
Notéc, R *Pol* **58B2**
Notikeuin *Can* **5G4**
Noto *Italy* **53C3**
Notodden *Nor* **39F7**
Noto-hantō, Pen *Japan* **75B1**
Notre Dams B *Can* **7E5**
Nottingham, County *Eng* **43D3**
Nottingham *Eng* **43D3**
Nottingham, I *Can* **6C3**
Nottingham Island *Can* **6C3**
Nouadhibou *Maur* **96A2**
Nouakchott *Maur* **97A3**
Nouméa *Nouvelle Calédonie* **107F3**
Nouna *U Volta* **97B3**
Nouveau Comptoir *Can* **7C4**
Nouvelle Anvers *Zaïre* **98B2**
Nouvelle Calédonie, I *S W Pacific O* **107F3**
Nova Caipemba *Angola* **98B3**
Nova Chaves *Angola* **100B2**
Nova Esparança *Brazil* **35A2**
Nova Friburgo *Brazil* **35C2**
Nova Gaia *Angola* **100A2**
Nova Granada *Brazil* **35B2**
Nova Horizonte *Brazil* **35B2**
Nova Lima *Brazil* **35C1**
Nova Londrina *Brazil* **35A2**
Nova Mambone *Mozam* **101C3**
Novara *Italy* **47C2**
Nova Scotia, Province *Can* **7D5**
Novato *USA* **22A1**
Nova Venécia *Brazil* **35C1**
Novaya Kakhovka *USSR* **60D4**
Novaya Zemlya, I *Barents S* **64G2**
Nova Zagora *Bulg* **54C2**
Novo Russas *Brazil* **31C2**
Nové Zámky *Czech* **54A1**
Novgorod *USSR* **60D2**
Novi Ligure *Italy* **47C2**
Novi Pazar *Bulg* **54C2**
Novi Pazar *Yugos* **54B2**
Novi Sad *Yugos* **54A1**
Novoalekseyevka *USSR* **61J3**
Novoanninskiy *USSR* **61F3**
Novocherkassk *USSR* **61E4**
Novograd Volynskiy *USSR* **60C3**
Novogrudok *USSR* **58D2**
Novo Hamburgo *Brazil* **30F4**
Novokazalinsk *USSR* **65H5**
Novokuznetsk *USSR* **65K4**
Novolazarevskaya, Base *Ant* **112B12**
Novo Mesto *Yugos* **52C1**
Novomoskovsk *USSR* **60E3**
Novorossiysk *USSR* **60E5**
Novosibirsk *USSR* **65K4**
Novosibirskye Ostrova I *USSR* **1B8**
Novotroitsk *USSR* **61J3**
Novo Uzensk *USSR* **61G3**
Novovolynsk *USSR* **59C2**
Novo Vyatsk *USSR* **61G2**
Novozybkov *USSR* **60D3**
Novyy Port *USSR* **64J3**
Novy Dwór Mazowiecki *Pol* **58C2**
Novyy Lyalya *USSR* **61K2**
Novyy Port *USSR* **64J3**
Novyy Uzem *USSR* **61H5**
Nowa Sól *Pol* **58B2**
Nowata *USA* **18A2**
Nowgong *India* **86C1**
Nowitna, R *USA* **12D2**
Nowra *Aust* **109D2**
Now Shahr *Iran* **90B2**
Nowshera *Pak* **84C2**
Nowy Sącz *Pol* **59C3**
Noyes I *USA* **12H3**
Noyon *France* **46B2**
Nsawam *Ghana* **97B4**
Nuba, Mts *Sudan* **99D1**
Nubian Desert *Sudan* **81B3**
Nuble, R *Chile* **34A3**
Nueces, R *USA* **9D4**
Nueltin L *Can* **5J3**
Nueva Gerona *Cuba* **26A2**
Nueva Imperial *Chile* **34A3**
Nueva Laredo *Mexico* **9C4**
Nueva Palmira *Urug* **34D2**
Nueva Rosita *Mexico* **24B2**
Nuevitas *Cuba* **26B2**
Nuevo Casas Grandes *Mexico* **24B1**
Nuevo Laredo *Mexico* **24C2**
Nugaal, Region *Somalia* **99E2**
Nûgâtsiaq *Greenland* **6E2**
Nugssuag, Pen *Greenland* **6E2**
Nûgussaq, I *Greenland* **6E2**
Nui Con Voi, R *Vietnam* **73A5**
Nukey Bluff, Mt *Aust* **108A2**
Nukhayb *Iraq* **93D3**
Nukus *USSR* **65G5**
Nulato *USA* **12C2**
Nullarbor Plain *Aust* **106B4**
Numan *Nig* **97D4**
Numata *Japan* **75B1**
Numatinna, R *Sudan* **98C2**
Numazu *Japan* **74D3**
Numfoor, I *Indon* **71E4**
Numurkah *Aust* **108C3**
Nunapitchuk *USA* **12B2**
Nunkun, Mt *India* **84D2**
Nuoro *Sardegna* **53A2**
Nurābād *Iran* **91B3**
Nure, R *Italy* **47C2**
Nuriootpa *Aust* **108A2**

Nuristan, Upland *Afghan* **84C1**
Nurlat *USSR* **61H3**
Nurmes *Fin* **38K6**
Nürnberg *W Germ* **57C3**
Nurri,Mt *Aust* **108C2**
Nusaybin *Turk* **93D2**
Nushagak, R *USA* **12C3**
Nushagak B *USA* **12C3**
Nushagak Pen *USA* **12C3**
Nushki *Pak* **84B3**
Nutak *Can* **7D4**
Nutzotin Mts *USA* **12F2**
Nuwakot *Nepal* **86A1**
Nuwara-Eliya *Sri Lanka* **87C3**
Nuyukjuak *Can* **6C3**
Nyack *USA* **16C2**
Nyahururu *Kenya* **99D2**
Nyah West *Aust* **108B3**
Nyai *USA* **4C3**
Nyainqentanglha Shan Mts *China* **68B3**
Nyakabindi *Tanz* **99D3**
Nyala *Sudan* **98C1**
Nyalam *China* **86B1**
Nyamlell *Sudan* **98C2**
Nyanda *Zim* **100C3**
Nyandoma *USSR* **64F3**
Nyanga, R *Gabon* **98B3**
Nyasa L *Malawi/ Mozam* **101C2**
Nyaunglebin *Burma* **76B2**
Nyazepetrovsk *USSR* **61J2**
Nyborg *Den* **39G7**
Nybro *Sweden* **39H7**
Nyda *USSR* **64J3**
Nyeboes Land, Region *Can* **6D1**
Nyeri *Kenya* **99D3**
Nyimba *Zambia* **101C2**
Nyingchi *China* **82D3**
Nyíregyháza *Hung* **59C3**
Nyiru,Mt *Kenya* **99D2**
Nykarleby *Fin* **38J6**
Nykøbing *Den* **39F7**
Nykøbing *Den* **39G8**
Nyköping *Sweden* **39H7**
Nylstroom *S Africa* **100B3**
Nymagee *Aust* **109C2**
Nynäshamn *Sweden* **39H7**
Nyngan *Aust* **109C2**
Nyon *Switz* **47B1**
Nyong, R *Cam* **98B2**
Nyons *France* **49D3**
Nysa *Pol* **59B2**
Nyssa *USA* **20C2**
Nyurba *USSR* **63D1**
Nzega *Tanz* **99D3**
Nzérékore *Guinea* **97B4**

O

Oaggsimiut *Greenland* **6F3**
Oahe Res *USA* **8C2**
Oahu, I *Hawaiian Is* **21C4**
Oakbank *Aust* **108B2**
Oakdale *USA* **22B2**
Oakey *Aust* **109D1**
Oakland, California *USA* **21A2**
Oakland, Oregon *USA* **20B2**
Oakland City *USA* **14A3**
Oak Lawn *USA* **14A2**
Oakley, California *USA* **22B2**
Oakridge *USA* **20B2**
Oakville *Can* **14C2**
Oamaru *NZ* **111B3**
Oates Land, Region *Ant* **112B7**
Oatlands *Aust* **109C4**
Oaxaca *Mexico* **23B2**
Oaxaca, State *Mexico* **23B2**
Ob', R *USSR* **65J3**
Obama *Japan* **75B1**
Oban *NZ* **111A3**
Oban *Scot* **44B3**
Obanazawa *Japan* **75C1**
Oberammergau *W Germ* **47D1**
Oberhausen *W Germ* **46D1**
Oberstdorf *W Germ* **47D1**
Obi, I *Indon* **71D4**
Obidos *Brazil* **33F4**
Obihiro *Japan* **74E2**
Obo *CAR* **98C2**
Obock *Djibouti* **99E1**
Oborniki *Pol* **58B2**
Oboyan *USSR* **60E3**
O'Brien *USA* **20B2**
Obshchiy Syrt, Mts *USSR* **61H3**
Obskava Guba, B *USSR* **64J3**
Obuasi *Ghana* **97B4**
Ocala *USA* **17B2**
Ocana *Colombia* **32C2**
Ocaño *Spain* **50B2**
Ocean C *USA* **12G3**
Ocean City, Maryland *USA* **15C3**
Ocean City, New Jersey *USA* **16B3**
Ocean Falls *Can* **5F4**
Oceanside *USA* **22D4**
Ocean Springs *USA* **19C3**
Ocher *USSR* **61H2**
Ochil Hills *Scot* **44C3**
Ochlockonee, R *USA* **17B1**
Ocho Rios *Jamaica* **27H1**
Ocmulgee, R *USA* **17B1**
Oconee, R *USA* **17B1**
Oconto *USA* **14A2**
Ocotlán, Jalisco *Mexico* **23A1**
Ocotlán, Oaxaca *Mexico* **23B2**
Oda *Ghana* **97B4**
Oda *Japan* **75A1**
Ódáðahraun, Region *Iceland* **38B2**
Odate *Japan* **74E2**
Odawara *Japan* **74D3**
Odda *Nor* **39F6**
Odemira *Port* **50A2**
Ödemiş *Turk* **55C3**
Odendaalsrus *S Africa* **101G1**
Odense *Den* **39G7**
Oder, R *Pol/E Germ* **56C2**
Odessa, Texas *USA* **9C3**
Odessa *USSR* **60D4**
Odessa, Washington *USA* **20C1**
Odienné *Ivory Coast* **97B4**
Odra, R *Pol* **59B2**
Oeiras *Brazil* **31C3**
Ofanto, R *Italy* **53C2**
Ofaqim *Israel* **94B3**
Offaly, County *Irish Rep* **45C2**
Offenbach *W Germ* **49D1**
Offenburg *W Germ* **49D2**
Oga *Japan* **74D3**
Ogaden, Region *Eth* **99E2**
Ogaki *Japan* **74D3**
Ogallala *USA* **8C2**
Ogasawara Gunto, Is *Japan* **69G4**
Ogbomosho *Nig* **97C4**
Ogden, Utah *USA* **8B2**
Ogdensburg *USA* **15C2**
Ogeechee, R *USA* **17B1**
Ogilvie *Can* **12G1**
Ogilvie Mts *Can* **4E3**
Oglethorpe,Mt *USA* **17B1**
Oglio, R *Italy* **47D2**
Ognon, R *France* **47B1**
Ogoja *Nig* **97C4**
Ogooué, R *Gabon* **98A3**
Ogre *USSR* **58C1**
Oguilet Khenachich, Well *Mali* **96B2**
Ogulin *Yugos* **52C1**
Ohai *NZ* **111A3**
Ohakune *NZ* **110C1**
Ohanet *Alg* **96C2**
Ohau,L *NZ* **111A2**
Ohio, State *USA* **10B2**
Ohio, R *USA* **14A3**
Ohopoho *Namibia* **100A2**
Ohre, R *Czech* **57C2**
Ohrid *Yugos* **55B2**
Ohridsko Jezero, L *Yugos/Alb* **55B2**
Ohura *NZ* **110B1**
Oiapoque *French Guiana* **33G3**
Oijiaojing *China* **68B2**
Oil City *USA* **14C2**
Oildale *USA* **21B2**
Oise, Department *France* **46B2**
Oise, R *France* **49C2**
Ōita *Japan* **74C4**
Ojai *USA* **22C3**
Ojinaga *Mexico* **24B2**
Ojitlán *Mexico* **23B2**
Ojiya *Japan* **75B1**
Ojos del Salado, Mt *Arg* **30C4**
Ojueloz *Mexico* **23A1**
Oka, R *USSR* **60E3**
Okahandja *Namibia* **100A3**
Okanagan Falls *Can* **20C1**
Okanagan L *Can* **13D2**
Okanogan *USA* **20C1**
Okanogan, R *USA* **20C1**
Okanogan Range, Mts *Can/USA* **20B1**
Okara *Pak* **84C2**
Okavango, R *Namibia/ Angola* **100A2**
Okavango Delta, Marsh *Botswana* **100B2**
Okaya *Japan* **74D3**
Okayama *Japan* **74C4**
Okazaki *Japan* **75B2**
Okeechobee *USA* **17B2**
Okeechobee,L *USA* **17B2**
Okefenokee Swamp *USA* **17B1**
Okene *Nig* **97C4**
Okha *India* **85B4**
Okha *USSR* **69G1**
Okhaldunga *Nepal* **86B1**
Okinawa, I *Japan* **69E4**
Okinawa gunto, Arch *Japan* **69E4**
Oki-shoto, Is *Japan* **74C3**
Oklahoma, State *USA* **9D3**
Oklahoma City *USA* **18A2**
Okmulgee *USA* **18A2**
Okondja *Gabon* **98B3**
Okoyo *Congo* **98B3**
Okpara, R *Nig* **97C4**
Oktyabr'sk *USSR* **61J4**
Oktyabr'skiy, Bashkirskaya *USSR* **61H3**
Okushiri-tō, I *Japan* **74D2**
Olafsvik *Iceland* **38A2**
Öland, I *Sweden* **39H7**
Olary *Aust* **108B2**
Olathe *USA* **18B2**
Olavarría *Arg* **29D3**
Olbia *Sardegna* **53A2**
Old Crow *Can* **12G1**
Oldenburg, Niedersachsen *W Germ* **56B2**
Oldenburg, Schleswig-Holstein *W Germ* **56C2**
Old Forge *USA* **15C2**
Oldham *Eng* **42C3**
Old Harbor *USA* **12D3**
Old Head of Kinsale, C *Scot* **41B3**
Old Lyme *USA* **16C2**
Olds *Can* **13E2**
Olean *USA* **15C2**
Olekma, R *USSR* **63E2**
Olekminsk *USSR* **63D1**
Olenegorsk *USSR* **38L5**
Olevsk *USSR* **58D2**
Ol'ga *USSR* **69F2**
Olifants, R *Namibia* **100A3**
Ólimbos, Mt *Greece* **55B2**
Olímpia *Brazil* **35B2**
Olinala *Mexico* **23B2**
Olinda *Brazil* **31E3**
Oliva *Arg* **34C2**
Olivares, Mt *Arg* **29C2**
Oliveira *Brazil* **35C2**
Oliver *Can* **13D3**
Ollague *Chile* **30C3**
Ollagüe, Mt *Bol* **30C3**
Olney *USA* **18C2**
Olochi *USSR* **68E1**
Olofstrom *Sweden* **39G7**
Olombo *Congo* **98B3**
Olomouc *Czech* **59B3**
Olonets *USSR* **60D1**
Olongapo *Phil* **79B3**
Oloron Ste Marie *France* **48B3**
Olovyannaya *USSR* **68D1**
Olpe *W Germ* **46D1**
Olsztyn *Pol* **58C2**
Olten *Switz* **47B1**
Oltul, R *Rom* **54B2**
Olympia *USA* **20B1**
Olympic Nat Pk *USA* **20B1**
Olympus,Mt *USA* **20B1**
Omachi *Japan* **75B1**
Omae-zaki, C *Japan* **75B2**
Omagh *N Ire* **45C1**
Omaha *USA* **18A1**
Omak *USA* **20C1**
Oman, Sultanate *Arabian Pen* **91C5**
Oman,G of *UAE* **91C4**
Omboué *Gabon* **98A3**
Omdurman *Sudan* **99D1**
Ometepec *Mexico* **23B2**
Omineca, R *Can* **13B1**
Omineca Mts *Can* **13B1**
Omiya *Japan* **75B1**
Ommaney,C *USA* **12H3**
Ommanney B *Can* **4H2**
Omo, R *Eth* **99D2**
Omsk *USSR* **65J4**
Omura *Japan* **74B4**
Ōmuta *Japan* **74C4**
Omutninsk *USSR* **61H2**
Onang *Indon* **78D3**
Onaping L *Can* **14B1**
Oncócua *Angola* **100A2**
Ondangua *Namibia* **100A2**
Ondava, R *Czech* **59C3**
Öndörhaan *Molgolia* **68D2**
One and Half Degree Chan *Indian O* **83B5**
Onega *USSR* **64E3**
Oneida L *USA* **15C2**
O'Neill *USA* **8D2**
Onekotan, I *USSR* **69H2**
Onema *Zaïre* **98C3**
Oneonta *USA* **15D2**
Onezhskoye Ozero, L *USSR* **64E3**
Ongiva *Angola* **100A2**
Ongjin *N Korea* **74B3**
Ongniud Qi *China* **72D1**
Ongole *India* **87C1**
Onieda L *USA* **15C2**
Onilahy, R *Madag* **101D3**
Onitsha *Nig* **97C4**
Onjüül *Mongolia* **68C2**
Ono *Japan* **75B1**
Ōnohara-jima, I *Japan* **75B2**
Onomichi *Japan* **74C4**
Onslow *Aust* **106A3**
Onslow B *USA* **17C1**
Ontake-san, Mt *Japan* **75B1**
Ontario, California *USA* **22D3**
Ontario, Oregon *USA* **20C2**
Ontario, Province *Can* **7A4**
Ontario,L *USA/Can* **15C2**
Onteniente *Spain* **51B2**
Oodnadatta *Aust* **106C3**
Ooldea *Aust* **106C4**

Oologah L *USA* **18A2**
Oostende *Belg* **46B1**
Oosterschelde, Estuary *Neth* **46B1**
Ootacamund *India* **87B2**
Ootsa L *Can* **13B2**
Opala *USSR* **69H1**
Opala *Zaïre* **98C3**
Opanake *Sri Lanka* **87C3**
Oparino *USSR* **61G2**
Opava *Czech* **59B3**
Opelika *USA* **17A1**
Opelousas *USA* **19B3**
Ophir *USA* **12C2**
Opochka *USSR* **58D1**
Opole *Pol* **59B2**
Opotiki *NZ* **110C1**
Opp *USA* **17A1**
Oppdal *Nor* **38F6**
Opunake *NZ* **110B1**
Oradea *Rom* **54B1**
Oraefajökull, Mts *Iceland* **38B2**
Orai *India* **85D3**
Oran *Alg* **96B1**
Orán *Arg* **30D3**
Orange *Aust* **109C2**
Orange, California *USA* **22D4**
Orange *France* **49C3**
Orange, Texas *USA* **19B3**
Orange, R *S Africa* **100A3**
Orangeburg *USA* **17B1**
Orange Free State, Province *S Africa* **101G1**
Orange Park *USA* **17B1**
Orangeville *Can* **14B2**
Oranienburg *E Germ* **56C2**
Oras *Phil* **79C3**
Orăstie *Rom* **54B1**
Oravita *Rom* **54B1**
Orbetello *Italy* **52B2**
Orbost *Aust* **109C3**
Orchies *France* **46B1**
Orco, R *Italy* **47B2**
Ord, R *Aust* **106B2**
Ord,Mt *Aust* **106B2**
Ordu *Turk* **93C1**
Ordzhonikidze *USSR* **61F5**
Örebro *Sweden* **39H7**
Oregon, State *USA* **8A2**
Oregon *USA* **14B2**
Oregon City *USA* **20B1**
Oregrund *Sweden* **39H6**
Orekhovo Zuyevo *USSR* **60E2**
Orel *USSR* **60E3**
Orenburg *USSR* **61H3**
Orense *Arg* **34D3**
Orense *Spain* **50A1**
Oresund, Str *Den/Sweden* **56C1**
Oreti, R *NZ* **111A3**
Orhaneli, R *Turk* **55C3**
Orhon Gol, R *Mongolia* **68C2**
Oriental *Mexico* **23B2**
Orientos *Aust* **108B1**
Orihuela *Spain* **51B2**
Orillia *Can* **15C2**
Orinoco, R *Ven* **33E2**
Orissa, State *India* **86A2**
Oristano *Sardegna* **53A3**
Orivesi, L *Fin* **38K6**
Oriximina *Brazil* **33F4**
Orizaba *Mexico* **23B2**
Orizona *Brazil* **35B1**
Orkney, I *Scot* **44C2**
Orlândia *Brazil* **35B2**
Orlando *USA* **17B2**
Orléanais, Region *France* **48C2**
Orléans *France* **48C2**
Orlik *USSR* **63B2**
Ormara *Pak* **82A3**
Ormoc *Phil* **79B3**
Ormond Beach *USA* **17B2**
Ornain, R *France* **46C2**
Ornans *France* **47B1**
Orne, R *France* **48B2**
Örnsköldsvik *Sweden* **38H6**
Orocué *Colombia* **32C3**
Oron *Israel* **94B3**
Oroquieta *Phil* **79B4**
Orosháza *Hung* **59C3**
Oroville, California *USA* **21A2**
Oroville, Washington *USA* **20C1**
Orsières *Switz* **47B1**
Orsk *USSR* **65G4**
Ørsta *Nor* **38F6**
Orthez *France* **48B3**
Ortigueira *Spain* **50A1**
Ortles, Mts *Italy* **47D1**
Ortoire, R *Trinidad* **27L1**
Oruro *Bol* **30C2**
Osa *USSR* **61J2**
Osage, R *USA* **18B2**
Osaka *Japan* **75B1**
Osa,Pen de *Costa Rica* **25D4**
Osceola, Arkansas *USA* **18C2**
Osceola, Iowa *USA* **18B1**
Osgood Mts *USA* **20C2**
Oshawa *Can* **15C2**
Ō-shima, I *Japan* **75B2**
Oshkosh *USA* **10B2**
Oshogbo *Nig* **97C4**
Oshosh *USA* **7B5**
Oshwe *Zaïre* **98B3**
Osijek *Yugos* **54A1**
Osinniki *USSR* **65K5**
Osipovichi *USSR* **58D2**
Oskaloosa *USA* **18B1**
Oskarshamn *Sweden* **60A2**
Oslo *Nor* **39G7**
Osmaniye *Turk* **92C2**
Osnabrück *W Germ* **56B2**
Osório *Brazil* **30F4**
Osorno *Chile* **29B4**
Osorno *Spain* **50B1**
Osoyoos *Can* **20C1**
Ospika, R *Can* **13C1**
Ossa,Mt *Aust* **107D5**
Ossining *USA* **16C2**
Ostashkov *USSR* **60D2**
Østerdalen, V *Nor* **38G6**
Östersund *Sweden* **38G6**
Ostfriesische Inseln, Is *W Germ* **56B2**
Östhammär *Sweden* **39H6**
Ostia *Italy* **53B2**
Ostiglia *Italy* **47D2**
Ostrava *Czech* **59B3**
Ostróda *Pol* **58B2**
Ostroleka *Pol* **58B2**
Ostrov *USSR* **60C2**
Ostrov Belyy, I *USSR* **64J2**
Ostrov Green Bell, I *Barents S* **64H1**
Ostrov Kolguyev, I *USSR* **64F3**
Ostrov Kunashir, I *USSR* **74F2**
Ostrov Mechdusharskiy, I *Barents S* **64F2**
Ostrov Ogurchinskiy, I *USSR* **90B2**
Ostrov Rudol'fa, I *Barents S* **64G1**
Ostrov Vaygach, I *USSR* **64G2**
Ostrov Vrangelya, I *USSR* **1B7**
Ostrów *Pol* **58B2**
Ostrowiec *Pol* **59C2**
Ostrów Mazowiecka *Pol* **58C2**
Osuna *Spain* **50A2**
Osweg *USA* **15C2**
Oswego *USA* **15C2**
Oswestry *Eng* **43C3**
Oświęcim *Pol* **59B2**
Ota *Japan* **75B1**
Otago Pen *NZ* **111B3**
Otaki *NZ* **110C2**
Otaru *Japan* **74E2**
Otavalo *Ecuador* **32B3**
Otavi *Namibia* **100A2**
Otawara *Japan* **75C1**
Othello *USA* **20C1**
Óthris, Mt *Greece* **55B3**
Otis, Massachusetts *USA* **16C1**
Otish Mts *Can* **10C1**
Otisville *USA* **16B2**
Otjiwarongo *Namibia* **100A3**
Otog Qi *China* **72B2**
Otorohanga *NZ* **110C1**
Otranto *Italy* **55A2**
Otranto,Str of, Chan *Italy/Alb* **55A2**
Otsego *USA* **14A2**
Otsu *Japan* **75B1**
Otta *Nor* **39F6**
Otta, R *Nor* **39F7**
Ottawa *Can* **15C1**
Ottawa, Kansas *USA* **18A2**
Ottawa, R *Can* **15C1**
Ottawa Is *Can* **7B4**
Otter Rapids *Can* **7B4**
Otto Fjord *Can* **6B1**
Ottosdal *S Africa* **101G1**
Ottumwa *USA* **18B1**
Ottweiler *W Germ* **46D2**
Oturkpo *Nig* **97C4**
Otusco *Peru* **32B5**
Otway,C *Aust* **108B3**
Otwock *Pol* **58C2**
Ötz *Austria* **47D1**
Otzal, Mts *Austria* **47D1**
Ou, R *Laos* **76C1**
Ouachita, R *USA* **19B3**
Ouachita,L *USA* **19B3**
Ouachita Mts *USA* **19B3**
Ouadane *Maur* **96A2**
Ouadda *CAR* **98C2**
Ouaddai, Desert Region *Chad* **98C1**
Ouagadougou *U Volta* **97B3**
Ouahigouya *U Volta* **97B3**
Ouaka *CAR* **98C2**
Oualam *Niger* **97C3**
Ouallen *Alg* **96C2**
Ouanda Djallé *CAR* **98C2**
Ouarane, Region *Maur* **96A2**
Ouargla *Alg* **96C1**
Ouarra, R *CAR* **98C2**
Ouarzazate *Mor* **96B1**
Ouassel, R *Alg* **51C2**
Oubangui, R *Congo* **98B2**
Oudenaarde *Belg* **46B1**
Oudtshoorn *S Africa* **100B4**
Oued Tlělat *Alg* **51B2**
Oued Zem *Mor* **96B1**
Ouesso *Congo* **98B2**
Ouezzane *Mor* **96B1**
Ouham, R *Chad* **98B2**
Ouidah *Benin* **97C4**
Oujda *Mor* **96B1**
Oulainen *Fin* **38J6**
Oulu *Fin* **38K5**
Oulu, R *Fin* **38K6**
Oulujärvi, L *Fin* **38K6**
Oum Chalouba *Chad* **95B3**
Oum Hadjer *Chad* **98B1**
Oum Haouach, Watercourse *Chad* **95B3**
Ounas, R *Fin* **38K5**
Ounianga Kébir *Chad* **95B3**
Our, R *W Germ* **46D1**
Ourcq, R *France* **46B2**
Ouricurí *Brazil* **31C3**
Ourinhos *Brazil* **35B2**
Ouro Prêto *Brazil* **35C2**
Ourthe, R *Belg* **46C1**
Ouse, R *Eng* **42D2**
Ouse, R *Eng* **43E3**
Outer Hebrides, Is *Is* **40B2**
Outer Santa Barbara, Chan *USA* **22C4**
Outjo *Namibia* **100A3**
Outokumpu *Fin* **38K6**
Ouyen *Aust* **108B3**
Ovada *Italy* **47C2**
Ovalle *Chile* **34A2**
Ovamboland, Region *Namibia* **100A2**
Ova Tyuleni, Is *USSR* **61H5**
Övertorneå *Sweden* **38J5**
Oviedo *Spain* **50A1**
Ovruch *USSR* **60C3**
Ovsyanka *USSR* **63E2**
Owaka *NZ* **111A3**
Owase *Japan* **75B2**
Owensboro *USA* **11B3**
Owens L *USA* **21B2**
Owen Sound *Can* **14B2**
Owen Stanley Range, Mts *PNG* **107D1**
Owerri *Nig* **97C4**
Owo *Nig* **97C4**
Owosso *USA* **14B2**
Owyhee, R *USA* **20C2**
Owyhee Mts *USA* **20C2**
Oxapampa *Peru* **32B6**
Oxelösund *Sweden* **39H7**
Oxford, County *Eng* **43D4**
Oxford *Eng* **43D4**
Oxford, Massachusetts *USA* **16D1**
Oxford, Mississippi *USA* **19C3**
Ox Mts *Irish Rep* **45B1**
Oxnard *USA* **22C3**
Oyama *Japan* **74D3**
Oyen *Can* **13E2**
Oyen *Gabon* **98B2**
Oykel, R *Scot* **44B3**
Øyre *Nor* **39F6**
Oyster B *Aust* **109C4**
Ozamiz *Phil* **79B4**
Ozark *USA* **17A1**
Ozark Plat *USA* **18B2**
Ozarks,L of the *USA* **18B2**
Ózd *Hung* **59C3**
Ozero Alakol, L *USSR* **65K5**
Ozero Balkhash, L *USSR* **65J5**
Ozero Baykal, L *USSR* **63C2**
Ozero Chany, L *USSR* **65J4**
Ozero Chudskoye, L *USSR* **60C2**
Ozero Il'men, L *USSR* **60D2**
Ozero Imandra, L *USSR* **38L5**
Ozero Issyk Kul', L *USSR* **82B1**
Ozero Khanka, L *USSR/China* **69F2**
Ozero Kovdozero, L *USSR* **38L5**
Ozero Kuyto, L *USSR* **38L5**
Ozero Pyaozero, L *USSR* **38L5**
Ozero Tengiz, L *USSR* **65H4**
Ozero Topozero, L *USSR* **38L5**
Ozero Zaysan *USSR* **65K5**
Ozuluama *Mexico* **23B1**

P

Paarl *S Africa* **100A4**
Pabbay, I *Scot* **44A3**
Pabianice *Pol* **58B2**
Pabna *Bang* **86B2**
Pabrade *USSR* **58D2**
Pacasmayo *Peru* **32B5**
Pachuca *Mexico* **23B1**
Pacific-Antarctic Ridge *Pacific O* **105K6**
Pacific Grove *USA* **22B2**
Pacitan *Indon* **78C4**
Pacuí, R *Brazil* **35C1**
Padang *Indon* **70B4**
Paderborn *W Germ* **56B2**
Padlei *Can* **5J3**
Padma, R *Bang* **86C2**

Padova *Italy* **47D2**
Padre I *USA* **9D4**
Padstow *Eng* **43B4**
Padthaway *Aust* **108B3**
Paducah, Kentucky *USA* **14A3**
Paducah *USA* **11B3**
Padunskoye More, L *USSR* **38L5**
Paengnyŏng-do, I *S Korea* **74A3**
Paeroa *NZ* **110C1**
Pafuri *Mozam* **100C3**
Pag, I *Yugos* **52B2**
Pagadian *Phil* **79B4**
Pagai Selatan, I *Indon* **70B4**
Pagai Utara, I *Indon* **70B4**
Pagan, I *Pacific O* **71F2**
Pagatan *Indon* **78D3**
Pagondhas *Greece* **55C3**
Pahiatua *NZ* **110C2**
Pahoa *Hawaiian Is* **21C4**
Pahokee *USA* **17B2**
Päijänna, L *Fin* **39K6**
Pailola Chan *Hawaiian Is* **21C4**
Painesville *USA* **14B2**
Painted Desert *USA* **9B3**
Paisley *Scot* **42B2**
Paita *Peru* **32A5**
Pajala *Sweden* **38J5**
Pakistan, Republic *Asia* **80E3**
Pak Lay *Laos* **76C2**
Pakokku *Burma* **86D2**
Pakowki L *Can* **13E2**
Pakrac *Yugos* **52C1**
Paks *Hung* **54A1**
Pak Sane *Laos* **76C2**
Pakse *Laos* **76D2**
Pakwach *Uganda* **99D2**
Pala *Chad* **98B2**
Palagruža, I *Yugos* **52C2**
Palaiseau *France* **46B2**
Palangkaraya *Indon* **78C3**
Palani *India* **87B2**
Palanpur *India* **85C4**
Palapye *Botswana* **100B3**
Palatka *USA* **17B2**
Palau Is *Pacific O* **71E3**
Palaw *Burma* **76B3**
Palawan, I *Phil* **79A4**
Palawan Pass *Phil* **79A4**
Palayankottai *India* **87B3**
Paldiski *USSR* **39J7**
Palembang *Indon* **78A3**
Palencia *Spain* **50B1**
Paleokhorio *Cyprus* **94A1**
Palermo *Italy* **53B3**
Palestine, Region *Israel* **94B3**
Palestine *USA* **19A3**
Paletwa *Burma* **86C2**
Pālghāt *India* **87B2**
Pāli *India* **85C3**
Pālitāna *India* **85C4**
Palk Str *India/Sri Lanka* **87B3**
Pallasovka *USSR* **61G3**
Pallastunturi, Mt *Fin* **38J5**
Palliser B *NZ* **111B2**
Palliser,C *NZ* **111C2**
Palma *Mozam* **101D2**
Palma de Mallorca *Spain* **51C2**
Palmares *Brazil* **31D3**
Palmar Sur *Costa Rica* **26A5**
Palmas,C *Lib* **97B4**
Palma Soriano *Cuba* **26B2**
Palm Bay *USA* **17B2**
Palm Beach *USA* **17B2**
Palmdale *USA* **22C3**
Palmeira dos Indos *Brazil* **31D3**
Palmer *USA* **12E2**
Palmer, Base *Ant* **112C3**
Palmer Arch *Ant* **112C3**
Palmer Land, Region *Ant* **112B3**
Palmerston *NZ* **111B3**
Palmerston North *NZ* **110C2**
Palmerton *USA* **16B2**
Palmetto *USA* **17B2**
Palmi *Italy* **53C3**
Palmira *Colombia* **32B3**
Palm Is *Aust* **107D2**
Palm Springs *USA* **21B3**
Palmyra, Missouri *USA* **18B2**
Palmyra, Pennsylvania *USA* **16A2**
Palmyras Pt *India* **86B2**
Palo Alto *USA* **22A2**
Paloh *Indon* **78B2**
Paloích *Sudan* **99D1**
Palomar Mt *USA* **21B3**
Palopo *Indon* **70D4**
Palu *Indon* **70C4**
Palu *Turk* **93C2**
Palwal *India* **84D3**
Pama *U Volta* **97C3**
Pamekasan *Indon* **78C4**
Pameungpeuk *Indon* **78B4**
Pamiers *France* **48C3**
Pamir, Mts *China* **82B2**
Pamir, R *USSR* **65J6**
Pamlico Sd *USA* **11C3**
Pampa *USA* **9C3**
Pampa de la Salinas, Salt pan *Arg* **34B2**
Pampa de la Varita, Plain *Arg* **34B3**
Pamplona *Colombia* **32C2**
Pamplona *Spain* **50B1**
Pana *USA* **18C2**
Panagyurishte *Bulg* **54B2**
Panaji *India* **87A1**
Panamá *Panama* **32B2**
Panama, Republic *C America* **32A2**
Panama Canal *Panama* **26B5**
Panama City *USA* **17A1**
Panamint Range, Mts *USA* **21B2**
Panamint V *USA* **21B2**
Panaro, R *Italy* **47D2**
Panay, I *Phil* **79B3**
Pancevo *Yugos* **54B2**
Pandan *Phil* **79B3**
Pandharpur *India* **87B1**
Pandie Pandie *Aust* **108A1**
Panevežys *USSR* **58C1**
Panfilov *USSR* **65K5**
Pang, R *Burma* **76B1**
Pangani *Tanz* **99D3**
Pangani, R *Tanz* **99D3**
Pangi *Zaïre* **98C3**
Pangkalpinang *Indon* **78B3**
Pangnirtung *Can* **6D3**
Pangtara *Burma* **76B1**
Pangutaran Group, Is *Phil* **79B4**
Panipat *India* **84D3**
Panjao *Afghan* **84B2**
P'anmunjŏm *N Korea* **74B3**
Panna *India* **86A2**
Panorama *Brazil* **35A2**
Pantelleria, I *Medit S* **53B3**
Pantepec *Mexico* **23B1**
Panuco *Mexico* **23B1**
Pánuco, R *Mexico* **23B1**
Pan Xian *China* **73A4**
Paola *Italy* **53C3**
Paola *USA* **18B2**
Paoli *USA* **14A3**
Papa *Hung* **59B3**
Papakura *NZ* **110B1**
Papaloapan, R *Mexico* **23B2**
Papantla *Mexico* **23B1**
Papa Stour, I *Scot* **44D1**
Papatoetoe *NZ* **110B1**
Papa Westray, I *Scot* **44C2**
Papua,G of *PNG* **107D1**
Papua New Guinea, Republic *S E Asia* **107D1**
Papudo *Chile* **34A2**
Papun *Burma* **76B2**
Para, State *Brazil* **33G4**
Pará, R *Brazil* **31B2**
Paraburdoo *Aust* **106A3**
Paracas,Pen de *Peru* **32B6**
Paracatu *Brazil* **35B1**
Paracatu, R *Brazil* **35B1**
Parachilna *Aust* **108A2**
Parachinar *Pak* **84C2**
Paracin *Yugos* **54B2**
Pará de Minas *Brazil* **35C1**
Paradise, California *USA* **21A2**
Paragould *USA* **18B2**
Paraguá, R *Bol* **33E6**
Paragua, R *Ven* **33E2**
Paraguai, R *Brazil* **30E2**
Paraguari *Par* **30E4**
Paraguay, Republic *S America* **30E3**
Paraguay, R *Par* **30E3**
Paraiba, State *Brazil* **31D3**
Paraiba, R *Brazil* **35B2**
Paraíba do Sul, R *Brazil* **35C2**
Parakou *Benin* **97C4**
Parakylia *Aust* **108A2**
Paramakkudi *India* **87B3**
Paramaribo *Surinam* **33F2**
Paramushir, I *USSR* **69H1**
Paraná, State *Brazil* **30F3**
Paraná *Urug* **34C2**
Paraná, R *Arg* **29E2**
Paranã, R *Brazil* **31B4**
Paraná, R *Brazil* **35A2**
Paranaguá *Brazil* **30G4**
Paranaíba *Brazil* **35A1**
Paranaiba, R *Brazil* **35A1**
Paranapanema, R *Brazil* **35A2**
Paranavai *Brazil* **35A2**
Parang *Phil* **79B4**
Paraope, R *Brazil* **35C1**
Paraparaumu *NZ* **110B2**
Parbhani *India* **87B1**
Pardes Hanna *Israel* **94B2**
Pardo *Arg* **34D3**
Pardo, R, Bahia *Brazil* **35D1**
Pardo, R, Mato Grosso do Sul *Brazil* **35A2**
Pardo, R, Minas Gerais *Brazil* **35B1**
Pardo, R, Sao Paulo *Brazil* **35B2**
Pardubice *Czech* **59B2**
Parece Vela, Reef *Pacific O* **69F4**
Parent *Can* **10C2**
Parepare *Indon* **70C4**
Parera *Arg* **34C3**
Pariaman *Indon* **70B4**
Paria,Pen de *Ven* **33E1**
Paris *France* **48C2**
Paris, Kentucky *USA* **14B3**
Paris, Texas *USA* **19A3**
Parkersburg *USA* **14B3**
Parkes *Aust* **109C2**
Parkesburg *USA* **16B3**
Park Forest *USA* **14A2**
Parksville *Can* **20B1**
Parli *India* **87B1**
Parma *Italy* **47D2**
Parma *USA* **14B2**
Parnaiba *Brazil* **31C2**
Parnaiba, R *Brazil* **31C2**
Párnon Óros, Mts *Greece* **55B3**
Pärnu *USSR* **60B2**
Paro *Bhutan* **86B1**
Paroo, R *Aust* **108B1**
Paroo Channel, R *Aust* **108B2**
Páros, I *Greece* **55C3**
Parpaillon, Mts *France* **47B2**
Parral *Chile* **34A3**
Parramatta *Aust* **109D2**
Parras *Mexico* **9C4**
Parry B *Can* **6B3**
Parry Is *Can* **4G2**
Parry Sd *Can* **7C5**
Parry Sound *Can* **14B1**
Parsberg *W Germ* **57C3**
Parsnip, R *Can* **5F4**
Parsons, Kansas *USA* **18A2**
Parsons, West Virginia *USA* **14C3**
Parthenay *France* **48B2**
Partinico *Italy* **53B3**
Partizansk *USSR* **74C2**
Paru, R *Brazil* **33G4**
Parys *S Africa* **101G1**
Pasadena, Texas *USA* **19A4**
Pasadena *USA* **22C3**
Pasangkayu *Indon* **78D3**
Pasawing *Burma* **76B2**
Pascagoula *USA* **19C3**
Paşcani *Rom* **54C1**
Pasco *USA* **20C1**
Pas-de-Calais, Department *France* **46B1**
Pasewalk *W Germ* **39G8**
Pashū'īyeh *Iran* **91C4**
Pasley,C *Aust* **106B4**
Paso de los Toros *Urug* **29E2**
Paso Limay *Arg* **29B4**
Paso Robles *USA* **21A2**
Passage West *Irish Rep* **45B3**
Passaic *USA* **16B2**
Passau *W Germ* **57C3**
Passo de los Libres *Arg* **30E4**
Passo di Stelvio, Mt *Italy* **47D1**
Passo Fundo *Brazil* **30F4**
Passos *Brazil* **35B2**
Passy *France* **47B2**
Pastaza, R *Peru* **32B4**
Pasteur *Arg* **34C3**
Pas,The *Can* **5H4**
Pasto *Colombia* **32B3**
Pastol B *USA* **12B2**
Pasubio, Mt *Italy* **47D2**
Pasuruan *Indon* **78C4**
Pasvalys *USSR* **58C1**
Pātan *India* **85C4**
Patan *Nepal* **86B1**
Patchewollock *Aust* **108B3**
Patea *NZ* **110B1**
Patea, R *NZ* **111B2**
Paterno *Italy* **53B3**
Paterson *USA* **16B2**
Paterson Inlet, B *NZ* **111A3**
Pathankot *India* **84D2**
Patiāla *India* **84D2**
Pativilca *Peru* **32B6**
Pátmos, I *Greece* **55C3**
Patna *India* **86B1**
Patnos *Turk* **93D2**
Patos *Brazil* **31D3**
Patos de Minas *Brazil* **35B1**
Patquia *Arg* **34B2**
Pátrai *Greece* **55B3**
Patrocinio *Brazil* **35B1**
Patta, I *Kenya* **99E3**
Pattallasang *Indon* **78D4**
Pattani *Thai* **77C4**
Patterson, California *USA* **22B2**
Patterson, Louisiana *USA* **19B4**
Patterson,Mt *Can* **12H2**
Patterson Mt *USA* **22C2**
Pattullo,Mt *Can* **13B1**
Patu *Brazil* **31D3**
Patuakhali *Bang* **86C2**
Patuca, R *Honduras* **25D3**
Patzcuaro *Mexico* **23A2**
Pau *France* **48B3**
Paulatuk *Can* **4F3**
Paulistana *Brazil* **31C3**
Paulpietersburg *S Africa* **101H1**

Pauls Valley *USA* **19A3**
Paungde *Burma* **76B2**
Pauri *India* **84D2**
Pauskie *Nor* **38H5**
Pavão *Brazil* **35C1**
Pavia *Italy* **47C2**
Pavlodar *USSR* **65J4**
Pavlovich *USSR* **63E2**
Pavlovka *USSR* **61J2**
Pavlovo *USSR* **61F2**
Pavlovsk *USSR* **61F3**
Pawan, R *Indon* **78C3**
Pawhuska *USA* **18A2**
Pawtucket *USA* **16D2**
Payerne *Switz* **47B1**
Payette *USA* **20C2**
Payne,L *Can* **7C4**
Paysandu *Urug* **34D2**
Pays-de-Bray, Region *France* **46A2**
Pazardzhik *Bulg* **54B2**
Peace, R *Can* **13D1**
Peace, R *USA* **17B2**
Peace River *Can* **13D1**
Peak District Nat Pk *Eng* **43D3**
Peake, R *Aust* **108A1**
Peak Hill *Aust* **109C2**
Peak Mandala, Mt *Indon* **71E4**
Peak,The, Mt *Eng* **42D3**
Pearl, R *USA* **19B3**
Pearl City *Hawaiian Is* **21C4**
Pearl Harbor *Hawaiian Is* **21C4**
Peary Chan *Can* **4H2**
Pebane *Mozam* **101C2**
Peć *Yugos* **54B2**
Peçanha *Brazil* **35C1**
Pecan Island *USA* **19B4**
Pechenga *USSR* **38L5**
Pechorskoye More, S *USSR* **64G3**
Pecoraro, Mt *Italy* **53C3**
Pecos *USA* **9C3**
Pecos, R *USA* **9C3**
Pécs *Hung* **59B3**
Pedirka *Aust* **108A1**
Pedra Azul *Brazil* **35C1**
Pedregulho *Brazil* **35B2**
Pedro Cays, Is *Caribbean* **26B3**
Pedro de Valdivia *Chile* **30C3**
Pedro Juan Caballero *Par* **30E3**
Pedro Luro *Arg* **34C3**
Pedro Mentova *Mexico* **23B1**
Pedro,Pt *Sri Lanka* **87C3**
Peebinga *Aust* **108B2**
Peebles *Scot* **42C2**
Pee Dee, R *USA* **17C1**
Peekskill *USA* **16C2**
Peel *Eng* **42B2**
Peel, R *Can* **12H1**
Peel Sd *Can* **4J2**
Peera Peera Poolanna, L *Aust* **108A1**
Peerless L *Can* **13E1**
Peg Arfak, Mt *Indon* **71E4**
Pegasus B *NZ* **111B2**
Pegu *Burma* **83D4**
Pegunungan Barisan, Mts *Indon* **78A3**
Pegunungan Iran, Mts *Malay Indon* **78C2**
Pegunungan Maoke, Mts *Indon* **71E4**
Pegunungan Meratus, Mts *Indon* **78D3**
Pegunungan Muller, Mts *Indon* **78C2**
Pegunungan Schwanet, Mts *Indon* **78C3**
Pogunungan Tigapuluh, Mts *Indon* **78A3**
Pegu Yoma, Mts *Burma* **76B2**
Pehuajó *Arg* **34C3**
Peixe, R, Sao Paulo *Brazil* **35A2**
Pei Xian *China* **72D3**
Pekalongan *Indon* **78B4**
Pekan *Malay* **77C5**
Pekanbaru *Indon* **78A2**
Pekin *USA* **18C1**
Pelabohan Kelang *Malay* **77C5**
Pelau Pelau Kangean, Is *Indon* **78D4**
Pelau Pelau Karimunjawa, Arch *Indon* **78C4**
Pelau Pelau Postilyon, Is *Indon* **78D4**
Peleaga, Mt *Rom* **54B1**
Peleduy *USSR* **63D2**
Pelee I *Can* **14B2**
Peleng, I *Indon* **71D4**
Pelican *USA* **12G3**
Pellegrini *Arg* **34C3**
Pello *Fin* **38J5**
Pelly, R *Can* **12H2**
Pelly Bay *Can* **6A3**
Pelly Crossing *Can* **12G2**
Pelly Mts *Can* **12H2**
Pelotas *Brazil* **30F5**
Pelotas, R *Brazil* **30F4**
Pelvoux, Region *France* **47B2**
Pemalang *Indon* **78B4**
Pematang *Indon* **78A3**
Pemba *Mozam* **101D2**
Pemba, I *Tanz* **99D3**
Pemberton *Can* **13C2**
Pembina, R *Can* **13D2**
Pembroke *Can* **15C1**
Pembroke *USA* **17B1**
Pembroke *Wales* **43B4**
Pemuco *Chile* **34A3**
Penambo Range, Mts *Malay* **78D2**
Penápolis *Brazil* **35A2**
Peñarroya *Spain* **50A2**
Penarroya, Mt *Spain* **51B1**
Peña Trevina, Mt *Spain* **50A1**
Pende, R *Chad* **98B2**
Pendelton,Mt *Can* **12J3**
Pendleton *USA* **20C1**
Pend Oreille, R *USA* **20C1**
Penedo *Brazil* **31D4**
Penganga, R *India* **85D5**
P'eng hu Lieh tao, Is *Taiwan* **73D5**
Penglai *China* **72E2**
Pengshui *China* **73B4**
Pengunungan Maoke, Mts *Indon* **71E4**
Península de la Guajiri Pen *Colombia* **26C4**
Península de Paria, Pen *Ven* **27E4**
Peninsular Malaysia *Malay* **77C5**
Penjamo *Mexico* **23A1**
Penner, R *India* **87B2**
Pennine Chain, Mts *Eng* **42C2**
Penns Grove *USA* **16B3**
Pennsylvania, State *USA* **10C2**
Penny Highlands, Mts *Can* **6D3**
Penola *Aust* **108B3**
Penong *Aust* **106C4**
Penrith *Eng* **42C2**
Pensacola *USA* **11B3**
Pensacola Mts *Ant* **80E**
Pensiangan *Malay* **78D1**
Penticton *Can* **13D3**
Pentland Firth, Chan *Scot* **44C2**
Pentland Hills *Scot* **42C2**
Penza *USSR* **61G3**
Penzance *Eng* **43B4**
Peoria *USA* **10B2**
Perabumulih *Indon* **78A3**
Perak, R *Malay* **77C5**
Perawang *Indon* **78A2**
Pereira *Colombia* **32B3**
Pereira Barreto *Brazil* **35A2**
Perelazovskiy *USSR* **61F4**
Perenosa B *USA* **12D3**
Pergamino *Arg* **34C2**
Peribonca, R *Can* **7C4**
Périqueux *France* **48C2**
Perlas Arch de, Is *Panama* **25E4**
Perm' *USSR* **61J2**
Pernambuco, State *Brazil* **31D3**
Pernatty Lg *Aust* **108A2**
Pernik *Bulg* **54B2**
Péronne *France* **46B2**
Perote *Mexico* **23B2**
Perpignan *France* **49C3**
Perris *USA* **22D4**
Perry, Florida *USA* **17B1**
Perry, Georgia *USA* **17B1**
Perry, Oklahoma *USA* **18A2**
Perry River *Can* **4H3**
Perrysburg *USA* **14B2**
Perryville, Alaska *USA* **12C3**
Perryville, Missouri *USA* **18C2**
Perth *Aust* **106A4**
Perth *Can* **15C2**
Perth *Scot* **44C3**
Perth Amboy *USA* **16B2**
Peru, Republic *S America* **32C6**
Peru *USA* **18C1**
Peru-Chile Trench *Pacific O* **103E5**
Perugia *Italy* **52B2**
Perušic *Yugos* **52C2**
Pervari *Turk* **93D2**
Pervomaysk, RSFSR *USSR* **61F3**
Pervomaysk, Ukraine SSR *USSR* **60D4**
Pervoural'sk *USSR* **61J2**
Pesaro *Italy* **52B2**
Pescadero *USA* **22A2**
Pescara *Italy* **52B2**
Peschiera *Italy* **47D2**
Peshawar *Pak* **84C2**
Peshkopi *Alb* **54B2**
Peshtigo *USA* **14A1**
Pestovo *USSR* **60E2**
Petah Tiqwa *Israel* **94B2**
Petaluma *USA* **21A2**
Pétange *Lux* **46C2**
Petatlån *Mexico* **23A2**
Petauke *Zambia* **101C2**
Peterborough *Aust* **108A2**
Peterborough *Can* **15C2**
Peterborough *Eng* **43D3**
Peterhead *Scot* **44D3**
Petermann Gletscher, Gl *Greenland* **6D1**
Petermann Range, Mts *Aust* **106B3**
Peteroa, Mt *Chile/Arg* **29B3**
Peter Pond L *Can* **13F1**
Petersburg, Alaska *USA* **12H3**
Petlād *India* **85C4**
Petlalcingo *Mexico* **23B2**
Peto *Mexico* **25D2**
Petomskoye Nagor'ye, Upland *USSR* **63D2**
Petorca *Chile* **34A2**
Petoskey *USA* **14B1**
Petral, Base *Ant* **112C2**
Petrolina *Brazil* **31C3**
Petropavlovsk *USSR* **65H4**
Petrópolis *Brazil* **35C2**
Petrovadovsk *USSR* **64E3**
Petrovsk *USSR* **61G3**
Petrovsk Zabaykal'skiy *USSR* **68C1**
Petrozavodsk *USSR* **64E3**
Petrus *S Africa* **101G1**
Petrusburg *S Africa* **101G1**
Pevek *USSR* **1B7**
Pfälzer Wald, Region *W Germ* **46D2**
Pforzheim *W Germ* **57B3**
Phagwara *India* **84D2**
Phalodi *India* **85C3**
Phalsbourg *France* **46D2**
Phaltan *India* **87A1**
Phangnga *Thai* **77B4**
Phanom Dang, Mts *Camb* **76C3**
Phan Rang *Viet* **76D3**
Phan Thiet *Viet* **76D3**
Phenix City *USA* **17A1**
Phet Buri *Thai* **76B3**
Phiafay *Laos* **76D3**
Philadelphia, Mississippi *USA* **19C3**
Philadelphia, Pennsylvania *USA* **16B2**
Philippeville *Belg* **46C1**
Philippine S *Pacific O* **71D2**
Philippines, Republic *S E Asia* **71D2**
Philippine Trench *Pacific O* **104E3**
Philipsburg, Pennsylvania *USA* **15C2**
Philip Smith Mts *USA* **12E1**
Phillipine S *Phil* **79B2**
Phillips B *Can* **6B1**
Phillipsburg, New Jersey *USA* **16B2**
Philpots Pen *Can* **6B2**
Phnom Penh *Camb* **76C3**
Phoenix, Arizona *USA* **9B3**
Phoenixville *USA* **16B2**
Phong Saly *Laos* **76C1**
Phu Bia, Mt *Laos* **76C2**
Phu Cuong *Viet* **76D3**
Phuket *Thai* **77B4**
Phulbāni *India* **86A2**
Phu Miang, Mt *Thai* **76C2**
Phu Set, Mt *Laos* **76D2**
Phu Tho *Viet* **76D1**
Phu Vinh *Viet* **77D4**
Piacenza *Italy* **47C2**
Pian, R *Aust* **109C2**
Pianosa, I *Italy* **52B2**
Pianosa, I *Italy* **52C2**
Piaseczno *Pol* **58C2**
Piatra-Neamţ *Rom* **54C1**
Piaui, State *Brazil* **31C3**
Piave, R *Italy* **47E2**
Pibor, R *Sudan* **99D2**
Pibor Post *Sudan* **99D2**
Picardie, Region *France* **46B1**
Picayune *USA* **19C3**
Pic de Rochebrune, Mt *France* **47B2**
Pichilemu *Chile* **34A2**
Pichi Mahuida *Arg* **34C3**
Pickering *Eng* **42D2**
Pickle Lake *Can* **7A4**
Pico, I *Açores* **96A1**
Pico Bernina, Mt *Switz* **47C1**
Pico de Anito, Mt *Spain* **51C1**
Pico del Infiernillo, Mt *Mexico* **24B3**
Pico Duarte, Mt *Dom Rep* **27C3**
Picos *Brazil* **31C3**
Picos de Europa, Mt *Spain* **50B1**
Picton *Aust* **109D2**
Picton *NZ* **111B2**
Pic Toussidé, Mt *Chad* **95A2**

Piedade *Brazil* **35B2**
Piedra *USA* **22C2**
Piedras Negras *Mexico* **24B2**
Pieksämäki *Fin* **38K6**
Pielinen, L *Fin* **38K6**
Piemonte, Region *Italy* **47B2**
Pierre *USA* **8C2**
Pieštany *Czech* **59B3**
Pietermaritzburg *S Africa* **101H1**
Pietersburg *S Africa* **100B3**
Piet Retief *S Africa* **101H1**
Pietrosu, Mt *Rom* **60B4**
Pietrosul, Mt *Rom* **54C1**
Pieve di Cadore *Italy* **47E1**
Pigeon L *Can* **13E2**
Piggott *USA* **18B2**
Pigüé *Arg* **34C3**
Pikangikum L *Can* **7A4**
Pikes Peak *USA* **8C3**
Piketberg *S Africa* **100A4**
Pikintaleq *Greenland* **6F3**
Pik Kommunizma, Mt *USSR* **82B2**
Pikounda *Congo* **98B2**
Pik Pobedy, Mt *China/USSR* **82C1**
Pila *Arg* **34D3**
Pila *Pol* **58B2**
Pilar *Par* **30E4**
Pilcomayo, R *Arg/Par* **30D3**
Pīlībhīt *India* **84D3**
Pilica, R *Pol* **59B2**
Pillar,C *Aust* **109C4**
Pílos *Greece* **55B3**
Pilot Point *USA* **12C3**
Pilot Station *USA* **12B2**
Pilottown *USA* **19C3**
Pimenta *Brazil* **33F4**
Pinang, I *Malay* **77C4**
Pinar del Rio *Cuba* **26A2**
Pinas *Arg* **34B2**
Pinche *Belg* **46C1**
Pincher Creek *Can* **13E2**
Pindaré, R *Brazil* **31B2**
Píndhos, Mts *Greece* **55B3**
Pine Bluff *USA* **19B3**
Pine Creek *Aust* **106C2**
Pinecrest *USA* **22C1**
Pinedale, California *USA* **22C2**
Pine Flat Res *USA* **22C2**
Pine Grove *USA* **16A2**
Pine Hills *USA* **17B2**
Pine I *USA* **17B2**
Pineland *USA* **19B3**
Pinellas Park *USA* **17B2**
Pine Point *Can* **5G3**
Pinerolo *Italy* **47B2**
Pines,Lo'the *USA* **19B3**
Pineville *USA* **19B3**
Pingdingshan *China* **72C3**
Pingguo *China* **73B5**
Pingliang *China* **72B2**
Pingluo *China* **72B2**
Pingtan Dao, I *China* **73D4**
P'ing tung *Taiwan* **73E5**
Pingwu *China* **72A3**
Pingxiang, Guangxi *China* **73B5**
Pingxiang, Jiangxi *China* **73C4**
Pinheiro *Brazil* **31B2**
Pini, I *Indon* **70A3**
Piniós, R *Greece* **55B3**
Pinjarra *Aust* **106A4**
Pink Mountain *Can* **13C1**
Pinnaroo *Aust* **108B3**
Pinos,Pt *USA* **21A2**
Pinotepa Nacional *Mexico* **23B2**
Pinrang *Indon* **70C4**
Pinsk *USSR* **60C3**
Pinta, I *Ecuador* **32J7**
Pinyug *USSR* **61G1**
Pioche *USA* **8B3**
Piombino *Italy* **52B2**
Piórsá *Iceland* **6H3**
Piotroków Trybunalski *Pol* **59B2**
Piper, Oilfield *N Sea* **44E2**
Piper Peak, Mt *USA* **21B2**
Pipmuacan Res *Can* **10C2**
Piqua *USA* **14B2**
Piracanjuba *Brazil* **35B1**
Piracicaba *Brazil* **35B2**
Piraçununga *Brazil* **35B2**
Piraí do Sul *Brazil* **35B2**
Piraiévs *Greece* **55B3**
Pirajui *Brazil* **35B2**
Piranhas *Brazil* **35A1**
Pirapora *Brazil* **35C1**
Pirdop *Bulg* **54B2**
Pirenópolis *Brazil* **35B1**
Pires do Rio *Brazil* **35B1**
Pírgos *Greece* **55B3**
Piripiri *Brazil* **31C2**
Pirmasens *W Germ* **46D2**
Pirot *Yugos* **54B2**
Pīr Panjāl Range, Mts *Pak* **84C2**
Piru *Indon* **71D4**
Piru Creek, R *USA* **22C3**
Pisa *Italy* **49E3**
Pisco *Peru* **32B6**
Písek *Czech* **57C3**
Pishin *Pak* **84B2**
Pissis, Mt *Arg* **30C4**
Pistoia *Italy* **49E3**
Pisuerga, R *Spain* **50B1**
Pit, R *USA* **20B2**
Pitalito *Colombia* **32B3**
Pitcairn, I *Pacific O* **105K5**
Pite, R *Sweden* **38H5**
Piteå *Sweden* **38J5**
Pitești *Rom* **54B2**
Pit Gorodok *USSR* **63B2**
Pitkyaranta *USSR* **38L6**
Pitlochry *Scot* **44C3**
Pitrutquén *Chile* **34A3**
Pitt I *Can* **13B2**
Pittsburg, California *USA* **22B1**
Pittsburg, Kansas *USA* **18B2**
Pittsburgh *USA* **14C2**
Pittsfield, Illinois *USA* **18B2**
Pittsfield, Massachusetts *USA* **16C1**
Pittsworth *Aust* **109D1**
Piuthan *Nepal* **86A1**
Pizzo Redorta, Mt *Italy* **47D1**
Pjórsá *Iceland* **38B2**
Pjura *Peru* **32A5**
Placentia B *Can* **7E5**
Placerville *USA* **22B1**
Plaine des Flandres, Plain *France/Belg* **46B1**
Plaine du Tidikelt, Desert, Region **96C2**
Plainview, Texas *USA* **9C3**
Planada *USA* **22B2**
Planalto de Mato Grosso, Plat *Brazil* **30F2**
Planalto do Borborema, Plat *Brazil* **31D3**
Planalto do Mato Grosso, Mts *Brazil* **32A1**
Plano *USA* **19A3**
Plantation *USA* **17B2**
Plant City *USA* **17B2**
Plasencia *Spain* **50A1**
Plast *USSR* **61K3**
Plastun *USSR* **69F2**
Plateau du Tademait *Alg* **96C2**
Plateau Lorrain, Plat *France* **46D2**
Plateaux de Limousin, Plat *France* **48C2**
Plateaux du Sersou, Plat *Alg* **51C2**
Plato *Colombia* **26C5**
Plato Ustyurt, Plat *USSR* **65G5**
Platte, R *USA* **8C2**
Plattsburgh *USA* **15D2**
Plattsmouth *USA* **18A1**
Plauen *E Germ* **57C2**
Plavsk *USSR* **60E3**
Playa Azul *Mexico* **23A2**
Playas *Ecuador* **32A4**
Playa Vicente *Mexico* **23B2**
Plaza de Moro Almanzor, Mt *Spain* **50A1**
Pleasanton, California *USA* **22B2**
Pleasantville *USA* **16B3**
Pleasure Ridge Park *USA* **14A3**
Pleiku *Viet* **76D3**
Plenty,B of *NZ* **110C1**
Pleszew *Pol* **58B2**
Pletipi,L *Can* **7C4**
Pleven *Bulg* **54B2**
Pljevlja *Yugos* **54A2**
Ploče *Yugos* **52C2**
Płock *Pol* **58B2**
Ploërmel *France* **48B2**
Ploiești *Rom* **54C2**
Płońsk *Pol* **60B3**
Plovdiv *Bulg* **54B2**
Plummer *USA* **20C1**
Plummer,Mt *USA* **12C2**
Plumtree *Zim* **100B3**
Plymouth, California *USA* **22B1**
Plymouth *Eng* **43B4**
Plymouth, Indiana *USA* **14A2**
Plymouth, Massachusetts *USA* **16D2**
Plymouth, Pennsylvania *USA* **15C2**
Plymouth Sd *Eng* **43B4**
Plynlimon, Mt *Wales* **43C3**
Plzeň *Czech* **57C3**
Pniewy *Pol* **58B2**
Pnyäselkä, L *Fin* **38K6**
Pô *U Volta* **97B3**
Po, R *Italy* **47E2**
Pobé *Benin* **97C4**
Pobedino *USSR* **69G2**
Pocatello *USA* **8B2**
Pocomoke City *USA* **15C3**
Pocos de Caldas *Brazil* **35B2**
Po di Volano, R *Italy* **47D2**
Podkamennaya, R *USSR* **63B1**
Podolsk *USSR* **60E2**
Podol'skaya Vozvyshennost', Upland *USSR* **59D3**
Podporozh'ye *USSR* **60D1**
Podyuga *USSR* **61F1**
Pofadder *S Africa* **100A3**
P'ohang *S Korea* **74B3**
Poinsett,C *Ant* **112C9**
Point *Aust* **108C2**
Pointe-à-Pitre *Guadeloupe* **27E3**
Pointe de Barfleur, Pt *France* **48B2**
Pointe Noire *Congo* **98B3**
Pointe Pongara, Pt *Gabon* **98A2**
Point Fairy *Aust* **108B3**
Point Fortin *Trinidad* **27L1**
Point Hope *USA* **4B3**
Point L *Can* **4G3**
Point Lay *USA* **12B1**
Point Pleasant, New Jersey *USA* **16B2**
Point Pleasant, W Virginia *USA* **14B3**
Point St Bernard, Mt *France* **47B2**
Poitiers *France* **48C2**
Poitou, Region *France* **48B2**
Poix *France* **46A2**
Pokaran *India* **85C3**
Pokataroo *Aust* **109C1**
Pokrovsk *USSR* **63E1**
Poland, Republic *Europe* **58B2**
Polatli *Turk* **92B2**
Polewali *Indon* **78D3**
Poligny *France* **47A1**
Poliny Osipenko *USSR* **63F2**
Políyiros *Greece* **55B2**
Pollāchi *India* **87B2**
Polollo Is *Phil* **79B3**
Polonnye *USSR* **59D2**
Polotsk *USSR* **58D1**
Poltava *USSR* **60D4**
Pölten *Austria* **52C1**
Poluostrov Kanin, Pen *USSR* **64F3**
Poluostrov Mangyshiak, Pen *USSR* **61H5**
Poluostrov Rybachiy, Pen *USSR* **38L5**
Poluostrov Yamal, Pen *USSR* **64H2**
Polyarnyy, Murmansk *USSR* **38L5**
Polyarnyy, Yakutskaya *USSR* **1B8**
Polynesia, Region *Pacific O* **105H3**
Pomabamba *Peru* **32B5**
Pomba, R *Brazil* **35C2**
Pomona *USA* **22D3**
Pomona Res *USA* **18A2**
Pompano Beach *USA* **17B2**
Pompton Lakes *USA* **16B2**
Ponca City *USA* **18A2**
Ponce *Puerto Rico* **27D3**
Ponce de Leon B *USA* **17B2**
Pondicherry *India* **87B2**
Pond Inlet *Can* **6C2**
Ponferrade *Spain* **50A1**
Pongo, R *Sudan* **98C2**
Pongola, R *S Africa* **101H1**
Ponnāni *India* **87B2**
Ponnyadoung Range, Mts *Burma* **86C2**
Ponoka *Can* **13E2**
Ponoy *USSR* **64F3**
Pons *France* **48B2**
Ponta da Baleia, Pt *Brazil* **35D1**
Ponta Delgada *Açores* **96A1**
Ponta do Padrão, Pt *Angola* **98B3**
Ponta dos Búzios, Pt *Brazil* **35C2**
Ponta Grossa *Brazil* **30F4**
Pontal *Brazil* **35B2**
Pont-à-Mousson *France* **46D2**
Ponta Pora *Brazil* **30E3**
Pontarlier *France* **49D2**
Pontchartrain,L *USA* **19B3**
Pontedera *Italy* **52B2**
Ponte Lecca *Corse* **52A2**
Pontevedra *Spain* **50A1**
Pontiac, Illinois *USA* **18C1**
Pontiac, Michigan *USA* **14B2**
Pontianak *Indon* **78B3**
Pontivy *France* **48B2**
Pontoise *France* **46B2**
Pontotoc *USA* **19C3**
Pontypool *Wales* **43C4**
Pontypridd *Wales* **43C4**
Poole *Eng* **43D4**
Pooncarie *Aust* **108B2**
Poopelloe,L, L *Aust* **108B2**
Poorman *USA* **12C2**
Popayán *Colombia* **32B3**
Poperinge *Belg* **46B1**
Popilta L *Aust* **108B2**
Poplar Bluff *USA* **18B2**
Poplarville *USA* **19C3**
Popndetta *PNG* **107D1**
Popocatepetl, Mt *Mexico* **23B2**
Popokabaka *Zaïre* **98B3**

Popondetta *PNG* 71F4
Popovo *Bulg* 54C2
Porbandar *India* 85B4
Porcher I *Can* 13A2
Porcupine, R *USA/ Can* 12F1
Poreč *Yugos* 52B1
Porecatu *Brazil* 35A2
Pori *Fin* 39J6
Porirua *NZ* 111B2
Porjus *Sweden* 38H5
Poronaysk *USSR* 69G2
Porrentruy *Switz* 47B1
Porsangen, Inlet *Nor* 38K4
Porsgrunn *Nor* 39F7
Portadown *N Ire* 45C1
Portage la Prairie *Can* 8D2
Port Alberni *Can* 13C3
Portalegre *Port* 50A2
Portales *USA* 9C3
Port Alfred *Can* 7C5
Port Alfred *S Africa* 100B4
Port Alice *Can* 13B2
Port Allen *USA* 19B3
Port Angeles *USA* 20B1
Port Antonio *Jamaica* 26B3
Portarlington *Irish Rep* 45C2
Port Arthur *USA* 19B4
Port Augusta *Aust* 108A2
Port-au-Prince *Haiti* 26C3
Port Austin *USA* 14B2
Port Campbell *Aust* 108B3
Port Canning *India* 86B2
Port Cartier *Can* 7D5
Port Chalmers *NZ* 111B3
Port Charlotte *USA* 17B2
Port Chester *USA* 16C2
Port Colborne *Can* 15C2
Port Credit *Can* 15C2
Port Davey *Aust* 109C4
Port-de-Paix *Haiti* 26C3
Port Dickson *Malay* 77C5
Port Edward *S Africa* 100C4
Porteirinha *Brazil* 35C1
Port Elgin *Can* 14B2
Port Elizabeth *S Africa* 100B4
Porter Pt *St Vincent* 27N2
Porterville *USA* 21B2
Port Fairy *Aust* 107D4
Port Gentil *Gabon* 98A3
Port Gibson *USA* 19B3
Port Graham *USA* 12D3
Port Hammond *Can* 20B1
Port Harcourt *Nigeria* 89E7
Port Hardy *Can* 13B2
Port Hawkesbury *Can* 7D5
Port Hedland *Aust* 106A3
Porthmadog *Wales* 43B3
Port Hope Simpson *Can* 7E4
Port Hueneme *USA* 22C3
Port Huron *USA* 14B2
Portimão *Port* 50A2
Port Jackson, B *Aust* 109D2
Port Jefferson *USA* 16C2
Port Jervis *USA* 16B2
Port Kembla *Aust* 109D2
Portland, Indiana *USA* 14B2
Portland, Maine *USA* 10C2
Portland, New South Wales *Aust* 109C2
Portland, Oregon *USA* 20B1
Portland, Victoria *Aust* 108B3
Portland Bight, B *Jamaica* 27H2
Portland Bill, Pt *Eng* 43C4
Portland,C *Aust* 109C4
Portland Canal *USA/ Can* 13A1
Portland I *NZ* 110C1
Portland Pt *Jamaica* 27H2
Port Laoise *Irish Rep* 45C2
Port Lincoln *Aust* 108A2
Port Loko *Sierra Leone* 97A4
Port Louis *Mauritius* 101E3
Port MacDonnell *Aust* 108B3
Port McNeill *Can* 13B2
Port Macquarie *Aust* 109D2
Port Moller *USA* 12B3
Port Moresby *PNG* 107D1
Port Nolloth *S Africa* 100A3
Port Norris *USA* 16B3
Port Novo *Benin* 89E7
Porto *Port* 50A1
Pôrto Alegre *Brazil* 30F5
Pôrto Artur *Brazil* 33F6
Pôrto 15 de Novembro *Brazil* 35A2
Pôrto E Cunha *Brazil* 30F3
Portoferraio *Italy* 52B2
Port of Spain *Trinidad* 27E4
Portomaggiore *Italy* 47D2
Porto Novo *Benin* 97C4
Port Orchard *USA* 20B1
Port Orford *USA* 20B2
Porto Santo, I *Medeira* 96A1
Pôrto Seguro *Brazil* 31D5
Porto Torres *Sardegna* 53A2
Porto Vecchio *Corse* 53A2
Pôrto Velho *Brazil* 33E5
Port Pegasus, B *NZ* 111A3
Port Phillip B *Aust* 108B3
Port Pirie *Aust* 108A2
Portree *Scot* 44A3
Port Renfrew *Can* 20B1
Port Royal *Jamaica* 27J2
Port Royal Sd *USA* 17B1
Portrush *N Ire* 45C1
Port Said *Egypt* 92B3
Port St Joe *USA* 17A2
Port St Johns *S Africa* 100B4
Port Saunders *Can* 7E4
Port Shepstone *S Africa* 100C4
Port Simpson *Can* 13A2
Portsmouth *Dominica* 27Q2
Portsmouth *Eng* 43D4
Portsmouth, Ohio *USA* 14B3
Portsmouth, Virginia *USA* 11C3
Port Stephens, B *Aust* 109D2
Port Sudan *Sudan* 95C3
Port Sulphur *USA* 19C3
Porttipahdan Tekojärvi Res *Fin* 38K5
Portugal, Republic *Europe* 50A2
Port Washington *USA* 14A2
Port Weld *Malay* 77C5
Porvenir *Bol* 32D6
Posadas *Arg* 30E4
Posadas *Spain* 50A2
Poschiavo *Switz* 47D1
Posheim Pen *Can* 6B2
Posht-e Badam *Iran* 90C3
Poso *Indon* 71D4
Postavy *USSR* 58D1
Post Clinton *USA* 14B2
Poste-de-la-Baleine *Can* 7C4
Postmasburg *S Africa* 100B3
Postojna *Yugos* 52B1
Pos'yet *USSR* 74C2
Potchetstroom *S Africa* 101G1
Poteau *USA* 19B2
Potenza *Italy* 53C2
Potgietersrus *S Africa* 100B3
Potiskum *Nig* 97D3
Potlatch *USA* 20C1
Potomac, R *USA* 15C3
Potosi *Bol* 30C2
Potrerillos *Chile* 30C4
Potsdam *E Germ* 56C2
Pottstown *USA* 16B2
Pottsville *USA* 16A2
Poughkeepsie *USA* 16C2
Pouso Alegre *Brazil* 35B2
Poverty B *NZ* 110C1
Povorino *USSR* 61F3
Povungnituk *Can* 7C4
Powder, R *USA* 8C2
Powell Creek *Aust* 106C2
Powell,L *USA* 9B3
Powell River *Can* 13C3
Power, R *USA* 8C2
Powys, County *Wales* 43C3
Poyang Hu, L *China* 73D4
Pozantı *Turk* 92B2
Poza Rica *Mexico* 23B1
Poznań *Pol* 58B2
Pozo Colorado *Par* 30E3
Pozzuoli *Italy* 53B2
Pra, R *Ghana* 97B4
Prachin Buri *Thai* 76C3
Prachuap Khiri Khan *Thai* 76B3
Praděd, Mt *Czech* 59B2
Pradelles *France* 49C3
Prado *Brazil* 35D1
Praha *Czech* 57C2
Praia *Cape Verde* 97A4
Prainha *Brazil* 33E5
Prairie Village *USA* 18B2
Prakhon Chai *Thai* 76C3
Prata *Brazil* 35B1
Prata, R *Brazil* 35B1
Prato *Italy* 49E3
Prattsville *USA* 16B1
Prattville *USA* 17A1
Prawle Pt *Eng* 48B1
Praya *Indon* 78D4
Predazzo *Italy* 47D1
Predivinsk *USSR* 63B2
Pregolyu, R *USSR* 58C2
Prek Kak *Camb* 76D3
Prenzlau *E Germ* 56C2
Preparis, I *Burma* 76A3
Preparis North Chan *Burma* 76A2
Přerov *Czech* 59B3
Presa del Infiernillo *Mexico* 23A2
Prescott, Arizona *USA* 9B3
Prescott, Arkansas *USA* 19B3
Prescott *Can* 15C2
Presidencia Roque Sáenz Peña *Arg* 30D4
Presidente Epitácio *Brazil* 35A2
Presidente Frei, Base *Ant* 112C2
Presidente Migúel Aleman, L *Mexico* 23B2
Presidente Prudente *Brazil* 35A2
Presidenté Vargas *Brazil* 30F3
Presidente Venceslau *Brazil* 35A2
Prešov *Czech* 59C3
Prespansko Jezero, L *Yugos* 55B2
Presque Isle *USA* 10D2
Preston *Eng* 42C3
Preston, Idaho *USA* 8B2
Preston, Missouri *USA* 18B2
Prestwick *Scot* 42B2
Prêto *Brazil* 31B6
Prêto, R *Brazil* 35B1
Pretoria *S Africa* 101G1
Préveza *Greece* 55B3
Prey Veng *Camb* 76D3
Price *USA* 8B3
Price I *Can* 13B2
Prichernomorskaya Nizmennost', Lowland *USSR* 60D4
Prickly Pt *Grenada* 27M2
Priekule *USSR* 58C1
Prieska *S Africa* 100B3
Priest L *USA* 20C1
Priest River *USA* 20C1
Prikaspiyskaya Nizmennost', Region *USSR* 61G4
Prilep *Yugos* 55B2
Priluki *USSR* 60D3
Primero, R *Arg* 34C2
Primorsk *USSR* 39K6
Primorsko-Akhtarsk *USSR* 60E4
Primrose L *Can* 13F2
Prince Albert *Can* 5H4
Prince Albert,C *Can* 4F2
Prince Albert Pen *Can* 4G2
Prince Albert Sd *Can* 4G2
Prince Charles I *Can* 6C3
Prince Charles Mts *Ant* 112B10
Prince Edward I *Can* 7D5
Prince George *Can* 13C2
Prince Gustaf Adolp, S *Can* 4H2
Prince of Wales, I *USA* 5E4
Prince of Wales I *Aust* 71F5
Prince of Wales I *Can* 4H2
Prince of Wales Str *Can* 4G2
Prince Patrick I *Can* 4F2
Prince Regent Inlet, Str *Can* 6A2
Prince Rupert *Can* 13A2
Princess Charlotte B *Aust* 107D2
Princess Royal I *Can* 13B2
Princes Town *Trinidad* 27L1
Princeton *Can* 13C3
Princeton, Kentucky *USA* 18C2
Princeton, Missouri *USA* 18B1
Princeton, New Jersey *USA* 16B2
Prince William *USA* 4D3
Prince William Sd *USA* 12E2
Principe, I *W Africa* 97C4
Prineville *USA* 20B2
Pringle,Mt *USA* 12E1
Prins Christian Sund, Sd *Greenland* 6F3
Prinsesse Astrid Kyst, Region *Ant* 112B12
Prinsesse Ragnhild Kyst, Region *Ant* 112B12
Prins Karls Forland, I *Barents S* 64B2
Prinzapolca *Nic* 25D3
Pripyat', R *USSR* 58D2
Priština *Yugos* 54B2
Pritzwalk *E Germ* 56C2
Privolzhskaya Vozvyshennost', Upland *USSR* 61F3
Prizren *Yugos* 54B2
Probolinggo *Indon* 78C4
Procatello *USA* 5G5
Proddatūr *India* 87B2
Progreso *Mexico* 25D2
Project City *USA* 20B2
Prokhladnyy *USSR* 61F5
Prokop'yevsk *USSR* 65K4
Proletarskaya *USSR* 61F4
Proliv Karskiye Vorota, Str *USSR* 64G2
Prome *Burma* 83D4
Propriá *Brazil* 31D4
Prospect, Oregon *USA* 20B2
Prosperine *Aust* 107D3
Prostějov *Czech* 59B3
Prøven *Greenland* 6E2
Provence, Region *France* 49D3
Providence *USA* 16D2
Provincetown *USA* 15D2
Provins *France* 49C2
Provo *USA* 8B2
Provost *Can* 13E2
Prudhoe Bay *USA* 4D2
Prudhoe Land *Greenland* 6D2
Pruszkow *Pol* 58C2
Prutul, R *USSR* 60C4
Pruzhany *USSR* 58C2
Pryor *USA* 18A2

Przemys'l *Pol* 59C3
Psará, I *Greece* 55C3
Pskov *USSR* 60C2
Ptich, R *USSR* 58D2
Ptolemaïs *Greece* 55B2
Pucallpa *Peru* 32C5
Pucheng *China* 73D4
Pucón *Chile* 34A3
Pudasjärvi *Fin* 38K5
Pudukkottai *India* 87B2
Puebla *Mexico* 23B2
Puebla, State *Mexico* 23B2
Puebla de Sanabria *Spain* 50A1
Puebla de Trives *Spain* 50A1
Pueblo *USA* 9C2
Puelches *Arg* 34B3
Puelén *Arg* 34B3
Puenta Ixbapa *Mexico* 23A2
Puente del Inca *Arg* 34B2
Puerta Aguja *Peru* 32A5
Puerta Coles *Peru* 30B2
Puerta de los Llanos *Arg* 34B2
Puerta do Calcanhar, Pt *Brazil* 31D3
Puerta Gallinas *Colombia* 32C1
Puerta Maldonado, Pt *Mexico* 23B2
Puerta Mariato *Panama* 32A2
Puerta Médanosa, Pt *Arg* 29C5
Puerta Mongrove *Mexico* 23A2
Puerta San Blas, Pt *Panama* 25E4
Puerta San Telmo *Mexico* 23A2
Puerto Aisén *Chile* 29B5
Puerto Armuelles *Panama* 25D4
Puerto Artur *Brazil* 33F6
Puerto Asis *Colombia* 32B3
Puerto Ayacucho *Ven* 32D2
Puerto Barrios *Guatemala* 25D3
Puerto Berrio *Colombia* 32C2
Puerto Cabello *Ven* 32D1
Puerto Cabezas *Nic* 25D3
Puerto Carreño *Colombia* 32D2
Puerto Cortes *Costa Rica* 25D4
Puerto Cortés *Honduras* 25D3
Puerto del Rosario *Canary Is* 96A2
Puerto E Cunha *Brazil* 30F3
Puerto Fijo *Ven* 32C1
Puerto Franco *Brazil* 31B3
Puerto Heath *Bol* 32D6
Puerto Juarez *Mexico* 25D2
Puerto la Cruz *Ven* 33E1
Puertollano *Spain* 50B2
Puerto Lopez *Colombia* 27C4
Puerto Madryn *Arg* 29D4
Puerto Maldonado *Peru* 32D6
Puerto Marquéz *Mexico* 23B2
Puerto Montt *Chile* 29B4
Puerto Murtinho *Brazil* 30E3
Puerto Natales *Chile* 29B6
Puerto Peñasco *Mexico* 24A1
Puerto Pirámides *Arg* 29D4
Puerto Plata *Dom Rep* 27C3
Puerto Princesa *Phil* 79A4
Puerto Rico *Colombia* 32B3
Puerto Rico, I *Caribbean* 27D3
Puerto Rico Trench *Caribbean* 27D3
Puerto San Juan de Lima *Mexico* 23A2
Puerto Santanga *Brazil* 33G4
Puerto Suárez *Bol* 30E2
Puerto Vallarta *Mexico* 24B2
Puerto Varas *Chile* 29B4
Puerto Villarroel *Bol* 30D2
Pugachev *USSR* 61G3
Pugal *India* 84C3
Puigcerdá *Spain* 51C1
Pukaki,L, L *NZ* 111B2
Pukch'ŏng *N Korea* 74B2
Pukekobe *NZ* 110B1
Puketeraki Range, Mts *NZ* 111B2
Pula *Yugos* 52B2
Pulaski, New York *USA* 15C2
Pulau Kolepom, I *Indon* 71E4
Pulau Pulau Batu, Is *Indon* 70A4
Pulawy *Pol* 58C2
Pulicat,L *India* 87C2
Pul-i-Khumri *Afghan* 84B1
Puliyangudi *India* 87B3
Pullman *USA* 20C1
Pulo Anna Merir, I *Pacific I* 71E3
Pulog,Mt *Phil* 79B2
Pulozero *USSR* 38L5
Pultusk *Pol* 58C2
Puna de Atacama *Arg* 30C4
Punakha *Bhutan* 86B1
Punch *Pak* 84C2
Pune *India* 87A1
Punéper *Mexico* 23A2
Punia *Zaïre* 98C3
Punitaqui *Chile* 34A2
Punjab, Province *Pak* 84C2
Punjab, State *India* 84D2
Puno *Peru* 30B2
Punta Abreojos, Pt *Mexico* 24A2
Punta Alice, Pt *Italy* 53C3
Punta Alta *Arg* 34C3
Punta Arenas *Chile* 29B6
Punta Baja, Pt *Mexico* 24A2
Punta Curaumilla, Pt *Chile* 34A2
Punta da Marca, Pt *Angola* 100A2
Punta de Barra Falsa, Pt *Mozam* 101C3
Punta del Este *Urug* 29F2
Punta Eugenia, Pt *Mexico* 24A2
Punta Gorda *Belize* 25D3
Punta Gorda *USA* 17B2
Punta Lavapié, Pt *Chile* 34A3
Punta Lengua de Vaca Pt *Chile* 34A2
Punta Licosa, Pt *Italy* 53B2
Punta Poroto, Pt *Chile* 34A1
Punta San Antonia, Pt *Mexico* 9B4
Punta Topocalma *Chile* 34A2
Puqi *China* 73C4
Purcell *USA* 19A2
Purcell Mt *USA* 12C1
Purcell Mts *Can* 13D2
Purén *Chile* 34A3
Puri *India* 86B2
Purna *India* 87B1
Pūrnia *India* 86B1
Pursat *Camb* 76C3
Puruandro *Mexico* 23A1
Purus, R *Brazil* 33E4
Purvis *USA* 19C3
Purwokerto *Indon* 78B4
Purworejo *Indon* 78C4
Pusad *India* 85D5
Pusan *S Korea* 74B3
Pushkin *USSR* 60D2
Pustochka *USSR* 58D1
Puta *Burma* 82D3
Putaendo *Chile* 34A2
Putaruru *NZ* 110C1
Putian *China* 73D4
Putnam *USA* 16D2
Puttalam *Sri Lanka* 87B3
Puttgarden *W Germ* 56C2
Putumayo, R *Ecuador* 32B4
Putussibau *Indon* 78C2
Puulavesl, L *Fin* 38K6
Puyallup *USA* 20B1
Puy de Sancy, Mt *France* 49C2
Puysegur Pt *NZ* 111A3
Pweto *Zaïre* 99C3
Pwllheli *Wales* 43B3
Pyapon *Burma* 76B2
Pyatigorsk *USSR* 61F5
P'yŏngyang *N Korea* 74B3
Pyramid Hill *Aust* 108B3
Pyramid L *USA* 21B1
Pyramid,Mt *NZ* 111A2
Pyrénées, Mts *France* 48B3
Pytalovo *USSR* 58D1
Pyu *Burma* 76B2

Q

Qabatiya *Israel* 94B2
Qā'el Hafīra, Mud Flats *Jordan* 94C3
Qa'el Jinz, Mud Flats *Jordan* 94C3
Qaidam Pendi, Salt Flat *China* 68B3
Qa Khanna, Salt Marsh *Jordan* 94C2
Qala'en Nahl *Sudan* 99D1
Qalat *Afghan* 84B2
Qal'at al Hisn *Syria* 94C1
Qal'at Bīshah *S Arabia* 81C3
Qal'at Sālih *Iraq* 93E3
Qamdo *China* 68B3
Qardho *Somalia* 99E2
Qara *Egypt* 95B2
Qaṣe Shīrīn *Iran* 90A3
Qaryat al Ulyā *S Arabia* 91A4
Qasr el Kharana *Jordan* 94C3
Qasr-e-Qand *Iran* 91D4
Qasr Farafra *Egypt* 95B2
Qaṭana *Syria* 94C2
Qatar, Emirate *Arabian Pen* 91B4
Qatrāna *Jordan* 94C3
Qattāra Depression *Egypt* 95B2
Qāyen *Iran* 90C3
Qazvīn *Iran* 90A2
Qena *Egypt* 95C2
Qeydār *Iran* 90A2
Qeys, I *Iran* 91B4
Qian Jiang, R *China* 73B5
Qian Shan, Upland *China* 72E1
Qidong *China* 72E3
Qijiang *China* 73B4
Qila Saifullah *Pak* 84B2
Qilian *China* 72A2
Qilian Shan *China* 68B3
Qin'an *China* 72B3
Qingdao *China* 72E2
Qinghai, Province *China* 72A2
Qinghai Hu, L *China* 68B3
Qingjiang, Jiangsu *China* 72D3
Qingjiang, Jiangxi *China* 73D4
Qing Jiang, R *China* 72B3
Qingshuihe *China* 72C2
Qingshui He, R *China* 72B2
Qingtonxia *China* 72B2
Qingyang *China* 72B2
Qingyuan, Liaoning *China* 74B2
Qingyuan, Zhejiang *China* 73D4
Qing Zang, Upland *China* 82C2
Qinhuangdao *China* 72D2
Qin Ling, Mts *China* 72B3
Qinzhou *China* 73B5
Qionghai *China* 76E2
Qionglai Shan, Upland *China* 73A3
Qiongzhou Haixia, Str *China* 76D1
Qiqihar *China* 69E2
Qiryat Ata *Israel* 94B2
Qiryat Gat *Israel* 94B3
Qiryat Shemona *Israel* 94B2
Qiryat Yam *Israel* 94B2
Qishon, R *Israel* 94B2
Qitai *China* 63A3
Qiyang *China* 73C4
Qog Qi *China* 72B1
Qolleh-ye Damavand, Mt *Iran* 90B2
Qom *Iran* 90B3
Qomisheh *Iran* 90B3
Qornet es Saouda, Mt *Leb* 94C1
Qôrnoq *Greenland* 6E3
Qorveh *Iran* 90A2
Qotābad *Iran* 91C4
Quabbin Res *USA* 16C1
Quakertown *USA* 16B2
Quam Phu Quoc, I *Viet* 77C3
Quang Ngai *Viet* 76D2
Quang Tri *Viet* 76D2
Quan Long *Viet* 77D4
Quanzhou, Fujian *China* 73D5
Quanzhou, Guangxi *China* 73C4
Qu' Appelle, R *Can* 5H4
Quarayyāt *Oman* 91C5
Quatsino Sd *Can* 13B2
Quchan *Iran* 90C2
Queanbeyan *Aust* 109C3
Québec *Can* 15D1
Quebec, Province *Can* 7C4
Quebra-Anzol, R *Brazil* 35B1
Quebracho *Urug* 34D2
Quedas do Iguaçu *Brazil/Arg* 30F4
Queen Anne *USA* 16A3
Queen Bess,Mt *Can* 13B2
Queen Charlotte, Is *Can* 5E4
Queen Charlotte Sd *Can* 13B2
Queen Charlotte Str *Can* 13B2
Queen Elizabeth Is *Can* 4H1
Queen Mary Land, Region *Ant* 112B9
Queen Maud G *Can* 4H3
Queen Maud Mts *Ant* 80E
Queens, Borough, New York *USA* 16C2
Queenscliff *Aust* 108B3
Queensland, State *Aust* 107D3
Queenstown *Aust* 109C4
Queenstown *NZ* 111A3
Queenstown *S Africa* 100B4
Queenstown *USA* 16A3
Quela *Angola* 98B3
Quelimane *Mozam* 101C2
Quemuquemú *Arg* 34C3
Quensel L *Can* 13C2
Quequén *Arg* 34D3
Quequén, R *Arg* 34D3
Querétaro *Mexico* 23A1
Queretaro, State *Mexico* 23A1
Quesnel *Can* 13C2
Quetta *Pak* 84B2
Quezaltenango *Guatemala* 25C3

Queziot *Israel* 94B3
Quezon City *Phil* 79B3
Quibala *Angola* 100A2
Quibaxe *Angola* 98B3
Quibdó *Colombia* 32B2
Quiberon *France* 48B2
Quicama Nat Pk *Angola* 98B3
Quijing *China* 73A4
Quilima *Chile* 34A2
Quilino *Arg* 34C2
Quillabamba *Peru* 32C6
Quillacollo *Bol* 30C2
Quillan *France* 48C3
Quill L *Can* 5H4
Quill Lakes *Can* 5H4
Quillota *Chile* 34A2
Quilon *India* 87B3
Quilpie *Aust* 108B1
Quilpué *Chile* 34A2
Quimbele *Angola* 98B3
Quimper *France* 48B2
Quimperlé *France* 48B2
Quincy, California *USA* 21A2
Quincy, Illinois *USA* 10A3
Quincy, Massachusetts *USA* 16D1
Quines *Arg* 34B2
Quinhagak *USA* 12B3
Qui Nhon *Viet* 76D3
Quintanar de la Orden *Spain* 50B2
Quintero *Chile* 34A2
Quinto, R *Arg* 34C2
Quirihue *Chile* 34A3
Quirima *Angola* 100A2
Quirindi *Aust* 109D2
Quissanga *Mozam* 101D2
Quissico *Mozam* 101C3
Quito *Ecuador* 32B4
Quixadá *Brazil* 31D2
Quorn *Aust* 108A2
Quseir *Egypt* 95C2
Qutdligssat *Greenland* 6E3
Qu Xian, Sichuan *China* 73B3
Qu Xian, Zhejiang *China* 73D4
Quynh Luu *Viet* 76D2
Quzhou *China* 72C2
Qüzü *China* 86C1

R

Raahe *Fin* 38J6
Raasay, I *Scot* 44A3
Raasay,Sound of, Chan *Scot* 44A3
Rab, I *Yugos* 52B2
Raba *Indon* 78D4
Rába, R *Hung* 59B3
Rabat *Mor* 96B1
Rabba *Jordan* 94B3
Rabigh *S Arabia* 80B3
Racconigi *Italy* 47B2
Race,C *Can* 7E5
Rachaya *Leb* 94B2
Rachel, Mt *W Germ* 57C3
Rach Gia *Viet* 76D3
Racine *USA* 14A2
Rădăuţi *Rom* 59D3
Radhanpur *India* 85C4
Radix,Pt *Trinidad* 27L1
Radom *Pol* 58C2
Radomsko *Pol* 59B2
Radviliškis *USSR* 58C1
Rae *Can* 4G3
Rāe Bareli *India* 86A1
Rae Isthmus *Can* 6B3
Rae L *Can* 4G3
Raetihi *NZ* 110C1
Rafaela *Arg* 34C2
Rafah *Egypt* 94B3
Rafai *CAR* 98C2
Rafhā Al Jumaymah *S Arabia* 93D3
Rafsanjān *Iran* 91C3
Raga *Sudan* 98C2
Ragged Pt *Barbados* 27R3
Raguba *Libya* 95A2
Ragusa *Italy* 53B3
Rahad, R *Sudan* 99D1
Rahimyar Khan *Pak* 84C3
Rāhjerd *Iran* 90B3
Raíces *Arg* 34D2
Rāichur *India* 87B1
Raigarh *India* 86A2
Rainbow *Aust* 108B3
Rainbow City *USA* 17A1
Rainier *USA* 20B1
Rainier,Mt *USA* 20B1
Rainy L *Can* 10A2
Rainy P *USA* 12D2
Rainy River *Can* 10A2
Raipur *India* 86A2
Rājahmundry *India* 87C1
Rajang, R *Malay* 78C2
Rajanpur *Pak* 84C3
Rājapālaiyam *India* 87B3
Rājasthan, State *India* 85C3
Rājgarh *India* 84D3
Rājgarh, State *India* 85D4
Rājkot *India* 85C4
Rājmahāl Hills *India* 86B2
Raj Nāndgaon *India* 86A2
Rājpīpla *India* 85C4
Rajshahi *Bang* 86B2
Rajur *India* 85D4
Rakaia, R *NZ* 111B2
Rakata, I *Indon* 78B4
Raka Zangbo, R *China* 82C3
Rakhov *USSR* 59C3
Rakops *Botswana* 100B3
Rakov *USSR* 58D2
Raleigh *USA* 11C3
Ralny L *Can* 7A5
Rama *Israel* 94B2
Ramallah *Israel* 94B3
Rāmanāthapuram *India* 87B3
Ramapo Deep *Pacific Oc* 69G3
Ramat Gan *Israel* 94B2
Rambouillet *France* 46A2
Rāmgarh, Bihar *India* 86B2
Rāmgarh, Rajosthan *India* 85C3
Rāmhormoz *Iran* 90A3
Ramla *Israel* 94B3
Ramlat Al Wahibah, Region *Oman* 91C5
Ramona *USA* 21B3
Rāmpur *India* 84D3
Rāmpura *India* 85D4
Rāmsar *Iran* 90B2
Ramsey *Eng* 42B2
Ramsey *USA* 16B2
Ramsey I *Wales* 43B4
Ramsgate *Eng* 43E4
Ramtha *Jordan* 94C2
Ramu, R *PNG* 71F4
Rancagua *Chile* 34A2
Rānchi *India* 86B2
Rānchi Plat *India* 86A2
Randers *Den* 39G7
Randfontein *S Africa* 101G1
Randolph, Vermont *USA* 15D2
Ranfurly *NZ* 111B3
Rangamati *Bang* 86C2
Rangiora *NZ* 111B2
Rangitaiki, R *NZ* 110C1
Rangitate, R *NZ* 111B2
Rangitikei, R *NZ* 110C1
Rangoon *Burma* 76B2
Rangpur *India* 86B1
Rānībennur *India* 87B2
Ranier,Mt, Mt *USA* 8A2
Rānīganj *India* 86B2
Rankins Springs *Aust* 109C2
Ranklin Inlet *Can* 6A3
Rann of Kachchh, Flood Area *India* 85B4
Ranong *Thai* 77B4
Rantauparapat *Indon* 70A3
Rantoul *USA* 18C1
Rapallo *Italy* 40D3
Rapel, R *Chile* 34A2
Raper,C *Can* 6D3
Rapid City *USA* 8C2
Rapid River *USA* 14A1
Rappahannock, R *USA* 15C3
Rapperswil *Switz* 47C1
Raritan B *USA* 16B2
Ras Abu Shagara, C *Sudan* 95C2
Ra's al 'Ayn *Syria* 93D2
Ra's al Hadd, C *Oman* 91C5
Ras al Kaimah *UAE* 91C4
Ras-al-Kuh, C *Iran* 91C4
Ra's al Madrakah, C *Oman* 81D4
Ra's az Zawr, C *S Arabia* 91A4
Rās Bânas, C *Egypt* 95C2
Ras Burûn, C *Egypt* 94A3
Ras Dashan, Mt *Eth* 99D1
Ra's-e-Barkan, Pt *Iran* 90A3
Râs el Kenâyis, Pt *Egypt* 92A3
Ra's Fartak, C *S Yemen* 81D4
Râs Ghârib *Egypt* 95C2
Rashad *Sudan* 99D1
Rashādīya *Jordan* 94B3
Rashîd *Egypt* 92B3
Rasht *Iran* 90A2
Ra's Jibish, C *Oman* 91C5
Ras Khanzira, C *Somalia* 99E1
Ras Koh, Mt *Pak* 84B3
Râs Muhammad, C *Egypt* 95C2
Ras Nouadhibou, C *Maur* 96A2
Rasshua, I *USSR* 69H2
Rasskazovo *USSR* 61F3
Ra's Tanāqib, C *S Arabia* 91A4
Ra's Tannūrah *S Arabia* 91B4
Rastatt *W Germ* 57B3
Ras Xaafuun, C *Somalia* 99F1
Ratangarh *India* 84C3
Rat Buri *Thai* 76B3
Rath *India* 85D3
Ratherow *E Germ* 56C2
Rathkeale *Irish Rep* 45B2
Rathlin, I *N Ire* 45C1
Ráth Luirc *Irish Rep* 45B2
Ratlām *India* 85D4
Ratnāgiri *India* 87A1
Ratnapura *Sri Lanka* 87C3
Ratno *USSR* 58C2
Rattenberg *Austria* 47D1
Rättvik *Sweden* 39H6
Ratz,Mt *Can* 12H3
Rauch *Arg* 34D3
Raukumara Range, Mts *NZ* 110C1
Raul Soares *Brazil* 35C2
Rauma *Fin* 39J6
Raurkela *India* 86A2
Ravānsar *Iran* 90A3
Rāvar *Iran* 90C3
Rava Russkaya *USSR* 59C2
Ravena *USA* 16C1
Ravenna *Italy* 52B2
Ravensburg *W Germ* 57B3
Ravenshoe *Aust* 107D2
Ravi, R *Pak* 84C2
Rawalpindi *Pak* 84C2
Rawicz *Pol* 58B2
Rawlinna *Aust* 106B4
Rawlins *USA* 8C2
Rawñdiz *Iraq* 93D2
Rawson *Arg* 29C4
Raya, Mt *Indon* 78C3
Rāyadurg *India* 87B2
Rayak *Leb* 94C2
Ray,C *Can* 7E5
Rāyen *Iran* 91C4
Raymond, California *USA* 22C2
Raymond, Washington *USA* 20B1
Raymond Terrace *Aust* 109D2
Ray Mts *USA* 12D1
Rayon *Mexico* 23B1
Razan *Iran* 90A2
Razgrad *Bulg* 54C2
Razim, L *Rom* 54C2
Reading *Eng* 43D4
Reading *USA* 16B2
Read Island *Can* 4G3
Readsboro *USA* 16C1
Real de Padre *Arg* 34B2
Realicó *Arg* 34C3
Rebiana, Well *Libya* 95B2
Rebiana Sand Sea *Libya* 95B2
Reboly *USSR* 38L6
Recherche,Arch of the Is *Aust* 106B4
Recife *Brazil* 31E3
Récifs D'Entrecasteaux *Nouvelle Calédonie* 107F2
Recklinghausen *W Germ* 46D1
Reconquista *Arg* 30E4
Red, R *USA* 19B3
Redang, I *Malay* 77C4
Red Bank, New Jersey *USA* 16B2
Red Bluff *USA* 21A1
Redcar *Eng* 42D2
Redcliff *Can* 13E2
Redcliffe *Aust* 109D1
Red Cliffs *Aust* 108B2
Red Deer *Can* 13E2
Red Deer, R *Can* 13E2
Redding *USA* 20B2
Red L *USA* 10A2
Red Lake *Can* 7A4
Redlands *USA* 22D3
Red Lion *USA* 16A3
Redmond *USA* 20B2
Red Oak *USA* 18A1
Redon *France* 48B2
Redondo Beach *USA* 22C4
Redoubt V *USA* 12D2
Red River Delta *Vietnam* 73B5
Red Sea *Africa/ Arabian Pen* 80B3
Redwater *Can* 13E2
Redwood City *USA* 22A2
Reed City *USA* 14A2
Reedley *USA* 22C2
Reedsport *USA* 20B2
Reefton *NZ* 111B2
Refahiye *Turk* 93C2
Regência *Brazil* 35D1
Regensburg *W Germ* 57C3
Reggane *Alg* 96C2
Reggio di Calabria *Italy* 53C3
Reggio Nell'Emilia *Italy* 47D2
Reghin *Rom* 54B1
Regina *Can* 5H4
Rehoboth *Namibia* 100A3
Rehoboth Beach *USA* 15C3
Rehovot *Israel* 94B3
Reicito *Ven* 32D1
Reigate *Eng* 43D4
Reims *France* 46C2
Reindeer, R *Can* 5H4
Reinosa *Spain* 50B1
Reisterstown *USA* 16A3
Reitz *S Africa* 101G1
Reliance *Can* 4H3
Remarkable,Mt *Aust* 108A2
Rembang *Indon* 78C4
Remeshk *Iran* 91C4
Remscheid *W Germ* 46D1
Rend,L *USA* 18C2
Rendsburg *W Germ* 56B2

Renfrew *Can* 15C1
Rengat *Indon* 78A3
Rengo *Chile* 34A2
Reni *USSR* 59D3
Renk *Sudan* 99D1
Renland, Pen *Greenland* 6H2
Renmark *Aust* 108B2
Rennell, I *Solomon Is* 107F2
Rennes *France* 48B2
Reno *USA* 21B2
Reno, R *Italy* 47D2
Renovo *USA* 15C2
Rensselaer *USA* 16C1
Renton *USA* 20B1
Reo *Indon* 70D4
Reprêsa de Furnas, Dam *Brazil* 35B2
Reprêsa Três Marias, Dam *Brazil* 35B1
Republic *USA* 20C1
Republic of Ireland *NW Europe* 41B3
Repulse Bay *Can* 6B3
Réservoir Baskatong, Res *Can* 15C1
Réservoire Cabonga, Res *Can* 7C5
Réservoire Gouin, Res *Can* 7C5
Réservoire Manicouagan, Res *Can* 10D1
Reshteh-ye Alborz, Mts *Iran* 90B2
Reshui *China* 72A2
Resistencia *Arg* 30E4
Resita *Rom* 54B1
Resolute *Can* 6A2
Resolution I *NZ* 111A3
Resolution Island *Can* 6D3
Ressano Garcia *Mozam* 101H1
Retamito *Arg* 34B2
Rethel *France* 46C2
Réthimnon *Greece* 55B3
Reunion, I *Indian O* 89K10
Reus *Spain* 51C1
Reuss, R *Switz* 47C1
Reutte *Austria* 47D1
Revda *USSR* 61K3
Revelstoke *Can* 13D2
Revillagigedo, Is *Mexico* 24A3
Revillagigedo I *USA* 12H3
Revin *France* 46C2
Revivim *Israel* 94B3
Rewa *India* 86A2
Rewari *India* 84D3
Rexburg *USA* 8B2
Reykjavik *Iceland* 38A2
Reynosa *Mexico* 24C2
Rezé *France* 48B2
Rezekne *USSR* 58D1
Rezh *USSR* 61K2
Rhätikon, Mts *Austria/Switz* 47C1
Rhazīr, Republic *Leb* 94B1
Rhein, R *W Europe* 56B2
Rheine *W Germ* 56B2
Rheinfielden *Switz* 47B1
Rheinland Pfalz, Region *W Germ* 49D2
Rheinwaldhorn, Mt *Switz* 47C1
Rhinebeck *USA* 16C2
Rhinelander *USA* 10B2
Rho *Italy* 47C2
Rhode Island, State *USA* 15D2
Rhode Island Sd *USA* 16D2
Rhône, R *France* 49C3
Rhyl *Wales* 43C3
Riachão do Jacuipe *Brazil* 31D4
Ria de Arosa, B *Spain* 50A1
Ria de Betanzos, B *Spain* 50A1
Ria de Corcubion, B *Spain* 50A1
Ria de Lage, B *Spain* 50A1
Ria de Sta Marta, B *Spain* 50A1
Ria de Vigo, B *Spain* 50A1
Riāsi *Pak* 84C2
Ribadeo *Spain* 50A1
Ribas do Rio Pardo *Brazil* 35A2
Ribauè *Mozam* 101C2
Ribble, R *Eng* 42C3
Ribeira *Brazil* 35B2
Ribeirão Prêto *Brazil* 35B2
Riberalta *Bol* 32D6
Rice L *Can* 15C2
Rice Lake *USA* 10A2
Richard's Bay *S Africa* 101H1
Richardson *USA* 19A3
Richardson Mts *Can* 12G1
Richfield *USA* 8B3
Richland *USA* 20C1
Richmond, California *USA* 22A2
Richmond, Natal *S Africa* 101H1
Richmond, New South Wales *Aust* 109D2
Richmond *NZ* 111B2
Richmond, Queensland *Aust* 107D3
Richmond, Virginia *USA* 10C3
Richmond Range, Mts *NZ* 111B2
Rideau,L *Can* 15C2
Ridgeland *USA* 17B1
Ridgway *USA* 15C2
Riecito *Ven* 27D4
Rienza, R *Italy* 47D1
Riesa *E Germ* 57C2
Riesco, I *Chile* 29B6
Riet, R *S Africa* 101F1
Rieti *Italy* 52B2
Rif, Mts *Mor* 50B2
Riga *USSR* 58C1
Riga,G of *USSR* 60B2
Rīgān *Iran* 91C4
Riggins *USA* 20C1
Rigolet *Can* 7E4
Riihimaki *Fin* 39J6
Rijeka *Yugos* 52B1
Rimbey *Can* 13E2
Rimbo *Sweden* 39H7
Rimini *Italy* 52B2
Rîmnicu Sârat *Rom* 54C1
Rîmnicu Vîlcea *Rom* 54B1
Rimouski *Can* 10D2
Rincón de Romos *Mexico* 23A1
Ringkøbing *Den* 39F7
Rio Benito *Eq Guinea* 98A2
Rio Branco *Brazil* 32D5
Rio Bravo del Norte, R *USA/Mexico* 24B1
Riochacha *Colombia* 32C1
Rio Claro *Brazil* 35B2
Rio Claro *Trinidad* 27L1
Rio Colorado *Arg* 34C3
Rio Cuarto *Arg* 34C2
Rio de Jacuipe *Brazil* 31D4
Rio de Janeiro *Brazil* 35C2
Rio de Janeiro, State *Brazil* 35C2
Rio de la Plata, Est *Arg/Urug* 29E3
Rio Gallegos *Arg* 29C6
Rio Grande *Arg* 29C6
Rio Grande *Brazil* 30F5
Rio Grande *Nic* 26A4
Rio Grande, R *Nicaragua* 25D3
Rio Grande, R *USA/Mexico* 24B2
Rio Grande de Santiago *Mexico* 23A1
Rio Grande do Norte, State *Brazil* 31D3
Rio Grande do Sul, State *Brazil* 30F4
Rio Grande Rise *Atlantic O* 103G6
Riohacha *Colombia* 26C4
Riom *France* 49C2
Riombamba *Ecuador* 32B4
Rio Mulatos *Bol* 30C2
Río Negro, State *Arg* 29C3
Rio Pardo *Brazil* 30F4
Rio Tercero *Arg* 34C2
Rio Theodore Roosevelt, R *Brazil* 33E6
Rio Turbio *Arg* 29B6
Rio Verde *Brazil* 35A1
Rio Verde *Mexico* 23A1
Ripley, Ohio *USA* 14B3
Ripley, West Virginia *USA* 14B3
Ripon *Eng* 42D2
Ripon *USA* 22B2
Rishon le Zion *Israel* 94B3
Rising Sun *USA* 16A3
Risør *Nor* 39F7
Ritenberk *Greenland* 6E2
Ritter,Mt *USA* 22C2
Ritzville *USA* 20C1
Rivadavia *Arg* 34B2
Rivadavia *Chile* 34A1
Rivadavia Gonzalez Moreno *Arg* 34C3
Riva de Garda *Italy* 47D2
Rivera *Arg* 34C3
Rivera *Urug* 29E2
Riverbank *USA* 22B2
River Cess *Lib* 97B4
Riverhead *USA* 16C2
Riverina *Aust* 108B3
Riversdale *NZ* 111A3
Riverside *USA* 22D4
Rivers Inlet *Can* 13B2
Riverton *NZ* 111A3
Riverton *USA* 8C2
Riviera Beach *USA* 17B2
Rivière aux Feuilles, R *Can* 7C4
Rivière de la Baleine, R *Can* 7D4
Rivière du Petit Mècatina, R *Can* 7D4
Rivigny-sur-Ornain *France* 46C2
Riyadh *S Arabia* 91A5
Rize *Turk* 93D1
Rizhao *China* 72D2
Rjukan *Nor* 39F7
Roanes Pen *Can* 6B2
Roanne *France* 49C2
Roanoke, Alabama *USA* 17A1
Roanoke, Virginia *USA* 11C3
Roanoke, R *USA* 11C3
Roaringwater B *Irish Rep* 45B3
Robertsforz *Sweden* 38J6
Robert S Kerr Res *USA* 19B2
Robertsport *Lib* 97A4
Roberval *Can* 7C5
Robinson Crusoe, I *Chile* 30H6
Robinvale *Aust* 108B2
Robson,Mt *Can* 13D2
Roca Partida, I *Mexico* 24A3
Rocas, I *Atlantic O* 103G5
Rocas, I *Brazil* 31E2
Rocha *Urug* 29F2
Rochdale *Eng* 42C3
Rochefort *France* 48B2
Rocher River *Can* 5G3
Rochester *Aust* 108B3
Rochester *Can* 7C5
Rochester *Eng* 43E4
Rochester, Minnesota *USA* 10A2
Rochester, New Hampshire *USA* 15D2
Rochester, New York *USA* 10C2
Rockford *USA* 10B2
Rock Hill *USA* 11B3
Rock Island *USA* 10A2
Rocklands Res *Aust* 108B3
Rockledge *USA* 17B2
Rock Springs, Wyoming *USA* 8C2
Rocks Pt *NZ* 110B2
Rock,The *Aust* 109C3
Rockville, Connecticut *USA* 16C2
Rockville, Indiana *USA* 14A3
Rockville, Maryland *USA* 16A3
Rocky Island L *Can* 14B1
Rocky Mountain House *Can* 13E2
Rocky Mts *Can/USA* 8B1
Rocky Pt *USA* 12B2
Rødbyhavn *Den* 56C2
Rodeo *Arg* 34B2
Rodez *France* 49C3
Ródhos *Greece* 55C3
Ródhos, I *Greece* 55C3
Rodi Garganico *Italy* 52C2
Rodopi Planina, Mts *Bulg* 54B2
Roebourne *Aust* 106A3
Roer, R *Neth* 46D1
Roermond *Neth* 46C1
Roeselare *Belg* 46B1
Roes Welcome Sd *Can* 6B3
Rogers *USA* 18B2
Rogers City *USA* 14B1
Rogue, R *USA* 20B2
Rohn *Pak* 85B3
Rohtak *India* 84D3
Roja *USSR* 58C1
Rolândia *Brazil* 35A2
Rolla *USA* 18B2
Roma *Aust* 109C1
Roma *Italy* 52B2
Romagnano *Italy* 47C2
Romain,C *USA* 17C1
Roman *Rom* 54C1
Romanche Gap *Atlantic O* 103H5
Romang, I *Indon* 71D4
Romania, Republic *E Europe* 60B4
Romano,C *USA* 17B2
Romans sur Isère *France* 49D2
Romblon *Phil* 79B3
Rome, Georgia *USA* 17A1
Rome, New York *USA* 15C2
Romilly-sur-Seine *France* 49C2
Romney *USA* 15C3
Romny *USSR* 60D3
Rømø, I *Den* 56B1
Romont *Switz* 47B1
Romoratin *France* 48C2
Ronda *Spain* 50A2
Rondônia *Brazil* 33E6
Rondônia, State *Brazil* 24F6
Rondonópolis *Brazil* 30F2
Rong'an *China* 73B4
Rongchang *China* 73B4
Rongcheng *China* 72E2
Rongjiang *China* 73B4
Rong Jiang, R *China* 73B4
Rongklang Range, Mts *Burma* 76A1
Rønne *Denmark* 39G7
Ronneby *Sweden* 39H7
Ronne Ice Shelf *Ant* 112B2
Ronse *Belg* 46B1
Ronthieu, Region *France* 46A1
Roof Butte, Mt *USA* 9C3
Roorkee *India* 84D3
Roosendaal *Neth* 46C1

Roosevelt I *Ant* **80E**
Roper, R *Aust* **106C2**
Roraima, State *Brazil* **33E3**
Roraime, Mt *Ven* **33E2**
Røros *Nor* **38G6**
Rorschach *Switz* **47C1**
Rørvik *Nor* **38G6**
Rosalie *Dominica* **27Q2**
Rosamond L *USA* **22C3**
Rosario *Arg* **34C2**
Rosário *Brazil* **31C2**
Rosario del Tala *Arg* **34D2**
Roscoff *France* **48B2**
Roscommon, County *Irish Rep* **45B2**
Roscommon *Irish Rep* **41B3**
Roscrea *Irish Rep* **45C2**
Roseau *Dominica* **27E3**
Rosebery *Aust* **109C4**
Roseburg *USA* **20B2**
Rosenberg *USA* **19A4**
Rosenheim *W Germ* **57C3**
Rosetown *Can* **13F2**
Rosiorii de Verde *Rom* **54B2**
Roskilde *Den* **39G7**
Roslavl' *USSR* **60D3**
Roslyatino *USSR* **61E2**
Ross *NZ* **111B2**
Ross, R *Can* **12H2**
Rossan, Pt *Irish Rep* **40B3**
Rossano *Italy* **53C3**
Ross Barnet Res *USA* **19C3**
Rosseau L, L *Can* **15C1**
Rossel, I *Solomon Is* **107E2**
Ross Ice Shelf *Ant* **80E**
Rossiyskaya S.F.S.R., Republic *USSR* **60D2**
Ross L *USA* **20B1**
Rossland *Can* **13D3**
Rosslare *Irish Rep* **45C2**
Ross,Mt *NZ* **111C2**
Rosso *Maur* **97A3**
Ross-on-Wye *Eng* **43C4**
Rossosh *USSR* **60E4**
Ross River *Can* **4E3**
Ross S *Ant* **112B6**
Rostāq *Iran* **91B4**
Rostock *E Germ* **56C2**
Rostov *USSR* **62E2**
Rostov-na-Donu *USSR* **61E4**
Roswell, Georgia *USA* **17B1**
Roswell, New Mexico *USA* **9C3**
Rota *Pacific O* **71F2**
Rotenburg, Niedersachsen *W Germ* **56B2**
Rothaar-Geb, Region *W Germ* **46E1**
Rothera, Base *Ant* **112C3**
Rotherham *Eng* **42D3**
Rothesay *Scot* **42B2**
Roti, I *Indon* **71D5**
Roto *Aust* **108C2**
Rotoiti,L *NZ* **111B2**
Rotoroa,L *NZ* **111B2**
Rotorua *NZ* **110C1**
Rotorua,L *NZ* **110C1**
Rotterdam *Neth* **56A2**
Roubaix *France* **46B1**
Rouen *France* **48C2**
Rough, Oilfield *N Sea* **42E3**
Round I *Mauritius* **101E3**
Round Mt *Aust* **109D2**
Roundup *USA* **8C2**
Rousay, I *Scot* **44C2**
Roussillon, Region *France* **48C3**
Rouyn *Can* **10C2**
Rovaniemi *Fin* **38K5**
Rovereto *Italy* **47D2**
Rovigo *Italy* **47D2**
Rovinj *Yugos* **52B1**
Rovno *USSR* **59D2**
Row'ān *Iran* **90A2**
Rowena *Aust* **109C1**
Rowley I *Can* **6C3**
Rowley Shoals *Aust* **106A2**
Roxao, Palawan *Phil* **79A3**
Roxas, Panay *Phil* **79B3**
Roxburgh *NZ* **111A3**
Royal Canal *Irish Rep* **45C2**
Royal Leamington Spa *Eng* **43D3**
Royal Oak *USA* **14B2**
Royal Tunbridge Wells *Eng* **43E4**
Royan *France* **48B2**
Roye *France* **46B2**
Royston *Eng* **43D3**
Rožňava *Czech* **59C3**
Rozoy *France* **46B2**
Rtishchevo *USSR* **61F3**
Ruaha Nat Pk *Tanz* **99D3**
Ruahine Range, Mts *NZ* **110C1**
Ruapehu,Mt *NZ* **110C1**
Rub al Khālī, Desert *S Arabia* **65D3**
Rubha Hunish *Scot* **44A3**
Rubinéia *Brazil* **35A2**
Rubtsoysk *USSR* **65K4**
Ruby *USA* **12C2**
Rudan *Iran* **91C4**
Rūdbār *Iran* **90A2**
Rudnaya Pristan' *USSR* **69F2**
Rudoka Planina, Mt *Yugos* **54B2**
Rudong *China* **72E3**
Rudyard *USA* **14B1**
Rue *France* **46A1**
Ruffec *France* **48C2**
Rufiji, R *Tanz* **99D3**
Rufino *Arg* **34C2**
Rufisque *Sen* **97A3**
Rufunsa *Zambia* **100B2**
Rugby *Eng* **43D3**
Rügen, I *E Germ* **39G8**
Ruhr, R *W Germ* **56B2**
Ruijin *China* **73D4**
Rujen, Mt *Bulg/Yugos* **54B2**
Rukwa, L *Tanz* **99D3**
Rum, I *Scot* **44A3**
Ruma *Yugos* **54A1**
Rumāh *S Arabia* **91A4**
Rumbek *Sudan* **98C2**
Rum Cay, I *Caribbean* **26C2**
Rumilly *France* **47A2**
Rum Jungle *Aust* **106C2**
Rumphi *Malawi* **101C2**
Runanga *NZ* **111B2**
Runaway,C *NZ* **110C1**
Rundu *Namibia* **100A2**
Rungwa *Tanz* **99D3**
Rungwa, R *Tanz* **99D3**
Rungwe, Mt *Tanz* **99D3**
Ruoqiang *China* **82C2**
Ruo Shui, R *China* **68C2**
Rupea *Rom* **54C1**
Rupert, R *Can* **7C4**
Rur, R *W Germ* **46D1**
Rurrenabaque *Bol* **32D6**
Rusape *Zim* **101C2**
Ruse *Bulg* **54C2**
Rushville, Illinois *USA* **18B1**
Rushworth *Aust* **108B3**
Rusk *USA* **19A3**
Ruskin *USA* **17B2**
Russell *NZ* **110B1**
Russellville, Arkansas *USA* **18B2**
Russellville, Kentucky *USA* **18C2**
Russian, R *USA* **21A2**
Russian Socialist Federated Soviet Rep *USSR* **60B3**
Rustavi *USSR* **93E1**
Rustenburg *S Africa* **101G1**
Ruston *USA* **19B3**
Rutana *Burundi* **99C3**
Rüthen *W Germ* **46E1**
Rutla *Mexico* **23B2**
Rutland *USA* **15D2**
Rutog *China* **84D2**
Ruvuma, R *Tanz/Mozam* **101D2**
Ruwenzori Range, Mts *Uganda/Zaïre* **99D2**
Ruya, R *Zim* **101C2**
Ružomberok *Czech* **59B3**
Rwanda, Republic *Africa* **99C3**
Ryazan' *USSR* **60E3**
Ryazhsk *USSR* **61F3**
Rybinsk *USSR* **60E2**
Rybinskoye Vodokhranilishche, Res *USSR* **60E2**
Rycroft *Can* **13D1**
Ryde *Eng* **43D4**
Rye *Eng* **43E4**
Rye Patch Res *USA* **20C2**
Ryl'sk *USSR* **60D3**
Ryn Peskt, Desert *USSR* **61G4**
Ryōtsu *Japan* **74D3**
Ryskany *USSR* **59D3**
Ryūkyū Retto, Arch *Japan* **69E4**
Rzeszów *Pol* **59C2**
Rzhev *USSR* **60D2**

S

Sa'ādatābād *Iran* **91B3**
Saale, R *E Germ* **56C2**
Saanen *Switz* **47B1**
Saar, R *W Germ* **46D2**
Saarbrücken *W Germ* **46D2**
Saarburg *W Germ* **46D2**
Saaremaa, I *USSR* **39J7**
Saarland, State *W Germ* **46D2**
Saarlouis *W Germ* **46D2**
Saavedra *Arg* **34C3**
Šabac *Yugos* **54A2**
Sabadell *Spain* **51C1**
Sabae *Japan* **75B1**
Sabah, State *Malay* **78D1**
Sabanalarga *Colombia* **26C4**
Sabang *Indon* **70A3**
Sabari, R *India* **87C1**
Sabastiya *Israel* **94B2**
Sabaya *Bol* **30C2**
Sab'Bi'ār *Syria* **93C3**
Sabhā *Jordan* **94C2**
Sabhā *Libya* **95A2**
Sabi, R *Zim* **101C3**
Sabinas *Mexico* **24B2**
Sabinas Hidalgo *Mexico* **24B2**
Sabine, R *USA* **19A3**
Sabine L *USA* **19B4**
Sabkhat Matti, Salt Marsh *UAE* **91B5**
Sabkhet El Bardawîl, Lg *Egypt* **94A3**
Sablayan *Phil* **79B3**
Sable,C *Can* **7D5**
Sable,C *USA* **17B2**
Sable I *Can* **7D5**
Sabzevār *Iran* **90C2**
Sacajawea Peak *USA* **20C1**
Sachigo, R *Can* **10A1**
Sachs Harbour *Can* **4F2**
Säckingen *W Germ* **47B1**
Sacramento *USA* **22B1**
Sacramento, R *USA* **22B1**
Sacramento, V *USA* **21A1**
Sacramento Mts *USA* **9C3**
Sa'dah *Yemen* **81C4**
Sadanski *Bulg* **54B2**
Sadiya *India* **82D3**
Sado, R *Port* **50A2**
Sado-shima, I *Japan* **74D3**
Sādri *India* **85C3**
Safed Koh, Mts *Afghan* **84A2**
Saffle *Sweden* **39G7**
Safi *Jordan* **92C3**
Safi *Mor* **96B1**
Safidabeh *Iran* **90D3**
Şāfītă *Syria* **94C1**
Şafwān *Iraq* **93F3**
Saga *Japan* **75A2**
Sagaing *Burma* **76B1**
Sagami-nada, B *Japan* **75B2**
Sāgar *India* **85D4**
Sag Harbor *USA* **16C2**
Saginaw *USA* **14B2**
Saginaw B *USA* **14B2**
Saglouc *Can* **6C3**
Sagua de Tánamo *Cuba* **26B2**
Sagua la Grande *Cuba* **26B2**
Saguenay, R *Can* **7C5**
Sagunto *Spain* **51B2**
Sahāb *Jordan* **94C3**
Sahagún *Spain* **50A1**
Sahara, Desert *N Africa* **96C2**
Saharanpur *India* **84D3**
Sahiwal *Pak* **84C2**
Şahrā al Hijārah, Desert Region *Iraq* **93D3**
Sahuayo *Mexico* **23A1**
Saibai I *Aust* **107D1**
Saïda *Alg* **96C1**
Säida *Leb* **94B2**
Sa'īdabad *Iran* **91C4**
Saidia *Mor* **51B2**
Saidpur *India* **86B1**
Saidu *Pak* **84C2**
Saigō *Japan* **75A1**
Saigon *Viet* **76D3**
Saiha *India* **86C2**
Saihan Tal *China* **68D2**
Saijo *Japan* **75A2**
Saiki *Japan* **74C4**
St Abb's Head, Pt *Scot* **42C2**
St Albans *Eng* **43D4**
St Albans, Vermont *USA* **15D2**
St Albans, West Virginia *USA* **14B3**
St Albans Head, C *Eng* **43C4**
St Albert *Can* **13E2**
St Amand-les-Eaux *France* **46B1**
St Amand-Mont Rond *France* **48C2**
St André, C *Madag* **101D2**
St Andrew B *USA* **17A2**
St Andrews *Scot* **44C3**
St Andrew Sd *USA* **17B1**
St Ann's Bay *Jamaica* **27H1**
St Anthony *Can* **7E4**
St Arnaud *Aust* **108B3**
St Augustine *USA* **17B2**
St Austell *Eng* **43B4**
St-Avold *France* **46D2**
St Bees Head, Pt *Eng* **42C2**
St-Bonnet *France* **47B2**
St Brides B *Wales* **43B4**
St-Brieuc *France* **48B2**
St Catharines *Can* **15C2**
St Catherine,Mt *Grenada* **27M2**
St Catherines I *USA* **17B1**
St Catherines Pt *Eng* **43D4**
St Chamond *France* **49C2**
St Charles, Missouri *USA* **18B2**
St Clair *USA* **14B2**
St Clair,L *USA/Can* **14B2**
St Clair Shores *USA* **14B2**
St Claud *France* **49D2**
St Cloud *USA* **10A2**
Ste Croix *Switz* **47B1**
St Croix, I *Caribbean* **27E3**
St Davids Head, Pt *Wales* **43B4**
St Denis *France* **46B2**
St Denis *Réunion* **101E3**
St Dizier *France* **46C2**
St Elias,Mt *USA* **12F2**
St Elias Mts *Can* **12G2**
Saintes *France* **48B2**

St Étienne *France* **49C2**
St Francis, R *USA* **18B2**
St Francis,C *S Africa* **100B4**
St Gallen *Switz* **47C1**
St-Gaudens *France* **48C3**
St George *Aust* **109C1**
St George, South Carolina *USA* **17B1**
St George, Utah *USA* **9B3**
St George I, Florida *USA* **17B2**
St George,Pt *USA* **20B2**
St-Georges *Can* **15D1**
St George's *Grenada* **27E4**
St Georges Chan *Irish Rep/Wales* **45C3**
St Germain-en-Laye *France* **46A2**
St-Gervais *France* **47B2**
St Gotthard, P *Switz* **47C1**
St Govans Head, Pt *Wales* **43B4**
St Helena *USA* **22A1**
St Helena, I *Atlantic O* **103H5**
St Helena B *S Africa* **100A4**
St Helena Sd *USA* **17B1**
St Helens *Aust* **109C4**
St Helens *Eng* **42C3**
St Helens *USA* **20B1**
St Helens,Mt *USA* **20B1**
St Helier *Jersey* **48B2**
St Hippolyte *France* **47B1**
St-Hubert *Belg* **46C1**
St-Hyacinthe *Can* **7C5**
St Ignace *USA* **14B1**
St Ives *Eng* **43B4**
St James, Missouri *USA* **18B2**
St James,C *Can* **5E4**
St Jean *Can* **15D1**
St Jean-d'Angely *France* **48B2**
St-Jean-de-Maurienne *France* **47B2**
St Jean,L *Can* **10C2**
St-Jérôme *Can* **15D1**
St Joe, R *USA* **20C1**
Saint John *Can* **7D5**
St John's *Can* **7E5**
St Johns, Michigan *USA* **14B2**
St Johns, R *USA* **17B2**
St Johnsbury *USA* **15D2**
St-Joseph *Can* **15D1**
St Joseph, Louisiana *USA* **19B3**
St Joseph, Michigan *USA* **14A2**
St Joseph, Missouri *USA* **18B2**
St Joseph *Trinidad* **27L1**
St Joseph, R *USA* **14B2**
St Joseph I *Can* **14B1**
St Joseph,L *Can* **7A4**
St Julien *France* **47B1**
St-Junien *France* **48C2**
St-Just-en-Chaussée *France* **46B2**
St Kilda, I *Scot* **4B2**
St Kitts, I *Caribbean* **27E3**
St-Laurent *France* **47A1**
St Lawrence, R *Can* **7D5**
Saint Lawrence,G of *Can* **7D5**
St Lawrence I *USA* **4A3**
St Lawrence Seaway *Can/USA* **15C2**
St Lô *France* **48B2**
St Louis *Sen* **97A3**
St Louis *USA* **11A3**
St Lucia, I *Caribbean* **27E4**
St Lucia,L *S Africa* **101H1**
St Magnus, B *Scot* **44D1**
St Malo *France* **48B2**
Ste Marie, C *Madag* **101D3**
St Maries *USA* **20C1**
St Martin, I *Caribbean* **27E3**
St Mary Peak, Mt *Aust* **108A2**
St Marys *Aust* **109C4**
St Marys *USA* **15C2**
St Marys, R *USA* **17B1**
Ste-Menehould *France* **46C2**
St Michael *USA* **12B2**
St Michaels *USA* **16A3**
St-Michel *France* **47B2**
St-Mihiel *France* **46C2**
St Moritz *Switz* **47C1**
St-Nazaire *France* **48B2**
St-Niklaas *Belg* **46C1**
St-Omer *France* **46B1**
St Paul *Can* **13E2**
St Paul, Minnesota *USA* **10A2**
St Paul, R *Lib* **97A4**
St Petersburg *USA* **17B2**
St Pierre *Can* **7E5**
St Pierre,L *Can* **15D1**
St-Pol-Sur-Ternoise *France* **46B1**
St Pölten *Austria* **59B3**
St Quentin *France* **46B2**
St Raphaël *France* **49D3**
St Sébastien, C *Madag* **101D2**
St Simons I *USA* **17B1**
St Stephen *USA* **17B1**
St Thomas *Can* **14B2**
St-Tropez *France* **49D3**
St Truiden *Belg* **46C1**
St-Valéry-sur-Somme *France* **46A1**
St Vincent, C *Madag* **101D3**
St Vincent, I *Caribbean* **27E4**
St Vincent,G *Aust* **108A2**
St-Vith *W Germ* **46D1**
St Wendel *W Germ* **46D2**
Saipan, I *Pacific O* **71F2**
Saiydabad *Afghan* **84B2**
Sajama, Mt *Bol* **30C2**
Sakai *Japan* **74D4**
Sakaidi *Japan* **75A2**
Sakaiminato *Japan* **75A1**
Sakākah *S Arabia* **93D4**
Sakami,L *Can* **10C1**
Sakania *Zaïre* **100B2**
Sakaraha *Madag* **101D3**
Sakarya, R *Turk* **60D5**
Sakasleja *USSR* **58C1**
Sakata *Japan* **74D3**
Saketél *Benin* **97C4**
Sakhalin, I *USSR* **69G1**
Sakishima gunto, Is *Japan* **69E4**
Sal, I *Cape Verde* **97A4**
Sal, R *USSR* **61F4**
Sala *Sweden* **39H7**
Saladillo *Arg* **34D3**
Saladillo, R *Arg* **34C2**
Salado, R, Buenos Aires *Arg* **34D3**
Salado, R, Mendoza/ San Luis *Arg* **34B3**
Salado, R, Sante Fe *Arg* **30D4**
Salaga *Ghana* **97B4**
Sala Hintoun *Camb* **76C3**
Salal *Chad* **98B1**
Şalālah *Oman* **81D4**
Salamanca *Chile* **34A2**
Salamanca *Mexico* **23A1**
Salamanca *Spain* **50A1**
Salamanca *USA* **15C2**
Salamat, R *Chad* **98B2**
Salamaua *PNG* **71F4**
Salamonica *USA* **15C2**
Salang *Indon* **78D1**
Salangen *Nor* **38H5**
Salar de Arizaro *Arg* **30C3**
Salar de Atacama, Salt Pan *Chile* **30C3**
Salar de Coipasa, Salt Pan *Bol* **30C2**
Salar de Uyuni, Salt Pan *Bol* **30C3**
Salasomaggiore *Italy* **47C2**
Salavat *USSR* **61J3**
Salayar *Indon* **70D4**
Sala y Gomez, I *Pacific O* **105L5**
Salazar *Arg* **34C3**
Salbris *France* **48C2**
Salcha, R *USA* **12E2**
Saldanha *S Africa* **100A4**
Saldhad *Syria* **94C2**
Saldungaray *Arg* **34C3**
Saldus *USSR* **58C1**
Sale *Aust* **109C3**
Salem, Illinois *USA* **18C2**
Salem *India* **87B2**
Salem, Massachusetts *USA* **16D1**
Salem, New Jersey *USA* **16B3**
Salem, Oregon *USA* **20B2**
Salembu Besar, I *Indon* **78C4**
Salen *Sweden* **39G6**
Salerno *Italy* **53B2**
Salford *Eng* **42C3**
Salgót *Hung* **54A1**
Salgótarjan *Hung* **59B3**
Salgueiro *Brazil* **31D3**
Salihli *Turk* **55C3**
Salima *Malawi* **101C2**
Salimaa, L *Fin* **39K6**
Salina, Kansas *USA* **18A2**
Salina, I *Italy* **53B3**
Salina Cruz *Mexico* **23B2**
Salina de Arizato *Arg* **30C3**
Salina Grande, Salt pan *Arg* **34B3**
Salina La Antigua, Salt pan *Arg* **34B2**
Salinas *Brazil* **35C1**
Salinas *USA* **22B2**
Salinas, R *USA* **22B2**
Salinas de Llancaneb, Salt Pan *Arg* **34B3**
Salinas Grandes, Salt Pan *Arg* **34B2**
Saline, R, Arkansas *USA* **19B3**
Salines,Pt *Grenada* **27M2**
Salinópolis *Brazil* **31B2**
Salins *France* **47A1**
Salisbury *Eng* **43D4**
Salisbury, Maryland *USA* **15C3**
Salisbury I *Can* **6C3**
Salisbury Plain *Eng* **43D4**
Salla *Fin* **38K5**
Sallanches *France* **47B2**
Sallisaw *USA* **18B2**
Sallyana *Nepal* **86A1**
Salmas *Iran* **93D2**
Salmi *USSR* **38L6**
Salmo *Can* **20C1**
Salmon *USA* **8B2**
Salmon Arm *Can* **13D2**
Salmon River Mts *USA* **8B2**
Salo *Fin* **39J6**
Salò *Italy* **47D2**
Salon-de-Provence *France* **49D3**
Salonta *Rom* **54B1**
Salpausselka, Region *Fin* **38K6**
Salsacate *Arg* **34B2**
Sal'sk *USSR* **61F4**
Salt *Jordan* **94B2**
Salta *Arg* **30C3**
Salta, State *Arg* **30C3**
Saltillo *Mexico* **24B2**
Salt Lake City *USA* **8B2**
Salto *Arg* **34C2**
Salto *Urug* **34D2**
Salto Angostura, Waterfall *Colombia* **32C3**
Salto da Divisa *Brazil* **35D1**
Salto del Angel, Waterfall *Ven* **33E2**
Salto del Guaira, Waterfall *Brazil* **30E3**
Salto Grande, Waterfall *Colombia* **32C4**
Salt Range, Mts *Pak* **84C2**
Salt River *Jamaica* **27H2**
Saluda *USA* **17B1**
Saluzzo *Italy* **47B2**
Salvador *Brazil* **31D4**
Salvador,L *USA* **19B4**
Salvatierra *Mexico* **23A1**
Salwah *Qatar* **91B5**
Salween, R *Burma* **76B1**
Sal'yany *USSR* **93E2**
Salzburg *Austria* **57C3**
Salzgitter *W Germ* **56C2**
Salzwedel *E Germ* **56C2**
Samagaltay *USSR* **68B1**
Samales Group, Is *Phil* **79B4**
Samaná *Dom Rep* **27D3**
Samandaği *Turk* **92C2**
Samangan *Afghan* **84B1**
Samar, I *Phil* **79C3**
Samarai *PNG* **107E2**
Samarinda *Indon* **78D3**
Samarkand *USSR* **80E2**
Sāmarr' *Iraq* **93D3**
Samar S *Phil* **79B3**
Sambalpur *India* **86A2**
Sambas *Indon* **78B2**
Sambava *Madag* **101E2**
Sambhal *India* **84D3**
Samboja *Indon* **78D3**
Sambor *USSR* **59C3**
Sambre, R *France* **46B1**
Samch'ŏk *S Korea* **74B3**
Same *Tanz* **99D3**
Samedan *Switz* **47C1**
Samer *France* **46A1**
Samfya *Zambia* **100B2**
Samka *Burma* **76B1**
Sam Neua *Laos* **76C1**
Sámos, I *Greece* **55C3**
Samothráki, I *Greece* **55C2**
Sampacho *Arg* **34C2**
Sampaga *Indon* **78D3**
Sampit *Indon* **78C3**
Sampit, R *Indon* **78C3**
Sam Rayburn Res *USA* **19B3**
Samrong *Camb* **76C3**
Samsø, I *Den* **56C1**
Samsun *Turk* **92C1**
San *Mali* **97B3**
San, R *Camb* **76D3**
San, R *Pol* **59C2**
Şan'ā' *Yemen* **81C4**
Sanaga, R *Cam* **98B2**
San Agustín *Arg* **29C2**
San Agustin,C *Phil* **79C4**
Sanandaj *Iran* **90A2**
San Andreas *USA* **22B1**
San Andrés Tuxtla *Mexico* **25C3**
San Angelo *USA* **9C3**
San Antioco *Sardegna* **53A3**
San Antioco, I *Medit S* **53A3**
San Antonio *Chile* **34A2**
San Antonio, New Mexico *USA* **9C3**
San Antonio *Phil* **79B2**
San Antonio, R, Texas *USA* **9D4**
San Antonio Abad *Spain* **51C2**
San Antonio,C *Cuba* **25D2**
San Antonio de los Banos *Cuba* **26A2**
San Antonio,Mt *USA* **22D3**
San Antonio Oeste *Arg* **29C4**
San Augustin *Arg* **34D3**
San Augustin de Valle Féril *Arg* **34B2**
Sanawad *India* **85D4**

San Bartolo *Mexico* 23A1
San Benedicto, I *Mexico* 24A3
San Benito, R *USA* 22B2
San Benito Mt *USA* 22B2
San Bernardino *USA* 22D3
San Bernardo *Chile* 34A2
San Blas,C *USA* 17A2
San Carlos *Chile* 34A3
San Carlos *Nic* 32A1
San Carlos *Phil* 79B2
San Carlos de Bariloche *Arg* 29B4
San-chung *Taiwan* 69E4
Sanchursk *USSR* 61G2
San Clemente *Chile* 34A3
San Clemente *USA* 22D4
San Clemente I *USA* 21B3
San Cristóbal *Arg* 34C2
San Cristóbal *Mexico* 25C3
San Cristóbal *Ven* 32C2
San Cristóbal, I *Ecuador* 32J7
San Cristobal, I *Solomon Is* 107F2
Sancti Spíritus *Cuba* 25E2
Sandai *Indon* 78C3
Sandakan *Malay* 70C3
Sanday, I *Scot* 44C2
Sanderson *USA* 9C3
Sandfly L *Can* 13F1
San Diego *USA* 21B3
Sandikli *Turk* 92B2
Sandīla *India* 86A1
Sandnes *Nor* 39F7
Sandnessjøen *Nor* 38G5
Sandø *Faroes* 38D3
Sandoa *Zaïre* 98C3
Sandomierz *Pol* 59C2
Sandpoint *USA* 20C1
Sandrio *Italy* 49D2
Sand Springs *USA* 18A2
Sandstone *Aust* 106A3
Sandu *China* 73C4
Sandusky *USA* 14B2
Sandviken *Sweden* 39H6
Sandy L *Can* 7A4
San Elcano *Arg* 34C2
San Felipe, Baja Cal *Mexico* 9B3
San Felipe *Chile* 34A2
San Felipe, Guanajuato *Mexico* 23A1
San Felipe *Ven* 27D4
San Feliu de Guixols *Spain* 51C1
San Felix, I *Pacific O* 28A5
San Fernando *Chile* 34A2
San Fernando *Phil* 79B2
San Fernando *Phil* 79B2
San Fernando *Spain* 50A2
San Fernando *Trinidad* 27E4
San Fernando *USA* 22C3
San Fernando *Ven* 32D2
Sanford, Florida *USA* 17B2
Sanford,Mt *USA* 12F2
San Francisco *Arg* 34C2
San Francisco *Dom Rep* 27C3
San Francisco *USA* 22A2
San Francisco B *USA* 22A2
San Francisco del Oro *Mexico* 24B2
San Francisco del Rincon *Mexico* 23A1
San Gabriel Mts *USA* 22D3
Sangamner *India* 85C5
Sangamon, R *USA* 18C2
Sangan, I *Pacific O* 71F2
Sangāreddi *India* 87B1
Sangeang, I *Indon* 78D4
Sanger *USA* 22C2
Sanggan He, R *China* 72C2
Sanggau *Indon* 78C2
Sangha, R *Congo* 98B2
Sanghar *Pak* 85B3
Sangkhla Buri *Thai* 76B3
Sangkulirang *Indon* 78D2
Sāngli *India* 87A1
Sangmélima *Cam* 98B2
San Gorgonio Mt *USA* 9B3
Sangre de Cristo, Mts *USA* 9C3
San Gregorio *Arg* 34C2
San Gregorio *USA* 22A2
Sangrūr *India* 84D2
San Ignacio *Arg* 30E4
San Isidro *Phil* 79B3
San Jacinto *Colombia* 32B2
San Jacinto Peak, Mt *USA* 21B3
San Javier *Chile* 34A3
San Javier, Sante Fe *Arg* 34D2
Sanjō, I *Japan* 74D3
San João del Rei *Brazil* 31C6
San Joaquin, R *USA* 22B2
San Joaquin Valley *USA* 22B2
San José *Costa Rica* 32A1
San José *Guatemala* 25C3
San Jose, Luzon *Phil* 79B2
San Jose, Mindoro *Phil* 79B3
San Jose *USA* 22B2
San José, I *Mexico* 9B4
San José de Chiquitos *Bol* 30D2
San José de Feliciano *Arg* 34D2
San José de Jachal *Arg* 34B2
San José de la Dormida *Arg* 34C2
San José do Rio Prêto *Brazil* 31B6
San José del Cabo *Mexico* 24B2
San Juan *Arg* 34B2
San Juan *Puerto Rico* 27D3
San Juan, State *Arg* 34B2
San Juan *Trinidad* 27L1
San Juan *Ven* 32D2
San Juan, Mt *Cuba* 26B2
San Juan, Mts *USA* 8C3
San Juan, R *Arg* 34B2
San Juan, R *Mexico* 23B2
San Juan, R *Nicaragua/Costa Rica* 25D3
San Juan Bautista *Mexico* 23B2
San Juan Bautista *Par* 30E4
San Juan Bautista *USA* 22B2
San Juan del Norte *Nic* 25D3
San Juan de los Cayos *Ven* 27D4
San Juan de loz Lagoz *Mexico* 23A1
San Juan del Rio *Mexico* 23A1
San Juan del Sur *Nicaragua* 25D3
San Juan Is *USA* 20B1
San Juan Tepozcolula *Mexico* 23B2
San Julián *Arg* 29C5
San Justo *Arg* 34C2
Sankuru, R *Zaïre* 98C3
San Leandro *USA* 22A2
San Lorenzo *Ecuador* 32B3
San Lorenzo *Arg* 34C2
San Lucas *USA* 22B2
San Luis *Arg* 34B2
San Luis, State *Arg* 34B2
San Luis de la Paz *Mexico* 23A1
San Luis Obispo *USA* 21A2
San Luis Potosi *Mexico* 23A1
San Luis Res *USA* 22B2
Sanluri *Sardegna* 53A3
San Maigualida, Mts *Ven* 33D2
San Manuel *Arg* 34D3
San Marcos *Chile* 34A2
San Marcos *Mexico* 23B2
San Marino, Republic *Europe* 52B2
San Martin, Mendoza *Arg* 34B2
San Martin, Base *Ant* 112C3
San Martino di Castroza *Italy* 47D1
San Martin Tuxmelucan *Mexico* 23B2
San Mateo *USA* 22A2
San Matias *Bol* 30E2
Sanmenxia *China* 72C3
San Miguel *El Salvador* 25D3
San Miguel, I *USA* 22B3
San Miguel del Allende *Mexico* 23A1
San Miguel del Monte *Arg* 34D3
San Miguel de Tucumán *Arg* 30C4
Sanming *China* 73D4
San Nicolas, I *USA* 9B3
San Nicolás de los Arroyos *Arg* 34C2
Sannieshof *S Africa* 101G1
Sanniquellie *Lib* 97B4
Sanok *Pol* 59C3
San Onofore *Colombia* 26B5
San Onofre *USA* 22D4
San Pablo *Phil* 79B3
San Pablo B *USA* 22A1
San Pedro, Buenos Aires *Arg* 34D2
San Pédro *Ivory Coast* 97B4
San Pedro, Jujuy *Arg* 30D3
San Pedro *Par* 30E3
San Pedro Chan *USA* 22C4
San Pedro de los Colonias *Mexico* 9C4
San Pedro Sula *Honduras* 25D3
San Pietro, I *Medit S* 53A3
San Quintin *Mexico* 24A1
San Rafael *Arg* 34B2
San Rafael *USA* 22A2
San Rafael Mts *USA* 22C3
San Remo *Italy* 49D3
San Salvador *Arg* 34D2
San Salvador, I *Caribbean* 26C2
San Salvador, I *Ecuador* 32J7
San Salvador de Jujuy *Arg* 30C3
San Sebastian *Spain* 51B1
San Severo *Italy* 53C2
Santa Ana *Bol* 30C2
Santa Ana *Guatemala* 25C3
Santa Ana *USA* 22D4
Santa Ana Mts *USA* 22D4
Santa Bárbara *Chile* 34A3
Santa Barbara *Mexico* 24B2
Santa Barbara *USA* 22C3
Santa Barbara, I *USA* 22C4
Santa Barbara Chan *USA* 22B3
Santa Barbara Res *USA* 22C3
Santa Catalina, I *USA* 22C4
Santa Catalina,G of *USA* 22C4
Santa Catarina, State *Brazil* 30F4
Santa Clara *Cuba* 26B2
Santa Clara *USA* 22B2
Santa Clara, R *USA* 22C3
Santa Cruz *Arg* 29C6
Santa Cruz *Bol* 30D2
Santa Cruz *Chile* 34A2
Santa Cruz *Phil* 79B3
Santa Cruz, State *Arg* 29B5
Santa Cruz *USA* 22A2
Santa Cruz, I *USA* 22C4
Santa Cruz Cabrália *Brazil* 35D1
Santa Cruz Chan *USA* 22C3
Santa Cruz de la Palma *Canary Is* 96A2
Santa Cruz del Sur *Cuba* 26B2
Santa Cruz de Tenerife *Canary Is* 96A2
Santa Cruz do Cuando *Angola* 100B2
Santa Cruz do Rio Pardo *Brazil* 35B2
Santa Cruz Mts *USA* 22A2
Santa Elena *Arg* 34D2
Santa Elena *Ven* 33E3
Santa Fe *Arg* 34C2
Santa Fe, State *Arg* 34C2
Santa Fe *USA* 9C3
Santa Helena de Goiás *Brazil* 35A1
Santai *China* 73B3
Santa Inés, I *Chile* 29B6
Santa Isabel, La Pampa *Arg* 34B3
Santa Isabel, Sante Fe *Arg* 34C2
Santa Isabel, I *Solomon Is* 107E1
Santa Lucia, Ra *USA* 21A2
Santa Lucia Range, Mts *USA* 21A2
Santa Luzia, I *Cape Verde* 97A4
Santa Margarita, I *Mexico* 9B4
Santa Margarita, R *USA* 22D4
Santa Maria *Brazil* 30F4
Santa Maria *Colombia* 26C4
Santa Maria *USA* 21A3
Santa Maria, I *Açores* 96A1
Santa Maria, R, Queretaro *Mexico* 23B1
Santa Maria del Rio *Mexico* 23A1
Santa Marta *Colombia* 32C1
Santa Monica *USA* 22C3
Santa Monica B *USA* 22C4
Santana do Livramento *Brazil* 29E2
Santander *Colombia* 32B3
Santander *Spain* 50B1
Santañy *Spain* 51C2
Santa Paula *USA* 22C3
Santa Quitéria *Brazil* 31C2
Santarem *Brazil* 33G4
Santarém *Port* 50A2
Santa Rosa, California *USA* 22A1
Santa Rosa *Honduras* 25D3
Santa Rosa, La Pampa *Arg* 34C3
Santa Rosa, Mendoza *Arg* 34B2
Santa Rosa, San Luis *Arg* 34B2
Santa Rosa, I *USA* 22B3
Santa Rosalía *Mexico* 24A2
Santa Rosa Range, Mts *USA* 20C2
Santa Talhada *Brazil* 31D3
Santa Teresa *Brazil* 35C1
Santa Teresa di Gallura *Sardegna* 53A2
Santa Ynez, R *USA* 22B3
Santa Ynez Mts *USA* 22B3
Santee, R *USA* 17C1
Santhia *Italy* 47C2
Santiago *Chile* 34A2
Santiago *Dom Rep* 27C3
Santiago *Panama* 32A2
Santiago *Phil* 79B2
Santiago, R *Peru* 32B4
Santiago de Compostela *Spain* 50A1

Santiago de Cuba *Cuba* **26B2**
Santiago del Estero *Arg* **30D4**
Santiago del Estero, State *Arg* **30D4**
Santiago Peak, Mt *USA* **22D4**
Santo, State *Brazil* **31C5**
Santo Anastatácio *Brazil* **35A2**
Santo Angelo *Brazil* **30F4**
Santo Antão, I *Cape Verde* **97A4**
Santo Antonio da Platina *Brazil* **35A2**
Santo Domingo *Dom Rep* **27D3**
Santos *Brazil* **35B2**
Santos Dumont *Brazil* **35C2**
Santo Tomé *Arg* **30E4**
San Valentin, Mt *Chile* **29B5**
San Vicente *Chile* **34A2**
Sanza Pomba *Angola* **98B3**
São Borja *Brazil* **30E4**
São Carlos *Brazil* **35B2**
São Félix, Mato Grosso *Brazil* **33G5**
São Fidélis *Brazil* **35C2**
São Francisco *Brazil* **35C1**
São Francisco, R *Brazil* **31D3**
São Francisco do Sul *Brazil* **30G4**
São Gotardo *Brazil* **35B1**
Sao Hill *Tanz* **99D3**
São João da Barra *Brazil* **35C2**
São João da Boa Vista *Brazil* **35B2**
São João da Ponte *Brazil* **35C1**
São João del Rei *Brazil* **35C2**
São Joaquim da Barra *Brazil* **35B2**
São Jorge, I *Açores* **96A1**
São José do Rio Prêto *Brazil* **35B2**
São José dos Campos *Brazil* **35B2**
São Luis *Brazil* **31C2**
São Marcos, R *Brazil* **35B1**
São Maria do Suaçui *Brazil* **35C1**
São Mateus *Brazil* **35D1**
São Mateus, R *Brazil* **35C1**
São Miguel, I *Açores* **96A1**
Saône, R *France* **49C2**
São Nicolau, I *Cape Verde* **97A4**
São Paulo *Brazil* **35B2**
São Paulo, State *Brazil* **35A2**
São Raimundo Nonato *Brazil* **31C3**
São Romão *Brazil* **35B1**
São Sebastia do Paraiso *Brazil* **35B2**
São Simão, Goias *Brazil* **35A1**
São Simão, Sao Paulo *Brazil* **35B2**
São Tiago, I *Cape Verde* **97A4**
São Tomé, I *W Africa* **97C4**
São Tomé and Principe, Republic *W Africa* **97C4**
Saoura, Watercourse *Alg* **96B2**
São Vicente *Brazil* **35B2**
São Vincente, I *Cape Verde* **97A4**
Sápai *Greece* **55C2**
Sape *Indon* **78D4**
Sapele *Nig* **97C4**
Sapporo *Japan* **74E2**
Sapri *Italy* **53C2**
Sapulpa *USA* **18A2**
Saqqez *Iran* **90A2**
Saquenay, R *Can* **10C2**
Sarāb *Iran* **90A2**
Sarafa *USSR* **54C1**
Sarajevo *Yugos* **54A2**
Sarakhs *Iran* **90D2**
Saraktash *USSR* **61J3**
Sarala *USSR* **63A2**
Saranac L *USA* **15D2**
Saranac Lake *USA* **15D2**
Sarandë *Alb* **55B3**
Sarangani Is *Phil* **79C4**
Saransk *USSR* **61G3**
Sarapul *USSR* **61H2**
Sarasota *USA* **17B2**
Saratoga Springs *USA* **15D2**
Saratok *Malay* **78C2**
Saratov *USSR* **61G3**
Saratovskoye Vodokhranilishche, Res *USSR* **61G3**
Sarawak, State *Malay* **67F4**
Saraykoy *Turk* **92A2**
Sarbīsheh *Iran* **90C3**
Sarca, R *Italy* **47D1**
Sardalais *Libya* **95A2**
Sar Dasht *Iran* **90A2**
Sardegna, I *Medit S* **52A2**
Sarektjåkkå, Mt *Sweden* **38H5**
Sargodha *Pak* **84C2**
Sarh *Chad* **98B2**
Sārī *Iran* **90B2**
Sarida, R *Isreal* **94B2**
Sarikamiş *Turk* **93D1**
Sarina *Aust* **107D3**
Sarine, R *Switz* **47B1**
Sar-i-Pul *Afghan* **84B1**
Sarir *Libya* **95B2**
Sarir Tibesti, Desert *Libya* **95A2**
Sariwŏn *N Korea* **74B3**
Sark, I *UK* **48B2**
Šarkišla *Turk* **92C2**
Sarmi *Indon* **71E4**
Sarmiento *Arg* **29C5**
Särna *Sweden* **39G6**
Sarnen *Switz* **47C1**
Sarnia *Can* **14B2**
Sarny *USSR* **58D2**
Saroaq *Greenland* **6E2**
Sarobi *Afghan* **84B2**
Sarolangun *Indon* **78A3**
Saronikós Kólpos, G *Greece* **55B3**
Saronno *Italy* **47C2**
Saros Körfezi, B *Turk* **55C2**
Sarpsborg *Nor* **39G7**
Sarralbe *France* **46D2**
Sarrebourg *France* **46D2**
Sarreguemines *France* **46D2**
Sarre-Union *France* **46D2**
Sarrion *Spain* **51B1**
Sartanahu *Pak* **85B3**
Sartène *Corse* **53A2**
Sarthe, R *France* **48B2**
Sarykamys *USSR* **61H4**
Sarysu, R *USSR* **65H5**
Sasarām *India* **86A2**
Sasebo *Japan* **74B4**
Saskatchewan, Province *Can* **5H4**
Saskatchewan, R *Can* **5H4**
Saskatoon *Can* **13F2**
Sasolburg *S Africa* **101G1**
Sasovo *USSR* **61F3**
Sassandra *Ivory Coast* **97B4**
Sassandra, R *Ivory Coast* **97B4**
Sassari *Sardegna* **53A2**
Sassnitz *E Germ* **56C2**
Sassuolo *Italy* **47D2**
Sastre *Arg* **34C2**
Sātāra *India* **87A1**
Satellite B *Can* **4G2**
Satengar, Is *Indon* **78D4**
Säter *Sweden* **39H6**
Satilla, R *USA* **17B1**
Satka *USSR* **61J2**
Satluj, R *India* **84D2**
Satna *India* **86A2**
Sātpura Range, Mts *India* **85C4**
Satu Mare *Rom* **54B1**
Sauce *Arg* **34D2**
Sauda *Nor* **39F7**
Saudi Arabia, Kingdom *Arabian Pen* **80C3**
Sauer, R *W Germ/Lux* **46D2**
Sauerland, Region *W Germ* **46D1**
Sauðárkrókur *Iceland* **38B1**
Saugatuck *USA* **14A2**
Saugerties *USA* **16C1**
Saugstad,Mt *Can* **13B2**
Sault Sainte Marie *Can* **7B5**
Sault Ste Marie *Can* **14B1**
Sault Ste Marie *USA* **14B1**
Saumlaki *Indon* **71E4**
Saumur *France* **48B2**
Saurimo *Angola* **98C3**
Sauteurs *Grenada* **27M2**
Sava, R *Yugos* **54A2**
Savalou *Benin* **97C4**
Savannah, Georgia *USA* **17B1**
Savannah, R *USA* **17B1**
Savannakhet *Laos* **76C2**
Savanna la Mar *Jamaica* **26B3**
Savant Lake *Can* **7A4**
Savarane *Laos* **76D2**
Savé *Benin* **97C4**
Save, R *Mozam* **101C3**
Sāveh *Iran* **90B3**
Saverne *France* **46D2**
Savigliano *Italy* **47B2**
Savigny *France* **46B2**
Savoie, Region *France* **49D2**
Savona *Italy* **49D3**
Savonlinna *Fin* **38K6**
Savoonga *USA* **4A3**
Savukoski *Fin* **38K5**
Savu S *Indon* **71D4**
Saw *Burma* **76A1**
Sawai Mādhopur *India* **85D3**
Sawang *Indon* **78A2**
Sawankhalok *Thai* **76B2**
Sawara *Japan* **75C1**
Sawknah *Libya* **95A2**
Sawtooth Mt *USA* **12E1**
Sawu, I *Indon* **106B2**
Say *Niger* **97C3**
Sayghan *Afghan* **84B1**
Sayhandulaan *Mongolia* **72B1**
Sayhūt *S Yemen* **91B5**
Saykhin *USSR* **61G4**
Saynshand *Mongolia* **68D2**
Say-Utes *USSR* **61H5**
Sayville *USA* **16C2**
Sayward *Can* **13B2**
Sázava, R *Czech* **57C3**
Sbisseb, R *Alg* **51C2**
Scafell Pike, Mt *Eng* **42C2**
Scalloway *Scot* **44D1**
Scapa Flow, Sd *Scot* **44C2**
Scarborough *Can* **15C2**
Scarborough *Eng* **42D2**
Scarborough *Tobago* **27E4**
Scarp, I *Scot* **44A2**
Scarriff *Irish Rep* **45B2**
Schaffhausen *Switz* **52A1**
Scharding *Austria* **57C3**
Scharteberg, Mt *W Germ* **46D1**
Schefferville *Can* **7D4**
Schelde, R *Belg* **46B1**
Schenectady *USA* **10C2**
Schio *Italy* **47D2**
Schleiden *W Germ* **46D1**
Schleswig *W Germ* **56B2**
Schleswig Holstein, State *W Germ* **56B2**
Schoharie *USA* **16B1**
Schouten, Is *PNG* **71F4**
Schreiber *Can* **7B5**
Schurz *USA* **21B2**
Schuykill Haven *USA* **16A2**
Schuylkill, R *USA* **16B2**
Schwabische Alb, Upland *W Germ* **57B3**
Schwarzwald, Mts *W Germ* **49D2**
Schwarzwald, Upland *W Germ* **57B3**
Schwatka Mts *USA* **12C1**
Schwaz *Austria* **47D1**
Schweinfurt *W Germ* **57C2**
Schweizer Reneke *S Africa* **101G1**
Schwerin *E Germ* **56C2**
Schwyz *Switz* **47C1**
Sciacca *Italy* **53B3**
Scioto, R *USA* **14B3**
Scone *Aust* **109D2**
Scoresby Sd *Greenland* **6H2**
Scotia Ridge *Atlantic O* **103F7**
Scotia S *Atlantic O* **103F7**
Scotland, Country *U K* **44B3**
Scott, Base *Ant* **112B7**
Scott,C *Can* **13B2**
Scott City *USA* **9C2**
Scott I *Ant* **112C6**
Scott Inlet, B *Can* **6C2**
Scott,Mt *USA* **20B2**
Scott Reef *Timor S* **106B2**
Scottsbluff *USA* **8C2**
Scottsboro *USA* **17A1**
Scottsdale *Aust* **109C4**
Scranton *USA* **10C2**
Scuol *Switz* **47D1**
Seal, R *Can* **5J4**
Sea Lake *Aust* **108B3**
Searcy *USA* **18B2**
Seaside, California *USA* **22B2**
Seaside, Oregon *USA* **20B1**
Seaside Park *USA* **16B3**
Seattle *USA* **20B1**
Sebastopol *USA* **22A1**
Sebez *USSR* **58D1**
Sebring *USA* **17B2**
Secretary I *NZ* **111A3**
Sedalia *USA* **18B2**
Sedan *France* **46C2**
Seddonville *NZ* **111B2**
Sede Boqer *Israel* **94B3**
Sederot *Israel* **94B3**
Sédhiou *Sen* **97A3**
Sedom *Israel* **94B3**
Seeheim *Namibia* **100A3**
Sefton,Mt *NZ* **111B2**
Segamat *Malay* **77C5**
Segorbe *Spain* **51B2**
Ségou *Mali* **97B3**
Segovia *Spain* **50B1**
Segre, R *Spain* **51C1**
Séguéla *Ivory Coast* **97B4**
Seguia el Hamra, Watercourse *Mor* **96A2**
Segundo, R *Arg* **34C2**
Seguntur *Indon* **78D2**
Segura, R *Spain* **50B2**
Sehwan *Pak* **85B3**
Seille, R *France* **46D2**
Seinäjoki *Fin* **38J6**
Seine, R *France* **48C2**
Seine-et-Marne, Department *France* **46B2**
Sekenke *Tanz* **99D3**
Selah *USA* **20B1**
Selaru, I *Indon* **71E4**
Selat Alas, Str *Indon* **78D4**
Selat Bangka, Str *Indon* **78B3**
Selat Berhala, B *Indon* **78A3**

Selat Dampier, Str *Indon* **71E4**
Selat Gaspar, Str *Indon* **78B3**
Selat Lombok, Str *Indon* **78D4**
Selat Sape, Str *Indon* **78D4**
Selat Sunda, Str *Indon* **78B4**
Selat Wetar, Chan *Indon* **71D4**
Selawik *USA* **12B1**
Selawik, R *USA* **12C1**
Selawik L *USA* **12B1**
Selby *Eng* **42D3**
Selçuk *Turk* **55C3**
Seldovia *USA* **12D3**
Selebi Pikwe *Botswana* **100B3**
Selfoss *Iceland* **6H3**
Selima Oasis *Sudan* **95B2**
Selkirk *Can* **5J4**
Selkirk *Scot* **42C2**
Selkirk Mts *Can* **13D2**
Selma, California *USA* **22C2**
Selouane *Mor* **50B2**
Selous,Mt *Can* **12H2**
Selta Karimata, Str *Indon* **78B3**
Selvas, Region *Brazil* **32C5**
Selwyn *Aust* **107D3**
Selwyn Mts *Can* **4E3**
Semarang *Indon* **78C4**
Semenov *USSR* **61E2**
Semidi Is *USA* **12C3**
Semiluki *USSR* **60E3**
Seminole, Oklahoma *USA* **19A2**
Seminole,L *USA* **17B1**
Semipalatinsk *USSR* **65K4**
Semirara Is *Phil* **79B3**
Semirom *Iran* **90B3**
Semitau *Indon* **78C2**
Semnān *Iran* **90B2**
Semois, R *Belg* **46C2**
Sempoala, Hist Site *Mexico* **23B2**
Sena Madureira *Brazil* **32D5**
Senanga *Zambia* **100B2**
Senatobia *USA* **19C3**
Sendai, Honshū *Japan* **74E3**
Sendai, Kyūshū *Japan* **74C4**
Sendwha *India* **85D4**
Seneca Falls *USA* **15C2**
Senegal, Republic *Africa* **97A3**
Sénégal, R *Maur Sen* **97A3**
Senekal *S Africa* **101G1**
Senhor do Bonfim *Brazil* **31D4**
Senigallia *Italy* **52B2**
Senj *Yugos* **52C2**
Senkaku Gunto, Is *Japan* **69E4**
Senlis *France* **46B2**
Sennar *Sudan* **99D1**
Senneterre *Can* **7C5**
Sens *France* **49C2**
Senta *Yugos* **54A1**
Sentery *Zaïre* **98C3**
Sentinel Peak, Mt *Can* **13C2**
Seoni *India* **85D4**
Separation Pt *NZ* **110B2**
Sepone *Laos* **76D2**
Sept-Iles *Can* **7D4**
Séquédine *Niger* **95A2**
Sequoia, Nat Pk *USA* **21B2**
Seram, I *Indon* **71D4**
Serang *Indon* **78B4**
Serasan, I *Indon* **78B2**
Serbia, Region *Yugos* **54A2**
Serdobsk *USSR* **61F3**
Seremban *Malay* **77C5**
Serengeti Nat Pk *Tanz* **99D3**
Serenje *Zambia* **100C2**
Seret, R *USSR* **59D3**
Sergach *USSR* **61G2**
Sergino *USSR* **65H3**
Sergipe, State *Brazil* **31D4**
Seria *Brunei* **78C2**
Serian *Malay* **78C2**
Sérifos, I *Greece* **55B3**
Serio, R *Italy* **47C2**
Serir Calanscio, Desert *Libya* **95B2**
Sermaize-les-Bains *France* **46C2**
Sermata, I *Indon* **71D4**
Sernovodsk *USSR* **61H3**
Serov *USSR* **65H4**
Serowe *Botswana* **100B3**
Serpa *Port* **50A2**
Serpukhov *USSR* **60E3**
Serra da Canastra, Mts *Brazil* **35B2**
Serra da Estrela, Mts *Port* **50A1**
Serra da Mantiqueira, Mts *Brazil* **35B2**
Serra da Mombuca *Brazil* **35A1**
Serra do Cabral, Mt *Brazil* **35C1**
Serra do Cachimbo, Mts *Brazil* **33F5**
Serra do Caiapó, Mts *Brazil* **35A1**
Serra do Cantu, Mts *Brazil* **35A2**
Serra do Caparaó, Mts *Brazil* **35C2**
Serra do Chifre *Brazil* **31C5**
Serra do Espinhaço, Mts *Brazil* **35C1**
Serra do Mar, Mts *Brazil* **35B2**
Serra do Mirante, Mts *Brazil* **35A2**
Serra do Navio *Brazil* **33G3**
Serra do Paranapiacaba, Mts *Brazil* **35B2**
Serra dos Caiabis, Mts *Brazil* **33F6**
Serra dos Dourados, Mts *Brazil* **35A2**
Serra dos Parecis, Mts *Brazil* **33E6**
Serra dos Pilões, Mts *Brazil* **35B1**
Serra Dourada, Mts *Brazil* **35A1**
Serra Formosa, Mts *Brazil* **33F6**
Sérrai *Greece* **55B2**
Serrana Bank, Is *Caribbean* **25D3**
Serrana de Cuenca, Mts *Spain* **51B1**
Serranópolis *Brazil* **35A1**
Serra Pacaraima, Mts *Brazil/Ven* **33E3**
Serra Parima, Mts *Brazil* **33E3**
Serra Tumucumaque *Brazil* **33G3**
Serre, R *France* **46B2**
Serrezuela *Arg* **34B2**
Serrinha *Brazil* **31D4**
Sermilik *Greenland* **6G3**
Serro *Brazil* **35C1**
Sertanópolis *Brazil* **35A2**
Sêrtar *China* **72A3**
Seruyan, R *Indon* **78C3**
Sesfontein *Namibia* **100A2**
Sesheke *Zambia* **100B2**
Sestriere *Italy* **47B2**
Setana *Japan* **74D2**
Sète *France* **49C3**
Sete Lagoas *Brazil* **35C1**
Sétif *Alg* **96C1**
Seto *Japan* **75B1**
Seto Naikai, S *Japan* **75A2**
Settat *Mor* **96B1**
Settle *Eng* **42C2**
Settler *Can* **5G4**
Sêtúbal *Port* **50A2**
Sevan,Oz, L *USSR* **93E1**
Sevastopol' *USSR* **60D5**
Severn, R *Can* **7B4**
Severn, R *Eng* **43C3**
Severnaya Zemlya, I *USSR* **1B9**
Severo-Baykalskoye Nagorye, Mts *USSR* **63C2**
Severo Donets *USSR* **60E4**
Severodvinsk *USSR* **64E3**
Severo Sos'va, R *USSR* **64H3**
Sevier, R *USA* **8B3**
Sevier L *USA* **8B3**
Sevilla *Spain* **50A2**
Sevlievo *Bulg* **54C2**
Sewa, R *Sierra Leone* **97A4**
Seward, Alaska *USA* **12E2**
Seward, Nebraska *USA* **18A1**
Seward Pen *USA* **12A1**
Sexsmith *Can* **13D1**
Seychelles, Is *Indian O* **89K8**
Seyðisfjörður *Iceland* **38C1**
Seyhan *Turk* **92C2**
Seym, R *USSR* **60E3**
Seymour *Aust* **108C3**
Seymour, Connecticut *USA* **16C2**
Seymour, Indiana *USA* **14A3**
Sézanne *France* **46B2**
Sfax *Tunisia* **96D1**
Sfînto Gheorghe *Rom* **54C1**
's-Gravenhage *Neth* **56A2**
Shaanxi, Province *China* **72B3**
Shabunda *Zaïre* **98C3**
Shache *China* **82B2**
Shackleton Ice Shelf *Ant* **112C9**
Shadadkot *Pak* **85B3**
Shādhām, R *Iran* **91B3**
Shaftesbury *Eng* **43C4**
Shag Rocks, Is *South Georgia* **29G8**
Shāhabād *Iran* **90A3**
Shahbā *Syria* **94C2**
Shahdap *Iran* **91C3**
Shahdol *India* **86A2**
Shāhīn Dezh *Iran* **90A2**
Shāh Kūh *Iran* **90C3**
Shahr-e Bābak *Iran* **91C3**
Shahr Kord *Iran* **90B3**
Shājābād *India* **87B1**
Shājahānpur *India* **84D3**
Shājāpur *India* **85D4**
Shakhty *USSR* **61F4**
Shakhun'ya *USSR* **61G2**
Shaki *Nig* **97C4**
Shaktoolik *USA* **12B2**
Shamary *USSR* **61J2**
Shambe *Sudan* **99D2**
Shamokin *USA* **16A2**
Shandaken *USA* **16B1**
Shandong, Province *China* **72D2**
Shangchuan Dao, I *China* **73C5**
Shangdu *China* **72C1**
Shanghai *China* **73E3**
Shangnan *China* **72C3**
Shangombo *Zambia* **100B2**
Shangra *China* **73D4**
Shangsi *China* **73B5**
Shang Xian *China* **72C3**
Shannon, R *Irish Rep* **41B3**
Shanqiu *China* **72D3**
Shansonggang *China* **74B2**
Shantarskiye Ostrova, I *USSR* **63F2**
Shantou *China* **73D5**
Shanxi, Province *China* **72C2**
Shan Xian *China* **72D3**
Shaoguan *China* **73C5**
Shaoxing *China* **73E4**
Shaoyang *China* **73C4**
Shapinsay, I *Scot* **44C2**
Shaqqā *Syria* **94C2**
Sharifābād *Iran* **90C2**
Sharjah *UAE* **91C4**
Shark B *Aust* **106A3**
Sharlauk *USSR* **90C2**
Sharon,Plain of *Israel* **94B2**
Sharya *USSR* **61G2**
Shashamanna *Eth* **99D2**
Shashi *China* **73C3**
Shasta L *USA* **20B2**
Shasta,Mt *USA* **20B2**
Shaṭṭ al Gharrat, R *Iraq* **93E3**
Shaubak *Jordan* **94B3**
Shaunavon *Can* **13F3**
Shaver L *USA* **22C2**
Shawangunk Mt *USA* **16B2**
Shawinigan *Can* **15D1**
Shawnee, Oklahoma *USA* **19A2**
Sha Xian *China* **73D4**
Shay Gap *Aust* **106B3**
Shaykh Miskīn *Syria* **94C2**
Shaykh 'Uthmān *S Yemen* **99E1**
Shchigry *USSR* **60E3**
Shchors *USSR* **60D3**
Shchuchinsk *USSR* **65J4**
Sheboygan *USA* **14A2**
Shebshi, Mts *Nig* **98B2**
Sheenjek, R *USA* **12F1**
Sheep Haven, Estuary *Irish Rep* **45C1**
Sheerness *Eng* **43E4**
Shefar'am *Israel* **94B2**
Sheffield *Eng* **42D3**
Shekhupura *Pak* **84C2**
Shelagyote Peak, Mt *Can* **13B1**
Shelburne Falls *USA* **16C1**
Shelby, Michigan *USA* **14A2**
Shelby, Montana *USA* **8B2**
Shelbyville, Indiana *USA* **14A3**
Sheldon,Mt *Can* **12H2**
Shelikof Str *USA* **12D3**
Shellharbour *Aust* **109D2**
Shelter Pt *NZ* **111A3**
Shelton *USA* **20B1**
Shemakha *USSR* **93E1**
Shenandoah *USA* **18A1**
Shenandoah, R *USA* **15C3**
Shenandoah Nat Pk *USA* **15C3**
Shendam *Nig* **97C4**
Shendi *Sudan* **95C2**
Shenmu *China* **72C2**
Shenyang *China* **72E1**
Shenzhen *China* **73C5**
Sheopur *India* **85D3**
Shepetovka *USSR* **59D2**
Shepparton *Aust* **108C3**
Sherard,C *Can* **6B2**
Sherborne *Eng* **43C4**
Sherbro I *Sierra Leone* **97A4**
Sherbrooke *Can* **15D1**
Shergarh *India* **85C3**
Sheridan, Arkansas *USA* **19B3**
Sheridan, Wyoming *USA* **8C2**
Sherman *USA* **19A3**
s-Hertogenbosh *Neth* **56B2**
Sheslay *Can* **12H3**
Shetland, Is *Scot* **40C1**
Shevchenko *USSR* **61H5**
Sheyk Sho'eyb, I *Iran* **91B4**
Shiashkotan, I *USSR* **69H2**
Shibarghan *Afghan* **84B1**
Shibata *Japan* **74D3**
Shibeli, R *Eth* **99E2**
Shibin el Kom *Egypt* **95C1**
Shibukawa *Japan* **75B1**
Shijiazhuang *China* **72C2**
Shikarpur *Pak* **84B3**
Shikoku, I *Japan* **67G3**
Shikoku-sanchi, Mts *Japan* **75A2**

Shiliguri *India* **86B1**
Shilka *USSR* **68D1**
Shilka, R *USSR* **68D1**
Shillington *USA* **16B2**
Shillong *India* **86C1**
Shilovo *USSR* **61F3**
Shimabara *Japan* **75A2**
Shimada *Japan* **75B2**
Shimanovsk *USSR* **69E1**
Shimizu *Japan* **74D3**
Shimoda *Japan* **75B2**
Shimoga *India* **87B2**
Shimonoseki *Japan* **74C4**
Shinano, R *Japan* **75B1**
Shināş *Oman* **91C5**
Shingū *Japan* **74D4**
Shinjō *Japan* **75C1**
Shinminato *Japan* **74D3**
Shinshār *Syria* **94C1**
Shinyanga *Tanz* **99D3**
Shiogama *Japan* **74E3**
Shiono-misaki, C *Japan* **75B2**
Shiping *China* **73A5**
Shippensburg *USA* **16A2**
Shiquan *China* **72B3**
Shirakawa *Japan* **75C1**
Shirane-san, Mt *Japan* **75B1**
Shirani-san, Mt *Japan* **75B1**
Shīraz *Iran* **91B4**
Shīr Kūh *Iran* **90B3**
Shirotori *Japan* **75B1**
Shirvān *Iran* **90C2**
Shishmaref *USA* **12A1**
Shishmaref Inlet *USA* **12A1**
Shishmaret *USA* **4B3**
Shitanjing *China* **72B2**
Shively *USA* **14A3**
Shivpuri *India* **85D3**
Shivta, Hist Site *Israel* **94B3**
Shiwa Ngandu *Zambia* **101C2**
Shiyan *China* **72C3**
Shizuishan *China* **72B2**
Shizuoka *Japan* **75B1**
Shkodër *Alb* **54A2**
Shoalhaven, R *Aust* **109D2**
Shobara *Japan* **75A2**
Shoranūr *India* **87B2**
Shorāpur *India* **87B1**
Shoshone Mts *USA* **21B2**
Shostka *USSR* **60D3**
Shreveport *USA* **19B3**
Shrewsbury *Eng* **43C3**
Shropshire, County *Eng* **43C3**
Shuanglia *China* **72E1**
Shuangyashan *China* **69F2**
Shubar kuduk *USSR* **61J4**
Shu He, R *China* **72D2**
Shuicheng *China* **73A4**
Shujaabad *Pak* **84C3**
Shujālpur *India* **85D4**
Shule He *China* **68B2**
Shumen *Bulg* **54C2**
Shumerlya *USSR* **61G2**
Shuncheng *China* **73D4**
Shungnak *USA* **12C1**
Shuo Xian *China* **72C2**
Shūr Gaz *Iran* **91C4**
Shurugwi *Zim* **100B2**
Shuswap L *Can* **13D2**
Shuya *USSR* **61F2**
Shuyak I *USA* **12D3**
Shwebo *Burma* **82D3**
Shwegyin *Burma* **76B2**
Siah Koh, Mts *Afghan* **84A2**
Siālkot *Pak* **84C2**
Siarao, I *Phil* **79C4**
Siaton *Phil* **79B4**
Šiauliai *USSR* **58C1**
Sibay *USSR* **65G4**
Sibayi L *S Africa* **101H1**
Šibenik *Yugos* **52C2**
Siberut, I *Indon* **70A4**
Sibi *Pak* **84B3**
Sibirskoye *USSR* **68C1**
Sibiti *Congo* **98B3**
Sibiti, R *Tanz* **99D3**
Sibiu *Rom* **54B1**
Sibolga *Indon* **70A3**
Sibsāgār *India* **86C1**
Sibu *Malay* **78C2**
Sibuguay B *Phil* **79B4**
Sibut *CAR* **98B2**
Sibuyan, I *Phil* **79B3**
Sibuyan S *Phil* **79B3**
Sichuan, Province *China* **73A3**
Sicilia, I *Medit S* **53B3**
Sicilian, Chan *Italy/ Tunisia* **53B3**
Sicuani *Peru* **32C6**
Siddhapur *India* **85C4**
Siddipet *India* **87B1**
Sidhi *India* **86A2**
Sidi Barrani *Egypt* **95B1**
Sidi bel Abbès *Alg* **96B1**
Sidlaw Hills *Scot* **44C3**
Sidley,Mt *Ant* **112B5**
Sidney *Can* **20B1**
Sidney, Nebraska *USA* **8C2**
Sidney, New York *USA* **15C2**
Sidney, Ohio *USA* **14B2**
Sidney Lanier,L *USA* **17B1**
Siedlce *Pol* **58C2**
Sieg, R *W Germ* **46D1**
Siegburg *W Germ* **46D1**
Siegen *W Germ* **46D1**
Siem Reap *Camb* **76C3**
Siena *Italy* **52B2**
Sierpc *Pol* **58B2**
Sierra Andrés Tuxtla *Mexico* **23B2**
Sierra Auca Mahuida, Mts *Arg* **34B3**
Sierra Blanca *USA* **9C3**
Sierra de Albarracin, Mts *Spain* **51B1**
Sierra de Alcaraz, Mts *Spain* **50B2**
Sierra de Cordoba, Mts *Arg* **34B2**
Sierra de Gredos, Mts *Spain* **50A1**
Sierra de Guadalupe, Mts *Spain* **50A2**
Sierra de Guadarrama, Mts *Spain* **50B1**
Sierra de Guara, Mts *Spain* **51B1**
Sierra de Gudar, Mts *Spain* **51B1**
Sierra de Juárez *Mexico* **23B2**
Sierra de la Ventana, Mts *Arg* **34C3**
Sierra del Codi, Mts *Spain* **51C1**
Sierra del Morro, Mt *Arg* **34B2**
Sierra del Nevado, Mts *Arg* **34B3**
Sierra de los Alamitos, Mts *Mexico* **24B2**
Sierra de los Filabres *Spain* **50B2**
Sierra de los Huicholes *Mexico* **23A1**
Sierra de Miahuatlán *Mexico* **23B2**
Sierra de Morones, Mts *Mexico* **23A1**
Sierra de Honda, Mts *Spain* **50A2**
Sierra de San Luis, Mts *Arg* **34B2**
Sierra de Segura, Mts *Spain* **50B2**
Sierra de Urbion, Mts *Spain* **50B1**
Sierra de Uspallata, Mts *Arg* **34B2**
Sierra de Valle Fértil, Mts *Arg* **34B2**
Sierra de Zongolica *Mexico* **23B2**
Sierra Grande, Mts *Arg* **34C2**
Sierra Leone, Republic *Africa* **97A4**
Sierra Leone,C *Sierra Leone* **97A4**
Sierra Madre, Mts *Phil* **79B2**
Sierra Madre del Sur, Mts *Mexico* **23A2**
Sierra Madre Occidental, Mts *Mexico* **24B2**
Sierra Malanzan, Mts *Arg* **34B2**
Sierra Mojada *Mexico* **9C4**
Sierra Morena, Mts *Spain* **50A2**
Sierra Nevada, Mts *Spain* **50B2**
Sierra Nevada, Mts *USA* **21A2**
Sierra Nevada de santa Marta, Mts *Colombia* **32C1**
Sierra Pié de Palo, Mts *Arg* **34B2**
Sierre *Switz* **47B1**
Sífnos, I *Greece* **55B3**
Sighet *Rom* **59C3**
Sighisoara *Rom* **54B1**
Siglufjörður *Iceland* **38B1**
Sigüenza *Spain* **50B1**
Siguiri *Guinea* **97B3**
Sihora *India* **85E4**
Siirt *Turk* **93D2**
Sikai Hu, L *China* **68B3**
Sīkar *India* **85D3**
Sikaram, Mt *Afghan* **84B2**
Sikasso *Mali* **97B3**
Sikeston *USA* **18C2**
Síkinos, I *Greece* **55C3**
Sikionía *Greece* **55B3**
Sikkim, State *India* **86B1**
Sil, R *Spain* **50A1**
Silandro *Italy* **47D1**
Silao *Mexico* **23A1**
Silay *Phil* **79B3**
Silchar *India* **86C2**
Silet *Alg* **96C2**
Silgarhi *Nepal* **86A1**
Silifke *Turk* **92B2**
Siling Co, L *China* **82C2**
Silistra *Bulg* **54C2**
Silkeborg *Den* **39F7**
Sillian *Austria* **47E1**
Siloam Springs *USA* **18B2**
Silsbee *USA* **19B3**
Siltou, Well *Chad* **95A3**
Šilute *USSR* **58C1**
Silvan *Turk* **93D2**
Silvania *Brazil* **35B1**
Silvassa *India* **85C4**
Silver City, Nevada *USA* **21B2**
Silver City, New Mexico *USA* **9C3**
Silver Lake *USA* **20B2**
Silver Spring *USA* **16A3**
Silverthrone Mt *Can* **13B2**
Silverton *Aust* **108B2**
Silvretta, Mts *Austria/ Switz* **47C1**
Simanggang *Malay* **78C2**
Simao *China* **76C1**
Simareh, R *Iran* **90A3**
Simav *Turk* **55C3**
Simav, R *Turk* **55C3**
Simcoe,L *Can* **15C2**
Simeulue, I *Indon* **70A3**
Simferopol' *USSR* **60D5**
Sími, I *Greece* **55C3**
Simla *India* **84D2**
Simmern *W Germ* **46D1**
Simoon Sound *Can* **13B2**
Simplon, Mt *Switz* **49D2**
Simplon, P *Switz* **47C1**
Simpson,C *USA* **4C2**
Simpson Desert *Aust* **106C3**
Simpson Pen *Can* **6B3**
Simrishamn *Sweden* **39G7**
Simushir, I *USSR* **69H2**
Sinadogo *Somalia* **99E2**
Sinai, Pen *Egypt* **92B4**
Sincelejo *Colombia* **32B2**
Sinclair,L *USA* **17B1**
Sind *Pak* **85B3**
Sind, R *India* **85D3**
Sindirği *Turk* **55C3**
Sindri *India* **86B2**
Sines *Port* **50A2**
Singa *Sudan* **99D1**
Singapore, Republic *S E Asia* **77C5**
Singapore,Str of *S E Asia* **77C5**
Singaraja *Indon* **78D4**
Singida *Tanz* **99D3**
Singkawang *Indon* **78B2**
Singleton *Aust* **109D2**
Singtep, I *Indon* **78A3**
Singu *Burma* **76B1**
Siniscola *Sardgena* **53A2**
Sinjár *Iraq* **93D2**
Sinkai Hills, Mts *Afghan* **84B2**
Sinkat *Sudan* **95C3**
Sinkiang, Autonomous Region **82C1**
Sinnamary *French Guiana* **33G2**
Sinop *Turk* **92C1**
Sintana *Rom* **54B1**
Sintang *Indon* **78C2**
Sintra *Port* **50A2**
Sinú, R *Colombia* **32B2**
Sinŭiju *N Korea* **74A2**
Siofok *Hung* **59B3**
Sion *Switz* **47B1**
Sioux City *USA* **8D2**
Sioux Falls *USA* **8D2**
Sioux Lookout *Can* **10A2**
Sipalay *Phil* **79B4**
Siparia *Trinidad* **27L1**
Siping *China* **69E2**
Siple, Base *Ant* **112B3**
Siple I *Ant* **112B5**
Sipocot *Phil* **79B3**
Sipora *Indon* **70A4**
Siquijor, I *Phil* **79B4**
Sira *India* **87B2**
Siracusa *Italy* **53C3**
Sirajganj *Bang* **86B2**
Sir Alexander,Mt *Can* **13C2**
Sīr Banī Yās, I *UAE* **91B5**
Sir Edward Pellew Group, Is *Aust* **106C2**
Siret, R *Rom* **54C1**
Sir James McBrien,Mt *Can* **12J2**
Sir Kālahasti *India* **87B2**
Sir Laurier,Mt *Can* **13D2**
Şirnak *Turk* **93D2**
Sirohi *India* **85C4**
Sironcha *India* **87B1**
Sironj *India* **85D4**
Síros, I *Greece* **55B3**
Sirri, I *Iran* **91B4**
Sirsa *India* **84D3**
Sir Sandford,Mt *Can* **13D2**
Sirsi *India* **87A2**
Sirt *Libya* **95A1**
Sirte Desert *Libya* **95A1**
Sirte,G of *Libya* **95A1**
Sisak *Yugos* **52C1**
Sisaket *Thai* **76C2**
Sisophon *Camb* **76C3**
Sissonne *France* **46B2**
Sistan, Region *Iran/ Afghan* **90D3**
Sisteron *France* **49D3**
Sistig Khem *USSR* **63B2**
Sītāpur *India* **86A1**
Sitía *Greece* **55C3**
Sitka *USA* **4E4**

Sitkalidak I *USA* **12D3**
Sitkinak, I *USA* **12D3**
Sittang, R *Burma* **76B2**
Sittard *Neth* **46C1**
Sittwe *Burma* **86C2**
Situbondo *Indon* **78C4**
Sivas *Turk* **92C2**
Siverek *Turk* **93C2**
Sivrihisar *Turk* **92B2**
Siwa *Egypt* **95B2**
Siwalik Range, Mts *India* **84D2**
Siwalik Range, Mts *Nepal* **86A1**
Siyang *China* **72D3**
Sjaelland, I *Den* **56C1**
Skagen *Den* **39G7**
Skagerrak, Str *Nor/ Den* **39F7**
Skagit, R *USA* **20B1**
Skagit Mt *Can* **20B1**
Skagway *USA* **4E4**
Skara *Sweden* **39G7**
Skarzysko-Kamlenna *Pol* **59C2**
Skeena, R *Can* **5F4**
Skeena Mts *Can* **13B1**
Skeenjek, R *USA* **4D3**
Skegness *Eng* **42E3**
Skellefte, R *Sweden* **38H5**
Skellefteå *Sweden* **38J6**
Skíathos, I *Greece* **55B3**
Skibbereen *Irish Rep* **45B3**
Skidegate *Can* **5E4**
Skiemiewice *Pol* **58C2**
Skien *Nor* **39F7**
Skikda *Alg* **96C1**
Skikoku, I *Japan* **74C4**
Skipton *Eng* **42D3**
Skíros, I *Greece* **55B3**
Skive *Den* **39F7**
Skjern *Den* **56B1**
Skjoldungen *Greenland* **6F3**
Skokie *USA* **14A2**
Skópelos, I *Greece* **55B3**
Skopje *Yugos* **54B2**
Skövde *Sweden* **39G7**
Skovorodino *USSR* **63E2**
Skwentna *USA* **4C3**
Skwierzyna *Pol* **58B2**
Skye, I *Scot* **40B2**
Slagelse *Den* **39G7**
Slaney, R *Irish Rep* **45C2**
Slatina *Rom* **54B2**
Slaung *Indon* **78C4**
Slav Brod *Yugos* **54A1**
Slave, R *Can* **5G3**
Slave Lake *Can* **13E1**
Slavgorod, Rossiyskaya *USSR* **65J4**
Slavuta *USSR* **59D2**
Slavyansk *USSR* **60E4**
Sleat,Sound of, Chan *Scot* **44B3**
Sleetmute *USA* **12C2**
Sleeve Bloom, Mts *Irish Rep* **45C2**
Slidell *USA* **19C3**
Slide Mt *USA* **16B2**
Sligo, County *Irish Rep* **45B1**
Sligo *Irish Rep* **41B3**
Sligo, B *Irish Rep* **41B3**
Sliven *Bulg* **54C2**
Slobozia *Rom* **54C2**
Slocan *Can* **13D3**
Slonim *USSR* **58D2**
Slough *Eng* **43D4**
Slough, R *USA* **22B2**
Slovensko, Region *Czech* **59B3**
Słubice *Pol* **56C2**
Sluch', R *USSR* **59D2**
Sludyanka *USSR* **68C1**
Słupsk *Pol* **58B2**
Slutsk *USSR* **58D2**
Slutsk, R *USSR* **58D2**
Slyne Head, Pt *Irish Rep* **41A3**
Slyudyanka *USSR* **63C2**
Smallwood Res *Can* **7D4**
Smara *Mor* **96A2**
Smederevo *Yugos* **54B2**
Smederevska Palanka *Yugos* **54B2**
Smela *USSR* **60D4**
Smethport *USA* **15C2**
Smith *Can* **13E1**
Smith Arm, B *Can* **4F3**
Smithers *Can* **13B2**
Smith I *Can* **7C3**
Smith Sd *Can* **13B2**
Smiths Falls *Can* **15C2**
Smithton *Aust* **109C4**
Smoky, R *Can* **13D1**
Smoky C *Aust* **109D2**
Smoky Lake *Can* **13E2**
Smøla, I *Nor* **38F6**
Smolensk *USSR* **60D3**
Smólikas, Mt *Greece* **55B2**
Smolyan *Bulg* **54B2**
Smorgon' *USSR* **58D2**
Smyrna, Delaware *USA* **16B3**
Smyrna, Georgia *USA* **17B1**
Snaefell, Mt *Eng* **42B2**
Snafell, Mt *Iceland* **38B2**
Snake, R *USA* **8B2**
Snake River Canyon *USA* **8B2**
Sneek *Neth* **56B2**
Sneem *Irish Rep* **45B3**
Snelling *USA* **22B2**
Sněžka, Mt *Pol/Czech* **59B2**
Snøhetta, Mt *Nor* **38F6**
Snohomish *USA* **20B1**
Snoqualmie P *USA* **20B1**
Snoul *Camb* **76D3**
Snowdon, Mt *Wales* **43B3**
Snowdonia Nat Pk *Wales* **43B3**
Snowdrift *Can* **4G3**
Snow Lake *Can* **5H4**
Snowtown *Aust* **108A2**
Snowy Mts *Aust* **109C3**
Snyder *USA* **9C3**
Soan-kundo, I *S Korea* **74B4**
Sobat, R *Sudan* **99D2**
Sobral *Brazil* **31C2**
Sochaczew *Pol* **58C2**
Sochi *USSR* **61E5**
Socorro *USA* **9C3**
Socorro, I *Mexico* **24A3**
Socos *Chile* **34A2**
Socotra, I *S Yemen* **81D4**
Sodankylä *Fin* **38K5**
Soddo *Eth* **99D2**
Soderhamn *Sweden* **39H6**
Södertälje *Sweden* **39H7**
Sodiri *Sudan* **99C1**
Soest *W Germ* **46E1**
Sofala *Mozam* **101C2**
Sofiya *Bulg* **54B2**
Sofu Gan, I *Japan* **69G4**
Sogamoso *Colombia* **32C2**
Sognefjorden, Inlet *Nor* **39F6**
Sog Xian *China* **82D2**
Sohâg *Egypt* **95C2**
Sohīpat *India* **84D3**
Soignies *Belg* **46B1**
Soissons *France* **46B2**
Sojat *India* **85C3**
Sŏjosŏn-man, B *N Korea* **74A3**
Söke *Turk* **92A2**
Sokodé *Togo* **97C4**
Sokol *USSR* **61E2**
Sokołka *Pol* **58C2**
Sokolo *Mali* **97B3**
Søkongens Øy, I *Greenland* **6H3**
Sokota *Eth* **99D1**
Sokoto *Nig* **97C3**
Sokoto, R *Nig* **97C3**
Solander I *NZ* **111A3**
Solano *Phil* **79B2**
Solapur *India* **87B1**
Solbad Hall *Austria* **47D1**
Sölden *Austria* **47D1**
Soldotna *USA* **12D2**
Soledad *Colombia* **26C4**
Solent, Sd *Eng* **43D4**
Solesmes *France* **46B1**
Soligorsk *USSR* **58D2**
Solikamsk *USSR* **61J2**
Solimões *Peru* **32C4**
Solingen *W Germ* **46D1**
Sol'Itesk *USSR* **65G4**
Sollefteå *Sweden* **38H6**
Sol'Iletsk *USSR* **61H3**
Solok *Indon* **70B4**
Solomon, Is *Pacific O* **105G4**
Solothurn *Switz* **47B1**
Soltau *W Germ* **39F8**
Solvang *USA* **22B3**
Solway Firth, Estuary *Scot/Eng* **42C2**
Solwezi *Zambia* **100B2**
Sōma *Japan* **75C1**
Soma *Turk* **55C3**
Somalia, Republic *E Africa* **81C5**
Sombor *Yugos* **54A1**
Somerset *Aust* **107D2**
Somerset, County *Eng* **43C4**
Somerset, Massachusetts *USA* **16D2**
Somerset, Pennsylvania *USA* **15C2**
Somerset East *S Africa* **100B4**
Somerset I *Can* **6A2**
Somers Point *USA* **16B3**
Somerville *USA* **16B2**
Somerville Res *USA* **19A3**
Somes, R *Rom* **54B1**
Somme, Department *France* **46B2**
Somme, R *France* **46B2**
Sommesous *France* **46C2**
Son, R *India* **86A2**
Sŏnch'ŏn *N Korea* **74A3**
Sønderborg *Den* **39F8**
Søndre Strømfjord *Greenland* **6E3**
Sondrio *Italy* **47C1**
Song Ba, R *Viet* **76D3**
Song Cau *Viet* **76D3**
Songea *Tanz* **101C2**
Songjiang *China* **73E3**
Songkhla *Thai* **77C4**
Songnim *N Korea* **74B3**
Sông Pahang, R *Malay* **77C5**
Songpan *China* **72A3**
Sonid Youqi *China* **72C1**
Son La *Viet* **76C1**
Sonmiani *Pak* **85B3**
Sonmiani Bay *Pak* **85B3**
Sonoma *USA* **22A1**
Sonora, California *USA* **22B2**
Sonora, R *Mexico* **24A2**
Sonoran Desert *USA* **9B3**
Sonora P *USA* **22C1**
Sonsonate *El Salvador* **25D3**
Sonsorol, I *Pacific O* **71E3**
Soo Canals *USA/Can* **10B2**
Sooke *Can* **13C3**
Sopot *Pol* **58B2**
Sopron *Hung* **59B3**
Soquel *USA* **22B2**
Sora *Italy* **53B2**
Sored, R *Israel* **94B3**
Sorel *Can* **15D1**
Sorell *Aust* **109C4**
Sorgun *Turk* **92C2**
Soria *Spain* **50B1**
Sørkjosen *Nor* **38J5**
Sørksop, I *Barents S* **64C2**
Sor Mertvyy Kultuk, Plain *USSR* **61H4**
Sorocaba *Brazil* **35B2**
Sorochinsk *USSR* **61H3**
Sorol, I *Pacific O* **71F3**
Sorok *USSR* **60C4**
Sorong *Indon* **71E4**
Sorong, Province *Indon* **71E4**
Soroti *Uganda* **99D2**
Sørøya, I *Nor* **38J4**
Sorrento *Italy* **53B2**
Sorsatunturi, Mt *Fin* **38K5**
Sorsele *Sweden* **38H5**
Sorsogon *Phil* **79B3**
Sortavala *USSR* **38L6**
Sŏsan *S Korea* **74B3**
Sosnowiec *Pol* **59B2**
Sos'va *USSR* **65H4**
Souanké *Congo* **98B2**
Soubré *Ivory Coast* **97B4**
Souderton *USA* **16B2**
Soufrière *St Lucia* **27P2**
Soufrière, V *St Vincent* **27N2**
Souillac *France* **48C3**
Souk Ahras *Alg* **96C1**
Soul *S Korea* **74B3**
Soummam, R *Alg* **51C2**
Sources,Mt aux *Lesotho* **101G1**
Sousa *Brazil* **31D3**
Sousse *Tunisia* **96D1**
South Africa, Republic *Africa* **100B4**
South Amboy *USA* **16B2**
Southampton *Can* **14B2**
Southampton *Eng* **43D4**
Southampton *USA* **16C2**
Southampton I *Can* **6B3**
South Atlantic O **28F6**
South Aulatsivik I *Can* **7D4**
South Australia, State *Aust* **106C3**
South Australian Basin *Indian O* **104E5**
Southaven *USA* **19C3**
South Bay *USA* **17B2**
South Baymouth *Can* **14B1**
South Bend, Indiana *USA* **14A2**
South Bend, Washington *USA* **20B1**
Southbridge *USA* **16D1**
South Carolina, State *USA* **11B3**
South China S *S E Asia* **70C2**
South Dakota, State *USA* **8C2**
South Deerfield *USA* **16C1**
South Downs *Eng* **43D4**
South East C *Aust* **109C4**
Southen Alps, Mts *NZ* **111A2**
Southend *Can* **5H4**
Southend-on-Sea *Eng* **43E4**
Southern Alps, Mts *NZ* **111A2**
Southern Cross *Aust* **106A4**
Southern Indian L *Can* **5J4**
Southfield *Jamaica* **27H2**
South Fiji Basin *Pacific O* **105G5**
South Fork, R, Alaska *USA* **12D2**
South Fork, R, California *USA* **22B1**
South Georgia, I *S Atlantic O* **28F8**
South Glamorgan, County *Wales* **43C4**
South Haven *USA* **14A2**
South Henik L *Can* **5J3**
South Honshu Ridge *Pacific O* **104F3**
South I *NZ* **111A2**
Southington *USA* **16C2**
South Korea, Republic *S E Asia* **74B3**
South Lake Tahoe *USA* **21A2**

South Magnetic Pole *Ant* 112C8
South Miami *USA* 17B2
South Mt *USA* 16A3
South Nahanni, R *Can* 4F3
South Negril Pt *Jamaica* 26G1
South Orkney, Is *Atlantic O* 103F8
South Platte, R *USA* 8C2
South Pole *Ant* 80E
Southport *Eng* 42C3
South Pt *Barbados* 27R3
South River *USA* 16B2
South Ronaldsay, I *Scot* 44C2
South Sandwich Trench *Atlantic O* 103G7
South San Francisco *USA* 22A2
South Saskatchewan, R *Can* 5H4
South Shields *Eng* 42D2
South Taranaki Bight, B *NZ* 110B1
South Uist, I *Scot* 44A3
South West C *Aust* 107D5
South West Pacific Basin *Pacific O* 105J5
South West Peru Ridge *Pacific O* 103D5
South Yemen, Republic *Arabian Pen* 81C4
South Yorkshire, County *Eng* 43D3
Sovetsk, RSFSR *USSR* 58C1
Sovetsk, RSFSR *USSR* 61G2
Soyo Congo *Angola* 98B3
Sozh, R *USSR* 60D3
Spa *Belg* 46C1
Spain, Kingdom 37
Spalding *Eng* 43D3
Spanish, R *Can* 14B1
Spanish Town *Jamaica* 26B3
Sparks *USA* 21B2
Spartanburg *USA* 11B3
Spartí *Greece* 55B3
Spassk Dal'niy *USSR* 69F2
Speightstown *Barbados* 27R3
Spenard *USA* 12E2
Spencer, Indiana *USA* 14A3
Spencer, Iowa *USA* 8D2
Spencer Bay *Can* 6A3
Spencer,C *Aust* 108A3
Spencer G *Aust* 108A2
Spencer I *Can* 6C3
Spenser Mts *NZ* 111B2
Sperrin, Mts *N Ire* 45C1
Spey, R *Scot* 44C3
Speyer *W Germ* 57B3
Speyside *Tobago* 27K1
Spiez *Switz* 47B1
Spike Mt *USA* 12F1
Spirit Lake *USA* 20C1
Spirit River *Can* 5G4
Spitsbergen, I *Barents S* 64C2
Spittal *Austria* 57C3
Spjelkavik *Nor* 38F6
Split *Yugos* 52C2
Splügen *Switz* 47C1
Spokane *USA* 20C1
Sporádhes, Is *Greece* 55C3
Spray *USA* 20C2
Spree, R *E Germ* 56C2
Springbok *S Africa* 100A3
Springdale *USA* 18B2
Springfield, Illinois *USA* 10B3
Springfield, Massachusetts *USA* 10C2
Springfield, Missouri *USA* 18B2
Springfield, Ohio *USA* 14B3
Springfield, Oregon *USA* 20B2
Springfield, Vermont *USA* 15D2
Springfontein *S Africa* 100B4
Springs *S Africa* 101G1
Spurn Head, Pt *Eng* 41D3
Squamish *Can* 13C3
Sredne-Russkaya Vozvyshennost, Upland *USSR* 60E3
Sredne Sibirskoye Ploskogorve, Tableland *USSR* 63B1
Sredniy Ural, Mts *USSR* 61J2
Srepok, R *Camb* 76D3
Sretensk *USSR* 68D1
Sre Umbell *Camb* 76C3
Sri Lanka, Republic *S Asia* 83C5
Srīnagar *Pak* 84C2
Srīvardhan *India* 87A1
Sroda *Pol* 58B2
Sta Clara, I *Chile* 30H6
Sta Cruz, I *Ecuador* 32J7
Stade *W Germ* 56B2
Staffa, I *Scot* 44A3
Stafford, County *Eng* 43C3
Stafford *Eng* 43C3
Stafford Springs *USA* 16C2
Stallworthy,C *Can* 6A1
Stalowa Wola *Pol* 59C2
Sta Maria, I *Ecuador* 32J7
Stamford, Connecticut *USA* 16C2
Stamford, New York *USA* 16B1
Stampriet *Namibia* 100A3
Standerton *S Africa* 101G1
Standish *USA* 14B2
Stanger *S Africa* 101H1
Stanislaus, R *USA* 22B2
Stanke Dimitrov *Bulg* 54B2
Stanley *Aust* 109C4
Stanley *Falkland Is* 29E6
Stanley Res *India* 87B2
Stann Creek *Belize* 25D3
Stanovoy Khrebet, Mts *USSR* 63E2
Stans *Switz* 47C1
Stanthorpe *Aust* 109D1
Starachowice *Pol* 59C2
Stara Planiná, Mts *Bulg* 54B2
Staraya Russa *USSR* 60D2
Stara Zagora *Bulg* 54C2
Stargard *Pol* 58B2
Starkville *USA* 19C3
Starnberg *W Germ* 57C3
Starogard Gdanski *Pol* 58B2
Starokonstantinov *USSR* 59D3
Start Pt *Eng* 43C4
Staryy Oskol *USSR* 60E3
State College *USA* 15C2
Staten I *USA* 16B2
Statesboro *USA* 17B1
Staunton *USA* 15C3
Stavanger *Nor* 39F7
Stavelot *Belg* 46C1
Stavropol' *USSR* 61F4
Stawell *Aust* 108B3
Stawno *Pol* 58B2
Stayton *USA* 20B2
Stebbins *USA* 12B2
Steele,Mt *Can* 12F2
Steelton *USA* 16A2
Steens Mt *USA* 20C2
Steenstrups Gletscher, Gl *Greenland* 6E2
Stefansson I *Can* 4H2
Stegi *Swaziland* 101H1
Steinach *Austria* 47D1
Steinback *Can* 8D2
Steinkier *Nor* 38G6
Stein Mt *Can* 13C2
Stemaco *Mexico* 23B2
Stenay *France* 46C2
Stendal *E Germ* 56C2
Stephens,C *NZ* 110B2
Stephens Creek *Aust* 108B2
Stephenson *USA* 14A1
Stephens Pass *USA* 12H3
Stephenville *Can* 7E5
Sterkstroom *S Africa* 100B4
Sterling, Colorado *USA* 8C2
Sterling Heights *USA* 14B2
Sterlitamak *USSR* 61J3
Stettler *Can* 13E2
Steubenville *USA* 14B2
Stevens Village *USA* 4D3
Stewart *Can* 13B1
Stewart *USA* 21B2
Stewart, R *Can* 12G2
Stewart Crossing *Can* 12G2
Stewart I *NZ* 111A3
Stewart Is *Solomon Is* 107F1
Stewart River *Can* 4E3
Stewartstown *USA* 16A3
Steyn *S Africa* 101G1
Steyr *Austria* 57C3
Stika *USA* 12G3
Stikine, R *Can* 12H3
Stikine Ranges, Mts *Can* 12H3
Stillwater, Oklahoma *USA* 18A2
Stillwater Range, Mts *USA* 21B2
Stirling *Aust* 108A2
Stirling *Scot* 44C3
Stockbridge *USA* 16C1
Stockerau *Austria* 59B3
Stockholm *Sweden* 39H7
Stockport *Eng* 42C3
Stockton, California *USA* 22B2
Stockton *Eng* 42D2
Stockton L *USA* 18B2
Stoke-on-Trent *Eng* 43C3
Stokkseyri *Iceland* 38A2
Stokmarknes *Nor* 38G5
Stolbtsy *USSR* 39K8
Stolin *USSR* 58D2
Stone Harbor *USA* 16B3
Stonehaven *Scot* 44C3
Stonewall *USA* 19A3
Stony, R *USA* 12D2
Storavan, L *Sweden* 38H5
Støren *Nor* 38G6
Storm B *Aust* 109C4
Stornoway *Scot* 44A2
Storozhinets *USSR* 59D3
Storrs *USA* 16C2
Storsjon, L *Sweden* 38G6
Storuman *Sweden* 38H5
Stoughton *USA* 16D1
Stowmarket *Eng* 43E3
Strablane *N Ire* 45C1
Strahan *Aust* 109C4
Stralsund *E Germ* 56C2
Stranda *Nor* 38F6
Strängnäs *Sweden* 39H7
Stranraer *Scot* 42B2
Strasbourg *France* 49D2
Strasburg *USA* 15C3
Stratford *Can* 14B2
Stratford, Connecticut *USA* 16C2
Stratford *NZ* 110B1
Stratford-on-Avon *Eng* 43D3
Strathalbyn *Aust* 108A3
Strathclyde, Region *Scot* 42B2
Strathmore *Can* 13E2
Streator *USA* 18C1
Stresa *Italy* 47C2
Stretto de Messina, Str *Italy/Sicily* 53C3
Stroboli, I *Italy* 53C3
Strømfjord *Greenland* 6E3
Stromness *Scot* 44C2
Strømø *Faroes* 38D3
Stromsburg *USA* 18A1
Stromsund *Sweden* 38H6
Ströms Vattudal, L *Sweden* 38G6
Stronsay, I *Scot* 44C2
Stroud *Eng* 43C4
Stroudsburg *USA* 16B2
Struma, R *Bulg* 54B2
Strumble Head, Pt *Wales* 43B3
Strumica *Yugos* 55B2
Stryy *USSR* 59C3
Stryy, R *USSR* 59C3
Strzelecki Creek, R *Aust* 108B1
Stuart, Florida *USA* 17B2
Stuart, R *Can* 13C2
Stuart I *USA* 12B2
Stuart L *Can* 13C2
Stubaier Alpen, Mts *Austria* 47D1
Stuch, R *USSR* 60C3
Stung Sen *Camb* 76D3
Stung Treng *Camb* 76D3
Stura, R *Italy* 52A2
Sturge I *Ant* 112C7
Sturgeon Bay *USA* 14A2
Sturgeon Falls *Can* 14C1
Sturgis, Kentucky *USA* 18C2
Sturgis, Michigan *USA* 14A2
Sturt Creek, R *Aust* 106B2
Sturt Desert *Aust* 108B1
Stuttemeim *S Africa* 100B4
Stuttgart *USA* 19B3
Stuttgart *W Germ* 57B3
Stykkishólmur *Iceland* 38A1
Styr, R *USSR* 59D2
Suaçuí Grande, R *Brazil* 35C1
Suakin *Sudan* 81B4
Su-ao *Taiwan* 73E5
Suardi *Arg* 34C2
Subi, I *Indon* 78B2
Subotica *Yugos* 54A1
Suceava *Rom* 60C4
Suck, R *Irish Rep* 45B2
Sucre *Bol* 30C2
Sucuriú, R *Brazil* 35A1
Sudan, Republic *Africa* 98C1
Sudbury *Can* 14B1
Sudbury *Eng* 43E3
Sudd, Swamp *Sudan* 99C2
Suddie *Guyana* 33F2
Sue, R *Sudan* 98C2
Suerdrup Is *Can* 4H2
Suez *Egypt* 92B4
Suez Canal *Egypt* 92B3
Suez,G of *Egypt* 92B4
Suffern *USA* 16B2
Suffolk, County *Eng* 43E3
Sugarloaf Pt *Aust* 109D2
Suhär *Oman* 91C5
Sühbaatar *Mongolia* 68C1
Sui *Pak* 84B3
Suide *China* 72C2
Suihua *China* 69E2
Suining *China* 73B3
Suippes *France* 46C2
Suir, R *Irish Rep* 41B3
Sui Xian *China* 73C3
Suizhong *China* 72E1
Sujāngarth *India* 85C3
Sukabumi *Indon* 78B4
Sukadana, Borneo *Indon* 78C3
Sukadana, Sumatra *Indon* 78B4
Sukagawa *Japan* 74E3
Sukaraya *Indon* 78C3
Sukhinichi Shchekino *USSR* 60E3
Sukhona, R *USSR* 61F2
Sukhumi *USSR* 61F5
Sukkertoppen *Greenland* 6E3
Sukkertoppen, L *Greenland* 6E3
Sukkozero *USSR* 38L6

Sukkur *Pak* 85B3
Sukma *India* 87C1
Sukses *Namibia* 100A3
Sukumo *Japan* 75A2
Sukunka, R *Can* 13C1
Sula, R *USSR* 60E3
Sulaiman Range, Mts *Pak* 84B3
Sulawesi, I *Indon* 70C4
Sulaymānīyah *Iraq* 93E3
Sulina *Rom* 54C1
Sulitjelma *Nor* 38H5
Sullana *Peru* 32A4
Sullivan *USA* 18B2
Sullivan Bay *Can* 13B2
Sullivan L *Can* 13E2
Sulmona *Italy* 52B2
Sulphur, Louisiana *USA* 19B3
Sulphur, Oklahoma *USA* 19A3
Sulphur Springs *USA* 19A3
Sultānpur *India* 86A1
Sulu Arch *Phil* 79B4
Sulu S *Philip* 70C3
Sumampa *Arg* 30D4
Sumba, I *Indon* 70C4
Sumbawa, I *Indon* 78D4
Sumbawa Besar *Indon* 78D4
Sumbawanga *Tanz* 99D3
Sumbe *Angola* 100A2
Sumburgh Head, Pt *Scot* 44D2
Sumenep *Indon* 78C4
Sumisu, I *Japan* 69G3
Summerland *Can* 13D3
Summit Lake *Can* 5F4
Summit Mt *USA* 21B2
Sumner,L *NZ* 111B2
Sumoto *Japan* 75A2
Sumter *USA* 17B1
Sumy *USSR* 60D3
Sunbury *USA* 16A2
Sunchales *Arg* 34C2
Sunch'ŏn *N Korea* 74B3
Sunch'ŏn *S Korea* 74B4
Sundargarh *India* 86A2
Sunderbans, Swamp *India* 86B2
Sunderland *Eng* 42D2
Sundre *Can* 13E2
Sundridge *Can* 15C1
Sundsvall *Sweden* 38H6
Sungaianyar *Indon* 78D3
Sungaisalak *Indon* 78A3
Sunnyside *USA* 20C1
Sunnyvale *USA* 21A2
Suntar *USSR* 63D1
Sunyani *Ghana* 97B4
Suō-nada, B *Japan* 75A2
Suonejoki *Fin* 38K6
Supaul *India* 86B1
Superior, Nebraska *USA* 18A1
Superior, Wisconsin *USA* 10A2
Superior,L *USA/Can* 10B2
Suphan Buri *Thai* 76C3
Süphan Dağ *Turk* 93D2
Supiori, I *Indon* 71E4
Suq ash Suyukh *Iraq* 93E3
Suqian *China* 72D3
Sūr *Oman* 91C5
Surabaya *Indon* 78C4
Suraga-wan, B *Japan* 75B2
Surakarta *Indon* 78C4
Surar, R *USSR* 61G3
Surat *Aust* 109C1
Sūrat *India* 85C4
Sūratgarh *India* 84C3
Surat Thani *Thai* 77B4
Surendranagar *India* 85C4
Surf City *USA* 16B3
Surgut *USSR* 64J3
Suriāpet *India* 87B1
Sürich *Switz* 49D2
Surigao *Phil* 79C4
Surin *Thai* 76C3
Surinam, Republic 33F3
Surrey, County *Eng* 43D4
Sursee *Switz* 47C1
Surtsey, I *Iceland* 38A2
Surulangan *Indon* 78A3
Susa *Italy* 47B2
Susa *Japan* 75A2
Susaki *Japan* 75A2
Susanville *USA* 21A1
Süsch *Switz* 47D1
Susitna, R *USA* 12E2
Susquehanna, R *USA* 16A3
Sussex *USA* 16B2
Sussex West *Eng* 43D4
Sustut Peak, Mt *Can* 13B1
Sutherland *S Africa* 100B4
Sutlej, R *Pak* 84C2
Sutter Creek *USA* 21A2
Sutton *USA* 14B3
Sutwik I *USA* 12C3
Suwa *Japan* 74D3
Suwałki *Pol* 58C2
Suwannee, R *USA* 17B2
Suweilih *Jordan* 94B2
Suwŏn *S Korea* 74B3
Su Xian *China* 72D3
Suzaka *Japan* 75B1
Suzhou *China* 73E3
Suzu *Japan* 74D3
Suzuka *Japan* 75B2
Suzu-misaki, C *Japan* 75B1
Svalbard, Is *Barents S* 64C2
Svalyava *USSR* 59C3
Svartisen, Mt *Nor* 38G5
Svay Rieng *Camb* 76D3
Sveg *Sweden* 38G6
Svendborg *Den* 39G7
Sverdlovsk *USSR* 65H4
Sverdrup Chan *Can* 6A1
Svetlaya *USSR* 69F2
Svetlogorsk *USSR* 58C2
Svetogorsk *USSR* 39K6
Svetozarevo *Yugos* 54B2
Svilengrad *Bulg* 54C2
Svir' *USSR* 58D2
Švitavy *Czech* 59B3
Svobodnyy *USSR* 69E1
Svolvaer *Nor* 38G5
Swain Reefs *Aust* 107E3
Swainsboro *USA* 17B1
Swakopmund *Namibia* 100A3
Swale, R *Eng* 42D2
Swallow Reef, I *S E Asia* 70C3
Swāmihalli *India* 87B2
Swan, I *Honduras* 25D3
Swanage *Eng* 43D4
Swan Hill *Aust* 108B3
Swan Hills *Can* 13D2
Swan Hills, Mts *Can* 13D2
Swan I *Caribbean* 26A3
Swan River *Can* 5H4
Swansea *Wales* 43C4
Swansea B *Wales* 43C4
Swartruggens *S Africa* 101G1
Swaziland, Kingdom *S Africa* 101H1
Sweden, Kingdom *N Europe* 39G7
Sweet Home *USA* 20B2
Sweetwater *USA* 9C3
Swellendam *S Africa* 100B4
Świdnica *Pol* 59B2
Swidwin *Pol* 58B2
Swiebodzin *Pol* 58B2
Swiecie *Pol* 58B2
Swift Current *Can* 5H4
Swindon *Eng* 43D4
Swinford *Irish Rep* 45B2
Świnoujście *Pol* 56C2
Switzerland, Federal Republic *Europe* 49D2
Swords *Irish Rep* 45C2
Syderø *Faeroes* 38D3
Sydney *Aust* 109D2
Sydney *Can* 7D5
Syktyvkar *USSR* 64G3
Sylacauga *USA* 17A1
Sylarna, Mt *Sweden* 38G6
Sylhet *Bang* 86C2
Sylt, I *W Germ* 56B1
Sylvania *USA* 14B2
Syowa, Base *Ant* 112C11
Syracuse, New York *USA* 10C3
Syracuse *USA* 15C2
Syrdal'ya, R *USSR* 65H5
Syria, Republic *S W Asia* 93C2
Sysert' *USSR* 61J2
Syzran' *USSR* 61G3
Szczecin *Pol* 56C2
Szczecinek *Pol* 58B2
Szczytno *Pol* 58C2
Szeged *Hung* 59C3
Székesfehérvar *Hung* 59B3
Szekszard *Hung* 59B3
Szolnok *Hung* 59B3
Szombathely *Hung* 59B3
Szprotawa *Pol* 58B2

T

Tabas *Iran* 90C3
Tabasco *Mexico* 23A1
Tabatinga *Brazil* 32D4
Tabelbala *Alg* 96B2
Tabeng *Camb* 76C3
Taber *Can* 13E2
Tablas, I *Phil* 79B3
Table Mt *S Africa* 100A4
Table Mt *USA* 12F1
Table Rock Res *USA* 18B2
Taboali *Indon* 78B3
Tábor *Czech* 57C3
Tabora *Tanz* 99D3
Tabou *Ivory Coast* 97B4
Tabrīz *Iran* 90A2
Tabūk *S Arabia* 92C4
Tacámbaro *Mexico* 23A2
Tacheng *China* 82C1
Tacloban *Phil* 79C3
Tacna *Peru* 30B2
Tacoma *USA* 8A2
Tadjoura *Djibouti* 99E1
Tādpatri *India* 87B2
Tadzhen *USSR* 65H6
Tadzhikskaya SSR, Republic *USSR* 82A2
Taebaek Sanmaek, Mts *S Korea* 74B3
Taegu *S Korea* 74B3
Taehŭksan, I *S Korea* 74B4
Taejŏn *S Korea* 74B3
Tafalla *Spain* 51B1
Tafasaset, Watercourse *Alg* 96C2
Taff, R *Wales* 43C4
Tafila *Jordan* 94B3
Tagant, Region *Maur* 97A3
Tagbilaran *Phil* 79B4
Taguenout Hagguerete, Well *Maur* 96B2
Tagula, I *Solomon Is* 107E2
Tagum *Phil* 79C4
Tahat, Mt *Alg* 96C2
Tahiti, I *Pacific O* 105J4
Tahlequah *USA* 18A2
Tahoe City *USA* 21A2
Tahoe,L *USA* 21A2
Tahoua *Niger* 97C3
Tahuna *Indon* 71D3
Tai'an *China* 72D2
Taibai Shan, Mt *China* 72B3
Taibus Qi *China* 72D1
T'ai-chung *Taiwan* 73E5
Taieri, R *NZ* 111B3
Taihang Shan *China* 72C2
Taihape *NZ* 110C1
Tai Hu, L *China* 72E3
Tailem Bend *Aust* 108A3
Tain *Scot* 44B3
T'ai-nan *Taiwan* 73E5
Taiobeiras *Brazil* 35C1
T'ai pei *Taiwan* 73E5
Taiping *Malay* 77C5
Taira *Japan* 75C1
Tais *Indon* 78A3
Taisha *Japan* 75A1
Taitao,Pen de *Chile* 29B5
T'ai-tung *Taiwan* 73E5
Taivelkoski *Fin* 38K5
Taiwan, Republic *China* 69E4
Taiyuan *China* 72C2
Taizhou *China* 72D3
Ta 'izz *Yemen* 81C4
Tajo, R *Spain* 50B1
Tak *Thai* 76B2
Takada *Japan* 74D3
Takahashi *Japan* 75A2
Takaka *NZ* 110B2
Takamatsu *Japan* 74C4
Takaoka *Japan* 74D3
Takapuna *NZ* 110B1
Takasaki *Japan* 74D3
Takayama *Japan* 75B1
Takefu *Japan* 74D3
Takeo *Camb* 76C3
Takeo *Japan* 75A2
Takestān *Iran* 90A2
Taketa *Japan* 75A2
Takingeun *Indon* 70A3
Takjvak L *Can* 4G3
Takkaze, R *Eth* 99D1
Takla L *Can* 13B1
Takla Landing *Can* 13B1
Takslesluk L *USA* 12B2
Taku Arm, R *Can* 12H2
Tala *Mexico* 23A1
Talabanya *Hung* 59B3
Talagang *Pak* 84C2
Talagante *Chile* 34A2
Talaimannar *Sri Lanka* 87B3
Talak, Desert, Region *Niger* 97C3
Talangbetutu *Indon* 78A3
Talara *Peru* 32A4
Talavera de la Reina *Spain* 50B2
Talca *Chile* 34A3
Talcahuano *Chile* 34A3
Tālcher *India* 86B2
Taldy Kurgan *USSR* 82B1
Taliabu *Indon* 71D4
Taligan *Afghan* 84B1
Tali Post *Sudan* 99D2
Taliwang *Indon* 78D4
Talkeetna *USA* 12D2
Talkeetna Mts *USA* 12E2
Talladega *USA* 17A1
Tall 'Afar *Iraq* 93D2
Tallahassee *USA* 17B1
Tall Bīsah *Syria* 94C1
Tallinn *USSR* 60B2
Tall Kalakh *Syria* 92C3
Tallulah *USA* 19B3
Tal'noye *USSR* 60D4
Talpaki *USSR* 58C2
Taltal *Chile* 30B4
Talwood *Aust* 109C1
Tamabo Range, Mts *Malay* 78D1
Tamale *Ghana* 97B4
Tamanrasset *Alg* 96C2
Tamanrasset, Watercourse *Alg* 96C2
Tamaqua *USA* 16B2
Tamazula, Jalisco *Mexico* 23A2
Tamazulapán *Mexico* 23B2
Tamazunchale *Mexico* 23B1
Tambacounda *Sen* 97A3
Tambov *USSR* 61F3
Tambre, R *Spain* 50A1
Tambura *Sudan* 98C2
Tamchaket *Maur* 97A3
Tamega, R *Port* 50A1
Tamiahua *Mexico* 23B1
Tamil Nādu, State *India* 87B2
Tamis, R *Rom* 54B1
Tam Ky *Viet* 76D2

Tampa *USA* 17B2
Tampa B *USA* 17B2
Tampere *Fin* 39J6
Tampico *Mexico* 23B1
Tamsagbulag *Mongolia* 68D2
Tamu *Burma* 86C2
Tamuis *Mexico* 23B1
Tamworth *Aust* 109D2
Tamworth *Eng* 43D3
Tana *Nor* 38K4
Tana, L *Eth* 99D1
Tana, R *Kenya* 99E3
Tana, R *Nor/Fin* 38K5
Tanabe *Japan* 75B2
Tanafjord, Inlet *Nor* 38K4
Tanahgrogot *Indon* 78D3
Tanahmerah *Indon* 71E4
Tanana *USA* 12D1
Tanana, R *USA* 12E2
Tanaro, R *Italy* 47C2
Tanch'ŏn *N Korea* 74B2
Tandaho *Eth* 99E1
Tandil *Arg* 34D3
Tandjong Datu, Pt *Indon* 78B2
Tandjung d'Urville, C *Indon* 71E4
Tandjung Layar, C *Indon* 78D3
Tandjung Lumut, C *Indon* 78B3
Tandjung Mangkalihet C *Indon* 78D2
Tandjung Sambar, C *Indon* 78C3
Tandjung Sirik, C *Malay* 78C2
Tandjung Vals, C *Indon* 71E4
Tando Adam *Pak* 85B3
Tando Muhammad Khan *Pak* 85B3
Tandou L *Aust* 108B2
Tāndūr *India* 87B1
Taneatua *NZ* 110C1
Tanen Range, Mts *Burma/Thai* 76B2
Tanezrouft, Desert Region *Alg* 96B2
Tang *Iran* 91C4
Tanga *Tanz* 99D3
Tanganrog *USSR* 60E4
Tanganyika,L *Tanz/Zaïre* 99C3
Tanger *Mor* 96B1
Tanggula Shan, Mts *China* 82C2
Tangjungpinang *Indon* 78A2
Tangra Yumco, L *China* 82C2
Tangshan *China* 72D2
Tangub *Phil* 79B4
Tanguy *USSR* 63C2
Tanjay *Phil* 79B4
Tanjong Bugel, C *Indon* 78C4
Tanjong Cangkuang, C *Indon* 78B4
Tanjong Puting, C *Indon* 78C3
Tanjong Selatan, C *Indon* 78C3
Tanjung *Indon* 78D3
Tanjungbalai *Indon* 70A3
Tanjung Jabung, Pt *Indon* 78A3
Tanjungpandan *Indon* 78B3
Tanjung Priok *Indon* 78B4
Tanjungredeb *Indon* 78D2
Tanjungselor *Indon* 78D2
Tank *Pak* 84C2
Tannu Ola, Mts *USSR* 68B1
Tano, R *Ghana* 97B4
Tanout *Niger* 97C3
Tanquián *Mexico* 23B1
Tan-shui *Taiwan* 73E4
Tansing *Nepal* 86A1
Tanta *Egypt* 95C1
Tan-Tan *Mor* 96A2
Tanunak *USA* 4B3
Tanzania, Republic *Africa* 99D3
Tao He, R *China* 72A3
Taolañaro *Madag* 101D3
Taole *China* 72B2
Taourirt *Mor* 96B1
Tapa *USSR* 60C2
Tapachula *Mexico* 25C3
Tapajós, R *Brazil* 33F4
Tapalquén *Arg* 34C3
Tapan *Indon* 70B4
Tapanui *NZ* 111A3
Tapauá, R *Brazil* 32D5
Tapi, R *India* 85D4
Taplejung *Nepal* 86B1
Tapuaeniku, Mt *NZ* 111B2
Tapuaritinga *Brazil* 35B2
Tapul Group, Is *Phil* 79B4
Tapurucuara *Brazil* 33E4
Tara *Aust* 109D1
Tara *USSR* 65J4
Tara, R *USSR* 65J4
Tara, R *Yugos* 54A2
Taraba, R *Nig* 97D4
Tarabuco *Bol* 30D2
Taracón *Spain* 50B1
Taradale *NZ* 110C1
Tarakan *Indon* 78D2
Taransay, I *Scot* 44A3
Taranto *Italy* 53C2
Tarapoto *Peru* 32B5
Tarare *France* 49C2
Tararua Range, Mts *NZ* 110C2
Tarat *Alg* 96C2
Tarawera *NZ* 110C1
Tarazona *Spain* 51B1
Tarbat Ness, Pen *Scot* 44C3
Tarbela Res *Pak* 84C2
Tarbert, Strathclyde *Scot* 42B2
Tarbert, Western Isles *Scot* 44A3
Tarbes *France* 48C3
Tarcoola *Aust* 106C4
Tarcoon *Aust* 109C2
Taree *Aust* 109D2
Tarfaya *Mor* 96A2
Tarhūnah *Libya* 95A1
Tarīf *UAE* 91B5
Tarija *Bol* 30D3
Tarikere *India* 87B2
Tarīm *S Yemen* 81C4
Tarime *Tanz* 99D3
Tarim He, R *China* 82C1
Tarim Pendi, Basin *China* 82C2
Tarin Kut *Afghan* 84B2
Tarkio *USA* 18A1
Tarlac *Phil* 79B2
Tarma *Peru* 32B6
Tarn, R *France* 49C3
Tarnobrzeg *Pol* 59C2
Tarnów *Pol* 59C3
Taroom *Aust* 107D3
Tarragona *Spain* 51C1
Tarraleah *Aust* 109C4
Tarrasa *Spain* 51C1
Tarrytown *USA* 16C2
Tarsus *Turk* 92B2
Tartan, Oilfield *N Sea* 44D2
Tartaro, R *Italy* 47D2
Tartu *USSR* 60C2
Tartūs *Syria* 92C3
Tarumirim *Brazil* 35C1
Tarutung *Indon* 70A3
Tarvisio *Italy* 52B1
Tashauz *USSR* 80D1
Tashigang *Bhutan* 86C1
Tashkent *USSR* 82A1
Tashtagol *USSR* 65K4
Tashtyp *USSR* 63A2
Tasikmalaya *Indon* 78B4
Tasīl *Syria* 94B2
Tasiussaq *Greenland* 6E2
Tasker, Well *Niger* 95A3
Tasman B *NZ* 110B2
Tasmania, I *Aust* 107D5
Tasman Mts *NZ* 111B2
Tasman Pen *Aust* 109C4
Tasman S *NZ Aust* 107E4
Taşova *Turk* 92C1
Tassili du Hoggar, Desert, Region *Alg* 96C2
Tassili N'jjer, Desert, Region *Alg* 96C2
Tata *Mor* 96B2
Tataouine *Tunisia* 96D1
Tatarsk *USSR* 65J4
Tatarskaya ASSR, Republic *USSR* 61G2
Tatarskiy Proliv, Str *USSR* 69G2
Tateyama *Japan* 75B1
Tathlina L *Can* 5G3
Tatitlek *USA* 12E2
Tatla Lake *Can* 13C2
Tatry, Mts *Pol/Czech* 59B3
Tatsuno *Japan* 75A2
Tatta *Pak* 85B4
Tatuí *Brazil* 35B2
Tatvan *Turk* 93D2
Tauá *Brazil* 31C3
Taubaté *Brazil* 35B2
Taumarunui *NZ* 110C1
Taung *S Africa* 101F1
Taungdwingyi *Burma* 76B2
Taung-gyi *Burma* 76B1
Taungup *Burma* 76A2
Taunsa *Pak* 84C2
Taunton *Eng* 43C4
Taunton *USA* 16D2
Taunus, Region *W Germ* 46E1
Taupo *NZ* 110C1
Taupo,L *NZ* 110C1
Taurage *USSR* 58C1
Tauranga *NZ* 110C1
Tauranga Harbour, B *NZ* 110C1
Tauroa Pt *NZ* 110B1
Tavani *Can* 7A3
Tavira *Port* 50A2
Tavistock *Eng* 43B4
Tavoy *Burma* 76B3
Tavoy Pt *Burma* 76B3
Tavsanli *Turk* 92A2
Tawa *NZ* 111B2
Tawakoni,L *USA* 19A3
Tawas City *USA* 14B2
Tawau *Malay* 70C3
Taweisha *Sudan* 98C1
Tawitawi, I *Phil* 79B4
Tawitawi Group, Is *Phil* 79B4
Taxco *Mexico* 23B2
Taxcoco *Mexico* 23B2
Tay, R *Scot* 44C3
Tayan *Indon* 78C3
Taylor, Alaska *USA* 12B1
Taylor *Can* 13C1
Taylor, Michigan *USA* 14B2
Taylor, Texas *USA* 19A3
Taylorville *USA* 18C2
Taymā' *S Arabia* 80B3
Taymura, R *USSR* 63B1
Tay Ninh *Viet* 76D3
Tayshet *USSR* 63B2
Tayshir *Mongolia* 68B2
Tayside, Region *Scot* 44C3
Taytay *Phil* 79A3
Tayyebat *Iran* 90D3
Taza *Mor* 96B1
Tazerbo, Region *Libya* 95B2
Tazlina L *USA* 12E2
Tazovskiy *USSR* 64J3
Tbilisi *USSR* 65F5
Tchibanga *Gabon* 98B3
Tchigai,Plat du *Niger* 95A2
Tchin Tabaradene *Niger* 97C3
Tcholliré *Cam* 98B2
Tczew *Pol* 58B2
Te Anau *NZ* 111A3
Te Anau,L *NZ* 111A3
Te Aroha *NZ* 110C1
Te Awamutu *NZ* 110C1
Tébessa *Alg* 96C1
Teboman *Mexico* 23A2
Tecailtlān *Mexico* 23A2
Tecate *Mexico* 21B3
Techa, R *USSR* 61K2
Tecolotlán *Mexico* 23A1
Tećpan *Mexico* 23A2
Tecuci *Rom* 54C1
Tecumseh *USA* 18A1
Tedzhen *USSR* 80E2
Tedzhen, R *USSR* 65H6
Tees, R *Eng* 42D2
Tefé *Brazil* 33E4
Tegal *Indon* 78B4
Tegineneng *Indon* 78B4
Tegucigalpa *Honduras* 25D3
Tehachapi Mts *USA* 21B3
Tehachapi P *USA* 21B2
Tehek L *Can* 4J3
Tehrān *Iran* 90B2
Tehuacán *Mexico* 23B2
Tehuantepec *Mexico* 23B2
Tehuitzingo *Mexico* 23B2
Teifi, R *Wales* 43B3
Tejo, R *Port* 50A2
Tejupilco *Mexico* 23A2
Tekapo,L *NZ* 111B2
Tekeli *USSR* 82B1
Tekirdağ *Turk* 92A1
Tekir Dağlari, Mts *Turk* 55C2
Teknaf *Bang* 86C2
Te Kuiti *NZ* 110C1
Tela *Honduras* 25D3
Tel Aviv Yafo *Israel* 94B2
Telén *Arg* 34B3
Telescope Peak, Mt *USA* 21B2
Teles Pires, R *Brazil* 33F5
Telfs *Austria* 47D1
Teli *USSR* 63A2
Tell el Meise, Mt *Jordan* 94B3
Teller *USA* 12A1
Tellicherry *India* 87B2
Telok Anson *Malay* 77C5
Tĕlok Darvel *Malay* 78D2
Tĕlok Flamingo, B *Indon* 71E4
Tĕlok Kumai, B *Indon* 78C3
T14elok Pelabuanratu, B *Indon* 78B4
Tĕlok Saleh, B *Indon* 78D4
Tĕlok Sampit, B *Indon* 78C3
Tĕlok Sukadona, B *Indon* 78B3
Teloloapán *Mexico* 23B2
Telšiai *USSR* 58C1
Telukbatang *Indon* 78C3
Teluk Berau, B *Indon* 71E4
Telukbetung *Indom* 78B4
Teluk Bone, B *Indon* 70D4
Teluk Cendrawasih, B *Indon* 71E4
Teluk Mandar, B *Indon* 78D3
Teluk Tolo, B *Indon* 71D4
Teluk Tomini, B *Indon* 70D3
Tĕluk Weda, B *Indon* 71D3
Temagami,L *Can* 14B1
Temascal *Mexico* 23B2
Tembesi, R *Indon* 78A3
Tembilahan *Indon* 78A3
Temblador *Ven* 27E5
Temerloh *Malay* 77C5
Temir *USSR* 65G5
Temirtau *USSR* 65J4
Temiscaming *Can* 15C1
Temora *Aust* 109C2
Tempe *USA* 9B3
Temple *USA* 19A3
Templemore *Irish Rep* 45C2
Tempoal *Mexico* 23B1
Temuco *Chile* 34A3

Temuka *NZ* 111B2
Tena *Ecuador* 32B4
Tenāli *India* 87C1
Tenancingo *Mexico* 23B2
Tenasserim *Burma* 76B3
Tenby *Wales* 43B4
Ten Degree Chan *Indian O* 83D5
Ténéré, Desert Region *Niger* 98B1
Tenerife, I *Canary Is* 96A2
Teng, R *Burma* 76B1
Tenggarong *Indon* 78D3
Tengger Shamo, Desert *China* 72A2
Tenkāsi *India* 87B3
Tenke *Zaïre* 100B2
Tenkodogo *U Volta* 97B3
Tennant Creek *Aust* 106C2
Tennessee, State *USA* 11B3
Tennessee, R *USA* 18C2
Teno *Chile* 34A2
Tenom *Malay* 78D1
Tenosique *Mexico* 25C3
Tenterfield *Aust* 109D1
Ten Thousand Is *USA* 17B2
Teocaltiche *Mexico* 23A1
Teófilo Otôni *Brazil* 35C1
Teotihiucan, Hist Site *Mexico* 23B2
Teotitlan *Mexico* 23B2
Tepatitlan *Mexico* 23A1
Tepehuanes *Mexico* 24B2
Tepeji *Mexico* 23B2
Tepic *Mexico* 23A1
Teplice *Czech* 57C2
Te Puke *NZ* 110C1
Tequila *Mexico* 23A1
Tequistepec *Mexico* 23B2
Ter, R *Spain* 51C1
Téra *Niger* 97C3
Teradomari *Japan* 75B1
Teramo *Italy* 52B2
Terceira, I *Açores* 96A1
Tereboviya *USSR* 59D3
Teresina *Brazil* 31C3
Teresópolis *Brazil* 35C2
Terme *Turk* 92C1
Termez *USSR* 80E2
Termoli *Italy* 52B2
Ternate *Indon* 71D3
Terni *Italy* 52B2
Ternopol *USSR* 59D3
Terrace *Can* 13B2
Terracina *Italy* 53B2
Terrafirma *S Africa* 100B3
Terre Adélie, Region *Ant* 112C8
Terre Bonne B *USA* 19B4
Terre Haute *USA* 14A3
Terrell *USA* 19A3
Terschelling, I *Neth* 56B2
Teruel *Spain* 51B1
Teshekpuk *USA* 4C2
Teshekpuk L *USA* 4C2
Teshio, R *Japan* 74E2
Tesiyn Gol, Mts *Mongolia* 68B2
Teslin *Can* 12H2
Teslin, R *Can* 12H3
Teslin L *Can* 12H2
Teslyn Gol, R *Mongolia* 63B3
Tessalit *Mali* 96C2
Tessaoua *Niger* 97C3
Tete *Mozam* 101C2
Tetela *Mexico* 23A2
Tetouan *Mor* 96B1
Tetyushi *USSR* 61G2
Teuco, R *Arg* 30D3
Teúl de Gonzalez Ortega *Mexico* 23A1
Teun, I *Indon* 71D4
Tevere, R *Italy* 52B2
Teviot, R *Scot* 42C2
Tevriz *USSR* 65J4
Te Waewae B *NZ* 111A3
Tewah *Indon* 78C3
Tewantin *Aust* 109D1
Têwo *China* 72A3
Texarkana *USA* 19B3
Texarkana,L *USA* 19B3
Texas *Aust* 109D1
Texas, State *USA* 9C3
Texas City *USA* 19B4
Texel, I *Neth* 56A2
Texoma,L *USA* 19A3
Teyateyaneng *Lesotho* 101G1
Teziutlán *Mexico* 23B2
Tezpur *India* 86C1
Tha *Laos* 76C1
Thabana Ntlenyana, Mt *Lesotho* 101G1
Thaba Putsoa, Mt *Lesotho* 101G1
Thagyettaw *Burma* 76B3
Thai Binh *Viet* 76D1
Thailand, Kingdom *S E Asia* 76C2
Thailand,G of *Thai* 76C3
Thai Nguyen *Viet* 76D1
Thakhek *Laos* 76C2
Thal *Pak* 84C2
Thale Luang, L *Thai* 77C4
Thallon *Aust* 109C1
Thames *NZ* 110C1
Thames, R *Eng* 43E4
Thanh Hoah *Viet* 76D2
Thanjavur *India* 87B2
Thar Desert *India* 85C3
Thargomindah *Aust* 108B1
Thásos, I *Greece* 55B2
Thaton *Burma* 76B2
Thayetmyo *Burma* 76B2
The Dalles *USA* 5F5
The Gulf *S W Asia* 91B4
Thelon, R *Can* 4H3
Theodore *Aust* 107E3
Theodore Roosevelt L *USA* 9B3
Thermaïkós Kólpos, G *Greece* 55B2
Thermopolis *USA* 8C2
Thesiger B *Can* 4F2
Thessalon *Can* 14B1
Thessaloníki *Greece* 55B2
Thetford *Eng* 43E3
Thetford Mines *Can* 15D1
Theunissen *S Africa* 101G1
Thibodaux *USA* 19B4
Thicket Portage *Can* 5J4
Thief River Falls *USA* 8D2
Thielsen,Mt *USA* 20B2
Thiers *France* 49C2
Thiès *Sen* 97A3
Thika *Kenya* 99D3
Thimphu *Bhutan* 86B1
Thionville *France* 49D2
Thíra, I *Greece* 55C3
Thirsk *Eng* 42D2
Thisted *Den* 39F7
Thívai *Greece* 55B3
Thiviers *France* 48C2
Thomaston, Georgia *USA* 17B1
Thomastown *Irish Rep* 45C2
Thomasville, Georgia *USA* 17B1
Thom Bay *Can* 6A2
Thompson *Can* 5J4
Thompson, R *USA* 18B1
Thompson Landing *Can* 4G3
Thompson R *Can* 13C2
Thompsonville *USA* 16C2
Thomson *USA* 17B1
Thomson, R *Aust* 107D3
Thon Buri *Thai* 76C3
Thongwa *Burma* 76B2
Thonon-les-Bains *France* 47B1
Thornhill *Scot* 42C2
Thouars *France* 48B2
Thousand Is *Can/USA* 15C2
Three Hills *Can* 13E2
Three Kings Is *NZ* 7G4
Three Pagodas P *Thai* 76B2
Three Rivers, Michigan *USA* 14A2
Three Sisters, Mt *USA* 20B2
Thule *Greenland* 6D2
Thun *Switz* 47B1
Thundar Bay *Can* 10B2
Thuner See, L *Switz* 47B1
Thung Song *Thai* 77B4
Thur, R *Switz* 47C1
Thüringen Wald, Upland *E Germ* 57C2
Thurles *Irish Rep* 45C2
Thursday I *Aust* 71F5
Thurso *Scot* 44C2
Thurston I *Ant* 112B4
Thusis *Switz* 47C1
Thylungra *Aust* 108B1
Tiandong *China* 73B5
Tian'e *China* 73B5
Tianjin *China* 72D2
Tianlin *China* 73B5
Tiân Shan, Mts *C Asia* 82C1
Tianshui *China* 72B3
Tianzhu *China* 72A2
Tiaret *Alg* 96C1
Tibagi, R *Brazil* 35A2
Tiberias *Israel* 94B2
Tiberias,L *Israel* 94B2
Tibesti, Mountain Region *Chad* 95A2
Tibet, Autonomous Region *China* 82C2
Tibooburra *Aust* 108B1
Tibrikot *Nepal* 86A1
Tiburón, I *Mexico* 24A2
Tichitt *Maur* 97B3
Tichla *Mor* 96A2
Ticino, R *Italy/Switz* 47C2
Ticonderoga *USA* 15D2
Ticul *Mexico* 25D2
Tidjikja *Maur* 97A3
Tiefencastel *Switz* 47C1
Tieling *China* 74A2
Tielt *Belg* 46B1
Tienen *Belg* 46C1
Tien Shan, Mts *USSR/China* 65J5
Tientsin *China* 72D2
Tierp *Sweden* 39H6
Tierra Blanca *Mexico* 23B2
Tierra Colorada *Mexico* 23B2
Tierra del Fuego, Territory *Arg* 29C6
Tierra del Fuego, I *Chile/Arg* 28C8
Tietê *Brazil* 35B2
Tiete, R *Brazil* 35A2
Tiffin *USA* 14B2
Tifton *USA* 17B1
Tigre, R *Peru* 32B4
Tigre, R *Ven* 33E2
Tigris, R *Iraq* 93E3
Tihuatlán *Mexico* 23B1
Tijuana *Mexico* 21B3
Tikamgarh *India* 85D4
Tikhin *USSR* 60D2
Tikhoretsk *USSR* 61F4
Tikrīt *Iraq* 93D3
Tiksi *USSR* 1B8
Tilburg *Neth* 46C1
Tilbury *Eng* 43E4
Tilcara *Arg* 30C3
Tilcha *Aust* 108B1
Tilin *Burma* 76A1
Tillabéri *Niger* 97C3
Tillamook *USA* 20B1
Tillia *Niger* 97C3
Tílos, I *Greece* 55C3
Tilpa *Aust* 108B2
Tiluá *Colombia* 32B3
Timaru *NZ* 111B2
Timashevsk *USSR* 60E4
Timbákion *Greece* 55B3
Timbalier B *USA* 19B4
Timbédra *Maur* 97B3
Timétrine Monts, Mts *Mali* 97B3
Timia *Niger* 97C3
Timimoun *Alg* 96C2
Timişoara *Rom* 54B1
Timmins *Can* 10B2
Timor, I *Indon* 106B1
Timor S *Aust/Indon* 106B2
Timote *Arg* 34C3
Tinaca Pt *Phil* 79C4
Tinaco *Ven* 27D5
Tindivanam *India* 87B2
Tindouf *Alg* 96B2
Tinfouchy *Alg* 96B2
Tin Fouye *Alg* 96C2
Tingmiarmiut *Greenland* 6F3
Tingo Maria *Peru* 32B5
Tingrela *Ivory Coast* 97B3
Tingri *China* 86B1
Tinian *Pacific O* 71F2
Tinogasta *Arg* 30C4
Tínos, I *Greece* 55C3
Tintagel Head, Pt *Eng* 43B4
Tin Tarabine, Watercourse *Alg* 96C2
Tintinara *Aust* 108B3
Tin Zaouaten *Alg* 96C2
Tioga P *USA* 22C2
Tioman, I *Malay* 77C5
Tione *Italy* 47D1
Tipperary, County *Irish Rep* 45C2
Tipperary *Irish Rep* 41B3
Tipton, Missouri *USA* 18B2
Tiptūr *India* 87B2
Tiquicheo *Mexico* 23A2
Tiranë *Alb* 55A2
Tirano *Italy* 47D1
Tiraspol *USSR* 60C4
Tirchchirāppalli *India* 87B2
Tire *Turk* 55C3
Tirebolu *Turk* 93C1
Tiree, I *Scot* 44A3
Tîrgovişte *Rom* 54C2
Tîrgu Jiu *Rom* 54B1
Tîrgu Mureş *Rom* 54B1
Tirich Mir, Mt *Pak* 84C1
Tiris, Region *Mor* 96A2
Tirlyanskiy *USSR* 61J3
Tîrnăveni *Rom* 54B1
Tírnavos *Greece* 55B3
Tirodi *India* 85D4
Tirol, Province *Austria* 47D1
Tirso, R *Sardegna* 53A2
Tiruchchendūr *India* 87B3
Tirunelveli *India* 87B3
Tirupati *India* 87B2
Tiruppattūr *India* 87B2
Tiruppur *India* 87B2
Tiruvannamalai *India* 87B2
Tishomingo *USA* 19A3
Tisīyah *Syria* 94C2
Tisza, R *Hung* 59C3
Titlagarh *India* 86A2
Titograd *Yugos* 54A2
Titovo Užice *Yugos* 54A2
Titov Veles *Yugos* 54B2
Titule *Zaïre* 98C2
Titusville *USA* 17B2
Tiverton *Eng* 43C4
Tivoli *Italy* 52B2
Tixtla *Mexico* 23B2
Tiyeglow *Somalia* 99E2
Tizayuca *Mexico* 23B2
Tizimin *Mexico* 25D2
Tizi Ouzou *Alg* 96C1
Tiznit *Mor* 96B2
Tizpan el Alto *Mexico* 23A1
Tlacolula *Mexico* 23B2
Tlacotalpan *Mexico* 23B2
Tlalchana *Mexico* 23A2
Tlalnepantla *Mexico* 23B2
Tlalpan *Mexico* 23B2
Tlaltenango *Mexico* 23A1
Tlancualpicán *Mexico* 23B2
Tlapa *Mexico* 23B2
Tlapacoyan *Mexico* 23B2

Tlaquepaque *Mexico* 23A1
Tlaxcala *Mexico* 23B2
Tlaxcala, State *Mexico* 23B2
Tlaxiaco *Mexico* 23B2
Tlemcem *Alg* 96B1
Toamasina *Madag* 101D2
Toay *Arg* 34C3
Toba *Japan* 75B2
Toba and Kakar Ranges, Mts *Pak* 84B2
Tobago, I *Caribbean* 27E4
Toba Inlet, Sd *Can* 13C2
Tobelo *Indon* 71D3
Tobermory *Can* 14B1
Tobermory *Scot* 44A3
Tobi, I *Pacific O* 71E3
Tobin,Mt *USA* 21B1
Tobol, R *USSR* 65H4
Toboli *Indon* 70D4
Tobol'sk *USSR* 65H4
Tocantins, R *Brazil* 31B2
Toccoa *USA* 17B1
Toce, R *Italy* 47C1
Tocopilla *Chile* 30B3
Tocorpuri, Mt *Chile* 30C3
Tocuyo, R *Ven* 32D1
Toda *India* 85D3
Tödi, Mt *Switz* 47C1
Todong *S Korea* 75A1
Todos Santos *Mexico* 9B4
Tofield *Can* 13E2
Tofino *Can* 13B3
Togiak *USA* 12B3
Togiak B *USA* 12B3
Togo, Republic *Africa* 97C4
Togtoh *China* 72C1
Tok *USA* 12F2
Tokachi, R *Japan* 74E2
Tokamachi *Japan* 75B1
Tokar *Sudan* 95C3
Tokara Retto, Arch *Japan* 69E4
Tokat *Turk* 92C1
Tŏkchŏk-kundo, Arch *S Korea* 74B3
Tok-do, I *S Korea* 75A1
Tokmak *USSR* 82B1
Tokomaru Bay *NZ* 110C1
Toku, R *Can/USA* 12H3
Tokung *Indon* 78C3
Tokuno, I *Japan* 69E4
Tokushima *Japan* 74C4
Tokuyama *Japan* 75A2
Tōkyō *Japan* 74D3
Tolaga Bay *NZ* 110C1
Toledo *Brazil* 30F3
Toledo *Spain* 50B2
Toledo *USA* 14B2
Toledo Bend Res *USA* 19B3
Toliara *Madag* 101D3
Toliman *Mexico* 23B1
Tolina, Mt *Colombia* 32B3
Tolosa *Spain* 51B1
Toltén *Chile* 29B3
Toluca *Mexico* 23B2
Tol'yati *USSR* 61G3
Tomakomai *Japan* 74E2
Tomani *Malay* 78D1
Tomaszów Mazowiecka *Pol* 58C2
Tombigbee, R *USA* 11B3
Tomboco *Angola* 98B3
Tombos *Brazil* 35C2
Tombouctou *Mali* 97B3
Tombua *Angola* 100A2
Tomé *Chile* 34A3
Tomelloso *Spain* 50B2
Tomer *Port* 50A2
Tomkinson Range, Mts *Aust* 106B3
Tommot *USSR* 63E2
Tomorrit, Mt *Alb* 55B2
Tomsk *USSR* 65K4
Toms River *USA* 16B3
Tonalá *Mexico* 25C3
Tonasket *USA* 20C1
Tonawanda *USA* 15C2
Tonga, Is *Pacific O* 105H4
Tongaat *S Africa* 101H1
Tongcheng *China* 73D3
Tongchuan *China* 72B2
Tongde *China* 72A2
Tongeren *Belg* 46C1
Tonggu Jiao, I *China* 76E2
Tonghai *China* 73A5
Tonghua *China* 74B2
Tongjosŏn-man *N Korea* 74B3
Tongkin,G of *Viet/China* 76D1
Tonglia *China* 72E1
Tongling *China* 73D3
Tongo *Aust* 108B2
Tongoy *Chile* 34A2
Tongren, Guizhou *China* 73B4
Tongren, Qinghai *China* 72A2
Tongsa *Bhutan* 86C1
Tongta *Burma* 76B1
Tongtian He, R *China* 68B3
Tongue *Scot* 44B2
Tong Xian *China* 72D2
Tongxin *China* 72B2
Tongzi *China* 73B4
Tonhil *Mongolia* 63B3
Tonich *Mexico* 9C4
Tonj *Sudan* 99C2
Tonk *India* 85D3
Tonkawa *USA* 18A2
Tonle Sap, L *Camb* 76C3
Tonopah *USA* 21B2
Tonsina *USA* 12E2
Tooele *USA* 8B2
Toogoolawah *Aust* 109D1
Toompine *Aust* 108B1
Toowoomba *Aust* 109D1
Topaz L *USA* 22C1
Topeka *USA* 18A2
Topolobampo *Mexico* 9C4
Toppenish *USA* 20B1
Torbali *Turk* 55C3
Torbat-e-Heydarīyeh *Iran* 90C2
Torbat-e Jām *Iran* 90D2
Torbay *Eng* 43C4
Torbert,Mt *USA* 12D2
Tordesillas *Spain* 50A1
Torgau *E Germ* 56C2
Torhout *Belg* 46B1
Tori *Eth* 99D2
Tori, I *Japan* 69G3
Torino *Italy* 47B2
Torit *Sudan* 99D2
Torixoreu *Brazil* 35A1
Tormes, R *Spain* 50A1
Tornado Mt *Can* 13E2
Torne, L *Sweden* 38J5
Torneträsk *Sweden* 38H5
Torngat, Mts *Can* 7D4
Tornio *Fin* 38J5
Tornquist *Arg* 34C3
Toronto *Can* 15C2
Toropets *USSR* 60D2
Tororo *Uganda* 99D2
Toros Dağlari, Mts *Turk* 92B2
Torrance *USA* 22C4
Torrão *Port* 50A2
Torreblanca *Spain* 51C1
Torre del Greco *Italy* 53B2
Torrelavega *Spain* 50B1
Torremolinos *Spain* 50B2
Torrens,L *Aust* 108A2
Torreón *Mexico* 24B2
Torre Pellice *Italy* 47B2
Torres Str *Aust* 107D2
Torres Vedras *Port* 50A2
Torrington, Connecticut *USA* 16C2
Torrington, Wyoming *USA* 8C2
Torrón *Mexico* 9C4
Torshavn *Faeroes* 38D3
Tortona *Italy* 47C2
Tortosa *Spain* 51C1
Torūd *Iran* 90C2
Toruń *Pol* 58B2
Tory, I *Irish Rep* 40B2
Torzhok *USSR* 60D2
Tosa *Japan* 75A2
Tosa-shimizu *Japan* 74C4
Tosa-wan, B *Japan* 74C4
To-shima, I *Japan* 75B2
Tosno *USSR* 39L7
Tosno *USSR* 60D2
Tosu *Japan* 75A2
Tosya *Turk* 92B1
Tot'ma *USSR* 61F1
Totnes *Eng* 43C4
Totness *Surinam* 33F2
Totolapan *Mexico* 23B2
Totona *Spain* 51B2
Tottenham *Aust* 109C2
Tottori *Japan* 74C3
Touba *Ivory Coast* 97B4
Touba *Sen* 97A3
Toubkal, Mt *Mor* 96B1
Tougan *U Volta* 97B3
Touggourt *Alg* 96C1
Tougué *Guinea* 97A3
Toul *France* 46C2
Toulon *France* 49D3
Toulouse *France* 48C3
Toumodi *Ivory Coast* 97B4
Toungoo *Burma* 76B2
Tourcoing *France* 46B1
Tourine *Maur* 96A2
Tournai *Belg* 46B1
Tours *France* 48C2
Towada *Japan* 74E2
Towada-ko, L *Japan* 74E2
Towanda *USA* 15C2
Townsville *Aust* 107D2
Towson *USA* 16A3
Towy, R *Wales* 43C4
Toyama *Japan* 74D3
Toyama-wan, B *Japan* 75B1
Toyohashi *Japan* 75B2
Toyonaka *Japan* 75B2
Toyooka *Japan* 75A1
Toyota *Japan* 74D3
Tozeur *Tunisia* 96C1
Traben-Trarbach *W Germ* 46D2
Trabzon *Turk* 93C1
Tracy, California *USA* 22B2
Traiguén *Chile* 34A3
Trail *Can* 13D3
Tralee *Irish Rep* 41B3
Tralee B *Irish Rep* 45B2
Tramore *Irish Rep* 45C2
Tranås *Sweden* 39G7
Trang *Thai* 77B4
Trangan, I *Indon* 71E4
Trangie *Aust* 109C2
Transalaskan Pipeline *USA* 12E2
Transvaal, Province *S Africa* 100B3
Trapani *Italy* 53B3
Traralgon *Aust* 109C3
Trarza, Region *Maur* 97A3
Trat *Thai* 76C3
Traveller's, L *Aust* 108B2
Travemünde *W Germ* 56C2
Traverse City *USA* 14A2
Traverse Peak, Mt *USA* 12C1
Travers,Mt *NZ* 111B2
Trebbia, R *Italy* 47C2
Třebíč *Czech* 59B3
Trebinje *Yugos* 54A2
Trebon *Czech* 57C3
Treinta y Tres *Urug* 29F2
Trelew *Arg* 29C4
Trelleborg *Sweden* 39G7
Tremadog B *Wales* 43B3
Tremblant,Mt *Can* 15D1
Trembleur L *Can* 13C2
Tremont *USA* 16A2
Trenčin *Czech* 59B3
Trenque Lauquén *Arg* 34C3
Trent, R *Eng* 43D3
Trentino, Region *Italy* 47D1
Trento *Italy* 47D1
Trenton *Can* 15C2
Trenton, Missouri *USA* 18B1
Trenton, New Jersey *USA* 16B2
Trepassey *Can* 7E5
Tres Arroyos *Arg* 34C3
Tres Corações *Brazil* 35B2
Três Lagoas *Brazil* 30F3
Tres Lomas *Arg* 34C3
Tres Pinos *USA* 22B2
Três Rios *Brazil* 35C2
Treviglio *Italy* 47C2
Treviso *Italy* 47E2
Trezzo *Italy* 47C2
Trichūr *India* 87B2
Trida *Aust* 108C2
Trier *W Germ* 46D2
Trieste *Italy* 52B1
Trim *Irish Rep* 45C2
Trincomalee *Sri Lanka* 87C3
Trinidad *Bol* 33E6
Trinidad *Urug* 29E2
Trinidad *USA* 9C3
Trinidad, I *Arg* 34C3
Trinidad, I *Caribbean* 27E4
Trindade, I *Atlantic O* 103G6
Trinidad & Tobago, Is Republic *Caribbean* 27E4
Trinity *USA* 19A3
Trinity, R *USA* 9D3
Trinity B *Can* 7E5
Trinity Is *USA* 12D3
Trion *USA* 17A1
Tripoli *Leb* 94B1
Tripoli *Libya* 95A1
Trípolis *Greece* 55B3
Tripura, State *India* 86C2
Tristan da Cunha, Is *Atlantic O* 103H6
Trivandrum *India* 87B3
Trnava *Czech* 59B3
Trobriand Is *PNG* 107E1
Trois-Riviéres *Can* 15D1
Troitsk *USSR* 65H4
Trollhättan *Sweden* 39G7
Trollheimen, Mt *Nor* 38F6
Tromelin, I *Indian O* 89K9
Tromsø *Nor* 38H5
Trondheim *Nor* 38G6
Trondheimfjord, Inlet *Nor* 38G6
Troon *Scot* 42B2
Tropic of Cancer 102J3
Tropic of Capricorn 103J6
Troudenni *Mali* 96B2
Trout L, Ontario *Can* 7A4
Troy, Alabama *USA* 17A1
Troy, New York *USA* 16C1
Troy, Ohio *USA* 14B2
Troyan *Bulg* 54B2
Troyes *France* 49C2
Trucial Coast, Region *UAE* 91B5
Truckee, R *USA* 21A2
Trujillo *Honduras* 25D3
Trujillo *Peru* 32B5
Trujillo *Spain* 50A2
Trujillo *Ven* 32C2
Trundle *Aust* 109C2
Truro *Can* 7D5
Truro *Eng* 43B4
Trust Territories of the Pacific Is *Pacific O* 71E3
Tsagaan Nuur, L *Mongolia* 68B2
Tsagan-Tologoy *USSR* 68B1
Tsaratanana *Madag* 101D2
Tsau *Botswana* 100B3
Tsavo *Kenya* 99D3
Tsavo Nat Pk *Kenya* 99D3
Tselinograd *USSR* 65J4
Tses *Namibia* 100A3
Tsetserleg *Mongolia* 68B2
Tsetserleg *Mongolia* 68C2
Tsévié *Togo* 97C4

Tshabong *Botswana* 100B3
Tshane *Botswana* 100B3
Tshela *Zaïre* 98B3
Tshibala *Zaïre* 98C3
Tshikapa *Zaïre* 98C3
Tshuapa, R *Zaïre* 98C3
Tsihombe *Madag* 101D3
Tsimlyanskoye Vodokhranilishche, Res *USSR* 61F4
Tsiroanomandidy *Madag* 101D2
Tsitsutl Peak, Mt *Can* 13B2
Tsna, R *USSR* 58D2
Tsogt Ovoo *Mongolia* 72B1
Tsu *Japan* 75B2
Tsubata *Japan* 75B1
Tsuchira *Japan* 74E3
Tsugaru-kaikyō, Str *Japan* 74E2
Tsumeb *Namibia* 100A2
Tsumis *Namibia* 100A3
Tsunugi *Japan* 75B1
Tsuruga *Japan* 74D3
Tsuruoka *Japan* 74D3
Tsushima *Japan* 75B1
Tsushima, I *Japan* 74B4
Tsuyama *Japan* 74C3
Tua, R *Port* 50A1
Tuam *Irish Rep* 45B2
Tuapse *USSR* 60E5
Tuatapere *NZ* 111A3
Tubarão *Brazil* 30G4
Tubas *Israel* 94B2
Tubbataha Reefs, Is *Phil* 79A4
Tübingen *W Germ* 57B3
Tubruq *Libya* 95B1
Tuckerton *USA* 16B3
Tucson *USA* 9B3
Tucumán, State *Arg* 30C4
Tucunuco *Arg* 34B2
Tucupita *Ven* 33E2
Tudela *Spain* 51B1
Tudmur *Syria* 93C3
Tugela, R *S Africa* 101H1
Tuggerah, L *Aust* 109D2
Tugidak, I *USA* 12D3
Tuguegarao *Phil* 79B2
Tugur *USSR* 63F2
Tuhai He, R *China* 72D2
Tuktoyaktuk *USA* 4E3
Tukums *USSR* 58C1
Tukuyu *Tanz* 99D3
Tukzar *Afghan* 84B1
Tula *USSR* 60E3
Tulancingo *Mexico* 23B1
Tulangbawang, R *Indon* 78A3
Tulcán *Colombia* 32B3
Tulcea *Rom* 60C5
Tuli *Zim* 100B3
Tulkarm *Israel* 94B2
Tulle *France* 48C2
Tullos *USA* 19B3
Tullow *Irish Rep* 45C2
Tulsa *USA* 18A2
Tulūl ash Shāmīyah, Desert Region *Syria/S Arabia* 93C3
Tulun *USSR* 63C2
Tulungagung *Indon* 78C4
Tumaco *Colombia* 32B3
Tumbarumba *Aust* 109C3
Tumbes *Ecuador* 32A4
Tumby Bay *Aust* 108A2
Tumen *China* 74B2
Tumkūr *India* 87B2
Tumpat *Malay* 77C4
Tumsar *India* 85D4
Tumu *Ghana* 97B3
Tumut *Aust* 109C3
Tumut, R *Aust* 109C3
Tunapuna *Trinidad* 27L1
Tunceli *Turk* 93C2
Tunduma *Zambia* 99D3
Tunduru *Tanz* 101C2
Tundzha, R *Bulg* 54C2
Tungabhadra, R *India* 87B1
Tung-Chiang *Taiwan* 68D4
Tungnafellsjökull, Mts *Iceland* 38B2
Tungsten *Can* 12J2
Tunguska, R *USSR* 63B1
Tuni *India* 87C1
Tunis *Tunisia* 96D1
Tunisia, Republic *N Africa* 88E4
Tunja *Colombia* 32C2
Tuntutuliak *USA* 12B2
Tununak *USA* 12B2
Tunuyán *Arg* 34B2
Tunuyán, R *Arg* 34B2
Tunxi *China* 73D4
Tuolumne Meadows *USA* 22C2
Tupã *Brazil* 35A2
Tupaciguara *Brazil* 35B1
Tupelo *USA* 19C3
Tupiza *Bol* 30C3
Tupper Lake *USA* 15D2
Tupungato *Arg* 34B2
Tupungato, Mt *Arg* 29C2
Tura *India* 86C1
Tura *USSR* 63C1
Tura, R *USSR* 61K2
Turān *Iran* 90C2
Turan *USSR* 63B2
Turayf *S Arabia* 93C3
Turbat *Pak* 80E3
Turbo *Colombia* 32B2
Turda *Rom* 54B1
Turfan Depression *China* 63A3
Turgay *USSR* 65H4
Turgen Uul, Mt *Mongolia* 63B3
Turgutlu *Turk* 92A2
Turhal *Turk* 92C1
Türi *USSR* 39K7
Turia, R *Spain* 51B2
Turinsk *USSR* 61K2
Turiy Rog *USSR* 69F2
Turkana,L *Kenya/Eth* 99D2
Turkestan, Region *C Asia* 80E1
Turkestan *USSR* 82A1
Turkey, Republic *W Asia* 92C2
Turkmenskaya, SSR, Republic *USSR* 80D1
Turkmenskiy Zaliv, B *USSR* 90B2
Turks Is *Caribbean* 27C2
Turku *Fin* 39J6
Turkwel, R *Kenya* 99D2
Turlock *USA* 22B2
Turlock L *USA* 22B2
Turnagain,C *NZ* 110C2
Turneffe I *Belize* 25D3
Turners Falls *USA* 16C1
Turnhout *Belg* 46C1
Turnor L *Can* 13F1
Turnu Măgurele *Rom* 54B2
Turnu-Severin *Rom* 54B2
Turpan *China* 63A3
Turquino, Mt *Cuba* 26B2
Turtkul' *USSR* 80E1
Turtle Creek Res *USA* 18A2
Turtle L *Can* 13F2
Turukhansk *USSR* 63A1
Turuntayevo *USSR* 68C1
Turvo, R, Goias *Brazil* 35A1
Turvo, R, São Paulo *Brazil* 35B2
Tur'ya, R *USSR* 58C2
Tuscaloosa *USA* 19C3
Tuscola *USA* 18C2
Tusharík *Iran* 90C3
Tuticorin *India* 87B3
Tutrakan *Bulg* 54C2
Tuttlingen *W Germ* 57B3
Tuul Gol, R *Mongolia* 68C2
Tuvalu, Is *Pacific O* 105G4
Tuvinskaya, Republic *USSR* 63B2
Tuxpan, Jalisco *Mexico* 23A2
Tuxpan, Nayarit *Mexico* 24B2
Tuxpan, Veracruz *Mexico* 23B1
Tuxtepec *Mexico* 23B2
Tuxtla Gutiérrez *Mexico* 25C3
Túy *Spain* 50A1
Tuy Hoa *Viet* 76D3
Tuz Gölü, Salt L *Turk* 92B2
Tuz Khurmātū *Iraq* 93D3
Tuzla *Yugos* 54A2
Tweed, R *Scot/Eng* 42C2
Tweed Heads *Aust* 109D1
Tweedsmuir Hills *Scot* 42C2
Twillingate *Can* 7E5
Twin Falls *USA* 8B2
Twins,The, Mt *NZ* 111B2
Two Rivers *USA* 14A2
Tygda *USSR* 63E2
Tyler *USA* 19A3
Tymovskoye *USSR* 69G1
Tyne, R *Eng* 42D2
Tyne and Wear, Metropolitan County *Eng* 42D2
Tynemouth *Eng* 42D2
Tynset *Nor* 38G6
Tyonek *USA* 12D3
Tyr *Leb* 94B2
Tyrone, County *N Ire* 45C1
Tyrrell,L *Aust* 108B3
Tyrrhenian S *Italy* 53B2
Tyumen' *USSR* 65H4
Tywyn *Wales* 43B3
Tzoumérka, Mt *Greece* 55B3

U

Uarsciek *Somalia* 99E2
Ubá *Brazil* 35C2
Ubaí *Brazil* 35C1
Ubangi, R *CAR* 98B2
Ubaye, R *France* 47B2
Ube *Japan* 75A2
Ubeda *Spain* 50B2
Ubekendt Ejland, I *Greenland* 6E2
Uberaba *Brazil* 35B1
Uberlândia *Brazil* 35B1
Ubon Ratchathani *Thai* 76C2
Ubort, R *USSR* 58D2
Ubundi *Zaïre* 98C3
Ucayali, R *Peru* 32C5
Uch *Pak* 84C3
Uchiura-wan, B *Japan* 74E2
Uchur, R *USSR* 63F2
Udaipur *India* 85C4
Udaipur Garhi *Nepal* 86B1
Udaquoila *Arg* 34D3
Uddevalla *Sweden* 39G7
Uddjaur, L *Sweden* 38H5
Udgir *India* 87B1
Udhampur *India* 84D2
Udmurtskaya, ASSR, Republic *USSR* 61H2
Udon Thani *Thai* 76C2
Udskaya Guba, B *USSR* 63F2
Udupi *India* 87A2
Ueda *Japan* 75B1
Uele, R *Zaïre* 99C2
Uelzen *W Germ* 56C2
Uere, R *Zaïre* 98C2
Ufa *USSR* 61J3
Ufa, R *USSR* 61J2
Ugab, R *Namibia* 100A3
Ugaila, R *Tanz* 99D3
Ugak B *USA* 12D3
Uganda, Republic *Africa* 99D2
Ugashik B *USA* 12C3
Ugashik L *USA* 12C3
Ugine *France* 47B2
Uglegorsk *USSR* 69G2
Uglich *USSR* 60E2
Ugra, R *USSR* 60E3
Uig *Scot* 44A3
Uige *Angola* 98B3
Uil *USSR* 61H4
Uinta Mts *USA* 8B2
Uitenhage *S Africa* 100B4
Ujfehértó *Hung* 59C3
Uji *Japan* 75B2
Ujiji *Tanz* 99C3
Ujina *Chile* 30C3
Ujjain *India* 85D4
Ujung Pandang *Indon* 70C4
Ukerewe, I *Tanz* 99D3
Ukhrul *India* 86C1
Ukiah, California *USA* 21A2
Ukiah, Oregon *USA* 20C1
Ukmerge *USSR* 58C1
Ukrainskaya, Republic *USSR* 60C4
Ulaanbaatar *Mongolia* 68C2
Ulaangom *Mongolia* 68B2
Ulaan Uul *Mongolia* 72C1
Ulangar Hu, L *China* 82C1
Ulan Ude *USSR* 68C1
Ulan Ul Hu, L *China* 68B3
Ulapes *Arg* 34B2
Ulchin *S Korea* 74B3
Ulcinj *Yugos* 54A2
Uldz *Mongolia* 68D2
Uliastay *Mongolia* 68B2
Ulla *USSR* 58D1
Ulladulla *Aust* 109D3
Ullapool *Scot* 44B3
Ullsfjorden, Inlet *Nor* 38H5
Ullswater, L *Eng* 42C2
Ullung-do, I *S Korea* 74C3
Ulm *W Germ* 57C3
Uloowaranie,L *Aust* 108A1
Ulsan *S Korea* 74B3
Ulster, Region *N Ire* 45C1
Ulungur He, R *China* 65K5
Ulungur Hu, L *China* 65K5
Ulva, I *Scot* 44A3
Ulverston *Eng* 42C2
Ulverstone *Aust* 109C4
Ulya, R *USSR* 63G2
Ul'yanovsk *USSR* 61G3
Uman *USSR* 60D4
Umanak *Greenland* 6E2
Umaria *India* 86A2
Umarkot *Pak* 85B3
Umaroona,L *Aust* 108A1
Umatilla *USA* 20C1
Umba *USSR* 38L5
Umba, R *Tanz* 99D3
Ume, R *Sweden* 38H6
Umea *Sweden* 38J6
Umfolozi, R *S Africa* 101H1
Umiat *USA* 4C3
Umm al Qaiwain *UAE* 91C4
Umm as Samīm, Salt Marsh *Oman* 91C5
Umm Bell *Sudan* 99C1
Umm Hagar *Eth* 99D1
Umm Keddada *Sudan* 98C1
Umm Ruwaba *Sudan* 99D1
Umm Sa'id *Qatar* 91B5
Umnaiti, R *Zim* 100B2
Umpqua, R *USA* 20B2
Umred *India* 85D4
Umtata *S Africa* 100B4
Umuarama *Brazil* 35A2
Una, R *Yugos* 52C1
Unai *Brazil* 35B1
Unalakleet *USA* 12B2
Unayzah *S Arabia* 80C3
Uncasville *USA* 16C2
Underberg *S Africa* 101G1
Unecha *USSR* 60D3
Uneisa *Jordan* 94B3
Ungava B *Can* 7D4
União de Vitória *Brazil* 30F4
Unión *Arg* 34B3
Union, Missouri *USA* 18B2
Union, S Carolina *USA* 17B1

Union City, Pennsylvania *USA* **14C2**
Union of Soviet Socialist Reps *Asia* **62C3**
Union Springs *USA* **17A1**
Uniontown *USA* **15C3**
United Arab Emirates *Arabian Pen* **91B5**
United Kingdom, Kingdom *W Europe* **36C3**
United States of America **2H4**
United States Range, Mts *Can* **6B1**
Unity *Can* **13F2**
Unity *USA* **20C2**
Unna *W Germ* **46D1**
Unnão *India* **86A1**
Unst, I *Scot* **44D1**
Unuk, R *USA* **13A1**
Ünye *Turk* **92C1**
Unzha, R *USSR* **61F2**
Upata *Ven* **33E2**
Upemba Nat Pk *Zaïre* **98C3**
Upernavik *Greenland* **6E2**
Upland *USA* **22D3**
Uplington *S Africa* **100B3**
Upper Arlington *USA* **14B2**
Upper Arrow L *Can* **13D2**
Upper Hutt *NZ* **111C2**
Upper Klamath L *USA* **20B2**
Upper L *USA* **20B2**
Upper Lough Erne, L *N Ire* **45C1**
Upper Manzanilla *Trinidad* **27L1**
Upper Seal,L *Can* **7C4**
Upper Volta, Republic *Africa* **97B3**
Uppsala *Sweden* **39H7**
Urad Qianqi *China* **72B1**
Urairah *S Arabia* **91A4**
Ural, R *USSR* **61H3**
Uralla *Aust* **109D2**
Ural'sk *USSR* **61H3**
Uralskiy Khrebet, Mts *USSR* **65G4**
Uranium City *Can* **5H4**
Urawa *Japan* **75B1**
Urbana, Illinois *USA* **18C1**
Urbana, Ohio *USA* **14B2**
Urbino *Italy* **52B2**
Ure, R *Eng* **42C2**
Uren' *USSR* **61G2**
Urfa *Turk* **93C2**
Urgench *USSR* **80E1**
Urgun *Afghan* **84B2**
Urla *Turk* **55C3**
Uroševac *Yugos* **54B2**
Uruaçu *Brazil* **31B4**
Uruapan *Mexico* **23A2**
Urucuia, R *Brazil* **35B1**
Uruguaiana *Brazil* **30E4**
Uruguay, Republic *S America* **29E2**
Uruguay, R *Urug* **29E2**
Ürümqi *China* **82C1**
Urup, I *USSR* **69H2**
Uruzgan *Afghan* **84B2**
Uryupinsk *USSR* **61F3**
Urzhum *USSR* **61H2**
Urziceni *Rom* **54C2**
Usa *China* **82C1**
Usa *Japan* **75A2**
Uşak *Turk* **92A2**
Usakos *Namibia* **100A3**
Ushashi *Tanz* **99D3**
Ush Tobe *USSR* **65J5**
Ushuaia *Arg* **29C6**
Ushumun *USSR* **63E2**
Usk, R *Wales* **43C4**
Üsküdar *Turk* **92A1**
Usol'ye Sibirskoye *USSR* **63C2**
Uspallata *Arg* **34B2**
Ussuriysk *USSR* **69F2**
Uster *Switz* **47C1**
Ustica, I *Italy* **53B3**
Ústi nad Labem *Czech* **57C2**
Ust'Ishim *USSR* **65J4**
Ustka *Pol* **58B2**
Ust'-Kamenogorsk *USSR* **65K5**
Ust Karabula *USSR* **63B2**
Ust'Katav *USSR* **61J2**
Ust'-Kut *USSR* **63C2**
Ust Labinsk *USSR* **61E4**
Ust'Maya *USSR* **63F1**
Ust'Nera *USSR* **1C8**
Ust'Nyukzha *USSR* **63E2**
Ust'Ordynskiy *USSR* **63C2**
Ust'Tsil'ma *USSR* **64G3**
Ust'Umal'ta *USSR* **63F2**
Usuki *Japan* **75A2**
Usumacinta, R *Guatemala/Mexico* **25C3**
Usutu, R *Swaziland* **101H1**
Utah, State *USA* **8B3**
Utah L *USA* **8B2**
Utena *USSR* **58D1**
Uthal *Pak* **85B3**
Utica *USA* **10C2**
Utiel *Spain* **51B2**
Utikuma L *Can* **13D1**
Utrecht *Neth* **56B2**
Utrecht *S Africa* **101H1**
Utrera *Spain* **50A2**
Utsjoki *Fin* **38K5**
Utsunomiya *Japan* **74D3**
Uttaradit *Thai* **76C2**
Uttar Pradesh, State *India* **86A1**
Uval *USSR* **65H4**
Uvéa, I *Nouvelle Calédonie* **107F3**
Uvinza *Tanz* **99D3**
Uvira *Zaïre* **99C3**
Uvkusigssat *Greenland* **6E2**
Uvsikaupunki *Fin* **39J6**
Uvs Nuur, L *China* **68B1**
Uwajima *Japan* **74C4**
Uxin Qi *China* **72B2**
Uyar *USSR* **63B2**
Uyuni *Bol* **30C3**
Uzbekskaya, S.S.R., Republic *USSR* **80E1**
Uzerche *France* **48C2**
Uzhgorod *USSR* **59C3**
Uzlovaya *USSR* **60E3**
Uzunköprü *Turk* **92A1**

V

Vaal, R *S Africa* **101F1**
Vaal Dam, Res *S Africa* **101G1**
Vaalwater *S Africa* **100B3**
Vaasa *Fin* **38J6**
Vác *Hung* **59B3**
Vacaria *Brazil* **30F4**
Vacaria, R, Minas Gerais *Brazil* **35C1**
Vacaville *USA* **21A2**
Vadodara *India* **85C4**
Vadsø *Nor* **38K4**
Vaduz *Leichtenstein* **47C1**
Va Gesell *Arg* **29E3**
Vågø *Faroes* **38D3**
Váh, R *Czech* **59B3**
Vaigai, R *India* **87B2**
Vâlcea *Rom* **60B4**
Valcheta *Arg* **29C4**
Valdagno *Italy* **47D2**
Valday *USSR* **60D2**
Valdayskaya Vozvyshennost', Upland *USSR* **60D2**
Val de la Pascua *Ven* **32D2**
Valdepeñas *Spain* **50B2**
Valdez *USA* **12E2**
Valdivia *Chile* **29B3**
Val d'Oise, Department *France* **46B2**
Valdosta *USA* **17B1**
Vale *USA* **20C2**
Valemount *Can* **13D2**
Valença, Bahia *Brazil* **31D4**
Valença, Rio de Janeiro *Brazil* **35C2**
Valence *France* **49C3**
Valencia, Region *Spain* **51B2**
Valencia *Spain* **51B2**
Valencia *Ven* **32D1**
Valencia, I *Irish Rep* **45A3**
Valencia de Alcantara *Spain* **50A2**
Valenciennes *France* **46B1**
Valenza *Italy* **47C2**
Valera *Ven* **32C2**
Valga *USSR* **39K7**
Valikiyo *USSR* **64E4**
Valjevo *Yugos* **54A2**
Valkeakoski *Fin* **39J6**
Valladolid *Mexico* **25D2**
Valladolid *Spain* **50B1**
Valle d'Aosta, Region *Italy* **47B2**
Valle de la Pascua *Ven* **27D5**
Valle de Santiago *Mexico* **23A1**
Valle d'Isére *France* **47B2**
Valledupar *Colombia* **32C1**
Vallée de l'Azaouak, V *Niger* **97C3**
Vallée Tilemis, V *Mali* **97C3**
Valle Grande *Bol* **30D2**
Vallejo *USA* **22A1**
Vallenar *Chile* **30B4**
Valley City *USA* **8D2**
Valley Falls *USA* **20B2**
Valleyfield *Can* **15D1**
Valleyview *Can* **13D1**
Valli di Comacchio, Lg *Italy* **47E2**
Valls *Spain* **51C1**
Valmiera *USSR* **58D1**
Valparaiso *Brazil* **35A2**
Valparaiso *Chile* **34A2**
Valparaiso *Mexico* **23A1**
Valparaiso *USA* **17A1**
Vals, R *S Africa* **101G1**
Valsād *India* **85C4**
Valuyki *USSR* **60E3**
Valverde del Camino *Spain* **50A2**
Vammala *Fin* **38J6**
Van *Turk* **93D2**
Vanavara *USSR* **63C1**
Van Buren, Arkansas *USA* **18B2**
Vancouver *Can* **13C3**
Vancouver *USA* **20B1**
Vancouver I *Can* **5F5**
Vancouver,Mt *Can* **12G2**
Vandalia, Illinois *USA* **18C2**
Vandalia, Ohio *USA* **14B3**
Vanderhoof *Can* **13C2**
Van Diemen G *Aust* **106C2**
Vänern, L *Sweden* **39G7**
Vänersborg *Sweden* **39G7**
Vangaindrano *Madag* **101D3**
Van Gölü, Salt L *Turk* **93D2**
Vang Vieng *Laos* **76C2**
Van Horn *USA* **9C3**
Vanier *Can* **15C1**
Vankarem *USSR* **1C6**
Vännäs *Sweden* **38H6**
Vannes *France* **48B2**
Vanoise, Mts *France* **47B2**
Vanrhynsdorp *S Africa* **100A4**
Vansittart I *Can* **6B3**
Vanuatu, Is *Pacific O* **105G4**
Van Wert *USA* **14B2**
Varallo *Italy* **47C2**
Varāmīn *Iran* **90B2**
Vārānasi *India* **86A1**
Varangerfjord, Inlet *Nor* **38K4**
Varangerhalvøya, Pen *Nor* **38K4**
Varazdin *Yugos* **52C1**
Varberg *Sweden* **39G7**
Varde *Den* **39F7**
Vardø *Nor* **38L4**
Varéna *USSR* **58C2**
Varenna *Italy* **47C2**
Varese *Italy* **47C2**
Varginha *Brazil* **35B2**
Varkaus *Fin* **38K6**
Varna *Bulg* **54C2**
Värnamo *Sweden* **39G7**
Varnville *USA* **17B1**
Várzea da Palma *Brazil* **35C1**
Varzi *Italy* **47C2**
Vascongadas, Region *Spain* **50B1**
Vasil'kov *USSR* **60D3**
Vassar *USA* **14B2**
Västerås *Sweden* **39H7**
Västervik *Sweden* **39H7**
Vasto *Italy* **52B2**
Vatnajökull, Mts *Iceland* **38B2**
Vatneyri *Iceland* **38A1**
Vatra Dornei *Rom* **54C1**
Vättern, L *Sweden* **39G7**
Vaughn *USA* **9C3**
Vaupés, R *Colombia* **32C3**
Vauxhall *Can* **13E2**
Vavunija *Sri Lanka* **87C3**
Växjö *Sweden* **39G7**
Vedia *Arg* **34C2**
Vega, I *Nor* **38G5**
Vegreville *Can* **13E2**
Vejer de la Frontera *Spain* **50A2**
Vejle *Den* **39F7**
Velebit, Mts *Yugos* **52C2**
Velenje *Yugos* **52C1**
Velhas, R *Brazil* **35C1**
Velikaya, R *USSR* **39K7**
Velikiye Luki *USSR* **60D2**
Velikiy Ustyug *USSR* **61G1**
Veliko Tŭrnovo *Bulg* **54C2**
Vélingara *Sen* **97A3**
Vellore *India* **87B2**
Vel'sk *USSR* **61F1**
Vembanad L *India* **87B3**
Venado Tuerto *Arg* **34C2**
Vençeslau Braz *Brazil* **35B2**
Vendôme *France* **49C2**
Venetie *USA* **12E1**
Veneto, Region *Italy* **47D2**
Venezia *Italy* **47E2**
Venezuela, Republic *S America* **32D2**
Vengurla *India* **87A1**
Veniaminof V *USA* **12C3**
Venkatagiri *India* **87B2**
Venlo *Neth* **56B2**
Venta, R *USSR* **58C1**
Ventersburg *S Africa* **101G1**
Ventspils *USSR* **58C1**
Ventuari, R *Ven* **32D3**
Ventura *USA* **22C3**
Vepsovskaya Vozvyshennost', Upland *USSR* **60D1**
Vera *Arg* **30D4**
Vera *Spain* **51B2**
Veracruz *Mexico* **23B2**
Veracruz, State *Mexico* **23B1**
Verāval *India* **85C4**
Verbania *Italy* **47C2**
Vercelli *Italy* **47C2**
Verde, R, Goias *Brazil* **35A1**
Verde, R, Jalisco *Mexico* **23A1**
Verde, R, Mato Grosso do Sul *Brazil* **35A1**
Verde, R, Oaxaca *Mexico* **23B2**
Verde Grande, R *Brazil* **35C1**
Verde,Pen *Arg* **34C3**
Verdon, R *France* **49D3**
Verdun *France* **46C2**
Vereeniging *S Africa* **101G1**
Vereshchagino *USSR* **61H2**
Verga,C *Guinea* **97A3**

Vergara *Arg* **34D3**
Verin *Spain* **50A1**
Verissimo Sarmento *Angola* **98C3**
Verkh Angara, R *USSR* **63D2**
Verkhneural'sk *USSR* **61J3**
Verkhnevilyuysk *USSR* **63E1**
Verkhoyansk *USSR* **1C8**
Vermelho, R *Brazil* **35A1**
Vermilion *Can* **13E2**
Vermont, State *USA* **10C2**
Vernalis *USA* **22B2**
Vernon *Can* **13D2**
Vernon *France* **46A2**
Vernon *USA* **9D3**
Vero Beach *USA* **17B2**
Veroia *Greece* **54B2**
Verolanuova *Italy* **47D2**
Verona *Italy* **47D2**
Versailles *France* **46B2**
Verulam *S Africa* **101H1**
Verviers *Belg* **46C1**
Vervins *France* **46B2**
Vesle, R *France* **46C2**
Vesoul *France* **49D2**
Vesterålen, Is *Nor* **38G5**
Vestfjorden, Inlet *Nor* **38G5**
Vestmannaeyjar *Iceland* **38A2**
Vesuvio, Mt *Italy* **53B2**
Veszprém *Hung* **59B3**
Vetlanda *Sweden* **39H7**
Vetluga, R *USSR* **61F2**
Veurne *Belg* **46B1**
Vevey *Switz* **47B1**
Vexin, Region *France* **46A2**
Veynes *France* **47A2**
Viana do Castelo *Port* **50A1**
Viareggio *Italy* **49E3**
Viborg *Den* **39F7**
Vibo Valentia *Italy* **53C3**
Vice-commodoro Marambio, Base *Ant* **112C2**
Vicenza *Italy* **52B1**
Vich *Spain* **51C1**
Vichada, R *Colombia* **32D3**
Vichuga *USSR* **61F2**
Vichy *France* **49C2**
Vicksburg *USA* **19B3**
Vicosa *Brazil* **35C2**
Victor Harbour *Aust* **106C4**
Victoria *Arg* **34C2**
Victoria *Can* **13C3**
Victoria *Chile* **34A3**
Victoria *Hong Kong* **73C5**
Victoria *Malay* **78D1**
Victoria, State *Aust* **108B3**
Victoria *USA* **9D4**
Victoria, R *Aust* **106C2**
Victoria, State *Aust* **107D4**
Victoria de las Tunas *Cuba* **26B2**
Victoria Falls *Zambia/Zim* **100B2**
Victoria I *Can* **4G2**
Victoria,L *Aust* **108B2**
Victoria,L *C Africa* **99D3**
Victoria Land, Region *Ant* **112B7**
Victoria,Mt *Burma* **86C2**
Victoria Nile, R *Uganda* **99D2**
Victoria Range, Mts *NZ* **111B2**
Victoria River Downs *Aust* **106C2**
Victoria Str *Can* **4H3**
Victoriaville *Can* **15D1**
Victoria West *S Africa* **100B4**
Victorica *Arg* **34B3**
Victorville *USA* **21B3**
Vicuña *Chile* **34A2**
Vicuña Mackenna *Arg* **34C2**
Vidalia *USA* **17B1**
Videle *Rom* **54C2**
Vidin *Bulg* **54B2**
Vidisha *India* **85D4**
Vidzy *USSR* **58D1**
Viedma *Arg* **29D4**
Viéjo *Costa Rica* **26A4**
Viella *Spain* **51C1**
Vienna, Illinois *USA* **18C2**
Vienna, W Virginia *USA* **14B3**
Vienne *France* **49C2**
Vienne, R *France* **48C2**
Vientiane *Laos* **76C2**
Vierwaldstätter See, L *Switz* **47C1**
Vierzon *France* **48C2**
Vieste *Italy* **53C2**
Vietnam, Republic *S E Asia* **70B2**
Vietri *Viet* **76D1**
Vieux Fort *St Lucia* **27P2**
Vigan *Phil* **79B2**
Vigevano *Italy* **47C2**
Vignemale, Mt *France* **48B3**
Vigo *Spain* **50A1**
Vijayawāda *India* **87C1**
Vijosë, R *Alb* **55A2**
Vik *Iceland* **38B2**
Vikhren, Mt *Bulg* **54B2**
Viking *Can* **13E2**
Vikna, I *Nor* **38G6**
Vila da Maganja *Mozam* **101C2**
Vila Machado *Mozam* **101C2**
Vilanculos *Mozam* **101C3**
Vila Real *Port* **50A1**
Vila Vasco da Gama *Mozam* **101C2**
Vila Velha *Brazil* **35C2**
Vileyka *USSR* **58D2**
Vilhelmina *Sweden* **38H6**
Vilhena *Brazil* **33E6**
Viljandi *USSR* **60C2**
Viljoenskroon *S Africa* **101G1**
Vilkovo *USSR* **59D3**
Villa Ahumada *Mexico* **9C3**
Villa Atuel *Arg* **34B2**
Villaba *Spain* **50A1**
Villa Carranza *Mexico* **23A2**
Villach *Austria* **52B1**
Villa Colon *Arg* **34B2**
Villa Constitución *Arg* **34C2**
Villa de Maria *Arg* **34C1**
Villa de Reyes *Mexico* **23A1**
Villa Dolores *Arg* **34B2**
Villafranca di Verona *Italy* **47D2**
Villa General Mitre *Arg* **34C2**
Villa General Roca *Arg* **34B2**
Villaguay *Arg* **34D2**
Villahermosa *Mexico* **25C3**
Villa Hidalgo *Mexico* **23A1**
Villa Huidobro *Arg* **34C2**
Villa Iris *Arg* **34C3**
Villa Maria *Arg* **34C2**
Villa Montes *Bol* **30D3**
Villaneuva *Mexico* **23A1**
Villa Nova de Gaia *Port* **50A1**
Villanueva de la Serena *Spain* **50A2**
Villanueva-y-Geltrú *Spain* **51C1**
Villa Regina *Arg* **34B3**
Villarreal *Spain* **51B2**
Villarrica *Chile* **29B3**
Villarrica *Par* **30E4**
Villarrobledo *Spain* **50B2**
Villa San José *Arg* **34D2**
Villa Valeria *Arg* **34C2**
Villavicencio *Colombia* **32C3**
Villefranche *France* **49C2**
Ville-Marie *Can* **7C5**
Villena *Spain* **51B2**
Villeneuve-St-Georges *France* **46B2**
Villeneuve-sur-Lot *France* **48C3**
Ville Platte *USA* **19B3**
Villers-Cotterêts *France* **46B2**
Villeurbanne *France* **49C2**
Villiers *S Africa* **101G1**
Villupuram *India* **87B2**
Vilnius *USSR* **58D2**
Vilyuy *USSR* **63D1**
Vilyuysk *USSR* **63E1**
Viña del Mar *Chile* **34A2**
Vinaroz *Spain* **51C1**
Vincennes *USA* **14A3**
Vindel, R *Sweden* **38H5**
Vindhya Range, Mts *India* **85D4**
Vineland *USA* **16B3**
Vineyard Haven *USA* **16D2**
Vinh *Viet* **76D2**
Vinh Cam Ranh, B *Viet* **76D3**
Vinh Loi *Viet* **77D4**
Vinh Long *Viet* **77D3**
Vinita *USA* **18A2**
Vinkovci *Yugos* **54A1**
Vinnitsa *USSR* **60C4**
Vinson Massif, Upland *Ant* **112B3**
Vioolsdrift *S Africa* **100A3**
Vipiteno *Italy* **47D1**
Virac *Phil* **79B3**
Virddhāchalam *India* **87B2**
Virei *Angola* **100A2**
Virgem da Lapa *Brazil* **35C1**
Virginia *S Africa* **101G1**
Virginia, State *USA* **10C3**
Virginia *USA* **10A2**
Virginia City *USA* **21B2**
Virgin Is *Caribbean* **27E3**
Virovitica *Yugos* **52C1**
Virton *Belg* **46C2**
Virudunagar *India* **87B3**
Vis, I *Yugos* **52C2**
Visalia *USA* **21B2**
Visayan S *Phil* **79B3**
Visby *Sweden* **39H7**
Viscount Melville Sd *Can* **4H2**
Višegrad *Yugos* **54A2**
Viseu *Port* **50A1**
Vishākhapatnam *India* **83C4**
Visp *Switz* **47B1**
Vissingen *Neth* **49C1**
Vista *USA* **21B3**
Vitavia, R *Czech* **57C3**
Vite *India* **87A1**
Vitebsk *USSR* **60D2**
Viterbo *Italy* **52B2**
Vitigudino *Spain* **50A1**
Vitim, R *USSR* **63D2**
Vitora *Spain* **50B1**
Vitória *Brazil* **31C6**
Vitória da Conquista *Brazil* **31C4**
Vitré *France* **48B2**
Vitry-le-Francois *France* **46C2**
Vittangi *Sweden* **38J5**
Vittoria *Italy* **53B3**
Vittorio Veneto *Italy* **47E2**
Vityaz Depth *Pacific O* **69H2**
Vivero *Spain* **50A1**
Vivi, R *USSR* **63B1**
Vivorata *Arg* **34D3**
Vizhne-Angarsk *USSR* **63C2**
Vizianagaram *India* **83C4**
Vladeasa, Mt *Rom* **54B1**
Vladimir *USSR* **65F4**
Vladimir Volynskiy *USSR* **59C2**
Vladivostok *USSR* **74C2**
Vlieland, I *Neth* **56A2**
Vlissingen *Neth* **46B1**
Vlorë *Alb* **55A2**
Vöcklabruck *Austria* **57C3**
Voeune Sai *Camb* **76D3**
Voghera *Italy* **47C2**
Vohibinany *Madag* **101D2**
Vohimarina *Madag* **101E2**
Voi *Kenya* **99D3**
Voinjama *Lib* **97B4**
Voiron *France* **49D2**
Volcán Baru, Mt *Panama* **26A5**
Volcán Citlaltepetl, Mt *Mexico* **23B2**
Volcán Lullaillaco, Mt *Chile* **30C3**
Volcáno Copahue, Mt *Chile* **34A3**
Volcáno Domuyo, Mt *Arg* **34A3**
Volcáno Lanin, Mt *Arg* **29B3**
Volcán Ollagüe, Mt *Chile* **30C3**
Volcáno Llaima, Mt *Chile* **34A3**
Volcáno Maipo, Mt *Arg* **34B2**
Volcáno Peteroa, Mt *Chile* **34A3**
Volcáno Tromen, V *Arg* **34B3**
Volcán Paracutin, Mt *Mexico* **23A2**
Volcán Puraće, Mt *Colombia* **32B3**
Volcán Tinguiririca, Mt *Chile/Arg* **34A2**
Volchansk *USSR* **61J2**
Volga, R *USSR* **61G4**
Volgodonsk *USSR* **61F4**
Volgograd *USSR* **61F4**
Volgogradskoye Vodokhranilishche, Res *USSR* **61G3**
Volkhov *USSR* **60D2**
Volkhov, R *USSR* **60D2**
Volkovysk *USSR* **58C2**
Volksrust *S Africa* **101G1**
Vologda *USSR* **61F2**
Volognes *France* **48B2**
Vólos *Greece* **55B3**
Vol'sk *USSR* **61G3**
Volta *USA* **22B2**
Volta Blanche, R *U Volta* **97B3**
Volta,L *Ghana* **97B4**
Volta Noire, R *U Volta* **97B3**
Volta Redonda *Brazil* **35C2**
Volta Rouge, R *U Volta* **97B3**
Volynskiy *USSR* **60C3**
Volzhskiy *USSR* **61F4**
Von Frank Mt *USA* **12D2**
Vopnafjörður *Iceland* **6J3**
Voralberg, Province *Austria* **47C1**
Vorder Rhein, R *Switz* **47C1**
Vordingborg *Den* **56C1**
Vorkuta *USSR* **64H3**
Vorma, R *Nor* **39G6**
Voronezh *USSR* **60E3**
Voron'ya, R *USSR* **38M5**
Voroshilovgrad *USSR* **60E4**
Võru *USSR* **39K7**
Vosges, Mt *France* **49D2**
Voshnyy Saytocan, Mts *USSR* **68B1**
Voss *Nor* **39F6**
Vostochnyy Sayan, Mts *USSR* **63B2**
Vostok, Base *Ant* **112B9**
Votkinsk *USSR* **61H2**
Vouziers *France* **46C2**
Voznesensk *USSR* **60D4**
Vranje *Yugos* **54B2**
Vratsa *Bulg* **54B2**
Vrbas *Yugos* **54A1**
Vrbas, R *Yugos* **52C2**
Vrbovsko *Yugos* **52B1**
Vrede *S Africa* **101G1**
Vreed en Hoop *Guyana* **33F2**
Vršac *Yugos* **54B1**
Vrtoče *Yugos* **52C2**
Vryburg *S Africa* **100B3**
Vryheid *S Africa* **101H1**

Vukovar *Yugos* **54A1**
Vulcan *Can* **13E2**
Vulcano, I *Italy* **53B3**
Vung Tau *Viet* **77D3**
Vuollerim *Sweden* **38J5**
Vyartsilya *USSR* **38L6**
Vyatka, R *USSR* **61H2**
Vyazemskiy *USSR* **69F2**
Vyaz'ma *USSR* **60D2**
Vyazniki *USSR* **61F2**
Vyborg *USSR* **60C1**
Vyrnwy, R *Wales* **43C3**
Vyshiy Volochek *USSR* **60D2**
Vyškov *Czech* **59B3**
Vytegra *USSR* **60E1**

W

Wa *Ghana* **97B3**
Wabasca *Can* **13E1**
Wabasca, R *Can* **5G4**
Wabasca L *Can* **13E1**
Wabash *USA* **14A2**
Wabash, R *USA* **14A3**
Wabowden *Can* **5J4**
Wabush *Can* **7D4**
Waccasassa B *USA* **17B2**
Wachusett Res *USA* **16D1**
Waco *USA* **19A3**
Wad *Pak* **85B3**
Waddān *Libya* **95A2**
Waddington,Mt *Can* **5F4**
Wadi al Bātin, Watercourse *Iraq* **93E4**
Wadi al Ghudāf, Watercourse *Iraq* **93D3**
Wadi al Harīr, V *Syria* **94C2**
Wadi al Mirah, Watercourse *S Arabia/Iraq* **93D3**
Wadi al Ubayyid, Watercourse *Iraq* **93D3**
Wadi Ar'ar, Watercourse *S Arabia* **93D3**
Wadi as Hsabā', Watercourse *S Arabia* **91A5**
Wadi as Sirhān, V *Jordan/S Arabia* **92C3**
Wadi az Zaydi, V *Syria* **94C2**
Wadi edh Dhab'i, V *Jordan* **94C3**
Wadi el 'Arish, V *Egypt* **94A3**
Wadi el Ghadaf, V *Jordan* **94C3**
Wadi el Hasa, V *Jordan* **94B3**
Wadi el Janab, V *Jordan* **94C3**
Wadi el Jeib, V *Israel/Jordan* **94B3**
Wadi el Milk, Watercourse *Sudan* **95B3**
Wadi el Natrun, Watercourse *Egypt* **92A3**
Wadi es Sir *Jordan* **94B3**
Wadi Fidan, V *Jordan* **94B3**
Wadi Hareidin, V *Egypt* **94B3**
Wadi Hawrān, R *Iraq* **93D3**
Wadi Howa, Watercourse *Sudan* **95B3**
Wadi Ibra, Watercourse *Sudan* **98C1**
Wadi Luhfi, Watercourse *Jordan* **94C2**
Wadi Mujib, V *Jordan* **94B3**
Wadi Qîtaiya, V *Egypt* **94B3**
Wadi Sha'it, Watercourse *Egypt* **80B3**
Wad Medani *Sudan* **99D1**
Wafra *Kuwait* **93E4**
Wager B *Can* **6B3**
Wager Bay *Can* **6A3**
Wagga Wagga *Aust* **109C3**
Wagin *Aust* **106A4**
Waha *Libya* **95A2**
Wahaiwa *Hawaiian Is* **21C4**
Wahoo *USA* **18A1**
Wahpeton *USA* **8D2**
Wai *India* **87A1**
Waiau *NZ* **111B2**
Waiau, R *NZ* **111A3**
Waiau, R *NZ* **111B2**
Waigeo, I *Indon* **71E3**
Waihi *NZ* **110C1**
Waikaremoana,L *NZ* **110C1**
Waikato, R *NZ* **110C1**
Waikerie *Aust* **108A2**
Waikouaiti *NZ* **111B3**
Wailuku *Hawaiian Is* **21C4**
Waimakariri, R *NZ* **111B2**
Waimate *NZ* **111B2**
Waimea *Hawaiian Is* **21C4**
Waingapu *Indon* **106B1**
Wainwright *Can* **13E2**
Wainwright *USA* **4B2**
Waipara *NZ* **111B2**
Waipukurau *NZ* **110C2**
Wairarapa,L *NZ* **111C2**
Wairau, R *NZ* **111B2**
Wairoa *NZ* **110C1**
Wairoa, R *NZ* **110C1**
Waitaki, R *NZ* **111B2**
Waitara *NZ* **110B1**
Waitomo *NZ* **110C1**
Waiuku *NZ* **110B1**
Wajima *Japan* **75B1**
Wajir *Kenya* **99E2**
Wakasa-wan, B *Japan* **75B1**
Wakatipu,L *NZ* **111A3**
Wakayama *Japan* **74D4**
Wakefield *Eng* **42D3**
Wakefield *Jamaica* **27H1**
Wakefield, Rhode Island *USA* **16D2**
Wakema *Burma* **76B2**
Wakkanai *Japan* **69G2**
Wakool, R *Aust* **108B3**
Walbrzych *Pol* **59B2**
Walcha *Aust* **109D2**
Walcz *Pol* **58B2**
Waldbröl *W Germ* **46D1**
Walden *USA* **16B2**
Waldia *Eth* **99D1**
Wales, Country *U K* **43C3**
Wales *USA* **12A1**
Wales I *Can* **6B3**
Walgett *Aust* **109C2**
Walgreen Coast, Region *Ant* **112B4**
Walikale *Zaïre* **99C3**
Walker, L *USA* **21B2**
Walkerton *Can* **14B2**
Wallace *USA* **8B2**
Wallaroo *Aust* **108A2**
Walla Walla *Aust* **109C3**
Walla Walla *USA* **20C1**
Wallingford *USA* **16C2**
Wallis and Futuna, Is *Pacific O* **105H4**
Wallowa *USA* **20C1**
Wallowa Mts, Mts *USA* **20C1**
Wallumbilla *Aust* **109C1**
Walnut Ridge *USA* **18B2**
Walouru *NZ* **110C1**
Walsall *Eng* **43D3**
Walsenburg *USA* **9C3**
Walsenburgh *USA* **9C3**
Walterboro *USA* **17B1**
Walter F George Res *USA* **17A1**
Waltham *USA* **16D1**
Walvis Bay *S Africa* **100A3**
Walvis Ridge *Atlantic O* **103J6**
Wamba *Nig* **97C4**
Wamba, R *Zaïre* **98B3**
Wamego *USA* **18A2**
Wana *Pak* **84B2**
Wanaaring *Aust* **108B1**
Wanaka *NZ* **111A2**
Wanaka,L *NZ* **111A2**
Wanapitei L *Can* **14B1**
Wandoan *Aust* **109C1**
Wanganella *Aust* **108B3**
Wanganui *NZ* **110B1**
Wanganui *NZ* **110C1**
Wanganui, R *NZ* **110C1**
Wangaratta *Aust* **109C3**
Wanle Weyne *Somalia* **99E2**
Wanning *China* **76E2**
Wanparti *India* **87B1**
Wanxian *China* **73B3**
Wanyuan *China* **73B3**
Wapiti, R *Can* **13D2**
Wappapello,L *USA* **18B2**
Wappingers Falls *USA* **16C2**
Warangal *India* **87B1**
Waratah *Aust* **109C4**
Waratah B *Aust* **108C3**
Warburton *Aust* **108C3**
Warburton, R *Aust* **108A1**
Ward, R *Aust* **109C1**
Warden *S Africa* **101G1**
Warder *Eth* **99E2**
Wardha *India* **85D4**
Ward,Mt *NZ* **111A3**
Ware *Can* **5F4**
Ware *USA* **16C1**
Wareham *USA* **16D2**
Warialda *Aust* **109D1**
Warin Chamrap *Thai* **76C2**
Warmbad *S Africa* **100B3**
Warminster *USA* **16B2**
Warm Springs *USA* **21B2**
Warnemünde *E Germ* **56C2**
Warner Mts *USA* **20B2**
Warner Robins *USA* **17B1**
Warracknabeal *Aust* **108B3**
Warrandirinna,L *Aust* **108A1**
Warrego, R *Aust* **107D3**
Warren, Arkansas *USA* **19B3**
Warren *Aust* **109C2**
Warren, Massachusetts *USA* **16D2**
Warren, Ohio *USA* **14B2**
Warren, Pennsylvania *USA* **15C2**
Warrenpoint *N Ire* **45C1**
Warrensburg *USA* **18B2**
Warrenton *S Africa* **101F1**
Warrenton *USA* **15C3**
Warri *Nig* **97C4**
Warrina *Aust* **108A1**
Warrington *Eng* **42C3**
Warrnambool *Aust* **108B3**
Warszawa *Pol* **58C2**
Warta, R *Pol* **59B2**
Warwick *Aust* **109D1**
Warwick, County *Eng* **43D3**
Warwick *Eng* **43D3**
Warwick, New York *USA* **16B2**
Warwick, Rhode Island *USA* **16D2**
Wasatch Range, Mts *USA* **8B3**
Wasbank *S Africa* **101H1**
Wasco *USA* **21B2**
Washburn L *Can* **4H2**
Wāshīm *India* **85D4**
Washington, District of Columbia *USA* **10C3**
Washington, Georgia *USA* **17B1**
Washington, Indiana *USA* **14A3**
Washington, Missouri *USA* **18B2**
Washington, New Jersey *USA* **16B2**
Washington, Pennsylvania *USA* **14B2**
Washington, State *USA* **8A2**
Washington Court House *USA* **14B3**
Washington Land *Can* **6D1**
Washington,Mt *USA* **15D2**
Wash,The *Eng* **43E3**
Washuk *Pak* **85A3**
Wasilla *USA* **12E2**
Waspán *Nic* **26A4**
Watampone *Indon* **70D4**
Waterbury *USA* **16C2**
Waterford, County *Irish Rep* **45C2**
Waterford *Irish Rep* **41B3**
Waterford Harbour *Irish Rep* **45C2**
Waterloo *Belg* **46C1**
Waterloo *USA* **10A2**
Watertown, New York *USA* **15C2**
Waterval-Boven *S Africa* **101H1**
Waterville, Maine *USA* **10D2**
Watervliet *USA* **16C1**
Waterways *Can* **5G4**
Watford *Eng* **43D4**
Watkins Bjerge, Mt *Greenland* **6H3**
Watkins Glen *USA* **15C2**
Watrous *Can* **8C1**
Watsa *Zaïre* **99C2**
Watson Lake *Can* **12J2**
Watsonville *USA* **22B2**
Wau *PNG* **71F4**
Wau *Sudan* **99C2**
Waua *Can* **7B5**
Wauchope *Aust* **109D2**
Wauchula *USA* **17B2**
Waukegan *USA* **14A2**
Wausau *USA* **10B2**
Wauwatosa *USA* **14A2**
Wave Hill *Aust* **106C2**
Waveney, R *Eng* **43E3**
Waverly, Ohio *USA* **14B3**
Wavre *Belg* **46C1**
Wawa *Can* **10B2**
Wāw Al Kabīr *Libya* **95A2**
Wāw an Nāmūs, Well *Libya* **95A2**
Wawona *USA* **22C2**
Waxahachie *USA* **19A3**
Waycross *USA* **17B1**
Waynesboro, Georgia *USA* **17B1**
Waynesboro, Mississippi *USA* **19C3**
Waynesboro, Pennsylvania *USA* **16A3**
Waynesboro, Virginia *USA* **15C3**
Waynesville, Missouri *USA* **18B2**
Wazi Khwa *Afghan* **84B2**
Weald,The, Upland *Eng* **43E4**
Wear, R *Eng* **42C2**
Weatherford, Texas *USA* **19A3**
Weaverville *USA* **20B2**
Webbwood *Can* **14B1**
Webster *USA* **16D1**
Webster Groves *USA* **18B2**
Weddell I *Falkland Is* **29D6**
Weddell S *Ant* **112C2**
Wedge Mt *Can* **13C2**
Weed *USA* **20B2**
Weenen *S Africa* **101H1**
Wee Waa *Aust* **109C2**
Weichang *China* **72D1**
Weiden *W Germ* **57C3**
Weifang *China* **72D2**
Weihai *China* **72E2**
Wei He, R, Henan *China* **72C3**
Wei He, R, Shaanxi *China* **72C2**
Weilmoringle *Aust* **109C1**
Weining *China* **73A4**
Weipa *Aust* **107D2**
Weirton *USA* **14B2**
Weiser *USA* **20C2**

Weishan Hu, L *China* **72D3**
Weissenfels *E Germ* **57C2**
Weiss L *USA* **17A1**
Welkom *S Africa* **101G1**
Welland *Can* **15C2**
Welland, R *Eng* **43D3**
Wellesley Is *Aust* **106C2**
Wellesley L *Can* **12G2**
Wellingborough *Eng* **43D3**
Wellington *Aust* **109C2**
Wellington, Kansas *USA* **18A2**
Wellington *NZ* **111B2**
Wellington Chan *Can* **6A2**
Wells *Can* **13C2**
Wells *Eng* **43C4**
Wellsford *NZ* **110B1**
Wells,L *Aust* **106B3**
Wels *Austria* **57C3**
Welshpool *Wales* **43C3**
Wembley *Can* **13D1**
Wenatchee *USA* **20B1**
Wenatchee, R *USA* **20C1**
Wenchi *Ghana* **97B4**
Wenden *China* **72E2**
Wenling *China* **73E4**
Wenman, I *Ecuador* **32J7**
Wenshan *China* **73A5**
Wenthaggi *Aust* **107D4**
Wentworth *Aust* **108B2**
Wen Xian *China* **72A3**
Wenzhou *China* **73E4**
Wenzhu *China* **73C4**
Wepener *S Africa* **101G1**
Wernecke Mts *Can* **12G1**
Werra, R *E Germ* **57C2**
Werris Creek *Aust* **109D2**
Wesel *W Germ* **56B2**
Weser, R *W Germ* **56B2**
Wessel Is *Aust* **106C2**
West Allis *USA* **14A2**
West Australian Basin *Indian O* **104C4**
West Australian Ridge *Indian O* **104C5**
West B *USA* **19C3**
West Bengal, State *India* **86B2**
West Bromwich *Eng* **43D3**
West Chester *USA* **16B3**
Westerburg *W Germ* **46D1**
Westerland *W Germ* **56B2**
Westerly *USA* **16D2**
Western Australia, State *Aust* **106A3**
Western Ghats, Mts *India* **87A1**
Western Isles *Scot* **44A3**
Western Sahara, Region *Mor* **96A2**
Western Samoa, Is *Pacific O* **105H4**
Westerschelde, Estuary *Neth* **46B1**
Westerwald, Region *W Germ* **46D1**
Westfalen, Region *W Germ* **49D1**
West Falkland, I *Falkland Is* **29D6**
Westfield, Massachusetts *USA* **16C1**
Westfield, New York *USA* **15C2**
West Frankfort *USA* **18C2**
Westgate *Aust* **109C1**
West Germany, Federal Republic *Europè* **57B2**
West Glamorgan, County *Wales* **43C4**
West Indies, Is *Caribbean S* **102E3**
Westlock *Can* **13E2**
West Lorne *Can* **14B2**
Westmeath, County *Irish Rep* **45C2**
West Memphis *USA* **18B2**
West Midlands, County *Eng* **43D3**
Westminster *Eng* **43D4**
Westminster, Maryland *USA* **16A3**
Westminster, S Carolina *USA* **17B1**
West Nicholson *Zim* **100B3**
Weston *Malay* **78D1**
Weston *USA* **14B3**
Weston-super-Mare *Eng* **43C4**
West Palm Beach *USA* **17B2**
West Plains *USA* **18B2**
West Point, California *USA* **22B1**
West Point, Mississippi *USA* **19C3**
West Point, New York *USA* **16C2**
West Point, Mt *USA* **12F2**
Westport *Irish Rep* **45B2**
Westport *NZ* **111B2**
Westray, I *Scot* **40C2**
West Road, R *Can* **13C2**
West Side, Oilfield *N Sea* **42E3**
West Virginia, State *USA* **11B3**
West Walker, R *USA* **22C1**
West Wyalong *Aust* **109C2**
West Yorkshire, County *Eng* **42D3**
Wetar, I *Indon* **71D4**
Wetaskiwin *Can* **13E2**
Wete *Tanz* **99D3**
Wetzlar *W Germ* **46E1**
Wewak *PNG* **71F4**
Wewoka *USA* **19A2**
Wexford, County *Irish Rep* **45C2**
Wexford *Irish Rep* **45C2**
Weyburn *Can* **5H5**
Weymouth *Eng* **43C4**
Weymouth *USA* **16D1**
Whakatane *NZ* **110C1**
Whakatane, R *NZ* **110C1**
Whalsay, I *Scot* **44D1**
Whangarei *NZ* **110B1**
Wharfe, R *Eng* **42D3**
Wharton *USA* **19A4**
Whataroa *NZ* **111B2**
Wheaton, Maryland *USA* **16A3**
Wheeler Peak, Mt, Nevada *USA* **8B3**
Wheeler Peak, Mt, New Mexico *USA* **9C3**
Wheeling *USA* **14B2**
Whistler *Can* **13C3**
Whitby *Can* **15C2**
Whitby *Eng* **42D2**
White, R, Arkansas *USA* **18B2**
White, R *Can* **12F2**
White, R, Indiana *USA* **14A3**
White, R, S Dakota *USA* **8C2**
White B *Can* **7E4**
White Cliffs *Aust* **108B2**
White Coomb, Mt *Scot* **40C2**
Whitecourt *Can* **13D2**
Whitefish Pt *USA* **14A1**
Whitegull L *Can* **7D4**
Whitehall, New York *USA* **15D2**
Whitehall, Pennsylvania *USA* **16B2**
Whitehaven *Eng* **42C2**
Whitehorse *Can* **12G2**
White I *NZ* **110C1**
White L *USA* **19B4**
Whitemark *Aust* **109C4**
White Mountain Peak, Mt *USA* **21B2**
White Mts, Alaska *USA* **12E1**
White Mts, New Hampshire *USA* **15D2**
White Plains *USA* **16C2**
White River *Can* **7B5**
White River Junction *USA* **15D2**
Whitesail L *Can* **13B2**
White Salmon *USA* **20B1**
Whiteville *USA* **17C1**
White Volta, R *Ghana* **97B4**
Whithorn *Scot* **42B2**
Whitmire *USA* **17B1**
Whitney,Mt *USA* **21B2**
Whittier, Alaska *USA* **12E2**
Whittier, California *USA* **22C4**
Wholdia L *Can* **5H3**
Whyalla *Aust* **108A2**
Wiarton *Can* **14B2**
Wichita *USA* **18A2**
Wichita Falls *USA* **9D3**
Wick *Scot* **44C2**
Wicklow, County *Irish Rep* **45C2**
Wicklow *Irish Rep* **45C2**
Wicklow, Mts *Irish Rep* **45C2**
Widgeegoara, R *Aust* **109C1**
Wied, R *W Germ* **46D1**
Wielun *Pol* **59B2**
Wien *Austria* **59B3**
Wiener Neustadt *Austria* **59B3**
Wieprz, R *Pol* **58C2**
Wiesbaden *W Germ* **46E1**
Wigan *Eng* **42C3**
Wiggins *USA* **19C3**
Wigtown *Scot* **42B2**
Wigtown B *Scot* **42B2**
Wil *Switz* **47C1**
Wilbur *USA* **20C1**
Wilcannia *Aust* **108B2**
Wildcat Peak, Mt *USA* **21B2**
Wildhorn, Mt *Switz* **47B1**
Wild Horse *Can* **13E2**
Wildspitze, Mt *Austria* **47D1**
Wildwood, Florida *USA* **17B2**
Wildwood, New Jersey *USA* **16B3**
Wilge, R *S Africa* **101G1**
Wilhelmshaven *W Germ* **56B2**
Wilkes-Barre *USA* **15C2**
Wilkes Land *Ant* **112B8**
Wilkie *Can* **13F2**
Willamette, R *USA* **20B2**
Willandra, R *Aust* **108B2**
Willapa B *USA* **20B1**
Willcox *USA* **9C3**
Willemstad *Curaçao* **27D4**
William Creek *Aust* **108A1**
William,Mt *Aust* **108B3**
Williams, California *USA* **21A2**
Williams Lake *Can* **13C2**
Williamsport *USA* **15C2**
Williamstown, Massachusetts *USA* **16C1**
Williamstown, W Virginia *USA* **14B3**
Willimantic *USA* **16C2**
Willingboro *USA* **16B2**
Willingdon,Mt *Can* **13D2**
Willis Group, Is *Aust* **107E2**
Williston, Florida *USA* **17B2**
Williston *S Africa* **100B4**
Williston L *Can* **13C1**
Willmar *USA* **8D2**
Willoughby,C *Aust* **108A3**
Willow, R *Can* **13C2**
Willow Ranch *USA* **20B2**
Willows *USA* **21A2**
Willow Springs *USA* **18B2**
Wilmington *Aust* **108A2**
Wilmington, Delaware *USA* **16B3**
Wilmington, N Carolina *USA* **17C1**
Wilnona *USA* **7A5**
Wilson *USA* **11C3**
Wilson, R *Aust* **108B1**
Wilson,C *Can* **6B3**
Wilson,Mt, California *USA* **22C3**
Wilson,Mt, Oregon *USA* **20B1**
Wilsons Promontory, Pen *Aust* **109C3**
Wiltshire, County *Eng* **43D4**
Wiltz *Lux* **46C2**
Wiluna *Aust* **106B3**
Winamac *USA* **14A2**
Winburg *S Africa* **101G1**
Winchendon *USA* **16C1**
Winchester *Can* **15C1**
Winchester *Eng* **43D4**
Winchester, New Hampshire *USA* **16C1**
Winchester, Virginia *USA* **15C3**
Windermere *Eng* **42C2**
Windhoek *Namibia* **100A3**
Windorah *Aust* **107D3**
Wind River Range, Mts *USA* **8C2**
Windsor *Aust* **109D2**
Windsor, Connecticut *USA* **16C2**
Windsor *Eng* **43D4**
Windsor, Nova Scotia *Can* **7D5**
Windsor, Ontario *Can* **14B2**
Windsor, Quebec *Can* **15D1**
Windsor Forest *USA* **17B1**
Windsor Locks *USA* **16C2**
Windward Is *Caribbean* **27E4**
Windward Pass *Caribbean* **26C3**
Winefred L *Can* **13E1**
Winfield, Kansas *USA* **18A2**
Wingham *Aust* **109D2**
Winifreda *Arg* **34C3**
Winisk, R *Can* **7B4**
Winisk L *Can* **7B4**
Winkana *Burma* **76B2**
Winlock *USA* **20B1**
Winneba *Ghana* **97B4**
Winnebago,L *USA* **14A2**
Winnemucca *USA* **20C2**
Winnfield *USA* **19B3**
Winnipeg *Can* **5J4**
Winnipeg,L *Can* **5J4**
Winnipegosis *Can* **5J4**
Winnipesaukee,L *USA* **15D2**
Winona, Minnesota *USA* **10A2**
Winona, Mississippi *USA* **19C3**
Winooski *USA* **15D2**
Winslow *USA* **9B3**
Winsted *USA* **16C2**
Winston-Salem *USA* **11B3**
Winterberg *W Germ* **46E1**
Winter Garden *USA* **17B2**
Winter Park *USA* **17B2**
Winters *USA* **22B1**
Winterthur *Switz* **47C1**
Winton *Aust* **107D3**
Winton *NZ* **111A3**
Wisbech *Eng* **43E3**
Wisconsin, State *USA* **10B2**
Wisconsin Rapids *USA* **7B5**
Wiseman *USA* **12D1**
Wisla, R *Pol* **58B2**
Wismar *E Germ* **56C2**
Witagron *Surinam* **33F2**
Witbank *S Africa* **101G1**
Witchita Falls *USA* **9D3**
Witham, R *Eng* **43D3**
Withernsea *Eng* **42E3**

Witney *Eng* **43D4**
Witten *W Germ* **46D1**
Wittenberg *E Germ* **56C2**
Wittenoom *Aust* **106A3**
Wittlich *W Germ* **46D1**
Wladyslawowo *Pol* **58B2**
Włocławek *Pol* **58B2**
Włodawa *Pol* **58C2**
Wodonga *Aust* **109C3**
Wohlen *Switz* **47C1**
Wokam *Indon* **71E4**
Woking *Eng* **43D4**
Woleai, I *Pacific O* **71F3**
Wolf Creek *USA* **20B2**
Wolf Point *USA* **8C2**
Wolfsberg *Austria* **57C3**
Wolfsburg *W Germ* **56C2**
Wollaston L *Can* **5H4**
Wollaston Lake *Can* **5H4**
Wollaston Pen *Can* **4G3**
Wollongong *Aust* **109D2**
Wolmaransstad *S Africa* **101G1**
Wolow *Pol* **59B2**
Wolseley *Aust* **108B3**
Wolverhampton *Eng* **43C3**
Womelsdorf *USA* **16A2**
Wondai *Aust* **109D1**
Wŏnju *S Korea* **74B3**
Wonominta, R *Aust* **108B2**
Wonowon *Can* **13C1**
Wŏnsan *N Korea* **74B3**
Wonthaggi *Aust* **108C3**
Woocalla *Aust* **108A2**
Woodbine *USA* **16B3**
Woodbridge *USA* **15C3**
Wood Buffalo Nat Pk *Can* **5G4**
Woodburn *Aust* **109D1**
Woodburn *USA* **20B1**
Woodbury *USA* **16B3**
Woodchopper *USA* **12F1**
Woodland, California *USA* **21A2**
Woodland, Washington *USA* **20B1**
Woodlark, I *PNG* **107E1**
Woodmera *Aust* **106C4**
Woodroffe,Mt *Aust* **106C3**
Woodstock, Ontario *Can* **14B2**
Woodstown *USA* **16B3**
Woodville *NZ* **110C2**
Woodville *USA* **19B3**
Woomera *Aust* **108A2**
Woonsocket *USA* **15D2**
Wooster *USA* **14B2**
Worcester *Eng* **43C3**
Worcester *S Africa* **100A4**
Worcester *USA* **16D1**
Wörgl *Austria* **47E1**
Workington *Eng* **42C2**
Worland *USA* **8C2**
Worms *W Germ* **46E2**
Worms Head, Pt *Wales* **43B4**
Worthing *Eng* **43D4**
Worthington *USA* **8D2**
Wowoni, I *Indon* **71D4**
Wrangell *USA* **12H3**
Wrangell I *USA* **12H3**
Wrangell Mts *USA* **12F2**
Wrath,C *Scot* **40B2**
Wrexham *Wales* **43C3**
Wrightsville *USA* **17B1**
Wrightwood *USA* **22D3**
Wrigley *Can* **4F3**
Wrocław *Pol* **59B2**
Wrzésnia *Pol* **58B2**
Wuchang *China* **69E2**
Wuchuan *China* **76E1**
Wuda *China* **72E2**
Wuding He, R *China* **72C2**
Wudu *China* **72A3**
Wugang *China* **73C4**
Wuhai *China* **72B2**
Wuhan *China* **73C3**
Wuhu *China* **73D3**
Wuhua *China* **73D5**
Wūjang *China* **84D2**
Wujia He, R *China* **72B1**
Wu Jiang, R *China* **73B4**
Wukari *Nig* **97C4**
Wuling Shan, Mts *China* **73B4**
Wum *Cam* **97D4**
Wumeng Shan, Upland *China* **73A4**
Wuppertal *W Germ* **46D1**
Wuqi *China* **72B2**
Wuqing *China* **72D2**
Würzburg *W Germ* **57B3**
Wurzen *E Germ* **57C2**
Wutai Shan, Mt *China* **72C2**
Wuvulu, I *Pacific O* **71F4**
Wuwei *China* **72A2**
Wuxi *China* **73E3**
Wuxing *China* **73E3**
Wuyang *China* **72C2**
Wuyi Shan, Mts *China* **73D4**
Wuyuan *China* **72B1**
Wuzhi Shan, Mts *China* **76D2**
Wuzhong *China* **72B2**
Wuzhou *China* **73C5**
Wyandotte *USA* **14B2**
Wyandra *Aust* **109C1**
Wye, R *Eng* **43C4**
Wylye, R *Eng* **43C4**
Wymondham *Eng* **43E3**
Wyndham *Aust* **106B2**
Wynne *USA* **18B2**
Wynniatt B *Can* **4G2**
Wynyard *Aust* **109C4**
Wyoming, State *USA* **8C2**
Wyoming *USA* **14A2**
Wyong *Aust* **109D2**

X

Xaidulla *China* **84D1**
Xai Moron He, R *China* **72D1**
Xai Xai *Mozam* **101C3**
Xaltinguis *Mexico* **23B2**
Xangongo *Angola* **100A2**
Xanten *W Germ* **46D1**
Xánthi *Greece* **55B2**
Xau,L *Botswana* **100B3**
Xenia *USA* **14B3**
Xiaguan *China* **68B4**
Xiahe *China* **72A2**
Xiamen *China* **73D5**
Xi'an *China* **72B3**
Xianfeng *China* **73B4**
Xiangfan *China* **73C3**
Xiang Jiang, R *China* **73C4**
Xiangtan, Province *China* **73C4**
Xianning *China* **73C4**
Xianyang *China* **72B3**
Xiao Shui, R *China* **73C4**
Xiapu *China* **73D4**
Xichang *China* **73A4**
Xicotepec *Mexico* **23B1**
Xieng Khouang *Laos* **76C2**
Xifeng *China* **73B4**
Xigazê *China* **86B1**
Xi He, R *China* **72A1**
Xiji *China* **72B2**
Xi Jiang, R *China* **73C5**
Xiliao He, R *China* **72E1**
Xilin *China* **73B5**
Xilitla *Mexico* **23B1**
Xinfeng *China* **73D4**
Xinghe *China* **72C1**
Xingning *China* **73D5**
Xingren *China* **73B4**
Xingtai *China* **72C2**
Xingu, R *Brazil* **33G4**
Xingxingxia *China* **68B2**
Xingyi *China* **73A4**
Xining *China* **72A2**
Xinjin, Liaoning *China* **72E2**
Xinjin, Sichuan *China* **73A3**
Xinwen *China* **72D2**
Xin Xian *China* **72C2**
Xinxiang *China* **72C2**
Xinyang *China* **73C3**
Xinyi, Guangdong *China* **73C5**
Xinyi, Jiangsu *China* **72D3**
Xi Ujimqin Qi *China* **72D1**
Xiuyan *China* **74A2**
Xochimilco *Mexico* **23B2**
Xuancheng *China* **73D3**
Xuanhan *China* **73B3**
Xuanhua *China* **72D1**
Xuanwei *China* **73A4**
Xuchang *China* **72C3**
Xuddur *Somalia* **99E2**
Xunhua *China* **72A2**
Xun Jiang, R *China* **73C5**
Xunke *China* **69E2**
Xunwu *China* **73D5**
Xupu *China* **73C4**
Xuwen *China* **76D2**
Xuwen *China* **76E1**
Xuyong *China* **73B4**
Xuzhou *China* **72D3**

Y

Ya'an *China* **73A4**
Yaapeet *Aust* **108B3**
Yabassi *Cam* **98B2**
Yablonovyy Khrebet, Mts *USSR* **68C1**
Yabrūd *Syria* **94C2**
Yachats *USA* **20B2**
Yacuiba *Bol* **30D3**
Yādgīr *India* **87B1**
Yafran *Libya* **95A1**
Yahualica *Mexico* **23A1**
Yahuma *Zaïre* **98C2**
Yaita *Japan* **75B1**
Yaizu *Japan* **75B2**
Yajiang *China* **73A4**
Yakima *USA* **20B1**
Yakima, R *USA* **20B1**
Yako *U Volta* **97B3**
Yakoma *Zaïre* **98C2**
Yakumo *Japan* **74E2**
Yakutat *USA* **12G3**
Yakutat B *USA* **12G3**
Yakutsk *USSR* **63E1**
Yala *Thai* **77C4**
Yalalag *Mexico* **23B2**
Yalinga *CAR* **98C2**
Yallourn *Aust* **109C3**
Yalong, R *China* **68B3**
Yalong Jiang, R *China* **73A4**
Yalova *Turk* **54C2**
Yalta *USSR* **60D5**
Yalu Jiang, R *China* **74B2**
Yamagata *Japan* **74D3**
Yamaguchi *Japan* **74C4**
Yamarovka *USSR* **68D1**
Yamba, New S Wales *Aust* **109D1**
Yamba, S Australia *Aust* **108B2**
Yambio *Sudan* **99C2**
Yambol *Bulg* **54C2**
Yamdena, I *Indon* **71E4**
Yamma Yamma,L *Aust* **108B1**
Yamuna, R *India* **85D3**
Yamzho Yumco, L *China* **86C1**
Yana, R *USSR* **63F1**
Yanac *Aust* **108B3**
Yanagawa *Japan* **75A2**
Yanam *India* **87C1**
Yan'an *China* **72B2**
Yanbu'al Bahr *S Arabia* **80B3**
Yancannia *Aust* **108B2**
Yancheng *China* **72E3**
Yanchi *China* **72B2**
Yandama, R *Aust* **108B1**
Yangambi *Zaïre* **98C2**
Yang He, R *China* **72C1**
Yangjiang *China* **73C5**
Yangquan *China* **72C2**
Yangshan *China* **73C5**
Yangtze Gorges *China* **73C3**
Yangtze,Mouths of the *China* **72E3**
Yangzhou *China* **72D3**
Yanhe *China* **73B4**
Yanji *China* **74B2**
Yanko, R *Aust* **108C3**
Yankton *USA* **8D2**
Yanqi *China* **68A2**
Yan Shan, Hills **72D1**
Yantabulla *Aust* **108B1**
Yantai *China* **72E2**
Yanzhou *China* **72D2**
Yaoundé *Cam* **98B2**
Yapen, I *Indon* **71E4**
Yap Is *Pacific O* **71E3**
Yaqui, R *Mexico* **24B2**
Yaransk *USSR* **61G2**
Yargon, R *Israel* **94B2**
Yari, R *Colombia* **32C3**
Yariga-dake, Mt *Japan* **74D3**
Yarkant He, R *China* **82B2**
Yarlung Zangbo Jiang, R *China* **86C1**
Yarmouth *Can* **7D5**
Yarmūk, R *Syria/Jordan* **94B2**
Yaroslavl' *USSR* **61E2**
Yarram *Aust* **109C3**
Yarraman *Aust* **109D1**
Yarrawonga *Aust* **109C3**
Yartsevo *USSR* **60D2**
Yartsevo *USSR* **63B1**
Yarumal *Colombia* **32B2**
Yashi *Nig* **97C3**
Yashikera *Nig* **97C4**
Yashkul' *USSR* **61F4**
Yasin *Pak* **84C1**
Yasinya *USSR* **59C3**
Yass *Aust* **109C2**
Yass, R *Aust* **109C2**
Yasugi *Japan* **75A1**
Yates Center *USA* **18A2**
Yatolema *Zaïre* **98C2**
Yatsushiro *Japan* **74C4**
Yatta *Israel* **94B3**
Yavari *Peru* **32C4**
Yavatmāl *India* **85D4**
Yawatahama *Japan* **74C4**
Ya Xian *China* **76D2**
Yazd *Iran* **90B3**
Yazd-e Khvāst *Iran* **90B3**
Yazoo, R *USA* **19B3**
Yazoo City *USA* **19B3**
Ye *Burma* **76B2**
Yedintsy *USSR* **59D3**
Yeelanna *Aust* **108A2**
Yefremoy *USSR* **60E3**
Yegorlyk, R *USSR* **61F4**
Yei *Sudan* **99D2**
Yelets *USSR* **60E3**
Yell, I *Scot* **40C1**
Yellandu *India* **87C1**
Yellowhead P *Can* **8B1**
Yellowknife *Can* **4G3**
Yellowmead P *Can* **5G4**
Yellow Mt *Aust* **109C2**
Yellow Sea *China/Korea* **69E3**
Yellowstone, R *USA* **8C2**
Yellowstone L *USA* **8B2**
Yelverton B *Can* **6B1**
Yelwa *Nig* **97C3**
Yemen, Republic *Arabian Pen* **81C4**
Yen Bai *Viet* **76C1**
Yendi *Ghana* **97B4**
Yengan *Burma* **76B1**
Yeniseysk *USSR* **63B2**
Yeniseyskiy Kryazh, Ridge *USSR* **63B1**
Yeniseyskiy Zai, B *USSR* **64J2**
Yentna, R *USA* **12D2**
Yeo, R *Eng* **43C4**
Yeoval *Aust* **109C2**
Yeovil *Eng* **43C4**

Yerbogachen *USSR* 63C1
Yerevan *USSR* 65F5
Yerington *USA* 21B2
Yermo *USA* 21B3
Yerofey *USSR* 63E2
Yerofey-Pavlovich *USSR* 69E1
Yeroham *Israel* 94B3
Yershov *USSR* 61G3
Yeşil, R *Turk* 92C1
Yesud Hama'ala *Israel* 94B2
Yetman *Aust* 109D1
Yetti *Maur* 96B2
Yevlakh *USSR* 93E1
Yevpatoriya *USSR* 60D4
Ye Xian *China* 72E2
Yeysk *USSR* 60E4
Yiannitsá *Greece* 55B2
Yibin *China* 73A4
Yichang *China* 73C3
Yichun *China* 69E2
Yijun *China* 72B2
Yıldızeli *Turk* 92C2
Yiliang *China* 73A5
Yinchuan *China* 72B2
Ying He, R *China* 72D3
Yingkou *China* 72E1
Yingshan, Hubei *China* 73D3
Yingshan, Sichuan *China* 72B3
Yingtan *China* 73D4
Yining *China* 82C1
Yin Shan, Upland *China* 72B1
Yirga Alem *Eth* 99D2
Yirol *Sudan* 99D2
Yirshi *China* 63D3
Yishan *China* 73B5
Yishui *China* 72D2
Yíthion *Greece* 55B3
Yivieska *Fin* 38J6
Yiyang *China* 73C4
Yli-Kitka, L *Fin* 38K5
Ylilornio *Sweden* 38J5
Yoakum *USA* 19A4
Yogope *Mexico* 23B2
Yogyakarta *Indon* 78C4
Yoho Nat Pk *Can* 13D2
Yokadouma *Cam* 98B2
Yokkaichi *Japan* 75B2
Yokohama *Japan* 75B1
Yokosuka *Japan* 75B1
Yonago *Japan* 74C3
Yonezawa *Japan* 74E3
Yong'an *China* 73D4
Yongchang *China* 72A2
Yŏngch'on *S Korea* 74B3
Yongchuan *China* 73B4
Yongdeng *China* 72A2
Yongding *China* 73D5
Yongding He, R *China* 72D2
Yŏngdŏk *S Korea* 74B3
Yŏnghŭng *N Korea* 74B3
Yongju *S Korea* 74B3
Yongning *China* 72B2
Yonkers *USA* 16C2
Yonne, R *France* 49C2
York *Eng* 42D3
York, Nebraska *USA* 18A1
York, Pennsylvania *USA* 16A3
York,C *Aust* 107D2
Yorke Pen *Aust* 108A2
Yorketown *Aust* 108A3
York Factory *Can* 7A4
Yorkshire Moors, Moorland *Eng* 41C3
Yorkshire Wolds, Upland *Eng* 42D2
Yorkton *Can* 5H4
Yosemite L *USA* 22B2
Yosemite Nat Pk *USA* 22C1
Yoshii, R *Japan* 75A2
Yoshino, R *Japan* 75A2
Yoshkar Ola *USSR* 61G2
Yŏsu *S Korea* 74B4
Youghal *Irish Rep* 41B3
Youghal Harb *Irish Rep* 45C3
You Jiang, R *China* 73B5
Young *Aust* 109C2
Young *Urug* 34D2
Young Range, Mts *NZ* 111A2
Youngstown *Can* 13E2
Youngstown, Ohio *USA* 14B2
Yountville *USA* 22A1
Youyang *China* 73B4
Yozgat *Turk* 92B2
Yreka *USA* 20B2
Ystad *Sweden* 39G7
Ystwyth, R *Wales* 43C3
Ythan, R *Scot* 44C3
Yuan Jiang, R, Hunan *China* 73C4
Yuan Jiang, R, Yunnan *China* 73A5
Yuanmu *China* 73A4
Yuanping *China* 72C2
Yuba City *USA* 21A2
Yūbari *Japan* 74E2
Yubi,C *Mor* 96A2
Yucatan, Pen *Mexico* 25D3
Yucatan Chan *Mexico/Cuba* 25D2
Yuci *China* 72C2
Yudoma, R *USSR* 63F2
Yudu *China* 73D4
Yuexi *China* 73A4
Yueyang *China* 73C4
Yugoslavia, Federal Republic *Europe* 54A2
Yu Jiang, R *China* 73B5
Yukon, R *USA/Can* 12C2
Yukon Territory *Can* 4E3
Yulin, Guangdong *China* 76E1
Yulin, Guangxi *China* 73C5
Yulin, Shaanxi *China* 72B2
Yuma *USA* 9B3
Yumen *China* 68B3
Yunan *China* 72D2
Yungay *Chile* 34A3
Yunkai Dashan, Hills *China* 73C5
Yunta *Aust* 108A2
Yunxi *China* 72C3
Yun Xian *China* 72C3
Yunyang *China* 73B3
Yurimaguas *Peru* 32B5
Yu Shan, Mt *Taiwan* 73E5
Yushkozero *USSR* 38L6
Yushu, Tibet *China* 82D2
Yuxi *China* 73A5
Yuzhno-Kuril'sk *USSR* 74F2
Yuzhno-Sakhalinsk *USSR* 69G2
Yuzh Ural, Mts *USSR* 61J3
Yvelines, Department *France* 46A2
Yverdon *Switz* 47B1

Z

Zaandam *Neth* 56A2
Zabakalskiy *USSR* 63C2
Zāb al Babir, R *Iraq* 93D2
Zāb as Şaghīr, R *Iraq* 93D2
Zabaykal'sk *USSR* 68D2
Zabreh *Czech* 59B3
Zabrze *Pol* 59B2
Zacapu *Mexico* 23A2
Zacatecas *Mexico* 24B2
Zacatepec, Morelos *Mexico* 23B2
Zacatepec, Oaxaca *Mexico* 23B2
Zacatlan *Mexico* 23B2
Zacoalco *Mexico* 23A1
Zacualtipan *Mexico* 23B1
Zadar *Yugos* 52C2
Zadetkyi, I *Burma* 76B3
Zafra *Spain* 50A2
Zagazig *Egypt* 95C1
Zagora *Mor* 96B1
Zagorsk *USSR* 60E2
Zagreb *Yugos* 52C1
Zagros Mts
Zāhedān *Iran* 91D4
Zahle *Leb* 94B2
Zahrez Chergui, Marshland *Alg* 51C2
Zainsk *USSR* 61H2
Zaïre, Republic *Africa* 98C3
Zaïre, R *Zaïre/Congo* 98B3
Zaječăr *Yugos* 54B2
Zakamensk *USSR* 68C1
Zakho *Iraq* 93D2
Zákinthos, I *Greece* 55B3
Zakopane *Pol* 59B3
Zalaegerszeg *Hung* 59B3
Zalău *Rom* 54B1
Zalew Szczeciński, Lg *Pol* 56C2
Zalingei *Sudan* 98C1
Zaliv Akademii, B *USSR* 63F2
Zaliv Kara-Bogaz Gol, B *USSR* 65G5
Zaliv Petra Velikogo, B *USSR* 74C2
Zaliv Turpeniya, B *USSR* 69G2
Zambesi, R *Mozam* 89H9
Zambezi *Zambia* 100B2
Zambezi, R *Zambia* 100B2
Zambia, Republic *Africa* 100B2
Zamboanga *Phil* 79B4
Zamboanga Pen *Phil* 79B4
Zambrów *Pol* 58C2
Zamora *Ecuador* 32B4
Zamora *Mexico* 23A2
Zamora *Spain* 50A1
Zamość *Pol* 59C2
Zamtang *China* 72A3
Zanaga *Congo* 98B3
Záncara, R *Spain* 50B2
Zanda *China* 84D2
Zanesville *USA* 14B3
Zangla *India* 84D2
Zanjān *Iran* 90A2
Zanjitas *Arg* 34B2
Zanjon, R *Arg* 34B2
Zanzibar *Tanz* 99D3
Zanzibar, I *Tanz* 99D3
Zaouatanlaz *Alg* 96C2
Zaozhuang *China* 72D3
Zap, R *Turk* 93D2
Zapadnaja Dvina, R *USSR* 39K7
Zapadno Dvina, R *USSR* 58C1
Zapadno-Sibirskaya Nizmennost', Lowland *USSR* 65H3
Zapadnyy Sayan, Mts *USSR* 63B2
Zapala *Arg* 34A3
Zaporozh'ye *USSR* 60E4
Zara *Turk* 93C2
Zaragoza *Mexico* 23A1
Zaragoza *Spain* 50B1
Zarand *Iran* 90B2
Zarand *Iran* 90C3
Zaranj *Afghan* 80E2
Zarara *Ven* 33D2
Zarasai *USSR* 58D1
Zárate *Arg* 34D2
Zard Kuh, Mt *Iran* 90B3
Zarembo I *USA* 12H3
Zarghun Shahr *Afghan* 84B2
Zargun, Mt *Pak* 84B2
Zaria *Nig* 97C3
Zarqa *Jordan* 92C3
Zarqa, R *Jordan* 94B2
Zaruma *Ecuador* 32B4
Zary *Pol* 58B2
Zarzis *Tunisia* 96D1
Zāskār, Mts *India* 84D2
Zāskār, R *India* 84D2
Zatara, R *Jordan* 94C2
Zatoka Gdańska
Zavitinsk *USSR* 69E1
Zawiercie *Pol* 59B2
Zawīlah *Libya* 95A2
Zayarsk *USSR* 63C2
Zaysan *USSR* 65K5
Zaysan *USSR* 82C1
Zayü *China* 82D3
Zayü, Mt *China* 68B4
Zduńska Wola *Pol* 58B2
Zeebrugge *Belg* 46B1
Zeelim *Israel* 94B3
Zeerust *S Africa* 101G1
Zefat *Israel* 94B2
Zegueren, Watercourse *Mali* 97C3
Zeila *Somalia* 99E1
Zeitz *E Germ* 57C2
Zekog *China* 72A2
Zelenodol'sk *USSR* 61G2
Zelenogorsk *USSR* 39K6
Zell *Austria* 47D1
Zelten *Libya* 95A2
Zemio *CAR* 98C2
Zemlya Aleksandry, I *Barents S* 64F1
Zemlya Frantsa Iosifa, Is *Barents S* 64F2
Zemlya Georga, I *Barents S* 64F1
Zemlya Vil'cheka, I *Barents S* 64H1
Zenning *China* 73B4
Zermatt *Switz* 47B1
Zeya *USSR* 63E2
Zeya, Res *USSR* 63E2
Zézere, R *Port* 50A1
Zghorta *Leb* 94B1
Zgierz *Pol* 58B2
Zhangjiakou *China* 72D1
Zhangping *China* 73D4
Zhangwei He, R *China* 72D2
Zhangwu *China* 72E1
Zhangye *China* 72A2
Zhangzhou *China* 73D5
Zhanjiang *China* 73C5
Zhanyi *China* 73A4
Zhaoqing *China* 73C5
Zhaotong *China* 73A4
Zhaoyang Hu, L *China* 72D2
Zharkamys *USSR* 61J4
Zhatay *USSR* 63E1
Zhdanov *USSR* 60E4
Zhejiang, Province *China* 73D4
Zhengou *China* 67F3
Zhengzhou *China* 72C3
Zhenjiang *China* 72D3
Zhenxiong *China* 73A4
Zhenyuan *China* 73B4
Zherdevka *USSR* 61F3
Zhicheng *China* 73C3
Zhigalovo *USSR* 68C1
Zhijin *China* 73B4
Zhitkovichi *USSR* 58D2
Zhitomir *USSR* 60C3
Zhlobin *USSR* 60D3
Zhmerinka *USSR* 60C4
Zhob *Pak* 84B2
Zhodino *USSR* 58D2
Zhongning *China* 72B2
Zhongshan *China* 73C5
Zhongwei *China* 72B2
Zhougdian *China* 68B4
Zhoushan Quandao, Arch *China* 73E3
Zhuanghe *China* 72E2
Zhugqu *China* 72A3
Zhushan *China* 73C3
Zhuzhou *China* 73C4
Zibo *China* 72D2
Ziel,Mt *Aust* 106C3
Zielona Gora *Pol* 58B2
Zigaing *Burma* 76A1
Zigong *China* 73A4
Ziguinchor *Sen* 97A3
Zihuatanejo *Mexico* 23A2
Zikhron Ya'aqov *Israel* 94B2
Žilina *Czech* 59B3

Ziller, R *Austria* **47D1**
Zillertaler Alpen, Mts *Austria* **47D1**
Zilupe *USSR* **58D1**
Zima *USSR* **63C2**
Zimapan *Mexico* **23B1**
Zimatlan *Mexico* **23B2**
Zin, R *Israel* **94B3**
Zinacatepec *Mexico* **23B2**
Zinapécuaro *Mexico* **23A2**
Zinder *Niger* **97C3**
Zi Shui *China* **73C4**
Zitácuaro *Mexico* **23A2**
Zittau *E Germ* **57C2**
Ziya He, R *China* **72D2**
Ziyang *China* **72A3**
Zlatoust *USSR* **61J2**
Zmeinogorsk *USSR* **65K4**
Znin *Pol* **58B2**
Znoimo *Czech* **59B3**
Zofinger *Switz* **47B1**
Zoigê *China* **72A3**
Zolochev *USSR* **59D3**
Zomba *Malawi* **101C2**
Zongo *Zaïre* **98B2**
Zonguldak *Turk* **92B1**
Zorzor *Lib* **97B4**
Zouerate *Maur* **96A2**
Zrenjanin *Yugos* **54B1**
Zug *Switz* **47C1**
Zugspitze, Mt *W Germ* **47D1**
Zújar, R *Spain* **50A2**
Zumbo *Mozam* **100C2**
Zumpango *Mexico* **23B2**
Zungeru *Nig* **97C4**
Zunyi *China* **73B4**
Zuo, R *China* **76D1**
Zuo Jiang, R *China* **73B5**
Zürich *Switz* **47C1**
Zürichsee, L *Switz* **47C1**
Zuwārah *Libya* **95A1**
Zuyevka *USSR* **61H2**
Zvishavane *Zim* **100B4**
Zvolen *Czech* **59B3**
Zvornik *Yugos* **54A2**
Zweibrücken *W Germ* **46D2**
Zweisimmen *Switz* **47B1**
Zwickau *E Germ* **57C2**
Zwolle *Neth* **56B2**
Zyrardów *Pol* **58C2**
Zyryanovsk *USSR* **65K5**
Żywiec *Pol* **59B3**
Zyyi *Cyprus* **94A1**